Global Asset Management

Also by Michael Pinedo

SCHEDULING: Theory, Algorithms and Systems
PLANNING AND SCHEDULING IN MANUFACTURING AND SERVICES
QUEUEING NETWORKS: Customers, Signals and Product Form Solutions (*with X. Chao and M.Miyazawa*)
OPERATIONAL CONTROL IN ASSET MANAGEMENT (*edited*)
CREATING VALUE IN FINANCIAL SERVICES: Strategies, Operations, and Technologies (*edited with E. Melnick, P. Nayyar and S. Seshadri*)

Also by Ingo Walter

THE COMMON MARKET: Economic Integration in Europe (*with F.B. Jensen*)
THE EUROPEAN COMMON MARKET: Growth and Patterns of Trade and Production
EXERCISES IN MACROECONOMICS (*with W.E. Mitchell and J.H. Hand*)
INTERNATIONAL ECONOMICS (*with K. Areskoug*)
INTERNATIONAL ECONOMICS OF POLLUTION
MULTINATIONALS UNDER FIRE: LESSONS IN THE MANAGEMENT OF CONFLICT (*with T.N. Gladwin*)
SECRET MONEY
GLOBAL COMPETITION IN FINANCIAL SERVICES: Market Structure, Protection and Trade Liberalization
INVESTMENT BANKING IN EUROPE: Restructuring for the 1990s (*with Roy C. Smith*)
GLOBAL FINANCIAL SERVICES (*with Roy C. Smith*)
UNIVERSAL BANKING IN THE UNITED STATES (*with A. Saunders*)
STREET SMARTS: Leadership, Professional Conduct and Shareholder Value in the Securities Industry (*with Roy C. Smith*)
POLITICAL ECONOMY OF FINANCIAL INTEGRATION IN EUROPE: The Battle of the Systems (*with J. Story*)
GLOBAL CAPITAL MARKETS AND BANKING (*with R.C. Smith*)
INVESTMENT BANKING IN THE EURO-ZONE (*with R.C. Smith*)
MERGERS AND ACQUISITIONS IN BANKING AND FINANCE – What Works, What Does Not, and Why?
GOVERNING THE MODERN CORPORATION (*with R.C. Smith*)
REGULATING WALL STREET (*with members of the faculty and co-edited with V. Acharya, T. Cooley and M. Richardson*)
GLOBAL BANKING (*with R.C. Smith and G. DeLong*)
INTERNATIONAL ECONOMIC RELATIONS (*edited with F.B. Jensen*)
STATE AND LOCAL FINANCE (*edited with W.E. Mitchell*)
THE UNITED STATES AND INTERNATIONAL MARKETS: Commercial Policy Options in an Age of Controls (*edited with R.G. Hawkins*)
READINGS IN MACROECONOMICS (*edited with W.E. Mitchell and J H. Hand*)
STUDIES IN INTERNATIONAL ENVIRONMENTAL ECONOMICS (*edited*)
RESOURCE CONSERVATION: Social and Economic Dimensions of Recycling (*edited with D.W. Pearce*)
REGIONAL DIMENSIONS OF ENVIRONMENTAL POLICY (*edited with H. Siebert and K. Zimmermann*)
RISK AND THE POLITICAL ECONOMY OF RESOURCE DEVELOPMENT (*edited with D.W. Pearce and H. Siebert*)
DEREGULATING WALL STREET – Commercial Bank Penetration of the Corporate Securities Market (*edited*)
HANDBOOK OF INTERNATIONAL BUSINESS (*edited*)
HANDBOOK OF INTERNATIONAL MANAGEMENT (*edited*)
EUROPEAN INDUSTRIAL RESTRUCTURING IN THE 1990s (*edited with K. Cool and D. Neven*)
RESTRUCTURING JAPAN'S FINANCIAL MARKETS (*edited*)
FINANCIAL SYSTEMS DESIGN: Universal Banking Considered (*edited with A. Saunders*)

Global Asset Management

Strategies, Risks, Processes, and Technologies

Edited by

Michael Pinedo

and

Ingo Walter

First published 2013 by
PALGRAVE MACMILLAN

Palgrave Macmillan in the UK is an imprint of Macmillan Publishers Limited,
registered in England, company number 785998, of Houndmills, Basingstoke,
Hampshire RG21 6XS.

Palgrave Macmillan in the US is a division of St Martin's Press LLC,
175 Fifth Avenue, New York, NY 10010.

Palgrave Macmillan is the global academic imprint of the above companies
and has companies and representatives throughout the world.

Palgrave® and Macmillan® are registered trademarks in the United States,
the United Kingdom, Europe and other countries

ISBN: 978–1–137–32947–9

This book is printed on paper suitable for recycling and made from fully
managed and sustained forest sources. Logging, pulping and manufacturing
processes are expected to conform to the environmental regulations of the
country of origin.

A catalogue record for this book is available from the British Library.

A catalog record for this book is available from the Library of Congress.

Contents

Part V   Operational Processes and Costs

Part VI   Operational Platforms and IT Strategies

Part VII   Future Challenges and Growth

List of Figures

List of Tables

Preface

This volume collects the thoughts of experts – insiders and outsiders with no axes to grind or services to sell – on the complex and dynamic issues that confront the global asset management industry.

What value is being created in the diverse asset management sector and how is that likely to change? What separates the winners from the losers in the various sectors of the industry? How and why did the industry fail to protect its clients in the financial crisis and what are the consequences going forward? What are the key risk issues confronting firms in the industry, notably operational and reputational risks, and how do they relate to governance and regulation?

If durable competitive distinction in fund performance is difficult or impossible to attain, then the name of the game has to be efficiency and costs – and their critical dependence technologies, systems architecture and client interface. The pivotal role of best-in-class transactions and information platforms is one of the few certainties in an otherwise uncertain industry context.

We have divided the volume into a logical sequence of parts discussing, respectively, broad asset management industry dynamics, the industry impact of the financial crisis of 2007–2009, and key risk and regulatory issues facing the industry – subsequently narrowing the focus on operational processes and cost structures as well as operational platforms and IT strategies.

The latter are of key importance. If competitive distinction cannot durably be achieved through persistent portfolio outperformance adjusted for risk, then the distinguishing factors between winners and losers in the industry depend heavily on costs and quality of service, as well as on optimizing the value of information both internally and externally.

The more technical chapters contained in this part of the volume are well worth the time and effort it takes to peruse them carefully. The last section of the book looks ahead to the future of the asset management industry and the strategic positioning and execution issues that will determine competitive success.

We intend this book to be the go-to reference on the asset management industry, with a substantial shelf life. It provides a serious resource for readers seeking greater depth and alternative opinions on specific industry developments, as well as access to breadth for specialists interests in the dynamics of the industry.

We are grateful to the authors of the chapters contained in this volume for the quality and timeliness of their work – as in any such collection of views, credit belongs to them. We are also thankful to SimCorp StrategyLab, SimCorp's private research institution, that through its extensive research program has transformed our idea into reality and made this publication possible.

We are also indebted to Mette Trier, who kept us on a tight leash in getting contributions in on time and in correct form, and handling the logistics of the project with her usual high level of efficiency and diplomacy. Responsibility for any remaining errors of omission or commission rest with the editors.

Michael Pinedo, Professor
Ingo Walter, Professor and President of
SimCorp StrategyLab
New York City, 15 April 2013

Notes on Contributors

Renée B. Adams is Professor of Finance and Commonwealth Bank Chair in Finance at the University of New South Wales. She is also the director of the Finance Research Network (FIRN), an affiliate of LSE's Financial Markets Group, and a member of the European Corporate Governance Institute (ECGI). She holds an MS in Mathematics from Stanford University and a PhD in Economics from the University of Chicago. Professor Adams's research focuses on corporate governance, corporate finance and the economics of organizations. She is an expert on corporate boards and the governance of financial institutions. She has published in top accounting, economics, finance and management journals including the *Journal of Accounting and Economics*, the *Journal of Finance*, the *Journal of Financial Economics*, *Management Science*, the *Review of Economic Studies and Strategic Management Journal*. Contact: renee.adams@unsw.edu.au.

Ümit Alptuna is Managing Director at Goldman Sachs Asset Management and COO of Goldman Sachs Investment Partners. Prior to joining Goldman Sachs in 2001, he was a manager in Business Assurance Services at PriceWaterhouse Coopers LLP in New York where he was responsible for overseeing audit engagements as well as for providing guidance on technical accounting matters. He is a graduate of the Stern School of Business at New York University, a licensed CPA and a CFA Charterholder. Contact: umit.alptuna@gs.com

Yakov Amihud is Ira Leon Rennert Professor of Entrepreneurial Finance at the Stern School of Business, New York University. His research focuses on the effects of the liquidity of stocks and bonds on their returns and values, and on the design and evaluation of securities markets trading systems. He has also advised the NYSE, AMEX, CBOE, CBOT and other securities markets. His research also includes the evaluation of corporate financial policies, dividend policy, mergers and acquisitions, initial public offerings, objectives of corporate managers and their risk taking, and law and finance. He is the co-author of a recently published book *Market Liquidity: Asset Pricing, Risk and Crises* and has published more than 80 research articles in professional journals and books. He has also edited and co-edited five books on topics such as LBOs, bank M&As, international finance and securities market design. Contact: yamihud@stern.nyu.edu

Anders Bidsted Andersen is Vice President and Head of Global Professional Services at SimCorp. His responsibilities include global regulatory service product development, value-creating packaged services and service-enabled solution innovations. With global teams and in cooperation with SimCorp's regional professional service managers, he drives development, launch and execution of global regulatory, business and operational services and solutions for clients in all markets serviced by SimCorp. With over 20 years' experience from executing and managing roles in Big-4 management consultancies and global high-performance organizations, his specialties are quantitative finance, regulatory change and acceleration of strategic and operational breakthroughs. Anders Bidsted Andersen holds an MBA from the University of Chicago Booth School of Business and a graduate degree in Computer Science. Contact: anders. andersen@simcorp.com

Mirzha de Manuel Aramendia is Research Fellow at the European Capital Markets Institute (ECMI) and the Centre for European Policy Studies (CEPS) in Brussels since September 2010. In this capacity, he set up a task force on 'Long-term Investing and Retirement Savings' in December 2012, the final report of which will be released in the Fall of 2013. Mirzha's research at CEPS focuses on public policy and market aspects in relation to investment management, retirement savings, broader asset management – including life insurance – and investor protection. It extends to connected aspects in the fields of financial stability, institutional settings and supervisory practices, economic growth and competitiveness, corporate governance, social inclusiveness, competition policy, market structure and industrial organization. Mirzha has an MA in European Economic and Legal Analysis from the College of Europe in Belgium (2010) and is a qualified lawyer from the Bar of Madrid. He holds a masters both in Business Economics and in Spanish and Common Law (2009) from the University of Valladolid (Spain). Contact: mirzha.demanuel@ceps.eu

John H. Biggs is Executive-in-Residence and Adjunct Professor of Finance at the Stern School of New York University. He served as President and then Chairman and CEO of TIAA-CREF, a multiline pension and insurance company for 14 years. He served as a director of many companies, in particular, JP MorganChase, a multiline financial institution, where he was a member of the audit committee. He is currently Chairman of the Audit Committee of Boeing, a multiline industrial company. He is a Fellow of the Society of Actuaries and earned a PhD in Economics. He has participated in and written on corporate governance, actuarial and general management issues. He is a director and former Chairman of the National Bureau of Economic Research. He served as the Chief Financial Officer of a life insurance company before becoming Vice-Chancellor of Washington University in St Louis in 1977. In these two institutions, he implemented the 'accountability center' management principles as described in this article. He has served as a trustee of the foundations overseeing FASB and the International Accounting Standards Board. He is currently a trustee of Washington University in St Louis and Chairman of its Investment

Management Company. He is a member of the American Academy of Arts and Sciences and the Council on Foreign Relations. Contact: jbiggs@stern.nyu.edu

Aaron Brown is a risk manager at AQR Capital Management and the 2011 Global Association of Risk Professionals Risk Manager of the Year. He is the author of *Red-Blooded Risk* (2012), *The Poker Face of Wall Street* (2006 – selected one of the ten best books of 2006 by Business Week) and *A World of Chance* (with Reuven and Gabrielle Brenner, 2008). In his 32-year Wall Street career he has been a trader, portfolio manager, head of mortgage securities and risk manager for institutions including Citigroup and Morgan Stanley. He has also served as a finance professor and was one of the top professional poker players in the world during the 1970s and 1980s. He holds degrees in Applied Mathematics from Harvard and Finance and Statistics from the University of Chicago respectively. Contact: Aaron.Brown@aqr.com

Stephen J. Brown is David S. Loeb Professor of Finance at the NYU Stern School of Business. He graduated from the University of Chicago, earning a PhD in 1976. Following successive appointments at Bell Laboratories and Yale, he joined the faculty of New York University in 1986. In 2002 he was appointed Professorial Fellow at the University of Melbourne. He has served as President of the Western Finance Association, was a founding editor of the *Review of Financial Studies* and is a managing editor of *The Journal of Financial and Quantitative Analysis*. He has testified on his research before a Full Committee Hearing of the US Congress House Financial Services Committee in March 2007. In 2010 he served as a member of the Research Evaluation Committee of the Excellence in Research Australia initiative on behalf of the Commonwealth Government of Australia. Contact: sbrown@stern.nyu.edu

Alistair Byrne is a senior investment consultant at Towers Watson in London, but writes here in a personal capacity. He advises a number of large, defined contribution pension plans on their investment approach and strategy. Alistair began his career in investment management at AEGON Asset Management UK, where he was investment strategist and head of equity research. He has also held academic positions at the University of Edinburgh and Strathclyde business schools, and has been a principal at Investit, the investment management consultancy. Alistair has a PhD in finance from the University of Strathclyde and is a CFA charterholder. Contact: alistair.byrne@btinternet.com

Lin-Sya Chao graduated from the Solvay Brussels School of Economics and Management with a major in finance. Having a special interest in strategic issues underlying the financial crisis, she completed a masters thesis on the topic 'Strategic Risk Management: The Next Challenge for Financial Institutions', under the supervision of Professor Mathias Schmit. Contact: l.chao@segora.be

Marcelo Cruz is the editor-in-chief of the *Journal of Operational Risk* and adjunct professor at the New York University. He is the head of Enterprise Risk Management and Operational Risk at E*TRADE. He was also the global head of operational risk at Morgan Stanley. Previously he was an associate partner at McKinsey & Co, Chief Risk Officer of Aviva plc and global head of operational risk at Lehman Brothers. Marcelo was the managing director and founder of RiskMaths, a boutique consultancy focused on risk management and strategy. Marcelo also worked at UBS AG, the Swiss bank, for three years as head of operational risk, having worked in London and New York. Before UBS he also worked as a chief economist/strategist for an investment bank and as a derivatives trader for JP Morgan where he was in charge of structuring and trading OTC products. Marcelo Cruz is author of *Modeling, Measuring and Hedging Operational Risk* (2002). He was a member of the Industry Technical Working Group that helped to develop the new Basel Accord. He was also a Trustee of the Board of GARP and currently sits on the Research Committee of PRMIA. Contact: marcelo.g.cruz@gmail.com

Khosrow Dehnad is Assistant General Manager and Head of Analytic and Quantitative Trading at Samba Financial Group. Before joining Samba, he was a managing director in the Structured Credit Products at Citigroup and in charge of Exotic Credit Trading. Previously, he was head of Fixed Income Derivatives Structuring and New Products. Prior to the merger of Citibank and Travelers Group, he was the Head of Hybrid Desk at Citibank where he created products such as Flexible Cap, Q-Cap, and Defensive Swap etc. Dr Dehnad received his BSc in Mathematics with first class honors from University of Manchester, England and his PhD in Mathematics from the University of California, Berkeley. After receiving his second doctorate in Applied Statistics from Stanford University, he joined AT&T Bell Labs where he published the book *Quality Control and Taguchi Method*. He has worked at the program trading firm of D.E. Shaw and Derivatives marketing and structuring group at Chase Manhattan Bank. For the past 14 years, Dr Dehnad has been an Adjunct Professor of Operations Research at Columbia University where he teaches Applied Financial Engineering and Forecasting. He has taught at University of California at Berkeley, San Jose State University, and Rutgers University. Contact: dehnad@aol.com

Jean Dermine received his Docteur des Sciences Economiques from the Université Catholique de Louvain and MBA from Cornell University. Jean Dermine is Professor of Banking and Finance at INSEAD, Fontainebleau. Author of articles on European banking markets, asset and liability management and the theory of banking, he has also published five books, including being *Bank Valuation and Value-Based Management-Deposit and Loan Pricing, Performance Evaluation and Risk Management*, 2009. He has been a Visiting Professor at

Lausanne, Louvain, New York University, the Stockholm School of Economics and the Wharton School. Contact: jean.dermine@insead.edu

Jacob Elsborg is Head of Technology for ATP's investment department since 2000 and is responsible for the department's operational platform. ATP is a statutory pension fund with over 4.7 million members – virtually the entire adult population in Denmark – and the country's largest fund. Group assets totaled around DKK629 billion at year-end 2012. He started his career as an IT economist for Danmark's National Bank from 1991 until 2000. Jacob has both an MSc in Mathematics and Economics from the Copenhagen Business School and an MBA from Henley Management College. Contact: jae@atp.dk

Johannes Elsner is a partner in McKinsey's Munich office. Since 2006 he has been working for clients in the European financial services industry with a focus on asset managers, investors and universal banks. Aside from his client activities, Elsner is a core member of McKinsey's European asset management practice leadership. He has co-authored several publications such as *Check or Checkmate – Game-changing Strategies for the Asset Management Industry* (2012). He studied law at the University of Munich in Germany (qualifying as state attorney) and economics at the London School of Economics. Contact: Johannes_Elsner@mckinsey.com.

Martin J. Gruber is Scholar in Residence and Professor Emeritus at the Stern School of Business at NYU. He has an SB in Chemical Engineering from MIT and both an MBA and PhD from Columbia University. He is the author of over 100 journal articles, many of which deal with mutual funds. His book *Modern Portfolio Theory and Investment Analysis* is going into its ninth edition and has been a best-seller for more than 30 years. Professor Gruber is currently a member of the board of several Daiwa and Aberdeen mutual funds. He has been a director of the DWS funds, the S.G. Cowen funds and TIAA-CREF, where he served as Chairman of the board. Contact: mgruber@stern.nyu.edu

Emmanuel D. (Manos) Hatzakis is a risk, structuring, and analytics expert, currently with UBS in New York, and earlier with Goldman Sachs and Merrill Lynch. Manos has built award-winning risk-management models, developed and validated sovereign debt restructuring proposals, and designed and implemented portfolio optimization programs for annuities and private investors. He has authored several articles, including 'Op-Eds' in *The New York Times* and *The Financial Times*, and edited academic journals. Manos earned a PhD in Operations Research at Wharton. He is a CFA Charterholder and FRM. Contact: manoshatzakis@aol.com

Martin Huber is a senior partner working in McKinsey's Cologne office. Since 1996 he has been working for several international clients in the European and

Middle-Eastern financial services industry. He serves asset managers, investors, insurance companies and private banks on a broad range of topics. Furthermore, he is the co-leader of McKinsey's global asset management practice and responsible for the annual pan-European survey on the economics of asset managers. Mr Huber also leads McKinsey's recruiting efforts in Germany. He received an MBA and holds masters and doctorate degrees in law from the University of Vienna, as well as an LLM from the University of Chicago. He is also a member of the New York bar. Contact:martin_huber@mckinsey.com.

John Hull is Maple Financial Professor of Derivatives and Risk Management at the Joseph L. Rotman School of Management, University of Toronto. He has written three books *Risk Management and Financial Institutions* (now in its third edition), *Options, Futures, and Other Derivatives* (now in its eighth edition) and *Fundamentals of Futures and Options Markets* (now in its seventh edition). The books have been translated into many languages and are widely used in trading rooms throughout the world. He has won many teaching awards, including University of Toronto's prestigious Northrop Frye award, and was voted Financial Engineer of the Year in 1999 by the International Association of Financial Engineers. He is co-director of Rotman's Master of Finance program. Contact: hull@rotman.utoronto.ca

Anders Kirkeby is global domain manager for System Architecture in the Strategic Research Department at SimCorp. He leads a team charged with setting and executing strategically focused changes in the SimCorp Dimension investment management software product. His specific focus areas include scalability, enterprise-wide cross-functional consistency and overall user experience. Prior to joining SimCorp, he served in software architecture and consultant roles focused on the Microsoft technology stack, as well as a three-year IT start-up engagement as technologist and product owner for an SaaS product. He earned his degree in computer science and human-computer interaction from the University of Aarhus, Denmark. Contact: anders.kirkeby@ simcorp.com

Philipp Koch is a partner working in McKinsey's Hamburg office. Since 2001 he has been working for clients in the banking and insurance industry, with a special focus on asset management. He is a core member of the European asset management practice. He served numerous asset managers and institutional investors worldwide on questions on strategy, PMM, distribution strategy, product development, alternative assets – in particular real estate – and organizational set-up. Prior to joining McKinsey, Dr Koch received a MSc from the London School of Economics in Political Science. He holds a PhD from the Helmut-Schmidt University Hamburg and his doctoral dissertation was entitled 'Optimizing Distribution Systems in the Asset Management

Sector – Institutional Arrangements as Key Factor of Success'. Contact: philipp_ koch@mckinsey.com.

Carsten Kunkel is Manager of the Legal Practices team in SimCorp's Central European market unit. The team has a regulatory compliance function with a number of specialized consultants dedicated to meeting the regulatory requirements of global asset managers. Carsten has been with SimCorp for more than seven years and prior to heading up the Legal Practices team from 2008, he worked as a presales consultant. Before joining SimCorp, he gained five years of consultancy experience in the financial services industry, focusing on banks and insurance companies in Germany. He earned his degree in economics from the University of Mannheim, Germany. Contact: carsten. kunkel@simcorp.com

David Lando is a Professor of Finance at Copenhagen Business School and Director of the Center for Financial Frictions (FRIC) funded by the Danish National Research Foundation. He holds a masters degree from the joint mathematics–economics program at the University of Copenhagen and a PhD in statistics from Cornell University. Lando's main area of research in finance is credit risk modeling and risk management and some of his work has appeared in *Econometrica, Journal of Financial Economics* and *Review of Financial Studies*. He is the author of a monograph on credit risk modeling published by Princeton University Press. Lando has been a visiting scholar at Princeton University, the Federal Reserve Board in Washington and The Federal Reserve Bank of New York. Before joining Copenhagen Business School, he was a Professor at the Department of Applied Mathematics and Statistics at the University of Copenhagen. Contact: dl.fi@cbs.dk

Karel Lannoo is Chief Executive of the Centre for European Policy Studies (CEPS), one of the leading independent European think tanks. He has published a number of books and numerous articles in specialized magazines and journals on general European policy, and specific financial regulation and supervision matters. He is an independent director of BME (Bolsas Y Mercados Espanoles), the listed company that manages the Spanish securities exchanges. Karel Lannoo directs the European Capital Markets Institute (ECMI) and the European Credit Research Institute (ECRI), both operated by CEPS. He holds a baccalaureate in philosophy and an MA in history from the University of Leuven, Belgium and obtained a postgraduate in European studies from the University of Nancy in France. Contact: klannoo@ceps.eu

Massimo Massa is the Rothschild Chair Professor of Banking and Finance at INSEAD, where he teaches international finance, corporate finance, information financial economics and behavioral finance in MBA, PhD and Executive programs. He graduated summa cum laude from the Department of Economics at the LUISS University of Rome, Italy. He has obtained an MBA from the Yale School of Management and an MA and PhD in Financial Economics from Yale University. His research interests include portfolio theory, theory of information in financial markets, behavioral finance, market microstructure and mutual funds. His articles have been published in academic journals such as *Review of Financial Studies, Journal of Finance, Journal of Financial Economics, Journal of Business, Journal of Financial and Quantitative Analysis, Journal of Financial Markets, Review of Finance, and European Journal of Financial Management.* Massimo has previously worked in the Bank of Italy in the Banking Division (1989–1992) and in the Research Department (Monetary and Financial Markets Division) (1993–1997), participating in the day-to-day running of monetary policy and on the analysis of the financial markets. Contact: Massimo.MASSA@insead.edu

Haim Mendelson is the Kleiner Perkins Caufield & Byers Professor of Electronic Business and Commerce, and Management at the Stanford Business School. His research areas include information technology and finance, and he has published more than 100 research papers, more than 30 company case studies, and three books in these areas. His most recent book (co-authored by Yakov Amihud and Lasse Pedersen) is *Market Liquidity: Asset Pricing, Risk, and Crises* (2013). Professor Mendelson has been a consultant and adviser to leading firms and startups in the areas of high technology, finance and entrepreneurship, and he has directed multiple executive education programs and research projects in these areas. Professor Mendelson has been elected Distinguished Fellow of the Information Systems Society in recognition of outstanding intellectual contributions to the Information Systems discipline. Contact: Mendelson_Haim@gsb.stanford.edu

Michael Pinedo has an Ir degree in Mechanical Engineering from the Delft University of Technology in the Netherlands, and MSc and PhD degrees in Operations Research from the University of California at Berkeley. He is currently the Julius Schlesinger Professor of Operations Management and Chair of the Department of Information, Operations and Management Sciences at the Stern School of Business at New York University. Pinedo's current research focuses on the modeling and analysis of service systems, with an emphasis on Total Quality Management (TQM) and operational risk. He has written numerous technical papers on these topics and is the author of several books. Pinedo has consulted extensively for manufacturing companies as well as financial services companies, for instance as a consultant for many years at Goldman Sachs, advising on issues involving operational risk. Currently, he is editor of the *Journal of Scheduling* (Springer) and associate editor of the *Journal of Operational Risk*. Contact: mpinedo@stern.nyu.edu

Ole Risager has a PhD degree and is a professor at Copenhagen Business School. He has published extensively on foreign exchange markets, stock markets, and macroeconomics. His work has appeared in international journals as well as in publications of the International Monetary Fund and the World Bank. He is currently chairman for Core German Residential II, a real estate investment company, vice chairman for Maj Invest, a mutual investment company, and member of APM Terminals' Executive Risk Management Committee. He has previously served as a senior economist to the IMF and as a consultant to the World Bank. He has also been Vice President – Chief Economist at A.P. Moller – Maersk. Contact: or.int@cbs.dk

Caspar Rose has a PhD degree and is a professor at Copenhagen Business School, Department of International Economics and Management. He holds a master of laws as well as a doctorate in finance and his research focuses on operational risk management, financial regulation, M&As as well as corporate governance – all issues about which he has published extensively in international journals. Caspar has worked in Dansk Industri (Confederation of Danish Industries) as special legal adviser as well as chief analyst at the Danske Bank, Group Operational Risk. He also serves as external consultant for financial institutions. Contact: car.int@cbs.dk

Howie San is the global Domain Manager for data management and connectivity for SimCorp. Starting at Coopers and Lybrand Associates, he is an industry veteran with over 25 years in finance and technology, working both for banks and vendors. He has, for the last 15 years, held a number of senior product management roles at various industry leaders including Citigroup Securities and Fund Services, Dealogic, GFI and Thomson Financial. He earned his degree in Business Administration from the University of Bath UK. He is both Pragmatic Marketing certified and a trained credit analyst. Contact: howie.san@simcorp.com

Adam Schneider is a Principal in Deloitte's Financial Services practice. He serves as Senior Advisor to the Deloitte Center for Financial Services. Adam is also Deloitte's Regional head of Banking and Securities, responsible for organizing services to a portfolio of major financial institutions. Adam works primarily in financial services and technology. He managed Deloitte's Securities Industry consulting practice from 1995–2001, Deloitte's Investment Industry consulting practice from 2001–2007, and has been the lead partner for several clients. Adam assists clients in major business transformations including product strategy, M&A, finance, technology implementation, operations improvement, regulatory response, and cost reduction. He managed Deloitte's Credit Crisis Task Force from 2008–2009 providing resources and knowledge to a wide range of clients. He is a Deloitte knowledge resource in many areas including capital markets, investment banking, investment management, home lending, retail banking, asset servicing, and transaction processing.

From 1991 to 1995, Adam was Managing Director responsible for technology, operations, and administration at an institutional asset management firm. Before 1991 he was also a Partner at Deloitte & Touche. Adam is extremely active professionally. He has authored numerous publications, contributed to industry reference books, and has given numerous presentations, roundtables, and speeches at industry conferences and at major business schools. Adam holds an MBA from the Columbia University Graduate School of Business and a BS from the Sloan School of the Massachusetts Institute of Technology. Contact: aschneider@deloitte.com

Mathias Schmit holds a PhD in finance from the Solvay Brussels School of Economics and Management (Brussels), where he is a part-time professor and member of the Emile Bernheim Research Centre. He has worked in banking and public affairs-related activities since 1995. Currently, he is conducting research and consulting activities in banking and risk management. He is also a regular speaker at major conferences around Europe on banking issues, with a special focus on financial analysis, risk management and strategic risks. Contact: m.schmit@sagora.eu or mschmit@ulb.ac.be.

Marc Schröter is Senior Vice President and Head of Strategic Research at SimCorp. With SimCorp since 1995, he has worked with a wide range of financial institutions in Europe. In that role he has experience with most business areas of buy-side investment managers across front, middle and back office. Prior to his current position, Schröter was Head of Professional Services at SimCorp. Since 2006, he has been managing the Strategic Research department, where he leads a team of 35 domain managers and senior business analysts and is responsible for the strategic direction of SimCorp's investment management solutions. Marc holds a masters in engineering and a bachelors in finance. Contact: marc.schroeter@simcorp.com

Steen Thomsen is director of the Center for Corporate Governance at Copenhagen Business School (CBS). He specializes in corporate governance as a teacher, researcher, consultant, commentator and practitioner. His academic publications include some 30 international journal articles and three books on the subject. His research is currently focused on industrial foundations – foundations that own business firms. Steen has served as a board member in several business companies and is currently a non-executive chairman of two consulting firms. He writes columns for the Danish business newspaper *Børsen*, and has served as a consultant and lecturer to several large companies and government organizations, including the EU, the UN, Copenhagen Stock Exchange, the Danish Central Bank and the Danish Venture Capital Association. He has also contributed to the Danish corporate governance code and other best practice codes. Contact: st.int@cbs.dk

Reha Tütüncü is a managing director in the Quantitative Investment Strategies business within Goldman Sachs (GS) Asset Management where he manages a team of strategists responsible for building the infrastructure and algorithms for quantitative portfolio construction and risk management. Prior to joining GS, he was an Associate Professor in the Department of Mathematical Sciences at Carnegie Mellon University. He received his PhD in Operations Research from Cornell University. He is the co-author of the book *Optimization Methods in Finance* and the author of many articles on the subjects of optimization and quantitative finance in academic and practitioner journals. Contact: reha.tutuncu@gs.com

Paul Verdin is Full Professor and Chair in Strategy and Organization at Solvay Business School (ULB, Brussels) and Professor of Strategy & International Management at KULeuven (B). Previously an Associate Dean at TiasNimbas (Tilburg University, NL), he was also on the INSEAD (F) faculty for over 15 years, notably as a 'Distinguished Visiting Professor' and at IESE Business School (E). After masters degrees in Law and in Economics (KULeuven, B), he obtained the MA and PhD in Economics from Harvard University, where he worked with Nobel Laureate Tom Schelling, and consulted with McKinsey & Co., Merrill Lynch Capital Markets, the IMF and the World Bank. Dr. Verdin's widely cited research focuses on the critical role of innovative company strategy and organization for long-term value creation, and how it interacts with industry dynamics and competence- and resource-based competition. For many years he has also been researching the strategic and organizational challenges of globalization and regional integration. He directs executive seminars and strategy workshops, and consults on strategy processes for a wide range of companies in a variety of industries and particularly in financial services. Contact: paul.verdin@econ.kuleuven.be

Ingo Walter is President of SimCorpStrategyLab and the Seymour Milstein Professor of Finance, Corporate Governance and Ethics at New York University Stern School of Business. His principal areas of academic and consulting activity include international banking and capital markets. Professor Walter is the author and/or editor of 28 books, most recently the third edition of *Global Banking*, published in 2012. He studied engineering at Lehigh University and received his PhD degree in economics from New York University. Contact:iwalter@stern.nyu.edu

Part I

Global Asset Management – Introduction and Overview

1
The Asset Management Industry Dynamics of Growth, Structure and Performance

Ingo Walter

1.1 Introduction

This chapter examines the industrial organisation and institutional development of the global asset management industry. Few industries have encountered as much 'strategic turbulence' in recent years as has the financial services sector in general and the asset management – the 'buy-side' of the capital markets – in particular. Indeed, there is ample evidence to suggest that the development of the asset management industry has much to do with capital allocation in national and global financial systems. That is, asset-gathering and deployment of savings affect the pace of capital formation and the economic growth process more broadly.

Consequently, the asset management industry will continue to be one of the largest and most dynamic parts of the global financial services sector, resuming its long-term growth after the impact of the global financial crisis of the 2000s – based on a number of underlying factors:

- A continued broad-based trend toward professional management of discretionary household assets in the form of mutual funds or unit trusts and other types of collective investment vehicles.
- The growing recognition that most government-sponsored pension systems, many of which were created wholly or partially on a pay-as-you-go (PAYG) basis, have become fundamentally untenable under demographic projections that appear virtually certain to materialise, and must be progressively replaced by asset pools that will throw off the kinds of returns necessary to meet the needs of growing numbers of longer living retirees.

- Partial displacement of traditional defined-benefit public- and private sector pension programs backed by assets contributed by employers and working individuals under the pressure of the evolving demographics, rising administrative costs, and shifts in risk-allocation by a variety of defined-contribution schemes.
- Substantial increases in individual wealth in a number of developed countries and a range of developing countries, as reflected in changing global shares in assets under management.
- Reallocation of portfolios that have – for regulatory, tax or institutional reasons – been overweight domestic financial instruments (notably fixed-income securities) toward a greater role for equities and non-domestic asset classes. These not only may provide higher returns but also may reduce the beneficiaries' exposure to risk due to portfolio diversification across both asset classes and economic and financial environments which are less than perfectly correlated in terms of total investment returns.
- A continued important role for alternative asset classes and special situations in real assets, private equity and certain hedge funds. However, a long period of mediocre performance and a dearth of investment opportunities – together with high fees, compliance problems and operational risks may/will continue to undermine some types of alternative assets going forward.

The chapter reviews the four main components of the asset management industry – pension funds, mutual funds, alternative asset pools such as hedge funds, and private client asset pools. The chapter then discusses key structural and competitive characteristics of the industry and its reconfiguration.

1.2   Mapping the global asset management industry

The layout of the global asset management industry can perhaps best be explained in terms of Figure 1.1. The right side of the diagram is the institutional side of the market for professional asset management and the left side is the individual side of the markets, although the distinctions are often heavily blurred.

First, retail clients have the option of placing funds directly with financial institutions such as banks or by purchasing securities from retail sales forces of broker-dealers, possibly with the help of fee-based financial advisers. Alternatively, retail investors can have their funds professionally managed by buying shares in mutual funds or unit trusts (again possibly with the help of advisers), which in turn buy securities from the institutional sales desks of broker-dealers (or maintain balances with banks).

Second, private clients are broken-out as a separate segment of the asset management market in Figure 1.1, and are usually serviced by private bankers who

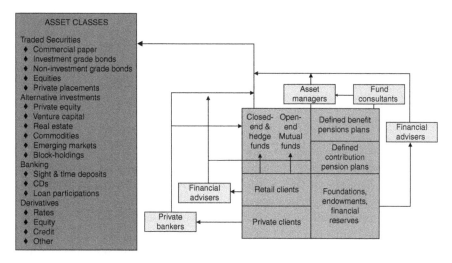

Figure 1.1 Mapping the global asset management architecture

bundle asset management with various other services such as tax planning, estates and trusts, placing assets directly into financial instruments, commingled managed asset pools, or sometimes publicly-available mutual funds and unit trusts.

Third, foundations, endowments, and financial reserves held by nonfinancial companies, institutions and governments can rely on in-house investment expertise to purchase securities directly from the institutional sales desks of banks or securities broker-dealers, use financial advisers to help them build efficient portfolios, or place funds with open-end or closed-end mutual funds.

Fourth, pension funds take two principal forms, those guaranteeing a level of benefits and those aimed at building beneficiary assets from which a pension will be drawn (see below). Defined-benefit pension funds can buy securities directly in the market, or place funds with banks, trust companies or other types of asset managers, often aided by fund consultants who advise pension trustees on performance and asset allocation styles. Defined-contribution pension programs may operate in a similar way if they are managed in-house, creating proprietary asset pools, and in addition (or alternatively) provide participants with the option to purchase shares in publicly-available mutual funds.

The structure of the asset management industry encompasses significant overlaps between the four types of asset pools to the point where they are sometimes difficult to distinguish. We have noted the linkage between defined-contribution pension funds and the mutual fund industry, and the association of the disproportionate growth in the former with the expansion of mutual fund assets under management. There is a similar but perhaps more limited linkage between private client assets and mutual funds, on the one hand, and pension funds, on the other. This is particularly the case for the lower-bound of private client business, which is often commingled with mass-marketed mutual funds, and pension benefits awarded to high-income executives, which in effect become part of the recipient's high net worth portfolio.

1.3 Pension funds

The pension fund market for asset management has been one of the most rapidly growing domains of the global financial system, and promises to be even more dynamic in the years ahead. Consequently, pension assets have been in the forefront of strategic targeting by all types of financial institutions, including banks, trust companies, broker-dealers, insurance companies, mutual fund companies, and independent asset management firms.

Pension fund assets in the OECD countries reached a record USD 20.1 trillion in 2011 but return on investment fell below zero, with an average negative return of –1.7% due to weak equity markets and low interest rates.[1] Roughly two-thirds of the assets covered private sector employees and the balance covered public sector employees. The growth rate of pension assets had been about 5% per year before the global financial crisis, but declined materially during the crisis. About 40% of global pension assets under management are in Europe and the United States, roughly evenly divided, while the rest of the world accounted for the balance – although the most rapidly growing, especially in Asia.

The basis for the projected growth of managed pensions continues to focus on the demographics of gradually aging populations, colliding with existing structures for retirement support which in many countries carry heavy political baggage. They are politically exceedingly difficult to bring up to the standards required for the future, yet doing so eventually is inevitable. The near-term focus of this problem will be Europe and Japan, with profound implications for the size and structure of capital markets, the competitive positioning and performance of financial intermediaries in general and asset managers in particular.

The demographics of the pension fund problem are straightforward, since demographic data are among the most reliable. Unless there are major unforeseen changes in birth rates, death dates or migration rates, the dependency ratio (population over 65 divided by the population age 16–64) will have doubled between 2010 and 2040, with the highest dependency ratios in the case of Europe being attained in Italy, Germany and the Netherlands, and the lowest in Ireland. Japan has dependency ratios even higher than Europe, while the US ratio is somewhat lower – with the lowest generally found in developing countries. Surprisingly close behind are major emerging markets like Korea and China. All are heading in the same direction.

While the demographics underlying these projections may be quite reliable, dependency ratios remain subject to shifts in working age start- and end-points. Obviously, the longer people remain out of the active labour force (e.g., for purposes of education), the higher the level of sustained unemployment; and the earlier the average retirement age, the higher will be the dependency ratio. The collision comes between the demographics and the existing structure of pension finance. There are basically three ways to provide support for the post-retirement segment of the population:

- Pay-as-you-go (PAYG) programs: Pension benefits under this approach are committed by the state based on various formulas – number of years worked and income subject to social charges, for example – and funded by current mandatory contributions of those employed (taxes and social charges) that may or may not be specifically earmarked to covering current pension payouts. Under PAYG systems, current pension contributions may exceed or fall short of current disbursements. In the former case a trust fund may be set up which, as in the case of US Social Security, may be invested in government securities. In the latter case, the deficit will tend to be covered out of general tax revenues, government borrowing, or the liquidation of previously accumulated trust fund assets.
- Defined-benefit programs: Pension benefits under such programs are committed to public or private sector employees by their employers, based on actuarial benefit formulas that are part of the employment contract. Defined-benefit pension payouts may be linked to the cost of living, adjusted for survivorship, etc., and the funds set aside to support future claims may be contributed solely by the employer or with some level of employee contribution. The pool of assets may be invested in a portfolio of debt and equity securities (possibly including the company's own shares) that are managed in-house or by external fund managers. Depending on the level of contributions and benefit claims, as well as investment performance, defined-benefit plans may be over-funded or under-funded. They may thus be tapped by the employer from time to time for general corporate purposes, or they may have to be topped-up from the employer's own resources. Defined-benefit plans may be insured (e.g., against corporate bankruptcy) either in the private market or by government agencies, and are usually subject to strict regulation – for example, in the United States under ERISA, which is administered by the Department of Labor.
- Defined-contribution programs: Pension fund contributions are made by the employer, the employee, or both into a fund that will ultimately form the basis for pension benefits under defined-contribution pension plans. The employee's share in the fund tends to vest after a number of years of employment, and may be managed by the employer or placed with

various asset managers under portfolio constraints intended to serve the best interests of the beneficiaries. The employee's responsibility for asset allocation can vary from none at all to virtually full discretion. Employees may, for example, be allowed to select from among a range of approved investment vehicles, notably mutual funds, based on individual risk–return preferences.

Most countries have several types of pension arrangements operating simultaneously – for example a base-level PAYG system supplemented by state-sponsored or privately-sponsored defined-benefit plans and defined-contribution plans sponsored by employers, mandated by the state or undertaken voluntarily by individuals.

The collision of the aforementioned demographics and heavy reliance on the part of many countries on PAYG approaches is at the heart of the pension problem, and forms the basis for the future growth of asset management. The conventional wisdom is that the pension problems that are today centred in Europe and Japan will eventually spread to the rest of the world. They will have to be resolved, and there are only a limited number of options in dealing with the issue:

- Raise mandatory social charges on employees and employers to cover increasing pension obligations under PAYG systems. This is problematic especially in countries that already have high fiscal burdens and increasing pressure for avoidance and evasion. A similar problem confronts major increases in general taxation levels or government borrowing to top up eroding trust funds or finance PAYG benefits on a continuing basis.
- Undertake major reductions in retirement benefits, cutting dramatically into benefit levels. The sensitivity of fiscal reforms to social welfare is illustrated by the fact that just limiting the growth in pension expenditures to the projected rate of economic growth from 2015 onward would reduce income-replacement rates from 45% to 30% over a period of 15 years, leaving those among the elderly without adequate personal resources in relative poverty.
- Apply significant increases in the retirement age at which individuals are eligible for full PAYG-financed pensions, perhaps to age 70 for those not incapacitated by ill health. This is not a palatable solution in many countries that have been subject to pressure for reduced retirement age, compounded by chronically high unemployment especially in Europe, which has been widely used as a justification for earlier retirements.
- Undertake significant pension reforms to progressively move away from PAYG systems toward defined-contribution and defined-benefit schemes such as those widely used in the US, Chile, Singapore, Malaysia, the UK, the

Netherlands and Denmark. These differ in detail, but all involve the creation of large asset pools that are reasonably actuarially sound.

Given the relatively bleak outlook for the first several of these alternatives, it seems inevitable that increasing reliance will continue to be placed on the last of these options. The fact is that future generations can no longer count on the present value of benefits exceeding the present value of contributions and social charges as the demographics inevitably turn against them in the presence of clear fiscal constraints facing governments. This bodes well for the future growth of the asset management industry emanating from the pension sector.

Whereas there are wide differences among countries in their reliance on PAYG pension systems and in the degree of demographic and financial pressure to build actuarially viable pension asset pools, there are equally wide differences in how those assets have been allocated.

The United States (not including the Social Security Trust Fund) and the United Kingdom have relied quite heavily on domestic equities – one result being that pension beneficiaries were seriously impacted during the financial crisis of 2007–09 and had to adjust their levels of living downward or put off retirement. Pension pools in many of the other European countries and Japan have relied more heavily on fixed-income securities and were not as adversely affected. Equity markets in many emerging markets outperformed the developed markets during this period, shielding pension beneficiaries from the worst consequences of the crisis.

The significant shift from defined-benefit to defined-contribution pension plans in the United States, as an example, has led to strong linkages between pension funds and mutual funds. Numerous mutual funds – notably in the equities sector – are strongly influenced by 401(k) and other pension inflows. At the end of 2012, about two-thirds of mutual fund assets represented retirement accounts of various types in the US. Conversely, 50% of total retirement assets were invested in mutual funds, up from about 1% in 1980 – one reason why US pension savers were so badly affected by the financial crisis of 2007–09 and putting an end to talk of replacing Social Security by defined contribution pension arrangements – at least until Social Security itself becomes financially impaired some time in the mid-century.[2]

In the most competitive parts of the pension sector, access to fund trustees often relies on consultants. Company-sponsored retirement plans often seek advice from pension investment consultants before awarding pension mandates, or include particular mutual funds or fund families in the menu they offer to employees in US-type 401k plans. Consultants are particularly useful in formal reviews of pension fund managers. Fund management companies may, and sometimes do, provide fee- or expense-reimbursement to consultants. In the case of pension funds, the investment manager quotes a single, all-in expense to be charged for services which is sufficient to cover expenses and the manager's profit. Pension fund trustees are able to apply the fund's bargaining power to the process.

To summarise, with respect to the pension component of growth in the asset management industry there is no single 'magic bullet' solution to supporting the retirement of the 'bulge' of baby boomers moving through population structures.

Countries that are taking action are using a multi-pronged approach consisting of:

- Increase working populations. Immigration and increased labour force participation rates help but cannot solve the problem. Some perverse incentive structures impede labour force participation rate improvements.
- Increase productivity. Strong productivity growth is the single most important factor in alleviating the burden of global aging. However, productivity growth is difficult if not impossible to predict, and aging countries cannot rely on it.
- Change the promise. Although it is politically difficult, countries are changing the minimum retirement age, modifying benefit levels and making it more tax advantageous for the elderly to work. As individuals realise that the benefit reductions already enacted and the future reductions will affect their retirement income, they may increase their savings.
- Change the funding. Those countries with healthy funded private pension funds are in a better position to support their elderly population than those that rely on unfunded PAYG systems. Some countries are establishing funded pension trusts or using the proceeds of privatisations to establish trust funds for future generations. Others are encouraging personal plans or increasing funding ceilings on existing personal pension plans.

The consensus seems to be that the latter option provides the best way forward, both for advanced countries as well as for emerging-market countries. And when this is combined with the shift from defined-benefit to defined-contribution approaches, discussed earlier, it should provide ample competitive opportunities for the asset management industry globally. The growth of the defined-benefit and defined-contribution pension plans worldwide forms the basis for the future growth of asset management, as these programs involve the creation of large asset pools.

Within this overall context, pension assets and the adequacy of old age provisioning in the developing countries have, in relative terms, outpaced those in many developed countries. There are several reasons for this.

First, they have relatively young populations and gradual aging, so that they have more time to develop pre-funded pension schemes without some of the friction burdens of countries with much older populations.

Second, they are much less reliant on PAYG pension systems with high and possibly unsustainable promises to pension beneficiaries. Most systems are defined-contribution and therefore pre-funded, although all such systems are prone to investment returns that may not meet expectations – as experienced in the major pension fund markets during the financial crisis of 2007–09. Most developing country pension plans are controlled by the state and offer only limited portfolio discretion for participants, limited reliance on private asset managers, and limited choice of asset classes.

Given that defined-contribution pension systems represent key pools of investible assets in these countries, increased choice and competition among asset managers – as well as increased choice among asset classes – could make a significant contribution to the development of pension schemes and to capital market development – and of course increase the risks associated with old age security provisioning.

1.4 Mutual funds

The mutual fund industry has enjoyed rapid growth in developed countries over many years, although there are wide differences among national financial markets in the pace of development, in the character of the assets under management, and in the nature of mutual fund marketing and distribution.

Mutual funds essentially take the form of collective investment vehicles in which the proceeds from share sales to investors are placed in securities of various types. They are usually 'mutual' in the sense that the investors own all of the assets in the fund, and are responsible for all of its operating costs. The funds are usually organised by a particular fund management company that undertakes the legal registration of the fund, nominates a board of directors for the fund, and arranges for the distribution and sale of fund shares to the public. The fund's board of directors contracts with an investment advisor (usually the same fund management company) to manage the assets and to handle ongoing operational details such as marketing, administration, reporting and compliance.

Legally, mutual funds in the US, for example, take the form of 'trusts' representing the undivided sum of assets held on behalf of the investors by the trustees (directors) of the fund. US mutual fund assets never belong to either the fund (trust) itself or to the management company. Rather, they are owned by the fund investors themselves, who can normally redeem their shares instantly at their net asset value (NAV). US mutual funds were created as successors to the investment trusts of the 1920s, which suffered large-scale asset losses during the stock market crash of 1929.

The principal legislation governing the modern mutual fund industry is the Investment Company Act of 1940, which covers both the qualifications and registration of management companies of mutual funds sold to the public, as well as the disclosure of pertinent information to investors in the form of selling prospectuses and periodic reporting. A mutual fund's investment adviser must comply with terms of the Investment Advisers Act of 1940 and various state laws.

Mutual funds in Europe, on the other hand, usually take the form of either 'co-property' (co-ownership) and 'company' structures. A typical example is France, where there are two types of mutual funds: Sociétés d'Investissement à Capital Variable (SICAVs) and Fonds Communs de Placement (FCPs). SICAVs invest accumulated capital subscribed by investors in shares, bonds, short-term paper, or other financial instruments. They are independent legal entities, governed by boards, and the investors are effectively shareholders who vote at annual shareholder meetings. FCPs consist of a 'common property' of assets. They are not separate, independent legal entities, but rather 'co-ownership entities, i.e., unit trusts which invest in different financial instruments – each investor is merely a co-owner of an undivided mass of assets of which he or she owns a percentage.

The SICAV model has been adopted under the EU's Undertakings for Collective Investments in Transferable Securities (UCITS) legislation, which governs how a fund can be marketed within the European Union and is designed to allow cross-border fund sales to investors of different nationalities. The objective of the original UCITS directive, adopted in 1985, was to allow for mutual funds investing in publicly issued securities to be subject to the same regulation in every EU member country, so funds authorised for distribution in one EU country could be sold to the public in all others without further authorisation, thereby furthering the goal of a single market for financial services in Europe. However in practice many EU member nations have imposed additional regulatory requirements that have impeded free operation with the effect of protecting local asset managers – varied marketing rules in each country created persistent obstacles to cross-border marketing of UCITS. In addition, the limited definition of permitted investments for UCITS weakened the single market initiative for mutual funds. So in the early 1990s proposals were developed to amend the 1985 Directive and more successfully harmonise laws throughout Europe. This led to a draft UCITS II directive, which was abandoned as being too ambitious and was followed by a new proposal (UCITS III) which contained (a) A management directive designed to give fund management companies a 'European passport' to operate throughout the EU, and widened the activities which they are allowed to undertake; (b) The concept of a simplified prospectus, which was intended to provide more accessible and comprehensive information in a simplified format to assist the cross-border marketing of UCITS throughout Europe; and (c) A Product Directive intended to remove barriers to the cross-border marketing of units of collective investment funds by allowing funds to invest in a wider range of financial instruments.

Under this directive, it is possible to establish money funds, derivatives funds, index-tracking funds, and funds of funds as UCITS.

UCITS IV was proposed in 2009 and was intended to remedy some of the remaining market-access barriers to mutual fund distribution in the market. This includes a Management Company Passport which will allow funds authorised in one member country to be managed remotely by management companies established in another country and be authorised by that country's regulatory body. It also focused on removal of administrative barriers for cross-border distribution of UCITS funds by improved among national regulators, the creation of a framework for mergers between UCITS funds and allows the use of 'master-feeder' structures to deal with cultural preference toward domestic funds, and the replacement of the previous simplified prospectus with a short two-page 'key investor information' document.

A new revision of the Directive (UCITS V) in 2012 focused on a clarification of the UCITS depositary duties and liabilities, a review of remuneration practices with the objective to align the interests of UCITS managers on the long-term interests of investors, as well as harmonising and strengthening UCITS sanctioning regimes.

As depicted in Figure 1.2, in the United States just prior to the global financial crisis there were about 8,000 mutual funds available to the public, compared to over 25,000 funds in Europe and 7,500 funds in Asia. US funds held assets of about $9.5 trillion, compared with $5.5 trillion in Europe and $900 billion in Asia. Consequently, the average US mutual fund held about $1.2 billion in assets under management, compared with $162 million in Europe and $108 million in Asia, presumably giving US-based funds a substantial cost and marketing advantage.

The number of US equity mutual funds was almost three times the number shares listed on the New York Stock Exchange. Equity mutual funds held 25% of US stock market capitalisation and 10% of bond market capitalisation.

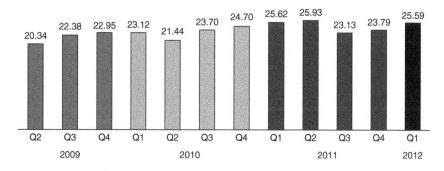

Figure 1.2   Assets of mutual funds worldwide, 2009–2012 trillions of US dollars

Mutual funds accounted for about 21% of US household net financial wealth in the mid-2000s – more than life insurance companies and about equal to the total household deposits in commercial banks.[3]

Competition for asset-gathering by mutual funds can be among the most intense within financial systems, marked by advertising and extensive media coverage – they are in effect mass-market investment vehicles involving 'branding' and public performance ratings by independent rating agencies. Mutual fund management companies have aggressively added banking-type services such as checking and cash management accounts, credit cards and overdraft lines.

Despite scale economies associated with the extraordinary growth in the size of mutual funds, costs investors have increased over the years. Mutual fund distribution efforts have targeted individual investors to attract them away from traditional banking and savings institutions – investors who are not particularly sophisticated about the fees, costs, performance metrics and expense reimbursement on the part of the fund management companies.

In Europe, mutual fund distribution through bank branches dominates in countries such as Germany (80%), France (70%) and Spain (61%), with UK distribution concentrated among independent advisers and Italian distribution roughly split between bank branches and independent sales forces. The dominance of universal banks, savings banks and cooperative banks as financial intermediaries in most of the continental European countries explains the high concentration of mutual fund distribution via branch networks.

In contrast, 90% of US mutual fund distribution has been concentrated in financial intermediaries – notably on full-service broker-dealers who maintain large retail sales forces capable of penetrating the household sector and which are compensated mainly on the basis of commissions earned and assets under management – as well as discount brokers who have compensated for reduced sales effort and limited investment advice by charging lower fees and expenses. Insurance agents account for 15% of US mutual fund distribution, focusing on mutual funds with an insurance wrapper such as fixed and variable annuities and guaranteed investment contracts (GICs). Bank branches have played a growing role in the US after deregulation in 1999, although they only account for about a 15% distribution share, while direct sales by independent fund managers have captured about 10% of sales.

As a result of the financial crisis of 2007–09, the acquisition of Merrill Lynch by Bank of America and Bear Stearns by JP Morgan Chase, the bankruptcy of Lehman Brothers and the conversion of the remaining investment banks (Goldman Sachs and Morgan Stanley) into bank holding companies has correspondingly altered the mutual fund landscape toward greater concentration.

Mutual fund managers offer a broad array of money market, fixed-income and equity funds, and invest heavily in technology platforms that enable efficient administration, custody and reporting functions in a customer-friendly manner. Some fund management companies manage dozens of mutual funds. The basis of competition in mutual fund management comprises five elements – perceived performance, fees for performance, expenses, direct and indirect costs of marketing and distribution, and service quality and technology.

- Investors must select from an array of investment types or styles based on asset classes (stocks, bonds, etc.). Fund managers are expected to remain true to their proclaimed investment objectives and attempt to optimise asset allocation in accordance with modern portfolio management concepts.
- Mutual fund managers incur a variety of operating costs and expenses in running their businesses, notably for personnel and facilities, commissions, and technology. The fund management company retained by the fund board enters into a contract for services in which it charges a fee for managing the assets, and its expenses, in part, are reimbursed. Combined, these fees are charged against the assets of the fund and comprise the fund's 'expense ratio'. Fund investors may also be subject to a sales charge when they invest (a 'front-end load'), or at a later point when they exit (a 'back-end load'), as well as a charge for marketing the fund to its investors. Funds generally subject investors to higher expense ratios when the fund size is smaller, the turnover is higher, or when the relative fund performance is better.
- Service quality in fund management involves ease of investment and redemptions, the quality and transparency of statements, cash management, tax computation and investment advice.
- Mutual fund management companies tend to invest heavily in IT platforms in order to improve service quality and cut costs, investments that must be paid for in the form of fees and expenses reimbursed by the funds.

One of the key issues relating to the mutual fund industry is assessing performance. Do fund managers, after expenses and fees, outperform available index funds or exchange-traded funds that reflect gains and losses of the market as a whole? Issues that need to be taken into account to address this question include the following:

- Time buckets (length, start/end periods) used for performance tracking.
- Index benchmark (e.g., S&P 500 vs. Russell 2000) against which performance is measured.
- Survivorship bias (upward bias in the performance of surviving managed funds as poor performers fail and no longer appear in the data).
- Sharpe ratio (performance adjusted for risk).
- Management fees.
- Front loads, back loads, digressive loads in annual return-equivalents.

- Fees and other charges which regulators permit to be loaded onto fund investors.
- Performance distribution over market cycles.
- Performance distribution relative to sector averages.
- The importance of fund names as reflecting investment styles, and the problem of style-drift.
- Persistence – do firms outperforming in one period continue to outperform in successive periods?

Confidence in mutual funds as transparent, efficient and fair investment vehicles was undermined with the uncovering of major scandals in 2003 and 2004, involving 'late trading' and 'market timing' in the shares of mutual funds with the knowledge and sometimes participation of the fund managers. The disclosures, legal proceedings and settlements led to extensive further investigations of mutual fund practices and governance procedures.

Late trading allows a favoured investor to illegally execute trades at the fund's 4 pm US daily closing net asset value (NAV) sometimes as late as 9 pm the same evening, enabling the investor to 'bet on yesterday's horse race' by profiting from news released domestically after the closing, or released overseas in different time-zones. Ordinary fund investors are obliged to trade at the 4 pm price until it is reset at 4 pm the following day. The practice, in effect, transfers wealth from ordinary shareholders to sophisticated hedge fund investors who had agreed to invest 'sticky assets' (i.e., incorporating high performance fees for the fund manager) in lucrative hedge funds to be sold to sophisticated buyers. For a fund management group to allow late trading is a major regulatory violation and a serious breach of fiduciary duty owed to the group's investors.

Market timing trades in mutual fund shares – a practice not illegal *per se* – involves rapid-fire trading by favoured investors in shares primarily of international mutual funds across time-zones. This practice skims the returns from the mutual fund shareholders, increases mutual fund expenses and requires them to hold large cash balances to meet abrupt withdrawals, costs which have to be borne by all investors, not just the market-timers. Investors permitted to engage in market timing trades by fund managers again promised to park 'sticky' assets with the fund management companies in their own hedge funds, in effect kicking-back some of their questionable market timing gains to the fund management companies, not to the shareholders of the mutual fund. Market timing trades were estimated to have cost long-term US mutual fund investors about $4 billion of dilution per year in the early 2000s.

By July 2005 prosecutors in the US had extracted over $2.8 billion in fines and penalties from some 24 mutual fund management companies in settlements in which those charged admitted no guilt. The funds managed by the investment groups that were named in the scandals suffered considerably more redemptions than firms that were not charged, including the industry's largest fund managers.

Some observers have argued that profit-making mutual fund managers' earnings are a function of the volume of assets under management, and so there is relentless pressure to grow those assets by offering an increasing variety of fund products to investors who benefit from their performance, liquidity and originality. Such pressure can cause fiduciary violations in all but mutually owned fund managers and index funds, and perhaps should be seen as an unwelcome but tolerable friction to be endured in an industry that has benefited millions of people otherwise unable to invest safely in financial markets. In any event, the late trading and market timing scandals were not seen to cause enough damage to seriously impair mutual funds as investment vehicles, but they did raise serious questions among regulators, policy advocates and prosecutors regarding conflicting interests between mutual fund investors and the fund management companies that invest the assets.

- Fund managers want independent directors who comply with the rules but are cooperative, supportive and not difficult to work with. Investors want directors who will robustly execute their fiduciary duties to the mutual fund shareholders.
- Fund managers want maximum fees and expense reimbursements. Investors want their fund directors to negotiate minimum total costs and for those costs to be fully disclosed.
- Fund managers want to ensure that they are reappointed. Investors want boards that act vigorously in their interests in selecting managers capable of top-flight risk-adjusted performance.
- Fund managers want to increase assets under management. Investors want optimum investment returns, after expenses and taxes.
- Fund managers want to promote their funds through brokers and financial advisers who need to be compensated. Investors do not want to pay these fees if they receive no benefits from them.
- Fund managers want to lower unreimbursed costs through soft dollar commissions from broker-dealers. Investors want best-price execution of trades and lowest commissions.
- Fund managers want to favour their own funds by obtaining 'shelf space' in distribution channels, while investors want access through brokers to the best and most appropriate funds for them.
- Fund managers want to be able to organise funds to assist other business interests of the firm, such as investment banking, and promoting investments in particular stocks. Investors want all investment decisions by the managers to be arm's length and objective.

These are some of the generic conflicts of interest with which the mutual fund industry will have to come to terms if it expects to be an enduring part of the financial architecture. Containing exploitation of these conflicts will invariably depend on a combination of market discipline and effective regulation. Failure in either domain will drive assets onto the balance sheets of banks and into alternative investment vehicles.

Mutual fund regulation requires a singular focus on management companies, as well as extensive disclosure of pertinent information. In the US, the National Securities Markets Improvement Act of 1996 makes the Securities and Exchange Commission responsible for overseeing investment advisers with over $25 million under management, with state regulators alone responsible for investment advisers with smaller amounts under management, advisers who had previously been co-regulated together with the SEC. The large investment advisers falling under SEC jurisdiction account for about 95% of US assets under management, although the vast majority of abusive practices and enforcement problems occur among the smaller firms.

A great deal of mutual fund information is in the public domain, which helps market discipline along with the aforementioned high degree of transparency with respect to fund performance and ample media coverage and vigorous competition among funds and fund managers. This means that investors today face a generally fair and efficient market in which to make their asset choices. Overall, the mutual fund business, at least in the more developed markets, is probably a good example of how regulation and competition can come together to serve the retail investor about as well as is possible.

Given the dynamics of the global mutual fund industry, there have been significant numbers of mergers, acquisitions and alliances among fund managers as well as between fund managers and commercial and universal banks, securities broker-dealers, and insurance companies. In general the effect of competition in the industry has been to make it more customer-friendly, technology-sensitive, adaptive – and more concentrated. In the mid-2000s, the US mutual funds industry had a five-firm ratio of 39%, a ten-firm ratio of 51% and a 25 firm ratio of 74% – these ratios were roughly constant for the previous 15 years and increased slightly following the crisis. Factors that seem to argue for greater industry concentration in the future are economies of scale and brand name recognition. Arguments against further concentration include shifts in performance track records and the role of mutual fund supermarkets in distribution, which increase the relative marketing advantage of smaller funds. One factor that may promote continued fragmentation of the mutual fund industry is that size itself can lead to significant performance problems.

Finally, mutual funds have come under pressure from passive funds and exchange-traded funds (ETFs) on the one hand, and hedge funds on the other. Figure 1.3 shows the size and growth of ETFs, which provide very low-cost

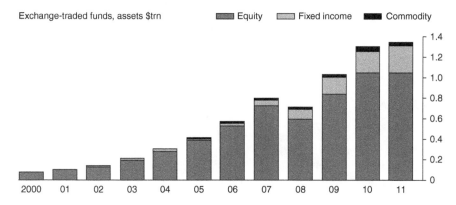

Figure 1.3   ETF assets

exposure to market risk. Given the certainty of mutual fund fees and their performance drag, and the uncertainty of persistent outperformance of individual funds, investors have increasingly moved to passive funds. Additional migration among relatively wealthy investors has been to alternative investment vehicles, notably hedge funds and private equity funds.

1.5   Hedge funds and private equity funds

Hedge funds gained substantial prominence as investment vehicles in the late 1990s and 2000s. At the end of 2007 there were estimated to be about 10,100 active hedge funds in existence worldwide, with assets under management approaching $2 trillion and growing at the time at about 20% per year. Both the number of funds and assets under management declined significantly during the global financial crisis – see Figure 1.4.

Hedge funds are lightly regulated investment vehicles – essentially closed-end investment pools with participations sold to wealthy individuals and institutional investors such as foundations, endowments and pension funds. Hedge funds originally sought to 'hedge' the underlying risk of the market using various strategies designed to identify underpriced assets and overpriced assets, taking both long and short positions in order to remain essentially neutral with respect to overall market risk. Various types of derivatives and leverage were used to neutralise market risk and increase the size of positions in order to benefit from often very small pricing imperfections. Consequently, performance of many hedge fund strategies, particularly relative value strategies, was not dependent on the direction of the bond or equity markets – unlike conventional equities or mutual funds, which are generally 'long only' and fully exposed to market risk.

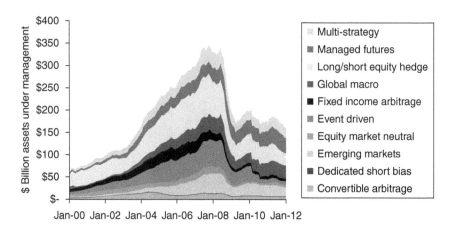

Figure 1.4   Hedge funds
Source: Prof. Stephen Brown (2012) Stern School of Business, New York University.

As the industry developed the classic hedging strategies evolved into a broad array of investment styles, so that hedge funds today are probably best described as 'special-purpose investment vehicles' which may or may not hedge their various exposures. Some strategies which try to be uncorrelated to equity markets are intended to deliver consistent returns with extremely low risk of loss, while others may be as or more volatile than mutual funds. Many, but not all, hedge fund strategies tend to hedge against downturns in the markets being traded. Most are flexible in their investment options and may use short selling, leverage, derivatives such as puts, calls, options and futures. The following are the principal investment styles that appear in the global hedge fund market today:

- Aggressive Growth: Invests in equities expected to experience acceleration in growth of earnings per share.
- Distressed Securities: Buys equity, debt, or trade claims at deep discounts of companies in or facing bankruptcy or reorganisation.
- Emerging Markets: Invests in equity or debt of emerging (less mature) markets which tend to have higher inflation and volatile growth.
- Fund of Funds: Mixes and matches hedge funds and other pooled investment vehicles. This blending of different strategies and asset classes aims to provide a more stable long-term investment return than any of the individual funds.
- Income: Invests with primary focus on yield or current income rather than solely on capital gains. May utilise leverage to buy bonds and sometimes fixed-income derivatives in order to profit from principal appreciation and interest income.

- Macro: Aims to profit from changes in global economies, typically brought about by shifts in government policy which impact interest rates, in turn affecting currency, stock, and bond markets.
- Market Neutral – Arbitrage: Attempts to hedge out most market risk by taking offsetting positions, often in different securities of the same issuer.
- Market Neutral – Securities Hedging: Invests equally in long and short equity portfolios generally in the same sectors of the market.
- Market Timing: Allocates assets among different asset classes depending on the manager's view of the economic or market outlook.
- Opportunistic: Investment theme changes from strategy to strategy as opportunities arise to profit from events such as IPOs.
- Multi Strategy: Investment approach is diversified by employing various strategies simultaneously to realise short- and long-term gains.
- Short Selling: Sells securities short in anticipation of being able to re-buy them at a future date at a lower price due to the manager's assessment of the overvaluation of the securities, or the market, or in anticipation of earnings disappointments often due to accounting irregularities, new competition, change of management, etc.
- Special Situations: Invests in event-driven situations such as mergers, hostile takeovers, reorganisations, or leveraged buy outs.
- Value: Invests in securities perceived to be selling at deep discounts to their intrinsic or potential worth.

Most hedge funds are highly specialised, relying on the specific expertise of the manager or management team. Consequently, hedge fund managers' remuneration is heavily weighted towards performance incentives (20% or more of investment gains), in an effort to attract the best fund management talent. However, hedge fund expense ratios are also high – up to 2% of assets under management – so that hedge fund managers can do very well regardless of performance. Lock-ups usually prevent investors from withdrawing their funds for various periods of time, in order to allow hedge fund managers to execute their strategies. At the same time, since size can be the enemy of hedge fund performance, many successful hedge fund managers limit the amount of capital they will accept.

As Figure 1.4 shows, as a result of the financial crisis of 2007–09, both the number of hedge funds and assets under management declined. It turned out that many hedge funds were not hedged against severe market declines, and the disappearance of liquidity, while others were unable to cope with systemic shocks and 'tail events' in the financial system. So, many hedge funds have had to rebuild their reputations, cut expenses and renegotiate management fees in order to survive. No doubt hedge funds will remain part of the global asset management architecture, but under much more disciplined conditions and greater scrutiny from regulators concerned about lack of transparency and possible systemic effects of a major hedge fund failure at some point in the future.

A second alternative class of investment vehicles comprises private equity funds, which probably originated in the late 18th century, when entrepreneurs in Europe and the US found wealthy individuals to back their projects on an *ad hoc* basis. This informal method of financing became an industry in the late 1970s and early 1980s when a number of private equity firms were founded. Private equity at that point became a recognised asset class.

In contrast to hedge funds, private equity is a broad term that refers to any type of equity investment in an asset in which the equity is not freely tradable on a public stock market. Categories of private equity investment include leveraged buyouts, venture capital, growth capital, angel investing, mezzanine capital and others.

Private equities are equity securities of companies that have not 'gone public' (companies that have not listed their stock on a public exchange), and are generally illiquid and considered a long-term investment. Private equity usually includes forms of venture capital and management buy-out (MBO) financing – i.e., both early-stage (venture) and later-stage (buy-out) investing. In some cases the term 'private equity' is used to refer only to the buy-out and buy-in investment sector. In other cases – for example in Europe but not the US – the term 'venture capital' is used to cover all stages, i.e. synonymous with 'private equity'. In the US 'venture capital' refers only to investments in early-stage and expanding companies.

Private equity investing reached a peak during the technology bubble of the late 1990s and subsequently focused more on investment opportunities where the business had proven potential for realistic growth in an expanding market,

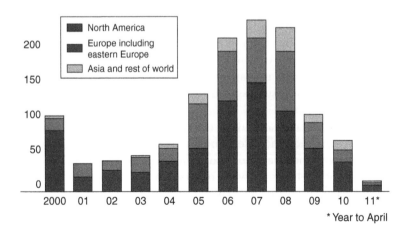

Figure 1.5   Buy-out fund-raising by region

backed by a well-researched and well-documented business plan and an experienced management team – ideally including individuals who had started and run a successful business before.

Private equity firms have been especially active in restructuring situations, where shifts in technologies, international comparative advantage, overcapacity, bankruptcies and government policy changes have made existing businesses economically non-viable. This includes privatisations and strategic divestitures by major corporations and conglomerates, with substantial activity in this respect in countries like Germany, Japan and China. In this activity, private equity firms – which consider their core competence to be in industrial and financial expertise and relatively long investment periods – have had to compete with hedge funds looking for pure financial plays.

Since private equity firms, notably those specialising in leveraged buyouts, were highly dependent on cheap and abundant debt financing, their growth in the 2000s was heavily fuelled by favourable market conditions. This allowed high returns to private equity investors due largely to the addition of leverage to target companies, facilitating early withdrawal of equity commitments but leaving the target companies with heavy debt loads and vulnerable to an economic downturn. When the financial markets abruptly turned during the financial crisis of 2007–09 returns to private equity investors plummeted, pending deals were cancelled, and bankruptcies multiplied among firms taken private in LBOs. In the period since 2010 much tighter credit conditions and a dearth of attractive projects in the sluggish global economy continued to drag on the global private equity industry. Nevertheless, as in the case of hedge funds, private equity will be a long-term feature of the financial landscape.

1.6 Insurance

Alongside pension funds, mutual funds and discretionary alternative asset funds, the fourth major player in asset management worldwide is the insurance industry. This industry manages assets both for its own account (reserves against life and non-life insurance claims) and off the balance sheet in the form of fiduciary assets managed on behalf of retail clients, usually in the form of annuities and other savings and retirement products that incorporate insurance features.

The principal activities of insurance companies consist of non-life insurance, life insurance, and asset management, although the differences between the last two areas have become increasingly blurred. Non-life insurance includes property, casualty, and health-related programs. Reinsurance adds a global activity that provides liability coverage for insurers themselves. Life insurance comprises whole life (life insurance that incorporates a savings or cash-value feature) and term life (pure life insurance) policies, and increasingly savings and pension products that are based on annuities.

The two traditional sources of insurance company income are earnings on policies – known as 'technical profits and losses' – and earnings on invested premiums from policyholders. Technical profits and losses refer to the difference between policy premiums earned and claims or benefits paid. In some countries, insurers are required to invest the majority of their premiums in government bonds, but most countries allow a range of high-quality, conservative assets, together with establishing a 'technical reserve' liability on their balance sheet. The technical reserve reflects the estimated cost of claims and benefit payments that the insurer would be ultimately required to make.

The non-life insurance industry tends to go through substantial underwriting cycles based on excess capital in times of low insured losses and the reverse when claims are high. Normally, substantial capital would be considered a strength, in terms of its role as a buffer against future losses, but in terms of industry performance an oversupply of capital can actually be dangerous. Since capital determines underwriting capacity, surplus capital creates overcapacity in the industry. Excess capacity leads to intensified underwriting activity, triggering price wars, which in turn undermines profitability and makes it difficult for weaker companies to survive.

Growth opportunities in life insurance have been more attractive than non-life due to the strong market growth since the early 1990s in retirement savings and pensions. In industrialised countries, the pensions business benefits from an aging population and threatened cutbacks in social security benefits, discussed earlier. However, life insurance has also been affected by a 'yield pinch', associated with asset allocation to fixed-income securities, mostly government bonds. With these traditional life products, insurers guaranteed their clients a fixed rate of return that was usually set by regulators. However, the spread between the insurer's investment yield and its guarantee to policyholders can be dramatically narrowed in periods of lower interest rates.

From time to time this situation has seriously damaged the profitability of both old and new life insurance business. The life of outstanding liabilities to policyholders often exceeded that of the underlying bond assets, which periodically matured and had to be rolled over at successively lower yields. For new policies, insurers could only invest new premiums at rates that were either close to or below those guaranteed to policyholders. This can be mitigated though profit-sharing agreements with clients and shifts to unit-linked products, where gains and losses are borne largely by policyholders.

Unit-linked products, also known as 'separate asset account' policies, are usually tied to the performance of equity investments. Unlike traditional life products bearing a guaranteed return, the investment risk under a unit-linked product is borne by the policyholder. Under this business model, income is earned from asset management fees rather than from participating in investment returns. The unit-linked product provides an important benefit by requiring lower capital reserves than traditional policies – sometimes as much as 25% of traditional products' capital requirements – since clients assume the risks directly.

Due in part to unit-linked life insurance, the industry basically reinvented itself into an increasingly asset management-based business. Indeed, some of the larger insurers adopted a strategy of asset management as a 'core' business by leveraging their investment expertise. These companies offered separate asset management products to satisfy demand from both retail and institutional clients and to compete with banks that had made inroads into life insurance with annuity-linked products. The insurance sector in 2012 controlled close to $25 trillion in assets worldwide.

Many life insurers traditionally operated as mutuals, in which ownership was vested in policyholders, not shareholders. Without shareholder pressure, mutual insurance companies are often less efficient than their shareholder-owned competitors. The mutual form of ownership also hinders consolidation through mergers and acquisitions, since a mutual is first required to demutualise after obtaining consent from its policyholders to become a stock company in order to use its shares as acquisition currency. By the late 1990s, the trend toward demutualisation was industry-wide.

The insurance industry had become increasingly consolidated both across and within national markets, and this trend is not likely to fade any time soon. Because of lower margins from intense competition, insurers feel increasingly pressured to diversify outside of their home markets to spread volatility risks and gain access to new business. Greater size advantage is perceived to provide economies of scale and tighter control of expenses through improved technology. Cost-cutting seems clearly more advantageous at the national level between domestic rivals than between companies based in different countries, or in financial sectors with few overlapping operations.

1.7   Private banking services

Private banking comprises financial and related services for wealthy individuals and households with more than a given threshold net worth. Terms such as 'core-affluent' and 'mass-affluent' are used to segment the market, focusing on assets under management (AUM). Private banking service providers range from proprietorships and partnerships, independent asset management firms and insurance companies to universal banks and financial conglomerates. Depending on the target market, the array of private banking services tends to be broad, ranging from high volume, standardised products commonly provided in the retail banking market to tailored advice and customised solutions to help resolve complex multi-generational family situations or interlinkages of personal and business wealth. The most successful private banking relationships are built on an intimate knowledge of the wealthy client, relationships built on trust, creative solutions, appropriate products, acceptable investment performance and flawless execution.

The private banking product suite is organised around four core functions – cash management, credit, investments, and trust services. For many wealthy clients, business finance is an important complement to personal finance, and connects private banking to commercial and investment banking. 'Personal services' help as a source of competitive distinction in delivering the private banking product suite. Key private banking functions include the following:

Cash management and fund services. A broad range of deposit and payments services are available to wealthy individuals – checking accounts, cash management accounts, brokerage sweep accounts, savings accounts, CDs, commercial paper, bankers acceptances, Treasury bills, and taxable and tax-exempt money market mutual funds. Most are generic services, available to retail clients as well. But here they are made available to private clients with a 'platinum' level of service – and in some cases with 'institutional' rather than 'retail' commissions and fees. This set of activities essentially comprises treasury services for wealthy clients.

Fiduciary and trust services. This includes wealth planning, trust and estate advisory services, and asset administration. There is usually an element of tactical investment planning (a subset of strategic wealth planning) which integrates both investment management with brokerage services. Liquid assets as well as alternative investments are covered, which may include real estate holdings, limited partnerships investing in start-up businesses or special situations, precious metals, currencies, emerging-market equities and commodities as well as private assets – for example, 'passion investments' like sports franchises and works of art.

Fiduciary services for private clients vary between and within institutions, depending on the type of investor and net worth. Smaller accounts are usually pooled, with many banks offering a variety of in-house and third-party managed funds across a broad range of investments. Larger accounts may be managed either on a discretionary basis or on an active advisory mandate with clients involved in key portfolio decisions.

Banks compete aggressively for both active and passive wealthy clients and tend to be particularly attracted to active investors, given a greater scope for value-added and fee income. That includes individuals in the wealth-building phase of their lives. By helping clients in the early stages of wealth accumulation, a bank may keep them later on. The wealth-deployment part of client lifecycles is attractive as well, with profitable opportunities in charitable activities and intergenerational wealth transfers.

Tax planning is another key private banking function, since changes in tax structures or altered client circumstances may mean that changes are needed in client balance sheets. Tax efficiency can be a key client objective, especially in the management of inheritances and estates.

Transactions and Custody Services. Traditional private client services include money transfers, custody services as well as conventional stockbrokerage services at a high level of quality.

Credit extension and personal lending. Commercial banking tends to be a key revenue source for a private bank. Everyone has credit cards and overdraft lines, and most borrow against their real estate and maintain credit lines to even out cash flows. Custom credit facilities provide private banks with the ability to differentiate themselves, although it comes with credit risk exposure and sometimes unusual collateral requiring specialised lending expertise. Unlike investor clients, credit clients will typically reveal their entire balance sheets to their bankers, and this provides private banks with marketing insight not otherwise accessible.

The need to borrow is particularly prevalent among wealthy entrepreneurs, who tend to be in the wealth-creating phase of their lives and relatively illiquid. They may rely on a private banker to find a way to structure a deal around an existing personal asset base, for example. Private client lending may also involve real estate purchases, temporary (bridge) credits pending a sale of assets, or the use of credit in tax planning, for example.

Business finance. The overlap between the personal and business needs of wealthy clients is of particular interest to some of the larger commercial and investment banking firms that have private banking units. It allows them to penetrate more deeply into the individual's finances and can open the door to attractive corporate banking activities. These include bankers acceptances, letters of credit, revolving lines of credit, and term loans on the commercial banking side, and initial and secondary public offerings, merger and acquisition services, and corporate finance advisory and transactions services on the investment banking side.

Conversely, IPOs often make people rich. That wealth needs to be managed, so a strong investment banking division can provide attractive opportunities for a firm's private bankers. Moreover, wealthy individuals are often interested in private equity participations, hedge funds and other alternative asset classes. Banks that are able to exploit links between the corporate and personal finance may find that familiarity with a wealthy individual's attitudes to risk, currencies, maturity, and liquidity requirements can provide a significant advantage in servicing his or her commercial and investment banking needs.

Personal services. In a business where quality of service is of paramount importance and where the fiduciary nature of the relationship is critical, private bankers provide personal services that are often atypical of mainstream banking. These can include personal introductions to celebrities, admission to exclusive schools for children or grandchildren, introductions to A-list political and social figures, invitations to sports and entertainment events, and many others – all provided with a good deal of style and discretion.

For the right clients, private banks try to supply so-called '360-degree coverage and execution', comprising active customer solicitation and retention based on a high level of intimacy and trust to achieve maximum 'share of wallet'. Seamless delivery starts with wealth planning and includes comprehensive tactical investment planning and asset allocation (passive, discretionary, and active fund management); brokerage (including Internet access options); real estate; art banking (authenticity, pricing, financing); access to IPOs and private equity participations; M&A services where appropriate; research; credit; structured products such as hedge funds and funds of funds; tax advice; estates and trusts; and a supporting array of personal services.

Wealthy clients tend to be quite loyal to their private banks and bankers, based on relatively high switching costs and the complexity of their personal financial holdings and estate structures. Client defections mainly occur as a result of consistently poor investment performance, personal disagreements, or serious administrative snafus, as well as migration of private bankers and their teams to competitors – raising the question of who owns the client. Conversely, wealthy clients are difficult to poach from competitors, so client acquisition depends on distinctive value propositions that can be put forward in a credible way. A new private banking relationship may attract a part of the client's business that can later be expanded, based on good service, investment performance and product integrity.

In larger institutions, client acquisition may also benefit from the ability to identify future wealthy clients early in the asset accumulation process and retaining the relationship later on. Wealthy private clients tend to maintain up to three significant relationships with competitive vendors, with each organisation striving to increase its share of fees. This behavioural pattern rewards clients by exposing them to market innovations and useful ideas, but tends to be generally 'sales' rather than 'client' driven.

Most firms focus on client segmentation based on potential fee income and product requirements, with maximum delivery of proprietary services.

The argument is twofold – first, it helps the institution structure a delivery model that is appropriate for the client opportunity, as well as leveraging multiple in-house capabilities, sharpening the application of specific expertise, helping to capitalise on global capabilities, and improving the firm's operating economics. An alternative approach focuses on the private client as a single continuous 'advisory project', using targeted teams led by a private banking generalist and emphasising best-in-class products, whether in-house or externally sourced, to facilitate client intimacy, maximise objectivity in fulfilling client needs, and broaden the product range – so-called 'open architecture'.

The argument for the second approach is that private clients need to be made aware of best products, regardless of source, on an objective basis (as against favouring in-house products) in the expectation that this will maximise relationship returns over the long term. It presupposes a fluid, capable, demanding, and diverse client base going forward, with much greater transparency in both performance and costs. It also presupposes a shift from product-linked fees (with advice provided virtually free) to advisory fees (with some products and transactions provided virtually free). In short, the idea is to offer private clients what they want, drawn from an array of benchmarked vendors through a highly capable client officer.

Bundling of private banking services makes it difficult for wealthy clients to evaluate the value/cost relationship of each component of the relationship – a lack of transparency that potentially allows the bank to extract higher fees. It is also likely that the client is less price-sensitive with respect to the purchase of bundled services than sourcing each of the products or services separately. While other parts of banking have been subject to a general unbundling as a result of a proliferation of new financial products and techniques, private banking remains an area where bundling seems to retain value, especially in the presence of firm-level cost- and revenue-economies of scope. These advantages may be offset, however, by real or perceived conflicts of interest facing wealthy clients banking with large and complex financial firms.

Figure 1.6 summarises key factors in executing a viable private banking business. High-quality execution should create barriers to client exit and financial promiscuity, thereby retaining assets during lifecycle changes and possibly over multiple generations. High-quality specialties such as art banking and real estate advisory services may help as well. Conversely, substandard service in administrative back-office functions can easily contaminate a private banking relationship.

As noted, private banking fees tend to be opaque, although revealed preference and strategic moves in the financial services industry suggest they can be very attractive, especially in terms of returns on invested capital.

There are basically three sources of private banking earnings. (1) A 'wrap' fee in the form of a percentage of AUM set at an agreed level (e.g., 1%) which covers overall financial and other advisory services provided to a client by the

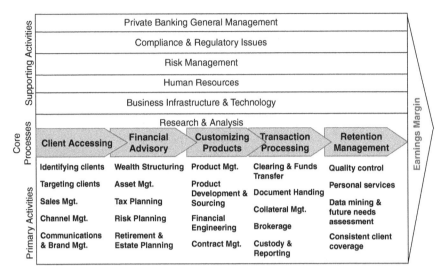

Figure 1.6   Schematic of the private banking value chain

private banking 'team', the relationship coverage generalist and the various financial, legal, tax and other specialists involved, with specific fulfillment often outsourced to the most competent providers in the open architecture model. (2) Fee-for-service pricing whereby individual services are separately priced and charged directly to the client. (3) Product-related fees, spreads and commissions generated in various parts of the firm and attributed to the private banking group, often under service level agreements (SLAs).

In many cases a wrap fee includes discounted brokerage fees and asset management charges, custody and other fees normally charged by the bank. Fees charged by others have to be paid by the client, with both wrap and service fees negotiable above a certain level of AUM. European private banks seem to rely more on fee-for-service pricing. In the US, industry sources suggest that most private banking income is driven by or hidden in products or bundled services, and that a pure advisory fee is rarely assessed.

All three revenue sources may apply in a given relationship with wealthy clients. Private banking 'boutiques' arguably rely more on the first two (most transparent) and financial conglomerates rely more on the third (least transparent) revenue source.

1.8   Structural change and competitive dynamics

Institutional asset management attracts competitors from an extraordinarily broad range of strategic groups. Commercial and universal banks, investment banks, trust companies, insurance companies, private banks, captive and independent pension fund managers, mutual fund companies, financial conglomerates and various types of specialist firms are all active in investment management.

This rich array of contenders, coming at the market from several very different starting points, competitive resources and strategic objectives, is likely to render the market for institutional asset management a highly competitive one even under conditions of large size and rapid growth. Securities firms (broker-dealers, some of which converted to bank holding companies after the global financial crisis) have also penetrated the mutual fund market, and so have insurance companies reacting to stiffer competition for their traditional annuities business. Commercial banks, watching some of their deposit clients drift off into mutual funds, have responded by launching mutual fund families of their own, or marketing those of other fund managers. Such cross-penetration among strategic groups of financial intermediaries, each approaching the business from a different direction, renders asset management markets highly competitive.

Competitors in asset management in many markets include domestic and foreign-based commercial banks and savings institutions, securities firms (full-service investment banks and various kinds of specialists), insurance companies, finance companies (including financial subsidiaries of nonfinancial companies, such as General Electric), investment and financial advisers, private banks, and independent mutual fund management companies. Members of each strategic group compete with each other, as well as with members of other strategic groups. Success or failure depends heavily on portfolio management skills and service quality as well as economies of scale, capital investment and key technologies.

Figure 1.7 shows the ownership structure of the asset management industry in Europe and the United States, and illustrates the substantial diversity of

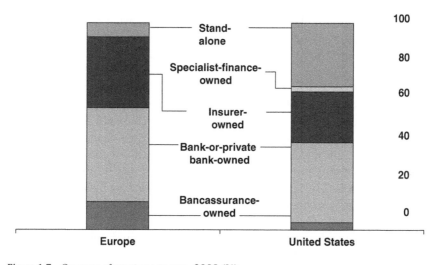

Figure 1.7   Owners of asset managers, 2009 (%)

firms active in the industry. Several ownership structures are solely on the 'buy-side', notably stand-alone and independent asset managers – some of which are either cooperatives or closely-held – and those controlled by insurance companies. The remainder is controlled either by banks or by financial conglomerates active in both banking and insurance. Such asset managers arguably suffer from potential conflicts of interest since their parent organisation may well be active on the capital-raising or 'sell-side' as well, and in any case may be subject to intense performance pressure which could turn out to be detrimental to the investor clients.

1.9   Summary

This chapter has identified the key components of the 'buy-side' of financial markets – the asset management industry in terms of its principal domains – pension funds, mutual funds, alternative asset classes, assets managed by insurance companies, and assets managed for wealthy clients. There are several other special categories not discussed here, including fiduciary assets managed on behalf of foundations, endowments, central banks, sovereign wealth funds and other large asset holders, as well as assets self-managed on behalf of seriously wealthy families – so-called family offices.

We have noted earlier that various kinds of financial firms have emerged to perform asset management functions – commercial banks, savings banks, postal savings institutions, savings cooperatives, credit unions, securities firms (full-service investment banks and various kinds of specialists), insurance companies, finance companies, finance subsidiaries of industrial companies, mutual fund companies, hedge funds financial advisers and various others. Members of each *strategic group* compete with each other, as well as with members of other strategic groups. There are two questions. First, what determines competitive advantage in operating distribution gateways to the end-investor? Second, what determines competitive advantage in the asset management process itself?

One supposition is that distribution of asset management services is both scope-driven and technology-driven. That is, asset management services can be distributed jointly with other types of financial services, and thereby benefit from cost economies of scope as well as demand economies of scope (cross-selling). Commercial banks may be able to cross-sell asset management services with banking products. Insurance companies may be able to cross-sell asset management services with insurance by incorporating insurance features in asset management products – like fixed and variable annuities. Broker-dealers may be able to cross-sell asset management services with brokerage services and use broker networks to distribute funds, benefiting in the process from greater earnings stability and possibly captive buy-side placing power for securities. Nonfinancial corporations may be able to incorporate asset management services into in-house pension plan management.

Such cross-links would tend to give retail-oriented financial services firms like commercial and universal banks, life insurance companies and savings institutions a competitive advantage in distribution. At the same time, more specialised firms may establish cost-effective distribution of asset management services using proprietary remote-marketing techniques like the mails, telephone selling or the Internet, or by 'renting' distribution through the established infrastructures of other financial intermediaries like banks, insurance companies or mutual fund supermarkets. They may also gain access through fund management consultants and financial advisers.

Asset management itself, of course, depends heavily on portfolio management skills as well as economies of scale, capital investment and technologies involved in back-office functions, some of which can be outsourced. Since fiduciary activities must be kept separate from other financial services operations that involve potential conflicts of interest, either through organisational separation or Chinese walls, there is not much to be gained in the way of economies of scope.

Inter-sectoral competition, alongside already vigorous intra-sectoral competition, is what makes asset management one of the most competitive areas of financial intermediation, even in the presence of rapid growth in the size of the market for asset management services. Certainly the dynamics of competition for the growing pools of defined-benefit and defined-contribution pension

Growth in AUM for Selected Asset Managers

Firm	AUM – 2007	AUM – June 2012	% Growth	
BlackRock	$2,366	$3,560	50%	
State Street	1,175	1,908	62%	**5-year Cohort Growth**
Fidelity	1,045	1,576	51%	
BNY Mellon	974	1,300	33%	
Legg Mason	809	632	–22%	42%
JPMorgan	668	1,347	101%	
Vanguard Group	656	1,600	144%	
Northern Trust	628	704	12%	
PIMCO	610	1,820	198%	
Wellington Management	587	720	23%	
Alliance Bernstein	508	406	–20%	

Figure 1.8 AUM size and growth – selected managers, 2007–2012
Source: 2012 SEC Quarterly Filings

Figure 1.9   Aggregating the top 15 asset managers
Source: CEB TowerGroup.

assets in various parts of the world, and its cross-linkage to the mutual fund business, has led to various strategic initiatives among fund managers. These include mergers, acquisitions and strategic alliances among fund managers as well as between fund managers, commercial and universal banks, securities broker-dealers, and insurance companies. Figures 1.8 and 1.9 show the existing state of play among the largest and most rapidly growing asset managers in the world.

Market valuations of asset management companies have traditionally been quite high in comparison with other types of firms in the financial services industry, and this has been reflected in prices paid in mergers and acquisitions (M&A) transactions. Besides gaining access to distribution and fund management expertise, the underlying economics of this deal-flow presumably have to do with the realisation of economies of scale and economies of scope, making possible both cost reductions and cross-selling of multiple types of funds, banking and/or insurance services, investment advice, high-quality research, etc., in a one-stop-shopping interface for investors despite a good deal of evidence that investors are quite happy to shop on their own with low-cost fund managers.

Notes

1. Source: OECD, http://www.oecd.org/daf/financialmarketsinsuranceandpensions/pri
   vatepensions/globalpensionstatistics.htm

2. Source: Investment Company Institute, Washington, DC, 2012.
3. Ibid.

Bibliography

Epstein, Neil, and Bruce R. Brewington, *The Investment Management Industry in the United States* (New York: Putnam, Lovell & Thornton, 1997).

Holzmann, Robert, *Pension Reform, Financial Market Development and Economic Growth: Preliminary Evidence from Chile* (Washington, DC: IMF Working Paper 96/94, August 1996).

Hurley, Mark P., Sharon I. Meers, Ben J. Bornstein and Neil R. Strumingher, *The Coming Evolution of the Investment Management Industry: Opportunities and Strategies* (New York: Goldman Sachs & Co., 1995).

Neave, Edwin, *The Economic Organization of a Financial System* (London: Routledge, 1992).

Patel, Jayendu, Richard J. Zeckhauser and Darryll Hendricks, 'Investment Fund Performance: Evidence from Mutual Funds, Cross-Border Investments, and New Issues', in Ryuzo Sato, Richard Levich and Rama Ramachandran (eds), *Japan, Europe and International Financial Markets: Analytical and Empirical Perspectives* (Cambridge: Cambridge University Press, 1994).

Reid, Brian, and Jean Crumrine, *Retirement Plan Holdings of Mutual Funds, 1996* (Washington, DC: Investment Company Institute, 1997).

Sittampalam, Arjuna, *Coming Wars in Investment Management* (Dublin: Lafferty Publications, 1993).

Smith, Roy C., Ingo Walter and Gayle De Long, *Global Banking, Third Edition* (New York: Oxford University Press, 2012).

Turner, John and Noriyasu Watanabe, *Private Pension Policies in Industrialized Countries* (Kalamazoo: W.E. Upjohn Institute for Employment Research, 1995).

Warther, Vincent A., 'Aggregate Mutual Fund Flows and Security Returns', *Journal of Financial Economics*, 39 (September 1995): 209–235.

2
What Do We Know About the Mutual Fund Industry?

Massimo Massa

2.1   Is there an engine in the car?

The Holy Grail in mutual funds literature has always been the analysis of performance. The literature has searched for answers to whether funds generate performance, whether they persist in doing so and whether it is enough to compensate for the fees that are charged. The answers have been mostly negative. Thus, a new question arises: if performance is not sizable and not persistent, what helps to justify the existence of the industry? The answer we will give in the following analysis is 'marketing'. We will see how marketing strategies help to disguise poor performance and attract clients by focusing on non-performance-related features.

2.1.1   The myth of measurability of performance

We start as the standard analysis of the asset management industry has always done: by focusing on performance. Mutual funds have always been considered self-standing entities engaged in a competition with each other to deliver higher performance ('alpha'). Performance has been defined as the ability to beat a 'benchmark' – i.e. deliver a return higher than the return of a portfolio which proxies for the investment in assets with similar risk as the fund. Various definitions of benchmarks have been provided. The first was the market portfolio – i.e. the return on a portfolio representing the main stocks in the market weighted according to their market capitalization. Next, a more sophisticated analysis has included other benchmarks: book to market and size portfolios. These represent the exposure to other classes of risk: the risk of investing in value stocks and the risk of investing in small stocks. Then, a third 'factor' has been considered: momentum. This proxies for the degree of autocorrelation of the returns of the assets in the relatively short period – momentum within a 6–12-month horizon and reversal beyond that period. Each new factor added to the benchmark was meant to proxy for new and different types of risk exposure of the fund (e.g., Carhart, 1997). However, as the ability to proxy for the degree of risk exposure improved, the quality of the detected performance deteriorated and quickly tipped to the negative side. More sophisticated models based on the observations of the actual stock holdings of the funds have not made the picture of the industry less bleak. The results in general have been dismal: mutual funds do not seem to outperform the market (e.g., Wermers, 2000). If we also include the fees charged by the fund, the picture gets gloomier: not only do funds not seem good at delivering superior performance, but after-fee they seem to underperform considerably.

Some trace of better performance could be found in some funds – extreme tail funds. However, this overperformance is very patchy and haphazard. Moreover, if we look at whether funds that overperform keep on doing it consistently over time, the answer seems to be negative. Mutual fund performance does not seem to persist, except in the case of negative performance. Some evidence of persistence of performance has been uncovered only recently. For example, funds with more incentive-loaded compensation structures for management seem to deliver better performance in a more consistent fashion (Massa and Patgiri, 2009).

Overall, skepticism remains. This is rooted in some of the characteristics of the process that generate performance: constraints on the ability to scale up the investment in profitable investment opportunities, negative size and organizational externalities. The existence of a directly observable link between fund-specific characteristics and performance would induce investors to flock to such funds, abnormally increasing their size and therefore, given these characteristics, limiting the ability of the funds to replicate such performance.

Given these considerations, it is instructive to look at how funds choose to present their performance and the benchmark they use. Funds characterize themselves in terms of investment styles. Performance is evaluated relative to the other competing funds operating in the same style. The idea is that, by using the other funds as a reference, investors can better identify fund managers' skills. For example, fund managers investing in value stocks should be judged relative to other managers investing in value stocks. However, any comparison with funds investing in growth stocks would be misleading, as investors, by choosing a value fund, have already decided to pass on the higher returns of growth stocks to obtain the relatively greater safety of the value ones.

Unfortunately, the use of relative performance evaluation directly affects the behavior of fund managers, making evaluation of performance illusory. Indeed, benchmarks are conveniently selected by the managers themselves and, when imposed by outside assessors – e.g. Morningstar and Lipper – managers enact timing and window-dressing techniques meant to get around them.

Managers react to the setting of investment-style benchmarks in two ways. On the one hand, they may position themselves close to their peer-group benchmark or just replicate their asset class. Alternatively, managers may focus less on their investment style average and take idiosyncratic bets in order to rank first in their investment style. In either case, the mere setting of a benchmark affects managerial behavior in a way that nullifies the role of the benchmark.

A nice case study about this is provided by the Lipper reclassification. In September 1999, Lipper Inc., a fund data vendor and a leader in fund ranking services, adopted a new fund classification methodology. Instead of asking the funds about their self-reported style, Lipper decided to reclassify the funds as a function of the style they actually belonged to by directly observing the fundamental characteristics of the securities held by the funds – e.g. value/core/growth and the small/mid/largecap. This reclassification has changed the way some funds were defined. For example, Fidelity's Magellan, a self-professed 'growth' fund in the old system, was reclassified as a 'large-cap growth' fund. It was joined in that new category by Janus Twenty, which previously was a 'capital appreciation' fund.

Fund managers reacted to the reclassification by increasing their loading on the stocks corresponding to their new Lipper classification and reducing their loading on the remaining stocks. For example, after the Lipper reclassification, 'large-cap growth' fund returns are more sensitive to the return of the stock index that tracks the returns of 'large-cap growth' stocks (i.e., the 'S&P/BARRA 500 Growth' stock index) and less sensitive to the other stocks. At the same time, however, this reclassification has induced funds to change their behavior vis-à-vis the other competing funds. The increased co-movement with their new peers – defined according to the new Lipper classification – has been accompanied by a lower co-movement with the peers defined according to their self-reported styles (Massa and Matos, 2005). The implication is clear. When the benchmark was self-reported, the funds were declaring they belonged to one style but were effectively investing as if they belonged to another style. The assignment of an exogenously imposed holding-based benchmark has forced them to change their behavior to more closely track the new style. However, this also induced them to increase idiosyncratic bets that allow them to be within the constraints of the new style but still diverge in terms of idiosyncratic risk-taking. This has unintended consequences in terms of risk-taking.

Also, the very fact that, after the reclassification, funds load on the size and value/growth factors in a way more similar to that of the corresponding stocks from each S&P/BARRA stock index has made funds less easily distinguishable on the basis of their return characteristics. In a sense, the classification grid has worked somewhat against itself and blurred the real difference between the size and value/growth orientation of funds.

Moreover, even if partially better, the setting of benchmarks based on holdings requires a truthful disclosure of information. However, such disclosure would negatively affect the information collection incentives of the funds by reducing the informational advantage of the good funds. Indeed, fund managers seem to condition their investment decisions on the information contained in the holdings of their peers. 'Copy-cat' funds purchasing the same assets as funds that disclose these asset holdings can earn returns similar to these actively managed funds (Myers et al., 2001). Funds investing in the stocks previously disclosed by other funds seem to display a positive persistence in future returns, while 'word-of-mouth' effects in fund holdings make managers more likely to hold a stock if other managers in the same city are holding that same stock (Hong et al., 2005).

2.1.2   The international dimension provides an answer

Is there some structural reason why funds may be able to overperform? To answer this question we need to look internationally. While most of our knowledge on the mutual fund industry is based on US data, recent evidence on international funds has also opened up new perspectives in determining where the sources of competitive advantage in the industry lie and what limits them. A caveat is required. Unlike traditional US mutual funds, international mutual funds can, in some instances, also invest in derivatives, borrow and go short. This should allow them to deliver higher gross-of-risk performance and higher risk.

International funds provide a way of studying the role of location as a source of comparative advantage. Traditionally, location has been seen as a source of performance, given the identification between proximity and information. If funds located closer to an asset have better information about it, closely-related managers may deliver better performance (Coval and Moskowitz, 1999 and 2001). This would suggest that international funds deliver a lower performance than the domestic ones.

However, location provides an even greater source of advantage: a negative correlation between flows in the fund and investment opportunities. One of the biggest problems for mutual funds is their liquidity management (Edelen, 1999; Massa and Phalippou, 2005).

Mutual funds suffer from liquidity problems. Mutual funds investors are entitled to redeem their shares at the market value of the fund at the end of the trading day. Mutual funds that suffer large outflows need to liquidate at ruinous prices, i.e. hold financial fire sales (Coval and Stafford, 2007). This is accentuated if a fund is forced to sell when the prices of the assets are tumbling, i.e., in the presence of a positive correlation between fund flows and returns of the stocks in which it invests. This implies that the higher the uncertainty of the flows, the more the fund should invest in liquid assets and therefore forefeit performance. That is, funds need to hold cash and liquid assets in order to be ready to meet withdrawals and redemption claims.

However, if a fund is located far away from the assets in which it invests, it may enjoy a lower correlation between its flows and the performance of these assets. For example, a fund that invests in Japanese stocks and is sold mostly to European investors will experience withdrawals from European investors, either if it underperforms or if its investors suffer liquidity shocks. European investors are less exposed to liquidity shocks that are correlated with the Japanese market than Japanese investors. In the ideal case of a negative correlation between its flows and the investment opportunities of the markets in which it invests – i.e., a negative correlation between the Japanese and European markets – the European fund will be able to buy Japanese stocks that are sold by Japanese investment funds when these funds experience outflows and sell at the times they receive inflows. In other words, the fact that the European fund targets European investors allows it to buy when the prices are low and sell when the prices are high.

This allows distantly located funds to outperform the domestic ones. In general, if the flows in the fund are scarcely – or even better, negatively – related to the performance of the assets the fund invests in, the fund will be investing in assets at the time in which their price is lower and selling at the time in which the price has increased. This provides a sort of insurance for the fund analogous to a 'natural hedge'. This hedge allows the fund to take more risk and to invest in assets at the right time, improving both timing and selectivity. Funds with a more negative correlation between flows and investment opportunities are able to exploit this strategic advantage by taking more risky positions and delivering higher performance. Indeed, the natural advantage provided by the negative correlation increases the fund's ability/willingness to take more risk. The funds do exploit their advantage by either loading up more on market risk or increasing their idiosyncratic risk by investing in more risky stocks than the market, or implementing a dynamic trading strategy and 'active management' (Ferreira et al, 2009).

While this can be seen also in the case of domestic funds, the lack of reliable identification of the location of fund flows makes it difficult to establish this point. However, the analysis of international funds allows a direct study of it. And indeed, it is very strongly the case that the correlation between the flows in the markets in which the fund sells its units and the markets in which it invests its assets (client–stock correlation) – i.e., the distance between the location of the investor in the fund and the location of the assets in which the fund invests – is directly and negatively related to performance.

This is a genuine source of performance that can be supported in equilibrium and that can explain the presence of fund performance both at home and internationally. However, this source of competitive advantage requires a segmentation between the financial markets in which the funds source and the financial markets in which the funds invest. The process of market integration, internationalization and direct competition from hedge funds will likely alter and destroy this advantage.

2.1.3   Some structural limits to the industry

If mutual funds are able to successfully use the patterns of flows they are endowed with as a source of strategic advantage and to generate performance, other players in the markets may do even better. These investors are the hedge funds.

The fact that hedge funds source from sophisticated institutional investors located across the globe makes the capital sourcing of the hedge funds more stable than that of the mutual funds. Indeed, a hedge fund specialized in Japanese market investments will not face major outflows when the Japanese market collapses, as its investors are more equally distributed around the world. Also, hedge funds have a series of instruments – lock-up clauses, clauses that defer the liquidation of the stake in the fund as well as its payment – that reduce the volatility of flows. Moreover, hedge funds sell to long-term institutional investors such as endowments, who have naturally fewer short-term liquidity needs. Finally, hedge funds have more freedom: they can borrow, invest in derivatives or sell short. All these elements provide hedge funds with a strong strategic advantage that allows them to better exploit the investment opportunities available in the market. In doing so, hedge funds limit the ability of the mutual funds to maneuver and to take clients away from them. The fact that much of the performance of the hedge funds can be attributed to their ability to exploit the locational stability of their flows confirms it.

Hedge funds can also even directly 'prey on' the mutual funds themselves, exploiting their fire sales. Indeed, hedge funds provide liquidity to the mutual funds when they most need it and reduce their liquidity risk. This risk takes different forms. One form of liquidity risk is simply related to the fact that the funds cannot promptly sell the assets in the market without incurring sizable transaction costs due to the market impact, or buy without moving the market. Alternatively, liquidity risk can be related to the co-movement with the market. Funds that suffer more outflows at the times in which liquidity is more expensive suffer more. Who stands to gain? The hedge funds do. They prey on mutual funds by investing in the assets sold by the mutual funds (Chen et al., 2008). While this activity generates returns for the hedge funds, it also provides liquidity to the market. This has two implications. The first implication is that the positive performance of the hedge funds can be seen as remuneration for the service of liquidity provision. That is, hedge funds act as sellers of put options that are exercised at times of liquidity pressure. This implies that we should expect hedge funds to deliver higher performance in areas/markets in which there are more mutual funds that are willing to pay for their services of liquidity provision. This, however, also implies that hedge funds represent a sort of limit to the expansion of the mutual funds. Indeed, by providing very expensive liquidity and preying on the mutual funds, they reduce the room to maneuver that the mutual funds have in terms of delivering higher performance and subtracting valuable clients. The second implication is more striking: by providing liquidity, hedge funds play a role of stabilization in the market and even more so in markets characterized by structural liquidity needs, i.e., less developed markets, markets with less financially-developed intermediation systems.

2.2   How do you sell a car with no engine?

2.2.1   Funds as differentiated products

The mutual fund industry has developed in a way that stressed product differentiation and market segmentation. One of the most striking features of the mutual fund industry is its market structure. This is based on a very high number of funds differentiated into market styles and belonging to relatively few families. In the US alone, the number of mutual funds is now higher than that of the stocks traded on NYSE, NASDAQ and AMEX added together. Over the period 1990–2000, the number of mutual funds grew from 3,081 to 8,171. At the end of 2008, it reached 16,262 mutual funds, closed-end funds, exchange-traded funds, and unit investment trusts managing $10.3 trillion in assets. The number of families has barely changed (from 361 to 431). At the same time, the degree of segmentation of the industry also grew, reaching roughly 33 different effective styles (Massa, 1998 and 2003).

All these facts can be hardly reconciled with the standard tenets of finance. In fact, the number of existing securities is already offering a sufficient degree of differentiation, and the existence of segmented funds makes it more difficult for the asset managers to generate absolute performance. Indeed, segmentation reduces the scope and range of activity of the manager and forces him to invest only in the assets specific to the fund's style, potentially hampering his market timing skills. For example, a manager with a mandate to invest in Asian stocks may see the arrival of the crisis in Asia, but cannot easily and swiftly reallocate investment to other areas of the world, as his investment mandate prevents him from doing so. This lack of ability to reorient the fund investments cannot be compensated for by superior investment skills of the investors in the funds or by a better ability to hedge investor-specific sources of uncertainty.

Market segmentation and fund proliferation are instead marketing strategies devised to exploit investors' heterogeneity. Funds can be seen as differentiated products sold by multiproduct firms – 'families' – engaged in product differentiation and marketing. Funds are differentiated in terms not only of fund-specific characteristics but also in terms of affiliation with families. For example, in the case of Magellan, the investors are likely to be equally affected by fund performance, fees and risk, as well as by its affiliation with a big family called Fidelity. Affiliation with a family provides a branding image in terms of quality as well as family-specific characteristics.

One typical example of these services is the possibility of moving money in and out of funds belonging to the same family at very low cost ('low switching fees'). This can be seen as an option the family provides to its investors that reduces the effective fees they pay. The higher the number of funds in the family, the greater the value of this option, because the effective fees decrease as a function of the number of funds. An investor who is considering investing for a long period of time and is planning to rebalance his portfolio between equity and bond funds will prefer, all else being equal, to invest in a big family, as this reduces the switching costs he will incur in the future when he rebalances his portfolio. A 'boutique' family, specialized in few equity funds, will have to offer a very significant superior performance in order to attract investors. And indeed, investors with a shorter or more volatile investment horizon tend to go for the funds with lower load fees that are parts of big families (Massa, 2003).

In fact, the existence of high load fees and low switching fees creates a sort of barrier to entry that protects big families and stimulates the existence of big families. The greater the value of the free-switching option, the lower the degree of competition between funds and the greater the segmentation of the industry. A family facing high costs in producing a decent level of performance will focus on other ways of attracting investors, such as playing with the fee structure and/or with the number of funds within the family.

A direct implication is that performance maximization is not necessarily the optimal strategy. In fact, the profit-maximizing mix of fees, performance and number of funds may even induce a level of performance that would otherwise be defined as 'inferior' in a standard performance evaluation analysis.

The fact that families are able to differentiate themselves in terms of non-performance-related characteristics makes performance *negatively* related to the degree of product differentiation in the style the fund is in and fund proliferation *positively* related to it. Styles characterized by a higher degree of product differentiation – i.e. a lower degree of competition – systematically provide lower performance and higher fund proliferations: in other words, each family offers more funds and each one of them is on average lower-performing.

2.2.2   The 'family model'

These few considerations have already suggested that a key role in the mutual fund industry is played by the families. Indeed, the mutual fund industry, unlike the hedge fund industry, has evolved adopting a model based on 'families' in charge of managing many funds. Mutual funds tend to organize themselves in big groups ('families'), while hedge funds tend to belong to much smaller groups if they have any affiliation at all. In the US, almost all the non-tiny mutual funds are affiliated with fund complexes, and the top 50 fund families have steadily concentrated over 80% of all the equity assets under management. Families help in terms of defraying fixed and research costs, by spreading them over many managed funds and by offering the potential for economies of scale and scope.

The family model is rooted in some main characteristics of the demand of mutual fund investors (Guedj and Papastaikoudi, 2004). The first characteristic is the convex flow-performance relationship: high performance attracts large inflows; bad performance does not deter outflows (Sirri and Tufano, 1998; Chevalier and Ellison, 1997 and 1999). A similar effect does not occur in the case of hedge funds: the flow-performance relationship is far more linear. The convex flow-performance relationship, plus the fact that the profits for the family are a function of the asset under management – given the linear ('fulcrum') fee structure – and are not directly linked to performance, increases the incentives for the families to 'play favourites'. Indeed, the expected assets of a family are higher if the family is able to produce one top-performing and one badly performing fund than it is if they have two funds whose performance is average. This creates the incentive to produce well-performing funds, even if it comes at the direct cost of generating badly performing ones (Gaspar et al., 2006).

The second characteristic of mutual fund investors' demand is the positive spillover externalities generated by having 'star funds'. Investors tend to select first a fund family and then the individual fund to invest in. In doing so, they use information about the family to draw inferences about the quality of the specific fund. This means that the good performance of an individual 'star fund' has disproportionately large effects on all the funds of the family. This effect is amplified by the fact that investors tend to see the positive performance of the best-performing funds of the family without being influenced by the underperforming ones. This makes a 'star' performing fund have a positive spillover effect on the inflows of the other funds in the same family, even if there seems to be no negative effect from poorly performing funds ('dogs') (Nanda et al., 2003). Incubation fund strategies are used by the families to amplify this effect (Evans, 2010).

The convex flow-performance relationship, linear fee structure and positive spillover externalities provide the rationale for the existence of families as well-structured marketing devices. Families generate many funds in order to capitalize on the convex flow-performance sensitivity and the positive sensitivity of profits to risk. Offering many funds is just like creating many options. The same way a portfolio of options is worth more than the option on a portfolio, a family offering many funds is worth more than an individual fund with a similar amount of assets under management. Enhanced risk-taking at the fund level and fund proliferation are related ways of implementing this strategy. Market segmentation and fund proliferation are marketing strategies used by families to exploit investors' heterogeneity, showing the positive spillover that having a 'star' fund provides to all the funds belonging to the same family. New mutual funds are added to the overall family menu as a function of economies of scale and scope, the family's prior performance, and the overall level of funds invested.

Families do also coordinate actions across funds in order to enhance the performance of the funds that are the most valuable to the family, even if this comes at the expense of the performance of other member funds. For example, families can charge different levels of fees on each of its member funds, making different funds contribute unequally to the total family profit. Alternatively, families may enhance the performance of funds likely to become stars or which are already the best-performing ones ('cross-subsidization') (Gaspar et al., 2006).

Evidence supports the existence of family cross-subsidization. This takes the form of enhancement of the performance of high-fee funds at the expense of low-fee ones; enhancement of the performance of currently high-performing funds – i.e., funds with high year-to-date performance likely to be well placed in fund rankings – at the expense of low-performing funds; and enhancement of the performance of young funds at the expense of old funds. This behavior is more prevalent at times when the styles of 'low-value' funds are doing relatively well, but is scaled down when the styles of these funds are underperforming, and this is more common in families that are large, manage many funds and are heterogeneous in terms of the size of the funds they offer.

How does this subsidization take place? One way is through cross-trades. The family directly coordinates the trades of its member funds so that the 'low-value' funds trade in the market to buffer the price pressure of orders by the 'high-value' fund, or directly cross-buy and cross-sell orders with the 'high-value' funds without going to the open market ('cross-trading'). Another way is through preferential allocation of the 'best deals' to the favored funds. For example, fund families allocate relatively more underpriced (hotter) IPOs to high-fee and high-past-performance funds.

Mutual funds are not just affiliated with complexes of mutual funds (families), but they often belong to broader financial conglomerates that exercise other activities, such as banking and insurance. In the US alone, approximately 40% of the mutual funds between 1990 and 2004 belonged to such financial conglomerates. This implies that the manager of a fund (e.g. ABN Amro Equity Plus Fund) is effectively working for a broader organization (ABN Amro) whose main interests may not be aligned with those of the fund holders. This phenomenon is magnified many times in the case of international funds for which the affiliation with big banking and insurance groups is more prevalent.

Affiliation with a financial conglomerate provides mutual funds with access to a broader set of resources, better research facilities, lower trans-action costs, and distribution externalities. For example, the manager of a fund affiliated with a group that also has a commercial bank may use the inside information acquired from the lending activity of the affiliated bank to select stocks. Knowledge of private trading forecasts, confidential reports, and presentations at bankers' meetings could be an invaluable resource that might help these funds in identifying the right stocks to invest in. A firm taking out a loan generally agrees to provide the lender with certain infor-mation, sometimes including monthly financial updates. Investors in a public company's stocks or bonds, by contrast, receive only quarterly reports. If a firm is considering whether to refinance debt or secure financing for a merger or acquisition, it could share those intentions with the lenders. Firms with problems threatening to break the terms of a loan must disclose them to the lenders.

While such sharing of information violates the law, and the Securities and Exchange Commission (SEC) has repeatedly tried to enforce it by sanctioning firms doing it, there is now ample evidence that this has not discouraged funds from taking advantage of it. US evidence documents the fact that funds con-dition their investment activity on the lending decisions of their affiliated banks. Mutual funds affiliated to lending banks, on average, increase their holdings in the stocks of borrowing firms around the initiation of the loan deal. This helps to boost fund net-of-risk performance (Massa and Rehman, 2008). This may just be the result of mutual funds being located in close geo-graphical proximity to their affiliated banks as opposed to a deliberate coordi-nated activity at the family level. However, this still makes it more convenient to have families.

What are the implications of the family model for the investors? It does not seem that investors benefit from such strategies in terms of subsequent period returns. However, the family model may help to explain the apparent incon-sistency between the performance results at the fund level and those at the family level. While there is no, or very scarce evidence of fund performance, there seems to be evidence of performance persistence at the family level. One way to reconcile these results is to argue that families purposefully allocate resources across funds in an unequal way.

2.2.3   The fund structure

A common adage in the industry is that 'fund management always involves more than one person and thus team management is primarily about what you tell the outside world.' According to some industry participants, stars are good for marketing, especially with retail investors, but (named) managers are more expensive to pay. The family model requires a coordinated behavior of the fund managers and a well-defined attribution of credit for performance. Therefore, the disclosure of the name of the fund manager becomes critical.

While almost any mutual fund is managed by the coordinated behavior of a team of experts, many funds have nonetheless been consistently marketed as sole-managed funds. That is, mutual fund families have traditionally chosen to identify a specific individual as the manager of each fund. For example, Fidelity's Magellan fund has been closely identified with Peter Lynch.

The choice between named and anonymous management is a strategic decision for the family. By linking the fund and its performance to a named manager, the family shares the credit for the fund performance with the manager. The better the performance, the higher the reputation of the manager is and thus also his bargaining power vis-à-vis the family. This makes the cost of the named manager higher and indirectly increases the fixed cost for the family.

Why would a family do it? For marketing reasons. By naming a manager, the family deliberately chooses the way it channels information to the market and exploits investor psychology. Investors tend to empathize with named managers, being more lenient in the case of negative performance and more bullish in case of positive performance. 'Regret' for having invested in a bad fund is attenuated if the fund manager is known. Nothing of this sort happens for team-managed funds.

This 'empathy' is magnified by the families that play the marketing card. Families buy ads in major newspapers and receive 'soft' media coverage as part of the deal. This coverage generates media mentions that are used to make the market aware of the managers as opposed to the funds themselves. Name-managed funds receive significantly more media mentions than comparable team-managed funds. This higher coverage boosts the fund flows by increasing the sensitivity of the flows to good performance and reducing the sensitivity to bad performance.

Moreover, as a part of a coordinated 'game', cross-family subsidization helps to boost the performance of the name-managed funds at the expense of the team-managed ones. This is due to both the effort to market the fund and the higher bargaining power of the named managers, who can appropriate more family resources. There is evidence of a broad concerted effort of strategic cross-subsidization of name-managed funds. For example, name-managed domestic equity funds receive more favorable allocations of underpriced initial public offerings, and name-managed international equity funds experience less dilution from market timing or late trading (Massa et al., 2010).

A second important aspect of the overall marketing strategy of the family is the choice of the distribution channel. Mutual funds are distributed through many channels and, when brokers are used, through many different brokers. In the US, an average mutual fund is distributed through 32 different independent brokers. This is over and above the direct distribution network directly managed by the family which the fund belongs to as well as the retail network of the branches of the affiliated bank. For example, Fidelity Contrafund is distributed by 34 independent brokers as well as the direct channel run by Fidelity. Unlike other industries, the mutual fund industry is characterized by the lack of exclusivity in the distribution channel.

This glut of brokers does not have cost-reducing goals. Indeed, it does not seem that having more brokers allows the fund to benefit from a lower cost of intermediation obtained by putting the different brokers in competition with one another. Nor does it help to simply increase flows. Indeed, a higher number of brokers, while it helps to attract more flows in the case of a positive performance, drastically increases outflows in the case of negative performance. Therefore, the use of a multiple-broker strategy can only be understood in terms of the overall family strategy.

Given that a good performance is amplified by the multiplicity of brokers, the availability of a multiple-broker channel increases the incentives to take risk and deliver higher performance. Funds with more brokers tend to take more risk, hold more illiquid assets and generate better performance. Also, it induces families to coordinate the multiple-broker strategy with their family 'coordination and cross-subsidization' strategy. The better performance of some 'subsidized' funds is enhanced by a multiple-broker strategy.

Broker multiplicity also allows the fund to approach and target different segments of the population. For example, some brokers are better at reaching Internet users, while other brokers are better at approaching households and so on. Approaching different clienteles of investors increases the disparity of fund investors' views and priors. Given that funds cannot be sold short, dispersion of opinions among investors increases the value of the fund, but only for the more optimistic investors, while the more pessimistic ones sit on the sidelines. Fund management companies are able to increase the dispersion of opinions by choosing to distribute the funds through many different brokers. Each broker caters to an alternative demand (Massa and Yadav, 2010).

Another key element of the family model is related to its internal organizational form. Consider a typical bond mutual fund. It is organized as a multilayer hierarchical ('vertical') structure. At the top is the CEO of the fund, below that the head of fixed income and below that again the portfolio manager. How do families choose between a more vertical and a flatter organizational structure? A more vertical structure lends itself to better risk management by helping reduce managerial moral hazard and lowering the incentives to take (un)necessary risk. However, a more vertical structure, by reducing the discretion of the portfolio manager, also lowers his incentive to collect difficult-to-transfer information ('soft information') – i.e., the information based on direct personal interaction with the managers of the firm in question – and to engage in proximity investment.

Given that performance is positively related to the collection of soft information on the firms located close by, more vertical structures, by reducing proximity investment and collection of information, deliver worse performance. Moreover, by forcing 'codification' of the information passed on to a portfolio manager's superiors and by reducing the direct attribution of the fund performance to the portfolio manager, a vertical structure increases the incentives of the manager to herd with the other fund managers and to hold less concentrated portfolios. Both more herding and a more limited collection of soft information result in more hierarchical funds with less concentrated portfolios.

Therefore the family faces a trade-off between better performance and flatter structures and between better risk/managerial control and more vertical structures. And indeed, more risk-conscious families tend to prefer more vertical structures. Overall, the organizational structure imposed by the family directly affects performance and impacts proximity investment, herding and portfolio concentration (Massa and Zhang, 2009).

2.3 A view to the future

The last decade has witnessed a growing threat to the family model. A main direct threat has come from the gradual disappearance of the main characteristics of the family model. The need to compete with cheap no-load index funds has reduced the ability of the families to impose high load fees. This has made it more difficult to remunerate a multibroker distribution channel. New solutions have involved cross-selling: families have started selling funds to each other. Big families now actually act like big supermarkets offering funds from other families as well.

However, the gradual reduction and/or disappearance of load fees and the rise of the 'fund supermarket approach' have also eliminated one of the main reasons for existence of the families themselves. Investors do not need to choose to invest in a big-family fund to take advantage of the free-switching option. In fact, investors can freely pick and choose the best funds available across the different families. If these funds are then offered on the same platform by a big fund supermarket, the investor 'free-shopping' attitude is reinforced and the barriers to entry that underpinned the family model collapse.

Also, the past decade has witnessed a decline in the number of name-managed funds. The incidence of anonymous management increased from 4% of the total in 1993 to more than 20% in 2004. One of the main reasons to explain this phenomenon is the increased competition for successful fund managers provided by the rising hedge fund industry. The hedge fund boom has multiplied the outside opportunities of successful named mutual fund managers and therefore increased the expected rent-sharing costs, to mutual fund firms, of naming their managers.

Finally, the recent scandals on market timing and late trading, as well as the contemporaneous investigations on insider trading in investment banks, have made it more difficult to keep pursuing cross-subsidization strategies or strategies based on the use of information from the other members of the group the fund is affiliated with.

A second and trickier threat has come from the competition. The family model has come under increasing attack by two alternative competitors: the index funds that provide cheap benchmark replication – i.e., beta strategies – and the hedge funds that provide better performance, i.e., alpha strategies. Greater financial sophistication of the investors and a refocusing of the interest of both hedge funds and mutual funds in big institutional clients such as endowments or pension funds have made it more difficult for families to keep playing the same marketing game.

Mutual funds suffer from legal constraints – inability to borrow, short-sell and use derivatives – as well as structural limitations from the shorter and more unstable investment horizons of its investors. These greatly hamper the ability of mutual funds to directly compete with the hedge funds in the alpha generation process. At the same time, however, the rise of index funds and more recently of exchange-traded funds (ETFs) has cornered the market in a low-cost game that heavy-structure high-fixed cost organizations such as mutual fund families cannot successfully play.

The combined effect of these direct and indirect developments has made it doubtful that the industry will proceed in the same way in the immediate future. There are two main alternative outcomes. The first is a blurring of the line between mutual funds and hedge funds. This may come from the mutual funds being allowed to operate in the same way as the hedge funds or from a new regulation forcing the hedge funds to behave like mutual funds. Allowing the mutual funds to operate like hedge funds involves allowing them to short, invest in derivatives and lever up. It may also involve lifting the restrictions on the classes of assets in which mutual funds can invest and on the way managers can be compensated. The alternative is to force upon the hedge funds the same regulations that now apply to every fund targeting retail investors. In terms of overall efficiency, clearly the former solution is the one that would increase the efficiency of the system.

For example, abolition of the imposition of fulcrum fees and a higher reliance on performance fees would not only increase the ability of the mutual funds to deliver better performance, but would also drastically change the incentives beyond the family model. Indeed, family affiliation would become important in terms of resource sharing – e.g. research – but the incentive to pursue marketing strategies based on fund proliferation would be reduced. The studies showing that more incentives reduce herding and therefore lower the incentive to ride the bubble also suggest that this change could be welfare enhancing, as it would reduce the excesses linked to the existence of a price bubble. However, after the more recent crisis, the second solution – a so-called 'retailization' of the hedge fund industry – is clearly becoming more likely. While less efficient and more demagogic, this solution seems the only one that is politically feasible.

The second scenario does not involve a blurring of the line between mutual funds and hedge funds. In this case, the better ability of the hedge funds to deliver performance – alpha – and of the index funds to deliver replication of risk factors – beta – would in the long run almost make it impossible for the mutual funds to support the competition. The industry answer would be an even greater stress on the family model and on marketing and branding. Mutual funds would offer additional – non-performance-related – features that would allow them to compete on other parameters, e.g., services and convenience. The application of this model to its extreme consequences would involve the transformation of the mutual fund families into providers of sophisticated advice to the retail investors. These investors would find it costly to invest directly in hedge funds, given the investment limits and given their lack of diffused distribution networks.

There are, however, two other factors that will help the industry and slow down its transformation. The first is the relationship with the banks. Outside the US, the dominant model sees a strict connection between commercial banking and mutual funds. This provides a unique distribution network that will 'push' the bank-affiliated funds through the local bank branches. This effectively segments the market, keeping unwanted competition at bay.

The second element is the role of the government. In most countries investors are forced to invest in poorly performing mutual funds simply because they are the only vehicles that can legally be used to defer capital gains. A typical example is France. A French investor willing to defer capital gains taxes can only invest in vehicles that are listed in France or the EU (the so-called *Plan d'Epargne en Actions,* or PEA).

If the investment is above a certain relatively low threshold (about 132,000 euros), the investment can only take the form of 'life insurance contracts', which are effectively a form of investing in the asset management industry with the possibility of deferring capital gains. However, they only allow investment in mutual funds; index funds and hedge funds are effectively ruled out. This segmentation created at the expense of the taxpayer will allow an underperforming industry to survive for a long time, with negative implications in terms of value destruction.

2.4   Policy and normative implications

The family model – and especially fund cross-subsidization or fund support – has relevant ethical and legal implications. Indeed, this model distorts the incentives of fund managers, possibly inducing them to sacrifice the interests of fund investors if the overall family stands to benefit. Even if the likely aggregate effect of cross-fund subsidization is zero, the gains accruing to investors in subsidized funds are still borne by subsidizing fund investors. This practice can represent a breach of fiduciary duty.

At the same time, however, practices such as the use of inside information accruing from separate parts of the same financial conglomerate are not detrimental to mutual fund investors and may actually be highly advantageous to them.

Finally, practices such as using some funds to smoothen the market impact of other funds with no systematic bias in the direction of specific funds may actually increase performance for all the investors in the funds of the family. And indeed, this is one of the arguments used by the mutual fund industry to argue in favor of lifting the restrictions on within-family cross-trades.

It is therefore difficult to pass judgment on the family model per se without properly accounting for both the pros – sizable economies of scales and scope, potentially better research and information, and the cons – cross-subsidization and excess wastage in marketing activities.

However, there is one dimension in which the 'social implications' of mutual fund behavior can be properly assessed: the impact on financial markets. This is rooted in the linkage between fund flows and fund portfolio strategy. The logic is simple. If a US fund holds equity of both Japanese firms and US firms, a shock to the US market may be transmitted to the Japanese market even if no direct shock takes place there. Indeed, the US funds facing redemption calls may sell Japanese stocks in order not to realize a loss by selling US assets whose price has collapsed. This behavior induces a transmission of the crisis that is not mere contagion, as very often no direct link exists between different assets in different countries or between different classes of assets – e.g., corporate bonds and ABS or MBS – except the joint ownership by financial investors.

A typical example on this transmission role of mutual funds is provided by the recent subprime crisis. As the crisis started, mutual funds were holding a lot of 'toxic' assets, i.e., ABS and MBS. In September 2007, their value collapsed and the market froze. The crisis almost immediately spread from the toxic market to the corporate bonds market. Yields on lower-quality bonds jumped, while high-quality bonds did not seem to be affected. Mutual fund investment behavior directly contributed to this transmission.

The drop in value of one class of assets – the toxic ones – induced the mutual funds to sell other assets in order to meet potential redemption claims. In particular, funds realized that selling toxic assets would have meant the realization of sizable capital losses, while selling liquid assets and holding the toxic ones would have allowed postponement of the loss. The ensuing drop in performance would have triggered outflows. They therefore decided to sell more liquid assets first, but not the very most liquid ones. In particular, mutual funds with short-term investor horizons did not sell their most liquid assets – above investment grade bonds – first, as a high probability of large future withdrawals induced them to store away liquidity for future needs (Manconi et al., 2012).

Mutual funds started out by first selling the more liquid assets, but they proceeded first with the assets that were relatively less liquid in order to store the most liquid ones for the future. Thus they sold mostly thinly traded bonds or bonds for which there was a paucity of readily-available counterparties in the market: the low-rated corporate bonds. This induced the crisis to spread from the financial sector – toxic assets – to the corporations, which had a real effect on their ability to raise sub-investment grade bonds. Therefore, the role of mutual funds in directly transmitting the crisis from the sector of toxic assets to the more liquid corporate bond market helps to explain the jump in the spread between low-quality bonds and high-quality bonds.

At the same time, however, and as we argued above, some funds also belong to financial conglomerates containing the banks that participate in the securitized debt markets and perform due diligence on the instruments. Affiliation with a bank provides the institutional investor with inside information acquired from the lending activity of the affiliated bank to select stocks. At the same time, however, affiliation with a conglomerate may constrain the fund manager and reduce his freedom to maneuver. The fund manager may be required to pursue the interests of the group at the expense of those of the investors, for example, by loading up on stocks of firms to which the banking arm of the group is lending in order to support the stock price of these firms.

Recent evidence suggests that, in the case of a crisis, institutional investors are constrained by their affiliation with the bank or actually use the inside information. Some fund-affiliated institutions are used in support of the overall policy of the bank of the group of which they are part, while other funds are helped by the use of inside information. Both behaviors affected the transmission mechanism in the crisis. Indeed, while the first set of considerations induced a short-term international institution to sell Japanese stocks even though the crisis originated in the US, banking affiliation reduced this incentive, slowing transmission of the crisis to the stocks of the firm to which the affiliated bank was lending.

Overall, the role of the investor flows in affecting mutual fund behavior has deep implications in terms of the role of international institutional investors (e.g. mutual funds, insurance companies, hedge funds and pension funds) in propagating financial market instability and on the mediating role of the banking sector. Indeed, turmoil in one class of assets trade in a geographical region propagates to other classes of assets in other regions.

References

Carhart, M.M. (1997) 'On persistence in mutual fund performance', *Journal of Finance*, 52(1): 57–82.

Chen, J., Hanson, S., Hong, H. and Stein, J. (2008) 'Do hedge funds profit from mutual-fund distress?', Working Paper.

Chen, J., Hong, H., Huang, M. and Kubik, J. (2004) 'Does fund size erode performance? Liquidity, organizational diseconomies and active money management', *American Economic Review*, 94: 1276–1302.

Chevalier, J. and Ellison, G. (1997) 'Risk taking by mutual funds as a response to incentives', *Journal of Political Economy*, 105: 1167–1200.

Chevalier, J. and Ellison, G. (1999) 'Career concerns of mutual fund managers', *Quarterly Journal of Economics*, 114: 389–432.

Coval, J.D. and Moskowitz, T.J. (1999) 'Home bias at Home: local equity preference in domestic portfolios', *Journal of Finance*, 54: 2045–2073.

Coval, J.D. and Moskowitz, T.J. (2001) 'The geography of investment: Informed trading and asset prices', *Journal of Political Economy*, 109: 811–841.

Coval, J. and Stafford, E. (2007) 'Asset fire sales (and purchases) in equity markets', *Journal of Financial Economics*, 86: 479–512.

Edelen, R.M. (1999) 'Investor flows and the assessed performance of open-end mutual funds', *Journal of Financial Economics*, 53: 439–466.

Evans, R. (2010) 'Mutual funds incubation', *Journal of Finance*, 65: 1581–1611.

Ferreira, M., Massa, M. and Matos, P. (2009), 'Strategic market coverage and mutual fund performance', Working Paper.

Gaspar, J., Massa, M. and Matos, P. (2006), 'Favoritism in mutual fund families? Evidence on strategic cross-fund subsidization', *Journal of Finance*, 73–104.

Guedj, I. and J. Papastaikoudi, J. (2004) 'Can mutual fund families affect the performance of their funds?', MIT Working Paper.

Hong, H., Kubik, J.D. and Stein, J. (2004) 'Social interaction and stock market participation', *Journal of Finance*, 59(1): 137–163.

Hong, H., Kubik, J.D. and Stein, J.C. (2005) 'Thy neighbour's portfolio: Word-of-mouth effects in the holdings and trades of money managers', *Journal of Finance*, 60(6): 2801–2824.

Manconi, M., Massa, M. and Yasuda, A. (2012) 'The role of institutional investors in propagating the financial crisis of 2007–2008', *Journal of Financial Economics*, 104: 491–518.

Massa, M. (1998) 'Why so many mutual funds? Mutual fund families, market segmentation and financial performance', INSEAD mimeo.

Massa, M. (2003) 'How do family strategies affect fund performance? When performance maximization is not the only game in town', *Journal of Financial Economics*, 67: 249–304.

Massa, M. and Matos, P. (2005) 'Beyond Grid? How style categorization affects mutual fund performance', Working paper.

Massa, M. and Patgiri, R. (2009) 'Incentives and mutual fund performance: Higher performance or just higher risk taking?', *Review of Financial Studies*, 22: 1777–1815.

Massa, M. and Phalippou, L. (2005) 'Mutual funds and the market for liquidity', Working Paper.

Massa, M. and Rehman, Z. (2008) 'Information flows within financial conglomerates: Evidence from the banks-mutual funds relationship', *Journal of Financial Economics*, 89: 288–306.

Massa, M. and Yadav, V. (2010) 'Mutual fund demand and multiple brokers', Working Paper.

Massa, M. and Zhang, L. (2009) 'The effects of organizational structure on asset management', Working Paper.

Massa, M., Reuter, J. and Zitzewitz, E. (2010) 'When should firms share credit with employees? Evidence from anonymously managed mutual funds', *Journal of Financial Economics*, 95: 400–424.

Myers, M., Poterba, J.M., Shackelford, D. and Shoven, J.B. (2001) 'Copycat funds: Information disclosure regulation and the returns to active management in the mutual fund industry', Working Paper.

Nanda, V., Wang, J. and Zheng, L. (2003) 'Family values and the star phenomenon', University of Michigan Working Paper.

Sirri, E. and Tufano, P. (1998) 'Costly search and mutual fund flows', *Journal of Finance*, 53: 1589–1622.

Wermers, R. (2000) 'Mutual fund performance: An empirical decomposition into stock-picking talent, style, transaction costs, and expenses', *Journal of Finance*, 55(4): 1655–1695.

Part II

The Crisis of 2007–2008 and its Aftermath

3
Macroeconomic Perspectives on the Financial Crisis and Its Aftermath

Ole Risager

3.1 Introduction

This chapter deals with the macroeconomic roots and consequences of the financial crisis. The roots of the crisis go back to the preceding period of low interest rates, excessive risk appetite and inadequate regulation. The combination of cheap finance and new financial products, including zero amortization loans, made it possible to buy real estate without any equity capital.[1] New home owners also often entered the market in the anticipation that house prices would continue to rise. The problem with this model became particularly obvious in the US subprime market in late 2006 and early 2007 when house prices began to flatten out and subsequently decline. At that time delinquency rates started to increase to levels not seen in many years and financial institutions began to report their first significant losses. This marked the beginning of the financial crisis. Once the crisis had struck, high leverage was the key to understanding why it became the worst crisis since the Great Depression. Following Lehman's crash on September 15, 2008, financial markets froze and highly leveraged financial institutions, including hedge funds, embarked on massive fire sales which led to plummeting stock markets and a fast contraction in real economic activity. Had policymakers not intervened and undertaken the necessary firefighting the crisis could very well have led the world into the Great Depression II since world industrial production, trade and stock markets were diving faster from April 2008 to early spring 2009 than during 1929–30, see Eichengreen and O'Rourke (2009).[2]

Following the outline of the crisis, we go on to discuss key consequences for G3 countries, including the significant output loss, the high unemployment and the soaring budget deficits and public debt. The last part discusses the Euro crisis and threats to the survival of the EMU in its present form. In this section we also discuss the outlook for the global economy.

The global outlook is bleak reflecting that G3 governments are cutting budget deficits and businesses are reducing capital spending. This also explains why major players including the Euro Area, Japan and the UK are in recession. The outlook is, however, also highly uncertain since it depends crucially on how policymakers manage to address difficult challenges including the fiscal cliff in the US, tensions and imbalances in the Euro Area and the persistent deflationary bias in Japan. If policymakers find sensible policy solutions, the global economy could perform better than anticipated by the majority of forecasters (IMF, 2012a).[3]

At this juncture risks seem, however, weighed to the downside as noted also by the IMF (2012a). Downside risks include the risk that the current G3 strategy of government belt tightening gets us trapped in a persistent high unemployment/low growth scenario. Moreover, there is a risk that this strategy will lead to political turmoil and nationalist movements in some regions of the world (Krugman, 2012). The pre-conditions for massive political turmoil seem evident in Southern Europe. Spain for example is now suffering from 26% general unemployment and a GDP that has been declining since the crisis struck. There is little doubt that the deep crisis in Southern Europe provides a threat to the survival of the Euro in its present form and therefore also a risk to the outlook for the global economy.

From a business point of view the lesson from the financial crisis is once again that it pays to have a strong focus on risk management, and this includes macroeconomic surveillance. Companies that are forward looking and know that the economic cycle is not only a fundamental characteristic of the world we live in but also sometimes a highly brutal 'beast' can take much better advantage of the business cycle than companies that disregard macroeconomic realities.[4]

3.2   Roots of the crisis: low interest rates, excessive risk appetite and the boom-bust global housing cycle

The roots of the financial crisis go back to the long period of low interest rates, excessive risk-taking and high leverage spurred by extensive shadow banking and new financial products. These meant that the financial sector's capital reserves were inadequate when the crisis struck.

In response to the 2001 recession, caused by the bursting of the stock market bubble and the sharp cutback in firms' capital spending, the US Federal Reserve reduced the Fed funds rate to 1%, down from a peak at 5.5% prior to the recession. The Fed's aggressive interest rate policy led a global monetary policy easing trend reflecting that other countries were also hit by the downturn in the US. Moreover, as the world economy operated with very little inflation pressure due to the integration of China and other low cost producers into the global supply chain, central banks could maintain low rates over a long period of time. This also mirrored the dominant view at the time that central banks should only worry about goods and services price inflation and not asset-price inflation, including booming housing prices. It is easier to clean up after a bubble has run its course than to identify and prick a bubble as the Fed Chairman Alan Greenspan put it.[5, 6]

There is little doubt that this long period of cheap global credit is an important explanation of the sharp run-up in house prices we saw in almost all advanced economies with the exception of Japan and Germany; see Figure 3.1 showing the development in the US[7] On top of this, mortgage institutions and banks undertook a number of innovations on a global scale that essentially made it possible to buy real estate with very little down payment, if any at all. The problems with some of the innovations in mortgage financing became particularly obvious in the US subprime market in late 2006 and early 2007. The subprime loans were often made in anticipation that house prices would continue to rise. In many cases subprime mortgage loans were so-called teaser loans with low and even negative repayments at the beginning of the loan.[8] The idea was basically that even though many of the new homeowners could not afford a house, rising house prices would eventually solve that problem. However, when prices flattened out in fall 2006 and later nosedived, the problems with this model escalated and this marked the beginning of the global credit crisis. At that time subprime had become an important source of mortgage financing accounting for more than 20% of annual mortgage financing in the US.

Figure 3.1 US house prices and the personal savings rate
Source: Case-Shiller and BEA.

Declining house prices combined with poor credit assessments eventually triggered a sharp increase in delinquency rates. In the subprime segment, delinquency rates rose to almost 30%, see Risager (2009).[9] Investors who had purchased these mortgage loans, often securitized, that is, sliced and packaged together with other credit instruments, started therefore to report large losses.[10] These investors were US and European banks, insurance companies, pension funds, and even local governments entities reported large losses.[11] As a result of the large losses in the banking sector, credit started to dry up and several top US investment banks, including Merrill Lynch and Bear Stearns, came under severe pressure and were close to collapsing, had they not been taken over by Bank of America and JPMorganChase, respectively.[12]

However, the prime mortgage market also suffered in response to declining house prices and increasing delinquency rates. Fannie Mae and Freddy Mac therefore had to take huge losses on their books. This explains why the world's largest mortgage institutions, endowed with too little equity capital, later had to be rescued by the US Treasury.

It was not only housing-related institutions and investment banks that came under water. AIG, the world's largest insurance company, which had extended its business into derivatives and other complex risk products, was rescued in September 2008 to avoid larger, systemic consequences.

Other sectors were also characterized by strong risk appetite spurred in some cases by the emergence of China and India, which led to new outsourcing opportunities. As a result of this, container shipping, tank and bulk companies invested heavily in new vessels which led to unprecedented increases in capacity. When the crisis struck, freight rates therefore plummeted and the whole industry suffered large losses; this is not yet over as there is still excess capacity in spite of 'slow steaming' and other attempts to reduce excess capacity. This sector of the global supply chain therefore continues to report unsatisfactory investment returns.

At the regional level this cycle witnessed a remarkable building boom in Dubai and other oil-rich countries driven by a high oil price and the desire to diversify these countries into tourism and banking.[13] As a result of this boom, real estate prices skyrocketed but prices fell more than 50% when the crisis struck and are currently far below previous peak levels.

Excessive risk-taking was also evident in corporate finance in general. Many companies used their cash flows to buy back shares of equity capital, which boosted earnings per share and hence made companies look more attractive through conventional price/earnings multiples. Following the outbreak of the crisis, companies started globally to reverse this process by raising new capital to make the balance sheet more robust. In some cases firms also used the funding to pay back banks and other creditors. Similarly, capital funds, often gearing their investments at unprecedented levels prior to the crisis, now also live a quieter life. For these investors the crisis in itself has also made it harder to obtain funding.

Large losses on housing-related assets and other loans led to collapses of some of the world's major financial institutions which in turn meant that the interbank market essentially dried up in the fall of 2008 with interbank rates soaring. The decision of the US authorities not to rescue Lehman Brothers and the subsequent collapse on September 15 was a further shock to the markets. The Lehman collapse led to a sharp decline in confidence globally and to a huge increase in perceived counterparty risks. Moreover, as other countries (including the UK, Germany, France, Australia, Sweden and Denmark) also suffered from their own financial crises, rooted in losses on housing-related credits, we had a full blown international financial crisis, the worst since 1929.

3.3   Macroeconomic consequences of the financial crisis

As a result of a near collapse of financial markets, advanced economies went into the deepest recession since the 1930s. The Great Recession in the advanced economies is illustrated in Figure 3.2, which shows GDP in the US, the Euro

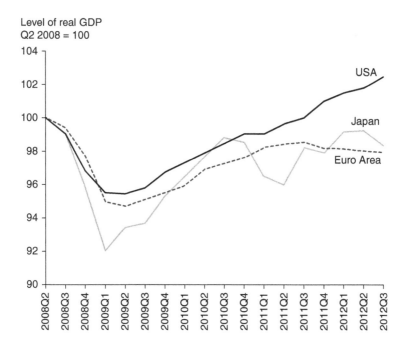

Figure 3.2   Real GDP for the US, Euro Area, and Japan
Source: EuroStat.

Area, and Japan. The downward spiraling of the G3 economies was amplified by financial institutions' desperate need for cash which not only led to a sudden stop in credit flows to businesses and consumers but also to fire sales of stocks and other financial assets. From Lehman's crash on September 15, 2008 to March 9, 2009 when the stock market bottomed out, the S&P 500 fell by 46%. Leading European and Japanese indexes fell by about the same. According to Eichengreen and O'Rourke (2009) stock markets, industrial production and global trade were diving faster from summer 2008 to spring 2009 than during 1929–30.

Plummeting asset prices and the fast contraction in real economic activity had the potential of triggering a 1930-like depression but due to timely and effective policies, the majority of advanced economies escaped this scenario, though not all. Figure 3.3 shows GDP for a subset of the battered PIIGS countries and contrasts their performances to Germany. As shown, the GDP in Portugal, Italy and Spain has continued to decline following the onset of the crisis. In Greece, the worst affected country, GDP is down 20%. Southern Europe was ill-prepared when the crisis struck due to structural problems including significant competitiveness problems reflecting much higher growth in unit labor costs than in Germany and in some cases also weak government finances. In Spain's case, there was also a huge housing bubble that started deflating prior to the onset of the financial crisis.

To avoid a repeat of the 1930s, leading central banks were quick in cutting policy rates and they also injected massive amounts of liquidity into money markets. Following the initial firefighting, central banks continued to ease

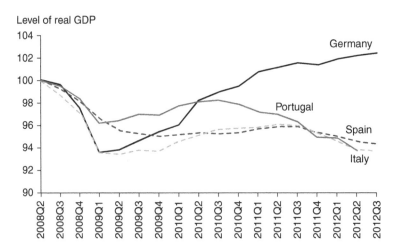

Figure 3.3   Real GDP for Portugal, Spain, Italy, and Germany
Source: EuroStat.

policy rates. By the end of 2008 leading interest rates in G3 countries were cut to emergency levels, where they have stayed since then. Moreover, it has also been announced that leading policy rates will remain ultra-low several years going forward. Governments soon followed course by undertaking large scale stimulus packages, which mitigated the consequences of the sharp contraction in private sector demand, see Buckley (2011). The majority of the advanced economies therefore slowly began to recover in Q2, 2009, but the recovery has been much weaker than what is normally observed after a recession. The advanced economies have therefore suffered large cumulative output losses which are obvious in the case of the Euro Area and Japan. However, the US has also experienced a big loss in real income in spite of Figure 3.2 displaying that the US has fared better than Japan and the Euro Area. To illustrate the large income losses, Figure 3.4 compares the US GDP path under the Great Recession to the case in which the downturn had resembled a typical recession, defined as the average recession since 1970. The area between the estimated GDP path following a normal recession and the actual GDP path captures the extraordinary income loss. From the start of the recession in Q1, 2008 to Q3, 2012 (the last quarter for which we have data), the cumulative extraordinary GDP loss amounts to USD 1,994 billion. Relative to all adult Americans (20 years or older), this loss amounts to USD 9,028 per person. However, since recessions are particularly brutal to low income individuals this number understates the real pain of the Great Recession.[14]

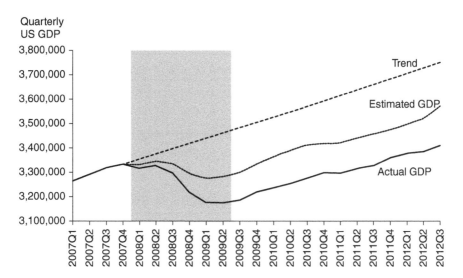

Figure 3.4   US GDP loss under the Great Recession relative to normal recession
Source: NBER and BEA.

As a consequence of the significant decline in GDP in 2008/09 and the weak recovery, government tax revenue has fallen in all economies. Moreover, as stimulus policies (enacted into law in 2008/09) were costly, government deficits were shooting up, see Table 3.1.

The sharp increase in budget deficits meant that public debt started spiraling up, see Table 3.2. The US debt burden is up by 40 percentage points since the crisis struck. Interestingly, Euro Area debt is up by less than 30 percentage points but the debt problem is highly uneven and reflects to a significant extent the PIIGS crisis. Japan's government debt has reached an unprecedented level but is entirely a domestic issue as Japanese government debt is held by domestic citizens unlike PIIGS countries who have also relied on foreign investors.

G3 countries, since 2009, have made significant progress in rolling back fiscal deficits. In spite of this, debt burdens will continue to increase over the coming years due to sizable deficits and weak growth.

As a result of the belt tightening, fiscal policy is now withdrawing spending in G3, which in part explains why global growth forecasts for 2013 have been marked significantly down. The point is that the fiscal multiplier has been underestimated by forecasters and the belt tightening has therefore had a more dampening growth effect than originally estimated, see the IMF (2012a) for a discussion. In addition, businesses are cutting investments in G3 countries probably because of weak aggregate demand and high uncertainty about the future. The risk that the US is falling out of the fiscal cliff in 2013 has been weighing heavily on the business outlook and the Euro crisis is also taking its

Table 3.1   Government deficits in G3, 2007–2012

	2007	2008	2009	2010	2011	2012
United States	–2.7	–6.7	–13.3	–11.2	–10.1	–8.7
Euro Area	–0.7	–2.1	–6.4	–6.2	–4.1	–3.3
Japan	–2.1	–4.1	–10.4	–9.4	–9.8	–10.0

Source: IMF (2012b).

Table 3.2   Government gross debt in percent of GDP in G3, 2007–2012

	2007	2008	2009	2010	2011	2012
United States	67.2	76.1	89.7	98.6	102.9	107.2
Euro Area	66.4	70.2	80.0	85.4	88.0	93.6
Japan	183.0	191.8	210.2	215.3	229.6	236.6

Source: IMF (2012b).

toll on business and investor confidence in this part of the world. And Japan, with a strong reliance on exports of manufactured goods, is negatively affected by the weak demand in Europe and the US.[15] As a result of the headwind, the Euro Area has not been able to escape recession yet and Japan has just entered a new recession, following a strong construction-driven upturn after the earthquake in 2011.

3.4   The outlook for the global economy

At this juncture the outlook for the global economy is therefore highly uncertain. The projections in Table 3.3 assume that the Euro Area and Japan move out of recession in 2013 and that the US manages to address the fiscal cliff in a sensible way, tightening the fiscal stance by around one percentage point of GDP.[16] If Europe fails on stabilizing the EMU and the US does not address the fiscal cliff problem in an appropriate way the outcome could get much worse than projected in Table 3.3, as noted also by the IMF (2012a). However, the outcome could also get better if leading governments globally implement wise policies, which in turn would stabilize expectations and lift the business sentiment. In addition, global private demand could recover more rapidly than envisaged in Table 3.3, led by the ongoing housing sector recovery in the US and by stronger than expected demand in emerging market economies, including in China.

Downside risks include the risk that the belt tightening in G3 could get us trapped in a depression-like situation. With G3 interest rates at historic lows this strategy cannot trigger the crowding-in of private sector investment, but this policy does lead to more subdued cost developments which, along with depreciating G3 currencies, could provide some relief through increased exports to EMs. However, since several EMs including China peg their currencies to the US dollar there is a risk that this approach will only trigger a currency war.

Table 3.3   GDP forecasts

			IMF	JPMorgan
GDP forecasts by the IMF and JPMorgan in percent				
	2011	2012 (est.)	2013	2013
USA	1.8	2.3	2.1	1.8
Eurozone	1.5	−0.4	0.2	0.0
Japan	−0.5	2.0	1.2	0.4
China	9.3	7.6	8.2	8.0

Source: IMF (2012a) and JPMorgan (2012).

At this juncture, the IMF (2012a) is arguing that if growth should get weaker than projected in Table 3.3, governments with room for maneuver should let the automatic stabilizers play out and hence accept higher deficits.

Others argue that it is too early for countries with room for maneuver to cut deficits since we run the risk of pushing all G3 regions into recession, see Krugman (2012). Currently we are close to this situation since it is only the US who is growing. The alternative view calls for stimulus spending in infrastructure, alternative energy and education, and the funding should primarily come from debt issuances taking advantage of the private sector's willingness to provide long-term funding at historic low interest rates. The alternative view argues that there is a high risk that austerity leads to political turmoil and radical nationalist movements like in the 1930s.

3.5   The Euro crisis and the depression in Spain

It is widely agreed that the survival of the Euro in its present form is highly dependent on developments in Italy and Spain. If policies in these countries fail to achieve debt sustainability and maintain support by the general public these countries could end up in default, which would result in massive losses for German and French banks and other creditors in the Euro Area in general and most likely to a breakup of the EMU in its present form.

The risk of this scenario has, however, been reduced significantly over the short-term by ECB President Draghi's statement this summer 'we will do whatever it takes to save the Euro' signaling that the ECB is now willing to act as the lender of last resort, under mild conditions, if Rome is burning. As a result of ECB's new strategy (supported by all ECB members except for Germany), the Italian and Spanish interest rates plummeted. However, in the medium/longer term the task is still the same: Italy and Spain have to bring their debt burdens onto a sustainable path, which is highly challenging for countries in deep recessions and who can only improve competitiveness through wage restraint and 'credibility gains' that kick in through a lower risk premium and hence financing costs.

To illustrate the challenges, consider the case of Spain. The most recent EU estimate of the 2012 government budget deficit is 8% and taking into account that GDP currently is shrinking by about 1.5%, Spain's debt burden will be up by more than 9 percentage points in 2012, that is, up from 80 to close to 90% of GDP. The projected deficit for 2013 is set to decline to 6% due to already implemented tax increases, including a hike in the VAT from 18 to 21%, and cuts in government spending. For 2013, Spain is therefore not planning to introduce new measures.[17] Because Spain is unlikely to achieve growth in 2013, Spain's debt burden is likely to further increase to more than 95% of GDP. Due to the high deficit in 2013, Spain needs substantial funding estimated to be around Euro 125 billion. It is therefore likely that Spain will ask the Troika for a program to facilitate financing via bond purchases by the ECB and the ESM.[18] A program will, however, set targets for further deficit reduction.

For Spain there is therefore more austerity in the pipeline. In a society with 26% unemployment in general and more than 50% youth unemployment this strategy could trigger political turmoil at a scale much higher than what has been seen so far. The point is that Spain's massive unemployment problem is not going to come down over the next couple of years. There is therefore a risk that the majority of the Spaniards will lose their patience with the political establishment and the current austerity strategy and decide to opt for a significant change. In addition, rising nationalist tendencies are evident in certain parts of Spain including Catalonia.[19] The pre-conditions for political turmoil and social unrest are therefore strong.

3.6   Conclusion

Crises are inevitable because long expansion periods almost always create excessive optimism and risk-taking, that is,'animal spirit', to use a phrase of Keynes (1936). This leads to too much debt creation and also often to asset-price inflation. Booming economies with overvalued asset prices and high debt are vulnerable to adverse shocks since this can easily trigger a sharp decline in asset prices. Plummeting asset prices lead banks to hold back on lending to reduce risks and to rebuild balance sheets, which pushes the economy further down the hole.

This boom–bust asset-price driven cycle is not new. What was unique this time was the magnitude of the leverage and risk-taking in the banking sector in the US and Europe. This was facilitated by an extended period of low interest rates, extensive shadow banking and the development of new financial products, which turned out to be much more risky than first perceived. With the benefit of hindsight it is also clear that inadequate regulation is part of the problem. This is particularly obvious in the case of the US subprime market, which should never have been allowed to become so big, as argued also by Shiller (2008). However, inadequate regulation was also part of the problem in a number of other markets.[20]

In spite of a *déjà vu* feeling of past boom–bust asset-price driven cycles it is important to mention that there has been some progress in policymaking. Most importantly the majority of G3 countries avoided Great Depression II thanks to timely and forceful policy interventions led by the US Federal Reserve and the US Treasury. The point is that this could have happened since stock markets, industrial production and trade were diving faster from summer 2008 to early 2009 than during 1929–30, see Eichengreen and O'Rourke (2009).

In spite of the successful crisis management in 2008/09, the cumulative GDP loss in G3 has been enormous even for the US who came out of the crisis faster than the Euro Area and Japan. The large decline in GDP, the weak recovery and the costly stimulus packages explain why all regions have experienced significant increases in government deficits and debt burdens.

G3 countries have, since 2009, made progress in rolling back the magnitude of the fiscal deficits. In spite of this, debt burdens will continue to increase over the coming years due to sizable deficits and weak growth. However, as a result of the belt tightening, fiscal policy is now withdrawing spending in G3, which in part explains why global growth forecasts for 2013 have been marked significantly down. In addition, businesses are cutting investments because of the weak aggregate demand and the high uncertainty about the future. The risk that the US is falling over of the fiscal cliff in 2013 has been weighing heavily on the business outlook and the Euro crisis is also taking its toll on business confidence whereas Japan, with the high reliance on exports, is affected by the bleak situation in Europe and the US. As a result, the Euro Area has not been able to escape recession yet, and Japan has just entered a new recession.

At this juncture the outlook for the global economy is not only bleak but also highly uncertain. The majority of forecasters project that the Euro Area and Japan will move out of recession in 2013 and that the US will manage to address the fiscal cliff in a sensible way tightening the fiscal stance by around one percentage point of GDP. However, there is a risk that the belt tightening in G3 could get us trapped in a depression-like situation. With interest rates at historic lows this type of policy cannot trigger any private sector investment crowding-in but does lead to more subdued cost developments which along with depreciating G3 currencies, driven by aggressive monetary policy, could provide some relief through increased exports to EMs. However, since several EMs including China are pegging their currencies to the US dollar there is a risk that this strategy will only trigger a currency war.[21]

Critics therefore argue that it is too early for G3 to aim at deficit cutting since we run the risk of pushing all regions into recession, see Krugman (2012). The alternative view calls for stimulus spending in countries with room for maneuver taking advantage of the private sector's willingness to provide long-term funding at historic low rates.[22] The alternative view argues that there is a high risk that austerity leads to political turmoil and radical nationalist movements like those of the 1930s. This risk seems particularly high in the battered Euro Area.

It is widely agreed that the survival of the Euro is highly dependent on Italy and Spain. If policies in these countries fail to achieve debt sustainability and maintain support by the general public these countries could end up in default and this would most likely trigger a breakup of the EMU. The risk of this scenario has been reduced significantly over the short-term by ECB President Draghi's statement this summer 'we will do whatever it takes to save the Euro' but Italy and Spain will still have to get their fiscal houses in order and they will also have to become more competitive in order to create jobs. Whether they can do this within the present institutional set-up is not yet clear. The task seems particularly challenging for Spain because of the country's high deficit, projected to be 6% in 2013, and because the country is trapped in a depression with 26% unemployment and shrinking GDP. However, due to the sheer size of the deficit, more austerity is in the pipeline and unemployment is therefore not likely to come down over the next couple of years. There is therefore a high risk that the majority of Spaniards will lose their patience with the austerity strategy and decide to opt for significant political change. In addition, rising nationalist tendencies are evident in certain parts of Spain, including in Catalonia. The pre-conditions for political turmoil and social unrest are therefore strong. It is safe to conclude that we do not know how this 'film' is going to end.[23]

Notes

1. The new financial products also included 'teaser' loans with negative amortization in the beginning.
2. April 2008 marks the peak of world industrial production.
3. We later discuss projections by the IMF and JP Morgan, respectively. Both assume that there will be some fiscal tightening in the US in 2013 but that the US will not fall out of the fiscal cliff, cf. below. The new agreement by Congress extends the income tax cuts for the majority of citizens but cancels the payroll tax cuts, which is broadly in line with expectations. An agreement has not yet been made on public expenditure including expenditure reforms.
4. Risk management including macroeconomic surveillance seems now also to have gained higher priority in the business world; see Risager (2009) for a short text on macroeconomic risk management.
5. This view was not shared by all economists. Roubini (2008), for example, warned against complacency and the risk of a large scale financial crisis and many of the predictions were spot on, see also Rajan (2005).
6. Amongst theoretical economists, Minsky has been writing extensively about financial crises, see e.g., Minsky (1977). His view is basically that investors in good times take on too much debt to finance aggressive asset expansions. Eventually, investors reach a point in time where the cash generated by their assets is insufficient to service the mountains of debt. This leads to fire sales and plummeting asset prices, which in turn lead to even more demand for cash, and therefore to a further decline in asset prices, and so on. When the economy has arrived at this point we are at the so-called Minsky moment, which captures very well the situation in the fall of 2008.
7. Econometric studies of real estate prices point in general to a large role of (nominal) interest rates as houses in many cases are purchased with an eye on current after-tax nominal mortgage costs; see also Buiter (2008).
8. See Shiller (2008) for more information on the subprime market including its growth.
9. Subprime loans were also known as liars' loans because of rosy income statements.
10. These asset-backed securities were rated by rating agencies, but with a flawed risk assessment.

11. Interestingly, the major sources of the financing of the US trade deficit including China, Japan and the OPEC countries were only minor victims of the collapse of the subprime market.
12. These deals were orchestrated by the Federal Reserve.
13. In this cycle, oil peaked at USD 147 per barrel.
14. Suppose we had not had the Great Recession but only a normal recession we would have been able to hand out USD 1,994 billion. Suppose the target was the 20% of adults with the lowest income. In this case their income could have been lifted by around USD 45,000 in total over the period 2008–2012.
15. Moreover, Japan's export to China is down by more than 10% in 2012 due to Chinese citizens' boycott of Japanese goods. In addition, the recent hike in the Japanese consumption tax is also weakening domestic spending. Japan's GDP declined by 3.5% in Q3, 2012. The weak macro performance has led to a change of government in December and the new government led by Mr. Abe has signaled a shift toward a much more expansionary monetary policy to end Japan's deflation.
16. The deal reached by the US Senate on December 31, 2012 seems in line with this but it is too early to draw firm conclusions since the House will also have to vote on the package. Moreover, issues on spending cuts have been postponed by a couple of months.
17. According to Financial Times, 14 November, 2012.
18. As Germany is set for an election in September 2013, a Spanish program request could come after this date. Funding pressures could, however, front load the initiative.
19. Catalonia, representing about 20% of Spain's GDP, is also the country's most indebted region, and has been forced to embark on a tough austerity program. Catalonia has requested a Euro 5bn credit line from Madrid to cover its debt service. In addition, Catalonia is playing hardball and is planning to have a referendum on independence. More than 600,000 have been reported to participate in pro-independence demonstrations in Barcelona. Andalucía, Spain's most populous region is also pressing for central government bailout and Valencia, another big region, has also asked Madrid for assistance.
20. See Dermines's analysis in this book and Soros (2008).
21. It is not only the US who is engaged in aggressive quantitative easing programs. It is likely that Japan will soon adopt a new initiative reflecting the victory of LDP in the December election and the UK is also pursuing this type of policy.
22. 10-year government bond interest rates in leading G3 countries are all significantly below 2%.
23. From a macroeconomic policy point of view this crisis should lead central banks to rethink the way they conduct monetary policy, see also IMF (2009a). Focus on inflation targeting is inadequate, that is, there is a call for putting more weight on preventing asset market bubbles, though this is not easy since bubbles are not always obvious and since political pressure could jeopardize attempts to burst bubbles. Progress in policymaking and the hard lessons learned from this crisis are likely to help in preventing large boom-bust cycles over the coming decade but it would be naive to think that it is a smooth ride from now on.

References

Buckley, A. (2011) *Financial Crisis*, UK: Prentice Hall.
Buiter, W.H. (2008) *Lessons from the North Atlantic financial crisis*, Unpublished Manuscript.

Eichengreen, B. and O'Rourke, K.H. (2009) *A Tale of Two Depressions*, Unpublished Manuscript.

Financial Times (2012) 'No further austerity for Spain', says Rehn. 14 November.

IMF (2009a) *Initial Lessons of the Crisis*, February, Washington DC.

IMF (2009b) *Global Financial Stability Report*, April, Washington DC.

IMF (2009c) *World Economic Outlook*, April, Washington DC.

IMF (2012a) *World Economic Outlook*, October, Washington DC.

IMF (2012b) *Fiscal Monitor*, October, Washington DC.

JPMorgan (2012) *Global Data Watch*, December.

Keynes, J.M. (1936) *The General Theory of Employment, Interest, and Money*, Macmillan, London.

Krugman, P. (2012) 'End this Depression Now', New York: W.W. Norton & Company.

Minsky, H. (1977) 'The Financial Instability Hypothesis', *Nebraska Journal of Economics and Business*.

Rajan, R.G. (2005) 'Has Financial Development Made the World Riskier?', Federal Reserve Bank of Kansas City, 313–369.

Risager, O. (2009) 'Managing Macro Financial Risks', *Journal of Applied IT and Investment Management*, April.

Risager, O. (2009) 'Macroeconomic Perspectives on the Financial Crisis', in S. Thomsen, C. Rose and O. Risager (eds), *Understanding the financial crisis*. SimCorp StrategyLab.

Rogoff, K. and Reinhart, C. (2009) *This Time is Different*. Princeton University Press.

Roubini, N. (2008) 'The Coming Financial Pandemic', Foreign Policy, March/April.

Shiller, R.J. (2008) *The Subprime Solution: How Today's Global Financial Crisis Happened, and What to Do about It*, Princeton, USA: Princeton University Press.

Soros, G. (2008) *The New Paradigm for Financial Markets*, New York, Public Affairs.

4

Some Lessons From CDO Markets on Mathematical Models

David Lando

4.1 Introduction

Bad mathematical models or over reliance on mathematical models is frequently cited as one of the culprits of the financial crisis. While models surely played a role, putting such a responsibility on models is giving too much credit to the influence that models have in the larger political decisions in financial institutions and in political decision making. Decisions to run banks with extreme leverage, to systematically try to loosen up capital constraints using off-balance sheet vehicles, searching-for-yield behavior by institutional and private investors, political desires to increase house ownership even at the cost of increasing riskiness in lending – these decisions are not deeply rooted in models. When they are, one is suspicious that the model selection has often been such that the decisions were justified in the selected models.

This does not mean that we should not again discuss the role that models play in financial decision making. The financial crisis adds new examples to frame this discussion and to help future decision makers understand the trade-offs and the dangers involved in using models. We cannot live without the models. Even if financial products become simpler and more transparent in the future, and if the financial architecture becomes simpler, we still depend critically on models. Below I will try to articulate why this is so.

Kac's (1969) statement remains one of the clearest affirmations of what mathematical modeling is all about:

> Models are for the most part, caricatures of reality, but if they are good, then like good caricatures they portray, perhaps in a distorted manner, some of the features of the real world. The main role of models is not so much to explain and to predict, though ultimately these are the main goals of science, as to polarise thinking and pose sharp questions

To most people working as researchers using mathematical models the statement is in a sense obvious. Models are indeed caricatures. But why only 'for the most part'? In physics there are a few natural laws whose empirical power and predictive ability make the models within which the laws are formulated seem like more than just good caricatures. The law of gravitation which states that the force of attraction between two bodies decreases with the square of the distance between them is an example of a law whose empirical validity has been established to an unbelievable degree of accuracy. We have become used to the power of this law along with Newton's laws of motion which allow us to send space ships to the moon and to predict exactly when a comet can be seen in the sky. Other models in physics have predicted the existence of subatomic particles. It is important to realize that there is simply no parallel to natural laws or models with this kind of extreme predictive ability in economics. In fact, even in physics, mathematical models are often caricatures with varying degrees of accuracy and predictive power. So the idea that mathematical models should be able to predict where prices are going and when a crisis will begin is hopeless – at least for the foreseeable future.

So why then are the models useful? One could give a loose sketch of why models are indispensable within many different areas, such as risk management, derivatives trading, managing and pricing of insurance and pensions, mortgage valuation, but I choose a different approach here. I will use a recurring example of modeling collateralized debt obligations (CDOs) to discuss the various roles models play. In connection with each role, I will briefly assess in what respects the models were useful and in what respects they were insufficient.

I will argue that even the basic model had plenty of room for understanding the risks involved in CDOs from several perspectives. It was possible using existing models to understand how pooling and tranching of large loan portfolios concentrate systematic risk and how this can be used to create bond-like securities with a low probability of default but a lot of systematic risk which therefore ought to result in high promised yields. It was possible to build models that in many cases captured the risks of CDOs on asset backed securities, that were already tranched, i.e. what basically are CDOs on CDOs. It was also possible to see at least some warnings that markets were beginning to price-in extreme events occurring with non-negligible probability.

One can always argue whether the models were calibrated to get the magnitude of the effects right, but one cannot question the models' ability to produce the right warnings to investors and risk managers investing in CDOs. The main shortcoming of the models arose from the scenarios that we are willing to make realistic outcomes of the models.

To help readers who are less familiar with CDOs, I will define the pay-off structure, somewhat idealized, of two such products and I will explain as nontechnically as possible the basic model structure in three types of approaches.

4.2   The modeling of cash flow CDOs and synthetic CDOs – a non-technical introduction

This section provides a non-technical and idealized description of how some main types of CDOs work. Readers familiar with these types of contracts can skip this section.

To understand the basic structure, imagine that a bank has 100 loans each with a principal of €1 million whose default risk the bank wishes to offload. The bank cannot or may not wish to terminate the relationship with the borrowers, but consistent with its 'originate-to-distribute' philosophy, wants to free up regulatory capital to develop business with new clients. The bank creates a company – a special purpose vehicle (SPV) that buys the loans from the bank. The loans form the collateral pool. The funding for this purchase is obtained by selling prioritized claims, so-called 'tranches', to the cash flows from the loans. As a very simple example, one could imagine that the loans are zero-coupon bonds and that they as well as the tranches mature in one year. Also, we may assume that here are three tranches: a senior tranche with a principal of €60 million, a junior tranche with a principal of €30 million and an equity tranche with a principal of €10 million. If the full principal of the loans is repaid, all of the tranches receive their full principal. But if losses occur in the collateral pool, the equity tranche is the first to be hit. All losses up to €10 million in the underlying collateral pool are born by the holders of the equity tranche. If losses exceed €10 million, the payment to holders of junior tranches is reduced by the amount by which the loss exceeds €10 million up until the loss hits more than €40 million, at which point the equity and junior tranches have lost everything and the senior tranche now begins to take losses. In practice, things are more complicated, of course. The underlying loans as well as the tranches pay coupons. Complicated so-called waterfall structures describe the precise way in which coupons from the underlying loans and recovery from losses that occur before maturity are distributed to the tranches. The waterfall structure is meant to ensure that cash is not paid to lower priority tranches unless the more senior tranches are still 'safe'. If necessary, the principal of senior tranches is reduced through prepayment when the value of the collateral pool starts eating its way down to threatening levels.

In the structure described above, the protection sellers are the buyers of the tranches; if there are defaults, they lose money. Furthermore, it is a funded structure in which the buyers of the tranches have to make an upfront payment or 'funding', which finances the purchase of the collateral pool. We could also use the loans merely as reference securities in an 'unfunded' transaction. This would work, again in an idealized structure, as follows: The protection buyer now buys protection on losses within a certain range in the reference pool. To be more concrete, one could imagine buying protection against losses between 3% and 6% in the reference pool. The principal of the contract can be any amount. The price of the protection is a periodic premium but there is no cash paid at the initiation of the contract. The seller of protection then compensates the buyer when losses in the reference pool exceed 3%. The contract terminates at maturity or when losses exceed 6%. At that point the entire principal of the contract has been paid from the protection seller to the protection buyer.

4.2.1 A simple modeling approach

The basic challenge in modeling prices of CDO tranches is to understand how they are affected by the default probabilities of the underlying reference names, by their recovery in default and by the correlation between default events. It is easy to convince oneself intuitively that these quantities all must have an effect. It is impossible without a model to give meaningful estimates of the magnitude of the effects.

We start by setting up what is arguably the simplest model which contains enough structure to provide interesting answers. Several of the more complicated models essentially build on the same structure. For pricing any tranche, we need to know the pay-off T_i to tranche i as a function of the number of defaults D in the pool and the probability that a given number of defaults occur. We are assuming that recovery rates are constant and the same for all loans, so that the pay-off to a tranche is indeed a function just of the number of defaults. The expected pay-off to a tranche is then simply obtained by weighing the pay-off as a function of the number of defaults with the probability that it occurs:

$$ET_i(D) = \sum_{k=0}^{N} T_i(k)P(D = k)$$

By using the appropriate discount rate (and using the market implied default probabilities from – say – CDS data) we have a pricing model. The challenge is modeling the distribution of the number of defaults.

The starting point for the simple model is the binomial distribution. Assume that the default probability of each name in the reference pool is p and that each loan pays back nothing in the event of default, i.e., there is zero recovery on the loans. If the default events of individual loans were independent, then the probability of having k defaults among N reference securities would be given from the binomial distribution:

$$P(D = k) = \sum_{k=0}^{N} \binom{N}{k} p^k (1-p)^{N-k}$$

The independence assumption makes the pure binomial distribution useless in a market that is all about correlation, but it requires a remarkably simple change of the model to fix this. Assume that instead of having a fixed default risk probability p, the default probability is a random variable taking values between 0 and 1. In the simplest possible case, the default probability can take on two different values, p_H and p_L, corresponding to a high and a low default probability state. If the high probability state has probability $f(p_H)$ we have that

$$P(D = k) = f(p_H)\sum_{k=0}^{N}\binom{N}{k}p_{H^k}(1 - p_H)^{N-k}$$
$$+ (1 - f(p_H))\sum_{k=0}^{N}\binom{N}{k}p_L^k(1 - p_L)^{N-k}$$

More generally, if $f(p)$ denotes the density function of the default probability, the probability if having k defaults is now given through the mixed binomial distribution as

$$P(D = k) = \int_0^1\sum_{k=0}^{N}\binom{N}{k}p^k(1 - p)^{N-k}f(p)dp$$

We interpret the model as follows: First, nature chooses an outcome of p. Conditional on this choice firms default independently. One can think of nature as choosing whether we end up in a downturn or an upturn. Firms are sensitive to the state of the cycle in that more default in a downturn, but there is no direct contagion: The actual default of one firm does not change the likelihood of another firm defaulting. Hence the source of correlation is the common dependence on the default probability p. And it is indeed the variation in p that determines to what extent defaults are correlated in this model. If we define X_i to be the indicator of default of firm i, i.e., a variable that is one if the company defaults and zero otherwise, then

$$Corr(X_i X_j) = \frac{var(p)}{\bar{p}(1 - \bar{p})}(i \neq j)$$

where $\bar{p}$ is the expected value of p.

Furthermore, when the number of firms N in the sample is large, the fraction of companies that default in the portfolio is entirely given by the distribution of p, i.e., when N is large

$$P\left(\frac{D_N}{N} \leq x\right) \cong F(x)$$

where F is the distribution function of p. This is what is known as the large homogeneous portfolio approximation. It literally just means that when the portfolio is large the frequency of companies that default is roughly equal to the realized default probability, simply because the law of large numbers applies once p is chosen. This is important for understanding how tranches concentrate systematic risk.

The model above is a useful toy model for understanding how changing the default probability and the correlation affects the pay-offs to different tranches. It assumes too much homogeneity which we will deal with later. A different problem is that the correlation between default indicator events is not easy to relate to more fundamental observables in the economy and it is also not that easy to interpret.

To obtain a clear economic interpretation, we introduce a way of generating the mixture distribution that also makes the model very easy to generalize to more realistic cases and which in essence contains the so-called Gaussian copula approach to modeling portfolio credit risk. We also take this opportunity to extend the model to deal with a time-to-maturity parameter T.

Define the event of the default of an individual issuer as follows: Let M and $\epsilon_i, \dots \epsilon_N$ denote standard normal random variables (i.e. with mean 0 and variance 1) which are independent of each other. Let default of firm i occur if

$$v_i \equiv \rho M \sqrt{1 - \rho^2} \epsilon_i < k_i(T)$$

where $K_i(T)$ is a threshold value chosen such that we obtain a particular probability $p_i(T)$ for firm i defaulting before time T. We have also adapted the model to a case where the default probability can be set to match that of each individual form in the sample, but we can make the model homogeneous by assuming that $K_i(T)$ and thus $p_i(T)$ are the same for all firms. The model is consistent with an interpretation going back to classical models of corporate bond pricing where we view default as happening when the market value of a firm's assets falls below a certain threshold. In these models, the logarithm of the market value of a firm's assets is normally distributed and default happens at a given horizon if firm asset value falls below the face value of debt maturing at the end of the horizon. To account for correlation, the model represents this logarithm as the sum of two shocks: one coming from the 'market', as represented by M and one coming from firm specific developments represented by ε_i. The loading of the firm's assets on the market is captured by the key parameter ρ. This parameter ρ controls the extent to which defaults tend to occur in clusters. If firms have high values of ρ, their asset values fluctuate together going either up or down at the same time. When ρ is small, they do not tend to cluster. The model is a special case of the mixed binomial distribution (see

Lando, chapter 9) where the mixture distribution for ρ is given by the distribution function

$$F(x) = N\left(\frac{1}{\rho}\sqrt{1-\rho^2}\,N^{-1}(x) - N^{-1}\overline{(p(T))}\right)$$

where N denotes the distribution function of a random normal variable, N^{-1} is the inverse of this function, and $\overline{p(T)}$ is the default probability of each firm in the homogeneous case.

The threshold value $K(T)$ is chosen for different time horizons so that the default probability of each firm is consistent with a term structure of estimated default probabilities (obtained from a statistical model) or a term structure of implied default probabilities (obtained from market data such as CDS contracts). The choice depends on whether the purpose is to make statements about the actual distribution of portfolio losses or to price derivatives with the loan portfolio as underlying assets. Even the correlation parameter can be estimated separately for each firm, but when using the model as a communication device this is often chosen to be the same across firms. With our maturity dependent structure, we can define the cumulative loss in a portfolio by time t as

$$L(t) = \sum_{i=1}^{N} 1(\tau_i \leq t)$$

If we assume that the recovery on each loan in the event of default is fixed and constant across firms, then the loss on the portfolio up to time t is a function of $L(t)$.

I will refer to the model with a common correlation parameter, a fixed recovery rate, but firm specific default probabilities, as the Gaussian copula model.

The Gaussian model is essentially a static model in that the dynamic evolution of default probabilities is not part of the model. A more sophisticated model looks at the simultaneous evolution of default probabilities of our collection of firms. For this advanced model, we need to define the notion of a stochastic intensity process. If a company has default intensity $\lambda(t)$ it means that given the firm has survived up to time t and given information $I(t)$ on the state of the economy at time t, the probability of the firm defaulting over the next little instant Δt is given by

$$P(\tau \leq t\Delta t\, \tau > t, I(t)) = \lambda(t)\Delta t$$

Here, τ denotes the default time of the firm. The relationship is actually only exact in the limit, but to give an idea of why intensities are useful, think of the following: if we model a distribution of the default time of a firm, and we imagine we can describe the distribution through a probability density function, then it is possible to represent the distribution of the default time using a so-called hazard function h as follows:

$$P(\tau \le t) = \exp(-\int_0^t h(s)ds)$$

If we model the survival distribution through a stochastic intensity, we have that

$$P(\tau \le t) = E\exp(-\int_0^t \lambda(s)ds)$$

Hence, we can think of the intensity as giving us a 'random set of hazard rates' over which we average to find the default probability. The intensity however, is a dynamic process whose value changes as we continuously learn about the state of the economy and the firm. The hazard function is a static function. For a more rigorous treatment of this framework, see Lando (2004).

For short maturities, the premium on a CDS with the firm as reference credit is roughly equal to the product of the (risk-neutral) intensity and the loss in default. Hence if we are willing to say what the loss in default is, then we can infer default intensities from CDS spreads. Now we can explain the structure of a dynamic intensity model: here, the default intensity of a firm depends on two factors, one factor μ that influences intensities of all firms in the pool that we are modeling and one v^i which is specific to each firm. In short,

$$\lambda^i(t) = \alpha^i\mu(t) + v^i(t)$$

The sensitivity of firm i's intensity to changes in the common factor is given by a parameter α^i. Both the process μ and each of the processes v^i are specified as either diffusion processes or jump-diffusion processes.

Again, we can define the cumulative loss on a portfolio of names as

$$L(t)\sum_{i=1}^N 1(\tau_i \le t)$$

This framework is from Mortensen (2006) who uses a small extension of Duffie and Garleanu (2001). I will refer to this model as the dynamic intensity model.

As shown in Mortensen (2006), when pricing CDO tranches in standardized CDO (based on the so-called CDX or iTraxx indices), the pricing problem can be reduced to knowing the distribution of the cumulative loss at all times, and using a small approximation, one can reduce the problem to looking at the cumulative loss at coupon dates only.

As a final example, consider a so-called 'top-down' model used by Longstaff and Rajan (2008). Let $L(t)$ denote the aggregate loss *including adjustment for recovery* – in the reference pool by time t, i.e., if the collateral pool consists of 100 loans of €1 million in size, 10 loans have defaulted by time t and the loss rate has been 0.6 on all loans, then the value of L(t) is €6 million. Longstaff and Rajan (2008) assume that losses of different (but fixed) sizes hit the pool with varying intensities. Formally stated the model assumes the following behavior of the loss on the reference pool in a standardized CDO:

$$L(t) = 1 - \exp(-\gamma_1 N_{1t}) \exp(-\gamma_2 N_{2t})(-\gamma_3 N_{3t})$$

Here, N_{it} is a Poisson-type jump-process which counts the number of events of type I that has hit the pool by time t. When γ_i is small, it roughly represents the fraction of the remaining part of the pool that is lost when an event of type I hits the pool. Each of the Poisson-type counting processes N_i has a stochastic intensity similar to the setup in the dynamic intensity model. But whereas intensities were used in the dynamic intensity model to represent the specific default intensity of each firm, intensities are now used to model sizes of losses to the aggregate pool. Since some of the losses in their model can be larger than the worst possible loss of one firm, we must interpret these events as simultaneous defaults of many firms in the collateral pool. Determining the number and the sizes of the different loss severities that give the best fit is a delicate problem. Longstaff and Rajan find that the assumptions that best fit a specific time interval of data on the CDX index, correspond to assuming three types of losses occurring with certain probabilities, under the probabilities used for pricing contracts, the so-called risk neutral probabilities: 40 bp loss on average every year, 6% loss on average every 40 years, and a 34.6% loss every 800 years. Note that in this kind of model there is no modeling of the underlying names.

The three models above will be our benchmarks for the following discussion of models.

4.2.2   Models as communication devices

One of the most important functions of models in the market place is their role as communication devices. Prices of similar instruments that differ in some simple dimension, such as maturity, are not easy to compare, and we therefore benefit from transforming prices into a common scale. We are used to comparing bonds in terms of their yields, since the yield is an easier quantity to compare than prices of bonds with different maturities and different coupons. For mortgage bonds, the notion of option adjusted spread is a model-dependent way of representing that part of a mortgage bond's excess yield over a treasury yield, which remains even when we correct for the options embedded in the callable mortgage bond. Transformations such as these are not unique to fixed-income markets. They are an integral part of derivatives markets as well.

A prominent example of such a model-based transformation device is the notion of implied volatility in options markets. In the Black-Scholes option pricing formula, the only input to the pricing formula that is not either directly observable or stipulated in the contract is the volatility of returns of the underlying security. Implied volatility is simply the value of the volatility one should plug into the Black-Scholes formula so that the model price matches the observed option price in the market. If the Black-Scholes model were a physical law, options with different strike prices and different maturities trading on the same underlying asset, would have the same implied volatility. The fact that the implied volatility is not constant across strikes or maturities is proof that the Black-Scholes model does not hold. Modelers, and traders know this. Yet the implied volatility still reveals how options of different strikes are priced compared to a Black-Scholes model and therefore relative to each other. The fact that there are 'smiles' in implied volatility curves, i.e., implied volatility for deep out-of-the-money puts is higher than for at-the-money puts, is a sign that investors in some sense are paying 'more' for these options, which in essence serve as insurance against steep losses.

When the market for CDOs began to grow, the search for a good pricing model was intense both in practitioner communities and among academics. A key success parameter was the ability of the model to serve as a communication device, and the Gaussian copula model delivered this possibility by having the common correlation parameter summarize the price of a tranche in a CDO once the default probabilities of the individual names are agreed upon. Unsurprisingly, just as implied volatility is not the same for different options even when the underlying security is the same, different correlations were needed to match different tranches in the same CDO. This is again proof that the model is wrong. But perhaps, just as with Black-Scholes, this does not matter. The transformation might still be useful. Unfortunately, it was evident early on that, in addition to having problems fitting real data, the model had some conceptual difficulties which showed that it would not have quite the same virtues as implied volatility.

First of all, for mezzanine tranches, the implied correlation is in general not unique. This is a consequence of the 'call spread' nature of the pay-offs to these tranches – that they are in essence a difference of two options whose prices are both increasing in correlation. Secondly, it quickly became clear that there were days when contracts traded, where the price of the tranches could not be inverted into an implied correlation. The observed prices were simply out of range of the pricing model

The non-uniqueness problem was addressed through a modification known as base correlations, explained for example in Willemann (2005), which essentially convert the inversion problem into looking at equity tranches only. But even this technique did not resolve the issue of non-existence. Also for base correlations, there were days when the measure could not be inverted from prices. This did not prevent the market from relying extensively on these measures for communication, and in that sense the model was successful. None of the other models had a chance of becoming the communication equivalent of the Black-Scholes model.

The intensity model has a very large number of parameters to estimate. We essentially model the dynamic evolution of each firm's CDS premium and how it is correlated with other firms' CDS premia. There can be both a diffusion part and a jump part. In the jump part we need to specify how often jumps occur, how large they are once they have occurred and to what extent they influence all firms simultaneously. These choices are critical for how strongly the default events of firms are correlated. There is no dynamic intensity model which is so simple to parameterize, that it can serve as a communication device along the lines of the Black-Scholes model or the Gaussian copula model. The top-down model is closer in its simplicity, but the key parameters that determine how many firms default simultaneously, and how often, are not robustly determined.

4.2.3 Interpolation and hedging

Another success of implied volatility is that it often performs well when computing an interpolated price based on using an interpolation of the implied volatilities. Even if base correlations extended the range of prices that could be reached by the model parameters, they did have problems with interpolation. As Willemann (2005) showed, when using base correlation as an interpolation device to price non-standard tranches, i.e. custom-made tranches for which there were no market quotes, it might sometimes produce negative prices of contracts whose cash flows were always non-negative.

There were other problems that made hedging problematic: Following Willemann (2005), if we assume we know the true default dynamics of underling firms in a fully specified model similar to the dynamic intensity model, what will happen to base correlations when we increase the tree correlation in the model? If the base correlation measure were indeed representing only correlation, it should increase as well. It does not necessarily do this. That is, we cannot know if an increase in base correlation is because of increasing correlation in the underlying names. Also, the model is essentially a static model which is used to try to calibrate data on a given day. In contrast, the parameters of the dynamic intensity model are determined not only from a static 'calibration' requirement, i.e., a requirement that the prices one computes on the various tranches fit at a specific point in time, but also on the time series behavior of the intensities. This means that the model is rich enough to answer all questions of hedging, risk premia, pricing of so-called 'bespoke' tranches, i.e., tranches that are not standard. This makes the model class well suited for understanding which drivers have the most important effects.

The top-down model is difficult to use for hedging, since it does not distinguish between whether a high default risk name or a low default risk name leaves the pool. It is also almost impossible to apply for interpolation when looking at bespoke tranches since it does not address the underlying firms' behavior and therefore makes it very hard to handle different loan portfolios with overlapping names.

The problems that followed from using the Gaussian copula model for hedging purposes had already become evident during the 'correlation' crisis, which hit in May 2005. The crisis is described in several papers, including Kherraz (2006). Without going into too much detail, the crisis was triggered by downgrades of Ford and GM by the major rating agencies, and this caused the large unwinding of positions which combined selling of equity protection with buying mezzanine protection, a trading strategy which suffered large losses as the unwinding of the positions caused losses both on the short and the long side of the deal. The failed hedge was a demonstration that the hedging based on the model surely did not work. There was no room in the model to allow for changes in the correlation. Attempts to fix the model, by altering the distributional assumptions gave better fits at any instant in time at the cost of using more parameters but it did not improve our understanding of the dynamic behavior of the markets and of the risk management implications.

The correlation crisis was a warning that the models for CDOs applied by the financial industry were insufficient. This was true even for standardized products that are easier to work with since there are good alternative sources of information on the underlying names from equity markets, corporate bond markets and CDS markets. The apparent lack of a good model did not prevent heavy trading in the products. One could have hoped that the intellectually more satisfying way to model prices of CDO tranches with a full dynamic model from the bottom up as in the dynamic intensity above would have fared better. But that would only potentially have worked if the model had included the possibility of changing correlations between the underlying CDS names.

The dynamic intensity model also had problems. One key problem is that it was hard for the model to capture the extreme volatility in the senior tranche premia. So even if the model is much better at addressing the mechanics that drive the different tranche prices, it still had problems capturing the current market conditions. Hence, the fact that it is hard to use as a simple communication device is not the only problem with the dynamic intensity model.

The aggregate loss model offers no solution. This model has many of the same shortcomings. How are we able to understand the changes in the dynamics of the loss process without understanding the components? That is, if we are looking at a market where we are trying to use the model to price contracts and not just calibrate to explain observed market prices in a liquid market, then we cannot avoid modeling the individual components. This is the biggest limitation of the top-down models. They are aimed at pricing derivatives on tranches but this market has more or less died out.

4.2.4   The danger of simplification – overextending the domain

There is a much more serious consequence of abolishing models that work from the bottom up. When the CDOs become very complicated because the collateral pool contains mortgage bonds with extremely complicated characteristics or tranches of other CDOs, then the Gaussian copula model becomes an oversimplification. As a minimum we have to address the fact that the mixtures of products underlying the structures have vastly different correlations, and when instruments in the collateral pool become tranches of other CDOs, it becomes very hard to attribute meaning to the correlation parameter in this model. In standardized CDOs as described above, we have the benefit of having more information on each name in the collateral pool. We can check if the correlations inputs are matches by correlations observed for the same entities in other markets.

It is worth noting, though, that even the Gaussian copula model (or simple extensions of it) could have been used to analyze more carefully what the effects are of 're-pooling' securities that are already tranches themselves. Even if the analysis of Hull and White (2010) was performed after the problems with ratings of CDOs based on asset backed securities based on subprime mortgages had become apparent, there is nothing in the analysis that could not have been carried out at a much earlier stage. Thus, even simple extensions of the Gaussian copula model that looked a little closer into the actual structure of the underlying pools would have revealed the problems with ratings of mezzanine ABS CDOs, i.e., CDOs in which the pooled securities were mezzanine tranches of mortgage securitizations.

The risk of over-simplification becomes larger the more complex the derivative. The complexity of some traded derivatives contracts can be a bit of a mystery to market outsiders. Who are the investors demanding the most exotic products? Surely, the financial institution structuring the deal in a derivatives contract has superior access to trading and hedging the contracts and essentially eliminates its side of the risk exposure, i.e., the institutions can engineer the pay-offs much less expensively than their clients. But the clients also have a very hard time judging whether the pricing of highly exotic derivatives is reasonable. Investors should be aware that when derivatives are very complex, financial institutions are taking compensation for the significant 'model risk' that arises from trading the contracts.

4.2.5   Interpreting signals and warnings in the market

In addition to their role as a tool for communication and for making comparisons, models are needed if we want to meaningfully assess what market prices are telling us. The market did not predict the crisis. Any price is an average over favorable and non-favorable outcomes, and ex post when the bad outcome has occurred it is easy to blame the model. But it is worth noting that both the Longstaff and Rajan (2008) paper and Mortensen (2006) in their calibration to market prices inferred that relatively extreme scenarios were priced in. We have already seen the probabilities of extreme losses reported in Longstaff and Rajan (2008) but Mortensen also showed that in quiet times jumps in CDS spreads of several hundred basis points were needed to calibrate to market prices. Of course, these probabilities are risk adjusted and not representative of real world probabilities, but they still force us to either think of extreme outcomes as very possible or, if we refuse to believe this, to have an opinion on why the market is so risk averse that it prices using much larger risk-adjusted probabilities of default than actual probabilities. Without models we can't even begin to ask these questions.

4.2.6   The choice of scenarios

It is important to realize that no model available could predict the spread movements we saw. Thinking about the models as predictors is confusing models with laws. As an illustration, consider the developments in the premium on different tranches in the standardized CDOs trading on names in the CDX index known as North American Investment Grade. This index consists of 125 investment grade companies across different sectors chosen on the basis of the liquidity of the CDS contracts trading on the companies. The development in these premia leading up to the crisis is shown in Figure 4.1. For example, premia on the 15–30% tranche went from a minimum around 2 basis points up to a maximum of more than 120 basis points. The premium on the 3–7% tranche went from around 60 basis points to almost 11%. Note the very quiet period before the subprime crisis.

The underlying pool consists of 125 investment grade companies in different sectors chosen according to the liquidity of the CDS contracts trading with the companies as reference credit. As an example, a premium of 1% on the senior 15–30% tranche means that a protection buyer had to pay an annual premium of 1%, divided into four quarterly payments, of the insured notional. The protection seller only has to pay when losses exceed 15% on the CDS

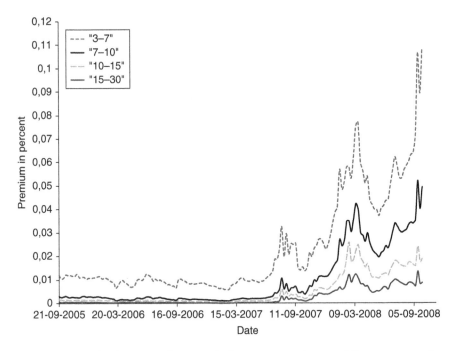

Figure 4.1 The development of premia for buying protection on different non-equity tranches on the North American Investment Grade companies in the so-called CDX index

contracts. If recovery is 40% in default, this means that more than 25% of the loans have to default within 5 years for there to be any payment from the protection seller. It is possible to include such extreme scenarios as possible scenarios in models. Ultimately, it is management and risk management who decide how much model inputs are to be stressed. Nothing prevents them from being conservative in the model inputs. Management must then decide whether capital should be put aside to withstand these extreme scenarios and subsequently explain to shareholders that this will cause expected returns to fall because of lower risk. Very few had the nerve or the power to do this in the quiet period.

4.2.7   The ability to pose sharp questions

Understanding how asset prices evolve in financial markets is a frustratingly complicated task and even if we have some rich theoretical frameworks in portfolio theory and in arbitrage pricing, there are many phenomena we do not understand. Still, there are certain insights that we believe are true. Carrying systematic risk carries a risk premium. We can disagree on how we measure systematic risk, but carrying a risk that is more closely correlated with a pervasive economic shock should be rewarded differently from carrying a highly idio-syncratic, firm specific risk.

The disagreements in the finance profession on how to quantify systematic risk and the inability to find a standard way of measuring it, should not serve as an excuse for investors not to pose sharp questions based on the premise that systematic risk should be priced. A consequence of this is that if two risks are presented as comparable in terms of actual probabilities of occurring, it does not mean that the risks are necessarily priced in the same way. Yet they are priced very differently. The investor should be skeptical about the under-lying structure and should ask questions as to the real source of the income. This is not to say that favorable deals cannot exist, but long persistent mispric-ings are rare. The extra return typically comes at a price. The informed investor should try hard to understand which price is paid in terms of risk-taking for any extra reward.

A selling point of CDO tranches was often that they were structured so that the yield on the tranche was high compared to the rating. It was not uncommon to offer AA-rated tranches yielding LIBOR plus several hundred basis points. Recall that LIBOR before the subprime crisis was an interbank rate offered by banks close to AA ratings. Even if we ignore the fact that models were probably underestimating the probability of a severe downturn in house prices, there are still important questions that could have been asked with the benefit of a good model. Brennan, Hein and Poon (2009), analyze the extent of the arbi-trage profit that can be earned for an arranger who buys the underlying bonds and sells tranched claims to the bonds' cash flows to unsophisticated investors who are willing to price CDO tranches of a given rating at the same level as a bond with a similar rating. Such investor behavior was not uncommon. In reality, investors did get more yield than a similarly rated underlying bond, but the selling argument that this is an 'arbitrage' does not hold.

The complexity of many CDO structures has undoubtedly helped mask the true risks of the structures and contributed to mispricing. An interesting question is whether tranches in standardized CDOs were also mispriced. This argument is made in Coval, Jurek and Stafford (2009), and their analysis is essentially based on the Gaussian copula model with the twist that the risk-neutral distribution of the market factor is not assumed Gaussian but is implied out from index options. If this is the case, we have a larger puzzle because the investors in these markets were and are, as argued in Collin-Dufresne, Goldstein and Yang (2012), sophisticated investors who certainly understood the link between options markets and CDS markets. These authors argue that a full calibration of implied state prices from an entire term-structure of index options gives a reasonably accurate pricing of CDO tranches in standardized CDOs. The skeptic could then argue that this shows that models can be used for anything. I would argue that the models force us to discuss the assumptions that lead to a certain pricing result. The model with the more reasonable assumptions makes a stronger case for its predictions.

4.2.8   Models as tools for structuring our data collection efforts

Good models structure the way we collect and interpret data. Even models that are caricatures are helpful in this respect if they do not assume away too much complexity. If models become too 'reduced-form' and in reality do not require the user to understand more fundamental dynamics of the model or the inputs to the model, then management has to be extra careful in relying too strongly on the conclusions. There is much black box modeling out there. If one insists on modeling the pay-offs to complicated CDOs from the bottom up, then one is forced to address the fine structure of the underlying pay-offs. There is no way around such efforts. For even if a modeler argues that a simplified model can do the job, then to confirm that this simplified model is not an oversimplification, it will have to prove its robustness to variations in the underlying sources of data. In other words, getting to the bottom of the payment streams in opaque structures is inevitable in good modeling practice so that one subsequently can explain the complications that have been ignored. Of course, the crisis also raises issues of entirely new classes of data that need to be collected, and there are already many examples of agencies being set up to collect data that will help us understand the system better. Interpreting these data will be very hard to do without modeling.

4.3   Conclusions

Mathematical models of CDOs did not cause the crisis. Attempts to blame the crisis on these models overestimate the influence of quantitative modeling in the financial industry in shaping decisions on capital structure of the banks, the choice of leverage, the systematic search for capital relief through creative accounting, and uncritical investors' searching for yield. This is not to say that there has not been plenty of misguided trading and investing where agents have relied too much on too simple models. Also, it is clear that insufficient understanding and measurement of the risks that were building up in the financial system are part of the reasons we had the crisis.

The crisis is an opportunity, with greater credibility perhaps, to repeat some warnings about models. Most importantly, mathematical models of financial markets, of economic systems in general, and indeed of almost any other area in which they are applied, are not laws. We cannot predict prices in financial markets with great accuracy. The changing nature of financial markets, their institutions and the rate of financial innovation, and the influence from events which truly fall outside our modeling territory, such as acts of war or terrorism, mean that prediction can never reach the level known from simple physical systems, such as planets moving around the sun. Macroeconomic models have become better at understanding some of the workings of the economy, but it is striking, and we must admit frustrating, that there is remarkably small consensus on even some of the most basic issues, such as the effects of fiscal policy, in macroeconomics as well.

Models can set up scenarios and we can use models to better understand the consequences of these scenarios, perhaps not down to the last penny, but when the models are good within the right order of magnitude. The scenarios we choose to include are grounded in history and experience but they are not the outcome of a model. Managers and regulators must decide whether a scenario that involves a repeat of the Great Depression should be a real possibility in the model i.e., an event with non-vanishing probability. Managers and regulators must decide whether capital should be set aside to withstand such an event. If that choice is made, shareholders must understand that this causes the stock to be less risky, thus sacrificing expected return.

If management decides that a return on equity should be very high, it inevitably involves higher risk-taking. Higher returns are typically connected with higher leverage, and higher leverage means higher risk. In boom times there will always be a tendency to disregard the disasters of the past arguing that 'we fixed the problem that generated the previous crisis.'

Models help us in understanding trade-offs in decision making but whenever we have a model, we should beware of stretching the model too far outside its domain.

Watch out for 'hyping' of models. The Gaussian copula model is an incredibly simple and crude model. The use of the word copula makes it sound more complicated than it is. It is really basically the old CreditMetrics approach in disguise. The basic structure is simple to explain. One should not be intimidated by models. If a quant or a risk manager cannot explain a model in simple terms, it is often a problem with the quant. Management and boards need people who are not intimidated by complicated models and who have enough training in modeling that they know when the problem is truly a communication problem on the part of the modeler.

Bad decision making leading up to the crisis came in part from ignoring economic insights that can best be articulated or learned from models. If every investor understands that systematic risk is concentrated in CDO tranches, then that investor will ask more critical questions on the reasons why high rated tranches seem to offer such high yields. And if the systematic risk cannot explain it, then the investor must ask whether the rating is wrong or whether the underlying cash flows are priced incorrectly. We can only ask such questions using models to fix our ideas and to understand orders of magnitude of effects.

References

Brennan, M., Hein, J. and Poon, S. (2009) 'Tranching and Rating', *European Financial Management*, 15(5): 891–922.

Collin-Dufresne, P., Goldstein, R. and Yang, F. 2012. 'On the Relative Pricing of long Maturity Options and Collateralized Debt Obligations', *Journal of Finance*, 67(6): 1983–2014.

Coval, J., Jurek, J. and Stafford, E. (2009) 'Economic Catastrophe Bonds', *American Economic Review*, 99(3): 628–666.

Duffie, D. and Garleanu, N. (2001) 'Risk and Valuation of Collateralised Debt Obligations', *Financial Analysts Journal*, 57(1): 41–59.

Hull, J. and White, A. (2010) 'The risk tranches created from residential mortgages', *Financial Analysts Journal*, 66(5): 54–67.

Kac, M. (1969) 'Some mathematical models in science', *Science*, 166(3906): 695–699.

Kherraz, A. (2006) 'The May 2005 correlation crisis: Did the models really fail?', Working Paper. Imperial College London.

Lando, D. (2004) *Credit risk modelling – theory and applications*. NJ: Princeton University Press.

Longstaff, F. and Rajan, A. (2008) 'An empirical analysis of the pricing of Collateralised Debt Obligations', *Journal of Finance*, 63(2): 529–562.

Mortensen, A. (2006) 'Semi-analytic valuation of basket credit derivatives in intensity-based models', *Journal of Derivatives*, 13(4): 8–26.

Willemann, S. (2005) 'An evaluation of the base correlation framework for synthetic CDOs', *Journal of Credit Risk*, 1(4): 180–190.

5

The Credit Crisis of 2007 and Its Implications for Risk Management[1]

John Hull

5.1 Introduction

The risk management profession has come under a great deal of criticism since July 2007. How could it not have anticipated the meltdown in financial markets? Were the tools that it had developed in the previous 20 years worthless? Was it too focused on historical data and not taking enough account of changing market conditions?

Although there is much that risk managers can learn from the credit crisis, many of the criticisms are unfair. Some risk management groups did realize that excessive risks were being taken during the period leading up to July 2007. At Merrill Lynch for example, Keishi Hotsuki, cohead of risk management, and David Rosenberg, chief North American economist, are on record as urging their employer to reduce its exposure to subprime mortgages. The reality of being a risk manager is that in good times, or times that appear to be good, you are usually ignored as being irrelevant. But, when disaster strikes, you get blamed.

This chapter builds on the analysis in Hull (2008, 2009, 2012) and Hull and White (2010). It examines the origins of the subprime crisis and the nature of the credit derivatives that were created. It looks at how the risks in credit derivatives were assessed and suggests areas that risk managers, the financial institutions they work for, and the bodies that regulate those financial institutions, should pay more attention to in the future.

5.2 The origins of the crisis

The first decade of the 21st century has been characterized by a period of leveraging that lasted from 2000 to 2006 and a period of deleveraging that started in 2007. During the leveraging period individuals and businesses found it relatively easy to borrow funds to buy assets. As a result, asset prices increased.

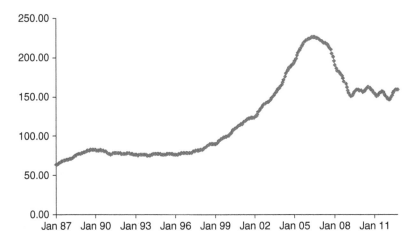

Figure 5.1   S&P/Case-Shiller Composite-10 Index of US Residential Real Estate 1987 to October 2012 (Not Seasonally Adjusted)

During the deleveraging period there was a scramble to sell assets and prices declined.

The US housing market, which is the root cause of the subprime crisis, exemplifies the leveraging/deleveraging periods well. Figure 5.1 shows the S&P/Case-Shiller composite-10 index for house prices in the US between January 1987 and October 2012. In about the year 2000, house prices started to rise much faster than they had in the previous decade. The very low level of interest rates between 2002 and 2005 was an important contributing factor, but the increase was for the most part fuelled by mortgage lending practices.

Mortgage lenders started to relax their lending standards in about 2000. This made house purchase possible for many families that had previously been considered to be not sufficiently creditworthy to qualify for a mortgage. These families increased the demand for real estate and prices rose. The mortgages were classified as subprime because they were much more risky than average. To mortgage brokers and mortgage lenders the combination of more lending and higher house prices was attractive. More lending meant bigger profits. Higher house prices meant that the mortgages were well covered by the underlying collateral. If the borrower defaulted the loss, if any, from the resulting foreclosure should not be large.

To keep house prices rising, lenders had to find ways of continuing to attract new entrants to the housing market. They did this by continuing to relax their lending standards. The amount lent as a percentage of the house price increased. Adjustable rate mortgages (ARMs) were developed where there was a low 'teaser' rate of interest that would last for two or three years. Lenders also became more cavalier in the way they reviewed mortgage applications. Indeed, the applicant's income and other information reported on a mortgage application were frequently not checked. If house prices increased, lenders expected borrowers to refinance at the end of the teaser rate period. This would be profitable for the lenders because pre-payment penalties were relatively high on subprime mortgages.

Mian and Sufi (2009) have carried out research confirming that there was a relaxation of the criteria used for mortgage lending. Their research defines 'high denial zip codes' as zip codes where a high proportion of mortgage applicants had been turned down in 1996, and shows that mortgage origination was high for these zip codes between 2000 to 2007. Moreover, their research shows that lending criteria were relaxed progressively through time rather than all at once because originations in high denial zip codes were an increasing function of time during the 2000 to 2007 period. Zimmerman (2007) provides some confirmation of this. He shows that subsequent default experience indicates that mortgages made in 2006 were of a lower quality than those made in 2005 and these were in turn of lower quality than the mortgages made in 2004.

Standard & Poor's has estimated that subprime mortgage origination in 2006 alone totalled US$421 billion. AMP Capital Investors estimate that there was a total of US $1.4 trillion of subprime mortgages outstanding in July 2007.

Residential mortgages in the US are non-recourse in many states. This means that, when there is a default, the lender is able to take possession of the house, but cannot seize other assets of the borrower. The result of this is that the borrower owns an American-style put option. He or she can at any time sell the house to the lender for the principal outstanding on the mortgage. (During the teaser-interest-rate period this principal is liable to increase, making the option more valuable.) Not surprisingly, many speculators attracted by the availability of non-recourse financing for close to 100% of the cost of a house, were active in the residential real estate market. The purchase of a house was a 'no-lose' proposition. If house prices went up, a speculator could sell the house at a profit; if house prices declined, the speculator could exercise the put option.

As Figure 5.1 illustrates, the house-price bubble burst during the 2006–2007 period. Many mortgage holders found they could no longer afford mortgages when teaser rates ended. Foreclosures increased. House prices declined. This led to other homeowners and speculators finding themselves in a negative equity position. They exercised their put options and 'walked away' from their houses and their mortgage obligations. This reinforced the downward trend in house prices. Belatedly mortgage lenders realized that the put options, implicit in their contracts, were liable to be very costly.

The United States was not alone in experiencing declining real estate prices. Prices declined in many other countries as well. The United Kingdom was particularly badly affected.

5.3   The products that were created

The originators of mortgages in many cases chose to securitize mortgages rather than fund the mortgages themselves. Securitization has been an important and useful tool in financial markets for many years. It underlies the 'originate-to-distribute' model that was widely used by banks prior to 2007.

Securitization played a part in the creation of the housing bubble. Research by Keys et al. (2010) shows that there was a link between mortgage securitization and the relaxation of lending standards. When considering new mortgage applications, the question was not, 'Is this a credit we want to assume?' Instead it was, 'Is this a mortgage we can make money on by selling it to someone else?'

When mortgages were securitized, the only useful information received about the mortgages by the buyers of the products that were created from the mortgages was the loan-to-value ratio (that is, the ratio of the size of the loan to the assessed value of the house) and the borrower's FICO score.[2] The reason why lenders did not check information on things such as the applicant's income, the number of years the applicant had lived at his or her current address, and so on, was that this information was considered irrelevant. The most important thing for the lender was whether the mortgage could be sold to others and this depended primarily on the loan-to-value ratio and the applicant's FICO score.

It is interesting to note in passing that both the loan-to-value ratio and the FICO score were of doubtful quality. The property assessors who determined the value of a house at the time of a mortgage application sometimes succumbed to pressure from the lenders to come up with high values. Potential borrowers were sometimes counseled to take certain actions that would improve their FICO scores.

We now consider the products that were created from the mortgages.

5.3.1   Asset backed securities

The main security created from pools of mortgages was an asset backed security (ABS). Figure 5.2 shows a simple example illustrating the features of an ABS. A portfolio of risky income-producing assets is sold by the originators of the assets to a special purpose vehicle (SPV) and the cash flows from the assets are allocated to tranches. In Figure 5.2, there are three tranches: the senior tranche, the mezzanine tranche, and the equity tranche. The portfolio has a principal of US$100m. This is divided as follows: US$75m to the senior tranche, US$20m to the mezzanine tranche, and US$5m to the equity tranche. The senior tranche is promised a return of 6%, the mezzanine tranche is promised a return of 10%, and the equity tranche is promised a return of 30%.

The equity tranche is much less likely to realize its promised return than the other two tranches. An ABS is defined by specifying what is known as a

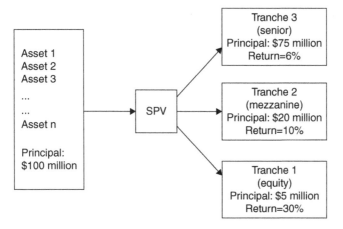

Figure 5.2 An asset backed security (simplified)

'waterfall'. This defines the rules for allocating cash flows from the income-producing assets to the tranches. Interest cash flows and cash flows which are the repayment of the principal are treated separately. Consider interest cash flows. Typically, these are allocated to the senior tranche until the senior tranche has received its promised return. Assuming that the promised return to the senior tranche is made in full, cash flows are then allocated to the mezzanine tranche. If the promised return to the mezzanine tranche is made in full and cash flows are left over, they are allocated to the equity tranche. Repayments of principal are similarly usually allocated to tranches in order of seniority. The precise waterfall rules are outlined in a legal document that is typically several hundred pages long.

The extent to which the tranches get their principal back depends on losses on the underlying assets. In the example in Figure 5.2, the first 5% of losses are borne by the equity tranche. If losses exceed 5%, the equity tranche loses its entire principal and some losses are borne by the mezzanine tranche. If losses exceed 25%, the mezzanine tranche loses its entire principal and some losses are borne by the senior tranche.

There are therefore two ways of looking at an ABS. One is with reference to the waterfall rules. Cash flows go first to the senior tranche, then to the mezzanine tranche, and then to the equity tranche. The other is in terms of losses. Losses of principal are first borne by the equity tranche, then by the mezzanine tranche, and then by the senior tranche.

The ABS is designed so that the senior tranche is rated AAA/Aaa. The mezzanine tranche is typically rated BBB/Baa. The equity tranche is typically unrated. Unlike the ratings assigned to bonds, the ratings assigned to the tranches of an ABS are what might be termed 'negotiated ratings'. The objective of the creator of the ABS is to make the senior tranche as big as possible without losing its AAA/Aaa credit rating. (This maximizes the profitability of the structure.) The ABS creator examines information published by rating agencies on how tranches are rated and may present several structures to rating agencies for a preliminary evaluation before choosing the final one.

5.3.2   ABS collateralized debt obligations

Finding investors to buy the senior AAA-rated tranches created from subprime mortgages was not difficult. Equity tranches were typically retained by the originator of the mortgages or sold to a hedge fund. Finding investors for the mezzanine tranches was more difficult. This led financial engineers to be creative; arguably too creative. Financial engineers created an ABS from the mezzanine tranches of different ABSs that were created from subprime mortgages. This is known as an ABS collateralized debt obligation (CDO) or mezzanine ABS CDO and is illustrated in Figure 5.3.

The senior tranche of the ABS CDO is rated AAA/Aaa. This means that the total of the AAA-rated instruments created in the example that is considered here is 90% (75% plus 75% of 20%) of the principal of the underlying mortgage portfolio. This seems high but, if the securitization were carried further with an ABS being created from the mezzanine tranches of ABS CDOs, and this type of re-resecuritization did happen, the percentage would be pushed even higher.

In the example in Figure 5.3, the AAA-rated tranche of the ABS would probably be downgraded in the second half of 2007. However, it is likely to receive its promised return if losses on the underlying mortgage portfolio are less than 25% because all losses of principal would then be absorbed by the more junior tranches. The AAA-rated tranche of the ABS CDO in Figure 5.3 is much more risky. It will get paid the promised return if losses on the underlying portfolio are 10% or less because in that case mezzanine tranches of ABSs

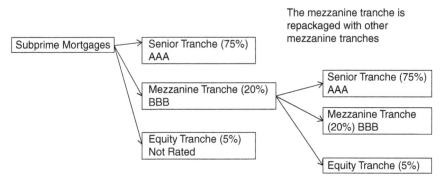

Figure 5.3   An ABS CDO (simplified)

have to absorb losses equal to 5% of the ABS principal or less. As they have a total principal of 20% of the ABS principal, their loss is at most 5/20 or 25%. At worst this wipes out the equity tranche and mezzanine tranche of the ABS CDO, but leaves the senior tranche unscathed.

The senior tranche of the ABS CDO suffers losses if losses on the underlying portfolios are more than 10%. Consider, for example, the situation where losses are 20% on the underlying portfolios. In this case, losses on the mezzanine tranches are 15/20 or 75% of their principal. The first 25% is absorbed by the equity and mezzanine tranches of the ABS CDO. The senior tranche of the ABS CDO therefore loses 50/75 or 67% of its value. These and other results are summarized in Table 5.1.

5.3.3   ABSs and ABS CDOs in practice

The examples we have considered so far illustrate how the products that were created worked. In practice more than three tranches were created at each level of securitization and many of the tranches were quite thin (in other words corresponded to a narrow range of losses). Figure 5.4 is an illustration, taken from Gorton (2009), of the type of structures that were created. The original source of the illustration is an article by UBS.

Two ABS CDOs are created in Figure 5.4. One is created from the BBB-rated tranches of ABSs (similarly to the ABS CDO in Figure 5.3); the other is from the AAA, AA, and A tranches of ABSs. There is also a third level of securitization based on the A and AA tranches of the mezzanine ABS CDO.

Many of the tranches in Figure 5.4 (for example, the BBB tranches of the ABS that cover losses from 1% to 4% and are used to create the mezzanine ABS CDO) appear to be very risky. In fact, they are less risky than they appear when the details of the waterfalls of the underlying ABSs are taken into account. In the arrangement in Figure 5.4, there is some over-collateralization with the face value of the mortgages being greater than the face value of the instruments that are created by the ABSs.

Table 5.1   Losses to AAA tranches of ABS CDO in Figure 5.3

Losses to subprime portfolios %	Losses to mezzanine tranche of ABS %	Losses to equity tranche of ABS CDO %	Losses to mezzanine tranche of ABS CDO %	Losses to senior tranche of ABS CDO %
10	25	100	100	0
15	50	100	100	33.3
20	75	100	100	66.7
25	100	100	100	100

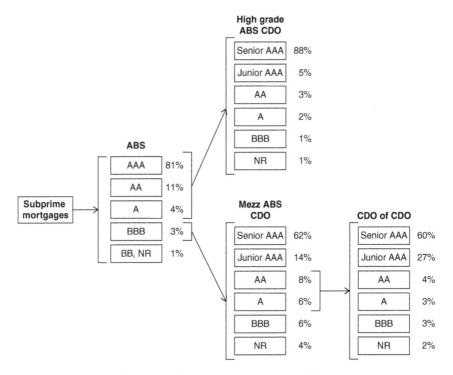

Figure 5.4   A more realistic example of the structures created from mortgages

Many banks have lost money investing in the senior tranches of ABS CDOs. The investments appeared attractive because they promised a return quite a bit higher than that available on other AAA-rated investments. Furthermore, because they were rated AAA, the capital requirements were minimal. In July 2008, Merrill Lynch agreed to sell senior tranches of ABS CDOs that had previously been rated AAA and had a principal of US$30.6 billion to Lone Star Funds for 22 cents on the dollar.[3]

The rating agencies played a key role in the securitization of mortgages. The traditional business of rating agencies is of course the rating of bonds. This is based largely on judgment. The rating process for instruments such as the tranches of ABSs and ABS CDOs was different from the rating of bonds because it was based primarily on models. The rating agencies published their models. Interestingly, different rating agencies used different criteria. Moody's criterion was expected loss. If a tranche's expected loss corresponded to the range of expected losses for a Aaa bond, it was rated Aaa. The S&P criterion was probability of loss. If the probability of loss for a tranche corresponded to the range of probabilities of default for a AAA bond, it was rated AAA.

5.4   Risk management

The promised return on the AAA/Aaa tranches of ABSs and ABS CDOs was higher than that on other assets rated AAA/Aaa. This should have served as a warning signal to financial institutions and their risk management groups. Financial markets do not usually increase expected return without there being an increase in risk. A reasonable assumption for risk managers is that there must be some risk that was not being taken into account by the models used by the rating agencies.

One key point is that rating agencies are concerned with is probability of loss and expected loss. They are not concerned with valuation. As has been well known for some time, valuation depends on systematic risk. A product with an expected loss of X and no systematic risk is worth more than one with the same expected loss and high systematic risk. The AAA tranches of ABS CDOs have high systematic risks (higher than bonds) because they experience losses only in states of the world where the market as a whole performs poorly. This point is discussed by, for example, Coval et al. (2009). Hull and White (2012) discuss other ways in which the criteria used by rating agencies misled investors and led to ratings arbitrage.

5.4.1   The role of models

Many financial institutions relied on the AAA/Aaa ratings of the senior tranches of ABSs and ABS CDOs without developing their own models or carefully examining the assumptions on which the models of the rating agencies were based. This was an unfortunate mistake. Only by developing a model, and critically examining the assumptions underlying the model, can a financial institution fully understand the nature of the risks being taken.

Without constructing a model, it is tempting to assume that a 25% to 100% tranche created from the BBB-rated tranches of an ABS, has the same risk as a 25% to 100% tranche created from BBB bonds. However, as Hull and White (2010) show, even a simple model very quickly reveals that this is not the case. Although the BBB tranches do not have a higher expected loss or probability of loss than bonds that are rated BBB, the probability distribution of the loss is quite different, and this has implications for the riskiness of the tranches created from them.

Two key factors determine the riskiness of the tranches of a mezzanine ABS CDO. These are the thickness of the underlying BBB tranches and the extent to which defaults are correlated across the different pools used to create the mezzanine ABS CDO. Consider an extreme situation where the underlying BBB tranches are very thin and the mortgages in all pools are perfectly correlated so that they have the same default rate.[4] The BBB tranches of all the underlying ABSs then have a probability, say p, of being wiped out and a probability $1-p$

of being untouched. All tranches of the ABS CDO are then equally risky. They also have a probability p of being wiped out and a probability $1-p$ of being untouched. It would be appropriate to give all of them the same rating as the underlying BBB tranches. This is an extreme example, but it illustrates why BBB tranches of ABSs should not be treated in the same way as BBB bonds when the second level of securitization is evaluated.

When a model is constructed, it is tempting to assume a constant recovery rate when credit derivatives are valued. This is dangerous. When the default rate is high, the recovery rate for a particular asset class can be expected to decline. This is because a high default rate leads to more of the assets coming on the market and a reduction in their prices.[5]

As is now well known, this argument is particularly true for residential mortgages. In a normal market a recovery rate of about 75% is often assumed for this asset class. If this is assumed to be the recovery rate in all situations, the worst possible loss on a portfolio of residential mortgages given by the model would be 25%, and the 25% to 100% senior tranche of an ABS created from the mortgages would be assumed to be totally safe. In fact, recovery rates on mortgages declined following 2007 and were in some cases as low as 25%.

5.4.2   Tail correlation

The standard market model for evaluating structures such as those in Figures 5.2 to 5.4 is the Gaussian copula model. This model is likely to be the starting point for a financial institution. However, the model has a serious weakness. It does not reflect a well-known feature of financial markets known as 'tail correlation'. This refers to the tendency for the correlation between two market variables to increase in extreme market conditions.

Tail correlation is a feature of credit markets. It explains why a relatively high correlation is used in the Gaussian copula model when the senior tranches of standard portfolios such as iTraxx and CDX are valued. These are tranches that provide pay-offs only in extreme market conditions. One way of handling tail correlation is to increase the correlation when risks are being evaluated. Another better approach is to examine the effect of using a model that incorporates tail correlation. Hull and White (2004) propose the use of a 'double t' copula. Anderson and Sidenius (2004) propose a copula where factor loadings depend on factor values. Both approaches provide a good fit to market data in the synthetic CDO market and are natural choices for understanding risks in the cash market.

Hull and White (2010) examine how expected losses on AAA-rated tranches are affected when the double t-copula is substituted for the Gaussian copula. They find that the ABS CDO tranches, and to a lesser extent the ABS tranches, that were rated AAA become much riskier.

5.4.3   Stress testing

The risk measures used by regulators, and by financial institutions themselves, are largely based on historical experience. For example, Value at Risk measures for market risk are typically based on the movements in market variables seen over the last one to four years. Credit risk measures are based on default experiences stretching back over a much longer period.

There can be no question that historical data provides a useful guide for risk managers. But historical data cannot be used in conjunction with models in a mechanistic way to determine if risks are acceptable. In risk management it is important that models be supplemented with managerial judgment. A risk management committee consisting of senior managers and economists should meet regularly to consider the key risks facing a financial institution. Stress tests should be based on the scenarios generated by these managers in addition to those generated from extreme movements that have occurred in the past. The risk committee should be particularly sensitive to situations where the market appears to be showing bouts of 'irrational exuberance'.[6]

Involving senior management in stress testing is important for two reasons. First, senior management can draw on a wealth of experience to propose credible scenarios for stress testing. Second, key decision-makers within a financial institution are more likely to take the results of stress testing seriously if their senior management colleagues have had a hand in generating the scenarios. It appears that the results of stress testing were not taken seriously during the period leading up to July 2007. In 2005 and 2006, many economists were forecasting a decline in house prices in the US. Risk management groups did consider this possibility in their scenario analysis. But it seems that few financial institutions took this into account in their decision making.

5.4.4   Liquidity and transparency

The management of liquidity risk is receiving more attention as a result of the credit crisis. Indeed Basel III has proposed two liquidity ratios that banks must meet. These are the liquidity coverage ratio (LCR) and the net stable funding ratio (NSFR). LCR is designed to ensure that a bank will survive a 30-day period of acute stress. The NSFR is designed to ensure that a bank's funding requirements on the asset side of the balance sheet are well matched by funding sources.

The crisis emphasizes the relationship between liquidity and transparency. ABSs and ABS CDOs are typically defined by a legal document several hundred pages long. They are extremely complex instruments. One structure frequently references many other structures. As mentioned earlier, many investors relied on credit ratings and did not analyze the structures for themselves. It is hardly surprising that, once the market lost confidence in subprime mortgages, it became impossible to trade ABSs and ABS CDOs at other than fire-sale prices. The key lesson from all this is that one way of managing liquidity is to focus on relatively simple structures where the cash flows in different future scenarios can be easily evaluated.

5.4.5   Collateral

Systemic risk is a major concern of regulators. One way of mitigating systemic risk is to ensure that all derivatives transactions are fully collateralized, regardless of the credit ratings of the two sides to the transactions. For example, the AIG debacle could have been avoided if AIG had been forced to post collateral on its transactions. Regulators seem to have taken steps to ensure that a high level of collateralization becomes the norm in derivatives markets, at least as far as transactions between financial institutions are concerned. New regulations require all standard derivatives (with a few exceptions) to be cleared through central clearing parties (CCPs). The CCPs (which are already well established for interest rate swaps and credit default swaps) operate similarly to the clearing houses used for exchange-traded products. Non-standard products will continue to be cleared bilaterally, but regulators are insisting (again with a few exceptions) on two-sided collateralization agreements where both an initial margin (also called an independent amount) and variation margin be posted with third parties. The objective is to ensure in both cases that there is enough collateral (margin) to cover losses with 99% certainty.

5.4.6   Compensation

Compensation schemes have a big impact on the risks being taken by financial institutions and risk management groups are becoming more involved in their design.

Employee compensation falls into three categories: regular salary, the end-of-year bonus, and stock or stock options. Many employees at all levels of seniority in financial institutions, particularly traders, receive much of their compensation in the form of end-of-year bonuses. This form of compensation tends to focus the attention of the employee on short-term results.

If an employee generates huge profits one year and is responsible for severe losses the next year, the employee will receive a big bonus the first year and will not have to return it the following year. The employee might lose his or her job as a result of the second year losses, but even that is not a disaster. Financial institutions seem to be surprisingly willing to recruit individuals with losses on their resumes. Imagine you are an employee of a financial institution buying tranches of ABSs and ABS CDOs in 2006. Almost certainly you would have recognized that there was a bubble in the US housing market and would expect that bubble to burst sooner or later. However, it is possible that you would decide to continue trading. If the bubble did not burst until after 31 December 2006, you would still receive a bonus for the year ending on that date.

It is not necessarily the case that salaries on Wall Street are too high. But they should be calculated differently. Many financial institutions are now recognizing that annual bonuses should be paid over a period of several years. If a good performance one year is followed by a bad performance the next year, part of the bonus for the first year is forfeited. Although not perfect, this type of plan potentially motivates employees to use a multiyear time horizon when making decisions.

5.5 Conclusions

Many factors contributed to the financial crisis that started in 2007. Mortgage originators used lax lending standards. Products were developed to enable mortgage originators to profitably transfer credit risk to investors. Rating agencies moved from their traditional business of rating bonds to rating structured products. The products bought by investors were complex and in many instances investors and rating agencies had inaccurate or incomplete information about the quality of the underlying assets.

There are a number of lessons for financial institutions and their risk management groups. Building models is important not only to value products but to understand the risks being taken and the dangers in the assumptions being made by traders. There is a tendency for Value at Risk calculations to assume that correlations observed in normal market conditions will apply in stressed market conditions. In practice, it is found that correlations almost always increase in stressed market conditions. Transparency is an important feature of a financial product. If the cash flows from a product cannot be calculated in a relatively straightforward way, the product should not be traded. Collateralization should become (and is becoming) a requirement in over-the-counter (OTC) markets. Compensation schemes should be chosen to better align the interests of traders with the long-term interest of the financial institutions they work for.

Notes

1. The author is grateful to Richard Cantor and Roger Stein for useful comments on an earlier draft. All views expressed are his own.
2. The Fair Isaac Corporation, known as FICO, created the first credit scoring system in 1958, for American Investments, and the first credit scoring system for a bank credit card in 1970, for American Bank and Trust.
3. Merrill Lynch agreed to finance 75% of the purchase price. When the value of the tranches fell below 16.5 cents on the dollar, Merrill Lynch found itself owning the assets again.

4. Many BBB tranches of ABS were only 1% wide. Figure 5.4 is a simplification. In practice, the 3% wide BBB tranche would actually consist of BBB+, BBB, and BBB- tranches, each about 1% wide.
5. The negative relationship between recovery rates and default rates has been documented for bonds by Altman et al. (2005) and Moody's Investors Service (2008).
6. Irrational exuberance was a term coined by Alan Greenspan during the bull market of the 1990s.

References

Altman, E.I., Brady, B., Resti, A. and Sironi, A. (2005) 'The link between default and recovery rates: implications for credit risk models and procyclicality', *Journal of Business*, 78(6): 2203–2228.

Andersen, L. and Sidenius, J. (2004) 'Extensions to the Gaussian Copula: Random Recovery and Random Factor Loadings', *Journal of Credit Risk*, 1(1): 29–70.

Coval, J.D., Jurek, J.W. and Stafford, E. (2009) 'Economic Catastrophe Bonds', *American Economic Review*, 99(3): 628–666.

Gorton, G. (2009) 'The Panic of 2007', in *Maintaining Stability in a Changing Financial System*, Proceedings of the 2008 Jackson Hole Conference, Federal Reserve Bank of Kansas City.

Hull, J.C. (2008) 'The Financial Crisis of 2007: Another Case of Irrational Exuberance', in *The Finance Crisis and Rescue: What Went Wrong? Why? What Lessons Can be Learned.* Toronto: University of Toronto Press.

Hull, J.C. (2012) 'Risk Management and Financial Institutions', 3rd edition, New York, New York: Wiley.

Hull, J.C. (2009) 'The Credit Crunch of 2007: What Went Wrong? Why? What Lessons Can Be Learned?', *Journal of Credit Risk*, 5(2): 3–18.

Hull, J.C. and White, A. (2004) 'Valuation of a CDO and an nth to Default Swap Without Monte Carlo Simulation', *Journal of Derivatives*, 12(2): 8–23.

Hull, J.C. and White, A. (2010) 'The Risk of Tranches Created from Mortgages', *Financial Analysts Journal*, (Sept/Oct Issue), 66(5): 54–67.

Hull, J.C. and White, A. 'Ratings Arbitrage and Structured Products', *Journal of Derivatives*, (Fall 2012), 20(1): 80–86.

Keys, B.J., Mukherjee, T., Seru, A. and Vig, V. (2010) 'Did Securitisation Lead to Lax Screening? Evidence from Sub-prime Loans', *Quarterly Journal of Economics*, 125(1): 307–362.

Mian, Atif R. and Amir Sufi. 2009. 'The Consequences of Mortgage Credit Expansion: Evidence from the 2007 Mortgage Default Crisis', *Quarterly Journal of Economics*, 124(4): 1449–1496.

Moody's Investors Service (2008) 'Corporate Default and Recovery Rates, 1920–2007', www.moodys.com/sites/products/DefaultResearch/.

Zimmerman, T. (2007) 'The Great Sub-prime Meltdown', *The Journal of Structured Finance*, Fall, 7–20.

6

After the Storm: Four Innovations Changing Investment Management

Adam Schneider

6.1 Introduction

After a long period of generally excellent financial performance, the investment management industry is now challenged by volatile markets, decreasing revenue and substantial client retention issues. As a result of the 2007–2009 credit crisis, many firms faced revenue declines, product performance issues and the need to adjust their strategies to changing conditions.

Four years after the beginning of the credit crisis, with many markets recovering, investment managers are shifting from reactive measures such as cost cutting to more innovative strategies focused on retaining clients and growing revenues. This chapter examines the implications for investment managers and specifically outlines a series of innovative strategies that firms can use to position themselves for growth.

After two years of struggling and with some light visible in the marketplace, can firms begin to go on the offensive?

6.1.1 The need for innovation

Our research has identified a series of market 'realities' that have been brought upon us by the credit crisis and subsequent events. As significant participants in the financial markets, the long-term effects of the credit crisis on the investment management businesses have been profound. These 'market trends' include the following:

1) An overall trend of financial institutions moving from relatively high-risk/high leverage businesses in search of higher financial returns toward a much less leveraged, potentially lower-return set of businesses. This has been directly encouraged by new regulation and capital requirements.
2) A formerly fragmented financial services marketplace that has moved rapidly toward consolidation.

3) The ending of a 'growth mindset' where firms previously managing for expansion are now finding themselves forced to manage in a no- or low-growth environment.
4) Significant failures in investment products, both in terms of some of the investments purchased by investment managers for portfolios and some of the investment products sold to clients.[1]

The magnitude of change has had significant effect on the entire financial services industry. Investment manager responses have included actions such as:

- Reducing costs. Numerous investment management firms have publicly announced they are undertaking cost-cutting activities.
- Improving risk management, especially in light of the failure of certain investment portfolios.
- Improving investment management processes, including product selection and compliance procedures.
- Improving governance, compliance, and regulatory response capabilities.
- Simplifying and consolidating channels and distribution strategies.

6.2   Innovation going forward

In our ongoing work with investment managers, we have seen a number of firms who are attempting to capitalize on the market change to their advantage. Typically this involves a very innovative approach to an existing problem. The following examples discuss how investment managers are using an innovative approach to deal with the market trends discussed above.

6.2.1   Market trend 1

Financial institutions such as banks and capital markets firms have been forced by recent events to raise capital and/or reduce assets, e.g., to lower balance sheet leverage. This has had the effect of moving many financial services firms toward a possibly lower-return set of businesses, and they are compensating by increasing their focus on select businesses and exiting or minimizing others. This resultant shrinkage of industry balance sheets has two major implications for investment managers:

- There are fewer total available funds in the marketplace to manage. Certain types of firms, such as hedge funds, have business models that are critically dependent on borrowing. The tightening of credit and the move toward 'less leveraged lower-return' businesses directly impacts firms who find it difficult to finance assets.

- Due to increased conservatism in the market, remaining assets under management (AUM) have moved to lower-margin products. In other words, clients who had a bad experience with 'high-risk/high-return' products are now more likely to seek 'lower-risk/lower-return' products. Unfortunately for investment managers, the fees for managing the higher-return products are often higher than those for the lower-return products, directly impacting revenues and profitability. As an example, in the institutional market, fees for managing a dollar of equity assets may be five to ten times as high as fees for managing a dollar of cash equivalent.

The net effect of these two types of impact on many investment firms is to structurally lower AUM and lower the fees obtained from those assets remaining.

In our discussions with a number of investment managers, we have seen several innovative ideas and strategies in response to this trend. These include two core techniques: resegmenting the market to focus on areas which can be profitably served and improving client pricing using optimization techniques.

Trend response: focus on segments which can be profitably served

In the years of market growth, many investment managers expanded into new market segments. In some cases, large numbers of clients were taken on without any detailed understanding of the cost to serve or profitability. Growth was the priority. However, not all clients are managed and treated equally.

Like many businesses, investment managers often have a small number of highly profitable relationships that subsidize an array of marginally profitable and unprofitable clients. To focus revenue-enhancing efforts where they can yield significant results, we believe it is essential to understand client profitability and the factors contributing to profitability.

Many business decisions drive variations in client profitability, including client tenure, product usage and mix, level of AUM, client adviser productivity, degree of price concessions, and service intensity. The variety of contributing factors makes it difficult to determine how profitable client relationships are today, let alone how profitable they could be if managed more effectively.

We have seen innovative investment management firms using analytic techniques to understand client profitability patterns and target specific clients for improvement. They use a holistic, analytical approach to understand:

- which clients are underperforming relative to their potential;
- what actions in what areas – service levels, pricing, product mix – might enhance these clients' performance;
- which clients are beyond repair and need to be terminated to free up resources to focus on higher-potential prospects.

A typical approach includes a five-step process of enhancing an investment manager's understanding of client profitability and its drivers. The five steps are discussed in detail in our other publications[2] but in summary include:

1. Quantify client profitability: The analysis of individual client profitability forms the foundation for improving performance, allowing firms to uncover the root causes of client profitability differences. In a related move, it is becoming common for firms to use and focus on advanced analytics to help drive this analysis.
2. Benchmark and identify underperformers: Profit performance is driven by many factors, which makes benchmarking a challenge. Traditional analytical approaches can be combined with modeling techniques to pinpoint under- and over-profit target clients or client segments.
3. Develop action plans: Client-specific action plans targeting the root causes of underperformance can help bring selected clients up to their profit-generating potential.
4. Monitor results: Effective monitoring and tracking of results provides feedback and allows definition of goals and metrics into performance incentives.
5. Expand focus beyond individual clients or segments: By examining aggregated client profitability information, a firm can gain insights about the profitability of client adviser, office, region and channels. The increased availability of analytic tools has helped this analysis significantly at many firms.

Trend response: improving client pricing using optimization techniques

In our experience and research, active management of pricing and price concessions is often neglected by investment managers.

Pricing is a key component of all businesses, and in theory pricing for investment management services should be quite simple. However, in our experience, there is pressure for price concessions at investment management firms, and these concessions often create significant revenue and profit leakage. Firms may have a general belief that all clients are profitable at the margin, and, as a result, over time and through individual negotiations, clients have received various forms of discounts, rebates and ad-hoc pricing structures.

In many firms, price concessions have become the norm rather than the exception. Our experience shows that margin leakage of 15–30% on gross profits is not uncommon. The prevalence of price concessions tends to feed on itself, as the current trend of more price transparency leads more demanding clients to ask for more frequent and greater concessions. We believe managing the process of granting price concessions is crucial because it directly affects the bottom line while having a disproportionately high impact on margin. In addition, pricing decisions, often the result of a one-time situation, can impact longer-term recurring revenues over a period of years.

Research indicates that although the rate of price concession generally correlates to AUM or total revenue per client, such concessions may vary greatly across clients, even those investing similar amounts in similar products. In fact, firms may have low-revenue clients receiving high concessions, and at times we have identified clients with negative margins. In many cases, price concessions are granted with an expectation of anticipated future opportunities (such as new assets), but afterwards they are seldom tracked to determine whether the expected future assets truly materialize.

As a result, there are often shortcomings in the management of price concessions that leave unrealized opportunities. Innovative firms are enhancing their price concession management to significantly drive profit improvement.

The first step to improving management of price concessions is to understand and create transparency in concessions already granted. Greater insight into the current situation almost always leads to improvement in pricing strategies. The insight derived can help drive tangible initiatives to improve the process. Innovative firms are undertaking actions such as:

- Establishing a comprehensive pricing database that supports reliable calculations of price concessions and provides a holistic view of clients.
- Deploying pricing tools to calculate gross prices for each product at a client or account level. This requires an in-depth understanding of the actual and often highly complex price structures in use.
- Performing in-depth analysis by product or service, by AUM tier, by channel or by region to identify drivers of profitability. The goal is to evaluate outliers, inconsistencies, high margin leakage patterns and current price sensitivity.
- Understanding the core reasons why price concessions are granted in specific situations. This can enable appropriate management action or countermeasures to be launched. For example, a particular client segment may be requesting and obtaining unreasonably large concessions. This information is then used to quantify the potential benefit of pricing and profitability management initiatives.

The second step is to identify required pricing strategy improvements. We have found that guidelines for price concession management should be tied to business strategies and objectives as well as on the insights gained through the above-mentioned analysis.

The third step is to enhance the execution of price concessions. This generally requires a set of tangible initiatives focused on the goal of significantly reducing margin leakage. Figure 6.1 below shows a scatter chart of client

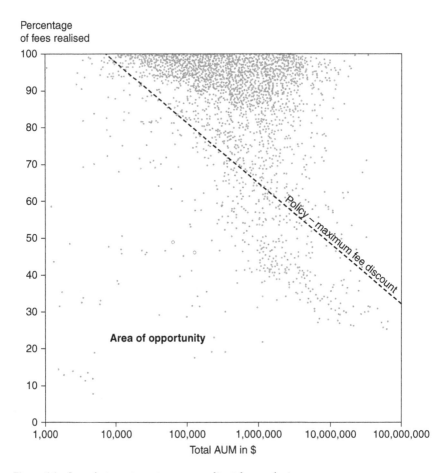

Figure 6.1   Sample investment manager client fee analysis
Source: Deloitte analysis, private wealth client.

accounts indicating what percentage of 'rack rate' fees are actually realized and plotted against asset size. With data of this sort, a firm can define specific initiatives at the account or client level to increase profitability. These initiatives can be sized based on their effectiveness in supporting strategic objectives and can then be prioritized in terms of their impact on client satisfaction, profit improvement, effort and risk. Following these three steps can provide a foundation for price execution and monitoring, and it is essential to express them in a clear-cut way.

In Figure 6.1, taken from an actual study at an investment management firm, we have compared fees received as a percentage of the 'list' price schedule versus client AUM. The firm had a policy for the maximum fee reduction it would offer depending on client negotiation, which is indicated by the dotted line. Clients with significant assets who are charged far below the fee policy are in the 'area of opportunity'.

While each investment manager is different, there are a number of innovative high-value practices that have been demonstrated to be effective.
Improve profitability strategy by:

• defining profitability targets
• defining objective criteria for concessions
• providing sales negotiation training to client advisers.

Define price concession process by:

• eliminating unauthorized price concessions
• resetting price concessions and limiting duration
• changing structure of price concessions
• defining concession structures and limits
• developing tracking system for negotiated terms.

Improve client profitability by:

• implementing profitability benchmarking and reporting
• including specific margin leakage KPIs in sales incentive systems
• implementing margin leakage reporting
• calculating roll-out price concession profit impact
• Obtain and assemble information on competitor pricing and concession strategy. Note that fees for some types of clients are on public record and that there is a wide variety of anecdotal information available in the marketplace.

A fourth step is to use analytics and modeling techniques to focus and organize the price concession process. Many investment managers enter client negotiations with little or no objective fact-based information upon which to base pricing decisions. Predictive modeling tools can help estimate a client's sensitivity to price and develop recommendations based on client, competitor and external market information. When implemented, this intelligence can be provided at the point of negotiation, maximizing its value.

Fifth, innovative investment managers make a systematic effort to monitor price concessions over time. A monitoring system can identify disruptive developments, determine the effectiveness of measures taken, and reveal opportunities for improvement. An internal profitability and price concession benchmarking analysis exposes over- and underperformers and helps to achieve better results by encouraging implementation of more effective practices across the firm.

Based on hands-on client experience, we have seen investment managers use strategies like these to obtain significant profit improvement. Improving management of price concessions can be started with relatively small investments, can be piloted initially and implemented quickly, and are generally effective within a short period of time.

6.2.2   Market trend 2

One result of recent market events has been significant consolidation across much of the financial industry. In a similar fashion in the investment industry we have seen the emergence of the large scale trillion-dollar AUM firms. This is a major change to the competitive landscape and there are direct implications for most investment managers:

- Scale has grown in importance. The strategies of many investment management firms have been to organize themselves as product- or sector-oriented boutiques and strive for outperforming benchmarks in those areas. However, with the growth of giant competitors, smaller firms have lost market share and are concerned they potentially may lose relevance.
- Increased activity in mergers and acquisitions (M&A) may be warranted as a way to increase product breadth, distribution or scale generally.
- The very largest firms can differentiate themselves and choose to compete on a different basis. For example, one firm may conclude its scale provides an ability to invest in market analysis tools to drive superior results. Another firm may seek to offer many different investment styles so that, as markets shift, they can induce clients to move assets across style, rather than seeing assets depart.

The effect is that firms must decide whether they want, or need, to grow. If scale is more important, what can investment management firms do to achieve it? Assuming investment performance is already a focus area, one innovative strategy is increasing the focus on client *service* satisfaction. Increasing the focus on client service should, other factors being equal, increase inflows, slow outflows, and generally make assets 'stickier'. However, this requires identifying what is important in servicing clients and optimizing the service and delivery mechanisms to provide that.

We believe that, in the investment industry, the factors driving client service are generally specific to each client segment. Specific recommendations for a set of defined investor segments are presented in Figure 6.2.

In general, the strategies focus on providing the following:

- Improved education so that clients can put their results in the context of historical returns.

Investor segment	Typical service priorities	Typical investment priorities	Potential retention strategy in light of market events
Mass affluent < $1m	– Convenience – Advice – Ease of access	– Accumulation	– Educate and communicate – Alternate advisory path
Affluent $1–5m	– Relationship – Service quality – Advice	– Preservation – Next generation	– Educate and communicate – 'Health check' portfolio – Alternate advisory path
High net worth (HNW) $5–25m	– Personal relationship – Service quality	– Preservation and innovation – Philanthropic – Next generation	– Educate and communicate – 'Health check' portfolio – Increase touchpoints
Ultra HNWI > $25m	– Personal relationship	– Preservation and innovation – Philanthropic – Next generation	– Educate and communicate – Increase touchpoints
Institutions	– Service quality – Enquiry response – Accuracy/types of reporting	– Defined expectations – Performance consistent with expectations	– Communicate – Focus on sector rotation and longer term returns

Figure 6.2   Improving client retention: strategies by investor segment
Source: Deloitte analysis.

- Additional communications and personal touch points (as may be economic) so that clients feel that they are getting the appropriate level of contact and support for their level of assets and situation.
- Developing a 'health check' process to confirm that clients are correctly receiving the right level of attention in light of their individual situation, current asset value and investment goals. The goal of the 'health check' is to take a fresh look at the investment portfolio and to indicate to the client that the investment manager is taking special care, given market volatility and ever-evolving client needs.
- In the retail servicing area, one innovative strategy being employed for clients that want to change advisers is to offer a revised, alternative advisory path. The thinking goes that many clients change adviser by changing firms – and it would be far better to build a process to find a new adviser within the firm rather than lose the client altogether.

Innovative investment managers have also expanded their client contact and calling programs to accomplish the above strategies. This includes creating the business reporting to confirm the program is effective. What may have been ad hoc and not monitored becomes a formal program with goals, methods, timelines and an assessment of effectiveness.

But trying harder is not enough. If improving service is indicated, a second innovative response is to recognize that the level of service offered to a client segment can be defined, measured and controlled. While the majority of investment managers strive for excellent service, many use informal mechanisms for defining service levels and do not measure service as delivered.

In our research across many industries, we have found that leading service organizations explicitly link their service strategy to their business strategy. The research indicates that service leaders bring together five building blocks to drive service delivery success. These are as follows:

- Service strategy definition: We have found that defining the goals and objectives for servicing is essential and that communicating a consistent service philosophy is common across all service excellence strategies. As part of that process, leadership needs to create a clear vision for service excellence and drives it through the organization. The importance of defining a firm's client service strategy cannot be overstated: firms with leading service cultures almost always explicitly state and manage to this goal. The goal should be explicit, service focused, and present throughout the organization.
- Employee/culture management: We have found that, regardless of industry or strategy, service leaders infuse a service culture into their employees. This includes training, development, use of performance guidelines, monitoring, feedback and leading by example.
- Measurement and incentives: Common parlance is that if something is not measured, then it did not happen. This requires defining standards for service and then tracking actual service performance. Our research indicates that measuring client service is an area of focus for most service leaders. In some cases this is routine: measurement and incentives are very commonly used in such settings as call centers. However, in our experience these types of measurements are rarely performed for institutional servicing, a key opportunity.
- Brand: In our research, all leading service organizations associate their brand with service quality to create a strong perception of quality and increase client expectations. This brand perception pervades externally and internally within the organization.
- Service delivery: We have found that service leaders focus on ensuring positive service interaction, emphasizing service recovery and a consistent client experience. This is best followed through a measurement mechanism

such as client satisfaction surveys. Again, these techniques are commonly used for retail call centre operations and are much less common for institutional servicing.

Most investment managers have an aggregate measurement of success: the inflow or outflow of AUM. Given that most firms focus on maximizing investment performance, the only other retention strategy available in many cases is to focus on client service.

6.2.3 Market trend 3

With the ending of the 'growth mindset', investment management firms are finding themselves managing in a no- or low-growth environment. The effect is that business models and organizational structures acceptable and affordable during the growth phase are likely less acceptable or perhaps unaffordable now. What are some of those practices suddenly in question?

- Allowing multiple investment organizations, possibly by strategy, to exist across the firm.
- Maintaining duplicative marketing/sales capabilities, generally by investment strategy or by subsidiary.
- Maintaining duplicative administrative functions such as finance or human resources.
- Maintaining duplicative back office and technology functions.
- Not exploring 'next generation' opportunities for back office and technology functions such as new technologies, offshoring, or outsourcing that can dramatically improve existing capabilities.

The lack of integration by investment managers in their business models is an interesting result of growth. Many firms have grown over the years through acquisition or combination, and often the duplication was deliberate, an outgrowth of the M&A process. It was common to promise individual firms or product areas significant autonomy.

The struggle is that business models that worked during a period of growth seem to be less viable going forward. Some firms are using this as an opportunity to pursue change. Much of this involves breaking down the structural silos that have formed and reorganizing/combining them with a shared services model. Often there are substantial synergy benefits but with substantial expense to change and transition.

Shared services is not an applicable approach for all areas at all times. Firms must balance their individual needs – for example, adding new strategies, offering new products, entering new client segments, or changing geographic focus – with the inevitable issues inherent in building a centralized, cost-effective service.

We consider opportunities of this sort to be 'deferred merger integration' and urge investment managers to balance the commitments made during the M&A process against the potential cost, functional, and scale synergies possibly available through consolidation of services or capabilities.

A related tactic taken by some investment managers is to more aggressively think through their operating model as a basis for reorganizing work. We have seen firms build and then implement a series of global operating principles. A typical principle might be 'there will be one functional capability (such as performance calculation) globally' or 'there will be one trade-clearing capability per geographic region', where the region in question might be defined as the Americas, Europe or Asia.

These principles are aimed at fostering coordination across the firm with a goal of optimizing processes, costs and capabilities. A typical outcome is that client service is also enhanced.

Regional or global integration efforts must be balanced with the need for local autonomy, especially in the areas of managing assets and in servicing clients. Also, some countries restrict the information that can 'leave'. So a typical structure would involve, say, country-by-country investment management, country-by-country client service, and many operational functions organizing into a regional or global hub. Trends observed in the market are summarized in Figure 6.3, but many firms use widely varying structures.

Investment managers are implementing governance at a global level to maximize economies of scale, apply consistent standards, encourage coordination and share scarce resources.

6.2.4 Market trend 4

The financial crisis has brought significant failures of investment products, both in terms of some securities purchased for portfolios and for products sold to clients. In the last few years, many of the allegedly misrepresented products have become the subject of litigation and negotiation. Firms that sponsored these products have been in some cases, cajoled, sued, or forced to otherwise make good on the original terms of the product.

Much has been made in the industry of the risks that have been uncovered during the credit crisis. In particular, a series of investment products failed in unprecedented amounts. Some examples include the following:

- Auction rate preferred securities sold as cash equivalents, where the risk of an auction failing was thought to be extremely small.
- Structured investment vehicles, where underlying long-term assets funded short-term cash such as investment returns, until the long-term assets lost value.

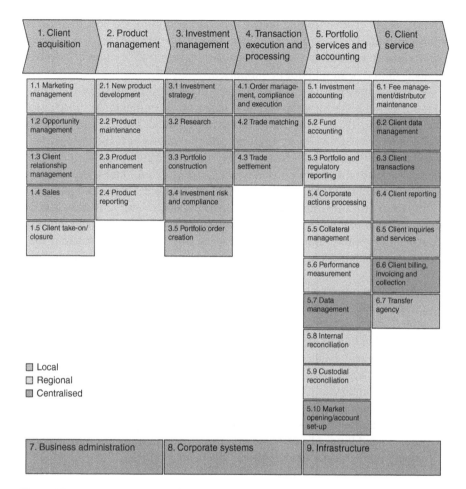

1. Client acquisition	2. Product management	3. Investment management	4. Transaction execution and processing	5. Portfolio services and accounting	6. Client service
1.1 Marketing management	2.1 New product development	3.1 Investment strategy	4.1 Order management, compliance and execution	5.1 Investment accounting	6.1 Fee management/distributor maintenance
1.2 Opportunity management	2.2 Product maintenance	3.2 Research	4.2 Trade matching	5.2 Fund accounting	6.2 Client data management
1.3 Client relationship management	2.3 Product enhancement	3.3 Portfolio construction	4.3 Trade settlement	5.3 Portfolio and regulatory reporting	6.3 Client transactions
1.4 Sales	2.4 Product reporting	3.4 Investment risk and compliance		5.4 Corporate actions processing	6.4 Client reporting
1.5 Client take-on/closure		3.5 Portfolio order creation		5.5 Collateral management	6.5 Client inquiries and services
				5.6 Performance measurement	6.6 Client billing, invoicing and collection
				5.7 Data management	6.7 Transfer agency
				5.8 Internal reconciliation	
				5.9 Custodial reconciliation	
				5.10 Market opening/account set-up	

☐ Local
☐ Regional
☐ Centralised

7. Business administration	8. Corporate systems	9. Infrastructure

Figure 6.3 Location trends for global investment management firms

- Money market funds, where one major fund ended up 'breaking the buck' due to exposure to commercial paper that fell in value.
- Tranches of subprime mortgage CDOs, which fell dramatically in value when the underlying mortgage cash flows were lower than expected.

While the risks inherent within these investment products were generally understood as something that 'could happen', they were also generally considered to be very low probability by the broker–dealers and investment managers involved. More significantly, the risks were considered so low that reserves or capital were not required to be held against them.

As the credit crisis unfolded, many firms stepped up to support their problematic products and funds. However, the market experienced significant uncertainty. It is clear that there are inconsistent standards for how a 'defective product' should or should not be supported.[3]

We expect the trend for 'product warranties' to continue. Let's contrast investment products to what happens when other products are purchased. One can go into an appliance store, buy a twenty dollar toaster, and generally receive a money-back warranty that protects the purchaser if the product fails within a given time period. The company manufacturing the product reserves for that warranty cost, and in fact may obtain insurance for an excessive rate of failure. Is there a similar process for investment products? Generally not.

This is a significant structural issue, in part because investment managers do not act like manufacturers and do not have businesses that operate in terms of a 'warranty'. However, some firms are debating whether there is a way to potentially resolve this problem. We believe there are two sets of core questions:

- For investment products purchased, such as subprime CDOs: is there a way to improve the investment process so that the true components of risk are better understood? For example, in this case the core issue was the cash flow of the underlying mortgage collateral, especially in light of an unexpected decrease in real estate value. Is there a structural way going forward to incorporate lessons of this type in the underwriting, ratings review, collateralization, and finally the investment process?
- For investment products that are cash equivalents, does the firm have a robust product management process so that underlying risks are identified, evaluated and if need be reserved against? Is there periodic monitoring on a frequent enough basis to alert a firm to a pending problem?

More generally: can product warranties be defined in a way that is structurally sound for the investor and the investment manager/issuer? As of this writing, this question remains open.

6.3   Conclusion

This chapter has summarized four market trends that have emerged from the credit crisis and innovative responses seen in the marketplace. The investment industry is robust and is intelligently focused on responding to what has happened. Key responses include the following:

1. The overall trend of deleveraging is being responded to by increasing focus on client service and client profitability.

2. The trend of a consolidating business environment is being responded to by an increasing focus on M&A and sensitivity to improving client service to maximize retention.
3. The ending of a 'growth mindset' is forcing changes in operating models such as regionalization, globalization or consolidation of functions into shared services capabilities.

Notes

1. The terminology of the investment business is often confusing, in part because while investment management firms may be relatively small, they work with significant asset values and are generally very complex entities. Investment managers have a full range of business functions (including marketing, sales, research, portfolio management, information technology, operations, finance and compliance); they generally manage multiple investment strategies (such as growth equity, fixed income or cash); and these strategies are packaged into a variety of products that clients can purchase (such as separate investment accounts, mutual funds or hedge funds).
2. This is a topic which is actively researched. Please see the series of publications located at www.deloitte.com/us/pricing.
3. As it turned out, most of the products that were ultimately supported were cash equivalent investment vehicles. While risks were often disclosed to investors, the analogy to government insured bank deposits led many of the product sponsors to support them for client relations reasons.

7
Avoiding International Financial Crises: An Incomplete Reform Agenda

Jean Dermine

7.1 Introduction

In this chapter, we argue that the set of reforms proposed recently by national and international groups to reduce the risk of future global banking crises constitutes an incomplete reform agenda. Three important issues remain, in our opinion, to be addressed:

- Accountability of bank supervisors and regulators
- An end to the Too-Big-To-Fail doctrine
- A satisfactory regime for the supervision and bailing out of international financial groups.

To address these issues, we first briefly review the origins of banking and the factors that contributed to the subprime crisis. This helps to evaluate the changes in regulations and financial market infrastructures proposed by various national and international institutions. It is then shown why these proposals, although useful, will not be sufficient to reduce significantly the risk of a future banking crisis.

7.2 The Origin of the 2007 financial crisis and the reform agenda

To understand the roots of the 2007 financial crisis and the remedies proposed to reduce the likelihood of future crises, it helps to understand first the developments in banking markets, with the creation of the modern bank in Italy in the 15th century, the interbank markets, securitization, and the market for credit risk guarantees.

7.2.1 The creation of banks

Let us travel back in time, three thousand years ago. There were no banks, no financial crises. As shown in Figure 7.1, an investment in a house (a cabin) had to be financed out of one's personal wealth (home equity) or through a loan made by a friend. A drop in the value of the house by 10 would imply a drop in the value of home equity by 10 (Figure 7.2). While allowing for transparency, the system was not efficient as it did not facilitate the mobilization of savings and the financing of real investment. Modern banking in Europe was created in Italy in 1406 (Banco di San Giorgio was founded in Genoa, several years before the founding in Siena in 1472 of the oldest surviving bank in the world, Banca Montei di Paschi[1]). As shown in Figure 7.3, short-term deposits, attractive to savers, are invested in longer-term loans (attractive to borrowers). Imagine what the system would be, if financing the purchase of a house with a short-term loan, one would have to refinance the funding every year. One refers to the maturity transformation role of banks, or, in modern economics, to the provision of liquidity insurance (Diamond and Dybvig, 1983; Allen and

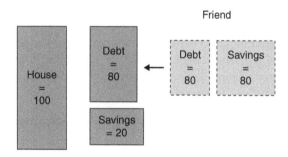

Figure 7.1 No banks

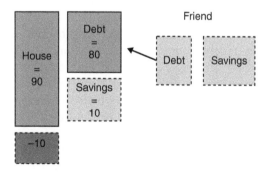

Figure 7.2 No banks. Reduction of value of real estate of 10

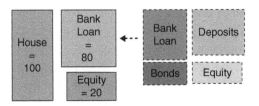

Figure 7.3   Bank financing

Gale, 2007). Whenever needed, depositors can withdraw money.[2] In addition, banks perform a useful role in screening and monitoring borrowers. Diamond (1984) has shown that the diversification of risks allows the reduction of overall bank risk, the risk borne by depositors, and the cost of monitoring the bank. Since the creation of modern banks in the 15th century, the system was inherently fragile as depositors could run away and illiquid loans could not be sold. For this reason, banks have been heavily regulated and safety nets, including emergency liquidity assistance by central banks or deposit insurance systems, have been created. Travellers in Brazil, South Africa or Russia will meet bankers who have experienced bank runs. The absence of major bank runs in the past 80 years in OECD countries was rather an exception. The observation that banking regulations and banking supervision have not been sufficient to prevent the 2007 banking crisis raised the question as to whether new regulations and supervisory models were needed or whether the enforcement of existing regulations was the issue.

7.2.2   The creation of interbank markets and securitization

As demand for loans was growing, banks short of cash started to borrow from other banks, often located in other countries. Such an example was the case of Icelandic banks borrowing from banks located in Germany. Another way to fund loans was to *securitize* them, that is, to sell them to investors. This is described in Figure 7.4. Due to an asymmetric information problem – the bank knows more about the quality of loans than investors – this was never going to be an easy affair. Financial engineers issued asset-backed securities differing in seniority: senior tranche, junior or mezzanine tranche, and equity tranche. The senior tranche is, to a large extent, protected from loan losses, which are covered by the junior and equity tranches. A question arises as to the size of junior and equity tranches needed to cover potential (unexpected) loan losses. Progress in statistics and credit risk modelling (Vasicek, 1987 and 2002) allows us to model the distribution of losses on a credit portfolio. Finally, rating agencies were invited to rate these issues. Note that securitization was not a completely new phenomenon, having been used by American government sponsored enterprises (GSEs), Fannie Mae and Freddie Mac, to securitize prime

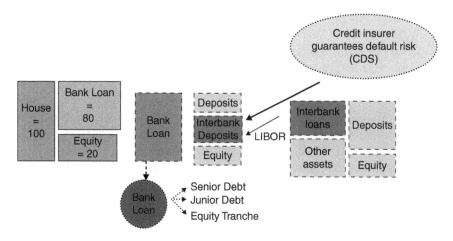

Figure 7.4   Banks, interbank markets, securitization, credit default swaps (CDS)

US mortgages for many years. What was new, in the period 2003–2007, was the securitization of increasingly large classes of risky assets, including US subprime loans (Calomiris, 2007; Gorton, 2008). Securitization reached $2 trillion in 2007, including 70% of recently issued US subprime loans.

7.2.3   Creation of credit default swaps (CDS)

A final type of financial innovation was the growth of a credit insurance market whereby one party would provide insurance coverage against the default (or downgrade) of another party. The market grew from $8 trillion in 2004 to $45 trillion in 2007. Looking at Figure 7.4, it is useful to remember that financial markets (financial assets and claims) are just a mirror image of the real assets (real estate, industrial assets) in an economy. When the housing market falls by 10, it becomes difficult to estimate the impact on the value of a bank's equity, on the value of a securitized asset, or on the value of a CDS. In other words, these credit transfer innovations have increased greatly the complexity and opacity in the market.

Apparently unnoticed by regulators was the fact that many of these securitization vehicles, so-called Structured Investment Vehicles (SIVs), involved the financing of long-term assets with short-term commercial paper (asset-backed commercial paper). The plan was that this short-term paper would be rolled over at maturity. One observes a financial structure similar to that of a bank, with long-term assets funded with short-term funding. A major difference is that this short-term funding was highly volatile, as it is not protected by a public safety net. This new system has been dubbed quite correctly 'shadow banking'. In July 2007, the US investment bank Bear Stearns had to step in to refinance one of its flagship SIVs, called the High-Grade Structured Credit Strategies Enhanced Leverage Fund. A second issue was that the statistics on portfolio credit risk (Vasicek, 1987, 2002) required the estimation of a critical variable, default correlation across loans. Few data on credit risk correlation at the time of a recession were available because the world economy had been expanding in the last ten years. Moreover, data were nonexistent in a new untested market, the US subprime mortgage market. Finally, information on the counterparty risk exposure of financial institutions to the credit insurance market was, at best, incomplete. The lack of information on counterparty risk and therefore on the domino consequence of a default of a large institution seems to have been the reason for the bailout in September 2008 of the giant insurance group, AIG.

Given the emphasis of this chapter on the regulatory reform agenda, we will not address the forces explaining the explosion of these markets, nor shall we discuss the various actions taken by public authorities to prevent a collapse of their banking systems. Progress in the statistics of credit risk, a savings glut with large surplus in several countries (China and the Middle Eastern countries in particular), a will of governments to facilitate home ownership, an acco-modating monetary policy with exceptionally low interest rates, market pressures to grow income applied to banks, asset managers and rating agencies, or simply greed and gullibility of investors are all likely to have contributed to the credit crisis (Hellwig, 2008; Greenspan, 2009). Following up on the bank run on Northern Rock in the United Kingdom in September 2007 (HM Treasury, 2009) and the default of Lehman Bros and Washington Mutual (WaMu) in September 2008 in the United States, various measures were taken around the world to restore the stability of banks. Actions were taken on the asset side (insurance of credit risk or sale of toxic or legacy assets in the United States with the private-public investment program (PPIP)) or on the liability side with public guarantees on bank debt and capital infusion around the world.

As stated above, the objective of the paper is to discuss the regulatory and supervision framework, the financial market architecture needed to reduce the risk of financial crises in the future. Various reports have addressed these issues: the Turner Review (2009) by the Chairman of the Financial Services Authority (FSA), the report by the Independent Banking Commission (2011) in the United Kingdom and the de Larosière (2009) and Liikanen (2012) Reports for the European Union. Others include a report by the Group of Thirty (2009) (the Volcker report), reports by the Financial Stability Forum (2008, 2009) and two communiqués by the Group of 20 (2008, 2009). A list of regulatory proposals, common to all these reports, includes regulation on liquidity risk, market (trading) risk, capital, counterparty risk, compensation schemes, systemic risk and systemic institutions, separation of commercial banking from investment banking and the control of cross-border financial institutions.

7.2.4   Control of liquidity risk

• Control liquidity risk with stress test.

7.2.5   Control of market (trading) risks

• Control market risk with stress test.
• Increase capital regulation on illiquid assets.
• Increase capital regulation on resecuritization (securitization of securitized tranches).

7.2.6   Control of capital

• Increase Core Tier 1 relative to Tier 2 securities. Impose a minimum leverage ratio (tier 1 capital over assets).
• Reduce the procyclicality of capital regulation. Due to loan losses in a recession, capital regulation becomes binding as a consequence of which is a reduction of lending activity which itself exarcerbates a recession. In reverse, due to larger profitability, capital regulation is not binding at a time of economic expansion, which facilitates lending, increasing the economic expansion and, possibly, bubbles in some asset markets. Following the approach adopted in Spain, proposals were made to create dynamic provisions and a capital buffer in periods of economic expansions.[3]

7.2.7   Control of counterparty risk

• Reduce counterparty risk by moving the CDS market to a central clearing counterparty with margin calls and daily settlements.

7.2.8   Control of compensation schemes

• Design financial incentives away from short-term profit to longer-term profit. Include clawback clauses in compensation schemes to introduce symmetry in the sharing of gains and losses.

7.2.9   Control of systemic risk

• Control of macro systemic risk. The view is that the micro control of the soundness of individual financial institutions is not sufficient, and that public authorities need to control systemic risk, a risk rarely defined. Our interpretation of systemic risk is the threat of economic shocks that could affect jointly several institutions (increasing correlation across the default risk of financial institutions). Examples of a shock are a bubble on the real estate market or the devaluation of a currency when domestic units are running a foreign exchange risk. The de Larosière report (2009) proposes to replace the Banking Supervisory Committee, a college of European supervisors who meet at the European Central Bank,[4] with a European Banking Authority and a European Systemic Risk Council (ESCR) presided by the

President of the European Central Bank.[5] The G20 meeting in London in April 2009 proposed to change the Financial Stability Forum (a club of Finance ministers) into a Financial Stability Board, in charge of monitoring systemic risk with the International Monetary Fund.

• Closer supervision for systemic institutions.

7.2.10   Separation of commercial banking from investment banking

It is felt that commercial banking activities that are vital for the functioning of the economy (deposit-taking and lending) should be insulated (ring-fenced) from potential losses that could occur in investment banking activities, such as trading or the creation of complex structured investment vehicles.

7.2.11   Control of cross-border financial institutions

Coordinate better the regulation and supervision of international financial groups. The de Larosière Report proposes to move progressively toward a European System of Financial Supervision (ESFS), with Level 3 committees[6] receiving more authority to arbitrate problems with the supervision of international groups. The G20 calls for the creation of colleges of national supervisors to coordinate the supervision of international groups. The European Commission (2012) proposes to move supervision of banks located in euro-countries from domestic authorities to the European Central Bank.

Additional measures of G20 are a curbing of tax havens and the supervision of systemic hedge funds, although neither of these seems to have been at the origin of the current crisis.

This long catalogue of measures to strengthen bank regulation and supervision is no doubt useful. But, one cannot refrain from asking two questions: are these proposals not addressing issues of the past (observed during the crisis)? Why were these measures not taken before the crisis? Evidently very few institutions saw the crisis coming. A few quotes from reports published before and during the crisis[7] by the European Central Bank, the International Monetary Fund and the Basel Committee of Banking Supervision (BCBS) are telling:

November 2006 (report by the Banking Supervision Committee (BSC) of the European System of Central Banks (ESCB), (ECB, 2006, p. 4): *'Vulnerability of the (banking) sector to adverse disturbances has diminished considerably.'*

November 2007 (report by the Banking Supervision Committee (BSC) of the European System of Central Banks (ESCB) (ECB, 2007a): *'Solvency should remain robust (p. 7), financial positions of large EU banks remained strong in the first half of 2007' (p. 11), 'Tier 1 capital ratio remains adequate to cope with unexpected losses' (p. 16), 'worsening earning prospects, but shock absorption capacity remains comfortable' (p. 37).*

The 2009 Turner Review in the United Kingdom (Turner Review, 2009) quotes the International Monetary Fund (Global Stability Report, April 2006, IMF):

> There is a growing recognition that the dispersion of credit risk by banks to a broader and more diverse group of investors, rather than warehousing such risk on their balance sheets, has helped make the banking system and overall financial system more resilient. The improved resilience may be seen in fewer bank failures and more consistent credit provision. Consequently the commercial banks may be less vulnerable today to credit or economic shocks.

Following the crisis, as discussed above, emphasis is put on strengthening regulations and supervision, such as those on liquidity risk and stress testing. The Basel II capital regulations are criticized for focusing too much on a single capital measure (Acharya and Richardson, 2009). However, a reading of Pillar 2 of the Basel II regulation finalized in June 2004 (BCBS, 2004) indicates explicitly that banking supervision must go beyond capital regulation:[8]

> # 738 Market risk: The assessment is based largely on the bank's own measure of Value-at-Risk or the standardized approach for market risk. Emphasis should also be placed on the institution performing stress testing in evaluating the capital to support the trading function. (BCBS, 2004, p. 161)

> # 741 Liquidity risk: Liquidity is crucial to the ongoing viability of any banking organization. Banks' capital positions can have an effect on their ability to obtain liquidity, especially in a crisis. Each bank must have adequate systems for measuring, monitoring and controlling liquidity risk. Banks should evaluate the adequacy of capital given their own liquidity profile and the liquidity of the markets in which they operate. (BCBS, 2004, p. 161)

One cannot help but observe that Basel II was asking explicitly for stress testing in market risk and liquidity risk. Why were these regulations not enforced? All the above proposals deal with emphasis on existing regulations or on new regulations, but they fail to address a central issue: the enforcement of regulations and conservative bank supervision. Moreover, the emphasis is almost exclusively on a reinforcement of public controls. No mechanism is suggested to develop private controls. In our opinion, three additional issues have to be addressed in a satisfactory manner in order to reduce significantly the risk of future global financial crises:

1. The accountability of banking supervisors. Banks were heavily regulated for many years. Why has the current supervision system allowed this crisis to happen?

2. The Too-Big-To-Fail doctrine. There is an accepted view that large, systemic institutions should not be allowed to fail. This creates a problem as the credit risk on these institutions is not priced properly by the market, creating a risk of moral hazard. As an outcome of the resolution of the crisis is creating even bigger institutions (such as the merger of Bank of America, Countrywide and Merrill Lynch, or BNP-Paribas and Fortis), this Too-Big-To-Fail doctrine must be reviewed.
3. The supervision of international banking groups needs specific attention.

These issues are discussed in the next section.

7.3   Three proposals to complete the reform agenda

7.3.1   Accountability of banking supervisors

It is a common observation that over the last two years, unlike the case of CEOs of banks, very few heads of national supervisory authorities have been invited to step down.[9] This raises the question of the accountability and independence of banking supervisors. An illustrative example is the case of several countries of Central and Eastern Europe (ECB, 2006, 2007a). Banks were allowed to lend massively in foreign currency (mostly Swiss francs, euro, and yen) on the individual mortgage market. This created a large source of systemic risk, as the devaluation of the local currency would raise the rate of default in the entire banking system. Why has this source of systemic risk been allowed to develop? It is not difficult to imagine that, for many ministers, a strong development in the real estate market was helping the economy, employment, and the public budget with increased tax receipts. One would have needed a very brave bank supervisor to put a break on foreign currency lending, slowing down the economy and hurting real estate developers. Another example is the risk division index imposed on mutual funds in some countries. So as to protect investors and provide them with minimum risk diversification, a mutual fund cannot invest more than 10% of its assets with the same counterparty. However, when money market funds were created in Europe, competing with bank deposits, banks lobbied successfully in some countries for an exception to this 10% rule. In Belgium, for example, money market funds can invest up to 25% of assets in money market certificates issued by the sponsoring bank (CBFA, 1991). For the sponsoring bank, the exception to the 10% risk rule was welcome in order to retain liquidity in the bank. The argument for the exception is that, regulated by competent authorities, the risk of bank default is minimal. Here, again is an example of how lobbying and a twist in regulation could harm the systemic stability of the financial system if worries about bank soundness start to migrate to the money market funds market.

Some (Rochet, 2008) are calling for truly independent banking supervisors who would be evaluated on their success in maintaining the stability and soundness of a banking system. In the same way as central banks have been given independence to conduct monetary policy to control inflation, independence would be given to banking supervisors to develop soundness in the banking system. One must recall that the independence of central banks is justified by the argument that, due to short cycles of political elections, Ministers of finance will be tempted to expand money supply to steer the economy in the short-term, at a cost of creating inflation and longer-term ills for the economy. To reduce the impact of lobbying or too short-term goals of public policy makers, independence was given to central banks to control inflation. Should banking supervision be given a similar independence?

The de Larosière report (2009, footnote 10, p. 47) is very explicit on this issue and the limited degree of independence that should be given to banking supervisors:

> As such, the supervisory authority must be empowered and able to make its own independent judgements (e.g., with respect to licensing, on-site inspection, off-site monitoring, sanctioning, and enforcement of the sanctions), without authorities of the industry having the right or possibility to intervene. Moreover, the supervisor itself must base its decision on purely objective and non-discriminatory grounds. However, supervisory independence differs from central banking independence (i.e., in relation to monetary policy), in the sense that the government (usually the Finance Minister) remains politically responsible for maintaining the stability of the banking system, and the failure of one or more financial institutions, markets or infrastructure can have serious implications for the economy and the tax payer's money.

The de Larosière report is very explicit on the limited independence of banking supervisors: day-to-day banking supervision should be independent, but, unlike monetary policy, the government is responsible for maintaining the stability of the banking system. Since this system seems to be prone to regulatory capture and/or short-term political interest, one wonders as to whether banking supervision should not receive the same degree of independence as that given to monetary policy and central banks. Note that the decision to bailout an institution with implications for taxpayers' money would still remain with the government. What would be given to the independent authority is the authority to pass regulation and to enforce supervision with the sole objective of preserving the stability and soundness of the banking system. In the author's opinion, given that it is not a lack of regulations but poor enforcement by banking supervisors that has contributed to the crisis, a reinforcement of the accountability of banking supervisors is a must. Independence with clearly set objectives – soundness of the banking system – would contribute greatly to accountability. The decision to bailout an institution would remain with the Ministry of Finance as it would likely involve the use of taxpayers' money. This system would be a second best as those who might face the cost of a bailout will complain that they were not in charge of supervision. Still, we take the view that the independence given to the supervisors will outweigh the cost if adequate governance rules create the incentives to establish a sound and stable banking system (Dermine, 2013). Institutional structures are moving in that direction in some countries. In Great Britain, the supervisory authority (FSA) is integrated into the independent Bank of England and, in the Eurozone countries, a proposal of the European Commission (2012) is to move banking supervision to the independent European Central Bank.

7.3.2   The too-big-to-fail doctrine

Several of the international proposals call for closer supervision of systemic institutions. Although not explicitly mentioned, as central banks have generally chosen to keep some ambiguity, there is an implicit recognition that the default of large institutions would cause systemic risk, and that, in case of distress, they would benefit *de facto* from some type of public support. A group of 26 global systemically important financial institutions (G-SIFIs) has been identified by the Basel Committee. As public support has often taken the form of public guarantees on the debt issued by these firms, the systemic institutions benefit from a significant source of competitive advantage: the ability to raise debt at a lower cost of funds. There is no doubt, in the author's opinion, that this state of affairs has facilitated the creation of very large financial institutions. And one is forced to recognize that the resolution of the crisis has created even larger systemic institutions. In the United States, Bank of America has purchased Countrywide and Merrill Lynch. In Europe, the Belgian government has sold Fortis Bank to the French BNP-Paribas. In the United Kingdom, Lloyds Banking Group has been formed with the merger of Lloyds TSB and HBOS. To resolve the moral hazard resulting from the implicit debt guarantee, the authorities are calling for a closer supervision of systemic institutions with a larger capital ratio, as, unregulated, they would not take into account the systemic cost of a failure. Again, we recognize the need to supervise closely systemic institutions. But as these institutions were identified long ago (Dermine, 2000), one is left wondering again why large institutions, such as Citigroup or UBS, were allowed by supervisors to grow so much and take such large risks. The previous proposal – granting more independence to supervisors – would reinforce their power and accountability. A complementary mechanism would be to increase private discipline. Several participants have claimed that private discipline has functioned properly during the crisis as shareholders of banks have been penalized dearly. But, this is not enough. Equity is a very small fraction of the funding of banks' assets. In most cases so far, bank debt – including non-insured deposits, interbank debt, subordinated debt – has been protected, often with explicit public guarantees. A way to increase scrutiny of banks, beyond that of supervisors, is to put bank debt at risk, that is to create the risk of bank failure. As these systemic institutions are vital for the proper functioning of the economy, one needs to design a bankruptcy system that allows for the benefits of default (increase in market discipline), with a maximum reduction of the cost of default (Dermine, 2003, 2006). To reduce the cost of the default of a large bank, three features must be met. The first is that the bank should be closed for only a few days (during a weekend). As depositors and consumers need to access their funds rapidly, the resolution of bankruptcy must be swift. Special resolution regimes must be able to enforce losses on 'bail-in' bonds or swap, very rapidly, debt for equity before the reopening of the bank. Second, to avoid the fear of domino effects (the failure of one bank causes the failures of other banks), credible information on counterparty risk must be available on the spot. Third, to reduce the risk of a bank run by uninsured short-term depositors and instability, a mechanism must be put in place to chase deposits who have run to avoid the default of the bank. Having no place to hide, they will have no incentive to run (Baltensperger and Dermine, 1987). An alternative is to have an authority that can force conversion of short-term debt into longer-term ones in the situation of liquidity crisis. In short, all banks should be able to meet the bankruptcy acid test: they can be put into bankruptcy. If it is not feasible, then the structure of the financial institution must be changed. With bank debt at risk, there will be much more pressure from private financial markets to limit bank risk. It seems to us that the current proposal calling for closer supervision of systemic banks could be a step in the wrong direction if it increases incentives for banks to become large and systemic.

Finally, a last recommendation on how to complete the international reform agenda, is to address more completely the supervision and corporate structure of international financial institutions.

7.3.3 The supervision of international banking groups

Both the G20 communiqués (2008, 2009) and the de Larosière Report (2009) have highlighted the need for an adequate supervision of international banking groups. The call is to create effective colleges of national supervisors to ensure better supervision of these groups. In the United Kingdom, the Turner Review (2009) also emphasizes a proper regulation of domestic and international banks operating in the UK. This followed the collapse of Icelandic banks which were collecting deposits through a branch network in the UK. Notice that an adequate supervision of international banks operating abroad with branches or subsidiaries is not a new issue. The collapse of the German Bank

Herstatt in 1974 prompted the *Basel Concordat* (BCBS, 1983). It called, in the case of branches, for regulation of capital by the home regulator of the parent, and liquidity regulation by the host state. Later on, the defaults of Banco Ambrosiano Holdings and BCCI called again attention to the supervision of international groups. Recent calls to improve the supervision of international financial firms confirm that the lessons of history have not yet delivered satisfactory responses. In the European Union, although the single market has been in place since 1992, the creation of significant cross-border banking groups is a relatively recent phenomenon (Schoenmaker and Oosterloo, 2004). It started with the creation of Nordea, the merger of four Nordic banks completed in 2000, the acquisition of Abbey National by Banco Santander in 2004, followed by Unicredit and HVB in 2005, and BNP-Paribas with BNL (2006) and Fortis (2009).

In the context of cross-border banking, one needs first to identify two specific issues. These issues concern, successively: 1. the presence of cross-border spillover effects, and 2. The financial ability of some countries to deal with bailout costs of large and complex financial institutions.[10] As the European Union is one of the more advanced cases of international banking integration, a discussion of the adequacy of current institutional structure follows. We then draw conclusions on the G20 world level proposals. In the European Union, the supervision of a bank operating through a branch network is supervised by the parent home supervisor, while a subsidiary is controlled by the host authority.

7.3.4   Two specific issues of international banking

The first and main issue concerns cross-border spillovers and the fear that the provision of financial stability (a public good) by national authorities might not be optimal. Four types of potential cross-border spillovers can be identified: i. cross-border cost of closure, ii. cross-border effects of shocks to banks' equity, iii. cross-border transfer of assets, iv. cross-border effects on the value of the deposit insurance liability.

i. **Cross-border cost of closure**. Imagine that a foreign bank buys a Dutch bank, and converts it into a branch. According to the EU rule on home country control, the Dutch branch would be supervised by the authority of the foreign parent.[11] However, Dutch authorities remain in charge of financial stability in the Netherlands. The Dutch treasury could be forced to bail it out for reasons of internal stability, but would not have the right to supervise the branch of a foreign bank because of home country control. Since the lender-of-last-resort and the treasury will be concerned primarily with their domestic markets and banks operating domestically,[12] and since they will bear the costs of a bailout, it is legitimate for insurers to keep some supervisory power on all institutions (branches and subsidiaries) operating domestically. That is, host country regulations could apply to limit the risks taken by financial institutions and the exposure of the domestic central bank or treasury in cases of bailing out.[13] In other words, home country control has to be complemented by some form of host control as long as the cost of bailing out remains domestic. This position appears to have been partly recognized by the European Commission which states that *'in emergency situations the host-country supervisor may – subject to ex-post Commission control – take any precautionary measures'* (Walkner and Raes, 2005, p. 37). This argument is again very present in the British Turner Review calling for effective supervision of all institutions operating in the UK. In this case, since the default of a large international bank could affect several countries, the optimal decision to bail out should take into account the interest of all parties–countries affected. As is discussed below, such a decision could be transferred to the European level or should at least require coordination among these countries.

ii. **Cross-border effects of shocks to banks' equity**. Peek and Rosengren (2000) demonstrated the impact on the real US economy of a drop in the equity of Japanese banks, resulting from the Japanese stock market collapse in the 1990s. The transmission channel runs through a reduction in the supply of bank credit. Since in a branch-type multinational bank, the home country will control solvency (through policy on loan-loss provisioning and validation of probability of default in the Basel II framework), it could have an impact on the real economy of the foreign country.[14] In the current crisis, a similar fear has been expressed by countries of Central and Eastern Europe having banking systems controlled largely by foreign banks.

iii. **Cross-border effects of transfer of assets**. In a subsidiary-type multinational, in which the host country retains supervision of the subsidiary, there could be a risk that the home country colludes with the parent bank to transfer assets to the parent bank. This risk has been discussed in the countries of Central and Eastern Europe. An example is the case of Lehman Brothers Holdings. The investment bank had the habit of centralizing cash operations in New York. In the case of Lehman Europe, the sweep had taken $8 billion out of the UK business the Friday before it collapsed.[15]

iv. **Cross-border effects on deposit insurance**. The general argument is related to diversification of risks in a branch-based multinational, which, because of coinsurance, reduces the value of the put option granted by deposit insurance (Repullo 2001, Dermine 2003). There is an additional dynamic consideration to take into account. A multinational bank could be pleased with its overall degree of diversification, while each subsidiary could become very specialized in local credit risk. This implies that banks in a given country could find themselves increasingly vulnerable to idiosyncratic shock. One could argue that, for reasons of reputation, the parent company will systematically bailout the subsidiaries as if they were branches. This could be true in many cases, but there will be cases where the balance of financial costs versus reputation costs may not be so favorable. Capital adequacy rules should be less stringent on branch-based structure. The more general point is that diversification should be rewarded with a less stringent capital adequacy ratio. Cross-border spillovers raise the question of whether coordination of national interventions will be optimal (Freixas, 2003). This will be discussed in our assessment of the European institutional architecture.

Bailing out costs: too big? too complex?

A second issue is that the bailout of a large bank could create a very large burden for the treasury or deposit insurance system of a single country (Dermine 2000, 2006). This was precisely the case of the Icelandic banks whose size vastly exceeded the insurance capability of the country. A related issue that has received much interest is that some banks have become too complex to fail. Imagine the case of a large European bank with significant cross-border activities and non-bank activities (such as insurance or asset management), which runs into financial distress. It would be very difficult to put this bank into receivership. Given the complex web of corporate subsidiaries and the various legal complexities, the uncertainty concerning the costs of a default is likely to be high, and this complexity might create a temptation for a bailout ('Too Big and Too Complex To Fail').

Two cross-border banking issues related to financial stability have been analyzed: cross-border spillover effects and the size and complexity of bailout. Let us now review the adequacy of the current EU institutional structure.

7.3.5   Adequacy of EU institutions

The EU institutional structure currently in place to deal with financial crises has received a great deal of attention (ECB, 2007b). A series of committees has been created to facilitate cooperation and exchange of information, and a directive on winding up financial institutions has been adopted.[16] The Brouwer reports (Economic and Financial Committee, 2000 and 2001) had very much validated the current EU institutional structure to deal with a financial crisis. They essentially argued that there would be no legal impediment to the transfer of information across borders, and recommended an additional effort to strengthen cooperation through a Memorandum of Understanding (MOU) dealing with crisis situations. [17] In May 2005, it was announced that an emergency plan for dealing with a financial crisis had been agreed by the

European Union finance ministers, central bankers and financial regulators. A Memorandum of Understanding (MOU) among the 25 EU members to facilitate the exchange of information was tested in 2005 and 2006 with a full scale simulation of a financial crisis.[18] But the ECB opposed a move to agree on *ex ante* sharing rules for the financing of a bailout. [19] The latest MOU on cooperation between the financial supervisory authorities, central banks and financial ministries of the European Union was signed on 1 June 2008. Signatories include 58 financial supervisory authorities, 28 central banks including the ECB, and 28 finance ministries (one for each of the 27 EU members, with the exception of Denmark which has a ministry of finance and a ministry of economics as signatories). The number of signatories (114 in total) is representative of the potential complexity in dealing with large international groups in the European Union. The 2008 MOU calls for a Voluntary Specific Cooperation Agreement (VSCA) on crisis management and resolution between the finance ministries, central banks and financial supervision authorities of countries A, B and C.

In the context of the Financial Services Action Plan, the directive on *Winding up of Credit Institutions*[20] was adopted in 2004, sixteen years after it was first proposed. It is consistent with the home regulator principle. When a credit institution with branches in other member states fails, the winding up process will be subject to the single bankruptcy proceedings of the home country. Note that, although recognized as a significant piece of legislation to avoid the complexity issue, it falls short of solving the subsidiaries issue.

Accepting a first–best accountability principle, according to which banking supervision, deposit insurance, and bailing out should be allocated to the same country, it appears that, in European banking, there are three approaches to allocate banking supervision: to the *host state*, to the *home country*, or to a *European entity*. The pros and cons of the three approaches are reviewed.

In the *host state* approach, adopted in New Zealand,[21] multinational banks operate with a subsidiary structure. The national central bank retains control of banking supervision, deposit insurance, and bailout.[22] This system suffers from three drawbacks. First, it does not allow banks to realize fully the operating benefits expected from branch banking (Dermine, 2003 and 2006). Second, a subsidiary structure contributes to the creation of large and complex financial institutions (LCFI). Subject to different bankruptcy proceedings, the closure of a large international bank would become very complex. In a branch structure, the European directive on Winding Up would be applicable, subjecting the bankruptcy proceedings of one country. Third, the resolution of a crisis could be hampered, as discussed above, by problems linked to transfer of assets from subsidiaries to the parent, or to problems of sharing of information. It appears that a host country-based system would not allow to realize fully the expected benefits of European integration.

The second approach, the *home country,* currently applicable to cross-border branches in the European Union, suffers from two drawbacks. The first is that small European countries, such as Ireland, Sweden, Belgium, Switzerland, or the Netherlands, may find it difficult to bear the cost of the bailout of a large international bank.[23] European funding might be needed. The second is related to the cross-border spillover effects. The decision to close a bank could affect other countries. In principle, cooperation among countries could take place in such a situation, but one can easily imagine that conflicts of interest between countries on the decision to close a bank will arise, and that the sharing of the bailing out costs among countries will not be simple (Schoenmaker and Oosterloo, 2004 ; Schoenmaker, 2009). These conflicts of interest could, at times, even limit the cross-border exchange of information among regulators. Freixas (2003) has called for *ex ante* rules to force this transfer of information. Goodhart and Schoenmaker (2009) explore *ex ante* mechanisms for fiscal burden sharing in a banking crisis in Europe.

The de Larosière Report is the first serious call on the lack of adequacy of the current arrangement to prevent and deal with financial crises. Besides the replacement of the Banking Supervisory Commitee (BSC) by a European Systemic Risk Council (ESRC), the Report proposed to move gradually to a European System of Financial Supervision (ESFS). This is in line with the G20 proposal of creating a college of national banking supervisors to supervise cross-border banks, but it goes further. It wants to give authority to the Committee of European Banking Supervisors to take decision and arbitrage eventual conflicts between national supervisors. In a first stage (2009–2010), the CEBS was transformed into a European Banking Authority. In a second stage, the European System of Financial Supervision was created. It includes the college of national supervisors, the newly created European Banking Authority and observers from the ECB.

In our opinion, the de Larosière proposal is not going far enough. An adequate public architecture for the proper functioning of financial markets must deal with four issues: regulation, supervision, special resolution regimes to enforce losses on private creditors and the rights to bailout (including financing with taxpayers' money). The creation of the ESFS is dealing with the first two issues, regulation and supervision. Instead of creating a European body, it relies on a college of supervisors and a banking authority that can arbitrage when necessary. As concerns the last issue, the decision to bailout, it is left to the national level. As such, it does not solve the problem of externality discussed earlier. It is therefore not a surprise that, although calling for international cooperation, the British Turner Review wants to strengthen host country supervision in the United Kingdom.

The lesson of the European Union with colleges of supervisors and memoranda of understanding is that it does not work satisfactorily at a time of a crisis. The G20 call for the creation of colleges of national supervisors ignores this EU experience. In the European Union, although progress is made in the de Larosière Report in dealing with the first two issues, regulation and supervision, a gap still exists with the bailout decision. The severity of the international crisis calls for more advanced solutions to cross-border banking.

The *home country* approach has served European banking well until now, because the scale of cross-border banking was limited and banks were operating abroad mostly with subsidiaries. Host country supervision was effectively taking place. The crisis has highlighted two facts: first, that branch banking was starting to take place limiting control by the host authority. Second, that in case of failure, international cooperation was not effective. The two drawbacks of the *home country* approach, discussed above, lead us to call again for a European-based system of banking supervision and deposit insurance for large international banks. An international bank would be defined either by its size, equity relative to the GDP of one country (say, 3%), or by its market share in a foreign country (say, 10%). Goodhart (2003) argued that a European supervisory agency cannot exist as long as the cost of the bailing out is borne by domestic authorities, with reference to a British saying '*He who pays the piper calls the tune*'. There is no disagreement with this accountability principle, but the recommendation to move banking supervision, deposit insurance, and bailing out to the EU is motivated first by the fact that, *de facto*, the bailout of large banks from small countries will be borne by European taxpayers, and, second, that spillover effects demand a coordinated resolution. A discussion of cross-border bailout will turn rapidly into an issue of taxpayers' money and into a constitutional debate. A discussion on the preference of citizens to define the border of a nation at the country or European level cannot and should not be avoided. It will guide the choice among *host country* or EU-wide control of international banks.

The proposal of the European Commission in 2012 to move banking supervision to the European Central Bank is a step in the right direction. However, it remains to be seen what will happen to deposit insurance, who will take the decision to bailout a bank, which special resolution regime will have the authority to enforce losses (Schillig, 2012), and in the case of public bailout, how the sharing of the financial burden will be shared among taxpayers. One should not take a piecemeal approach: transfer of supervision to ECB first and a decision on other issues at a later stage. To create confidence in the new European banking system, the allocation of rights to special resolution regimes and a system to allocate losses to taxpayers should be defined explicitly. One should not put the cart before the horse.

Globally, it seems that very strong host supervision should prevail. This is very much the case as international banking often develops with subsidiaries (Dermine, 2003).

7.4   Conclusion

Following the international banking crisis, a series of proposals have been made to reinforce the quality of banking supervision. They concern: liquidity, trading risk, capital and provisioning, compensation policies, systemic risk, and college of national supervisors. It is the author's opinion that, although useful, these proposals stop short of addressing three main issues: how to increase the accountability of supervisors? How to limit the Too-Big-To-Fail doctrine? How to supervise international groups?

It is striking to observe that pre-crisis regulation, such as Basel II, was already calling for stress tests on liquidity and market risk. The supervision issue in the crisis was not a lack of regulation but a lack of enforcement of regulation and effective supervision. How to increase accountability of bank supervision seems to be the issue. The second issue is the existence of systemic banks. Their existence seems to be taken for granted, with a need to guarantee their debt and, as a consequence, to supervise them closely to limit moral hazard. An alternative would be to design an adequate bankruptcy process for these institutions. The fear of bankruptcy would raise private incentives of debt holders to monitor bank risks. Finally, the G20 proposal of a college of supervisors will not help much if one examines the experience of the European Union. The *home country* approach has served European banking integration well until now because most banks were operating across borders with subsidiaries (regulated by host authorities). Cross-border banking with branches and spillover effects caused by bank failures call for European cooperation. And, in addition, small European countries may not be able, as the extreme case of Iceland illustrates, to bailout their large international banks. This raises the issue of transferring the cost of bailing out, deposit insurance and banking supervision of large international banks to a European entity. The proposal of the European Commission to transfer bank supervision to the ECB is a step in the right direction. However, in the case of international banks, it needs imperatively to be complemented by an explicit allocation of rights to special resolution regimes, by an identification of the authority that will decide the need for a bailout, and by a clear understanding of the distribution of eventual losses to taxpayers.

Notes

1. In March 2009, Montei di Paschi received Italian government funding, after the ill-timed decision to buy Banca Antonveneta from the Spanish Santander in November 2007 (WSJ, 26 March 09).
2. A similar role of liquidity insurance is the offering of lines of credit, allowing borrowers to call money on demand.
3. On the issue of dynamic loan-loss provision and capital, some clarity appears to be needed. Provisions should be set to evaluate at the fair value of assets (taking

into account the probability of default and a loss-given default). The objective is to evaluate the net economic value of a financial institution. Capital should be set to cover unexpected losses, to keep the net economic value positive, that is to ensure the survival and lending capacity of the bank in periods of severe recession. One would like to avoid the manipulation of provisions which reduce transparency and accountability of management. In Dermine (2008), we call to the attention that too severe capital regulation can have the unintended effect of forcing banks to divest of safe assets with too low a margin.

4. Dermine, 2006.
5. Note that according to ECB (2007b), the Banking Supervisory Committee (BSC) was already contributing to the macro-prudential and structural monitoring of the EU financial system.
6. With reference to the Lamfalussy process (Dermine, 2006), Level 3 committees, such as the European Banking Authority (formerly the Committee of European Banking Supervisors, CEBS), advise the European Commission with steps to harmonize European banking regulations.
7. Public information on the risk of a crisis on the US subprime market can be dated to February 2007 with the announcement by HSBC of large loan losses in its US consumer finance subsidiary, Household International.
8. Basel II regulations were applied in the European Union in 2008.
9. Exceptions include the head of banking supervision in Ireland, or the president of the central bank in Iceland.
10. A third issue of a more technical nature is deposit insurance coverage and the ability to reimburse depositors rapidly in case of bank closure (Dermine, 2006).
11. Although Iceland is not a Member of the European Union, the provisions of the single market applies to it due to its membership in the European Economic Area (EEA). This is the reason why branches of Icelandic banks were allowed to operate in the UK with apparently minimum supervision by the British authorities (Turner Review, 2009).
12. It is well known that the Bank of Italy did not intervene to prevent the collapse of the Luxembourg-based Banco Ambrosiano Holding, because it created little disruption to the Italian financial markets.
13. Bailing out would occur if the failure of a branch of a foreign bank led to a run on domestic banks.
14. The Basel Committee on Banking Supervision (2004) discusses the respective role of host and home country in validation of PDs. It calls for adequate cooperation between host and home authorities, and a lead role for the home country authority. In the case of Nordea, the Swedish supervisory authority has the final control of PDs across the group. This is in line with a recommendation by the European Union (ECB, 2007b).
15. FT 15 April 2009.
16. There are currently four potential forums for coordination. The *European Banking Committee* assists the European Commission in preparing new banking community legislation. The *Committee of European Banking Supervisors (CEBS)* is concerned with the application of EU regulations. At the *EU Groupe de Contact (GdC)*, national supervisors of banks meet regularly to exchange information. At the European Central Bank, the *Banking Supervisory Committee* (BSC) works in the context of the Eurosystem's task of contributing to the smooth conduct of policies pursued by the competent national authorities relating to the supervision of credit institutions and the stability of the financial system (article 105 (5) of the Treaty on European Union).

17. One cannot fail to notice the excess of optimism in these reports. Indeed, de Larosière (2009) reports the lack of resources and authority of the Committee of European Banking Supervisors (CEBS) and the inadequate cooperation in the case of handling the crisis of the Belgian–Dutch Fortis (despite the existence of an MOU between the Dutch and Belgian authorities (ECB, 2007b)).
18. Financial Times 16 May 2005 and 10 April 2006. ECB (2007b).
19. Financial Times 23 April 2007 and 17 September 2007; ECB (2007b).
20. Official Journal 125, 05 May 2001.
21. According to Schoenmaker and Oosterloo (2004), to allow them to exercise control, authorities in New Zealand require some overseas banks to establish locally incorporated subsidiaries, instead of operating as branches.
22. It must be observed that the host country= approach is applied as well in Europe when banks operate abroad with subsidiaries.
23. Note that large European countries might prefer the *status quo* to make the expansion of banks from smaller countries more difficult. One observes that the resolution of the banking crisis with public funding has increased the public debt of small countries, with a significant impact on the spread paid on this debt.

References

Acharya, V.V. and Richardson, M. (2009) *Restoring Financial Stability.* Wiley Finance.

Allen, F. and Gale, D. (2007) *Understanding Financial Crises.* Oxford University Press.

Baltensperger, E. and Dermine, J. (1987) 'Banking Deregulation in Europe', *Economic Policy*, 4: 63–110.

Basel Committee of Banking Supervision (1983) *Principles for the supervision of banks' foreign establishments.* Basel Concordat.

Basel Committee of Banking Supervision (2004) 'International Convergence of Capital Measurement and Capital Standards', (comprehensive version published in June 2006), Bank for International Settlements, Basel.

de Larosière, J. (2009) *The High-Level Group on Financial Supervision in the EU.* European Commission, Brussels, 1–85.

Calomiris, C.W. (2007) 'The Subprime Turmoil: What's old, What's New, and What's Next ?', Federal Reserve Bank of Kansas City, the Jackson Hole Conference, 1–112.

Dermine, J. (2000) 'The Economics of Bank Mergers in Europe, the Public Policy Issues', *Journal of Common Market Studies*, 38: 409–425.

Dermine, J. (2003) 'European Banking, Past, Present, and Future', in V. Gaspar, P. Hartmann and O. Sleijpen (eds), *The Transformation of the European Financial System* (Second ECB Central Banking Conference), ECB, Frankfurt.

Dermine, J. (2006) 'European Banking Integration, Don't Put the Cart before the Horse', *Financial Markets, Institutions and Instruments*, 15(2): 57–106.

Dermine, J. (2008) 'Blueprint for a New International Financial Order', INSEAD Knowledge, (http://knowledge.insead.edu/NewFinancialOrder081104.cfm).

Dermine, J. (2013) 'Bank Corporate Governance, Beyond the Global Banking Crisis', Forthcoming, *Financial Markets, Institutions and Instruments*.

Diamond, D.W. (1984) 'Financial Intermediation and Delegated Monitoring', *Review of Financial Studies*, 51: 393–414.

Diamond, D. and Dybvig, P. (1983) 'Bank Runs, Deposit Insurance and Liquidity', *Journal of Political Economy*, 91: 401–419.

Economic and Financial Committee (2000) 'Brouwer Report on Financial Stability', *Economic Papers*, 143: 1–33.

Economic and Financial Committee (2001) 'Report on Financial Crisis Management', *Economic Papers*, 156: 1–32.

European Central Bank (2006) 'EU Banking Sector Stability', November.

European Central Bank (2007a) 'EU Banking Sector Stability', November.

European Central Bank (2007b) 'The EU Arrangements for Financial Crisis Management', *ECB Monthly Bulletin*, February, 73–84.

European Commission (2012) 'A Road Map Towards a Banking Union', Communication from the Commission to the European Parliament and the Council, COM, 510 final, 1–10.

European Union (2008) Memorandum of Understanding on Cooperation between the Financial Supervisory Authorities, Central Banks and Finance Ministries of the European Union, ecfin/cefcpe(2008)rep/53106rev rev, 1 June.

Financial Stability Forum (2008) 'Report of the Financial Stability Forum on Enhancing Market and Institutional Resilience', April 1–70.

Financial Stability Forum (2009) 'Report of the Financial Stability Forum on Enhancing Market and Institutional Resilience – Update on Implementation', April, 1–17.

Freixas X. (2003) 'Crisis Management in Europe', in J. Kremers, D. Schoenmaker and P. Wierts (eds), *Financial Supervision in Europe*. Cheltenham: Edward Elgar, 102–119.

G20 (2008) 'Summit Communique', 16 November, Washington D.C.

G20 (2009) 'Summit Communique', 2 April, London.

Goodhart, C. (2003) 'The Political Economy of Financial Harmonization in Europe', in J. Kremers, D. Schoenmaker, and P. Wierts (eds) *Financial Supervision in Europe*. Cheltenham: Edward Elgar, 129–138.

Goodhart, C. and Schoenmaker, D. (2009) 'Fiscal Burden Sharing in Cross-Border Banking Crises', *International Journal of Central Banking*, forthcoming, 1–16.

Gorton G. (2008) 'The Panic of 2007', Federal Reserve Bank of Kansas City, the Jackson Hole Conference, August, 1–91.

Greenspan, A. (2009) 'The Fed Didn't Cause the Housing Bubble', *Wall Street Journal*, 12 March.

Group of Thirty (2009) 'Financial Reform, a Framework for Financial Stability', Washington DC, 1–70.

Hellwig, M. (2008) 'Systemic Risk in the Financial Sector: An Analysis of the Subprime-Mortgage Financial Crisis', Max Planck Institute for Research, November, 1–73.

HM Treasury (2009) 'The Nationalization of Northern Rock', National Audit Office, 20 March, 1–58.

Independent Commission on Banking (2011) Final Report, available at www.banking-commission.independent.gov.uk, London, 1–358.

Liikanen, E. (2012) 'High-level Expert Group on Reforming the Structure of the EU Banking Sector', Final Report, Brussels, 1–139.

Peek J. and Rosengren, E. (2000) 'Collateral Damage: Effects of the Japanese Banking Crisis on Real Activity in the United States', *American Economic Review*, 90(1): 30–45.

Repullo, R. (2001) 'A Model of Takeovers of Foreign Banks', *Spanish Economic Review*, 3: 1–21.

Rochet, J-C. (2008) 'Why are there so many banking crises? The politics and policy of banking regulation', Princeton University Press.

Schillig, M. (2012) 'Bank Resolution Regimes in Europe (II): Resolution Tools and Powers', mimeo, School of Law, King's College, London, 1–47.

Schoenmaker, D. (2009) 'The Trilemma of Financial Stability', VU Report (Free University of Amsterdam), 1–21.

Schoenmaker, D. and Oosterloo, S. (2004) 'Cross-border Issues in European Financial Supervision', forthcoming in D. Mayes and G. Wood (eds), *The Structure of Financial Regulation*, London: Routledge.

Vasicek, O.A.(1987) 'Probability of Loss on Loan Portfolio', Working Paper, KMV Corporation, 1–4.

Vasicek, O.A. (2002) 'Loan Portfolio Value », *Risk*, December, 160–162.

Walkner, C. and Raes, J.P. (2005) 'Integration and Consolidation in EU Banking, an Unfinished Business', *European Economy*, 226, April, 1–4.

Part III

Key Risk Factors in Asset Management

8
Managing Growth and Strategic Risk

Mathias Schmit and Lin-Sya Chao

8.1   Introduction

The financial crisis has caused multibillion dollar losses and put an end to a long period of strong and steady growth in the investment management industry. More importantly, the crisis has revealed the weaknesses and unsustainability of the growth achieved by several financial institutions.

Well known examples include Merrill Lynch's market share push in CDOs, Northern Rock's liquidity crisis, Fortis' hazardous acquisition of ABN Amro, and the disastrous rapid international expansion of Icelandic banks. As apparent from Figure 8.1, which shows extracts from their annual reports, these financial institutions pursued a strategy focused on growth. They made the common mistake of neglecting the strategic risk associated with their growth strategy, and this can be one of the most serious causes of value destruction.

In this turbulent context, the aim of this chapter is to discuss how sustainable growth in the financial industry can be achieved through effective management of the strategic risks. By reviewing the literature and exploring how the world's top 50 banks recognize strategic risks in their annual reports, this chapter highlights that these risks are not adequately perceived by the financial world and draws lessons from the current situation. Furthermore, this chapter suggests a clear definition of strategic risk and points out that uncontrolled growth is a major potential source of strategic risk and increases the vulnerability of an organization. Finally, this chapter discusses a number of key factors that need to be taken into account to manage growth risk effectively in order to secure sustainable value growth.

8.2   Literature overview

8.2.1   Definition

Currently, the literature on strategic risk is extremely limited compared to the literature on other types of risk. Moreover, we find a wide variety of

Year	Northern Rock	Kaupthing	Fortis	Merrill Lynch
2005	'The Northern Rock strategy encompasses efficiency, *growth* and value for both customers and shareholders... By growing lending and improving the mix of higher margin products, Northern Rock aims to *grow earnings* and improve returns to shareholders, at the same time as providing innovative and consumer friendly products to our customers.'[1]	'In recent years, Kaupthing Bank has been *one of the fastest growing financial groups in Europe*. The Bank's expansion has been achieved through *sound organic growth and a number of strategic acquisitions*.'[2]	'There are three strategic axes to the new strategy we launched at the beginning of 2005... Drive organic growth through sharpened customer focus... Increase focus outside Benelux [and] seize non-organic growth opportunities.'[3]	'Our goal is simple... establish a foundation from which we can continue to invest for growth in revenues and profits while producing strong, consistent financial performance; attract and retain top talent; and, above all, add more value to every client relationship.'[4]
2006		'Year of Organic Growth. Kaupthing Bank reported net earnings of ISK 85.3 billion (€972m) in 2006, an increase of 73% from the previous year. Earnings per share amounted to ISK 127.1, increasing by 69% from 2005. Return on shareholders' equity was 42.4% in 2006, which is well above the Bank's long-term target of 15%.'[5]	'Our success in the past two years has given us the confidence to reconfirm and accelerate our strategy of growing this company into a leading European provider of high-quality financial services.'[6]	'Our rapidly expanding franchise outside of the US generated revenue growth of 42% in 2006, increasing non-US operating revenues to 37% of total, the highest proportion in our history. Since 2004, we have announced more than 30 acquisitions, alliances and other strategic investments to accelerate our growth across a broad range of businesses and geographies.'[7]

Figure 8.1   Extracts from annual reports of several banks pursuing a strategy focused on growth

1. Northern Rock, 2005 and 2006 Annual Report, p. 1.
2. Kaupthing Bank, 2005 Annual Report, p. 2.
3. Fortis Holding, 2005 Management Report, p. 2.
4. Merrill Lynch, 2005 Annual Report, p. 2.
5. Kaupthing Bank, 2006 Annual Report, p. 5.
6. Fortis Holding, 2006 Annual Review, p. 1.
7. Merrill Lynch, 2006 Annual Report, p. 3.

Source: Banks' annual reports.

approaches, with a multitude of definitions and interpretations of strategic risk.

Jorion (2001) was one of the first authors to provide a definition of strategic risk as the 'result of fundamental shifts in the economy or political environment',[1] thus implying that strategic risk arises from *external sources* and is not under the control of the firm. Similarly, the definitions given by Slywotzky (2005) ('the array of external events and trends that can devastate a company's growth trajectory and shareholder value'[2]) and Allen (2007) ('external risks to the viability of the business arising from unexpected adverse changes in the business environment with respect to the economy [business cycle]; the political landscape; law and regulation; technology; social mores; and the actions of competitors'[3]) take into account only external sources of risks. Although most other researchers follow a similar approach, a few also consider internal sources of strategic risk.

STRATrisk,[4] for example, suggests that strategic risks are 'those "big picture" risks which can destroy shareholder value and even threaten the very survival of organizations'[5] and distinguishes a number of *internal sources* of strategic risk ('Strategy, Structure, Systems, Skills, Staff, Style, Shared Values') from the *external sources* ('Political, Economic, Social, Technological, Environmental, Ethical, Legal'). Beasley et al. (2007) also uphold the view that strategic risk can originate from internal as well as external events. While not considering internal sources of strategic risk, Emblemsvåg and Kjolstad (2002), for their part, make the link between external and internal factors in strategic risk management. They argue that while many strategic risks may arise from the organization's environment and hence be external, how these external risks are managed is determined by the organization's internal characteristics and competencies.

Several researchers highlight the relationship between *strategic risk and the firm's strategy, strategic decisions and/or strategy implementation*. For instance, Raff (2001) provides a definition based on strategic decisions: 'All strategic decisions induce and impose constraints on the types of risk banks traditionally monitored and managed. ... Strategic decisions also impose a new type of risk... which also needs to be analyzed, monitored, and controlled.'[6] The definition proposed by Emblemsvåg and Kjolstad (2007), 'the risks that arise in pursuit of business objectives',[7] also suggests a link with the organization's strategy. Gilad (2004) introduces the term 'strategic risk' to describe factors that can erode a company's ability to implement its business plan and that appear when the strategy does not fit the market reality anymore. Asher and Gale (2007) also uphold this view: 'We define strategy as preparation or investing for success, and for our purposes define strategic risk as the risk that these preparations will fail, or – perhaps more often – that insufficient preparation will be made for optimal decisions in future. We therefore see these risks as a by-product of strategy.'[8] In agreement with Asher and Gale, Mango defines strategic risk as 'unintentional risks as by-products of strategy planning or execution'.[9]

Definitions often indicate the potentially *devastating nature of strategic risk*, as in the definitions of Slywotzky and STRATrisk,[10] both of which present strategic risk as the *risk to the sustainability and viability* of the company. Similarly, in the above-mentioned definition, Allen (2007) emphasizes the potentially devastating nature of strategic risks ('external risks to the viability of the business arising from unexpected adverse changes in the business environment'[11]). Likewise, Drew et al. define strategic risks as those risks that 'threaten a firm's long-term competitive success and survival: risk to its market position, critical resources, and ability to innovate and grow'.[12]

As shown later in this chapter, the lack of a unique and recognized definition of strategic risk plays a key role in its misunderstanding by financial institutions, and hence in its inappropriate management.

8.2.2   Sources of strategic risk

In addition to defining strategic risk, several authors have classified the sources of strategic risks (see Figure 8.2). Using classic strategic tools, as suggested by STRATrisk (2005) and Allen and Beer (2006), four strategic risk categories can be distinguished: the macro-economic environment (using a PESTEL), the micro-environment (using Porter's five forces), the internal environment (using McKinsey 7S framework) and 'Others' – which include strategic risks not included in previous categories, as well as the SWOT matrix suggested by Emblemsvåg and Kjolstad (2002) and Allen and Beer (2006).

Figure 8.2 shows that strategic risks are mainly considered as arising from the external (macro- and micro-)environment and hence not under the control of the firm. In the macro-environment, strategic risks related to technology are the most widely recognized type of strategic risks, followed by risks related to the political, social, economic and legal/regulatory environment. As regards the micro-environment, the most frequently mentioned strategic risks are those resulting from competition, followed by the risks arising from customers and new entrants. Again, strategic risks are seldom considered as arising from the internal environment; only STRATrisk (2005) and Allen and Beer (2006) include internal sources of strategic risks.

This literature overview suggests that strategic risk can arise from a wide variety of sources, making it even more difficult to apprehend and to manage.

8.3   A suggested definition of strategic risk

For the purposes of this chapter, and working on the basis of our review of the available literature (despite its scarcity and the disparity between the approaches of different authors), we have defined strategic risk as follows:

		Authors									
Source of strategic risk		Emblemsvag and Kjolstad (2002)	Sadgrove (2005)	Drew et al. (2005)	Gilad (2004)	Allen (2007)	Van den Brink (2007)	Slywotzky (2005)	STRAtrisk (2005)	Allen and Beer (2005)	**Total**
Macro-environment	Political		•		•	•	•		•	•	6
	Economical					•	•		•	•	4
	Social				•	•	•		•	•	5
	Technological		•	•	•	•	•	•	•	•	8
	Environmental								•	•	2
	Ethical								•	•	2
	Legal/regulatory				•	•			•	•	4
Market environment	Suppliers			•				•	•	•	4
	Customers	•		•				•	•	•	5
	Competition	•		•	•	•		•	•	•	7
	Substitutes			•				•	•	•	4
	New entrants			•	•			•	•	•	5
Internal environment	Strategy/projects							•	•	•	3
	Style								•	•	2
	Structure								•	•	2
	Systems								•	•	2
	Staff			•			•		•	•	4
	Skills								•	•	2
	Shared values								•		1
	Brand									•	1
Others	Stagnation							•			1
	Critical resources			•							1
	Other stakeholders						•				1
	SWOT	•								•	2

Figure 8.2   Sources of strategic risk identified in existing literature

Strategic risk is the risk to the sustainability and viability of an organization as a result of inadequate strategic decisions or improper implementation of strategic decisions by the organization's management body, or lack of responsiveness of the management body in relation to the internal and/or the external environment.[13]

This definition is based on three dimensions: the level, the sources and the magnitude of the impact of strategic risk.

Firstly, following the approach of Raff (2001), we believe that strategic risk arises from inadequate strategic decisions or lack of responsiveness to developments, strategic decisions being decisions taken at a high level in the organization, i.e. at the board of directors and/or top management level. For example, the decision to pursue growth objectives or to enter into a merger or an important acquisition is a decision taken at the level of the management body and hence might induce strategic risk. As in the case of Mango (2007), our definition states that the implementation of strategic decisions can create strategic risks, but in our view this is so only if strategy implementation is decided/conducted at the level of the management body. In order to avoid any confusion and overlap, we believe that risks arising from strategy implementation not conducted by the management body should be categorized as operational risks.[14]

Secondly, we believe that the sources of strategic risk are both internal and external, as suggested by STRATrisk (2005), Allen and Beer (2006) and Beasley et al. (2007). This point is especially important when we consider that internal sources of strategic risk, though often neglected, can be an important cause of value destruction, as shown later in this chapter. Figures 8.3 and 8.4

Event type	Definition	Example
Strategy/project	Losses due to inappropriate decision or lack of decision concerning plans to reach identified goals	Overreliance on a category of customers, decision to outsource a crucial activity, mismanagement of financial aspects of a growth strategy
Critical resources: capability and availability	Losses due to inappropriate decision or lack of decision concerning the allocation and management of the firm's scarce and critical resources: human, financial and technical resources.	Insufficient training to compensate for skills gap, inadequate recruitment process causing skills gap
Structure	Losses due to inappropriate decision or lack of decision concerning the way the firm is organised regarding the hierarchy, communication channels, cooperation, decision-making process, etc.	Lack of coordination between multiple hierarchical layers, inefficient communication channels causing loss of information
Systems and processes (incl. models)	Losses due to inappropriate decision or lack of decision concerning internal rules, processes and systems such as remuneration schemes, models (for pricing, valuation, risk management, etc.) and IT systems	Choice of an inadequate model to measure market risk, use of non-precise project valuation model
Style	Losses due to inappropriate decision or lack of decision concerning management and leadership style	Authoritarian leadership preventing participation
Shared values	Losses due to inappropriate decision or lack of decision concerning values, work ethics and corporate culture	Lack of clear and strong shared values

Figure 8.3 Sources of strategic risk arising from the internal environment

Event type	Definition	Example
Political	Losses due to inappropriate decisions or lack of responsiveness to changes in the political environment: subsidies, government policy, public investment, trade restrictions, tariffs, tax policy etc.	Governmental decisions not to rescue a major bank
Economic	Losses due to inappropriate decisions or lack of responsiveness to changes in the economic environment: economic growth or recession, inflation etc.	Inadequate response to the economic recession
Social	Losses due to inappropriate decisions or lack of responsiveness to changes in the social environment: ageing population, population growth rate, cultural trend etc.	No initiative to attract and retain the ageing population
Technological	Losses due to inappropriate decisions or lack of responsiveness to changes in the technological environment: R&D investment, technological shift, automation etc.	Investment in the wrong new technology
Environmental and ethical	Losses due to inappropriate decisions or lack of responsiveness to changes in the environmental and ethical environment: climate change, fair trade etc.	Missed opportunity to offer green investment products
Legal and regulatory	Losses due to inappropriate decisions or lack of responsiveness to changes in the legal environment: discrimination law, competition law, employment law, consumer law, antitrust law etc.	Lack of responsiveness to a new regulation facilitating the entrance of nontraditional competitors (ex. MiFID)
Competitors	Losses due to inappropriate decisions or lack of responsiveness to changes in the competitive environment: new competitor, substitute, rising competitor, switching cost etc.	Retailers beginning to offer financial services
Customers	Losses due to inappropriate decisions or lack of responsiveness to changes in consumer behaviour: buyers' incentives, price sensitivity, brand awareness etc.	Not realising that customers are changing behaviour
Suppliers	Losses due to inappropriate decisions or lack of responsiveness to changes in suppliers: forward integration, switching cost, suppliers concentration etc.	Bankruptcy of one of the main suppliers

Figure 8.4   Sources of strategic risk arising from the external environment

summarize the different kinds of factors – in both the internal and external environments – that can induce important strategic risks.

Lastly, in agreement with most definitions found in the available literature, we state that strategic risk can have a devastating impact on a company's value and viability. This destructive characteristic was confirmed in a survey conducted in 2006 by The Conference Board *(The Role of U.S. Corporate Boards in Enterprise Risk Management)*, which found that 53% of board members believe strategic risk poses the greatest threat to the company, while only 15.7% identify financial risk as a key concern. Similarly, Funston's (2004) study of the 100 companies with the largest stock-price losses from 1995 to 2004 concluded that 66% of the companies suffered strategic risk while 37% were harmed by financial risk.

Having defined strategic risk, we now turn to examine how strategic risk is defined and managed in the financial industry.

8.4   The world's top 50 banks and strategic risk

8.4.1   Methodology

The analysis of strategic risk definition and management was conducted among the world's top 50 banks (source: FT Global 500, ranked by market value)[15] on the basis of their annual reports and public information.

8.4.2   Strategic risk definition

A preliminary analysis shows that only 56% of banks (28 out of 50) recognize strategic risk. Moreover, of these 28 banks, a mere 15 clearly define strategic risk, while the others just list it among their risk factors or mention it without further explanation (Figure 8.5).

A closer examination of the definitions used by these 15 banks enables us to draw up the following comparative in Figure 8.6. The dimensions selected are based on the literature overview and include the level at which strategic risk is considered, the recognized sources of strategic risk, and the perceived extent of the impact of strategic risk on the organization.

Confirming the findings of the literature overview, our analysis shows that the majority of banks analyzed (13 out of 15) place strategic risk at the level of strategy definition. Only seven of these 13 banks also set strategic risk at the strategy implementation level. This reflects the prevailing confusion concerning the level at which to deal with strategic risk.

With regard to the sources of strategic risk, Figure 8.6 shows that of the 15 banks that clearly define strategic risk, a majority (12) view strategic risk as something arising from the external environment. Only five of the world's top 50 banks recognize internal sources of strategic risk. This very low proportion is in line with the literature, although internal sources of strategic risk can be a severe cause of value destruction, as described later in this chapter.

Banks recognising strategic risk		Banks clearly defining strategic risk
Wells Fargo	Unicredito Italiano	Bank of America
Bank of America	Standard Chartered	BNP Paribas
Royal Bank Canada	China CITIC Bank	Commonwealth Bank of Australia
Westpac Banking	Mizuho Financial	Credit Suisse
BNP Paribas	Nordea Bank	Intesa Sanpaolo
Commonwealth	Hang Seng Bank	Toronto Dominion Bank
Bank of Australia	➡	UBS
Credit Suisse	Banco Brasil	Deutsche Bank
Intesa Sanpaolo	Shanghai Pudong	Unicredito Italiano
	Dev Bank	Nordea Bank
Toronto Dominion	Barclays	Banco Brasil
Bank		Barclays
Bradesco	Lloyds Banking Group	Lloyds Banking Group
UBS	Resona Holdings	Bank of Montreal
National Australia	Bank of Montreal	CIBC
Bank		
Bank of Nova Scotia	CIBC	
Deutsche Bank	Northern Trust	

Figure 8.5   Banks recognizing and clearly defining strategic risk among world's top 50 banks

Interestingly, most banks (five out of seven) that include strategy implementation in their definition of strategic risk also consider internal sources of strategic risk. Furthermore, half of the banks (four out of eight) that recognize external sources of strategic risk consider only strategy definition – and not strategy implementation – in their definition of strategic risk. These observations might be explained by the fact that strategy definition is seen by these banks as being determined by the external environment, while strategy implementation is seen as an internal source of strategic risk.

Finally, the extent of the impact of strategic risk is rather unclear: seven banks believe that strategic risk can impact the company's value, while seven believe that it can impact the company's profits (with four of the latter group considering the impact on profits only).

8.4.3   Sources of strategic risk

In line with the literature overview, we found it interesting to identify the main sources of strategic risk recognized by the world's top 50 banks. Our findings are summarized in Figure 8.7 which – following the same template as for the literature overview – shows that the world's top 50 banks recognize a wide range of strategic risks.

Again confirming the findings of the literature overview, it is apparent that the surveyed banks mainly recognize external sources of strategic risk. In the macro-environment, strategic risks associated with economic factors are the most frequently mentioned category, followed by technological, legal/

Company	Level		Source		Impact	
	Strategy definition	Strategy implementation	External	Internal	Impact on value	Impact on profits
Bank of America	•	•	•			
BNP Paribas	•				•	
Commonwealth Bank of Australia	•		•		•	
Credit Suisse	•	•	•	•		
Intesa Sanpaolo	•				•	
Toronto Dominion Bank	•	•	•		•	
UBS	•		•			
Deutsche Bank			•			•
Unicredito Italiano	•		•			
Nordea Bank			•			•
Banco Brasil	•		•		•	•
Barclays	•	•	•	•		•
Lloyds Banking Group	•	•	•	•	•	•
Bank of Montreal	•	•	•	•	•	•
CIBC	•	•		•		•
Total	13	7	12	5	7	7

Figure 8.6   Analysis of definitions of strategic risk among world's top 50 banks

regulatory, political and social factors. In the micro-environment, competition is again the most frequently mentioned source of strategic risk.

Given that the number of banks recognizing internal sources of strategic risk is even lower, we found even fewer banks providing examples or categories. The internal sources of strategic risk mentioned are mainly related to the organization's strategy or major projects (mergers, acquisitions and growth), while strategic risks related to systems and staff were mentioned only once.

Only Lloyds provides a longer list of internal sources of strategic risks, and it is also the bank with the most comprehensive categorization of such sources:

The Group's portfolio of businesses exposes it to a number of internal and external factors:

– Internal factors: resource capability and availability, customer treatment, service level agreements, products and funding and the risk appetite of other risk categories;

													Total
Macro-environment	Political								•	•	•	•		4
	Economical	•	•		•		•	•	•	•	•			8
	Social		•						•	•	•			4
	Technological			•		•			•	•	•	•		6
	Environmental/ ethical								•	•				2
	Legal/ regulatory		•	•					•	•	•			5
Market environment	Suppliers													0
	Customers	•				•				•				3
	Competition/ new entrants	•	•	•	•	•	•	•	•	•	•			10
	Substitutes	•								•				2
Internal environment	Strategy/ projects			•						•			•	3
	Style													0
	Structure													0
	Systems									•				1
	Staff			•										1
	Skills													0
	Shared values													0
	Others										•			1

Figure 8.7 Analysis of the sources of strategic risk recognized by the world's top 50 banks

   – *External factors: economic, technological, political, social and ethical, environmental, legal and regulatory, market expectations, reputation and competitive behaviour.*[16]

Interestingly, Barclays and CIBC clearly mention that their growth strategy can induce strategic risk:

   The Group devotes substantial management and planning resources to the development of strategic plans for organic growth and identification of possible acquisitions, supported by substantial expenditure to generate growth in customer business. If these strategic plans are not delivered as anticipated, the Group's earnings could grow more slowly or decline.[17]

   Strategic risk arises from ineffective business strategies or the failure to effectively execute strategies. It includes, but is not limited to, potential financial loss due to the failure of acquisitions or organic growth initiatives.[18]

8.5   Impacts of uncontrolled growth on strategic risks

As shown in the previous section and the introduction, the banks surveyed mainly recognize external sources of strategic risk, including economic, technological, legal/regulatory, political and social factors. However, only five out of the 50 surveyed banks recognize internal sources of strategic risk, and only two banks (i.e. Barclay's and CIBC) mention growth impact as a source of possible strategic risk in their annual reports.

Furthermore, when we look at the main risks reported in the Banking Banana Skins surveys[19] between 1996 and 2010,[20] we find that concerns have changed over the period. Towards the end of the 1990s, the main perceived risks concerned poor management/strategy, competition, poor grasp of technology and poor product design. When we consider the past two years, the main perceived risks relate to more specific and external sources such as political interference, credit risk, over-regulation, credit spreads and macroeconomic trends. In short, over the past decade, perceived sources of risk have shifted from strategic issues to factors originating in the external environment.

These observations illustrate that strategic risk awareness suffers from blind spots. In fact, the sustainability of an institution can be threatened because risks concerning the availability of required resources are not adequately identified and assessed in relation to strategic objectives, given the external factors that may occur. This can obviously happen when the financial system is under pressure. Growth and its management entail risk management issues, in part because many executives see growth as something to be maximized and not to be restrained. However, experience shows that, from a management perspective, growth is not always a piece of good fortune.

Indeed, rapid growth can put considerable strain on a company's resources (financial and human), and unless management is aware of this effect and takes active steps to control it, rapid growth can lead to disasters, especially in the event of exogenous shocks such as sudden adverse business cycles. For example, it is a common tendency to over-rely on credit institutions when markets (particularly the wholesale market) are liquid. This was the case with the Icelandic banks that relied on the unlimited availability of strong currencies.

Looking at another example, hedge funds can be subject to massive losses. A key source of value – and, simultaneously, a source of risk – lies in leverage increasing *de facto* with the growth objectives. In normal market conditions, leverage – including short selling or repo transactions – provides extra liquidity to the financial market and allows expansions. A survey of global prime brokers by Fitch Ratings Ltd. found that leverage for some credit strategies could be as much as 20 times the assets under management. However, in times of turbulence, to meet leverage ratio, hedge funds are forced to liquidate assets and unwind positions at a rapid pace, thus generating massive losses for investors, combined with a possible contagion effect. The problem can be aggravated by the fact that hedge funds are taking illiquid positions, especially in instruments like CDOs and CDS. When they need cash to meet commitments like margin calls from creditors, hedge funds fall into a vicious circle, since they are unable to liquidate their assets and cannot find additional funding. Nowadays, to mitigate these potential risks, some hedge funds are starting to look for permanent funding such as IPOs, debt offerings and committed lending facilities. Examples include GLC Partners, Blue Bay Asset Management, Fortress and Britain's Man Group.

In order to reduce the frequency and impact of strategic risks, it is necessary to establish an effective risk assessment and management system based on a causality-driven approach as discussed in Ayadi et al. (2008). Although it is supposed to be well-defined by regulators and risk managers, risk delimitation remains a puzzle for a number of institutions, especially when it comes to strategy formulation and implementation. One of the main problems is the definition of boundaries between the different types of risk, leading to potential inefficiencies when assessing them.

There is a case, therefore, for developing an up-to-date risk taxonomy based on a causality methodology to distinguish between different types of risks and thus determine at which level of the company they should be tackled. The implementation of such a framework by financial institutions would help to prevent the use of unsuitable risk assessment and management methods that are based exclusively on the classification of events (effects) without taking into consideration either the causes or the possible misalignment between resources and growth objectives. This approach would have been most helpful in identifying and analyzing the risks that led to the recent failure of major institutions. For example, funding or asset liquidity risk was mistakenly viewed as a primary source of risk dictated by the environment instead of being dealt with as one factor resulting from the strategic risk associated with the decisions taken at the highest level of the institution.

Uncontrolled growth leads institutions to follow a biased logic: the faster they grow, the more profitable they become from an accounting point of view, but the more vulnerable they become in terms of liquidity. Of course, leverage can be increased until investors refuse additional lending, particularly when market pressures are strong. However, as already pointed out by Higgins (1977), all of these problems can be prevented if the management body realizes that growth above the company's sustainable growth rate creates financial challenges that must be anticipated and managed. The sustainable growth rate is the maximum rate at which a company may grow given the possible resources available under various scenarios. Management must anticipate any gap between actual growth and sustainable growth. To manage that disparity, the challenge is first to recognize it and, secondly, to implement a viable mitigation plan to manage it. Furthermore, it should be kept in mind that, when a company grows at a rate in excess of the sustainable growth rate, it is imperative for it to respond to the situation by adopting appropriate investment policies.

In this regard, given that the management body is ultimately responsible for the sustainability and viability of the financial institution, there is a need for an overall (strategic) assessment of resources at the management body level. Indeed, the management body should clearly define the institution's risk strategies and risk profile, which have to be translated into business objectives. Therefore, an adequate understanding, on the part of directors, of risk factors and the potential impacts faced by the institution is vital.

Once this high-level task has been carried out, it is essential to update the institution's risk prevention and management policies continuously on the basis of effective risk assessment methods in order to optimize the implementation strategy, especially in terms of availability of essential resources. In the event that a risk assessment system proves to be flawed when faced with an uncommon (not necessarily exceptional) environment, a financial institution should be able to take timely corrective action, such as increasing its essential resources or strengthening its risk management processes and control systems.

Of course, strategic risk management also has to rely on fair judgment from management bodies and experts within the framework of better governance structures, increased transparency and increased risk-control capabilities to meet the (standard) risk governance requirements. In addition to appropriate incentives for banks to establish institution-wide risk assessment systems, regulatory measures are required to ensure that the development of institutions can be effectively monitored and evaluated, and to impose limitations on business expansion when available resources prove to be insufficient in relation to the institution's overall risk profile.

8.6   Conclusion

The current market turmoil is the result of an exceptional boom in credit growth and leverage in the financial system, based on a long period of low interest rates and a high level of liquidity combined with the lack of a strategic risk management framework. In addition to causing multibillion dollar losses among financial institutions, the financial crisis has revealed the weaknesses and unsustainability of the long-term growth achieved by certain financial institutions. It has emphasized the importance of a resilient and stable strategic risk management framework whose main aim should be to create the right incentives to improve the long-term viability of institutions that rely primarily on short-term funding.

As explained in this article, the sources of strategic risk are multiple. However, the key focus of this study is the strategic risk of financial institutions whose growth objectives and business models imply a high dependency on short-term wholesale market funding and high leverage. The sudden drying up of liquidity in markets has had serious consequences for these financial institutions. We suggest that financial institutions may have suffered from a tragic short-sightedness in the rapid-growth environment of the pre-2007 era.

Indeed, beyond 'growth targets' and 'growth achieved', the key challenge for long-term success is the ability to identify the relevant external and internal drivers of risks, including specifically those linked to the availability of the resources required in various stressed scenarios. To manage and thus sometimes to limit growth in order to meet sustainability objectives in the event of a stressed scenario is a difficult exercise for board members, executive managers and operating managers.

In our view, ensuring that strategic risks are managed at the highest level of the company is the main prerequisite for sustainable growth. We suggest that strategic risk management should rely on a methodical approach for coping with internal and external sources of uncertainty and should be a process at the core of decision making. In fact, the primary aim of strategic risk management is to support the achievement of the mission and the objectives of the organization while at the same time ensuring its long-term viability. The methodical approach aims to mobilize sufficient resources and time from the management body to ensure that significant strategic risks are effectively identified and appropriately managed. The response to strategic risks should consist of decisions taken by the management body on the basis of careful consideration of each situation, rather than result from a strong focus on economic capital allocation.

Finally, based on these conclusions, we strongly recommend calling on the relevant EU institutions and bodies to work toward developing sound and legally binding principles for strategic risk management and its governance. In our view, supervisors should provide high-level guidelines on the implementation, validation and assessment of strategic risk to ensure that it is adequately dealt with, instead of focusing inadequately on technically complex systems to assess capital levels, since such systems and their underlying approach do not ensure the availability of the required resources and may themselves generate additional risks, as is apparent from the current crisis.

Appendix World's top 50 banks

Sector rank	Global rank 2009	Global rank 2008	Company	Country	Continent	Market value $m	Net income $m	Total assets $m	P/E ratio	Dividend yield (%)	Year end
1	4	6	Indl & Coml Bank of China	China	Asia	187,885.4	16,196.2	1,425,722.0	10.8		31-12-2008
2	13	20	China Construction Bank	China	Asia	133,228.6	13,530.6	1,104,009.0	9.7	5.0	31-12-2008
3	21	26	Bank of China	China	Asia	115,243.1	9,404.3	1,015,785.0	9.1	5.7	31-12-2008
4	27	31	JPMorgan Chase	US	North America	99,885.4	5,605.0	2,175,052.0	30.9	3.2	31-12-2008
5	29	15	HSBC	UK	Europe	97,408.9	5,728.0	2,527,465.0	12.0	12.6	31-12-2008
6	54	64	Wells Fargo	US	North America	60,345.9	2,655.0	1,309,639.0	20.3	9.1	31-12-2008
7	62	40	Banco Santander	Spain	Europe	56,198.9	11,671.4	1,380,206.0			31-12-2008
8	64	67	Mitsubishi UFJ Financial	Japan	Asia	56,136.7	6,340.7	1,922,182.0	7.9	2.9	31-03-2008
9	83	23	Bank of America	US	North America	43,657.4	4,008.0	1,817,943.0	12.2	8.2	31-12-2008
10	88	142	Itau Unibanco	Brazil	South America	42,580.8	3,577.6	290,079.8	12.8	3.6	31-12-2008
11	91	114	Royal Bank Canada	Canada	North America	41,129.2	3,711.3	589,775.3	10.5	5.6	31-10-2008
12	94	105	Bank of Communications	China	Asia	40,409.7	4,148.8	392,034.4	8.2	4.2	31-12-2008
13	100	204	Westpac Banking	Australia	Oceania	38,605.0	2,765.8	315,033.1	9.0	7.7	30-09-2008
14	107	68	BNP Paribas	France	Europe	37,686.4	3,631.9	2,729,231.0	10.2	3.2	31-12-2008
15	108	157	Commonwealth Bank of Australia	Australia	Oceania	36,649.6	3,433.8	349,452.8	9.3	7.9	30-06-2008
16	110	118	Credit Suisse	Switzerland	Europe	36,110.3	-7,097.2	1,010,317.0		0.3	31-12-2008
17	113	69	Intesa Sanpaolo	Italy	Europe	34,360.0	3,357.0	836,478.6	10.5	3.2	31-12-2008
18	122	103	China Merchants Bank	China	Asia	32,729.7	2,227.3	191,499.0	11.5	2.3	31-12-2007

19	132	78	BBVA	Spain	Europe	30,404.7	6,601.0	713,553.8	4.6	8.1	31-12-2008
20	137	186	Toronto Dominion Bank	Canada	North America	29,363.1	3,123.0	458,887.3	8.7	5.6	31-10-2008
21	141	143	Bradesco	Brazil	South America	28,301.7	3,493.6	208,329.6	8.8	0.4	31-12-2008
22	145	113	UBS	Switzerland	Europe	27,596.3	−18,038.4	1,740,274.0			31-12-2008
23	149	152	Sumitomo Mitsui Financial	Japan	Asia	27,242.7	4,596.8	1,115,064.0	58.4	0.3	31-03-2008
24	153	179	National Australia Bank	Australia	Oceania	26,789.9	3,251.0	470,741.3	7.4	10.0	30-09-2008
25	163	131	U.S. Bancorp	US	North America	25,642.6	2,946.0	265,912.0	9.0	11.6	31-12-2008
26	170	182	Bank of Nova Scotia	Canada	North America	25,002.6	2,558.4	413,595.3	9.9	6.3	31-10-2008
27	171	115	Deutsche Bank	Germany	Europe	24,976.9	−5,128.3	2,895,504.0		1.6	31-12-2008
28	176	149	Credit Agricole	France	Europe	24,569.8	1,346.5	2,173,890.0	16.3	5.4	31-12-2008
29	185	70	Unicredito Italiano	Italy	Europe	23,683.3	7,838.6	1,343,554.0	2.3	20.7	31-12-2007
30	186	214	ANZ Banking	Australia	Oceania	23,616.5	2,378.8	337,592.6	9.0	8.9	30-09-2008
31	187	163	Standard Chartered	UK	Europe	23,565.6	3,408.0	435,068.0	6.1	5.5	31-12-2008
32	190	260	China CITIC Bank	China	Asia	23,317.1	1,216.0	147,755.3	11.2	2.1	31-12-2007
33	198	127	Societe Generale	France	Europe	22,745.6	2,401.1	1,485,890.0	8.8	4.0	31-12-2008
34	210	199	Mizuho Financial	Japan	Asia	21,278.1	3,099.7	1,537,921.0	7.5	5.2	31-03-2008
35	222	264	Al Rahji Banking	Saudi Arabia	Middle East	20,697.7	1,719.8	33,300.9	10.8	3.6	31-12-2007
36	236	194	Nordea Bank	Sweden	Europe	19,986.7	3,512.2	623,380.3	3.7	5.3	31-12-2008
37	240	97	Royal Bank of Scotland	UK	Europe	19,794.4	−34,449.9	3,514,578.0	89.7		31-12-2008
38	246	249	Hang Seng Bank	Hong Kong	Asia	19,254.1	1,819.4	98,356.0	10.6	8.1	31-12-2008

Continued

Appendix   Continued

Sector rank	Global rank 2009	Global rank 2008	Company	Country	Continent	Market value $m	Net income $m	Total assets $m	P/E ratio	Dividend yield (%)	Year end
39	252	259	Banco Brasil	Brazil	South America	18,797.1	4,035.8	238,982.1	4.7	7.1	31-12-2008
40	269	422	Shanghai Pudong Dev Bank	China	Asia	18,159.9	803.1	133,697.7	17.4	0.7	31-12-2007
41	277	119	Barclays	UK	Europe	17,783.6	6,412.6	3,004,331.0	2.4	8.8	31-12-2008
42	292		Industrial Bank	China	Asia	16,814.0	1,224.4	121,411.2			31-12-2007
43	297	153	Lloyds Banking Group	UK	Europe	16,563.9	1,198.5	638,090.7	4.8	18.4	31-12-2008
44	327		Resona Holdings	Japan	Asia	15,119.4	3,016.0	397,558.9	56.2	0.1	31-03-2008
45	349	411	Bank of Montreal	Canada	North America	14,178.8	1,611.6	338,983.2	8.5	8.7	31-10-2008
46	350	419	China Minsheng Banking	China	Asia	13,992.8	925.7	134,401.4	10.6	1.0	31-12-2007
47	355	373	CIBC	Canada	North America	13,897.1	-1,678.4	288,369.9		7.8	31-10-2008
48	358	53	Citigroup	US	North America	13,854.8	-27,684.0	1,938,470.0		44.3	31-12-2008
49	371		Northern Trust	US	North America	13,367.4	794.8	82,053.6	16.9	1.9	31-12-2008
50	372	365	State Bank of India	India	Asia	13,346.4	1,792.4	205,482.0	6.2	2.0	31-03-2008

Notes

1. Jorion, P. (2001) *Value at Risk*, McGraw-Hill, p. 3.
2. Slywotzky, A. and Drzik, J. (2005) 'Countering the Biggest Risk of All', *Harvard Business Review*, April.
3. Allen, B. (2007) 'Strategic risk: The best-laid plans...', *Risk – London*, 20(7): 142.
4. The STRATrisk research project is a collaborative venture between a professional institution, two universities (Bath and Bristol) and industry, aimed at, firstly, gaining an understanding of how strategic risk is identified and managed in UK construction companies and, secondly, providing a toolkit for company boards to better understand and manage those strategic risks and opportunities.
5. *STRATrisk* (2005), interim report, available at www.stratrisk.co.uk.
6. Raff, D. (2001) 'Risk Management in an Age of Change', working paper, Reginald H. Jones Center – The Wharton School (University of Pennsylvania), p. 2.
7. Emblemsvåg, J. and Kjolstad, L.E. (2002) 'Strategic risk analysis – a field version', *Management Decision*, 40(9): 846.
8. Asher, A. and Gale, A. (2007) 'Strategic Risk Management: Mapping the commanding heights and hazards', *The Institute of Actuaries of Australia*, p. 2.
9. Mango, D. (2007) 'An Introduction to Insurer Strategic Risk – Topic 1: Risk Management of an Insurance Enterprise', *Enterprise Risk Analysis*, Guy Carpenter & Company, LLC, p. 145.
10. See footnotes 4 and 5.
11. Allen, B. (2007) 'Strategic risk: The best-laid plans...', *Risk – London*, 20(7): 142.
12. Drew, S., Kelley, P. and Kendrick, T. (2006), 'CLASS: Five elements of corporate governance to manage strategic risk', *Business Horizons*, 49(2): 128.
13. We use the same definition of 'management body' as in the CEBS (Committee of European Banking Supervisors) Guidelines on the Application of the Supervisory Review Process under Pillar 2 (CP03 revised), p. 6: 'The term "management body", which represents the top management level of an institution, is used in this document to embrace different structures, such as unitary and dual boards.'
14. Operational risk is defined in Basel II as 'the risk of loss resulting from inadequate or failed internal processes, people and systems, or external events. This definition includes legal risk, but excludes strategic and reputational risk.'
15. For a complete list of the world's top 50 banks analyzed in this study, see the appendix, pp. 162–164.
16. Lloyds, Annual Report 2008, p. 48.
17. Barclays, Annual Report 2008, p. 74.
18. CIBC, Annual Report 2008, p. 82.
19. The surveys aim to describe the risks faced by the global banking industry as perceived by a wide range of bankers, banking regulators and close observers of the banking scene around the world.
20. Lascelles, D. (2010), 'Banking Banana Skins 2010', CSFI, p. 10.

References

Allen, N. and Beer, L. (2006) 'Strategic Risk: It's all in your head', University of Bath working paper.
Allen, B. (2007) 'Strategic risk: The best-laid plans...', *Risk*, 20(7): 142–143.

Asher, A. and Gale, A. (2007) 'Strategic Risk Management: Mapping the commanding heights and hazards', The Institute of Actuaries of Australia.

Ayadi, R., Nieto, M., Musch, F. and Schmit, M. (2008) 'Basel II Implementation: In the Midst of Turbulence', Center for European Studies.

Beasley, M., Frigo, M. and Litman, J. (2007) 'Strategic Risk Management: Creating and Protecting Value', *Strategic Finance*, 88(11): 24.

Brancato, C., Hexter, E., Newman, K. and Tonello, M. (2006) 'The Role of US Corporate Boards in Enterprise Risk Management', Conference Board with McKinsey and KPMG.

Drew, S., Kelley, P. and Kendrick, T. (2006) 'CLASS: Five elements of corporate governance to manage strategic risk', *Business Horizons*, 49(2):127–138.

Emblemsvåg, J. and Kjolstad, L.E. (2002) 'Strategic risk analysis – a field version', *Management Decision*, 40(9): 842–852.

Funston, R. (2004) 'Avoiding the Value Killers', *Treasury and Risk Management*, April, p. 11.

Gilad, B. (2004) 'Early Warning: Using Competitive Intelligence to Anticipate Market Shifts, Control Risk, and Create Powerful Strategies', Amacom.

Higgins, R.C. (1977) 'How much growth can a firm afford?', *Financial Management*, 6(2):7–16.

Jorion, P. (2001)'Value at Risk', McGraw-Hill, p. 3.

Lascelles, D. (2010) 'Banking Banana Skins 2010', CSFI.

Mango, D. (2007) 'An Introduction to Insurer Strategic Risk – Topic 1: Risk Management of an Insurance Enterprise', Enterprise Risk Analysis, Guy Carpenter & Company, LLC, p. 144–172.

Merritt, R., Linnell, I. and Grossman, R. (2005) 'Hedge Funds: An Emerging Force in the Global Credit Markets', FitchRatings Special Report.

Raff, D. (2001) 'Risk Management in an Age of Change', working paper, Reginald H. Jones Center – The Wharton School (University of Pennsylvania), p. 2.

Sadgrove, K. (2005) 'The Complete Guide to Business Risk Management', Gower.

Slywotzky, A. and Drzik, J. (2005) 'Countering the Biggest Risk of All', *Harvard Business Review*, April, p. 78–88.

STRATrisk Research on strategic risk in the construction industry, University of Bath, available at http://www.stratrisk.co.uk/.

Van den Brink (2007) 'Strategic Risk: can it be measured?', available at http://www.financeventures.nl.

9

Wall Street's Management of Risk: Why It Failed

John H. Biggs

9.1 Introduction

A little-discussed aspect of the 2007–2008 global financial crisis has been the failure of risk management systems in a variety of large financial companies. Preceding this global crisis an extraordinary amount of money was spent on 'risk management' and an equally extraordinary amount of verbiage was said to shareholders and regulators about management's focus on risks. As formal risk management systems are largely a creation of the last two decades, institutions did not have the benefit of the foresight they could provide prior to previous crashes. In addition, since 2008, two risk management system failures produced a massive bankruptcy in the case of MFGlobal and an embarrassing large loss for JPMorgan Chase's previously successful risk management system.

The purpose of this chapter is to analyze these failures by contrasting the highly centralized Wall Street Style, used by most of the failed institutions, with the Accountability Model which relies much more heavily on risk responsibility distributed into the basic businesses of the companies, which appears to be the model for JPMorgan Chase and Goldman Sachs and most large US non-financial companies. (See also Chapter 12 in this volume by Dehnad, who identifies various shortcomings of risk management systems related to the governance observations in this chapter).

During the late 1990's and the first decade of the 21st century, centralized risk management with a 'Chief Risk Officer' and staff became de rigueur for virtually all major financial institutions. The highly quantitative, company-wide approach to risk management accelerated after the *VaR* methodology was adopted by JPMorgan in 1994 and then marketed by them through their spin-off company, Riskmetrics. *VaR* is a quantitative risk management device that attempts to combine all, or major segments, of a company's financial risks in a single metric. By 2000, virtually all major financial companies used this measure, because of regulatory pressure, in their presentations of quantitative risk data to regulators as well as to shareholders.

Perhaps as much as anything, this company-wide comprehensive statistic led to a concentration of risk control at the top of the company, along with an explosive growth of quantitative risk management staff. A few firms even created Risk Committees at the Board level to monitor risk.

The assignment of risk responsibility to a high-level unit, involving the CEO, CFO and Board was characteristic of what in this chapter is referred to as the 'Wall Street Style'. This management style also has been used for other major management functions such as technology and cost management. Its flaws became especially obvious in the 2007–2008 collapse.

Another powerful force leading to highly centralized risk management was the growing use of complex hedging strategies to offset several new accounting standards. For example, as accounting for mortgage servicing moved to a market valuation of this 'asset' (representing the present value of future servicing fees), companies set up hedges against the assumptions used in modeling those values. This hedging responsibility was originally assigned to the CFO staff. In only a few companies has this responsibility devolved upon line managers as they became more familiar with difficult accounting standards issued by accounting standard setters.

It is interesting to review annual letters from CEOs to shareholders accompanying their 10-Ks, to see the excessive boasts about 'discipline', 'comprehensiveness' and 'senior management's hands on devotion to risk control'.

The Appendix to this paper provides examples of statements made by CEOs in the year before they went bankrupt, or were forced by regulators to be acquired by others, or had to receive emergency 'bailout' funds from the federal government. The similarity in wording, emphasis on top management involvement, and uniform confidence is striking. For example: Richard Fuld, the CEO of Lehman in his 2007 Annual Report says: 'We benefited from our senior level focus on risk management, and, more importantly, from a culture of risk at every level of the firm.' Martin Sullivan, the then CEO of AIG, in his 2006 letter to shareholders, wrote: 'AIGFP actively manages its exposures to limit financial losses'. Note that the AIGFP unit of AIG had an extraordinary $500 billion exposure to credit default insurance that ended up causing $40 billion of losses in 2008. The AIG comments are especially serious, since their inconsistency seems to indicate that some early statements were misleading.

Given the extraordinary apparent commitment and funds expended on risk management, one might think that the events of 2007–2009 could have been anticipated and the firm-destroying losses could have been avoided. An important question is how did this failure occur, and what should be the focus of management, regulators, creditors, auditors, consultants and shareholders in the future to avoid similar enormous errors?

Were these risk controls statements just window-dressing? Did a 'culture of risk combined with complex models of risk management increase the risk appetite from the traditional investment banking business to high volume, complex trades' as asserted in Business Week's cover story of June 12, 2006?[1] Or was Joe Nocera right in his *New York Times*, January 2, 2009 Op-ed arguing that using a *VaR*-type methodology as a primary tool misled senior managers? [2] Were the highly compensated managers and directors of all these companies simply incompetent in their use of the celebrated risk management systems? Or did poorly designed compensation systems encourage inappropriate risk-taking that overwhelmed feeble risk management controls?

Or is the solution that was encouraged by regulators, auditors and management consultants in engaging directors, CEO's and senior management on centralized high-level risk controls, simply not up to the job of risk management in these exceedingly complex financial institutions?

This chapter will argue that the risk management practices of large Wall Street firms, defined as major financial institutions that have been described as Too Big To Fail, or Too Interconnected To Fail, or, more generally, Too Systemic To Fail, were a result of an excessive centralization of the risk management function, at too high a level in the company to be effective.

In some cases the executives at the top failed to understand the risks their businesses were taking, and risk management accountability was not embedded in the businesses. In others the CEOs overrode clear warnings coming from those directly engaged in their businesses.

As Jamie Dimon, CEO of JPMorgan Chase (JPM) put it in a Wall Street Journal Op-Ed piece in June 27–28, 2009: 'There must be a relentless focus on risk management that starts at the top of the organization and permeates down to the entire firm. *This should be business-as-usual, but at too many places it wasn't.*' (Emphasis by author.)[3] Dimon further stated in February 2008, 'It's not the risk manager's job. It is the boss' job to manage risk.'

In spite of a JPM risk system relying heavily on risk management accountability embedded in the businesses, one of those businesses, with a seasoned and trusted leader, created an extremely large loss – but not one that put the company itself at risk. Subsequently I will discuss what occurred as an example of the dangers of complex risks mitigated by an environment well designed to prevent such losses. And also how the unusual severe response of the company to those managing that 'business' strengthened their system of accountability.

PriceWaterhouse conducted a study of effective Risk Management in Financial Services which stressed centralized oversight, but also argued that 'embedding risk managers within individual business lines lead to greater understanding and awareness of risk and its link to performance'. Their survey of 400 senior executives in financial services found 61% supporting embedding risk management into individual lines of business but only 1 in 8 thought their own organization's business units and risk management were well integrated.[4]

A classic analytic model of corporate risk management assumes that the safeguards against excessive risk consist of three lines of defense:

1. First, the business unit itself is responsible for controlling risk.
2. The second line of defense consists of committees and staff groups, formed by senior management, that are devoted to the management of risk. This includes the Board Audit and, if one exists, a Board Risk Committee.
3. The outside auditors and regulators constitute the third and last line of defense.

The failures of the second and third lines of defense in the cases of the troubled financial services firms that have been bailed out suggest that future progress in risk management will come from building into company cultures a strong commitment and accountability for managing risk in the crucial first line of defense.

9.2   The Wall Street style

I will use the term 'Wall Street Style' for the highly centralized corporate governance systems that pervade most, but not all, large, multiline and complex financial institutions that have needed federal government support in the recent crisis – for example, Merrill Lynch, AIG, Lehman Brothers, Bear Stearns, Morgan Stanley, Citibank, Bank of America, Prudential, and Hartford Insurance. This is probably also the style of many other financial companies of similar size, but did not generate headline failures.

These companies, based on self-reporting and the available research, relied on a common management model that included a strong role for *centralized risk management*. As will be seen in the Appendix, several paid 'lip-service' to the idea that risk control permeated their organization.

A strong Chief Financial Officer (CFO) with major responsibility for firm-wide cost control, as well as corporate financing is typical. The budget of the company, if one exists, is prepared by such a CFO with narrow inputs, if any, from line management. Evidence of the importance of this position to external eyes derives from how much interest is displayed by regulators, the media and equity analysts whenever personnel changes occur in the CFO function. Media attention to line managers in Wall Street Firms is minimal, and usually buried in later page stories.

A 'Corporate Risk Officer' (CRO) almost always exists with a substantial staff of highly skilled technical people to oversee the total risk of the company – including investment, credit, excessive exposures and, in some assignments, operational risks. A large highly regulated firm would face severe scrutiny if it could not claim that it had addressed the concerns about risk in such a manner.

For many companies the corporate governance scandals of 2000–2002 led to hasty and poorly implemented risk management programs. Certainly, a CRO with a large staff of mathematicians could be a quick fix to meet shareholder skepticism and regulatory demands. The long and arduous work of developing a culture permeating the entire enterprise and accompanying policies to support a risk control mentality at the operating level appears not to have been part of 'risk control'. Arguably the most essential and difficult piece of this work would have been imposing a longer-term, risk recognizing policy when rewarding high performance people in trading, banking and product development groups.

Compensation policies for traders, investment bankers and other risk-taking functions rose significantly in the 2002–2007 period, leading to an 'epidemic of false alpha – that is, short-term excess returns as the basis for the current bonus pool'.[5]

The most fundamental way to implement a risk control culture is to avoid such short-term casino incentives. Human Resource practices that result in company–employee loyalty should have been implemented in order to avoid high turnover and a short-term profit culture.

Blame does not only lie with institutions, as regulators, auditors and consultants often push for top level involvement in risk control. They heap praise on Boards of Directors and CEOs for their hands-on efforts concerning risk management. Anyone with experience in overseeing a large complex financial institution would know that such senior management efforts may create a tone-at-the-top commitment to risk management but have little practical hope of controlling risks taken by traders, bankers and others who are in line jobs.

Also common in centrally-managed firms is a 'Corporate Technology Officer' (CTO), not to be confused with a 'Corporate Investment Officer' (CIO). The CIO is more likely to have a major role overseeing investments and related risks in the alternate Accountability Center governance model, described hereafter. The CTO will have centralized responsibility for at least all the data centers and possibly also (in most Wall Street Style companies) for all the development or purchase of information systems. He will be the undisputed leader, agenda setter and decision maker on all technological issues. He will hire the staff and formulate the strategy and implementation methods with regard to technology. Everyone working in the company in technology will report to the CTO.

Such a CTO will be responsible for all development of systems as well as for their testing and implementation. Final decisions on priorities within lines of businesses, modes of development, and choices of software vendors, will rest with the CTO and not with line managers.

Finally, in a few companies, the responsibility for risk lies with a long tenured and very active CEO – AIG is an example of such a model where risk management appears to have failed seriously after the forced retirement of such a CEO.

9.3   The accountability model

The more common model for most non-financial businesses is one where responsibility for risk, cost control and technology gradually evolves away from the central core operations to the line managers, to the 'Presidents' of separate major business activities or lines. As typical companies grow in scope as well as in scale, whether through organic growth or, more typically, through acquisition of new businesses, it is a natural evolution to see accountability, responsibility and control placed in the hands of people who know their businesses, and who know their businesses' needs, opportunities and risks.

Companies that exemplify this model include most multiline industrial firms, most 'conglomerate' types of companies and a few financial institutions. Berkshire Hathaway is the best example of such a financial business. JPM appears to have evolved under Jamie Dimon's leadership into this model, but clearly the heritage JPMorgan Company, prior to its acquisition by Chase, had an accountability culture in the 1990s, (see example hereafter). JPMorganChase's huge 2012 trading loss which was a failure within an accountability system, and the company response which clearly reflected its accountability structure. Also, Goldman Sachs appears to have weathered the recent storm through their culture of managing serious risks at the operating level.

The Accountability Model involves much smaller staffs, if any, at the top of the organization. If such staffs exist, their function is limited. For example, in the case of the CFO, the job may be devoted primarily to the capital financing of the company and the management of significant investment assets such as the pension plan or, in the case of a bank CFO, the core asset management function. (Note that in the JPM structure the investment management function for investments of the core was considered a separate 'business' led by a senior executive who was responsible for risk management of that business.)

In an Accountability Model, the CFO, and also the CTO and CRO, if they exist, coordinate, monitor and audit functions in the various lines of businesses but leave major accountability to the line managers. The CFO provides a planning and budgetary framework, which requires *comprehensive* budgeting and financial management by the line operations. He or she also provides substantial oversight of the operating units, advising an engaged CEO in regular discussions with the leadership responsible for cost control, technology and risk management. The CFO in an accountability-oriented company may insist on common financial planning and reporting documents that address the key concerns of senior management.

Given the growing innovation in hedging instruments, another legitimate role for the CFO in both the Wall Street and the Accountability Model, is the oversight of the hedging of all the company's risks. This leads in the first place to centralization, but for financial entities committed to embedding risk management in their business, the CFO would find ways to educate and outsource this critical function to business leaders, as was the case at JPMorganChase. If hedging continues to cover transactions across lines of businesses, this function could stay with the CFO, but would probably not require a high-level highly compensated CRO.

9.4   Sources

Since it is difficult to do quantitative research on this subject, most of the sources are qualitative. For example, Gillian Tett's 'Fool's Gold' describes the culture of the heritage at JPMorgan and the people and events leading to the development of Credit Default Swaps. Tett also describes how the risk control mode as well as the successful curtailment of risk by line managers concerning extensions of the JPMorgan innovation of credit default swaps worked in an Accountability model. The detailed reporting by Robert O'Harrow and Dennis Brady for the Washington Post in 2008 and January 2009 on the development of Credit Default Swaps at AIG is another source. Michael Lewis's excellent essay on AIG in the July 2009 Vanity Fair describes how the central risk managers of AIG were unaware of the exposure in their reckless credit default swap business, but a line officer in their subsidiary company finally stopped the mindless, but already disastrous exposure, from becoming still greater. Ron Shelp's book on Hank Greenberg and AIG gives a clear description of how risk was controlled during Greenberg's build-up of the company[6] (see Tett, Shelps, Lewis and O'Harrow references). Jamie Dimon's quotes in the 2008 JPM Annual Report and the 2011 MDA section of the 10-K describe the important role of line managers in risk management.[7]

The analysis of MFGlobal's structure relies heavily on the bankruptcy Trustee's extensive report.

The next three sections of this chapter describe in more detail how the Wall Street Style works compared to the Accountability Style. The two systems are described in their extreme forms; however, they can be found in many enterprises in a blended form.

9.5   Risk management

A multibusiness financial services firm has multiple kinds of opportunities and related risks. Asset management, investment banking, credit cards, retail banking, custodial services, property casualty and life insurance, and reinsurance, all have substantially different risk characteristics.

It is hard to imagine how a centralized risk management staff could oversee the multiple types of risks encountered by such a variety of financial services. Certainly, a CRO would have to be broadly experienced, and with a staff of knowledgeable and well-trained professionals. The impulse to move toward highly quantified measurement devices is hard to resist and especially when, in a highly regulated environment, they become de rigueur. The fact that such an approach to risk management has utterly failed in so many major financial companies deserves intense scrutiny.

The late Peter L. Bernstein in his introduction to his book 'Against the Gods: The Remarkable Story of Risk' wrote: 'The story that I have to tell is marked by a persistent tension between those who assert that the best decisions are based on quantification and numbers, determined by the patterns of the past, and those who base their decisions on more subjective degrees of belief about the uncertain future. This is a controversy that has never been resolved.'

Perhaps one can attribute the failure of the Wall Street centralized quantitative approach for its inability to resolve this 'persistent tension'. The risk managers failed to find ways to incorporate the common sense of 'subjective degrees of belief about the uncertain future'.

In an Accountability Model, risk management is a fundamental responsibility of the line managers. In asset management, a line Chief Investment Officer has the responsibility to manage risk with the appropriate and usual methodologies – risk concentrations, tracking error to the overall market and other classic forms, covered widely in finance and investment theory. Risk in insurance businesses requires a line actuarial staff, and perhaps a designated Chief Actuary, to oversee the complex and varied natures of insurance risk. Property casualty requires a different kind of actuarial training to that of life insurance actuaries.

Gary Cohn of Goldman Sachs (GS) in 2007, said *'risk management is not a science but an art'* and attributed Goldman Sachs' success to the embedding of risk management in its 'business principles and culture'.

The first sentence in the JPMorgan Chase's 2011 10-K on Risk Governance is 'The Firm's risk governance structure is based on the principle that each line of business is responsible for managing the risk, inherent in its business, albeit with appropriate corporate oversight.'

Perhaps the most difficult risk area to manage is investment banking, where continuous innovations force a constant re-examination of risk. Line officers use many tools to monitor risk: 'reputation' committees, upward review of new products and transitions, concentration measurement and, the newly acknowledged 'systemic' risk. Those at the creation of an innovation are in the best position to understand its risks. It is important to have cautious and thoughtful leadership embedded in such units. Trying to oversee those risks from high above is impossible. (From my personal experience, I have observed how difficult it is to induce directors of major financial institutions to serve on audit committees. This is not only due to the inherent difficulty and time-consuming aspect of the work, but also due to the perceived legal liability attached to it.)

In the accountability model, all these types of risks are managed on a local basis, close to the actual business. The key personnel judgments of CEOs in appointing heads of each of these businesses is not only whether the leaders understand the business but also whether they have the values and the character to enable them to say no when necessary. Overlaying a centralized CRO is a weak solution.

When reviewing the detail of how companies avoided extreme risk (for example, subprime mortgages underlying complex structured products, excessive exposure to credit default risk, too aggressive marketing of credit cards) the common sense of line managers often can be much more effective than centralized risk managers. As sophisticated as the centralized computer models may be, they will not reflect the complex content and context of the realities at business ground zero.

Following are two interesting examples of how line managers identified risks and took action, without any apparent leadership from a centralized risk management function.

9.5.1   Example 1: insuring collateralized debt obligations in 2005–2007 at AIG

An ironically 'good' example of Accountability Center or decentralized risk management judgment is the AIG Financial Products decision in 2005 to *stop* writing credit default swaps on CDO's funding subprime mortgages. Gene Parks, an AIGFP employee in Connecticut was asked to take over marketing of the AIG default swaps business in mid-2005. Before taking the position, he investigated what the underlying collateralized assets were and was astonished to find that 90% of the assets were subprime mortgages. Others in the company were unaware of how the product mix had changed. Parks went to the dominating leader of AIGFP, Joe Cassano and made the case that they should stop writing more (they already had written protection on $500 billion of CDOs!). Cassano reluctantly agreed and, without Hank Greenberg or any central risk management group's assistance, they made a very hard decision[8] (see Michael Lewis in Vanity Fair reference).

The CDO desks at other banks, with highly centralized Wall Street models of risk management, continued to plunge ahead, creating and often holding on their balance sheets such CDOs, without the benefit of credit default protection from AIG or anyone else.

Citigroup was one of the largest issuers, $28 billion in 2005, $33 billion in 2006, and $40 billion in 2007. Since Citi's higher rated tranches were rated *AAA*, they did not show up in the central risk group's *VaR* analysis.[9]

Merrill Lynch's CDO desk also invested $54 billion in 2006 and $38 billion in 2007. With risk management centralized and not concerned with *triple A* tranches, no longer insured by AIG, Merrill entered the start of the financial crisis with over $70 billion of the subprime mortgage CDOs on its balance sheet. Jeffrey Kronthal, an experienced trader, recommended limits on CDO exposure at Merrill in 2006.[10] The centralized risk managers ignored him and he was later fired (see Wall Street Journal, April 16, 2008).

It may be ironic to use AIG, the most severely affected by the subprime mortgage CDO collapse, as an example, but at least in 2005 Gene Parks in his line operation, got them to stop.

9.5.2   Example 2: JP Morgan in the late 90s

Another good example of risk avoidance by line officers is the decision by the original JP Morgan company in the late 1990s to stay away from CDOs based on mortgage loans[11] (see Gillian Tett reference).

The JP Morgan derivatives staff invented the Credit Default Swap in the 90s and successfully deployed it as a device for insuring against credit risk for JP Morgan Bank's portfolio. The first CDOs were collateralized by a book of several hundred corporate issuers. AIG willingly wrote credit default swaps on those CDOs and they have been very profitable for AIG.

Structured mortgage-backed securities had been in place for several years at that time and seemed a natural extension of the corporate-issuer backed CDO. JP Morgan did several mortgage-backed securities transactions but then backed away from the business largely because of the substantial risk involved.

Bill Demchak, the head of the Derivatives group was willing to push ahead but Krishna Varikooty, a statistician in his group put up a warning stating that his models did not provide good inputs for mortgages. Corporate loans distress cycles were well known and were intuitively sensible, with substantial but not total independence from loss contagion. Demchak supported Varikooty's analysis and JP Morgan avoided a major risk. The rapid decline in house prices did finally illustrate Varikooty's concern but the other Wall Street firms issued billions of such CDOs and put their companies' survival at risk. Demchak and Varikooty were supported by the leadership of JP Morgan but the risk avoidance impulse came from the business line itself.

It is interesting to observe that in a relatively short time the present JPMorgan Chase company was formed from four very different banking cultures: JPMorgan and BancOne, which had an 'accountability center' culture, and Chase Bank with a Wall Street management style and the Chemical Bank which was well managed with a mixed style. The resulting entity, now led by Jamie Dimon moved strongly to the accountability model[12] (see references to Jamie Dimon Op-ed and the JP Morgan Chase 2008 Annual Report).

JP Morgan prior to the merger with Chase had rejected financing Enron and WorldCom on the basis of a line banker's skepticisms. Centralized risk management at Chase did not protect it from the commitments that ended up very costly.

9.6   Steps to take to embed risk management in the line organization

Arguably the most essential element of embedding good long-term risk views is to make sure the compensation system for high performing line employees does not give perverse incentives (as do many of the very short-term, one year measurements and payouts characteristic of most Wall Street firms). A multiple year 'bonus/malus' system would be a much better model.[13]

The presence in a creative line operation of some cautious, skeptical and courageous risk managers with the statistical background of a Krishna Varikooty would be extremely valuable.

Another useful custom would be a training of the line financial managers in the complex accounting standards. They create traps in new products and demand caution in compliance. Requiring certification in the new standards before permitting their use is another support mechanism. The auditing firm and the CFO could lead such training that would permit hedging to migrate to the accountability centers.

Academic writers could well provide a textbook on risk management successes, where the Gene Parks and Krishna Varikooty achievements might be described. (We have already an abundance of texts on statistical models of centralized risk management systems.)

Constant interaction between the line operation areas and the CFO and CRO functions, along with rotation of risk-oriented staff between the various areas, is common in industrial firms. In any event, centralized risk management models have a long track record of failure. Our regulators and managers need to move in new directions.

In Dehnad's chapter in this volume, *A Stitch in Time*..., he describes elegant and effective ways to control trading in an asset management operation. Clearly these ideas require technical understanding of the business of trading, which would have to be devised and introduced by risk managers with deep technical skills in trading. They would not be devised by audit committees, CEOs or high-level CROs of comprehensive asset management businesses. In short, the trading operation needs its own traders and embedded risk managers.

9.7   JPM's 2012 $6 billion hedging loss and MF global's 2011 bankruptcy

The biggest surprise since the 2007–2008 crash was the major loss in 2012 by JPM due to a risky hedging position in the management of its own assets. JPM was almost alone in surviving the 2007–2008 debacle without requiring a government bailout (it did accept TARP funds at the insistence of the Secretary of the Treasury to make it clear that everyone was participating and not taking reputational advantage over other banking institutions).

CEO Dimon bluntly called the loss 'stupid' and an 'isolated incident'. It occurred in an office (or a business in JPM terms) that invests excess deposits for the bank and hedges interest rate risk. It was headed by a senior executive with extensive successful experience in the job, with the title Chief Investment Officer.

In the bank's 'accountability model' she was the primary monitor of that unit's activity. Given her past performance over 30 years there was great confidence in her judgment.

For reasons not known clearly from outside the company she and her colleagues made a huge error in judgment. The details of the trades and the failed hedges are not important for seeing how the Dimon model of risk management worked.

First she, rather than the Chief Risk Officer, was directly responsible for the failure. There was no ambiguity. She understood her role and the Board, the CEO and CRO all had confidence in her.

Second, she and her colleagues were immediately identified and held responsible, and were fired, in spite of long and previously successful tenures.

Third, two years of compensation are being 'clawed back', representing roughly $30 million for the Chief Investment Officer. It is significant that the company had the claw back right included in the contracts of the affected employees. This is an extremely important feature in the 'accountability model' and not apparently employed in most Wall Street Models.

Fourth, no action or criticism was publicly directed at the central risk management staff since their role was oversight and monitoring.

Fifth, and most important, the swift and publicly humiliating response clearly gives a message within the firm to all the business managers that they are accountable for risks and rewards in their businesses. Over time, these actions make the accountability model credible.

It is interesting to note that regulators and the media are all asking the wrong questions. For example, they ask where was Dimon himself, as if he were expected to monitor this specific risk himself. Also there was immediate criticism of the Risk Committee of the Board – where were the other Risk monitors in the company? The answer is that they all did their jobs; it was the Chief Investment Officer leading the unit and her colleagues who had the responsibility. They failed, and swiftly and publicly paid high personal prices for their failure.

In short, a well-designed risk management system cannot guarantee zero failure. But it should have far fewer failures than the Wall Street model that brought significant failure, if not ruin, to so many companies in the 2007–2008 financial crisis.

The second example, MF Global, was the most serious failure of risk management since the 2007–2008 crisis. Its failure led not only to bankruptcy but also, apparently, to the misappropriation of customer funds that were required to be held in custody and protected from the other assets of the company.

We know a great deal about what happened in MF Global from the exhaustive report, a 175 page 'autopsy' by the bankruptcy trustee, James W. Giddens. (Submitted to the Bankruptcy Judge in June 2012.)

MF Global's risk management system is the most extreme form of the Wall Street model, with all risk oversight devolving to the control of the CEO, in spite of having a nominal Chief Risk Officer.

The trustee reported that when Corzine became the CEO he quickly transformed a former small but longstanding, Futures Commission Merchant and broker–dealer into a full service global investment bank. Dramatic changes then followed, including significant changes in personnel, lines of business and markets into which Corzine expanded the business.

Few of the new people knew the business well enough to evaluate risk, but several did and warned Corzine. They were ignored and several key people left the firm.

In effect the Wall Street Model degenerated into control by one individual whose avowed purpose was to increase revenue quickly by dramatically increasing risk. Apparently, according to the report, Corzine took a direct personal role in trading the distressed European debt that ultimately brought down the company.

Furthermore, as the European bet turned against him, he forced reluctant employees to transfer customer funds to company accounts.

The trustee also reported that the back office of the firm had not been strengthened to match the expanded scope and scale of the firm. Accordingly, there was no business know-how where a risk management responsibility could be embedded.

MF Global is an extreme case. Had Corzine wanted to build an accountability system he would have had to go far more slowly and patiently. Perhaps it is a characteristic of the Wall Street model that CEOs in a hurry find that model the only way they can accomplish what they want or are charged to do.

9.8 Summary and conclusion

The hypothesis of this paper is that the highly centralized management model of the Wall Street firms may be responsible for many of the failures and weakening of financial firms in the recent crisis.

The Wall Street Style or centralized management seems modeled on 'command and control' as practiced in the military, and historically in single

Table 9.1   Questions that suggest a Wall Street style, centralized management model

Question	Answer
Who is accountable for risk management in the company?	The risk management group reporting to the CEO or CFO
When the company side-stepped the subprime crisis, who received bonus increases?	The Risk Management staff
Who gets blamed for the bankruptcy or coerced take-over of failed Wall Street companies?	CFO

line, simple, and founder managed entities – the Accountability Model is an 'incentive-based' system more in accordance with modern corporate governance principles.

The evolution into a true Accountability Model is difficult, time consuming, and requires substantial forbearance by the CEOs who may prefer more direct control through a centralized model. The full Accountability Model and its concomitant culture, may take a decade to develop before it would show any significant results. It may be argued that market valuations and CEO survival cannot wait that long as apparently assumed by Jon Corzine at MF Global.

However, the downside of the Wall Street Style is the creation of 'imperial CEOs and CFOs', high costs, spasmodic management of changes in costs and personnel, failure to embed in the organization a deep respect for and a disciplined control of risk, and long run failures or at least, substantially less profit than in better managed companies.

The recent financial crisis and the collapse of major Wall Street firms should raise fundamental questions about how these firms have been managed. Failed risk managements have brought down or called in federal survival money for too many Wall Street firms to be ignored. The primary motivation of this paper is to ask why the structures collapsed.

The term 'Potemkin Village' has been used to describe fake structures designed to fool observers about the truth. It derives from the Russian commissar who allegedly built fake villages to deceive Catherine the Great in Russia in 1787. The fake trading stations of Enron have been called Potemkin Villages. Perhaps this is the best description of the risk control systems described in the Appendix of the paper. They were meant to deceive regulators, shareholders and creditors. Maybe they also deceived naïve CEOs and board audit committees.

Surely, since the events of 2008–2009, it's time for thoughtful regulators, audit committees as well as management to examine the governance and culture of risk management in their companies.

Appendix: Selected comments on risk management in public reports of Wall Street firms

1. Lehman Brothers (Bankrupt in 2008)

   Excerpt from 2007 Annual Report, Richard Fuld, Lehman CEO writes:

   'The Global Risk Management Division is independent of the trading areas. The Division includes credit risk management, market risk management, quantitative... sovereign and operational management.'

   'We benefited from our senior level focus on risk management, and, more importantly, from culture of risk at every level of the firm.'

   August 2008, Eric Callan, Lehman CFO writes:

   'From a risk management perspective, we continued to operate in our disciplined manner we're known for.'

2. AIG (Loss of $100 billion dollars in 2008)

   Excerpt from 2005 AIG Annual Report (after Greenberg removal), Martin Sullivan, AIG former CEO writes:

   'AIG has strengthened the position of the Chief Risk Officer, responsible for enterprise-wide credit, market and operational risk management and oversight of the corresponding functions of the business unit level and has empowered the Chief Risk Officer to work more closely with top executives at the corporate and major business unit levels to identify, assess, quantify, manage and mitigate risks to AIG.'

   'AIG has established an Operational risk department, reporting to the Chief Risk Office to engage in expanded risk self-assessment processes for more effective identification and management of operational and reputational risks.'

   Excerpt from 2006 AIG Annual Report, Martin Sullivan, former CEO writes:

   'AIG's senior management establishes the framework, principal responsibility for establishing and implementing risk management processes, responding to individual needs..., *including risk concentration within their business segments* (Emphasized by author).'

   'AIGFP actively manages its exposures to limit financial losses.'

   Excerpt from 2009 Congressional testimony of Martin Sullivan, former CEO:

   '... many years AIG has been a – has had a centralized risk management function that oversees the market, credit and operational risk management units in each of our businesses as well as at the parent company.

   ' We have our arms around what is happening through AIG and believe we have demonstrated this through timely and comprehensive disclosure and accuracy in our reporting.'

Excerpt from the same 2006 Annual Report by Kevin McGinn, AIG's Chief Credit Officer:

'But essentially every single super senior transaction does come down to our Committee. … some of them are of a size that requires the further sign off by…, if they go into very high amounts, by Martin Sullivan.'

But,

Excerpt from Edward Liddy, CEO in 2009 Congress:

'We had risk management practices in place. They generally were not allowed to go up into the financial products business.'

3. Bear Stearns (Forced by Federal Government to be taken over by JPMorgan Chase in 2008)

Excerpt from Bear Stearns 2006 Annual report:

'Our commitment to risk management is evident from the boardroom to every trading desk in the firm.'

'…comprehensive risk management procedures have been established to identify, monitor and control each of these major risks.'

'The Executive Committee is the most senior management committee of the Company. The ultimate approval of decisions regarding the Company's risk appetite and risk-taking capacity rests with the Executive Committee.'

Excerpt from James Cayne, CEO in August 2007 after Bear Stearns' ratings downgrade:

'The risk management infrastructure and processes remain conservative and consistent with past practices. This structure and strong risk management culture has allowed the firm to operate for all of its history as a public company without ever having an unprofitable quarter.'

4. Merrill Lynch (Forced by the Federal Government to be taken over by Bank of America)

Stanley O'Neal in the 2006 Annual report:

'The Executive Committee, a group comprised of executive management, approves the risk tolerance levels established by ROC and receives regular updates from the ROC (Risk Oversight Committee)…. The Executive Committee pay particular attention to risk concentrations – the ROC is chaired by our Chief Financial Officer…. The ROC works to ensure that the risks we assume are managed within their tolerance levels…and that we implement appropriate processes to identify, measure, monitor and manage our risks.'

John Thain excerpt from 2008 Annual Report:

'We have taken a number of steps to reinforce a culture of disciplined risk-taking. First, in September 2007, we integrated the independent control functions of market and credit risk in the new Global Risk Management group under a single Chief Risk Officer, the former head of Global Credit and Commitments, who now reports directly to the Chief Executive Officer.'

5. Morgan Stanley (continued requiring Federal Support in 2009):
   John Mack, CEO in 2008 Letter to Shareholders:
   'We put in place a new senior management team, including our new
      Co-Presidents as well as Mitch Petrick, the new Global Head of Sales and
      Trading. We reorganized and enhanced our risk management function
      by moving it to report directly to Chief Financial Officer Colm Kelleher,
      bringing in more talent and creating an additional risk-monitoring func-
      tion within the trading business.'
   Excerpt from Management Discussion and Analyses in 2008 10-K: 'The
      Chief Risk Officer, a member of the Firm's Risk Committee who reports
      to the Chief Executive Officer, oversees compliance with Company
      risk limits; approves certain excessions of Company risk limits; reviews
      material market, credit and operational risks; reviews results of risk man-
      agement processes with the Audit Committee.'
6. Citicorp (Federal Government became major shareholder in 2009)
   Excerpt from Vikram Pandit, CEO, in his 2007 Letter to Shareholders:
   'This is my top priority, and I am aggressively building a new risk culture
      at Citi. We have named a new Chief Risk Officer and I will stay actively
      involved in strengthening our risk philosophy and strategy. My goal is
      to have the best risk management in the business, to transform it into a
      key competitive advantage driving bottom-line results.'
   Excerpt from Citicorp 2007 10-K: 'Citigroup's risk management framework
      is designed to balance strong corporate oversight with well-defined inde-
      pendent risk management functions within each business. The Citigroup
      Chief Risk Officer is responsible for:

   • Establishing standards for the measurement and reporting of risk,
   • Identifying and monitoring risk on a Company-wide basis,
   • Managing and compensating the senior independent risk managers,
   • Ensuring that the risk function has adequate staffing, analytics and ex-
     pertise, and
   • Approving business-level risk management policies.

   'The risk managers supporting each of our businesses are responsible for
      establishing and implementing risk management policies and practices
      within their business, overseeing and critically evaluating the risk in
      their business and for applying risk control policies that enhance and
      address the requirements of the business.'
7. Prudential (Applied for Federal Support in 2009)
   Excerpt from Arthur Ryan's Annual Letter 2007:
   'Primary responsibility for strategy, performance and risk controls lies with
      the Prudential PLC board of Directors (the Board), the Group Chief
      Executive and the chief executives of each business unit. Additionally,

the Board has delegated responsibility to the Approvals Committee to approve actions which could significantly change the risk profile of any business, capital commitments and divestments within defined materiality thresholds, and certain legal matters involving trademarks, contracts, material guarantees and specific interactions with third parties.'

8. Hartford Insurance (Applied for Federal Support in 2009)

   Ramani Ayer, Chairman and CEO in his 2007 Letter to Shareholders:

   'The Company has a well-developed culture of financial discipline and astute capital and risk management. Together, these add up to a strong balance sheet, attractive returns, and a history of rational pricing and financial guarantees.'

Notes

1. Business Week cover story, June 12, 2006.
2. New York Times, Joe Nocera, January 2, 2009.
3. Wall Street Journal Op-ed reference, June 27–28, 2009.
4. PricewaterhouseCooper, Briefing Programme, March 2, 2007, See Pricewaterhouse-Coopers, March 2, 2007,http:/www.pwc.com/extweb/pwcpublications.nsf./docid/4 7A1B25A679C22D18525729400182A60/$File/fs_risk_briefing.pdf).
5. Chapter 8 on Compensation in *Restoring Financial Stability* by Acharya, V. and Richardson, M (2009) .
6. Tett, Shelps, Lewis and O'Harrow references.
7. JPMorgan Chase 2008 Annual Report reference.
8. Michael Lewis in Vanity Fair, August 2009 issue.
9. Chapter 8, Restoring Financial Stability.
10. Wall Street Journal, April 16, 2008.
11. Gillian Tett Reference
12. Jamie Dimon Op-ed and the JPMorgan Chase 2008 Annual Report.
13. Chapter 8, *Restoring Financial Stability.*

References

Acharya, V. and Richardson, M. (eds) (2009) *Restoring Financial Stability,* J. Wiley & Sons, Inc.

Dimon, J. (2009) *A Unified Regulator is a Good Start,* Wall Street Journal, June 27–28.

Giddens, J.W. (2012) Trustee for the SIPA Liquidation of MF Global Inc, Report of the Trustee's Investigation and Recommendations, June 2012, to the United States Bankruptcy Court, Southern District of New York.

Inside Wall Street's Culture of Risk, June 12, 2006, Cover Story, BusinessWeek.

JPMorgan Chase (2008) *Annual Report.*

JPMorgan Chase (2011) 10-K.

Lewis, M. (2009) *The Man Who Crushed the World,* Vanity Fair.

Nocera, J. (2009) *Risk Mismanagement, New York Times,* January 2.

O'Harrow R. Jr. and Brady, D. (2008) *Downgrades and Downfall*, The Crush: What Went Wrong, Washington Post, December 31.

PricewaterhouseCoopers (2007) *Effective Risk Management in Financial Services*, PwC Briefing Programme, March.

Pulliam, S., Ng, S. and Smith, Randall (2008) *Merrill Upped Ante as Boom in Mortgage Bonds Fizzled*, Wall Street Journal, April 16.

Shelp, R. (2006) *Fallen Giant, the Amazing Story of Hank Greenberg of AIG*. Hoboken, NJ: John Wiley & Sons, Inc.

Tett, G. (2009) *Fool's Gold*. Simon and Schuster, Inc.

10
Reputational Risk and the Financial Crisis

Ingo Walter[1]

10.1 Introduction

The global financial crisis of 2007–2009 was associated with an unprecedented degree of financial and economic damage. For investors and financial intermediaries, the estimates seem to have risen to over $4 trillion or so worldwide by the time things began to stabilize, according to the International Monetary Fund (2009). Along with the financial damage has come substantial reputational damage for the financial services industry, for financial intermediaries and asset managers, and for individuals.

At the industry level, for example, Josef Ackermann, CEO of Deutsche Bank and Chairman of the International Institute of Finance, noted in April 2008 that the industry was guilty of poor risk management with serious overreliance on flawed models, inadequate stress-testing of portfolios, recurring conflicts of interest, and lack of common sense, as well as irrational compensation practices not linked to long-term profitability – with a growing perception by the public of 'clever crooks and greedy fools'. He concludes that the industry has a great deal of work to do to regain its reputation.[2]

Crisis-driven reputational damage at the firm level can be inferred from remarks by Peter Kurer, former Supervisory Board Chairman of UBS AG, who noted at the bank's annual general meeting in April 2008 that 'We shouldn't fool ourselves. We can't pretend that there has been no reputational damage. Experience says it goes away after two or three years.'[3] Perhaps it does, perhaps not, but the hemorrhage of private client withdrawals at the height of the crisis suggests severe reputational damage to the world's largest private bank – to the point that it was surpassed in assets under management by Bank of America (after its acquisition of Merrill Lynch) in 2009.

The number of financial firms – ranging from Santander in Spain to Citigroup in the US and Union Bancaire Privée in Switzerland – that reimbursed client losses from the sale of bankrupt Lehman bonds, collapsed auction-rate securities, and investments in Bernard Madoff's fraudulent scheme, suggests the importance of reputational capital and the lengths to which financial firms must go to maintain it. And at the individual level the world is full of disgraced bankers whose hard work, career ambitions, and future prospects lie in tatters. At this writing, early in 2013, the following roster of reputation-sensitive financial firm allegations seemed to suggest that management considered it acceptable to:

- Mis-sell worthless payment protection insurance to retail mortgage and credit card customers.
- Push in-house products against superior (better performance or cheaper) third-party products.
- Allow hedge funds to trade in mutual funds' shares after the NAV fixing at the close of market.
- Invade segregated customer accounts and borrow the money for your own operations.
- Facilitate wealthy clients' evasion of taxes.
- Sell securities to institutional clients which sales staff know will collapse.
- Use an investment advisory relationship to earn kickbacks from vendors.
- Advise an M&A client to sell his company without conducting appropriate "due diligence" on the buyer.
- Design off-balance-sheet structures for clients solely for purposes of financial misrepresentation.
- Launder money for drug cartels and terrorist networks.
- Exceed trading exposure limits and cover your tracks.
- Submit false Libor numbers and trade against them.
- Redefine a central exposure hedging platform into a profit center.
- Provide inside corporate client information to selected investor clients.

This drumbeat of allegations, legal settlements and criminal charges convinced many that the 'culture' of financial intermediaries was broken, or at least severely strained. Among the reasons offered for the rash of reputation-sensitive revelations were:

- Changing competitive market structure.
- Fiduciary obligation – redefinition from client to transaction counterparty.
- Product complexity and erosion of transparency.
- Institutional size – too big to manage.
- Institutional complexity – too broad to be trusted.
- Acquisitions-driven growth and poor merger integration.
- Boardroom shortfalls:
  – Industry knowledge of directors.
  – Imperial chairmen.

– Sociology of boards.
– Institutional proxy voting.
- Underinvestment in compliance.
- Underinvestment in risk management.
- Asymmetry of revenues vs. risk management in key decisions.
- Compensation systems design – bonus vs. malus.
- External regulatory capabilities and ineffective penalties in no-contest pleas.

There were calls for the removal of an entire generation of senior management, recalibrating compensation programs, reform of corporate governance, strengthened compliance and external regulation and other measures to address illegal and unethical conduct on the part of financial firms, and in some cases to break them up into units that suffer from fewer conflicts of interest and are more easily supervised and regulated.

Section 10.2 of this chapter considers the 'special' nature of financial services and traces the roots of the reputational risk that firms in the industry invariably encounter. Section 10.3 defines what reputational risk is and outlines the sources of reputational risk facing financial services firms. Section 10.4 considers the key sources of reputational risk in the presence of transactions costs and imperfect information.[4] Section 10.5 surveys available empirical research on the impact of reputational losses imposed on financial intermediaries, including the separation of reputational losses from accounting losses. Section 10.6 considers managerial issues encountered in dealing with reputational risk issues, notably from a corporate governance perspective. Section 10.6 concludes with some governance and managerial implications.

10.2   The special character of financial services

Financial services comprise an array of 'special' businesses. They are special because they deal mainly with other people's money, and because problems that arise in financial intermediation can trigger serious external costs. In recent years, the roles of various types of financial intermediaries have evolved dramatically. Capital markets and institutional asset managers have taken a greater portion of the intermediation function from banks. Insurance activities conducted in the capital markets – such as credit default swaps and weather derivatives – compete with classic reinsurance functions. Fiduciary activities for institutional and retail clients are conducted by banks, broker-dealers, life insurers, and independent fund management companies. Intermediaries in each cohort compete as vigorously with their traditional rivals as with players in other cohorts, competition that has been intensified by deregulation and rapid innovation in financial products and processes. Market developments have periodically overtaken regulatory capabilities intended to promote stability and fairness as well as efficiency and innovation. The regulatory arbitrage that can result has a great deal to do with the dynamics of the financial crisis, and is being addressed in many of the regulatory measures that have been proposed and are being implemented.

It is unsurprising that these conditions would give rise to significant reputational risk exposure for all financial firms. For their part, investors in banks and other financial intermediaries are sensitive to the going-concern value of the firms they own, and hence to the governance processes that are supposed to work in their interests. Regulators, in turn, are sensitive to the safety, soundness, and integrity of the financial system and, from time to time, will recalibrate the rules of the game. Market discipline, operating through the governance process, interacts with the regulatory process in ways that involve both costs and benefits to market participants and are reflected in the value of their business franchises.

10.3   What is reputational risk?

There are substantial difficulties in defining the value of a financial firm's reputation, the extent of damage to that reputation, the origins of that damage, and, therefore, the sources of reputational risk. Reputation itself may be defined as the opinion (more technically, a social evaluation) of the public toward a person, a group of people or an organization. It is an important factor in many fields, such as education, business, online communities, and social status. In a business context, reputation helps drive the excess value of a business firm and such metrics as the market-to-book ratio. However, both precise definition and data are found to be lacking. Arguably many deficiencies in both definition and data can be attributed to the fact that theory development related to corporate reputation has itself been deficient. Such problems notwithstanding, common sense suggests some sources of gain/loss in reputational capital:

- The cumulative reputation of the firm, including its self-promoted ethical image.
- Economic performance – market share, profitability, and growth.
- Stakeholder interface – shareholders, employees, clients, and suppliers.
- Legal interface – civil and criminal litigation and enforcement actions.

Consequently, proximate symptoms of sources of loss in reputational capital include:

- Client flight and loss of market share.
- Investor flight and increase in the cost of capital.

- Talent flight.
- Increase in contracting costs.

For practical purposes, reputational risk in the financial services sector is therefore associated with the possibility of loss in the going-concern value of the financial intermediary, which is to say the risk-adjusted value of expected future earnings. Reputational losses may be reflected in reduced operating revenues as clients and trading counterparties shift to competitors, increased compliance and other costs required to deal with the reputational problem – including opportunity costs – and an increased firm-specific risk perceived by the market. Reputational risk is often linked to operational risk, although there are important distinctions between the two. According to Basle II, operational risks are associated with people (internal fraud, clients, products, business practices, employment practices, and workplace safety), internal processes and systems, and external events (external fraud, damage or loss of assets, and force majeure). Operational risk is specifically *not* considered to include strategic and business risk, credit risk, market risk or systemic risk, or reputational risk.[5]

If reputational risk is bracketed-out of operational risk from a regulatory perspective, then what is it? A possible working definition is as follows: 'Reputational risk comprises the risk of loss in the value of a firm's business franchise that extends beyond event-related accounting losses and is reflected in a decline in its share performance metrics. Reputation-related losses reflect reduced expected revenues and/or higher financing and contracting costs. Reputational risk, in turn, is related to the strategic positioning and execution of the firm, conflicts of interest exploitation, individual professional conduct, compliance and incentive systems, leadership, and the prevailing corporate culture. Reputational risk is usually the consequence of management *processes* rather than discrete *events*, and, therefore, requires risk control approaches that differ materially from operational risk.'

According to this definition, a reputation-sensitive event might trigger an identifiable monetary decline in the market value of the firm. After subtracting from this market capitalization loss the present value of direct and allocated costs, such as fines and penalties and settlements under civil litigation, the balance can be ascribed to the impact on the firm's reputation. Firms that promote themselves as reputational standard-setters will, accordingly, tend to suffer larger reputational losses than firms that have taken a lower profile – that is, reputational losses associated with identical events according to this definition may be highly idiosyncratic to the individual firm.

In terms of the overall hierarchy of risks faced by financial intermediaries, reputational risk is perhaps the most intractable. In terms of Figure 10.1, market risk is usually considered the most tractable, with adequate time-series and cross-sectional data availability, appropriate metrics to assess volatility and correlations, and the ability to apply techniques such as value at risk (*VaR*) and risk-adjusted return on capital (RAROC). Credit risk is arguably less tractable, given that many credits are on the books of financial intermediaries at historical values. The analysis of credit events in a portfolio context is less tractable than market risk in terms of the available metrics, although many types of credits have over the years become 'marketized' through securitization structures such as asset-backed securities (ABS) and collateralized loan obligations (CLOs), as well as derivatives such as credit default swaps (CDS). These financial instruments are priced in both primary and secondary markets, and transfer some of the granularity and tractability found in market risk to the credit domain. Liquidity risk, on the other hand, has both pluses and minuses in terms of tractability. In continuous markets, liquidity risk can be calibrated in terms of bid-offer spreads, although in times of severe market stress and flights to quality, liquidity can disappear.

If the top three risk-domains in Figure 10.1 show a relatively high degree of manageability, the bottom three are frequently less manageable. Operational risk is a composite of highly manageable risks with a robust basis for suitable risk metrics together with risks that represent catastrophes and extreme values – tail events that are difficult to model and, in some cases, have never actually been observed. Here management is forced to rely on either simulations or external data to try to assess the probabilities and potential losses. Meanwhile, sovereign risk assessment basically involves applied political economy and relies on imprecise techniques, such as stylized facts analysis, so that the track record of even the most sophisticated analytical approaches is not particularly strong – especially under conditions of macro-stress and contagion. As in the

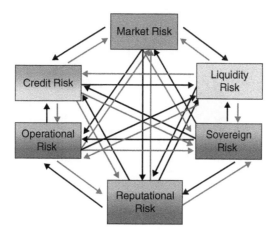

Figure 10.1   A hierarchy of risks confronting financial intermediaries

case of credit risk, sovereign risk can be calibrated when sovereign foreign-currency bonds and sovereign default swaps (stripped of non-sovereign attributes like external guarantees and collateral) are traded in the market. This leaves reputational risk as perhaps the least tractable of all – with poor data, limited usable metrics, and strong 'fat tail' characteristics.

The other point brought out in Figure 10.1 relates to the linkages between the various risk-domains. Even the most straightforward of these – such as the linkage between market risk and credit risk – are not easy to model or to value, particularly in a bidirectional form. There are 36 such linkages, exhibiting a broad range of tractability. It can be argued that the linkages which relate to reputational risk are among the most difficult to assess and to manage.

10.4   Sources of reputational risk

Where does reputational risk in financial intermediation originate? It may emanate in large part from the intersection between the financial firm and the competitive environment, on the one hand, and from the direct and indirect network of controls and behavioral expectations within which the firm operates, on the other, as depicted generically in Figure 10.2.[6] The franchise value of a financial institution as a going concern is calibrated against these two sets of benchmarks. One of them, market performance, tends to be relatively transparent and easy to reward or punish. The other, performance against corporate conduct benchmarks, is far more opaque but potentially more critical as a source of risk to shareholders.

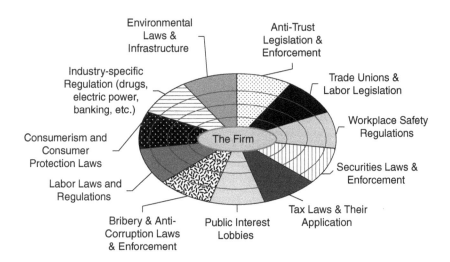

Figure 10.2   Reputational risk and the external control web

Management must work to optimize with respect to both sets of bench-marks. If it strays too far in the direction of meeting the demands of social and regulatory controls, it runs the risks of poor performance in the market, punishment by shareholders, and possibly a change in corporate control. If it strays toward unrestrained market performance and sails too close to the wind in terms of questionable market conduct, its behavior may have disas-trous results for the firm, its managers, and its shareholders. Such are the rules of the game, and financial intermediaries have to live with them. But they are not immutable. There is constant tension between firms and regulators about appropriate constraints on corporate conduct. Sometimes financial intermedi-aries win battles (and even wars) leading to periods of deregulation. Sometimes it is possible to convince the public that self-regulation and market discipline are powerful enough to obviate the need for external control. Sometimes the regulators can be convinced, one way or another, to go easy. Then along comes another major transgression, and the constraint system reacts and creates a spate of new regulations. A wide array of interests gets into this constant battle to define the rules under which financial business gets done – managers, politi-cians, the media, activists, investors, lawyers, and accountants – and eventually a new equilibrium gets established which will define the rules of engagement for the period ahead.

There are some more fundamental factors at work as well. Laws and regula-tions governing the market conduct of firms are not created in a vacuum. They are rooted in social expectations as to what is appropriate and inappropriate, which in turn are driven by values embedded in society. These values are rather basic. They deal with lying, cheating, and stealing, with trust and honor, with what is right and wrong. These are the *ultimate* benchmarks against which conduct is measured and which may be the origins of key reputational losses.

But fundamental values in society may or may not be reflected in people's *expectations* as to how a firm's conduct is assessed. There may be a good deal of slippage between social values and how these are reflected in the public expectations of business conduct. Build-up of adverse opinion in the media, the formation of special-interest lobbies and pressure-groups, and the general tide of public opinion with respect to one or another aspect of market conduct, can be reputationally debilitating.

Moreover, neither values nor expectations are static in time. Both change. But values seem to change much more gradually than expectations. Indeed, fundamental values such as those noted above are probably as close as one comes to 'constants' in assessing business conduct. But even in this domain, things do change. As society becomes more diverse and mobile, for example, values tend to evolve. They also differ across cultures. And they are sometimes difficult to interpret. Is lying to clients or to trading counterparties wrong? What is the difference between lying and bluffing? Is the *context* necessary to determine how particular behavior is assessed? The same conduct may be interpreted differently under different circumstances, so that interpretations may change significantly over time and differ widely across cultures, giving rise to unique contours of reputational risk.

There is additional slippage between society's expectations and the formation of public policy on the one hand, and the activities of public interest groups on the other. Things may go on as usual for a while despite occasional media commentary about inappropriate behavior of a firm or an industry in the marketplace. Then, at some point, some sort of social tolerance limit is reached. A firm goes too far. A consensus emerges among various groups concerned with the issue. The system reacts through the political process, and a new set of constraints on firm behavior develops, possibly anchored in legislation, regulation, and bureaucracy. Or the firm is subject to class action litigation.[7] Or its reputation is so seriously compromised that its share price drops sharply.

As managers review the reputational experiences of their competitors, they cannot escape an important message. Most financial firms can endure a credit loss or the cost of an unsuccessful trade or a broken deal, however large, and still survive. These are business risks that the firms have learned to detect and limit their exposure before the damage becomes serious. Reputational losses may be imposed by external reactions that may appear to professionals as unfocused or ambiguous, even unfair. They may also be new – a new reading of the rules, a new finding of culpability, something different from the way things were done before. Although regulators and litigants, analysts, and the media are accepted by financial professionals as facts of life, such outsiders can be influenced by public uproar and political pressure, during which times it is difficult to defend an offending financial firm.[8]

In the United States, for example, tighter regulation and closer surveillance, aggressive prosecution and plaintiff litigation, unsympathetic media and juries, and stricter guidelines for penalties and sentencing make it easier to get into trouble and harder to avoid serious penalties. Global brokerage and trading operations, for example, involve hundreds of different, complex, and constantly changing products that are difficult to monitor carefully under the best of circumstances. Doing this in a highly competitive market, where profit margins are under constant challenge and there is considerable temptation to break the rules, is even more challenging. Performance-driven managers, through compensation and promotion practices, have sometimes unwittingly encouraged behavior that has inflicted major reputational damage on their firms and destroyed some of them.

The reality is that the value of financial intermediaries suffers from such uncertain reputation-sensitive conditions. Since maximizing the value of the firm is supposed to be the ultimate role of management, its job is to learn how to run the firm so that it optimizes the long-term trade-offs between profits

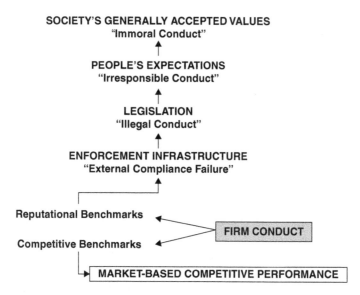

Figure 10.3   Performance gaps, competition and conflict

and external control. It does no good to plead unfair treatment – the task is for management to learn to live with it, and to make the most of the variables it can control.

The overall process can be depicted in Figure 10.3, which represents the firm and its internal governance processes in the center and various layers of external controls affecting both the firm's conduct and the reputational consequences of misconduct, ranging from 'hard' compliance components near the center to 'soft' but potentially vital issues of 'appropriate' conduct on the periphery. Clearly, serious reputational losses can impact a financial firm even if it is fully in compliance with regulatory constraints and its actions are entirely legal. The risk of reputational damage incurred in these outer fringes of the web of social control are among the most difficult to assess and manage. Nor is the constraint system necessarily consistent. There are important differences in regulatory regimes (as well as expectations regarding responsible conduct) across markets in which a firm is active, so that conduct which is considered acceptable in one environment may give rise to significant reputational risk in another.

10.5   Valuing reputational risk

Recent research has attempted to quantify the impact of reputational risk on share prices during the 1980s and 1990s.[9] Given the nature of the problem, most of the evidence has been anecdotal, although a number of event studies has been undertaken in cases where the reputation-sensitive event was 'clean' in terms of the release of the relevant information to the market.

Figure 10.4 summarizes shareholder value losses in a reputation-sensitive situation involving the aforementioned sources of loss: (1) client defections and revenue erosion; (2) increases in monetary costs comprising accounting write-offs associated with the event, increased compliance costs, regulatory fines and legal settlements, as well as indirect costs related to loss of reputation, such as higher financing costs, contracting costs, and opportunity costs; and (3) increases in firm-specific (unsystematic) risk assigned by the market as a result of the reputational event in question. In order to value the pure reputational losses, it is necessary to estimate the overall market value loss of the firm to a reputation-sensitive event, and then deduct the monetary losses identified in italics in Figure 10.4.

Consider the following example.[10] On December 28, 1993, the Bank of Spain took control of the country's fourth largest bank, Banco Español de Crédito (Banesto). Subsequently, shares of JP Morgan & Co., a US bank holding company closely involved with Banesto, declined dramatically. Such a reaction appeared inconsistent with market rationality, given that the impact of the event on Morgan's bottom line was trivial inasmuch as the accounting loss to Morgan was unlikely to exceed $10 million after taxes. Perhaps something more than the underlying book value of JP Morgan & Co. was moving the price of the stock. In particular, the central bank takeover of Banesto may have affected the value of Morgan's corporate franchise in some of the firm's core business areas, notably securities underwriting, funds management, client advisory work, and

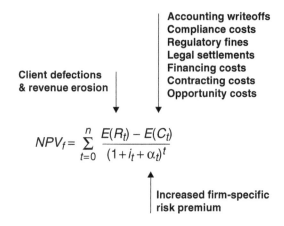

$$NPV_f = \sum_{t=0}^{n} \frac{E(R_t) - E(C_t)}{(1+i_t+\alpha_t)^t}$$

Figure 10.4 Reputation-sensitive events in a simple going-concern valuation framework

its ability to manage conflicts of interest that can accompany such activities in non-transparent environments.

JP Morgan was involved in Banesto in four ways, in addition to normal interbank transactions relationships.[11] (1) In May 1992, it began raising funds for the Corsair Partnership, L.P., aimed at making non-controlling investments in financial institutions. By February 1993, Morgan had raised over $1 billion from 46 investors, including pension funds and private individuals. Morgan served as general partner and fund manager, with an investment of $100 million. The Corsair Partnership's objective was to identify troubled financial institutions and, by improving their performance, earn a significant return to shareholders in the fund. The Corsair Partnership's first investment, undertaken in February 1993, was a share purchase of $162 million in Banesto, thereby giving Morgan a $16.2 million equity stake in the Spanish bank. (2) A vice-chairman of JP Morgan served on the Spanish bank's board of directors. (3) Morgan was directly advising Banesto on its financial and business affairs. (4) As part of an effort to recapitalize Banesto, Morgan was lead underwriter during 1993 of two stock offerings that totaled $710 million.

Corsair Partnership, L.P., was intended to search for troubled financial institutions in the United States and abroad. The objective was to restructure such institutions by applying Morgan's extensive expertise and contacts. Morgan indicated that Corsair investors could expect a 30% annual return over ten years. Although Morgan had a separate investment banking subsidiary (JP Morgan Securities, Inc.), Corsair was believed to be the first equity fund organized and managed by Morgan since the Glass-Steagall Act separated banking and securities activities in 1933, a separation which ended in 1999. The business concept of searching for troubled financial institutions emerged from a time of turmoil in the US and foreign banking sectors. When the US banking industry started to improve as a result of a favorable interest rate environment, Corsair ventured abroad. Corsair's first stake in Banesto was taken in February 1993. By August 1993, it had invested $162 million (23 % of the funds raised) in the Spanish bank. The overall JP Morgan – Banesto relationship is depicted in Figure 10.5.

Banesto's problems stemmed from rapid growth and a convoluted structure of industrial holdings, followed by a serious downturn in the Spanish economy. The bank's lending book decreased from Pta.4 trillion in 1988 to Pta2.3 trillion in 1991, a period when its competitors were growing at a quarter of that rate. Banesto bid aggressively for deposits, increasing interest rates by 51% while competitors increased theirs by 40%. When the Spanish economy weakened, the bank was stuck with an array of bad loans and losses on its industrial holdings. In October 1992, after a partial audit, the Bank of Spain was forced to lend the troubled institution 'a substantial amount'. A full audit released at the end of December 1993 revealed that Banesto assets of Pta5.5 trillion ($385 billion) were overvalued in excess of Pta50 billion ($3.5 billion). In April 1994, Banesto

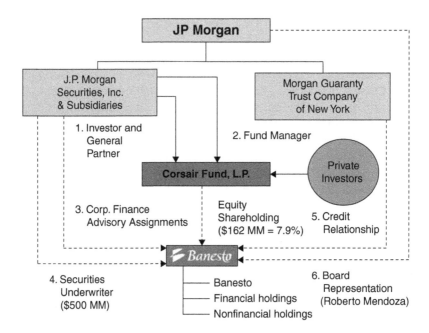

Figure 10.5 Reputational risk exposure – JP Morgan and Banco Español de Crédito 1993

was bought for $2.05 billion by Banco Santander, leaving costs of $3.7 billion to be borne by the Spanish banks and by taxpayers.

Morgan had been advising Banesto on various deals since 1987. In July 1992, Morgan's involvement became more extensive when it began advising Banesto on how to raise capital. By August 1993, Morgan had assisted Banesto in two rights issues to raise $710 million. During the period of these rights issues, Corsair invested $162 million in Banesto. In a letter dated December 27, 1993, Morgan wrote to the Bank of Spain's Governor, outlining how Banesto could continue to raise capital, including a bond issue that Morgan was planning to launch in the first quarter of 1993.

Instead, the Bank of Spain took control of Banesto on the following day, December 28, 1993. Citing mismanagement and reckless lending, the Governor justified the action as being necessary to avoid a run on the deposits of the bank, whose share prices were falling sharply on the Madrid Exchange. Given Morgan's multifaceted involvement in Banesto and potential conflicts embedded in that relationship, the announcement of the takeover could have had a large effect on the value of Morgan's reputation and business franchise and hence its stock price.

In order to test the impact of the Banesto case on the JP Morgan share price, the authors of a study of this case use conventional event study methodology.[12]

They create a sample prediction of returns on Morgan stock and compare the predicted returns with actual returns on Morgan shares after the Banesto event announcement.[13] The difference is considered the excess return attributable to the event, which is to say the difference between what shareholders would have received had they sold their shares in the market 50 days prior to the announcement and what they would have received if they had sold them on subsequent days. If the reputation-effect hypothesis is correct, the market response to the Bank of Spain's announcement on 28 December 1993 should have significantly exceeded the firm's book exposure to Banesto.[14]

Prior to the announcement, Morgan stock behaved as predicted, based on its behavior during the 250 days before the event period. A few days before the announcement, the stock price began to decline. Thereafter, an essentially steady decline occurred. A cumulative loss of 10% of shareholder equity value is apparent 50 days after the announcement translates into a loss in JPM market capitalization of approximately $1.5 billion versus a maximum direct loss of only $10 million from the Banesto failure. This analysis suggests that the loss of an institution's franchise value can far outweigh an accounting loss when its reputation is called into question, a finding similar to that of Smith (1992) in the case of Salomon Brothers, Inc.

Reasons for the adverse market reaction can only be conjectured. The takeover of Banesto could have been seen as compromising Morgan's reputation in precisely those areas key to its future. Inability to turn Banesto around may have called into question Morgan's ability to successfully advise clients. Banesto, as the dominant participant in the Corsair portfolio, may have suggested flaws in Morgan's ability to organize and manage certain equity funds. Difficulties with underwriting stock issues and placing shares with important investor clients raises questions about its ability to judge risks in underwriting securities. Service on Banesto's board suggests problems with monitoring, and the configuration of Morgan's various involvements with Banesto suggests the potential for conflicts of interest or lack of objectivity. Whatever the linkages, here was a case of a financial services firm of exceedingly high standing, which in no way violated legal or regulatory constraints but whose shares nevertheless appeared to have been adversely affected by the market reaction to the way a high-profile piece of business was handled.

In recent years, event studies such as this have yielded a growing body of evidence about share price sensitivity to reputational risk. For example, Cummins, Lewis, and Wei (2006) undertook a large sample study of operational and reputational events contained in the Fitch OpVar™ database. Figure 10.6 shows the results in terms of the magnitude of the losses using three-factor estimation models in terms of cumulative abnormal returns (CARs) and number of trading days before and after the announcement. The authors, however, do not distinguish between operational losses and reputational losses, as defined above.

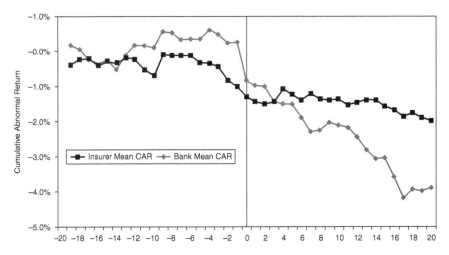

Figure 10.6 Cumulative Abnormal Returns (CARs) for banks and insurers in a large sample study of operational and reputational events (three-factor models)

De Fontnouvelle et al. (2006) use loss data from the Fitch OpVar™ and SAS OpRisk™ databases to model operational risk for banks that are internationally active. In a series of robust statistical estimates, they find a high degree of regularity in operational losses that can be quantified. This would justify maintaining significant capital reserves against operational risk – see Figures 10.7 and 10.8. The paper also segments the losses by event type and by activity line, as well as whether or not the operational losses occurred in the United States. The largest losses involved retail and commercial and retail/private banking activities in terms of the type of event. As in the case of other studies, the authors do not distinguish the associated accounting losses due to legal settlements, fines, penalties, and other explicit operational risk-related costs from reputational losses. As such, these estimates are relevant from a regulatory perspective but probably materially understate the losses to shareholders.

In a pilot study of 49 reputation-sensitive events, using the aforementioned definition and excluding operational events, we find negative mean CARs of up to 7% and $3.5 billion, depending on the event windows used.[15] Figure 10.9 shows the results graphically, and the tables in Figures 10.10 and 10.11 show the numerical results. The results do not, however, distinguish between the associated monetary losses and the pure reputational losses.[16]

The only study to date which attempts to identify pure reputational losses is that of Karpoff, Lee, and Martin (2006). The authors attempt to distinguish book losses from reputational losses in the context of US Securities and Exchange Commission enforcement actions related to earnings restatements or 'cooking

Event Type	SAS OpRiSk % of All Losses[a]	Percentiles ($M) 50%	75%	95%	Fitch Op Var % of All Losses[a]	Percentiles ($M) 50%	75%	95%	Wilcoxon Test
All Event Types	100.0%	6	17	88	100.0%	6	17	93	90.2%
Internal Fraud	23.0%	4	10	42	27.0%	6	16	110	1.2%
External Fraud	16.5%	5	17	93	16.6%	4	12	70	33.2%
EPWS	3.0%	4	14	–	3.3%	5	11	–	95.0%
CPBP	55.5%	7	20	95	48.1%	7	20	99	96.3%
Damage Phys. Assets	0.4%	18	–	–	0.3%	20	–	–	92.9%
BDSF	0.2%	36	–	–	0.4%	10	–	–	38.0%
EDPM	1.3%	9	27	–	4.2%	4	11	–	14.6%
Kruskal-Wallis Test	6.4E-06				9.1E-05				
Panel B. Losses that occurred outside the US									
All Event Types	100.0%	10	36	221	100.0%	13	46	288	16.7%
Internal Fraud	48.5%	9	35	259	42.9%	15	62	381	1.5%
External Fraud	15.3%	7	27		21.6%	10	28	136	27.3%
EPWS	0.8%	7			1.6%	2	7		75.3%
CPBP	32.6%	14	51	374	28.6%	13	51	359	99.6%
Damage Phys. Assets	0.0%	–	–	–	0.3%	163	–	–	–
BOSE	0.8%	7	–	–	0.5%	3	–	–	42.3%
EDP1v1	1.9%	29	–	–	4.6%	5	19	–	8.1%
Kruskal-Wallis Test	11.8%				5.5E-05				

Figure 10.7 Operational losses by event type

Source: De Fontnouvelle, Patrick, Virginia DeJesus-Rueff, John S. Jordan and Eric S. Rosengren (2006). 'Capital and Risk: New Evidence on Implications of Large Operational Losses', Federal Reserve Bank of Boston. Working Paper. September.

the books'. The authors review 2,532 regulatory events in connection with all relevant SEC enforcement actions from 1978 to 2002 and the monetary costs of these actions in the ensuing period through 2005. These monetary costs are then compared with the cumulative abnormal returns estimated from event studies to separate them from the reputational costs. The results are depicted in Figure 10.12. Note that the reputational losses (66%) are far larger than the cost of fines (3%), class action settlements (6%) and accounting write-offs (25%) resulting from the events in question.

It is likely that the broader the range of a financial intermediary's activities, (1) the greater the likelihood that the firm will encounter exploitable conflicts of interest and reputational risk exposure, (2) the higher will be the potential

Business Line	SAS OpRisk				Fitch Op Var				Wilcoxon Test
	% of All Losses[a]	Percentiles ($M)			% of All Losses[a]	Percentiles ($M)			
		50%	75%	95%		50%	75%	95%	
All Business Lines	100%	6	17	88	100%	6	17	93	90.2%
Corporate Finance	6%	6	23	–	4%	8	23	–	55.8%
Trading & Sales	9%	10	44	334	9%	10	27	265	89.2%
Retail Banking	38%	5	11	52	39%	5	12	60	73.1%
Commercial Banking	21%	7	24	104	16%	8	28	123	13.3%
Payment & Settlement	1%	4	11	–	1%	4	11	–	65.8%
Agency Services	2%	22	110	–	3%	9	28	–	10.3%
Asset Management	5%	8	20	–	6%	8	22	165	80.8%
Retail Brokerage	17%	4	12	57	22%	4	13	67	98.0%
Kruskal-Wallis Test	2.9E-07				1.0E-12				
Panel B. Losses that occurred outside the US									
All Business Lines	100%	10	36	221	100%	13	46	288	16.7%
Corporate Finance	2%	13	–	–	3%	12	27	–	69.3%
Trading & Sales	9%	30	125	–	12%	25	66	–	33.3%
Retail Banking	41%	6	27	101	44%	9	29	272	10.4%
Commercial Banking	30%	15	42	437	21%	35	91	323	2.4%
Payment & Settlement	1%	5	–	–	1%	13	–	–	17.7%
Agency Services	2%	45	–	–	3%	20	77	–	49.6%
Asset Management	3%	5	47	–	5%	7	23	–	90.1%
Retail Brokerage	12%	10	42	–	11%	8	34	–	42.6%
Kruskal-Wallis Test	6.6E-04				1.1E-05				

Figure 10.8   Operational losses by business line

Source: De Fontnouvelle, Patrick, Virginia DeJesus-Rueff, John S. Jordan and Eric S. Rosengren (2006). 'Capital and Risk: New Evidence on Implications of Large Operational Losses', Federal Reserve Bank of Boston. Working Paper. September.

agency costs facing its clients, and (3) the more difficult and costly will be the safeguards necessary to protect the value of the franchise. If this proposition is correct, costs associated with reputational risk mitigation can easily offset the realization of economies of scope in financial services firms, scope

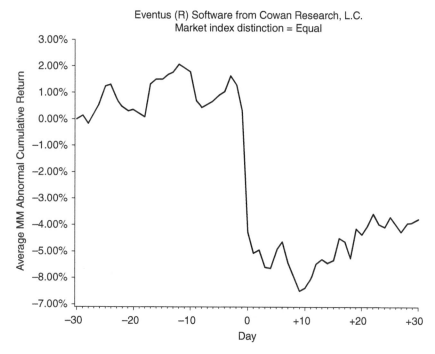

Figure 10.9 Reputational impact and share prices

Source: Gayle De Long, Antony Saunders and Ingo Walter, "Pricing Reputation-Sensitive Events in Banking and Financial Services," New York University, Department of Finance Working Paper (in draft).

economies that are supposed to generate benefits on the demand side through cross-selling (revenue synergies) and on the supply side through more efficient use of the firm's business infrastructure (cost synergies). As a result of conflict exploitation, the firm may win and clients may lose in the first instance, but subsequent adverse reputational and regulatory consequences (along with efficiency factors such as the managerial and operational cost of complexity) can be considered diseconomies of scope.

Breadth of engagement with clients may create conflicts of interest that can be multidimensional and involve a number of different stakeholders at the same time. Several examples came to light during the corporate scandals in the early 2000s. Following the $103 billion bankruptcy of WordCom in 2002, for example, it appeared that Citigroup, a multifunctional, global financial conglomerate, was serving as equity analyst, supplying assessments of WorldCom to institutional and (through the firm's brokers) retail clients, while simultaneously advising WorldCom management on strategic and financial matters. Citigroup's equity analyst at times participated in WorldCom's board meetings.

Cumulative Abnormal Returns – Statistical Summary				
Event window	(–5,3)	(–5,10)	(–1,3)	(–1,10)
MEAN	–6.24%	–7.02%	–6.79%	–7.57%
Patell Z-score	–10.02	–7.63	–14.37	–9.41
MEDIAN	–4.59%	–4.92%	–4.55%	–4.96%
Bottom 95% loss	–38.17%	–44.97%	–35.88%	–44.37%
Bottom 99% loss	–62.57%	–47.52%	–63.78%	–48.73%
90% skew	–1.0907	0.1740	–1.2563	0.0538
90% kurtosis	0.0696	–4.6151	0.9144	–4.7431

Figure 10.10   Relative CARs – reputational loss pilot study

Source: Gayle De Long, Antony Saunders and Ingo Walter, "Pricing Reputation-Sensitive Events in Banking and Financial Services," New York University, Department of Finance Working Paper (in draft).

Reputational Losses in Market Capitalization – Statistical Summary				
Event window	(–5,3)	(–5,10)	(–1,3)	(–1,10)
MEAN	–$3,300,009	–$3,485,131	–$1,765,038	–$1,950,161
p-value	0.0000	0.0013	0.0007	0.0049
MEDIAN	–$984,421	–$555,256	–$700,940	–$616,721
Bottom 95% loss	–$14,875,021	–$24,140,182	–$10,704,029	–$13,227,960
Bottom 99% loss	–$18,375,026	–$28,360,334	–$13,971,351	–$20,261,036
90% skew	–1.5269	0.2562	–0.5088	–1.3309
90% kurtosis	2.4720	–0.4915	0.1960	1.6990

Figure 10.11   Absolute CARs — reputational loss pilot study

As a major telecommunications-sector commercial and investment banking client, Citigroup maintained an active lending relationship with WorldCom and successfully competed for its securities underwriting business. At the same time, Citigroup served as the exclusive pension fund adviser to WorldCom and executed significant stock option trades for WorldCom executives, while at the same time conducting proprietary trading in WorldCom stock and holding a significant position in the company's stock through its asset management unit. Additionally, Citigroup advised the WorldCom CEO, financed his margin purchases of company stock, and provided loans for one of his private businesses.

On the one hand, Citigroup was very successfully engaged in the pursuit of revenue economies of scope (cross-selling), simultaneously targeting both the asset and liability sides of its client's balance sheet, generating advisory fee income, managing assets, and meeting the private banking needs of WorldCom's CEO. On the other hand, that same success caught the firm in

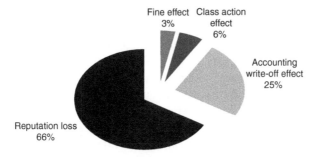

Data: All SEC enforcement actions 1978-2002 – 2,532 regulatory events
Actions & penalties tracked through 15 November 2005
Mean CAR –38.06% = mean market value loss $397 million (24% higher for surviving firms)
Partitioned for sample:
Fines imposed on firms $5.01 million
Class action payments $ 8.59 million
Accounting write-off $37.4 billion
Reputation loss $101.5 billion

Figure 10.12   Decomposing CARs related to earnings restatements

Source: Karpoff, Jonathan M., Lee, D.Scott and Martin, Gerald., "The Cost to Firms of Cooking the Books" (March 8, 2006).

simultaneous conflicts of interest relating to retail investors, institutional fund managers, WorldCom executives, and shareholders, as well as Citigroup's own positions in WorldCom credit exposure and stock trades. WorldCom's bankruptcy triggered a large market capitalization loss for Citigroup's own shareholders, only about a third of which can be explained by a $2.65 billion civil settlement the firm reached with investors in May 2004.[17]

It seems plausible that the broader the range of services that a financial firm provides to a given client in the market, and the greater the cross-selling pressure, the greater the potential likelihood that conflicts of interest and reputational risk exposure will be compounded in any given case, and, when these conflicts of interest are exploited, the more likely they are to damage the market value of the financial firm's business franchise once they come to light. Similarly, the more active a financial intermediary becomes in principal transactions such as affiliated private equity businesses and hedge funds, the more exposed it is likely to be to reputational risk related to conflicts of interest.

10.6   Conclusions

This chapter attempts to define reputational risk and to outline the sources of such risk facing financial services firms. The chapter then considers the key drivers of reputational risk in the presence of transactions costs and imperfect information, and goes on to survey empirical research on the impact of reputational losses of financial intermediaries. We conclude that market discipline, through the reputation effects on the franchise value of financial intermediaries, can be a powerful complement to regulation and civil litigation. Nevertheless, market discipline-based controls remain controversial. Financial firms continue to encounter serious instances of reputation loss due to misconduct despite its effects on the value of their franchises. This suggests material lapses in the governance and management process.[18]

Dealing with reputational risk can be an expensive business, with compliance systems that are costly to maintain and various types of walls between business units and functions that impose significant opportunity costs due to inefficient use of information within the organization. Moreover, management of certain kinds of reputational exposure in multifunctional financial firms may be sufficiently difficult to require structural remediation. On the other hand, reputation losses can cause serious damage, as demonstrated by reputation-sensitive 'accidents' that seem to occur repeatedly in the financial services industry. Indeed, it can be argued that such issues contribute to market valuations among financial conglomerates that fall below valuations of more specialized financial services businesses. (Laeven and Levine, 2005; Schmid and Walter, 2006).[19]

Managements and boards of financial intermediaries must be convinced that a good defense is as important as a good offense in determining sustainable competitive performance. This is something that is extraordinarily difficult to put into practice in a highly competitive environment for both financial services firms and for the highly skilled professionals that comprise the industry. A good defense requires an unusual degree of senior management leadership and commitment (Smith and Walter, 1997). Internally, there have to be mechanisms that reinforce the loyalty and professional conduct of employees. Externally, there has to be careful and sustained attention to reputation and competition as disciplinary mechanisms. In the end, it is probably leadership more than anything else that separates winners from losers over the long-term – the notion that appropriate professional behavior reinforced by a sense of belonging to a quality franchise constitutes a decisive comparative advantage.

Notes

1. Acknowledgements: The author is grateful for helpful comments by John Boatright and Ed Hartmann on earlier drafts of this chapter, which draws on 'Reputational Risk and the Financial Crisis', in John R. Boatright, *Business Ethics*, (ed.), London: John Wiley & Sons, 2010.
2. For the ensuing report, see http://www.iasplus.com/crunch/0804iifbestpractices.pdf
3. See http://careers.hereisthecity.com/front_office/corporate_and_investment_banking/press_releases/124.cntns

4. Earlier studies focusing on reputation include Chemmanur and Fulghieri (1994), Smith (1992), Walter and De Long (1995), and Smith and Walter (1997).
5. Basle II at http://www.bis.org/publ/bcbs107.htm.
6. For an early discussion of external conduct benchmarks, see Galbraith (1973).
7. For a discussion, see Capiello (2006).
8. For a full examination of these issues, see Smith and Walter (1997).
9. For one of the early studies, see Smith (1992).
10. Walter and DeLong (1995)
11. For a journalistic account, see *The Wall Street Journal* (1994) and *Euromoney* (1994).
12. De Long and Walter (1994). For event study methodology, see Brown and Warner (1985).
13. In order to create this prediction, we regress the daily return of Morgan stock on the daily return on the market index as well as on an industry–group index. The industry–group index included 20 financial institutions with characteristics showing some degree of overlap with those of JP Morgan. This is the unweighted average of share prices for Banc One, BankAmerica, Bank of Boston, Bank of New York, Bankers Trust NY, Barnett Bank, Bear Stearns, Chase Manhattan, Chemical Bank, Citicorp, Continental Bank, First Chicago, First Fidelity Bancorp, First Virginia, Merrill Lynch, Morgan Stanley Group, NationsBank, Paine Webber Group, Salomon Inc. and Wells Fargo. We use data from 300 days to 50 days prior to the announcement date (December 28, 1993). The resulting coefficients are then multiplied by the returns on the market and industry indices from 50 days prior to 50 days after the announcement, in order to obtain an estimation of the daily stock return during this period. Then, the excess return is calculated at the 'predicted' return minus the actual Morgan stock returns for the period, and the cumulative excess return is plotted. In order to translate these results into the monetary effect on JP Morgan stock, the cumulated excess return is multiplied by the total market value of equity (shares outstanding times price per share) 50 days before the announcement.
14. We regressed Morgan's stock returns against the value-weighted NYSE index and the industry group composed of 20 banking and securities firms. While autocorrelation can be a problem in using daily stock returns, JP Morgan stock was heavily traded, so that daily carryover is unlikely to be significant. Indeed, when we controlled the industry for this potential problem by including the lagged market index as a regression, the resulting coefficient was negative and statistically insignificant. We obtained the following model, estimated over days -300 to -50 prior to the announcement date: $RJPMt = -0.00014 + 0.5766*RMt + 0.2714*RGt + ut$ where $RJPMt$ = Return on JP Morgan stock; RMt = Return on NYSE composite (value-weighted) index; RGt = Return on group of companies in the same industry. The excess return attributable to the event is the calculated residual (ut) from 50 days prior to 50 days after the announcement.
15. Based on an ongoing empirical study of reputational risk being conducted at the Stern School of Business, New York University.
16. Ongoing empirical work on reputation-sensitive financial services events with Gayle De Long and Anthony Saunders.
17. Similar issues surfaced in the case of the 2001 Enron bankruptcy. See Batson (2003) and Healy and Palepu (2003).
18. These issues are explored in Daniel Hoechele, Markus Schmid, Ingo Walter, and David Yermack, 'Corporate Governance and the Diversification Discount', available at http://papers.ssrn.com/sol3/papers.cfm?abstract_id=1341006.
19. See also Kanatas and Qi (2003) and Saunders and Walter (1997).

References

Batson, N. (2003) *Final Report*, Chapter 11, Case No. 01-16034 (AJG), United States Bankruptcy Court, Southern District of New York, July 28.

Brown, S.J. and Warner, J.B. (1985) 'Using Daily Stock Returns: The Case of Event Studies', *Journal of Financial Economics*, (14): 3–31.

Capiello, S. (2006) 'Public Enforcement and Class Actions Against Conflicts of Interest in Universal Banking – The US Experience Vis-à-vis Recent Italian Initiatives', Bank of Italy, Law and Economics Research Department, Working Paper.

Chemmanur, T.J. and Fulghieri, P. (1994) 'Investment Bank Reputation, Information Production, and Financial Intermediation', *Journal of Finance*, March, (49): 57–86.

De Fontnouvelle, P., DeJesus-Rueff, V., Jordan, J.S. and Rosengren, E.S. (2006) 'Capital and Risk: New Evidence on Implications of Large Operational Losses', Federal Reserve Bank of Boston. Working Paper. September.

De Long, G. and Walter, I. (1994) 'J.P. Morgan and Banesto: An Event Study', New York University Salomon Center. Working Paper. April.

Galbraith, J.K. (1973) *Economics and the Public Purpose* (New York: Macmillan).

International Monetary Fund, Global Financial Stability Report (2009) Washington, DC: IMF, April.

Kanatas, G. and Jianping Qi (2003) 'Integration of Lending and Underwriting: Implications of Scope Economies', *Journal of Finance*, 58(3): 1167–1191.

Laeven, L. and Levine, R. (2005) 'Is there a diversification discount in financial conglomerates?', *Journal of Financial Economics*, (85): 331–367.

Saunders, A. and Walter, I. (1997) *Universal Banking In the United States: What Could We Gain? What Could We Lose?* New York: Oxford University Press.

Schmid, M.M. and Walter, I. (2006) 'Do Financial Conglomerates Create or Destroy Economic Value?', *Journal of Financial Intermediation*, 14(2): 78–94, May 2009.

Smith, C.W. (1992) 'Economics and Ethics: The Case of Salomon Brothers', *Journal of Applied Corporate Finance*, (5)2: 23–28, Summer.

Smith, R.C. and Walter, I. (1997) *Street Smarts: Linking Professional Conduct and Shareholder Value in the Securities Industry*. Boston: Harvard Business School Press.

Walter, I. and DeLong, G. (1995) 'The Reputation Effect of International Merchant Banking Accidents: Evidence from Stock Market Data', New York University Salomon Center, Working Paper.

11
Risk Management for Pension Funds and Endowments

Aaron Brown

11.1 Motivation and goals

Earlier this year, I was asked to speak at a luncheon for holders of the Financial Risk Manager professional designation who worked for pension funds and endowments. After my remarks, a discussion ensued in which it became clear that there was no consensus on best practice for how to be a risk manager in these types of organizations. The principles of modern financial risk management were developed in proprietary trading organizations; and later adapted first to commercial banking, then to investment banking and finally to agency asset management – that is, the business of managing money for others in return for a fee.

Pension funds and endowments are similar in some respects to agency asset management companies, but differ in one important respect. They work directly for the beneficial owners of the funds they invest. They share that characteristic with proprietary traders.

This spurred me on to do some research on the issue.[1] I read what I could find, and spoke to the authors. I looked at organizations in which I had personal contacts. The result confirmed the impression from the lunch, there is no consensus on best practice. There are a number of overlapping models, but most of them do not incorporate the insights from modern financial risk management. Some are based on older fiduciary legal concepts, others on Modern Portfolio Theory, and still others are based on accumulated practical experience with little theory. Moreover, even among people who agreed on basic outlook, details of practice varied considerably.

I am not qualified to set a best practice standard for risk managers in pension funds and endowments, but I believe I am in a position to describe how the principles of modern financial risk management apply logically. As far as I know, no risk manager works precisely as described here, and it is possible that some practices I recommend would conflict with the specific rules of some organizations. So this chapter is neither descriptive nor proscriptive. I attempt only to describe a high-level framework for risk managers to think about incorporating the theoretical advances and accumulated practical wisdom of the last quarter century in financial risk management.

11.2   A generic pension fund/endowment[2]

There is a wide variety of pension funds and endowments, and an even wider variety of staff organizations to manage them. For ease of exposition, the generic structure specified below is assumed. Individual readers can map it to their funds.

The organization is composed of the following parts:

- A pool of assets.
- A liability stream. In many cases this is an actuarially projected set of future benefit payments. In other cases it may be a less well-defined mandate to support the activities of a university or charity, or the needs of a family. The key point is the goal of the managers is not simply to make the pool of assets grow as much as possible, nor to keep the pool of assets as safe as possible, but to support specific liabilities or activities, which may be more or less precisely defined. It will be assumed that this can involve both short-term liquidity needs and long-term value needs. The organization may also have a non-investment income stream, say from contributions of future beneficiaries. At our level of generality these are just negative liabilities.
- A board of directors, which is assumed to be experienced and involved, but not composed of financial experts. Some funds will have other legal structures, but there is almost always some kind of external oversight to the fund management.
- An executive who will be called the Chief Investment Officer, although s/he may have another title. This person is assumed to have authority over all fund decisions, subject to legal guidelines and oversight of the board. In some funds there may be a high-level staff to consider things like investment strategy and asset allocation, in other funds the CIO may cover these areas directly. Also, in many funds there may be a large staff charged with administering contributions and benefits, it may be much larger than the investment staff. In this case the fund is considered only up to the level of CIO.[3]
- Investment analysts responsible for selecting and overseeing third party managers. In some funds this can be a large staff, in smaller funds the CIO may do this personally, or the work may be performed by independent consultants. If there are in-house managers, they will be treated as third-party managers for the purposes of this chapter. Obviously they will present another set of issues for the fund risk manager, but these issues are well

understood. There are plenty of books and chapters about risk management of portfolio managers and traders.

- Due diligence personnel responsible for investigating and approving third-party managers, both new manager candidates prior to selection, and existing managers on an ongoing basis. In some funds the investment analysts may be responsible for their own due diligence, in other funds it may be contracted to independent consultants. But either way, for risk management purposes it is important to separate due diligence conceptually from investment selection.
- Administrative staff, which is used as a catch-all for everyone else at the fund. This may include lawyers, accountants, operations staff and others. Obviously these are crucial functions, whether performed in-house or by third parties, but they can be treated similarly by the risk manager.

11.3   Why is an independent risk manager needed?[4]

Looking at the list of people above, which may include dozens of in-house staff and consultants or a single person, it is not immediately clear what a risk manager is supposed to do. The CIO is balancing risk and expected return when constructing the portfolio, and the investment analysts are monitoring risk and return of their subportfolios. Due diligence personnel examine non-investment risks, as do the administrative staff in their various capacities. Risk will always be one of the foremost concerns of the board.

A common failing of inexperienced or untrained people who find themselves with the risk manager title is to try to do other people's jobs for them: kibitzing about portfolio strategy or being a Monday morning quarterback on due diligence decisions. Even worse are people who go around looking worried all the time and fighting any decision that might be criticized in retrospect. These activities are annoying and useless at best, and corrosive at worst.

Modern financial risk management is a technical field with well-defined tools and techniques that have no overlap with the portfolio, investment or operational risk approaches that are the responsibility of other people in the fund. It is complementary work, not duplicative. In smaller funds, the risk manager might help out with, or even be responsible for, other tasks such as evaluating portfolio risk or performing due diligence. However in that case, it is important to separate the two tasks so that the risk management can be performed with some independence. Even CIOs and traders who act as their own risk managers benefit from setting aside time to dedicate to pure risk management rather than trying to wear both hats all the time.

As implied in the paragraph above, independence is a state of mind, not a line on an organization chart. Experienced and assertive risk managers will be independent whatever the rules say, and organization charts will not give independent voices to inexperienced timid people. Even in the extreme case of a CIO acting as her own risk manager, experience and discipline can produce an acceptable degree of independence. Expensive trial-and-error has demonstrated two things, however. The more independent risk management is, the more effective it is, and the best single way to facilitate independence is for the risk manager to report directly to the board.

The need for independence has nothing to do with conflict, contrary to some popular belief. A risk manager who causes excessive conflict is not doing a good job. The problem is that if the risk manager reports to someone, say the CIO, he will necessarily begin to share some of her assumptions and worldview. The CIO will influence how the risk manager works, how he allocates his time and how he acts on his conclusions. This is true however hands-off the CIO tries to be. It is hard enough to maintain genuinely independent perspectives when two people work together every day, it is twice as difficult if one reports to the other.

11.4   End to end

If a Martian observed a typical pension or endowment fund at work, it would probably conclude that the main function of the organization would be to aggregate, compile and redistribute data. Numbers from existing investments, potential future investments, the economy, liabilities and other sources flow into the office and are transformed into complex decision tools and presentations.

Bitter experience has shown how fragile this process is in all organizations. It is designed piecemeal. Each person who needs to do a job grabs the requisite data and transforms it in ways that make sense for the problem at hand, this transformation then becomes the input data for someone else. Inconsistencies abound. Numbers compiled under one set of assumptions, or one as-of date, are combined with essentially different numbers. Precise definitions are blurred. Approximations and guesses solidify into hard numbers. Ancient rules of thumb outlive their value. Errors propagate. People paper over inconsistencies (computers are extremely helpful for this). None of this is intended badly, in fact there may be no practical alternative to getting work done. But someone has to know the difference between data and information.[5]

There are some exceptions to this state of affairs. Some organizations have the discipline and IT skills to manage core data in end-to-end valid ways. Unfortunately, few of these organizations are pension funds or endowments, which usually cannot get exactly the data they want, do not have the IT budget to do things right and have too diverse a set of stakeholders to agree on a single data model. And even if the organization gets its core data right, noncore data is very important as well.

An independent organization-wide risk manager is usually the only person interested in coordinating all the data everyone uses. In the early 1990s, when this was developed for consolidated trading organizations, risk measures like duration (fixed-income desk), Beta (equity desk), Delta (options desk) and many others had to be combined. Positions with different data fields (coupon rate for a bond, strike price for an option) had to be aggregated and it often was the case that the same position was represented differently by different desks. There were prices set at different times of day, and some were bids, others were last transactions and others were from models. All of these data were available in different aggregations, it was usually impossible to go back to the source for granular reporting. It took the financial accounting folks months to produce reliable enough estimates for audited annual reports, we needed up-to-the-second information.

Attacking these problems was extremely expensive, literally hundreds of billions of dollars were spent, and the results were far from perfect. However, much of the expense was due to rigid regulatory or legal requirements. Getting the right information for real-time top-level risk management decisions was expensive, but tens of millions of dollars worth of expensive, not hundreds of billions.[6]

Even the largest and most complex pensions and endowment funds do not have this level of data requirements, but getting really good, timely, reliable information is still an enormous – and expensive – challenge. An unfortunate tendency is to spend more energy and money on analytics for the data than in getting the data right in the first place. Having good, clear, accurate, up-to-date simple data is essential for any kind of risk management, fancy analytics are just icing on the cake. Fancy analytics based on average quality data are worse than useless.

11.5 Getting data right

The first step is to set reasonable expectations. Every number cannot be checked at the lowest level of granularity, with all approximations and errors in the aggregation eliminated. Attempting to do that leads to burn-out, in fact, it is probably the biggest reason people do not do anything at all. The trick is to try to make the data a little better every day, not perfect in some distant future.

One important rule is to always go 'one level deeper' than the day-to-day managers. This will not catch all errors, but it gives some degree of independent check. Also, as this is done, the day-to-day managers will gradually deepen their own data sources, to keep up with risk management; then risk management can go another level deeper. Going more levels deeper sounds better, but it is usually too difficult and can leave risk management too far away from the day-to-day managers to communicate effectively.

Going one level deeper is done by taking note of the data sources people actually use as risk management reviews the organization. Risk managers do not rely on what a report says, they find out the real source. For example, a data item may be labeled as coming from an annual report, but it is actually downloaded from a financial information provider, and may include errors or adjustments. Or information on what looks like a custodian's report may actually be supplied by the investment manager.

Once risk management finds the source, it finds the source for that source and arranges to get that data directly. This cannot be done for every bit of data used by the organization, so risk managers pick the ones that are most important for risk management. When in doubt, they go with simplicity and ease of integration. Risk managers would rather have less relevant information of which they can be more certain, and which they can integrate with other information, than have more relevant and more doubtful or isolated information. A day-to-day manager may need the additional relevance and may not care about integrating across the organization, but the risk manager is in a different position. By the way, this is one important reason why you need an independent risk manager – one person usually cannot keep two different versions of the same information in mind at the same time.

The goal is to build up a simplified data model of the organization that is robust and reliable. It will not be as precise as the data used to run the organization, but it will have fewer errors. It will be less accurate on normal days, but – hopefully – it will be a more accurate guide on the big days that really matter for risk. It will not be free of biases, assumptions and the madness of crowds; but it will be one layer closer to reality.

11.6   Constant, rigorous, exact, objective verification

The next problem is that data tells you only about the past, while the effect of any risk management decisions will be realized in the future. The past is connected to the future through validation. The best-known method for this in risk management is Value at Risk (VaR). VaR was discovered accidentally in the late 1980s and early 1990s as the first generation of modern risk managers struggled with this issue.

The central idea of VaR is not a percentile of profit and loss, it is that a daily prediction is made that can be validated objectively, and its performance is tracked. The discipline of daily predictions and backtests forces improvements to data and systems, and that advantage would accrue even if the VaR were discarded after backtesting, or computed on something irrelevant to risk decisions. Another advantage is producing a VaR makes risk managers humble, they will realize how little they know about risk even on ordinary days. Humility is a giant leap on the path to sound risk management.

VaR, and validation in general, can be applied to all aspects of an organization, but the canonical VaR is on the daily profit or loss of beginning-of-the-day positions, assuming normal markets and no trading. For a 95% one-day VaR, the actual loss should exceed the VaR on 5% of days, one day in 20, no more and no less, and the VaR breaks (days with losses greater than VaR) should be independent in time (there should be as many VaR breaks the day after a break as when there has not been a break for six months) and independent of the level of VaR (there should be as many breaks when VaR is low as when VaR is high). More generally, it should be impossible for anyone to make money betting for or against VaR breaks at 19 to 1 odds, but the three tests mentioned are the most important.

Clearly VaR has nothing to do with tail risks. About one VaR break per month is expected, and VaR does not include the risks from trading or abnormal markets. A high VaR does not mean more risk than a low VaR, in fact a high VaR means there is a wider range of outcomes in which there can be some confidence in models. VaR is a discipline to improving data and systems, and a way to demonstrate understanding of center risks, not a measure of tail risk.

The CIO is likely to ask investment managers for exposure information and volatility measures, as well as more sophisticated analytics. None of that is very useful for the risk manager. The risk manager would rather have a daily Value at Risk, sent every day before trading begins, including on days when systems are down or data unavailable, and the daily pro forma profit or loss of initial positions. If managers refuse to supply such detailed information in real time, getting it with delay, or just getting the backtest statistics are still useful. The risk manager should not care what the VaR number is, he should care how rigorously the manager performs backtests.

The same principle applies to all data used for risk. The risk manager wants numbers that can be objectively validated, these are the only reliable foundations for risk decisions. They will not be the precise data people want, but better to make decisions based on reliable information of moderate relevance than unreliable information of perfect relevance. All useful numbers in the world are compromises between what we want to know and what we can measure.

11.7 Conclusion

If I leave you with one thought, it is that being a risk manager has nothing to do with reports or metrics or checklists. It has everything to do with independence, consistency and objective validation. You cannot predict or prevent disaster, in fact people who try to predict are the enemies of risk management, and the way to prevent disaster is to minimize risk which prevents success more effectively than it prevents disaster. You can improve the information in your organization and ground it more thoroughly in reality. You can bring independent views to risk decisions, and a broader decision is a better decision. And one final advantage is you can plug your organization into the network of risk managers at asset managers, dealers and other funds and organizations. The network is even more firmly grounded in reality than any individual risk manager can be.

Notes

1. The most comprehensive published account I found was Susan Mangiero's Pension Risk Management: Derivatives, Fiduciary Duty and Process, Society of Actuaries Joint Pension Research Project Working Paper, October 2008. http://www.soa.org/research/research-projects/pension/research-pen-risk-mngt.aspx. Another extensive discussion can be found in Jon Hatchett, David Bowie and Nick Forrester, Risk Management for Pension Funds, Staple Inn Actuarial Society, 2010. http://www.google.com/url?sa=t&rct=j&q=&esrc=s&frm=1&source=web&cd=12&ved=0CEMQFjABOAo&url=http%3A%2F%2Fwww.sias.org.uk%2Fdata%2Fmeetings%2FOctober2010%2Fattachment%2Fat_download&ei=nrD-UIvZGonB0QGJlYCIBQ&usg=AFQjCNFsmH_nM4ldbcDkHsiIKjBuThSbgw&sig2=fEfmt-ObzDGto0AexWONHQ&bvm=bv.41248874,d.dmQ
2. For an excellent summary that is still reasonably up-to-date, see Brizendine, Virginia S., Public Pension Plan Operations and Administration, Government Finance Officers Association, Chicago, 1992.
3. Miller, Girard, Pension Fund Investing, Government Finance Officers Association, Chicago, 1987.
4. Risk Standards for Institutional Investment Managers and Institutional Investors, Risk Standards Working Group, 1996.
5. Control Objectives for Information and Related Technology, Information Systems Audit and Control Foundation, Chicago, 1996.
6. Doherty, Stephen A., Trading Control, The Institute of Internal Auditors, Altamonte Springs, FL, 1998.

12
A Stitch in Time...

Kosrow Dehnad

12.1 Introduction

To discuss ways of reducing costs and increasing efficiencies in an asset management operation, it may be useful to develop first a simple model that captures the main features of such an operation. Figure 12.1 presents a model for an asset management operation.

In comparing the above scheme to a production process, 'Data and Information' may be regarded as similar to raw materials; 'Research and Analysis' and 'Trade Ideas' play the role of research and development; and 'Execution and Booking' are analogous to the production and servicing of products. Similarly, 'Outsized Positions' are akin to 'Overproduction' of a product relative to market demand; and implementing a 'New System or Trading Algorithm' without properly testing them is like installing 'New Machinery' or rolling out a new product without properly evaluating its performance. Quality improvement and reduction of rework correspond to the elimination of errors in the execution and booking of trades (5). The last two topics are the main focus of this chapter. In general, the risk of an error or chance of a defect is proportional to the 'number of parameters' times the 'degree of variability' of an item. In manufacturing, the 'number of parameters' corresponds to the number of components in a product. (This number may be very large; a car, for example, may be made

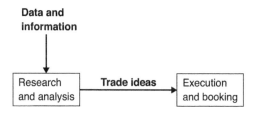

Figure 12.1   A basic model for an asset management operation

up of 14,000–20,000 different components). On the other hand, these components are very similar from one car to another; two Toyota Camrys have many components in common, with only a small number of exceptions, such as color, material of the seats and some other, mainly cosmetic, items. To monitor the quality of such end products, inspection of each item is often impractical because of the large 'number of parameters'. In such cases, sampling is a feasible alternative due to the low 'degree of variability' of components. The sampling technique, however, is not applicable to a trading operation because trades are generally non-homogeneous, and two trades rarely have many parameters in common while the total number of such parameters – size, maturity, counterparty etc. – rarely exceeds 20 to 30. For this reason, the quality improvement techniques for trading operations, basically error-detecting procedures, have to be designed and implemented in such a way that they can be efficiently applied to each trade. In the next section, we present several examples of such techniques. In the last section of this chapter, we digress into a discussion of the behavioral aspect of risk management in large financial institutions – a topical subject these days, given the relatively recent meltdown of the credit markets and the enormous losses suffered by some major financial institutions. This last section suggests that the shortcomings of risk management in these institutions reflect flaws in their promotion culture, which often elevates people to positions of chief risk officer (CRO) who lack the necessary technical and trading skills required to lead such efforts and foresee extreme financial events.

12.2   Examples of quality control and error-detection techniques

An asset management operation that invests in liquid assets such as foreign exchange (FX) may execute a large number of trades every day (10,000 trades a day is not uncommon for a major financial institution) (Chorafas, 1992). These trades must be entered into the firm's IT system for confirmation, P&L reconciliation, collateral settlement and a host of other actions. Delays and errors in entering trade information could have major undesirable consequences. One way of improving data entry processes is to institute procedures and safeguards that can reduce and detect errors early on. In the manufacturing world, such procedures are often referred to as 'poka-yoke' techniques.

Consider, for example, a simple transaction of buying euro forward. Any of the following parameters of the trade can be entered incorrectly into the firm's systems:

1. Trade date
2. Maturity date

3. Size (notional)
4. Level (price)
5. Counterparty
6. Long vs. short
7. Currency

If such mistakes are not caught and corrected early on, it may take a long time before they are discovered, and this delay could have a tremendous impact on the bottom line of the company. Suppose the direction of the trade is entered incorrectly and the trade is long-dated and of a large size; moreover, it is also part of a larger and more complex transaction which is dumped into the black hole of a large portfolio that is risk managed on a 'portfolio basis'. Unless such an error is caught early on, it will become increasingly difficult to detect and make the necessary corrections. Moreover, since the cash flow of the trade occurs in the distant future, the market can move significantly against the position and in the meantime the trading book can show a profit (because of the error) which, at the maturity of the trade, turns out to be a significant loss. At that point, usually the blame game starts: people may be looking for scapegoats; heads may roll. Management, in order to show its resolve and to demonstrate that it will not tolerate a repeat of such mistakes, will force some people to pursue interests outside of the firm.

As in manufacturing industries, very simple rules of thumb can go a long way in reducing the probabilities of errors and in improving the efficiencies of operations in the financial services industry. Some of these rules can also help risk managers gauge the overall risks that the organization will face should an extreme event happen. These rules complement the VaR calculations (in vogue these days), which are based on some restrictive assumptions that may not hold when markets are in distress. In what follows, we present examples of such very simple rules.

12.2.1   Trade parity checks

This is a simple test for high-volume operations where a trade either opens a new position or closes an existing one. The test can indicate the possibility of certain errors in the recording of new trades. Let the number of trades in the system at the close of yesterday, close of today and number of new trades be denoted by $N_{yesterday}$, N_{today} and $N_{new.trades}$ respectively. If

$$N_{yesterday} + N_{today} + N_{new.trades}$$

is odd, then not all new trades have been entered into the system, or the direction of at least one new trade is recorded incorrectly. This simple test can be applied at the desk or the trader level.

12.2.2 Trade profiling

Using historical data about the types of assets and the sizes and maturities of the trades the firm has executed in the past, management can establish a profile about single and joint distributions of these parameters at the firm, department, desk and even trader level. All new trades will be compared against these profiles and 'outlier' trades will be elevated for further review. Many firms try to accomplish the above by requiring trades larger than certain size, say $50 million or longer than a certain maturity, say five years, to be reviewed and signed off by management. The above approach makes the process of detecting outlier trades more efficient because, say a three-year CHF/AUD FX forward can be viewed as a long-dated transaction while a five-year interest rate swap in USD is not. Similarly, a three-year interest rate swap for an emerging market country with lesser developed capital markets can be a very long-dated trade from a practical and risk management point of view. Trade profiling can also bring to the attention of management large losing positions that a trader may be trying to hide by rolling and increasing his positions. A case in point is that of Nick Leeson, who singlehandedly brought down Barings Bank by making increasingly losing bets against the Nikkei (Fay, 1997). Another example is the embarrassing loss of more than $2 billion at Sumitomo Corporation because of disastrous copper trades by Yasuo Hamanaka, the so-called 'Mr. Copper'(Time International, 1996). A more recent case is that of 'London Whale' trader at JPMorgan who took an outsized position in a credit derivative index that eventually resulted in a loss exceeding USD 6 billion. Trade profiling would have revealed the outlier size of these trades and positions. Another technique, 'super stress testing', which is described later in the chapter, would also have revealed the enormous risks that the institutions were taking on(Wall Street shokku, 1995).

12.2.3 Batch-matching

This is a simple method for an easy comparison of a batch of trades on the company's books with those provided by a counterparty. It can help management discover discrepancies and detect possible phantom trades when trades exist on the company's books but not on the counterparty's. Such trades occurred in the Daiwa Bank scandal, when the bond trader Toshihide Iguchi, over a period of ten years, lost more than $1.1 billion in Treasury bond trading while managing to hide these losses. He was able to do this by being in charge of both the front office and the back office, where he could change the statements that were being received from Bankers Trust. The idea of batch-matching is based on the use of a simple algorithm to assign numbers to open trades received by the counterparty and to those in the company's books, so that management can quickly review a large number of trades for possible discrepancies. Let us illustrate this method through a simple example.

Suppose we receive a list of our open positions with a counterparty and would like to compare it against our records. For the sake of simplicity, assume the trades are FX forwards in the following seven major currencies: USD, JPY, EUR, GBP, CHF, AUD and CAD. Let us indicate these currencies by numbers 1 to 7. To each trade, we assign a number with digits:

$$BST_1T_2T_3T_4M_1M_2M_3M_4N_1N_2N_3$$

B is the currency being bought and S is the currency being sold. Year and month of trade and maturity dates are indicated by T_1T_2, T_3T_4, M_1M_2 and M_3M_4 respectively. Finally, the size of the trade, rounded to the nearest million, is indicated by $N_1N_2N_3$. For example, buying GBP 15.45m forward against USD in February 2009 with maturity a year and a half from the trade date, in August 2010, will be assigned the number 4109021008015, where the digits are determined based on the above rule, namely: 4 (GBP), 1 (USD), 09 (trade year 2009), 02 (trade month February), 10 (maturity year 2010), 08 (maturity month) and 015 (size of the trade rounded to the nearest million). Having assigned numbers to each trade in both batches, we simply sort these numbers and compare the result. In particular, if the data are available in spreadsheets, assigning the numbers, sorting and comparing the two batches is very simple and involves only a few key strokes.

12.2.4 Super stress test

Warren Buffet once said that 'when the tide recedes, everyone can see who has been swimming naked' – the recent Ponzi scheme of Bernie Madoff and the outsized CDS trades at JPM are cases in point. The goal of 'super stress test' is to make 'financial tides' really recede in order to expose the 'hot spots' of risks in a portfolio or in a firm. Financial firms, on a regular basis, stress-test various trades and portfolios by considering two or three standard deviation moves within various parameters. For example, to calculate the credit exposure of an interest rate swap, the yield curve is simulated and the maximum exposure is calculated with, say, a 99% confidence interval. These tests, however, are based on certain distributional assumptions that may not hold during times of market stress and are quite computationally intensive. Super stress testing simplifies this process, so that it can be easily applied to all trades and large portfolios.

Super Stress Test values trades and positions using extreme levels of market parameters. These levels, though sometimes unrealistic and improbable from an economic point of view, can reveal the main features of a trade or portfolio and alert management to potential risks or mistakes. In this test, each parameter takes, at most, four values, and the orthogonal array methodology (Hedayat et al., 1999) is used as a systematic way of reducing the number of cases to be considered. We illustrate this approach by using a simple example. Consider a $10 million long JPY call that matures in one year with a strike of 95. The following are the trade parameters and their super stress levels:

$/¥ exchange rate	Volatility	Counterparty Credit
$¥_L$ (1$ = 1000¥)	Vol_L (0.01%)	$Crdt_L$ (Default)
$¥_H$ (1$ = 1¥)	Vol_H (200%)	$Crdt_H$ (AAA)

Rather than valuing the option under all eight combinations of market parameters, we use the 2^3 orthogonal array and value the trade for the following four scenarios only:

Scenario	$/¥	Volatility	Credit	Option Value
1	$¥_L$	Vol_L	$Crdt_L$	(95) Credit loss
2	$¥_L$	Vol_H	$Crdt_H$	95
3	$¥_H$	Vol_L	$Crdt_H$	0
4	$¥_H$	Vol_H	$Crdt_L$	0

The 'Option value' column in the above table indicates that the trade is booked as a long option position, and there is counterparty risk.

Super stress testing of a portfolio can involve many parameters, and we again use orthogonal array techniques to minimize the number of cases to be considered. By way of illustration, suppose a portfolio consists of interest rate swaps in the following currencies: USD, EUR, GBP, JPY and CAD. We consider four types of yield curves for each currency, and these yield curves are assumed to be linear – flat and low (L), flat and high (H), steep (S) and inverted (N) – as shown below:

	1 month	30 years
Flat low (L)	1 bps	1 bps
Flat high (H)	50%	50%
Steep (S)	1 bps	50%
Inverted (N)	50%	1 bps

Instead of valuing the portfolio for all 1,024 possible combinations of the yield curves, it is sufficient to perform the valuation for the following 16 scenarios that are based on orthogonal array:

Scenario	$	€	¥	£	CAD
1	$_L$	€_L*	¥_L	£_L	CAD_L**
2	$_L$	€_H	¥_H	£_H	CAD_H
3	$_L$	€_S	¥_S	£_S	CAD_S
4	$_L$	€_N	¥_N	£_N***	CAD_N
5	$_H$	€_L	¥_H	£_S	CAD_N
6	$_H$	€_H	¥_L	£_N	CAD_S
7	$_H$	€_S	¥_N	£_L	CAD_H
8	$_H$	€_N	¥_S	£_H	CAD_L
9	$_S$	€_L	¥_S	£_N	CAD_H
10	$_S$	€_H	¥_N	£_S	CAD_L
11	$_S$	€_S	¥_L	£_H	CAD_N
12	$_S$	€_N	¥_H	£_L	CAD_S
13	$_N$	€_L	¥_N	£_H	CAD_S
14	$_N$	€_H	¥_S	£_L	CAD_N
15	$_N$	€_S	¥_H	£_N	CAD_L
16	$_N$	€_N	¥_L	£_S	CAD_H

* $€_L$ – The scenario in which banks can borrow in euros for 1 week, 1 month, 2 months etc. ... up to 30 years at 1 bps.

** CAD_L – Flat low-yield curve for the Canadian dollar.

*** $£_L$ – The scenario in which banks can borrow in pounds sterling for 1 month at 50%; for one year, say 45%; and for 30 years at 1 bps.

For example, super stress testing would have revealed the magnitude of risk taken by banks that were issuing CDOs and carrying the super-senior tranches (85% and above) on their trading books at, say, LIBOR + 35 bps. The trading books were showing significant gains when they were marked to market at LIBOR + 15 bps-spread of so-called 'super triple A'. A Super Stress Test, however, by moving the credit spread to 1,000 bps (which actually did happen), would have revealed the extraordinary amount of risk buried in these books.

The most effective way to implement error-detection techniques such as those described in the four examples above is through automation. Automation reduces human intervention, a major source of error, and enables management to efficiently monitor the firm's operations. Human error is the primary source of operational errors. Moreover, unlike machines, human beings tend to make more mistakes when under pressure. In other words, if the chance of a machine to produce a defective item is p, then the expected number of defects when the machine produces n items is pn. On the other hand, the probability of errors by humans rises with an increase in their workload and work pressure. This increase can be modeled as $a\, e^{-ß/n}$, where a is inversely proportional to the average prowess, the level of experience and the efficiency of the team handling the operation, and where ß represents the resources available for that operation. Automation tends to reduce a and increase $ß$. Consequently, if management expects the number of trades (n) to increase, then it should, in order to prevent increases in error rates, either increase the resources ($ß$) or the experience level ($1/a$) of those running the operation, or both. Through automation they can achieve both simultaneously. Historical data can be used to estimate a and $ß$ of an operation in the firm.

12.2.5 'Algo' testing and operational risk

In the rush to automate and take advantage of IT as a competitive edge, asset managers should ensure that all new systems are adequately tested and all checks and balances are in place regarding operational risk particularly when a system goes into production (Cormen, 2007). For example, Algorithmic trading is an area of finance that has experienced rapid growth in recent years. This is partly due to the phenomenal growth and degree of innovation in Information Technology which has given birth to High Frequency Trading and Algorithmic (Algo) order execution. In academia, also, it has renewed interest in the microstructure of the markets and the study of the impact of asymmetry of information on the functioning of the markets. Some Algos try, by observing trading patterns, to improve the accuracy of their forecasts and take advantage of the next market move and to front-run futures trades and make the bid/ask spread that at times can be a fraction of a penny. However, when such trades are done a large enough number of times it becomes a profitable proposition. The success of such an approach to trading has been the reason that some sell-side counterparties offer asset managers direct access to markets and the use of their Algos. Some asset managers have even started to develop Algos of their own. A shocker came when it was revealed that on August 1, 2012 a dormant system at Knight Capital Group started multiplying stock trades by 1,000 and its staff had to look through eight sets of software before determining what was happening. The error caused wild swings in the shares of almost 150 companies. Besides disrupting trading, the orders left Knight Capital nursing a loss of more than USD$400 million in less than an hour – three times the profit it made the year before.

It has been claimed that the problem was an infrastructure issue more related to network than using quantitative tools to trade. If this is the case, then Knight Capital's management has a major operational risk issue on its hands. This incident, however, brings to the fore the challenge of determining the viability of such Algos before they are subjected to real life trading situations. Traditionally, the testing of software follows a protocol that: given such and such input the output should be such and such. For example if the price rises in the last five trades and the volume also increases it is a signal to buy, and a bid at such and such level should be submitted to the market. These protocols, however, do not have a good handle on the ways to test the long-run performance of the software. One explanation could be the difficulty of testing such software, that has to deal with streaming data and evaluating their performance under yet unknown and unknowable market conditions. As the first step in testing of Algos under real market conditions we propose to evaluate their performance under some generic scenarios: Trending and Mean Reverting markets. This is very similar to subjecting a new forecasting technique to two simple tests by observing its performance when the quantity to be forecasted is either constant or trends on a straight line. A reasonable forecasting technique should have a satisfactory performance at least in these two simple cases. Similarly asset managers should ensure that any trading Algo they intend to use is stable if the price actions follow the next two general and generic families of trending and mean reverting processes:

> Let the changes in price at each step be either a tic up or a tic down – no gapping – where the size of a ticdepends on the asset. For example, a tic for S&P mini futures is 0.25 while a tick for a number of stocks is1 cent. Let P_i, P_{i-1}, P_{i-2} be the last three trades and define
>
> $$Pr\{P_{i+1} > P_i \,|\, P_i, P_{i-1}, P_{i-2}\} = P_{up}$$
> $$Pr\{P_{i+1} < P_i \,|\, P_i, P_{i-1}, P_{i-2}\} = P_{down}$$

We consider three classes of price action:

* Random walk:
  $P_{up} = P_{down} = \frac{1}{2}$.
* Simple Up Trending:
  If $P_i > P_{i-1} > P_{i-2}$ then $P_{up} > \frac{1}{2}$;
  otherwise $P_{up} = P_{down} = \frac{1}{2}$.
* Simple Down Trending:
  If $P_i < P_{i-1} < P_{i-2}$ then $P_{down} > \frac{1}{2}$;
  otherwise $P_{up} = P_{down} = \frac{1}{2}$.
* Simple Mean reversion:
  If $P_i > P_{i-1} > P_{i-2}$ then $P_{up} < \frac{1}{2}$;
  if $P_i < P_{i-1} < P_{i-2}$ then $P_{down} < \frac{1}{2}$;
  otherwise $P_{up} = P_{down} = \frac{1}{2}$.

We test the Algo under all the above scenarios with different probabilities. For example, in the case of simple up trending where $P_{up} > \frac{1}{2}$, we consider following cases $P_{up} = 0.55, 0.65, 0.75, 0.85, 0.95, 1$ – the last one being a steady rise in price. Passing these simple tests is the first step to ensure that the Algo will not create a positive feedback loop reinforced by its own actions similar to what happened in the case of Knight Capital Group. The test will also ensure that the software has features to limit the total size of any position which brings us to the question of position size and liquidity.

12.2.6 Liquidity risk

The great recession of 2008 has driven home once again the importance of liquidity in asset management particularly when there is a shock to the market and investors run for the exit and start a vicious circle of selling that reinforces itself through positive feedback. In such times liquidity, i.e., the ability to quickly exchange an asset for cash, becomes of paramount importance and immediacy of a trade takes precedence over its profitability. In fact during the credit crisis some hedge funds that faced a deluge of redemption could not honor them because lack of liquidity made closing a position impossible or very costly. The question of liquidity can also arise under normal market conditions if the position is disproportionally large compared to market liquidity. Attempts to quickly unwind such positions can move the prices significantly and result in major losses due to slippage. This phenomenon is aptly demonstrated by the major loss that JPMorgan suffered in its investment portfolio due to the outsized position in an illiquid credit index by one of the bank's traders nicknamed 'London Whale' because of his large trades. The loss initially was dismissed as a tempest in a tea pot but later the estimate was revised up to about $2 billion when the management realized absence of market liquidity for flattening such a large position particularly when the market got wind of the size of the position and extracted a price for providing liquidity. The final loss ballooned to more than $6 billion. (*The New York Times* June 28, 2008).

Attempts to unwind an outsized position could also alert 'Algos' that a large position is being closed and they will try to front-run the asset manager. For example, in November of 2012 SEC brought charges of insider trading against a former employee of SAC hedge fund. The hedge fund had accumulated large positions in two pharmaceutical companies, Elan and Wyeth, that were developing a drug for Alzheimer's Disease. At its height the positions were $373 million of Wyeth stock and $328 million of Elan stock. After the trader was tipped off about the disappointing results of a clinical trial, the company decided to unwind its position and go short those stocks. The head trader was instructed to 'begin selling the Elan position, and to do so in a way so as not to alert anyone else, inside or outside of the hedge fund'. The trader used algorithms, which are programs that disguise orders and keep them from being exploited by faster traders and algorithms. A few days later the head trader reported that 'This was executed quietly and effectively over a 4-day period through Algos and darkpools and booked into two firm accounts that have very limited viewing access. This process clearly stopped leakage of info from either in [or] outside the firm and in my viewpoint saved us some slippage.'

Often very large positions go hand in hand with a high degree of leverage and as the saying goes 'Enough leverage can turn any safe investment into a time bomb.' Leverage magnifies the loss due to slippage and impedes the speed with which liquidity can return to the market-resilience of liquidity. This phenomenon of liquidity slowly returning to the market is very similar to the speed with which water seeps back into a well and replenishes the water that has been taken out of it. Sometimes governments become providers of liquidity of last resort. For example during the recent credit crisis when companies such as GE capital had a hard time placing their commercial paper (CP), it was the Federal Reserve that stepped in and provided the needed liquidity to the CP market through its Commercial Paper Funding Facility. This action of the Fed is very similar to that of the government of Hong Kong during the 1997 Asian Financial Crisis where it supported the Hong Kong stock market by purchasing shares of companies, thus providing liquidity to that market.

Liquidity determines the trade-off between immediacy and volatility. A position can be closed quickly and incurring slippage, in return reducing exposure to price fluctuation, i.e., volatility. Alternatively a position can be closed over time with reduced slippage but exposure to price fluctuations. Consequently asset managers should be cognizant of the size of a position relative to liquidity of the market and quantify potential financial impact of forced liquidation of that position, keeping in mind that the liquidity of a stock is not constant and varies over time. The liquidity is a function of factors such as price, number of shares outstanding, time of the day, day of the week, general market sentiment etc. For example, the liquidity for after-hours trading or during holidays is much less than liquidity half an hour before the close of the market say at 3:30 on a business day. For illustration, following are the bid and ask quotes and the corresponding round lots offered for Bank of America (BAC) stock on Wednesday November 28, 2012 according to Bloomberg;

5:00 AM	9.58/9.73 6×18
6:00 AM	9.60/9.73 50×18
7:00 AM	9.62/9.65 10×4
8:00 AM	9.62/9.63 27×40
9:00 AM	9.59/9.60 547×305
9:30 AM	9.52/9.58 331×260
10:00 AM	9.52/9.53 969×562

We propose a simple and practical way of using market information to estimate the impact of liquidity on a position if it is to be closed quickly. The approach is particularly applicable to equity markets that are quote driven, i.e., at any instant there is a bid price P_b and bid size S_b and similarly an ask price P_a and ask size S_a and we assume

$$P_a > P_b$$

The above condition excludes transient states such as

$$P_a = P_b \text{ ('locked market')}$$

or

$$P_a < P_b \text{ ('crossed market')}.$$

We assume a change in price ΔP causes a change in liquidity ΔS i.e., higher prices bring more sellers into the market and similarly lower prices bring more buyers into the market. Since investing deals with returns rather than prices, we model the above relationship as

$$\Delta S = \lambda(t,P,S)\, \Delta P/P$$

where t is the time.

As the first approximation we assume λ to be constant. Solving the differential equation $\Delta S = \lambda \Delta P/P$ results in

$$S = \lambda Ln(P) + C$$

In this model $S > 0$ is interpreted as the size that is being offered for sale while $S < 0$ is the bid size. For example if there is a bid for 200 round lots then in this model it is represented as $S = -200$ while if this was the number of shares being offered then $S = 200$.

We use market data to determine λ and C. Assume the actual number shown in the market for the bid and ask prices and sizes are P_b, S_b and P_a, S_a respectively. Substituting these values in the solution gives

$$-S_b = \lambda Ln(P_b) + C$$
$$S_a = \lambda Ln(P_a) + C$$

Solving these equations yields

$$S_a + S_b = \lambda Ln(P_a) - \lambda Ln(P_b)$$

or

$$S_a + S_b = \lambda Ln(P_a/P_b)$$

Let

$$P_a = (1+d)\, P_b$$

If we assume bid/ask spread to be relatively small i.e., d<<1 then

$$Ln(P_a/P_b) = Ln(1+d) \approx d$$

or

$$\lambda \approx (S_a+S_b)/d$$

and

$$C = -S_b - \lambda\, Ln(P_b) + C$$

or for the current market conditions the liquidity at price P would be

$$S = (S_a+S_b)/d\ Ln(P/P_b) - S_b$$

where S > 0 indicates an offer and S < 0 indicates a bid.

It is easy to verify that the above relationship is consistent with what is currently observed in the market. For illustration, suppose we have 1,000,000 shares of BAC (10,000 round lots) and decide to close this position. At what levels can we expect to do this according to the above model? Recall liquidity determines the trade-off between immediacy and volatility, i.e., a position can be closed quickly by incurring slippage while reducing exposure to price fluctuations, i.e., volatility. Alternatively the slippage can be reduced by closing the position over time while increasing exposure to price fluctuations. Clearly this position should be closed during hours when NYSE is open and the market has liquidity. The question is to estimate the cost of unwinding the position given market liquidity say on Wednesday November 28, 2012 at 10 am. At this time following were the sizes and prices offered in the market

10:00 AM   9.52/9.53   969×562

The question is how low the price is expected to be so that the liquidity in the market will be sufficient to sell 10,000 round lots. In other words if we accept a slippage of d% then we expect to be able to fairly quickly sell the following number of shares at prices not worse than (1+d%)9.52

$$S = (969 + 562)Ln(1+d)/0.01 - 969$$

For S to be more than 10,000 round lot the slippage d = -6%, i.e., Price = 9.52 * (1–6%) = 8.95. For this price, the liquidity is expected to be

$$S = (969 + 562)Ln(1-6\%) - 969 = -10442$$

i.e., we should be able to unwind the whole position at a slippage that should not exceed 6%.

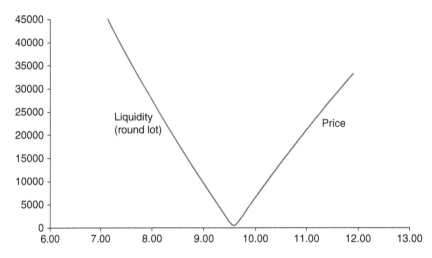

Figure 12.2   Liquidity function

In practice, an asset manager should gauge the resiliency of the liquidity at the time of execution to decide whether it would be better that the orders are worked into the market. For example, suppose we do not wish to have a slippage that exceeds 1%. In this case

$$S= (969+562)Ln(1-1\%)-969 = -2508$$

i.e., a fourth of our position.

In the absence of resiliency in the liquidity it should take less than four days to close the position with little slippage, keeping in mind that we will run the risk that prices could change dramatically from one day to the next. The asset manager's decision of balancing immediacy vs exposure to volatility will require an estimate of resiliency of liquidity, stock price volatility, and size of the float – a topic that is beyond the scope of this chapter.

Figure 12.2 is the graph of the above liquidity function when lot size for bid/ask are both shown as positive numbers (recall in the model the bid size is negative)

12.3   Conclusion

In conclusion, let us digress to the topic of the recent meltdown in credit markets and the fact that a number of risk managers did not see the freight train coming. This failure is a typical case of risk being underpriced because of over-reliance on mathematical models and a lack of attention to market realities. For example, most CDO models of rating agencies were developed by 'quants' who had never traded, were narrowly focused and who were clueless about the workings of credit and mortgage markets. They were oblivious to the fact that all the models were based on the assumption of 'liquidity', which can dry up rapidly and cause the models to break down. Unfortunately, some CROs also relied on these flawed models, since some CROs lacked the trading experience and technical expertise to challenge the models and their assumptions and conclusions. This lack of knowledge and skill on the part of risk managers is, to some extent, a reflection of a prevailing culture in many large financial institutions. In most investment houses, traders and risk takers are usually among the best-paid employees. Since trading is essentially a solitary activity, traders are often introverts, and not among those with the best interpersonal skills, who can schmooze and build their power bases. Moreover, successful traders, by their mid-careers, have made enough money to enable them to leave the world of finance and pursue their real interests. Consequently, very few CROs have a strong trading background and may also lack technical knowledge, since people with good quantitative skills often end up in research and support roles. Consequently, the major forte of some CROs is their presentation and 'people' skills. The result is that, during boom years, traders and marketers, who are bringing in the deals, generating revenue and perhaps acting like prima donnas, intimidate the risk officers by accusing them of killing the business and being an obstacle to the profitability of the firm. In such cases, a risk officer who lacks strong technical knowledge and trading experience will have a hard time arguing his/her case. New Basel III Capital Rules and provisions of the Dodd-Frank should put some regulatory barriers and a defense mechanism against imprudent risk taking. These barriers together with the use of automation to encode some of the hard-earned risk experiences of the firms that will survive the current crisis will go a long way in helping risk officers prevent another train wreck, when the bull market returns and pundits start talking again about 'new paradigms' or the 'Dow at 36,000' or 'rational exuberance', and sales and trading people go back to their bullying habits. A stitch at that time by the CRO and regulators may save more than the proverbial nine...

References

Chorafas, D.N. (1992) 'Treasury Operations and the Foreign Exchange Challenge: A Guide to Risk Management Strategies for the New World Markets', NewYork: Wiley Finance.

Cormen, T.H., Leiserson, C.E., Rivest, R.L. and Stein, C. (2007) 'Introduction to Algorithms', 3rd edition, MIT Press.

Fay, S. (1997) 'The Collapse of Barings', New York: W.W. Norton & Company.

Hedayat, A.S., Sloane, N.J.A. and Stufken, J. (1999) 'Orthogonal Arrays', New York: Springer Verlag.

Tapiero, C.S. (1996) 'The Management of Quality and its Control', Chapman and Hall.

Time International (1996) 'A Top Trader at Japan's Sumitomo Created a Disaster. How Did He Hide it for 10 Years?', *Time International*, 26 (147), 24 June 1996.

Wall Street shokku (1995) 'Daiwa Bank's U.S. Securities Trading Losses', *The Economist*, 30 September 1995.

Part IV

Regulations and Governance

13
Corporate Governance and the Financial Crisis

Steen Thomsen

13.1 Introduction

The financial crisis of 2007–2009 which devastated global capital management is often partly attributed to bad corporate governance. For example, the OECD Steering Committee on Corporate Governance argues that 'the financial crisis can to an important extent be attributed to failures and weaknesses in corporate governance' (Kirkpatrick, 2009). The standard story appears to be that weak boards tolerated the rise of a culture of greed and excessive pay, which led financial executives to take the risks that ultimately caused the financial crisis (see for instance Obama, 2009). In this chapter I examine the rationale for this assertion.

The literature is still quite limited. Cheffins (2009) and Adams (2009) provide some of the first academic research on the subject. Cheffins examines governance characteristics of 37 firms removed from the S&P 500 index during 2008, including companies like Lehman Brothers, Countrywide and Bear Stearns. He finds little evidence of Enron-style fraud, but notes that boards were criticized for lacking sufficient financial expertise and for not challenging the CEO's dominant position. Moreover, pay in many cases was very high and criticized for being excessive. However boards did react when financial distress became apparent and in many cases replaced top executives. Thus he concludes that corporate governance worked reasonably well and warns against fundamental reforms on this shaky foundation.

Adams (2009) examines governance structures at organizations ranging from banks and nonbank financial institutions to non-financial firms. She finds that bank boards are not obviously worse than those of non-financial firms. In fact their governance appears to be as good or better in terms of board independence and other important characteristics. Moreover, banks with more independent boards were more, not less, likely to become financially distressed during the crisis.

In this chapter I employ a different approach by relating current governance research to the issues raised by the financial crisis. Corporate governance can be defined as the mechanisms by which companies are directed and controlled. These mechanisms include active ownership, board supervision, managerial incentives, company law and informal mechanisms such as reputation. The question then is whether, and to what extent, the financial crisis was caused by failure in one or more of these mechanisms. This chapter reviews what is known about the performance of these mechanisms during the crisis. I focus mainly, but not exclusively on banks and financial institutions.

13.2   Agency problems in financial institutions

The classic agency problem, which corporate governance is expected to address, is that between a group of weak, dispersed shareholders and a strong CEO. The shareholders want maximum returns for a given level of risk, while the CEO has an interest in high pay, corporate expansion, high levels of expenditure and absence of control (Williamson, 1964). Corporate governance mechanisms then work to control CEO behavior (Tirole, 2006). For example, boards can negotiate sufficiently low executive pay and fire a nonperforming CEO. Shareholders can rebel at the annual meeting and elect a new board, or a hostile raider such as a private equity fund can take control, fire the CEO and clean up the company. Other agency problems like fraud, self-dealing or insider trading are assumed to be handled by law or regulation. Yet others are supposed to be overcome by performance-related pay. Even reputation can be a governance mechanism because it induces managers to perform well for fear of reputational loss. However, despite many governance mechanisms agency problems cannot be eliminated altogether (Tirole, 2006).

In principle, agency problems in financial institutions are no different from those of other corporations. They are known to depend on the nature and level of information asymmetries between managers and shareholders, the level of uncertainty in the business as well as the risk preferences and incentive sensitivity of managers. However, financial institutions are special because they have many residual risk-takers, so-called 'principals', including shareholders, debt holders, who are particularly involved in financial institutions because of their high degree of leverage, and governments, which pay the bills in bailout situations, not to speak of the general public who suffer during system breakdowns. The systemic character of financial institutions has led to extensive regulation of their governance including, depending on their jurisdiction, monitoring by government agencies, mandatory procedures for board approval of major loans, government appointed board members, limitations on directorships in other corporations and solvency rules.

However, during the past decades agency problems in financial institutions may have become worse. Their increasing size and complexity has made it hard for boards, shareholders and regulators to understand what they do. This refers to such things as the creation of financial supermarkets and their increasing globalization as well as the increasing sophistication of financial products like credit derivatives, swaps and so forth (Acharya et al. 2009). Complexity has grown because deregulation made it possible for banks and other institutions to diversify into related activities like mortgages or insurance and to organize a substantial share of their activities in off-balance sheet operations. Moreover, financial globalization has made it possible to diversify risk to a greater extent, which has added to the complexity while reducing the incentives to monitor individual institutions and products. Under Basel II, banks were given the responsibility for assessing the risks of their loan portfolios. The assessments were based on statistical models which were subject to approval by regulators. Self-reporting however involves obvious agency problems because managers could have a short-term incentive to free up capital and the regulators found it difficult to assess their increasingly sophisticated risk models, which were anyhow based on fairly recent data from the boom period. The problems were aggravated because mark-to-market accounting under the new international accounting standards forced many of them to reduce their hidden reserves and post better short-term results. All of this made financial institutions increasingly difficult to control and shifted much responsibility to boards and other governance mechanisms.

Similar, although perhaps less severe, problems arose in non-financial firms although the risks they took were related to overinvestment and borrowing rather than to lending and guaranteeing complex financial products. High economic growth, record profits and abundant credit made it easier to finance CEOs' desire for expansion and bid up share prices on the tacit assumptions that growth would continue, short-term funding would always be available and share prices would continue to rise. New financial institutions like private equity and hedge funds contributed to the trend. This put a strain on corporate governance to restrain executive growth ambitions and limit unsound leverage.

13.3 Executive pay

Executive pay is widely blamed for contributing to the crisis. This section will examine the justification for this assertion. Quoting Barack Obama (2009): 'We're going to examine the ways in which the means and manner of executive compensation have contributed to a reckless culture and quarter-by-quarter mentality that in turn have wrought havoc in our financial system.'

The standard argument is that excessive risk-taking in banks and other corporations was partly caused by dysfunctional managerial incentives such as stock options and short-term bonuses. This is a view shared by the OECD (Kirkpatrick, 2009) and the Financial Stability Forum (2008, 2009). For example, the Financial Stability Forum (2008) states that 'compensation schemes in financial institutions encouraged disproportionate risk-taking with insufficient regard to longer-term risks'. This argument has led to a series of proposed policy changes. For example that 'Compensation must be adjusted for all types of risk...Two employees who generate the same short-run profit but take different amounts of risk on behalf of their firm should not be treated the same by the compensation system ... Compensation outcomes must be symmetric with risk outcomes ... Bonuses should diminish or disappear in the event of poor firm, divisional or business unit performance ... Payments should not be finalized over short periods where risks are realized over long periods' (Financial Stability Forum, 2009). However, the Financial Stability Forum declines to take positions on the level and performance orientation of executive pay arguing that 'one size does not fit all'.

The case for intervention has been argued by Bebchuck and Fried (2004), who see high pay levels in the US as evidence of rent extraction, that is, that managers have been able to extract excessive pay substantially above their marginal productivity. The high compensation levels of failed financial institutions have been cited as anecdotal evidence (Chung et al. 2008). For example Angelo Mozilo, CEO of Countrywide, reportedly received $52 million in 2006, branding him the 'poster child of financial services excess'. In 2007 he got only $10.8 million, but made a further $121.5 million from cashing in stock options. Stan O'Neal, former CEO, Merrill Lynch, got $162 million before the company was sold to Bank of America. Richard Fuld of Lehman Brothers got $34.4 million in 2007 before his company went bankrupt. Charles Prince of Citigroup is said to have received $25.9 million in 2006, plus severance pay of $40 million in 2007. However, others have argued that the 'fat cat' theory is too simplistic (Holmstrom, 2005; Hubbard, 2005; Murphy and Zábojník, 2004). For example, CEO pay appears to have increased across the world reflecting a scarcity of talent, and the demand for talent in financial services during the boom years was no doubt exceptional. Moreover, the perceived value of additional risky equity compensation may have been quite low given their already substantial wealth and effort levels.

Moreover, the extremes are obviously extremes. Taking into consideration that banks are large firms, they should be compared with other large firms. Adams (2009) finds that bank CEOs have lower overall pay and less equity-based pay than their counterparts in non-financial firms. Thus it is not clear that bank managers' pay is particularly out of line. However, she did find that equity-based compensation was associated with an increased probability of government bailout.

In any case the responsibility for executive pay rests with boards. Jack Welch has argued that pay excesses are caused by weak boards (Welch and Welch, 2006). If executive pay has been excessive, attention is therefore directed at board structure.

13.4 Board supervision

Boards of banks and other corporations could in principle have prevented the excessive risk-taking which led to the credit crunch. According to the OECD, risk policy which is 'a clear duty of the board' failed because of insufficient information and insufficient monitoring by bank boards (Kirkpatrick, 2009).

Unfortunately, there is no consensus on what constitutes a good board. Hermalin and Weisbach (2003) review empirical studies of board structure and company performance and find no systematic effects except a negative association between board size and firm value. Even this negative finding has subsequently been questioned by Coles et al. (2011) and particularly for banks by Adams and Mehran (2008). Staggered boards and busy boards with many interlocks to other boards have also been claimed to have negative effects, but again there are significant problems involved in assessing the direction and magnitude of causal effects. One obvious problem is endogeneity: board structure is influenced by many other factors, which may also co-vary with company performance (Adams et al. 2010). Another, highly pertinent problem is that it is difficult to monitor risk when measuring bank and company performance. Many of the high performers of the bubble period turned out to be financially fragile because they had taken on too much risk. Thus the financial crisis has made it painfully clear that accounting numbers and market values were often not trustworthy because they did not take into consideration substantial underlying risks.

Adams (2009) finds that bank governance is generally fairly good compared to non-financial firms. She finds that banks have on average more independent and larger boards, fewer outside directorships, higher total CEO compensation and lower director compensation than non-financial firms although these results turn out to be sensitive to firm size. Allowing for size, nonbank financial firms have less independent and smaller boards, fewer outside directorships and lower director compensation than non-financial firms. Altogether, she concludes that the governance of banks and financial institutions was not obviously worse than that of other businesses. This is perhaps not surprising given the intensive regulation and public visibility of financial firms. See, for example, the fit and proper tests required by board members in financial institutions, FSA 2004. It is not clear, therefore, that the financial crisis was caused by particularly bad governance of financial institutions. It may be that financial institutions were particularly exposed during the crisis or that higher standards of corporate governance are necessary in financial institutions precisely because they are occasionally subjected to financial crises. However, Adams (2009) also shows that the boards of banks receiving bailout money were more, rather than less independent than those of other banks. Thus independence is no guarantee of effective risk management. On the contrary, effective risk governance may require that nonexecutive directors know more about the financial industry, which makes it attractive to recruit former financial executives. The OECD argues that nonexecutive board members may have had insufficient expertise in banking and finance (Kirkpatrick, 2009). Adams (2009) found that bank non-executive director pay is some 30% lower than in non-financial firms, and Adams speculates that this may have made it difficult to attract highly qualified board members.

Altogether, it is not clear that the board structures of banks and other financial institutions are particularly bad as compared to other firms, but it is clear that their boards were not good enough to protect them from financial distress. In this respect they were a failure.

13.5   Information systems

Case studies of leading financial institutions demonstrate that the boards were often inadequately informed about their overall risk profile (Kirkpatrick, 2009). Moreover, risk management practices and executive compensation were often unrelated to, and inconsistent with, fundamental strategic decisions. One reason for this was no doubt the complexity of evaluating complex financial assets and liabilities. Another reason appears to have been the 'silo' approach according to which individual divisions of complex financial institutions managed their own financial risk without regard to the overall financial position of the institution. In addition, risks related to liquidity, reputation and system effects appear to have been underestimated. Thus, there is room for improvement in the information provided to company boards.

Nordgard (2009) reviews how information technology can strengthen emerging practices in governance, risk and compliance (GRC). He envisions that risk measures will be introduced at all levels in the organization and quantified as 'risk budgets' that is to say, maximum acceptable risk. Compliance controls must then check that different internal units stay within their risk budget. Reporting and suitable analysis will then allow efficient aggregation of information to assess overall risks at the board level, as well as efficient disaggregation of risk targets to individual units. However, he emphasizes that the right foundations with regard to, for example, timely and accurate reporting must be in place before sophisticated analytical tools can create value.

13.6   Active ownership

Active ownership by self-interested shareholders might have prevented some of the value destruction during the crisis. Compared to non-financial firms, banks have quite dispersed ownership and therefore weak shareholders, partly because many agency concerns are already addressed by financial regulation (Demsetz and Lehn, 1985). Some have argued that empowering shareholders might provide better discipline in the future. For example it has been recommended that the US adopts a more British governance model with greater accountability to shareholders. However British banks have not done better than US banks during the crisis, nor is it clear that banks with higher ownership concentration have been better at handling risk. It is not evident that empowered shareholders would necessarily induce banks to take less risk, since there may be conflicts of interests between shareholders and debt holders. Shareholders may potentially gain by taking on more risk while debt holders lose.

It is interesting that some of the most highly leveraged institutions, the US investment banks, were historically closely held partnerships, in which high leverage was combined with a substantial equity stake by senior employees in the future of the business and thus counterbalanced excessive risk-taking. In many institutions this structure was replaced by public listing and separation of ownership and management, which may have lessened the incentive for managers to take downside risk into consideration. Moreover, it may be no accident that many financial institutions across the world are not publicly listed companies, but cooperatives, financial mutuals and the like. While these firms may be less profitable during boom periods, they also appear to be more financially stable (Hesse and Cihák, 2007).

While past ownership structure may have been problematic, nationalization of banks, which many countries have resorted to as a response to the crisis, is also far from ideal. Government ownership of banks is believed to be associated with slower subsequent financial development and lower growth of productivity and per capita income (La Porta et al. 2002). One important problem is that government ownership is often associated with political interference in lending decisions (Spanienza, 2004).

13.7   Capital structure

With equity to asset ratios of 10% or less, banks and financial institutions are highly leveraged compared to other companies. They are therefore *prima facie* cases of debt-governed corporations as envisioned by Jensen and Meckling (1976). Creditors have an obvious incentive to safeguard their interests by assessing and monitoring management in the companies that they finance, including, in particular, their risk policies. However, several factors may have diminished the vigilance of creditor monitoring. First, deposit insurance and the likelihood of government bailout, the so-called 'Greenspan put' may have acted as an implicit guarantee which dulled the incentives of creditors to monitor financial institutions and their management. Secondly, the 'originate to distribute' business model which involved repackaging, securitization and reselling of loans to take them off-balance sheet, may also have led to less monitoring. It is a paradox, however, that the risks of these loans turned out, as a matter of fact, not to have been outsourced partly because put options and reputation risks brought them back to bank balance sheets when the crisis materialized. In fact a large part of the outsourcing went to other, similar financial institutions rather than to pension funds and other agents that might have been better able to carry the risk. Third, the increasing size and complexity of financial institutions and their products also made it more difficult for creditors to understand and monitor the risks they were getting into. Finally, outsourcing of the monitoring function to rating agencies appears to have failed.

The risks of high leverage in financial institutions are obviously exacerbated if they themselves invest in leveraged assets like hedge funds or commercial property. An added concern is that fair value, mark-to-market accounting and individual risk weights estimated over relatively short periods of time may provide financial managers and their boards with a false sense of solvency security and thereby increase their risk appetite.

13.8   Reputation

Reputation concerns can work as a corporate governance mechanism by deterring excessive compensation and risk-taking or poor board monitoring (Adams et al. 2010; Fama, 1980). It is well known that reputation can help overcome incentive problems in long-term relationships, but also that reputation is no panacea. Reputation is obviously not a very precise instrument when there are large information asymmetries and the media distort the flow of information. Holmstrom (1999) argued that reputation concerns could cause managers to become overly risk adverse. Walter (2009, this volume) tries to make precise the concept of reputation risk for financial institutions. He notes that financial institutions are particularly vulnerable to reputation risk because they depend so much on confidence and provides a specific illustration of the magnitude of operational risk.

It is unclear to what extent the crisis can be attributed to a dilution of reputation concerns. It is known, however, that reputation mechanisms may break down when information signals are distorted, when there are strong incentives for opportunistic behavior and when players have short-time horizons. It seems possible that the increasingly opaque nature of complex financial products has made it more difficult for shareholders and depositors to assess the risk profiles of financial institutions and to punish offenders with a decline in reputation. Moreover, it seems plausible that the short-term bias of pay structures in investment banking and other financial firms came to dominate the concern for long-term reputation.

13.9 Conclusion

Many of the popular stories of the financial crisis make little sense. For example it is not very credible that the crisis was caused by a sudden epidemic of greed in the financial community. The major piece of evidence for this story appears to be that executive pay in some of the leading firms rose to very high levels, but this is insufficient. The alternative story that greed evolved over many years only to be exposed by the crisis indicates that it was caused by other factors such as easy money, deregulation and inadequate corporate governance. A simple alternative interpretation is that decades of rising asset prices led to expectations of continuing high returns, search for yield and increasing risk-taking which was reinforced by performance-based pay.

Corporate boards failed to prevent excessive leverage both among borrowers and lenders. It is not evident that the corporate governance of financial institutions was worse than that of non-financial firms or that it suddenly changed for the worse before the crisis. However, financial institutions have doubtlessly become more difficult to control and agency problems have become worse because of their increasing size, complexity and leverage as well as financial deregulation. Moreover, the credit expansion following lax monetary policy in the period 2003–2006 and the global savings glut, no doubt reinforced moral hazard and adverse selection problems by pushing up asset prices and providing easy money for all sorts of projects. Evidently, the governance of banks and other financial institutions was not up to the challenge. Reforms and regulations are therefore to be expected.

Among the current proposals for reform we highlight the following:

- Executive pay in banks and other financial institutions should be restructured to include more long-term components including restricted stock to be held over a long time period, inclusion of debt as well as equity, bonus accounts which can be reduced if long-term performance fails to meet expectations and by monitoring risk in calculating capital costs when assessing managerial performance. Thus reform proposals do not aim to cap executive pay nor even its performance orientation but rather its time horizon.
- Changes in ownership structure are in order. Government ownership of banks is known to be problematic. Nationalized financial institutions

should therefore be privatized as soon as the macroeconomic climate allows. In the long-term new ownership structures may be called for in order to counterbalance risk-taking. For example, greater ownership concentration and more downside risk may, to some extent, counterbalance risk-taking. Alternatively, unlisted financial mutuals may be more financially stable than listed entities (Hesse and Cihák, 2007).

- The boards of financial institutions should be upgraded to include more members with financial industry expertise, such as former bankers, as well as greater financial literacy. For example, if boards are to take charge of risk management or executive pay, new competencies are needed (Financial Stability Forum 2009).
- Information systems should be upgraded to provide an overall view of financial and strategic risks that can be integrated into both risk management and executive compensation schemes. To govern, boards must have a comprehensive, accurate and updated view of activities and risks including off-balance sheet activities and the like. If this is too complex to do in practice, financial institutions may become ungovernable and the complexity should probably be reduced by restructuring.
- Regulators should devise ways to provide incentives for creditor monitoring with the necessity of bailing out financial institutions in times of crisis. Increased solvency is not necessarily the solution because this may push retail banks to take on more risks to get a competitive return on equity.

With these reform proposals there is an obvious danger that regulators will attempt to fight the last war. The situation now is fundamentally different to what it was before the crisis. A generation of financial executives has learned some hard lessons, and there is currently little need to reinforce the lessons learned. For example, risk-taking and leverage are not the problems that they used to be and curbing them further may do more harm than good to the rest of the economy. However, history shows that it is necessary to act now, while the memory of the crisis is still fresh, if major reforms in financial regulation are to take place.

References

Acharya, V. and Richardson, M. (eds) (2009) *Restoring Financial Stability: How to Repair a Failed System*, Hoboken, NJ: J. Wiley & Sons.

Acharya, V., Carpenter, J., Gabaix, X., Kose, J., Richardson, M., Subrahmanyam, M., Sundaram, R. and Zemel, E. (2009) 'Corporate Governance in the Modern Financial Sector', Chapter 7, in V. Acharya and M. Richardson (eds), *Restoring Financial Stability: How to Repair a Failed System*, Hoboken, NJ: J. Wiley & Sons.

Adams, R. (2009) 'Governance and the Financial Crisis', in S. Thomsen, C. Rose and O. Risager (eds), *Understanding the Financial Crisis: Investment, Risk and Governance.* SimCorp StrategyLab.

Adams, R.B., Hermalin, B.E. and Weisbach, M.S. (2010) 'The Role of Boards of Directors in Corporate Governance: A Conceptual Framework and Survey', *Journal of Economic Literature*, 48(1): 58–107.

Adams, R. and H. Mehran, H. (2008) 'Corporate Performance, Board Structure and its Determinants in the Banking Industry', University of Queensland Working Paper, 2008.

Akerlof, G.A. and Shiller, R.J. (2009) *Animal Spirits: How Human Psychology Drives the Economy, and Why It Matters for Global Capitalism*. Princeton: Princeton University Press.

Bebchuk, L.A. and Fried, J.M. (2004) *Pay Without Performance: The Unfulfilled Promise of Executive Compensation*, Cambridge, MA: Harvard University Press.

Bicksler, J.L. (2008) *The Subprime Mortgage Debacle and Its Linkages to Corporate Governance*. International Journal of Disclosure and Governance, 5: 295–300.

Caprio, G., Laeven, L. and Levine, R. (2003) 'Governance and bank valuation', NBER Working Paper 10158.

Cheffins, B.R. (2009) 'Did Corporate Governance 'Fail' During the 2008 Stock Market Meltdown? The Case of the S&P 500', (May). Available at SSRN: http:// ssrn.com/ abstract=1396126.

Chung, J., Farrell, G., Guererra, F. and Scholtes, S. 2008. 'The Fallen Giants of Finance', *Financial Times*. 23 December.

Clementi, G.L., Cooley, T.F., Richardson, M. and Walter, I. (2009) 'Rethinking Compensation in Financial Firms', Chapter 8, in V. Acharya, and M. Richardson (eds), *Restoring Financial Stability: How to Repair a Failed System*, Hoboken, NJ: J. Wiley & Sons.

Coles, J.L., Lemmon, M.L. and Meschke, J.F. (2011) 'Structural Models and Endogeneity in Corporate Finance: The Link between Managerial Ownership and Corporate Performance', *Journal of Financial Economics*, 103(1): 149–168.

Demsetz, H. and Lehn, K. (1985) 'The structure of corporate ownership: causes and consequences', *Journal of Political Economy*, 93(6): 1155–1177.

Fama, E.F. (1980) 'Agency Problems and the Theory of the Firm,' *Journal of Political Economy*, 88(2): 288–307.

Financial Stability Forum (2008) *Report of the Financial Stability Forum on Enhancing Market and Institutional Resilience* (399 KB PDF), Basel, Switzerland: FSF, 7 April.

Financial Stability Forum (2009) *FSF Principles for Sound Compensation Practices* (87 KB PDF). Basel, Switzerland: FSF, 2 April.

FSA (2004) *The Fit and Proper test for Approved Persons. Chapter 2. Main assessment criteria.* http://www.fsa.gov.uk/pubs/hb-releases/rel27/rel27fit.pdf. FSA Handbook.

Hermalin, B.E. and Weisbach, M.S. (2003) 'Boards of Directors as an Endogenously Determined Institution: A Survey of the Economic Literature', *Economic Policy Review*, April, 9(1): 7–26.

Hesse, H. and Cihák, M. (2007) 'Cooperative Banks and Financial Stability' (January), IMF Working Paper No. 07/02. Available at SSRN: http:// ssrn.com/abstract=956767.

Holmstrom, B. (2005) 'Pay without Performance and the Managerial Power Hypothesis: A Comment', *Journal of Corporation Law*, 30(4): 703–715.

Holmstrom, B. (1999) 'Managerial Incentive Problems – A Dynamic Perspective', *Review of Economic Studies*, January 1999, 66(226): 169–182.

Hubbard, R. (2005) 'Pay without Performance: A Market Equilibrium Critique', *Journal of Corporation Law*, 30(4): 717–720.

Jensen, M. and Meckling, W. (1976) 'Theory of the Firm: Managerial Behavior, Agency Costs and Ownership Structure', *Journal of Financial Economics* 3(4): 305–60.

Kirkpatrick, G. (2009) 'The Corporate Governance Lessons from the Financial Crisis', *Financial Market Trends*. OECD.

La Porta, R., Lopez-De-Silanes, F. and Shleifer, A. (2002) 'Government Ownership of Banks', *Journal of Finance*, 57(1): 265–301.

Murphy, K. and Zábojník, J. (2004) 'CEO Pay and Appointments: A Market-Based Explanation for Recent Trends', *American Economic Review*, 94(2): 192–196.

. (2009) 'Governance, risk and compliance in the financial sector: an IT perspective in light of the recent financial crisis', in S Thomsen, C. Rose and O. Risager (eds), *Understanding the financial crisis: investment, risk and governance*. SimCorp StrategyLab.

Obama, B., (2009) Speech on Executive Compensation. http://www.cnbc.com/id/29014485/. CNBC.com 4 February 2009.

Sapienza, P. (2004) 'The Effects of Government Ownership on Bank Lending [Abstract]', *Journal of Financial Economics*, May, 72(2): 357–384.

Thomsen, S. (2008) *An Introduction to Corporate Governance*. Copenhagen: Djoef Publishing.

Tirole, J. (2006) *Corporate Governance. Chapter 1. The Theory of Corporate Finance*. Princeton: Princeton University Press.

Walter, I. (2009) 'Reputational Risk and The Financial Crisis', in T. Steen, C. Rose, and O. Risager (eds), *Understanding the Financial Crisis: Investment, Risk and Governance*. SimCorp.

Welch, J. and Welch, S. (2006) 'Paying big-time for failure: Who is really to blame for those fat severance packages given to CEO's who falter?', *Business Week*, 10 April.

Williamson, O.E. (1964) 'The Economics of Discretionary Behavior: Managerial Objectives in a Theory of the Firm', Englewood Cliffs, NJ: Prentice-Hall.

14

Governance and the Financial Crisis: More Convergence, Less Risk?[1]

Renée Adams[2]

14.1 Introduction

Based on measures of world industrial output, world trade and stock markets, Eichengreen and O'Rourke (2009) argue that the current financial crisis may be worse than the Great Depression on a global scale. Perhaps no one would have been surprised if a crisis of this magnitude originated in an emerging market. Bordo and Eichengreen (2003) provide evidence that most financial crises occur in emerging markets. They describe 139 financial crises between 1973 and 1997, 95 of which occurred in emerging market countries.

There are many reasons why investors may lose confidence in emerging markets. If such markets are characterized by weak institutions and poor firm-level governance, then capital outflows and stock market crashes may occur. This is what Johnson, Boone, Breach and Friedman (2000), amongst others, argue happened in the Asian crisis of 1997–1998. But the current financial crisis originated in the United States, a country that is commonly held up as a role model in terms of institutional strength and good governance. For example, the US achieves the highest score on La Porta, Lopez-de-Silanes, Shleifer and Vishny's (1998) anti-director rights index, which measures how well the legal system protects minority shareholders against managers or dominant shareholders.[3] In addition, La Porta et al. (1997) show that common law countries, such as the US, and countries that score higher on their measure of anti-director rights have more developed capital markets. The explanation is that in countries with better protection of shareholders, financiers are willing to invest more money and on better terms for entrepreneurs.

Not only is the US seen as having relatively strong legal institutions, but recent regulation designed to strengthen firm-level governance, the Sarbanes-Oxley Act of 2002 (SOX) and new exchange listing requirements at the NYSE and Nasdaq, have served as models for governance reform around the world. Adams (2011) documents that 16 countries published new or revised important governance codes or passed laws on governance in 2003 alone. Moreover, significantly more countries instituted governance reforms after 2002 than in the preceding 10 years.

The Sarbanes-Oxley Act and the new listing requirements were a reaction to a series of dramatic corporate and accounting scandals including those at Enron, Tyco and Worldcom. Much of the blame for these scandals was put on boards of directors. For example, in its report on Enron's collapse, the US Senate argued that by not questioning management about the complicated financial transactions Enron was engaging in, the board had failed in its fiduciary duties to shareholders (US House, 2002). Accordingly, both SOX and the NYSE and Nasdaq listing requirements contain a series of provisions designed to strengthen board oversight of management in publicly-traded firms.

Currently, for example, a company listed on the NYSE would have to have a majority of independent directors (new NYSE listing standard), an independent audit committee consisting of at least three members (NYSE) and a financial expert or a reason not to have a financial expert (SOX), a completely independent nominating/corporate governance committee (new NYSE listing standard), a completely independent compensation committee (new NYSE listing standard), regularly scheduled meetings of the non-management directors (new NYSE listing standard) and an annual meeting of the independent directors (new NYSE listing standard). Nasdaq listed companies are subject to similar requirements, although they do not have to have a separate compensation or nominating committee. In addition, SOX, NYSE and Nasdaq have tightened the definition of independent director.[4]

To a certain extent, the fact that the US is considered to have strong investor protection and good governance may help explain why the financial crisis was predicted by so few. But it raises the question whether and to what extent governance can be considered to be a cause of the financial crisis. The resignations of high profile finance executives, e.g., Stan O'Neal at Merrill Lynch, Charles Prince at Citigroup and Marcel Ospel at UBS, and the recommendations by proxy advisers against the re-election of the board at Citigroup, among others (see e.g., Moyer, 2008) is direct evidence that boards are, at least partly, being blamed for the crisis.

The OECD Steering Group on Corporate Governance goes further. It argues that weak governance is a major cause of the financial crisis (Kirkpatrick, 2009). It places much of the blame on board failures in financial firms, in particular,[5] and has launched an action plan to improve corporate governance.[6] Although the UK generally also scores highly on measures of investor protection, bank governance in the UK is also, at least partly, being blamed for the financial crisis. As a result, Sir David Walker was commissioned to recommend measures to improve board-level governance at banks to the government (Walker, 2009).

A measure of the importance of this review is that it serves as a basis for the 2010 UK Governance code.[7]

How can it be that governance problems still exist in the US despite strong shareholder protection mechanisms and recent governance reforms? Can boards of financial firms be to blame for the crisis when publicly-traded financial firms have to abide by the same governance requirements in SOX and the same listing rules as nonfinancial firms? And will governance reform measures resulting from the crisis achieve their goals of reducing the likelihood of future crises? This article first tries to shed more light on the extent to which the crisis can be attributable to bad financial firm governance, in particular board structure and incentives. Next, I ask whether governance reform will lead to a reduction in risk. If not, abiding by regulation alone will not be enough for asset managers to have effective internal governance.

Both because the financial crisis originated in the US and because of data limitations, this article focuses on publicly-traded financial firms in the US. Because financial firms around the world have different activities and structures and face different regulatory constraints, providing an overview of financial firm governance across multiple countries is a complex task that is beyond the scope of this article.[8] In Section 14.2, I discuss what one might expect a well-governed financial firm to look like. In Section 14.3, I examine whether recent regulatory reform in the US had an impact on firms' governance structures and compare measures of governance structure across financial and nonfinancial firms in the US. In Section 14.4, I discuss whether bad governance contributed to the crisis. In Section 14.5, I show that diversity in governance practices has decreased following SOX and the Dodd-Frank Act of 2010. I discuss some lessons for the future in Section 14.6.

14.2 What is a well-governed financial firm?

Descriptions in the media of what appear to be egregious governance failures at financial institutions have heightened the impression that governance failures play a large part in the financial crisis. For example, boards are being blamed for what appear to be excessive pay packages that executives of financial firms received even while their firms were failing or being bailed out by the government. Morgenson (2009) reports that executives at seven major financial institutions that are in distress received $464 million in performance pay since 2005, while reporting losses of $107 billion since 2007. However, it is important to keep in mind that the media stories often describe individual cases, not the industry as a whole. To understand the role governance plays in the financial crisis, it is important to get a broader perspective of potential governance problems in the financial industry. Certainly any broad-based policy reform should not be based on the consideration of isolated cases.

Ideally, the academic governance literature would provide guidance on the question of whether financial institutions are well-governed or not. However, because of the special nature of financial services, most academic papers exclude firms in the financial services from their data and focus on the governance of nonfinancial firms. Thus, to obtain a picture of the state of governance in the financial services industry, it is useful to directly examine some data on board characteristics and executive compensation. Before turning to the data, however, it is important to have a picture of what the board of a well-governed financial firm should look like.

Boards of financial firms have the same legal responsibilities as boards of nonfinancial firms, i.e., the duty of care and loyalty. In addition, publicly-traded financial firms have to abide by SOX and exchange listing requirements. However, understanding what constitutes an effective governance structure for a financial firm is complicated by several factors. First, as Adams (2010) and Adams and Mehran (2003) describe, boards of financial firms may face more pressure to satisfy non-shareholder stakeholders than boards of nonfinancial firms. Regulators, for example, expect boards to act to ensure the safety and soundness of the financial institution, an objective that may not necessarily be in shareholders' best interests. Consistent with the idea that regulators and owners' interests may diverge, Laeven and Levine (2009) find in a cross-country analysis that the impact of regulation on bank risk-taking depends on a bank's ownership structure. Adams and Mehran (2003, endnote 6) provide some examples of additional duties which regulators impose on bank boards for the purpose of ensuring soundness, which include the adoption of real estate appraisal and evaluation policies (Federal Reserve Board Commercial Bank Examination Manual) and the annual approval of bank risk management policies (Federal Reserve Board Trading Activities Manual).

Second, financial firms are regulated by several different regulators. Investment banks are regulated by the Securities and Exchange Commission (SEC). Until recently, thrifts were regulated by the Office of Thrift Supervision.[9] All banks with FDIC-insured deposits are subject to FDIC regulations. Because banks can choose to have a national or state charter and whether or not to be a member of the Federal Reserve, they effectively choose their regulatory authority. National banks are regulated by the OCC, while state banks are regulated either by the Federal Reserve or the FDIC. The presence of a regulator raises the question of whether regulatory scrutiny complements or substitutes for board-level governance. There is as yet no satisfactory answer to this question. Furthermore, it is not known whether regulators differ in the intensity with which they scrutinize the boards of the firms they examine. Some have argued that regulators may engage in a race to the bottom in order to attract banks with lax restrictions (see e.g., Rosen, 2003, 2005; and Whalen, 2002). Thus, it is possible that some regulators are more lenient in evaluating bank board behavior than others. For example, even though Federal Reserve Banks in theory penalize directors for poor attendance behavior, Adams and Ferreira (2011) find that the attendance behavior of directors of bank holding companies (BHCs) at board meetings is worse than in nonfinancial firms. Heterogeneity of regulators suggests that board-level governance may not be the same across all types of financial firms and the governance of each type of firm may need to be considered separately.

Third, the financial services industry underwent many changes recently that are likely to impact board governance. The banking industry underwent an intense period of consolidation in the 1990s through M&A activity. M&A activity affects board structure in several ways. First, it is common to add directors of target firms to the board of the acquirer in friendly acquisitions, as most banking M&As are. Adams and Mehran (2011) show that M&A activity leads to an increase in BHC board size. Second, M&A activity may have disciplining effects even if it is friendly. Thus, an active market for corporate control may improve board effectiveness. In the 1990s, banks were also increasingly allowed to engage in investment banking activities (culminating with the passage of the Gramm-Leach-Bliley Act in 1999). This created competition for investment banks, which may have put pressure on their boards. Consistent with this idea, Altınkılıç, Hansen and Hrnjić (2007) find that investment banks do not appear to have been ineffectively governed during the 1990–2003 period.

Notwithstanding these three factors, the literature generally argues that the same standards should apply to boards of financial firms as to the boards of nonfinancial firms, because their duties to shareholders are the same. The three most commonly studied features of board structure are board independence, board size and the number of other directorships directors hold. The literature generally argues that boards that are more independent, i.e., they contain more directors without social or business connections to management, should be more effective (see Adams, Hermalin and Weisbach, 2010, for a survey of the board literature). Smaller boards should be more effective because decision-making costs are lower in smaller groups. Because directors may become too busy when they hold more outside directorships, the literature argues that boards are more effective when directors hold fewer outside directorships.

Other features of boards that may be important for good governance are the attendance behavior of directors and the fraction of female directors on the board. The OECD's report on governance lessons from the crisis states that 'boards' access to information is key' (Kirkpatrick, 2009, p. 23). In order to obtain information, directors need to attend board meetings.

Although it is not clear that having more female directors necessarily improves firm performance, Adams and Ferreira (2009) provide evidence that boardroom gender diversity may improve several important aspects of board behavior, for example director attendance at board meetings. Moreover, Harriet Harman, UK Labour Party's number 2, famously argued that the financial crisis would have been less severe if Lehman Brothers had been Lehman Sisters (Morris, 2009). Similarly, EU commissioner Michel Barnier suggested that having more women on bank boards would end the kind of 'group-think' that exacerbated the crisis (Treanor, 2011).

It is less clear from the literature what effective CEO and director compensation should look like. To align their incentives with those of shareholders, CEOs and directors should receive a certain amount of performance-based pay in the form of equity. In addition, holding performance-pay constant, total compensation should increase as risk increases. However, equity incentives may induce managers to take excessive risks. In addition, poorly governed firms may be more likely to overpay their directors. Thus it is not always clear whether a given compensation contract is effective or not. Using an industry study, Philippon and Reshef (2009) argue that bankers were overpaid during the mid-1990s to 2006, however, they do not control for individual firm characteristics, such as size or risk which may influence compensation packages.

Since in theory the same general governance standards apply to boards of both financial and nonfinancial firms, the governance of nonfinancial firms may serve as a useful benchmark for evaluating the governance of financial firms. Since the academic literature has studied the governance of nonfinancial firms in more depth, the governance of nonfinancial firms may be closer to an 'ideal' governance structure simply because of greater scrutiny and external pressure. If governance failures at financial firms are partly to blame for the financial crisis, we might therefore expect that financial firms have worse governance in terms of board characteristics and incentives than nonfinancial firms. In a sample of data on 35 BHCs ending in 1999, Adams and Mehran (2003) find that BHCs have larger boards, more independent directors and lower performance-based pay for CEOs than nonfinancial firms. Thus, in their sample banks could be considered to be better governed than nonfinancial firms in some aspects (independence) but worse in other aspects (board size and performance pay). Since their sample predates the Gramm-Leach Bliley Act of 1999 which may have influenced governance structures in the industry, it is worthwhile making a similar comparison in a larger sample of more recent data, as I do in the next sections.

I choose eight governance characteristics (Independence, Board size, Number of directorships, Fraction of directors with attendance problems at board meetings, Fraction of female directors, Total CEO compensation, Fraction of equity-based pay for the CEO and Director compensation) and compare them across financial institutions and nonfinancial firms in a large sample of data. The arguments I describe above are frequently used to predict how these characteristics are related to governance quality. But, academics do not all agree on these predictions. Thus, for the sake of the argument, I categorize increases (or decreases) in a governance characteristic as a governance quality improvement if there is a regulation or regulatory recommendation promoting increases (or decreases) in that particular characteristic.

For example, SOX and the NYSE and Nasdaq exchange listing standards promote greater board independence. The UK's Walker Review (2009) suggests that bank board size should be reduced. In France and Germany, there are limits on the number of directorships directors can hold. The Federal Reserve System emphasizes the importance of attending board meetings in the bank director training book published by the Federal Reserve Bank of Kansas (2010). This book lists attendance at board meetings as the second most important managerial function of bank directors (p. 50). Numerous countries are implementing boardroom gender quotas (see Deloitte, 2011). Finally, the provisions in the 2010 Dodd-Frank Act concerning shareholders' right to a 'say-on-pay' can be interpreted as advocating lower executive pay and less incentive pay. For example, Protess (2011) writes that 'Lawmakers are hoping to discourage companies from awarding lucrative packages that encourage risky behavior'. Although I am unaware of any regulation specifically focusing on director compensation, by analogy with CEO compensation one can argue that decreasing director pay is seen to be a sign of better governance. Table 14.1 summarizes how governance quality increases according to these regulations.

14.3   The governance of financial firms-what are the facts?

In this section, I examine whether potential governance failures of financial firms in the US can be attributed to the fact that they were noncompliant with SOX and the listing standards. Next I examine whether financial firms complied with some aspects of governance standards but were so much worse on other governance dimensions that their overall governance was weak. But first I describe the data I use.

14.3.1   Data

To compare board characteristics and incentives in financial firms and nonfinancial firms, I use subsamples of the Riskmetrics director database from 1996 to 2011.[10] This is an unbalanced panel of director-level data for Standard & Poor's (S&P) 500, S&P MidCaps, and S&P SmallCap firms. It contains information on directors from company proxy statements or annual reports, such as whether the director is classified as independent, and the number of other directorships each director holds. I merge this data to Compustat to obtain SIC codes, which I use to identify financial firms and banks. I obtain

Table 14.1   Definition of 'good governance'

Governance characteristic	Regulatory policy concerning characteristic	Reference for column II	According to policy in column II, governance improves as characteristic…	Governance index-7	Governance index-5
I	II	III	IV	V	VI
Board independence	SOX, NYSE & Nasdaq listing standards		Increases	1 if above sample median, otherwise 0	1 if above sample median, otherwise 0
Board size	UK's Walker Review	Walker (2009)	Decreases	1 if below sample median, otherwise 0	1 if below sample median, otherwise 0
# Directorships	France's New Economic Regulation of 2001, German company law, Article 100	http://www.practicallaw.com/5-107–01847q= &qp=&qo=&qe=, http://www.aktiengesetz.de/	Decreases	1 if below sample median, otherwise 0	1 if below sample median, otherwise 0
Fraction attendance problems	Federal Reserve System	Federal Reserve Bank of Kansas City (2010)	Decreases	1 if below sample median, otherwise 0	1 if below sample median, otherwise 0
Fraction female	Numerous country-level quotas on boardroom gender diversity, also proposed quota on bank boards by Michel Barnier, EU Internal Markets Commissioner	Deloitte (2011), Treanor (2011)	Increases	1 if above sample median, otherwise 0	1 if above sample median, otherwise 0
Total CEO compensation	Dodd-Frank Act of 2010	Protess (2011)	Decreases	1 if below sample median, otherwise 0	–
Fraction equity-based pay CEO	Dodd-Frank Act of 2010	Protess (2011)	Decreases	1 if below sample median, otherwise 0	–
(Non-executive) Director compensation	–	–	Decreases (by analogy with CEO compensation)	–	–

This table describes how eight governance characteristics affect governance quality according to various regulatory movements concerning governance. For each characteristic in column I, column II describes the regulatory policy or recommendation discussing that characteristic. Column III provides a reference for the policy or recommendation. I provide no reference for SOX or the exchange listing standards, as these are well-documented in numerous sources. I provide no information for Director compensation in column II, as I am unaware of policy specifically concerning outside director compensation. Column IV describes how the governance characteristic is supposed to improve governance quality. In columns V and VI, I describe how I use the information in column IV to construct governance indices. To construct Governance index-7, I assign each characteristic in each firm-year a dummy variable which is equal to 1 if the characteristic is in the direction of good governance according to column IV. I use median levels of the characteristic to define the cut-offs for good governance. Governance index-7 is simply the sum of 7 dummy variables. Governance index-5 is defined similarly, except that I exclude CEO compensation variables due to missing data. I do not consider Director compensation in the construction of the governance indices because it is only available as an average number for 2006 and 2007 in Execucomp.

data on financial characteristics and CEO and director compensation from ExecuComp.

Using this data, I construct a firm-level dataset containing 24,727 firm-year level observations. I define Fraction of directors with attendance problems to be the fraction of directors who attended fewer than 75% of meetings they were supposed to attend in the prior fiscal year. Total CEO compensation is Execucomp item TDC1. Fraction equity-based pay CEO is (1-(salary+bonus))/TDC1. All compensation numbers are adjusted to 2007 dollars using the CPI-U. Director compensation is only available from 2006 on, due to changes in reporting requirements. Return on assets, ROA, is Execucomp item ROA. Tobin's Q is (book value of assets-book value of equity+market value of equity)/book value of assets ((assets-commeq+mktval)/assets). All other variables are described in Table 14.2. I define Board size, Assets, Total CEO Compensation and Director Compensation to be missing if they are less than 3, 0 or non-positive, respectively.

Financial firms comprise 14.94% of the overall sample (3,694 observations). Of the financial firm observations, 1,473 observations belong to banks. Table 14.2 shows summary statistics for firm characteristics and the eight governance characteristics. The number of observations varies across rows because of missing data.

All of the firms in this database are publicly-traded firms, thus this data does not allow me to shed any light on the governance of private financial firms. The number of banks represented in the sample varies over time from a low of 76 in 2007 to a high of 105. The number of nonbank financial firms varies from 92 to 178. Although the number of banks in the sample is small relative to the banking industry, the banks in this sample represent a large fraction of industry assets. For example, according to the FDIC, in 2007 there were 7,282 FDIC-insured commercial banks in the US with a total of $11,176 billion in assets. In 2007, there are 93 banks in my sample with assets comprising 49.86% of total commercial bank assets ($5,572,369 million). Thus, although the comparisons I make and conclusions I draw need not apply to all banks or nonbank financial firms, they are relevant for understanding potential governance failures at financial firms that are likely to matter the most for the crisis.

14.3.2 Did financial firms comply with SOX and the listing standards?

If financial firms in the US did not comply with SOX and the listing standards, then this would be a simple explanation why governance may have contributed to the financial crisis. Although a large literature examines the implications of SOX and the listing standards for nonfinancial firms, less is known about the effects of these reforms on financial firms. A full examination of compliance by financial firms is beyond the scope of this chapter. However, I can provide some suggestive evidence on this issue by examining changes in one

Table 14.2 Summary statistics

Variable	Obs	Mean	Std. Dev.	Min	Max
		Panel A: firm characteristics			
Assets	23060	14002.440	74216.000	6.268	2265792
Ln(Assets)	23060	7.705	1.678	1.835	14.633
ROA	21872	2.341	14.201	−587.973	70.325
Tobin's Q	21331	1.909	1.587	0.404	77.635
		Panel B: firm-level governance characteristics			
Board independence	24727	0.683	0.177	0	1
Board size	24725	9.608	5.156	3	170
# Directorships	21699	0.816	0.589	0	4.786
Fraction attendance problem	24727	0.016	0.047	0	0.546
Fraction female	24709	0.097	0.093	0	1
Total CEO compensation	21768	5.103	17.625	7.86E-07	2193.705
Fraction equity-based pay CEO	21768	0.575	0.279	0	1
Director compensation	8042	5563.950	7001.441	0.001	148807.8

The data for panels A-C consists of an unbalanced panel of 24,727 firm-year level observations for S&P 1500 firms for the period 1996–2011 which were in the Riskmetrics Director Database. Data on assets and SIC codes are from Compustat. Ln(Assets) is the natural logarithm of assets. Data for return on assets (Execucomp item: ROA), Tobin's Q, Volatility (Execucomp item: bs_volatility) and CEO and director compensation is from Execucomp. Tobin's Q is defined to be assets-commeq+mktval)/assets. SIC codes were used to classify firms into financial firms, banks and nonfinancial firms. Financial firm is a dummy equal to 1 if the firm is a financial firm. Riskmetrics classifies directors as independent if they have no business relationship with the firm, are not related or interlocked with management and are not current or former employees. Board independence is the number of independent directors on the board divided by board size. Board size is set to missing if it is less than 3. # Directorships is the average number of directorships in other for-profit companies per director. Fraction attendance problems is the fraction of directors who attended fewer than 75% of the meetings they were supposed to attend during the previous fiscal year. Fraction female is the fraction of female directors. Total CEO compensation (Execucomp item: TDC1) is the sum of Salary, Bonus, Other Annual, Total Value of Restricted Stock Granted, Total Value of Stock Options Granted (using Black-Scholes), Long-Term Incentive Payouts, and All Other Total. Total CEO compensation is set to missing if it is 0. Fraction equity-based pay CEO is 1-(Salary+Bonus)/ Total CEO Compensation. Director compensation is only available for the years 2006 onwards and is the average compensation for (generally non-executive) directors. Total CEO compensation is measured in millions. Director compensation is measured in thousands. All compensation figures have been converted to 2007 dollars using the CPI-U. Assets are measured in millions. Observations vary because of missing data.

governance characteristic emphasized in SOX and the listing standards, which I label US reforms, namely board independence.

In Table 14.3, I compare board independence in the years after 2002 to board independence prior by regressing board independence on a dummy variable,

Post-US Reform, which is equal to 1 for all years after and including 2002. In column I, I show the regression for the full sample. In columns II–IV, I divide the sample into nonfinancial firms, banks and nonbank financials. The regressions in columns V–VII replicate those in II–IV, except with firm fixed-effects. The coefficients on Post–US Reform are positive and significant at greater than the 1% level across all columns.

The results for nonfinancial firms are consistent with the findings from prior literature that the US reforms led to an increase in board independence. The results for financial firms suggest that the same is true for financial firms. The magnitudes of the coefficients on Post–US Reform are always highest for nonbank financial firms and are the lowest for banks. This indicates that nonbank financial firms increased board independence the most, and banks the least, following the implementation of SOX and the listing standards. However, the magnitudes of the coefficients on the constant terms indicate that banks had the highest level of board independence prior to the US reforms which explains their smaller average response to the reforms.

These results are suggestive evidence that financial firms complied with the US reforms emphasizing board independence. However, it is possible that financial firms performed poorly alongs other governance dimensions leading their overall governance quality to be weak. To examine this hypothesis, I compare the governance of financial firms to that of nonfinancial firms in the next section.

14.3.3 Comparing the governance of financial firms to that of nonfinancial firms

Because of the reasons outlined in Section 14.2, I compare the governance characteristics of banks and nonbank financials to those of nonfinancial firms separately. Table 14.4 provides comparisons for banks and nonfinancial firms. Table 14.5 provides the same comparisons for nonbank financial firms (NBFFs). Columns I–XV of Table 14.4 show comparisons of means of the eight governance characteristics from Table 14.1 (Independence, Board size, Number of directorships, Fraction of directors with attendance problems at board meetings, Fraction of female directors, Total CEO compensation, Fraction equity-based pay for the CEO and Director compensation) for banks and nonfinancial firms. To better highlight the differences in governance, I choose to compare the characteristics in the year 2000 before any governance reform (Columns I–VII), and just prior to the crisis, in 2007 (Columns VIII–XV). Because data on director compensation as reported in 2007 is not available in 2000, I exclude director compensation from the year 2000 comparison. Observations vary because of missing data. The coefficient on 'Bank' ('NBFF') is the coefficient on a 'Bank' ('NBFF') dummy variable in an OLS regression with the respective governance characteristic as the dependent variable. Results vary across panels

Table 14.3 Board independence post-governance reform in the US and pre-crisis

				Board independence			
	I	II	III	IV	V	VI	VII
Post–US Reform	0.105***	0.107***	0.036***	0.128***	0.094***	0.029***	0.115***
	[41.15]	[38.39]	[4.34]	[14.66]	[27.45]	[2.67]	[8.17]
Constant	0.604***	0.603***	0.680***	0.564***	0.609***	0.683***	0.570***
	[349.57]	[317.79]	[119.40]	[91.70]	[384.74]	[130.32]	[81.92]
Sample type	Full sample	Nonfinancial firms	Banks	Nonbank financials	Nonfinancial firms	Banks	Nonbank financials
Firm-Fixed effects?	No	No	No	No	Yes	Yes	Yes
Obs.	18839	15852	1134	1568	15852	1134	1568
R-squared	0.082	0.085	0.016	0.121	0.156	0.022	0.182

The table shows OLS regressions of board independence on a dummy variable (Post–US Reform) which is equal to 1 for all years after and including 2002. The data set in consists of Riskmetrics data from 1996–2007. The columns vary by the type of firms and the inclusion of firm fixed-effects (columns V-VII). The sample in column I consists of the full sample of Riskmetrics data as described in Table 14.2. The sample in columns II and IV consists of nonfinancial firms. The sample in columns III and VI consists of banks. The sample in columns III and VII consists of nonbank financial firms. The classification of firms into categories is described in Table 14.2. Observations vary because of missing data. Absolute values of t-statistics are in brackets. Standard errors are heteroskedasticity-corrected in columns V-VII. Asterisks indicate significance at 0.01 (***), 0.05 (**), and 0.10 (*) levels.

due to the inclusions of different control variables in the regressions. In Panel A, regressions contain no control variables. In Panel B, regressions contain Ln(Assets) as a proxy for firm size and standard errors are heteroskedasticity robust. In Panel C, I include Ln(Assets), ROA, Tobin's Q and year dummies and standard errors are heteroskedasticity robust. Asterisks indicate statistical significance, with ***, ** and * indicating significance at the 1%, 5% and 10% level, respectively.

From Columns I–VII of Table 14.1, Panel A we see that banks have on average more independent boards, larger boards and fewer outside directorships. While board size is larger in banks, Adams and Mehran (2011) do not find that larger bank board size has detrimental effects on shareholder value. Thus, on average banks do not appear to be worse governed than nonfinancial firms.

It is possible that the results are skewed because banks are generally much larger than nonfinancial firms in terms of assets. Thus, in Panel B, I perform the same comparisons after controlling for firm size, as proxied by the natural logarithm of the book value of assets. The picture looks slightly different now. Controlling for size, bank boards are still larger, with fewer outside director-ships. However, they now have a smaller fraction of female directors. But they also have less total CEO compensation and less incentive pay for the CEO. These results hold even in the 2007 data in which director compensation is also lower for banks. Clearly, firm size is an important factor influencing gov-ernance characteristics, consistent with findings in Boone, Fields, Karpoff and Raheja (2007), Coles, Daniel and Naveen (2008), Lehn, Patro and Zhao (2009) and Linck, Netter and Yang (2008). For example, the coefficient on 'Bank' in the board size comparison decreases by roughly 50% in Column II after con-trolling for firm size and the compensation numbers decrease significantly. These results are robust to controlling for additional firm characteristics in Panel C.

Based on these comparisons, it would be difficult to argue that banks are clearly poorly governed. In particular, much of the media attention focuses on 'excessive' total pay and performance pay in financial firms, yet, *on average,* bank CEOs earn less and have less performance pay than CEOs of nonfinancial firms of similar size. Because banks perform worse on some dimensions of gov-ernance (according to Table 14.1) and better on other dimensions than nonfi-nancial firms, I summarize their overall governance performance relative to nonfinancial firms using a governance score. For each characteristic for which the coefficient on 'Bank' is significant at greater than the 10% level, I define the governance score to be 1 if banks appear better governed according to column IV of Table 14.1, otherwise the score is defined to be 0. For each sample and each panel in Table 14.4, 'Total governance score for banks' shows the sum of the scores divided by the number of significantly different coefficients on 'Bank' for that sample and panel.

Table 14.4 Comparison of selected governance characteristics of banks to nonfinancial firms

	2000 data only							2007 data only							
	Board independence	Board size	# Directorships	Fraction attend. problems	Fraction female	Total CEO comp.	Fraction equity-based pay CEO	Board independence	Board size	# Directorships	Fraction attend. problems	Fraction female	Total CEO comp.	Fraction equity-based pay CEO	Director comp.
	I	II	III	IV	V	VI	VII	VIII	IX	X	XI	XII	XIII	XIV	XV
Panel A: OLS regressions of governance characteristics on the bank dummy in sample of banks and nonfinancial firms															
Bank	0.056***	5.287***	-0.307***	0.004	0.001	-0.355	0.027	-0.008	3.133***	-0.484***	-0.004	0.008	-0.868	-0.076**	-65.561***
	[2.70]	[17.05]	[-4.14]	[0.64]	[0.10]	[-0.16]	[0.81]	[-0.64]	[13.04]	[-8.57]	[-0.97]	[0.73]	[-0.75]	[-2.16]	[-3.17]
Obs.	1,370	1,370	1,370	1,370	1,370	1,316	1,316	1268	1268	1268	1268	1268	702	702	698
Score	1	0	1	NA	NA	NA	NA	NA	0	1	NA	NA	NA	1	1
				Total governance score for banks: 2/3								Total governance score for banks: 2/4			
Panel B: OLS regressions of governance characteristics on the bank dummy and Ln(Assets), robust standard errors															
Bank	0.009	2.768***	-0.879***	0.004	-0.042***	-7.380***	-0.117***	-0.036***	1.419***	-0.797***	-0.003	-0.027***	-6.845***	-0.204***	-127.855***
	[0.53]	[5.97]	[-15.12]	[0.61]	[-4.73]	[-4.70]	[-3.83]	[-3.05]	[5.10]	[-18.98]	[-1.02]	[-2.94]	[-8.66]	[-5.68]	[-9.02]
Obs.	1,368	1,368	1,368	1,368	1,368	1,316	1,316	1259	1259	1259	1259	1259	702	702	698
Score	NA	0	1	NA	0	1	1	0	0	1	NA	0	1	1	1
				Total governance score for banks: 3/5								Total governance score for banks: 4/7			
Panel C: OLS regressions of governance characteristics on the bank dummy, Ln(Assets), ROA, Tobins' Q, robust standard errors															
Bank	0.003	2.626***	-0.874***	0.005	-0.041***	-6.896***	-0.104***	-0.039**	1.126***	-0.744***	-0.004	-0.034**	-6.492***	-0.189***	-116.560***
	[0.19]	[5.66]	[-15.04]	[0.75]	[-4.59]	[-4.39]	[-3.40]	[-2.36]	[2.85]	[-11.27]	[-1.31]	[-2.40]	[-8.10]	[-5.26]	[-8.13]
Obs.	1,338	1,338	1,338	1,338	1,338	1,289	1,289	701	701	701	701	701	701	701	697
Score	NA	0	1	NA	0	1	1	0	0	1	NA	0	1	1	1
				Total governance score for banks: 3/5								Total governance score for banks: 4/7			

The table compares selected governance characteristics for banks and nonfinancial firms by regressing governance characteristics on a dummy variable ('Bank') equal to 1 if the sample firm is a bank. The panels vary by the control variables included in the regressions. The sample and governance characteristics are described in Table 14.2. Observations vary because of missing data. The coefficients on the control variables and the constant are omitted for the sake of brevity. Standard errors are corrected for heteroskedasticity in Panels B and C. Asterisks indicate significance at 0.01 (***), 0.05 (**), and 0.10 (*) levels. For each characteristic for which the coefficient on 'Bank' is significant at greater than the 10% level, 'Score' is defined to be 1 if banks appear better governed according to column IV of Table 14.1, otherwise 'Score' is defined to be 0. If the coefficient on 'Bank' is insignificant, 'Score' is equal to NA. For each sample and each specification 'Total governance score for banks' shows the sum of 'Score' divided by the number of significantly different coefficients on 'Bank' for that sample and specification. Thus, 'Total governance score for banks' is an index measuring the relative strength of bank governance as compared to nonfinancial firm governance according to Table 14.1. The panel on the left shows data for year 2000. The panel on the right shows data for year 2007.

The 'Total governance score for banks' varies from a low of 2/4 for Panel A, 2007 data to a high of 2/3 in Panel A, 2000 data. But in all cases, this score indicates that banks are generally equally, if not better, governed than nonfinancial firms. Although this measure is ad hoc because it gives equal weight to each dimension of governance, it illustrates that understanding potential governance failures at banks is not straightforward.

The picture looks slightly different when we compare nonbank financial firms (NBFF) to nonfinancial firms in Table 14.5. Comparing Panel A to Panel B for 2000 data, it is clear that firm size again has a significant effect on governance characteristics. After controlling for firm size, nonbank financial firms have less independent boards, fewer outside directorships, a lower fraction of female directors, lower Total CEO Compensation and less equity-based pay. Moreover, the governance score for NBFF changes from 0/3 to 2/4 after controlling for firm size. Similar to the scores for banks, the governance score for NBFFs indicate for all but Panel A, 2000 data that NBFF are at least as well-governed as nonfinancial firms.

Some conclusions one can draw from the discussion in this section are as follows: First, banks and nonbank financial firms do not have exactly the same governance characteristics. Second, although executive pay in financial firms may appear larger than in nonfinancial firms, much of this difference is driven by differences in firm size. Of course, CEOs at *some* financial firms may have received what many consider to be unfair or excessive pay. However, *on average* financial CEO pay does not seem to be excessive relative to CEO pay in nonfinancial firms. Moreover, the phenomenon of 'excess pay' for CEOs appears to be driven by nonbank financial firms. Third, although financial firms score worse on some governance characteristics than nonfinancial firms, on average they appear to be *better governed* than nonfinancial firms. Nevertheless, it is possible that the differences in governance I document are still partly to blame for the problems facing financial firms. I turn to this issue in the next section.

A final and potentially very important observation is that director pay is significantly lower in banks, even without controlling for firm size. This fact is also pointed out in Adams and Ferreira (2011). From Table 14.4, Panel A, Column XV, one can see that in 2007 average bank director compensation is lower than average nonfinancial director compensation by $65,561. Average director compensation in non-financials in 2007 is $193,931, so bank director compensation is 33.8% lower. This may have serious consequences for governance. If the pool of director candidates is the same for financial firms and nonfinancial firms, then the better qualified candidates may prefer to join the boards of firms that pay more. Of course, factors other than pay play a role in an individual's decision to join a board, but this finding raises the possibility

Table 14.5 Comparison of selected governance characteristics of non-bank financial firms to nonfinancial firms

	2000 data only							2007 data only							
	Board independence	Board size	# Directorships	Fraction attend. problems	Fraction female	Total CEO comp.	Fraction equity-based pay CEO	Board independence	Board size	# Directorships	Fraction attend. problems	Fraction female	Total CEO comp.	Fraction equity-based pay CEO	Director comp.
	I	II	III	IV	V	VI	VII	XIII	IX	X	XI	XII	XIII	XIV	XV
Panel A: OLS regressions of governance characteristics on the nonbank financial dummy in sample of nonbank financial firms and nonfinancial firms															
NBFF	-0.043**	1.487***	0.031	0.006	-0.002	3.696*	0.038	-0.031***	0.932***	-0.081*	-0.005*	-0.005	0.93	-0.038	2.208
	[-2.32]	[5.68]	[0.49]	[1.00]	[-0.21]	[1.80]	[1.23]	[-3.24]	[4.91]	[-1.81]	[-1.70]	[-0.53]	[1.06]	[-1.47]	[0.15]
Obs.	1,400	1,400	NA	1,400	1,400	1,334	1,334	1335	1335	1335	1335	1335	751	751	747
Score	0	0	NA	NA	NA	0	NA	0	0	1	1	NA	NA	NA	NA
Total governance score for NBFFs: 0/3								**Total governance score for NBFFs: 2/4**							
Panel B: OLS regressions of governance characteristics on the nonbank financial dummy and Ln(assets), robust standard errors															
NBFF	-0.071***	-0.002	-0.300***	0.006	-0.027***	-1.079	-0.05*	-0.053***	-0.166	-0.269***	-0.004**	-0.028***	-2.521***	-0.105***	-32.723**
	[-3.59]	[-0.01]	[-4.92]	[0.92]	[-3.36]	[-0.56]	[-1.66]	[-5.56]	[-0.83]	[-6.00]	[-2.30]	[-3.56]	[-3.06]	[-3.59]	[-2.79]
Obs.	1,398	1,398	1,398	1,398	1,398	1,334	1,334	1324	1324	1324	1324	1324	751	751	747
Score	0	NA	1	NA	0	NA	1	0	NA	1	1	0	1	1	1
Total governance score for NBFFs: 2/4								**Total governance score for NBFFs: 5/7**							
Panel C: OLS regressions of governance characteristics on the nonbank financial dummy, Ln(assets), ROA, Tobins' Q, robust standard errors															
NBFF	-0.076***	-0.014	-0.296***	0.007	-0.025***	-2.389	-0.061**	-0.051***	-0.296	-0.213***	-0.002	-0.025**	-2.304***	-0.096***	-25.964**
	[-3.76]	[-0.05]	[-4.79]	[1.18]	[-3.06]	[-1.32]	[-2.08]	[-4.32]	[-1.11]	[-3.55]	[-0.89]	[-2.38]	[-2.80]	[-3.31]	[-2.28]
Obs.	1,365	1,365	1,365	1,365	1,365	1,305	1,305	750	750	750	750	750	750	750	746
Score	0	NA	1	NA	0	NA	1	0	NA	1	NA	0	1	1	1
Total governance score for NBFFs: 2/4								**Total governance score for NBFFs: 4/6**							

The table compares selected governance characteristics for nonbank financial firms and nonfinancial firms by regressing governance characteristics on a dummy variable (NBFF) equal to 1 if the sample firm is a financial firm that is not a bank. The panels vary by the control variables included in the regressions. The sample and governance characteristics are described in Table 14.2. Observations vary because of missing data. The coefficients on the control variables and the constant are omitted for the sake of brevity; t-statistics are in brackets. Standard errors are corrected for heteroskedasticity in Panels B and C. Asterisks indicate significance at 0.01 (***), 0.05 (**), and 0.10 (*) levels. For each characteristic for which the coefficient on NBFF is significant at greater than the 10% level, 'Score' is defined to be 1 if nonbank financials appear better governed according to column IV of Table 14.1, otherwise 'Score' is defined to be 0. If the coefficient on NBFF is insignificant, 'Score' is equal to NA. For each sample and specification 'Total governance score for NBFFs' shows the sum of 'Score' divided by the number of significantly different coefficients on NBFF for that sample and specification. Thus, 'Total governance score for NBFFs' is an index measuring the relative strength of nonbank financial firm governance as compared to nonfinancial firm governance according to Table 14.1. The panel on the left shows data for year 2000. The panel on the right shows data for year 2007.

that the pool of bank directors may be worse along some dimensions than the pool of nonfinancial firm directors.

14.4   Is governance to blame for the problems at banks?

In the previous section, I showed that the governance of financial firms differs from that of nonfinancial firms. Although financial firms do not appear worse governed, a natural question is whether these differences may still have contributed to the problems financial firms faced during the crisis. In general, this is not an easy question to answer. One way of trying to answer it is to compare the governance characteristics of financial firms that received bailout money from the Federal Government to those that did not. The Troubled Assets Relief Program (TARP) was designed to strengthen the financial system by enabling the government to purchase or insure up to $700 billion in troubled assets. Although the US treasury did not describe it as a bailout program (see http://www.financialstability.gov/roadtostability/capitalpurchaseprogram.html), many observers referred to it as such (see, e.g., the TARP entry on Wikipedia). Moreover, it is clear that recipients of TARP money faced some financial difficulties. Thus, a comparison of firms with and without TARP assistance may be illustrative. In addition, I can eliminate firms that failed or were acquired from my sample to ensure that I am comparing institutions that were essentially healthy that did not receive bailout funds to those that did.

As of April 10, 2009 only six nonbank financial firms received TARP assistance. Thus, I limit the comparison to banks. To determine which of the banks in my sample received TARP funds, I matched their names and locations to the names and locations in the list of TARP recipients maintained by the *New York Times* (http://projects.nytimes.com/creditcrisis/recipients/table). Of the 93 banks in my sample in 2007, 56 received bailout funds in either 2008 or beginning of 2009 (until April 10, 2009). To determine whether any of the remaining institutions failed or were acquired, I first merge my sample to data from Osiris gathered on April 8, 2009. This dataset contains information about the current status of institutions. For the 16 institutions whose status I was unable to verify using Osiris, I checked institutional histories on the National Information Center's website,[11] a website containing information on banks collected by the Federal Reserve System. Four institutions in my sample disappeared by 2009. Two were acquired (Wachovia and National City Corp), one closed (Downey Financial Corp) and one failed (Franklin Bank Corp). I eliminate these observations from my sample. In Table 14.6, I perform a similar comparison for 2007 as in Table 14.4 after restricting my sample to banks. The coefficients on 'Bailout' measure differences in governance characteristics for banks that received TARP money in 2008 and 2009 to those that did not. Because the sample is so small, I do not also report the results after controlling

Table 14.6 Comparison of selected governance characteristics for sample banks receiving bailout money to surviving sample banks that did not

				2007 data only				
	Board independence	Board size	# directorships	Fraction attend. problems	Fraction female	Total CEO comp.	Fraction equity-based pay CEO	Director compensation
	I	II	III	IV	V	VI	VII	VIII
Bailout	0.037*	1.340**	0.265***	0.006	0.029	3.449*	0.163*	-3.699
	[1.68]	[2.13]	[2.66]	[1.21]	[1.59]	[1.79]	[1.97]	[-0.14]
Constant	0.745***	11.303***	0.246***	0.002	0.106***	3.152*	0.517***	131.295***
	[42.67]	[22.64]	[3.11]	[0.60]	[7.44]	[1.98]	[7.59]	[5.98]
Obs.	89	89	89	89	89	44	44	44
R-sq.	0.031	0.049	0.075	0.017	0.028	0.071	0.085	<0.001

The table shows a comparison of selected governance characteristics in 2007 between sample banks that received bailout money from the US government in 2008 and beginning of 2009 (up until April 10, 2009) and sample banks that survived until April, 2009 and did not receive bailout money. I define a bank to have received bailout money if it received funds from the US government under the Troubled Asset Relief Program (TARP). The underlying sample is described in Table 14.2. To determine which of the banks in my sample received TARP funds, I matched their names and locations to the names and locations in the list of TARP recipients maintained by the *New York Times* (http://projects.nytimes.com/creditcrisis/recipients/table). Of the 93 banks in my sample in 2007, 56 received bailout funds in either 2008 or the beginning of 2009 (until April 10, 2009). To determine whether any of the remaining institutions failed or were acquired, I first merge my sample to data from Osiris gathered on April 8, 2009. This dataset contains information about the current status of institutions as of the beginning of 2009. For the 16 institutions whose status I was unable to verify using Osiris, I checked institutional histories on the National Information Center's website, a website containing information on banks collected by the Federal Reserve System. Four institutions in my sample that did not receive TARP funds disappeared by 2009. Two were acquired, one closed and one failed. I eliminate these observations from my sample. Governance characteristics in columns I–VIII are defined as in Table 14.2. Bailout is a dummy variable equal to 1 if the sample firm received bailout money from the US government. Observations vary because of missing data, t-statistics are in brackets. Asterisks indicate significance at 0.01 (***), 0.05 (**), and 0.10 (*) levels.

for firm size. They are similar in sign, although less significant, except for director compensation which becomes significantly negative.

Table 14.6 indicates that banks with TARP funds have more independent boards, larger boards, more outside directorships, greater total CEO pay and greater incentive pay for CEOs. Some of these results are consistent with the idea that TARP banks have worse governance. In particular, the fact that TARP banks had higher performance pay for CEOs is consistent with the idea that performance pay may have led executives of banks to take on too much risk. The coefficient on the number of directorships is also consistent with potentially worse governance since taking on too many directorships can lead directors to become too unfocused. The fact that TARP banks have larger boards is also a potential indication of worse governance.

Perhaps the most surprising result, however, is the finding that TARP banks have boards that are more independent. What is going on here? There are several possible explanations. For example, it is possible that the governance of TARP banks is not much worse than that of non-TARP banks. However, given that a large part of the problems at banks was caused by securitization, another explanation is possible. An independent director, by definition, is a director who has not worked for the bank and has no business dealings with the bank. Because of potential conflicts of interests, independent directors are generally not employees of other financial firms. What this means is that independent directors are less likely to have an in-depth knowledge of the internal workings of the banks on whose boards they sit. They are also less likely to have the financial expertise to understand the complexity of the securitization processes banks were engaging in or to assess the associated risks banks were taking on. Thus, although board independence is generally seen to be a good thing, in the case of banks, greater independence may be a bad thing because a more independent board will not have sufficient expertise to monitor the actions of the CEO. This finding is also consistent with Guerrera and Larsen (2008) who describe that more than two-thirds of the directors at eight large US financial institutions did not have any significant recent experience in the banking industry and more than half had no financial service experience at all.

If we accept that independence may be a sign of poor governance, then the conclusion to be drawn from Table 14.6 is that it appears that TARP banks were indeed governed worse than non-TARP banks. However, because the messages from Tables 14.4 and 5 are mixed, i.e., banks and financial firms do not necessarily appear to be worse governed than nonfinancial firms, it is not obvious what the policy implications are. Nevertheless, many countries implemented governance policies as a direct response to the crisis. I discuss some implications of these policies in the next section.

14.5   Variation in governance practices decreased following governance reform

The previous sections illustrate that financial firms have different governance structures than nonfinancial firms. Regardless of whether governance was a cause of the crisis or not, many policy responses to the crisis targeted governance. What most of these policies have in common is that they do not distinguish between financial and nonfinancial firms. They also do not distinguish between banks and nonbank financial firms. What are the implications of uniform regulation? An obvious answer is uniform governance. Table 14.7 provides some evidence for this by showing regressions of yearly standard deviations in governance measures (except director compensation) for banks (Panel A) and nonbank financial firms (Panel B) on a Post–US Reform dummy and a Post Dodd-Frank Act of 2010 dummy (a dummy that is one in years 2010 and 2011).

What is noticeable from Table 14.7 is that almost all coefficients on the two policy dummy variables are negative, albeit not always significant. Panel A shows that for banks the standard deviations in board independence, board size, number of directorships and the fraction of attendance problems decreased after 2002. The standard deviations in board size and number of directorships decreased even further following the Dodd-Frank Act. The variation in the fraction of women and compensation variables did not change much following the US Reforms or Dodd-Frank. One reason may be that for banks there is simply not that much variation in these variables in the first place. Consistent with the idea that there may be more variation in the compensation packages for CEOs of nonbank financials, we observe from Panel B that CEOs of nonbank financials experienced a decrease in variation in their compensation packages following governance reform. The variation in total CEO pay decreased following 2002 and the standard deviation of the fraction of equity pay decreased following Dodd-Frank. In addition, variation in board independence and the fraction of attendance problems decreased after 2002 and the Dodd-Frank Act.

Recent work by Cai, Saunders and Steffen (2012) documents that banks with similar loan portfolios are more interconnected and have greater systemic risk. It is plausible that financial firms with more similarity in governance structures may also be more interconnected. Moreover, uniformity in decision-making structures may lead to uniform responses to challenges facing the financial services industry, which in turn could lead to more risk. Although more research on this topic needs to be done, I believe it is intuitive that cookie-cutter governance will not suit all asset management firms and that asset management firms will need to be more proactive in designing new governance structures

Table 14.7 Variation in governance practices

	Stddev. Board independence	Stddev. Board size	Stddev. # directorships	Stddev. Fraction attend. problems	Stddev. Fraction female	Stddev. Total CEO comp.	Stddev. Fraction equity-based pay CEO
	I	II	III	IV	V	VI	VII
				Panel A: Banks			
Post–US Reform	-0.018**	-1.122***	-0.116***	-0.020***	0.004	1.059	0.021*
	[-2.20]	[-4.59]	[-3.78]	[-3.09]	[1.27]	[0.84]	[1.78]
Post Dodd-Frank	-0.019	-0.903**	-0.101**	-0.009	-0.001	-1.274	0.005
	[-1.54]	[-2.52]	[-2.55]	[-0.91]	[-0.31]	[-0.69]	[0.30]
Constant	0.146***	4.441***	0.685***	0.056***	0.079***	5.459***	0.230***
	[23.05]	[24.02]	[27.41]	[11.36]	[33.30]	[5.70]	[25.84]
Obs.	16	16	14	16	16	16	16
R-sq.	0.029	0.426	0.266	0.001	0.089	0.073	0.111
				Panel B: Nonbank financials			
Post–US Reform	-0.062***	1.376	-0.134***	-0.027***	0.011**	-4.601**	0.002
	[-6.65]	[0.65]	[-4.87]	[-4.31]	[2.80]	[-2.30]	[0.29]
Post Dodd-Frank	-0.027*	-1.712	-0.001	-0.017*	0.013**	2.797	-0.036***
	[-1.94]	[-0.55]	[-0.03]	[-1.85]	[2.18]	[0.95]	[-3.74]
Constant	0.197***	3.364*	0.684***	0.061***	0.082***	11.818***	0.275***
	[27.82]	[2.09]	[30.54]	[12.68]	[26.61]	[7.80]	[54.94]
Obs.	16	16	14	16	16	16	16

The table examines variation in governance practices by regressing yearly standard deviations of selected governance characteristics (16 years maximum) on a Post–US Reform dummy variable and Post Dodd-Frank 2010 dummy variable. In Panel A, the standard deviations are calculated for the bank sample. In Panel B, they are calculated for the nonbank financial sample. Observations vary because of missing data, t-statistics are in brackets. Asterisks indicate significance at 0.01 (***), 0.05 (**), and 0.10 (*) levels.

to suit the requirements of their businesses. Simply abiding by regulatory governance requirements will not be enough to reduce risk.

14.6   What lessons can we learn?

Because it is the duty of the board to oversee management and many bank and financial firm managers led their banks to the brink of failure, boards of financial firms clearly share some responsibility for the crisis. But the question is how much of the blame should they shoulder? Popular opinion, fueled by stories of what seems to be excessive executive compensation at financial firms, might argue: a lot. However, it is important to keep several facts in mind, particularly when considering potential policy implications.

First, few people predicted the financial crisis. Rushe (2008) describes, for example, how little attention was paid to Nouriel Roubini's prediction that problems in the subprime mortgage market would trigger a financial crisis. While the boards of financial firms should have better information than outsiders, directors are generally not experts on the economy. Thus, it seems unreasonable to expect that they should have been better able to predict the problems financial firms would face than academics, regulators and financial analysts. Rodrik (2009) argues in his blog that blame should be spread more widely than bankers to the broader economics and policymaking community.

Second, financial firms are regulated. It is still not clear whether regulators substitute or complement board-level governance. However, it is possible that directors *perceive* a substitution effect. It is not hard to imagine that a bank director does not understand all risk implications of particular transactions but agrees to them anyhow, because he assumes that regulators would identify any potential problems.

Third, the data in this chapter show that governance in financial firms is, *on average*, not *obviously*, worse than in nonfinancial firms. While financial firm governance may appear worse in some dimensions, it appears better in others. Ex post, it is easy to argue that governance problems occurred, but ex ante it is not clear that boards of financial firms were doing anything much different from boards in other firms. Even the issue of executive compensation is not as clear cut as it appears at first. CEOs of nonbank financial firms do earn significantly more than CEOs of nonfinancial firms, but this is no longer true once firm size is accounted for.

However, two particular findings suggest that banking firms governance may have been worse, but in ways that might not have been predicted ex ante. Banks receiving bailout money had boards that were more independent and bank directors earned significantly less compensation than their counterparts in nonfinancial firms. What this suggests is that board independence may not necessarily be beneficial for banks. Independent directors may not always have the expertise necessary to oversee complex banking firms.

The fact that bank directors earn so much less than their counterparties in nonfinancial firms raises the possibility that the pool of bank directors is different from the pool of directors of nonfinancial firms. Further research is needed to examine why director pay is so low in banking.[12] However, regardless of whether low pay is a sign of a governance problem or not, it seems clear that if it is not increased it will be difficult to attract candidates to bank director positions given the additional duties expected of them in the future.

While representing a large fraction of banking industry assets, the sample in this chapter is relatively small compared to the number of institutions in the financial sector. Furthermore, many more factors affect governance characteristics than the ones I considered here. Thus, much more research is needed to understand the extent to which governance contributed to the financial crisis. Nevertheless, the simple analysis in this chapter is still suggestive that board-level governance of publicly-traded financial firms *may* have played a part in the crisis. However, it also suggests that the recent governance reform movement embodied in SOX and the NYSE and Nasdaq listing standards may be as much to blame. SOX and the listing standards place a lot of emphasis on director independence. However, it is not clear that director independence is always beneficial because independent directors lack information (see also the arguments in Adams and Ferreira, 2007). The problem may be exacerbated for financial firms because of the complex nature of their businesses. This is a point the OECD Steering Committee on Corporate Governance (Kirkpatrick, 2009) also makes. It argues that independence at financial firms may have been overemphasized at the expense of qualifications. Guerrera and Larsen (2009) also discuss the fact that SOX made it more difficult for financial firms to hire suitable directors with financial expertise because of the perception of conflicts of interests.

Some tentative policy implications that can be drawn are as follows: By placing too much emphasis on independence SOX and recent listing standards may have worsened board governance at publicly-traded financial firms. Not only are financial firms complex, but the financial industry is complex due to the existence of different regulators. Until the governance of financial firms is better understood, it may be better not to impose restrictions on the governance of financial firms. Further regulating governance may have unintended negative side-effects, as SOX may have had. These arguments suggest that, by emphasizing independence, section 952 of the Dodd-Frank Act mandating fully independent compensation committees seems unlikely to prevent governance failures and may even contribute to them. Moreover, compliance with such regulations is costly. For example, Leuz, Triantis and Wang (2008) find that compliance with SOX was a significant factor in companies' decisions to delist in 2002–2004. These costs may be particularly large for small firms. Since the majority of firms in the banking sector are relatively small, at this point in time it is not clear how imposing additional restrictions on their governance can help prevent future crises.

An additional problem is that governance policy imposes uniform standards. By decreasing the variation in governance practices across financial firms, policies may actually lead to more uniformity in decision-making and potentially more risk.

It seems clear that it may be beneficial for financial firms to try to increase the financial sophistication of their boards, either through hiring new directors or through additional education. Because financial firms, such as Citigroup, already changed their boards, it is not clear that increasing the financial sophistication of the board requires regulation, for example by allowing shareholder access to the proxy. Regardless of their expertise, it is likely that directors of financial firms will not need any regulatory prodding to ask tougher questions to management in the future.

One problem that remains is the issue of director compensation. To ensure that financial firms retain good directors and attract good candidates, directors of financial firms should be adequately compensated for the difficulties of their duties and the additional costs they bear in undertaking any additional training. However, it may be difficult to institute pay raises for directors of financial firms given the outrage over executive compensation following the crisis. It remains to be seen whether the provisions for greater oversight of executive compensation provided for in the Dodd-Frank Act will have a positive influence on director compensation.

Finally, financial firms will need to take extra care to differentiate themselves from other financial firms to ensure independence of thought. One possible way of doing this is to enhance the diversity of the board.

Notes

1. A large part of the material in this chapter appeared previously in Adams, Renée (2012) 'Governance and the Financial Crisis', *International Review of Finance*, (12)1: 7–38.
2. Contact information: School of Banking and Finance, Australian School of Business, University of New South Wales, Sydney, NSW 2052, Australia. E-mail: renee.adams@ unsw.edu.au.
3. La Porta, Lopez-de-Silanes, Shleifer and Vishny (1998) create this index for 49 countries. The other countries with scores as high as the US are Canada, Chile, Hong Kong, India, Pakistan, South Africa and the United Kingdom.
4. Regardless of exchange listing, all public companies are supposed to abide by SOX which requires that boards are responsible for internal control, audit committees consist entirely of independent directors, audit committees have at least one

financial expert, management certifies financial statements and board members face large penalties for corporate accounting fraud.

5. But, it also identifies governance in large, complex nonfinancial firms as a problem.
6. See http://www.oecd.org/document/48/0,3343,en_2649_34813_42192368_1_1_1_3 7439,00.html.
7. See http://www.hm-treasury.gov.uk/press_10_09.htm.
8. Laeven and Levine (2009) provide insights into the governance role of bank ownership structure across various countries.
9. Section 312 of the Dodd-Frank Act mandated the merger of the OTS into other regulatory bodies.
10. I use this data only after extensive cleaning.
11. http://www.ffiec.gov/nicpubweb/nicweb/NicHome.aspx.
12. It is possible that regulators do not look favorably on pay raises for directors.

References

Adams, R. (2010) 'Governance at Banking Institutions', Chapter 23 in R. Anderson and H.K. Baker (eds),*Corporate Governance*, Wiley & Sons .

Adams, R. (2011) 'Corporate Governance', to appear in the *Encyclopedia of Financial Globalization*, Gerard Caprio (ed.), Thorsten Beck, Charles Calomiris, Takeo Hoshi, Peter Montiel, and Garry Schinasi (assoc. eds), Elsevier.

Adams, R. (2012) 'Governance and the Financial Crisis', *International Review of Finance*, 12(1): 7–38.

Adams, R. and Ferreira, D. (2007) 'A Theory of Friendly Boards', *Journal of Finance*, 62(1): 217–250.

Adams, R. and Ferreira, D. (2009) 'Women in the Boardroom and their Impact on Governance and Performance', *Journal of Financial Economics*, 94(2): 291–309.

Adams, R. and Ferreira, D. (2011) 'Does Regulatory Pressure Provide Sufficient Incentives for Bank Directors? Evidence from Directors' Attendance Records', forthcoming, *International Review of Finance*.

Adams, R. and Mehran, H. (2003) 'Is Corporate Governance Different for Bank Holding Companies?', *Economic Policy Review*, 9(1): 123–142.

Adams, R. and Mehran, H. (2011) 'Bank Board Structure and Performance: Evidence from Large Bank Holding', forthcoming, *Journal of Financial Intermediation*.

Adams, R., Hermalin, B. and Weisbach, M. (2010) 'The Role of Boards of Directors in Corporate Governance: A Conceptual Framework and Survey', *Journal of Economic Literature*, 48(1): 58–107.

Altınkılıç, O., Hansen, R. and Hrnjić, E. (2007) 'Investment Bank Governance', Tulane University Working Paper.

Boone, A., Field, L., Karpoff, J. and Raheja, C. (2007) 'The determinants of corporate board size and composition: An empirical analysis', *Journal of Financial Economics*, 85: 66–101.

Bordo, M. and Eichengreen, B. (2003) 'Crises now and then: What lessons from the last era of financial globalization?', in Paul Mizen (ed.) *Monetary History, Exchange Rates and Financial Markets : Essays in Honor of Charles Goodhart*. Vol 2, Cheltenham: Edward Elgar.

Cai, J., Saunders, T. and Steffens, S. (2012) 'Syndication, Interconnectedness, and Systemic Risk', New York University Working Paper.

Coles, J., Daniel, N. and Naveen, L. (2008) 'Boards: Does one size fit all?', *Journal of Financial Economics*, 87: 329–356.

Deloitte, 2011, 'Women in the boardroom – A global perspective', EU calls for women to make up one-third of bank directors, January.

Eichengreen, B. and O'Rourke, K. (2009) 'A Tale of Two Depressions', http://www.voxeu.org/index.php?q=node/3421, April 6.

Federal Reserve Bank of Kansas City (2010) Basics for Bank Directors, www.BankDirectorsDesktop.org.

Guerrera, F. and Larsen, P. (2008) 'Gone by the board? Why bank directors did not spot credit risks', *Financial Times*, June 25.

Johnson, S., Boone, P. Breach, A. and E. Friedman (2000) 'Corporate Governance in the Asian Financial Crisis', *Journal of Financial Economics*, 58: 141–186.

Kirkpatrick, G. (2009) 'The Corporate Governance Lessons from the Financial Crisis,' *Financial Markets Trends*, 2009/1, OECD.

La Porta, R., Lopez-de-Silanes, F., Shleifer, A. and Vishny, R. (1997) 'Legal Determinants of External Finance', *Journal of Finance*, 52(3): 1131–1150.

La Porta, R., Lopez-de-Silanes, F., Shleifer, A. and Vishny, R. (1998) 'Law and Finance', *Journal of Political Economy*, 106(6): 1113–1155.

Laeven, L. and Levine, R. (2009) 'Corporate Governance, Regulation, and Bank Risk Taking', *Journal of Financial Economics*, 93(2): 259–275.

Lehn, K., Patro, S. and Zhao, M. (2009) 'Determinants of the Size and Composition of US Corporate Boards: 1935–2000', *Financial Management*, 38(4), 747–780.

Leuz, C., Triantis, A. and Wang, T. (2008) 'Why Do Firms Go Dark? Causes and Economic Consequences of Voluntary SEC Deregistrations', *Journal of Accounting and Economics*, 45: 181–208.

Linck, J., Netter, J. and Yang, T. (2008) 'The determinants of board structure', *Journal of Financial Economics*, 87(2): 308–328.

Morgenson, G. (2009) 'After Huge Losses, a Move to Reclaim Executives' Pay', *New York Times*, p. BU1, February 22.

Morris, N. (2009) 'Harriet Harman: If only it had been Lehman Sisters', *The Independent*, August 4, http://www.independent.co.uk/news/uk/home-news/harriet-harman-if-only-it-had-been-lehman-sisters-1766932.html.

Moyer, L. (2008) 'Off with their heads', Forbes.com, available at http://www.forbes.com/2008/04/11/shareholders-banking-iss-biz-wallcx_lm_0411proxy.html, April 4.

Philippon, T. and Reshef, A. (2009) 'Wages and Human Capital in the US Financial Industry: 1909–2006', NBER Working Paper No. 14644.

Protess, B. (2011) 'In Split Vote, S.E.C. Adopts Corporate Pay Rules', http://dealbook.nytimes.com/2011/01/25/s-e-c-adopts-say-on-pay-rules/, January 25.

Rodrik, D. (2009) 'Simon Johnson's morality tale', http://rodrik.typepad.com/dani_rodriks_weblog/2009/03/simon-johnsons-morality-tale.html, March 30.

Rosen, R. (2003) 'Is three a crowd? Competition among regulators in banking', *Journal of Money, Credit, and Banking*, 35: 967–998.

Rosen, R. (2005) 'Switching primary federal regulators: Is it beneficial for US banks?', *Economic Perspectives 29*, 2005.

Rushe, D. (2008) 'Nouriel Roubini: I fear the worst is yet to come', *The Sunday Times*, October 26.

Treanor, J. (2011) 'EU calls for women to make up one-third of bank directors', http://www.guardian.co.uk/business/2011/jun/21/eu-women-bank-directors, June 21.

US House (2002) 'The role of the board of directors in Enron's collapse', Committee on Governmental Affairs, Permanent Subcommittee on Investigations,

Walker, Sir D., (2009) 'A review of corporate governance in UK banks and other financial industry entities', Final recommendations, 26 November, http://www.hm-treasury.gov.uk/d/walker_review_261109.pdf .

Whalen, G. (2002) 'Charter Flips by National Banks', Office of the Comptroller of the Currency, E&PA Working Paper 2002–1.

15
Financial Regulation and Risk Governance

Caspar Rose

15.1 Introduction

The financial crisis has revealed that the current legislative framework has proved insufficient. As a consequence, many commentators have argued that there is a need for new regulation in order to reduce the pro-cyclicality of the existing Basel Capital Accord solvency rules as well as avoiding moral hazard problems from deposit insurance. The use of off-balance items such as structured investment vehicles (SIV) as well as the lack of transparency regarding over-the-counter (OTC) transactions has also come in for particular scrutiny. The role of credit rating agencies facilitating complicated structured financial products without proper due diligence has also been heavily debated. In other words, many of the fundamental building blocks in the global financial system have been seriously questioned following the crisis. However, perhaps most fundamentally, the existing regulatory framework as well as complicated risk management models failed to prevent the crisis that emerged from financial institutions' liquidity problems.

15.2 New regulation often follows a crisis

Financial institutions as well as financial markets have been heavily regulated for several years. It was started by the US with the introduction of the Securities Act of 1993 and the Securities and Exchange Act of 1934 following the crash of 1929. These acts, once enacted were followed by depressed markets for several years. Since many investors had lost money, both houses of Congress conducted lengthy hearings to find the cause and the culprits. The hearings were marked by sensationalism and wide publicity and the two acts were the direct result of the congressional hearings. The two acts were later supplemented by several other laws, which were enacted following other financial crises; Weston, Mitchell and Mulherin (2004) provide an overview. The latest example is the comprehensive Sarbanes-Oxley Act of 2002, which deals with issues such as: enhanced financial disclosure, auditor independence, conflicts of interest, and corporate fraud among other things. Europe has followed the legislative initiatives from the US by implementing regulation in the form of various directives.

Today we are witnessing a similar situation with the current financial crisis where politicians feel strong public pressure to do something. In other words everyone expects that politicians as well as financial authorities will introduce new legislative initiatives combined with tougher enforcement of existing regulation. This prompts a crucial question: how should we go ahead and redesign the regulatory framework? One may argue that future regulation should not be based on fear and control. Instead there is a need to create the right incentives through 'smart' laws.

15.3 The many faces of the regulatory failure

The regulatory failure has manifested itself in several ways. However, there are a number of large failures that have especially attracted their attention. First, the legal vacuum of credit default swaps (CDS) has been criticized by many commentators. A CDS involves a buyer who makes periodic payments to a seller, and in return receives a payout if an underlying financial instrument defaults. CDS contracts have been compared with insurance contracts because the buyer pays a premium and in return, receives a sum of money if one of the specified events occurs. However, there are a number of differences between CDS and insurance. For example a seller need not be a regulated entity and a buyer of a CDS does not need to own the underlying security or other form of credit exposure. In fact the buyer does not even have to suffer a loss from the default event, see www.wikipedia.org/wiki/Credit_default_swap for a description.

CDSs allow investors to speculate on changes in an entity's credit quality, since generally CDS spreads will increase as credit-worthiness declines, and decline as credit-worthiness increases. Despite the fact that the CDS market was enormous it remained completely unregulated. The market activity in 2008 amounted to $55 trillion and it had significant effects on ordinary regulated markets, see www.wikipedia.org/wiki/Credit_default_swap. The CDS market was characterized by herd behavior and banks' top managements did not always fully understand the products' risks. Or as Tom Wilson, Chief Risk Officer at Allianz SE says, 'when the music started to play people started to dance'.

Moreover, the lack of transparency in these instruments contributed significantly to uncertainty in the market. A main reason is that there were no legal requirement for disclosure surrounding credit default swaps, either to the

SEC or any other agency. As a consequence, the SEC (in 2008) worked with the financial services industry to develop one or more central counterparties, clearance, and settlement systems, and trading platforms for this market. The US capital markets regulator the Securities and Exchange Committee (SEC) will now work with Congress to make CDSs more transparent while 'giving regulators the power to rein in fraudulent or manipulative trading practices' and help ordinary investors to better assess the risks involved. The EU is currently contemplating how to strengthen the supervision of financial institutions.

There is no doubt that the regulation of credit rating agencies failed. This is a very serious problem, since rating agencies had played a key role in recent years especially with mortgage backed securities (MBS) and collateralized debt obligations (CDO), see www.wikipedia.org/wiki/Credit_rating_agency. After assigning, between 2004–2007, high ratings to these products, including subprime ones, rating agencies began to rapidly downgrade these instruments. This not surprisingly raised the question about the quality of the credit ratings with regard to structured products. It is a fact that high ratings encouraged investors to buy securities backed by subprime mortgages, helping finance the housing boom. The reliance on agency ratings and the way ratings were used to justify investment decisions led many investors to treat securitized products, some based on subprime mortgages, as equivalent to higher quality securities, see p. 32 in Financial Stability Forum (2008).

This was exacerbated by the SEC's removal of de facto regulatory barriers and its reduction of disclosure requirements. Critics allege that the rating agencies suffered from conflicts of interest, as they were paid by investment banks and other firms that organize and sell structured securities to investors. The SEC has now approved measures to strengthen oversight of credit rating agencies, following a ten-month investigation that found 'significant weaknesses in ratings practices', including conflicts of interest. See also SEC (2008) 'Summary Report of Issues Identified in the Commissions Staffs Examinations of Select Credit Rating Agencies'.

This naturally raises the question of whom to blame. Between Q3 2007 and Q2 2008, rating agencies lowered the credit ratings of $1.9 trillion in MBSs. Financial institutions felt they had to lower the value of their MBS and acquire additional capital so as to maintain capital ratios. If this involved the sale of new shares of stock, the value of the existing shares was reduced. Thus ratings downgrades lowered the stock prices of many financial firms. Arnold Kling told Congress that a high-risk loan could be 'laundered' by Wall Street and returned to the banking system as a highly-rated security for sale to investors, obscuring its true risks and avoiding capital reserve requirements (*Financial Times*).

As a result, following the findings of the Financial Stability Forum one may argue that the credit rating agencies should:

- provide disclosure on their due diligence performed on the underlying assets;
- disclose their track records as a test of their rating capabilities;
- offer mandatory information requirements emphasizing that investors should not overly rely on ratings.

Naked short selling has become a major problem for regulators especially in the US where it poses a serious threat to the trust in the financial markets. Naked short selling entails that sellers do not borrow stocks before an execution of a short sale, a practice that becomes evident once the stock is not delivered. Such trades can generate unlimited orders, overwhelm buyers and drive down prices. Failure to deliver can be used to manipulate markets. Harvey Pitt, a former SEC chairman calls it 'fraud'. There are strong indications that naked short selling contributed to the fall of both Lehman Brothers and Bear Stearns (*Financial Times*).

Until recently the SEC has been quite reluctant to act. An SEC report showed that of about 5,000 emailed tips related to naked short selling received from January 2007 to June 2008, 123 were forwarded for further investigation, but none led to actions (Bloomberg). Kotz, who is inspector general in the SEC said that the enforcement division 'is reluctant to expand additional resources to investigate complaints'.

The following situations illustrate the magnitude of the problem with naked short selling. On 30 June 2008, someone started a rumor that Barclays Plc. was ready to buy Lehman for 25% less than the day's price. The purchase did not materialize. On the previous trading day, 27 June, the number of shares sold without delivery jumped to 705,103 from 20,690, a 23-fold increase on 26 June. On 17 September, two days after Lehman Brothers filed for Chapter 11 bankruptcy protection, the number of failed trades climbed to 49.7 million, 23% of overall volume in the stock according to Bloomberg. The next day SEC announced a ban on shorting financial companies, which several jurisdictions around the world decided to follow, see SEC Press Release 211 (2008).

Following such instances, it is not surprising that the SEC at the start of 2009 is playing tough. For instance, the SEC Enforcement Division has announced what will be the largest settlements in the history of the SEC for investors who bought auction rate securities from Citigroup, UBS, Merrill Lynch and Bank of America. The Commission has finalized the Citi and UBS settlements. It has charged a number of Wall Street brokers with defrauding their customers when making more than $1 billion in unauthorized purchases of subprime-related auction rate securities. The SEC has also charged five California brokers for pushing homeowners into risky and unsustainable subprime mortgages, and then fraudulently selling them securities that were paid for with the mortgage proceeds. More importantly, it has charged Fannie Mae and Freddie Mac with accounting fraud in 2006 and 2007 respectively, and the companies paid more than $450 million in penalties to settle the SEC's charges, see SEC Press Release 211 (2008).

The ban on short selling may be seen as a bit of a paradox as modern textbook finance theory shows that short sale is not merely relevant if seller expects the shares to decline in value and wishes to profit from the decline. Another reason is to decrease the sensitivity of a portfolio to market movements, see Elton and Gruber (1995). Since the return on a short sale is the opposite of the return on a long position, a portfolio that includes short sales as well as long positions reduces its exposure to market movements.

The ability to short sell is a key ingredient in many theoretical asset pricing models see Huang and Litzenberger (1988) as well as more simple models such as capital asset pricing models (CAPM) that are used extensively in practice. This is indeed a paradox as prohibiting short sales may question if we can still rely on our fundamental financial asset pricing models such as CAPM which relies on the ability for investors to short sale in order to create a more risky portfolio with a higher expected return. Moreover, introducing short sales constraints creates additional challenges for the theoretical asset pricing models, see Duffie (1996) for an overview.

15.4   Why we cannot live without financial regulation

Ideally, the purpose of financial regulation is to internalize the social costs of potential bank failures via capital adequacy rules, the so-called Basel 'pillars', see Brunnermeier et al. (2009), or more precisely:

- to constrain the use of monopoly power and distortions to competition;
- to protect the essential needs of ordinary people in cases where information is hard or costly to obtain;
- to reduce substantial externalities i.e., the total costs of market failure exceed both the private costs of failure and the extra costs of regulation.

Contrary to other markets for goods and services, financial markets cannot entirely rely on there being completely free markets because they are not sufficient to sustain the financial system. Financial markets participants deal with other people's money. Economists designate it the principal agency relationship, which may create moral hazard problems, as financial markets are characterized by substantial informational asymmetries.

Contrary to nonfinancial firms there are severe externalities if financial institutions fail. To illustrate, the failure of a bank weakens the other banks and financial markets with which they are involved, whereas failure of, say, a car manufacturer tends to strengthen the remaining car companies as a competitor is removed. If, however, Lehman Brothers fails, due to a maturity mismatch between liabilities and assets, then investors might believe that Merrill Lynch is similar to Lehman, so lenders and depositors will lose confidence and withdraw their funds. This creates a liquidity problem, which restricts Merrill Lynch's access to funds. Thus, interest rates increase, which spread to other banks and eventually to the real economy, see Brunnermeier et al. (2009).

Bank failures may also have serious impacts on customers as nobody today can live without a bank. Externalities may consist of loss of access to future funding for the failed bank's customers. A client of a failed bank can always transfer his business to a surviving bank, but the new bank will have less direct information on this client so the start-up terms will be much tougher. Consequently, it is not a question of whether or not to have financial regulation, but instead how to regulate in a way that matters.

15.5 The regulatory framework for risk management

The Basel Committee on Banking Supervision is a standing committee of the Bank of International Settlements (BIS). It formulates broad supervisory standards and guidelines and recommends statements of best practice in banking supervision such as the Basel II Accord, expecting that member authorities and other nations' authorities will take steps to implement them through their own national systems, including the EU, whether in statutory form or otherwise. The purpose of the committee is also to encourage convergence toward common approaches and standards. For more, see www.bis.org/bcbs.

The EU Capital Requirements Directive (CRD) was formally adopted on 14 June 2006 building on the new Basel Accord. It affects banks and building societies and certain types of investment firms. The new framework consists of three pillars. Pillar 1 of the new standards sets out the minimum capital requirements firms will be required to meet for credit, market, and operational risk.

Moreover, the Basel Committee (2009) provides a forum for regular cooperation on banking supervisory matters. Its objective is to enhance understanding of key supervisory issues and improve the quality of banking supervision worldwide. It seeks to exchange information on national supervisory issues, approaches and techniques, with a view to promoting common understanding. At times, the Committee uses this common understanding to develop guidelines and supervisory standards in areas where they are considered desirable, see www.bis.org/bcbs/. In this regard, the Committee is best known for its international standards on capital adequacy; the Core Principles for Effective Banking Supervision; and the Concordat on cross-border banking supervision.

The Committee encourages contacts and cooperation among its members and other banking supervisory authorities. It circulates to supervisors throughout the world both published and unpublished papers providing guidance on banking supervisory matters. Contacts have been further strengthened by an International Conference of Banking Supervisors (ICBS) which takes place every two years.

On 29 May 2009, a proposal from the European Commission advocated the creation of a European Systemic Risk Council, to assess and warn about threats to financial stability in the region and a 'European System of Financial Supervisors' to oversee individual banks and financial firms. The European Systemic Risk Council would be headed by the president of the European Central Bank (ECB) and would include governors of the EU's 27 central banks. The panel would monitor broad risks in the region's financial system and intervene if necessary. Commission President Jose Manuel Barroso (2009) said, 'It's now or never, if we cannot reform the financial sector when we have a real crisis, when will we?' – see SPEECH/09/273.

Basel II mainly focused on three areas i.e., data management, model development, and system implementation. However, the general impact of these initiatives was rather small. As a consequence, the new initiatives in Basel III were much more significant as the new initiatives are expected to impact banks much more. A key driver is that regulatory capital is being defined as much more restrictive. Furthermore, based on the lessons of the financial crisis, Basel III also contains two liquidity ratios (a short and a long ratio) in combination of leverage ratios. Moreover, Basel III introduces a stressed VaR as well as enhanced counterparty risk measures.

The EU has a long tradition of following the accords of the Basel Committee and therefore the Capital Requirements Directive CRD IV closely follows the ideas of the Basel III.

15.6   Tougher regulation under way for EU banks

Following the global financial crisis, the Basel Committee developed Basel III which is the biggest regulatory initiative in decades. In order to bring the accords into hard law and binding rules, the European Union has drafted its Capital Requirements Directive or CRD IV. The overall objective is to foster enhanced risk management among financial institutions, as the financial crisis revealed that insufficient risk management was a key driver for the crisis. The CRD IV has been under way in the EU legislative system for years and was supposed to be implemented January 1, 2013. However, the directive has not yet been implemented, but instead it is expected that the new rules are going to be introduced as 'phase-in' arrangements over the coming year.

15.6.1   Increasing the quality of corporate governance

The EU Commission published an impact assessment in July 2011 which is normal in case of new EU initiatives. In fact the EU Commission issued two complement impact assessments.

The first impact assessment focuses on reinforcing sanction regimes in the financial sector. The background to this assessment is that sanction regimes vary a lot in size and with respect to proportionality within different Member States. The Commission emphasizes that: '*This situation may result in a lack of compliance with the EU rules, create distortions of competition in the Internal Market and have a negative impact on financial supervision, undermining proper functioning of banking markets, which can be detrimental to the protection of deposit-holders and investors and to the confidence in the financial sector.*' A uniform convergence of national sanctioning is also necessary if financial institutions are not to engage in forum shopping.

The Commission points at a number of key corporate governance areas which the Commission finds were among the factors responsible for the financial crisis. Specifically, the Commission states that inadequate risk oversight by boards was a major problem as several boards suffered from insufficient time commitment in combination with a lack of reporting lines of risk management to the board. Instead the Commission argues that boards spent too much time and effort to pursue growth which eventually resulted in excessive risk-taking. Moreover, the Commission intends to strengthen the corporate governance framework by:

- increasing the effectiveness of risk oversight by Boards
- improving the status of the risk management function
- ensuring effective monitoring by supervisors of risk governance

More concretely, the Commission suggests that corporate governance is improved in several ways: First, the Commission proposes to improve time commitment of board members. Even most corporate governance codes recommend that board meeting activities are published, including the number of board meetings held. However, such a number may not convey much information about how much time the board members spend on their board membership. The effectiveness of board meetings may also depend on the agenda as well as board members preparation before a meeting. Improved expertise of board members is also suggested e.g., by specifying criteria that board members must possess individually and collectively with regard to appropriate skills and expertise or by mandatory nomination committee. These measures are necessary to increase board effectiveness but it might be in combination with prohibiting cumulative mandates of the chairman and the CEO in the same credit institution.

More surprisingly, the Commission also argues for increased diversity in boards' compositions e.g., by requiring credit institutions to have a diversity policy .As such, it is not new that the Commission want to promote diversity, especially in relation to breaching glass ceilings and helping women to access leadership positions. However, there is no clear indication that insufficient board diversity resulted in poor corporate governance in financial institutions in general. It is a very legitimate goal to promote diversity in financial institutions but there is not yet (if possible) any scientific evidence that e.g., a male dominated board in a financial institution leads to increased risk-taking. This is mainly due to the fact that women only constitute a quite small proportion of members in the boards of financial institutions.

The Commission also suggests the need to improve risk management in boards e.g., by improving ownership by boards of risk strategy and priority given to risk issues. Moreover, boards in financial institutions should improve the information flows to boards with regard to risk matters and in particular, ensure efficient monitoring of risk governance by supervisors. The latter could be fulfilled by requiring that corporate governance is part of a supervisory review, or that suitability of board members is subject to specific supervisory review or to review of agendas and supporting documents for meetings of the board.

It is difficult to assess the exact impact of all these governance measures, but the main problem associated with the new governance initiatives is that the effects are difficult to measure and quantify in a scientific way.

15.6.2   More efficient sanctions in the Member States

Besides seeking to improve corporate governance in financial institutions, the Commission is considering the launch of the following initiatives on sanctioning regimes:

- Publication of sanctions as a general rule;
- Minimum common rules on the type of administrative sanctions to be available to competent authorities;
- Minimum common rules on maximum level of pecuniary administrative sanctions;
- List of key factors to be taken into account when determining the administrative sanctions;
- Obligation to provide for the application of administrative sanctions to both individuals and credit institutions;
- Publication of sanctions as a general rule;
- Internal whistle-blowing procedures in credit institutions;
- Requirement of Member States to set up systems for the protection of whistle-blowers.

As can be seen from the list, the Commission intends to harmonize and raise the bar regarding sanctions considerably. In retrospect such an initiative is difficult to ignore as there is some evidence that not all Member States are capable of enforcing sanctions that deter unlawful financial activities.

15.6.3   Increased capital quantity as well as quality

The Commission states in its second impact assessment that 'The EU banking system entered the crisis with capital of insufficient quantity and quality' where the Commission especially refers to hybrid capital instruments (featuring both debt and equity). The existing regulatory capital setup also revealed other shortcomings such as the treatment of counterparty credit risks as well as the issue of pro-cyclicality of lending which tend to follow the direction of and amplify the economic cycle. The reason in the latter case is that the current risk-based minimum capital requirements vary over the economic cycle. Furthermore, the Commission mentions that there were too many options and discretions in the existing regulatory setup, thus creating a high degree of divergence.

According to the Commission, the overall objectives of the new rules are to:

- Enhance the financial stability,
- Enhance safeguarding of depositors' interests,
- Ensure international competitiveness of the EU banking sector,
- Reduce pro-cyclicality of the financial system.

In order to improve financial stability the Commission intends to decrease liquidity risks by imposing two new ratios i.e., a Liquidity Coverage Ratio (LCR) from 2015 as well as an NSFR, i.e., Net Stable Funding Ratio from 2018. The latter is a consequence of the inherent asset-liability mismatch all banks face.

The Commission also intends to tighten criteria for eligibility of capital instruments for the different layers of regulatory capital. It is estimated that for Group 1 banks, revised regulatory adjustments reduce eligible common equity Tier 1 (CET1) by 42%, whereas for Group 2 banks the number is 33%. This is mainly a result of the reduction of the use of goodwill, material investments as well as deferred tax assets that are all less liquid and thus rely on a going concern assumption. Specifically, the new CET1 and Tier 1 will be implemented gradually from 2013 and by 2015 reaching 4.5% and 6% respectively.

Furthermore, the Commission plans to review some rules in relation to counterparty risks such as putting in place higher own funds requirements for bilateral derivative contracts which is supported by the Regulation on OTC derivatives adopted by the Commission in September 2010.

As mentioned, the Commission intends to reduce pro-cyclicality of the system by imposing a capital conservation buffer in combination with a countercyclical capital buffer. In the former case this equals a buffer of 2.5% of risk-weighted assets (RWA) aimed at ensuring banks' capacity to absorb losses in stressed periods. Thus, the counter cyclical capital buffer is supposed to protect the financial system from situations with a boom-bust behavior in aggregate credit growth by adjusting the conservation buffer with an additional 2.5%.

Finally, the Commission plans to introduce a nonrisk-based leverage ratio, although this is not expected within the next five years.

With regard to ensuring the international competitiveness of the EU banking sector, this is much more difficult to achieve with increased regulation as regulation does often put constraints on the growth of markets. Therefore this objective must be regarded as a more general statement.

With regard to the protection of the depositors, the EU extended the old DGS 1994 Directive in July 2010 by increasing payout coverage in EU Member States, so that all deposits below 100,000 euro are secured. However, on the other hand this is also the maximum amount secured. The objective of a deposit scheme with a high payout coverage is, for political reasons, to calm depositors and show commitment, see Gerhardt and Lannoo (2011) for an overview of the EU deposit rules.

15.6.4   Common EU banking supervision

After more than 13 hours of negotiation, all 27 EU Member States reached an agreement in which the EBC receives supervisory powers over the banks in the Eurozone. As part of the banking union the ECB receives substantial powers to monitor the performance of 6,000 banks in the Eurozone beginning from 2014. The ECB would take over tasks such as authorizing banks and other credit institutions, ensuring they have enough (liquid) capital to continue operating even when sustaining losses and monitoring the activities of financial conglomerates. If a bank breaches – or is at risk of breaching – capital requirements, the ECB would be able to ask the bank to take corrective action. National supervisors would meanwhile continue to carry out day-to-day checks.

The new EU initiative is vital, '*Ensuring that bank supervision and resolution across the Euro Area meets high standards will reassure citizens and markets that a common, high level of prudential regulation is consistently applied to all banks. If banks get into difficulties in the future, the public should have the confidence that ailing banks will be restructured or closed while minimizing costs for the taxpayer. This future system will help build the necessary trust between Member States, which is a pre-condition for the introduction of any common financial arrangements to protect depositors and support orderly resolution of failing banks*'. (COM, 2012: 510)

15.6.5   Consequences of the new rules

The EU, together with the ECB, has been heavily involved in restoring the European financial system in the years after the crisis. Therefore it seems natural that the EU has launched several new initiatives.

There is no doubt that the cumulative impact of the new CRD rules will be to increase RWA, although this is difficult to quantify for certain. For sure, the new rules will contribute to a reduction in bank leverage and therefore put pressure on the ability to leverage their returns. In short, banks are in general expected to earn a lower return, paying a price for decreasing the probability of a similar financial crisis to that which emerged in the autumn of 2008. However, it is doubtful that increasing liquidity and capital buffers may create a much more stable financial system. The reason for this is that history has taught us that business as well as financial cycles come and go, but they are very difficult to predict.

Protecting the interests of the depositors is necessary to avoid bank runs and create sufficient trust in financial institutions. However, on the other hand there is an inherent moral hazard problem as management may be tempted to engage in activities considered to be too risky as depositors to a large extent are immune from bankruptcy and therefore lack incentives to monitor and control management.

There is a risk that introducing the new EU banking supervision body may create additional bureaucracy and less transparency. After all, the new ECB body must rely on data from the Member States' own FSA and any decision can never be better than the data supplied. Trying to coordinate and avoid the situation where national FSAs are put under national political pressure is a positive move, as the ECB is expected to take a broader perspective less affected by Member States' own national interests. However, this does not completely neglect the risk that this new body becomes another EU 'paper tiger' consisting of civil servants isolated from the real world in their nice Frankfurt building.

15.7   How to move forward

The current regulatory framework has been heavily criticized following the crisis, especially due to a number of spectacular financial scandals. As US Treasury Secretary Hank Paulson says, 'The cost to our nation will be even larger if we do not overhaul our regulatory system', see the *Financial Times*. AIG was the largest insurance firm in the world and reported a loss of nearly $170 billion in March 2008 which affected several other large financial institutions. Bernanke told the Senate that AIG *de facto* served as a hedge fund. It had made a huge amount of irresponsible bets and losses due to a failure in financial regulation. President Barack Obama's administration reacted angrily to news that the AIG group, which is now 80%-owned by US taxpayers after it received federal bailouts of more than $150 billion, is to pay $165 million in bonuses to top executives. The bulk of the bonuses are expected to go to staff in AIG's London-run financial products unit, the very business division that got the institution into trouble last year. Lawrence Summers, Obama's senior economic adviser, called AIG's behavior 'outrageous', but said that the company was obliged to pay because of legally binding contracts made during the boom years, see the *Financial Times*.

This raises the crucial questions: should the government always pick up the pieces even if it creates a moral hazard problem and how should we design a new type of regulation that avoids similar events without creating excessive overregulation?

Ideally, I find that the goals of new regulation should concentrate on:

- fostering market stability while maintaining capitalism;
- creating regulation that facilitates on long-term incentives;
- building a regulatory structure organized by objectives;
- focusing on risk across the financial system, minimizing systemic risk;
- fostering increased transparency, which is necessary to fully understand financial products and their associated risks;
- avoiding excessive rules and bureaucracy as the lessons from the Sarbanes Oxley Act have shown that massive new rules may not offer any real degree of protection;
- producing rules based on substance rather than on form;
- providing regulators with the right incentive structures as well as independence.

Moreover, it is highly uncertain if the new initiatives from the Basel III and the CRD IV are sufficient to avoid future crises or to guarantee the stability of the financial system. However, much regulation is often the result of a political process that may not be completely in line with the principles just outlined above.

References

Barroso, J.M. (2009) SPEECH/09/273 by EU President Barroso, Brussels, 27 May.

Basel Committee on Banking Supervision, see also http://www.bis.org/bcbs/

Basel Committee (2009) 'Sound stress testing principles issued by Basel Committee', 20 May 2009, see http://www.bis.org/press/p090520.htm

Brunnermeier, M., Crocket, A., Goodhart, C., Persaud, A.D. and Hyun, Shin (2009) 'The Fundamental Principles of Financial Regulation', Geneva Reports on the World Economy 11.

Duffie, D. (1996) 'Dynamic Asset Pricing Theory', New York: Princeton.

Elton, E. and Gruber, M. (1995) 'Modern Portfolio Theory and Investment Analysis', Fifth Edition, New York: John Wiley.

European Commission, Communication from the Commission to the European Parliament and the Council – A roadmap towards a Banking Union, COM (2012) 510 Final.

European Commission, Impact Assessment SEC (2011) 950 Final.

European Commission, Impact Assessment SEC (2011) 953 Final.

European Commission, Proposal for Directive (CRD IV), COM (2011) 453 Final.

European Commission, Proposal for a Regulation (on prudential requirements for credit institutions and investment firms), COM (2011) 0452.

Financial Stability Forum (2008) 'Report of the Financial Stability Forum on Enhancing Market and Institutional Resilience', 7 April.

Gerhardt, M. and Lannoo, K. (2011) Options for reforming deposit protection schemes in the EU, ECRI Policy Brief No. 4, March.

Huang, C. and Litzenberger, R.H. (1988) 'Foundations for Financial Economics', New York: Elsevier Science, Ltd.

SEC (2008) 'Summary Report of Issues Identified in the Commissions Staffs Examinations of Select Credit Rating Agencies'.

SEC Press Release 211 (2008) 'SEC Halts Short Selling of Financial Stocks to Protect Investors and Markets', see http://www.sec.gov/news/press/2008/2008-211.htm.

Weston, J.F., Mitchell, M.L. and Mulherin, J.H. (2004) 'Takeovers, Restructuring and Corporate Governance', Fourth edition, Prentice Hall.

16

Game Change in Asset Management

Karel Lannoo and Mirzha de Manuel Aramendía

16.1 Introduction

The context for the European asset management industry changed more drastically after the crisis than was initially thought. Claims that the industry did not cause the crisis did not contribute to seeing the new peaks emerging after dawn. On the contrary, they may still today prevent managers from realizing how much has changed: new rules concerning hedge funds and private equity, on which no European framework existed before; restrictions on remuneration; tighter rules for depositaries; a more aligned supervisory framework; and everything else that is still expected to appear out of the 'shadow banking' hat. But great opportunities are opening to the asset management industry as Europe seeks to reduce the reliance on bank funding and the pension gap.

In regulatory terms, the wider asset management industry as such does not exist. Rather, the rules applicable depend upon the particular license that the financial institution in question possesses. One may be licensed as a fund management company, a bank, an insurance undertaking, a pension fund, or a broker, which immediately raises the question of possible inconsistencies, duplication and arbitrage among regimes. For certain segments of the asset management business, there will be no question of which regulatory regime applies, as they unambiguously fall into one of the aforementioned categories; for others, however, the vertical regulatory framework does not lend itself well to the range of activities they undertake. The crisis has however not helped calls for more alignment along regimes; on the contrary, the vertical segmentation of the industry, for systemic and prudential reasons, seems to be appropriate.

This segmentation of the financial industry implies that the diversity across the EU of the institutional framework will continue to be with us for some time to come. The crisis has strengthened financial disintegration considerably, reducing the pressure for regulatory convergence, although asset allocation patterns may have become more aligned across countries. The differences in consumer preferences, cultural habits and institutional heritage will thus remain a fundamental part of the European financial markets for the fore-seeable future.

The introduction of the EU's alternative investment fund managers directive (AIFMD) should bring more EU-wide convergence to the regulation of the typical activities of asset managers: discretionary management, mandates and alternative investment funds. Hence, UCITS (undertakings for collective investments in transferable securities) remains the traditional investment fund regime, while a new pillar has been added for alternatives, meaning non-UCITS.

In this chapter, we will start with a review of the changes in the EU's asset management markets as a result of the crisis. A second part discusses the new regulatory framework for asset management and the challenges ahead. We focus primarily on the new alternative investment fund managers directive (AIFMD), the consolidation of the UCITS regime and its recent changes, and challenges ahead. We will make reference to the links with other regulatory frameworks, primarily Solvency II and the markets in financial instruments directive (MiFID) as necessary.

16.2   The asset management industry

The crisis fundamentally altered the face of the asset management industry, allowing the insurance industry to re-emerge as the leading player. Of the three traditional groups of institutional investors – investment funds, insurance companies and pension funds – the first has dominated the sector in terms of total asset since 2004. By the end of 2011, net assets under management by the European industry totalled €13.8 trillion, a sum that has remained the same since the end of 2007, when they totalled €13.6 trillion. Approximately half of this corresponds to mandates and half to investment funds – of which about 70% or €5 trillion are long-term UCITS, that is, UCITS excluding money market funds. By comparison, the insurers' investment portfolio has increased in value from €5.9 trillion in 2007 to an estimated €7.7 trillion in 2011 (of which over 80% is in life insurance), while assets in occupational (2nd pillar) pension funds surpassed €3 trillion in the same year.[1] The largest part of the investment portfolios of insurers and pension funds however is administered by asset managers, mainly as mandates, as reflected in Figure 16.1.

The dramatic decline in the European investment fund industry in 2008 was a reflection of the extraordinary events in financial markets following the bankruptcy of Lehman Brothers, with huge declines in global stock markets, big outflows of money from the financial system, and out of equity investment funds in particular. In the retail space, the loss of confidence in managers was

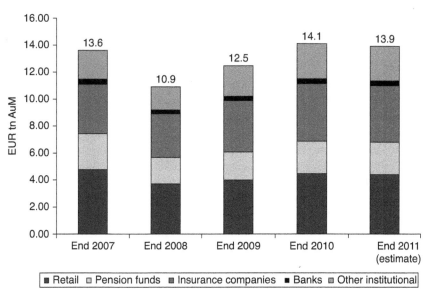

Figure 16.1 Total assets under management by client type in both investment funds and investment mandates managed by the European asset management industry
Sources: EFAMA and authors' own elaboration.

coupled with extended sovereign guarantees on bank deposits, prompting a flight to safety. This decline was prolonged in Europe as a result of the sovereign debt crisis, which led to a repatriation of assets and a return to the home bias, and seems only since the second half of 2012 to have started to attenuate. By comparison, the European insurance industry, which also manages long-term savings plans in life insurance products and group insurance plans, on its balance sheet, managed to consolidate its image as a truly long-term institutional investor. The asset management industry is striving to follow suit.

The growth of the European and US fund industry had been fairly comparable up until the crisis, but the recent decline was more pronounced in the EU, and the recovery in the US. Assets managed by the EU and US fund industry still amount to 69% of the global fund management industry (BCG, 2011).

Events in financial markets had a direct bearing on the investment fund industry, and on its future structure. The demise of Lehman Brothers revealed the uncertainty of holdings trapped in bankruptcy procedures and the nonmarket risks linked to the use of derivatives. Some banks had also made use of structured instruments (CDOs) to support guaranteed equity products. The large-scale fraud by Bernard Madoff, blown wide open by the end of 2008, was a further setback for the fund industry, which revealed the shortcomings prevalent in custody chains and their regulation, and the need for action at global level. Several European managers had invested in Madoff funds (mostly through funds of funds or feeder structures) but had not taken proper measures to ensure a complete separation between fund managers and depositaries, as required under UCITS. Industry and regulators then woke up to counterparty and custody risks in asset management.

The decline in the European fund industry emphasized even more the need for further consolidation, as the average size per fund declined. The average size of a UCITS today is ten times that of an average US mutual fund, although the top 10% largest funds concentrate 65% of assets (de Manuel and Lannoo, 2012). The sub-optimal average UCITS size brings about higher operational costs for investment management, a high total expense ratio (TER) and duplication of infrastructure. In this sense, the European asset management industry today still performs below its potential, the cost of which is passed on to the investor. The main causes are to be found in the high level of fragmentation, the absence among investors and firms of a European market concept and the remunerative *niche* markets that funds can target, exploiting differences in tax and regulatory regimes across Europe. The UCITS IV amendments, discussed below, address these challenges but only partially. Another revision of the directive (UCITS VI, not yet proposed) is expected to further remove barriers to market integration.

The long-term implications of the financial crisis for the fund industry remain unchanged. Too many funds were too closely managed or distributed by deposit-taking banks as an alternative savings instrument. Even today most funds are distributed by banks in Europe, a situation that raises questions in terms of competition and market structure. The situation prevails so despite the recent growth in passive and exchange-traded investing, the development of alternative distribution platforms and the forced sales of asset management subsidiaries by several banks in Europe, following the financial crisis and the conditions linked to state aid. Measures need to be elaborated to support the separation between banks and fund managers and to come to a more genuine application of the open architecture framework. This calls for, inter alia, a stricter application of conflict of interest rules, as enshrined in MiFID, but this is a moving objective. Furthermore, in particular, it raises the question whether the cost of investment advice needs to be fully separated from management fees, as is being implemented in the United Kingdom and the Netherlands.

16.3   The UCITS regime

UCITS accounts today for almost a third of global assets in traditional investment funds, a quarter of which are sourced outside Western Europe. With changes in the course of implementation and others still in the pipeline, the UCITS regime has reached a high degree of maturity, but at the same time complexity. UCITS IV allows greater market integration for the fund industry, UCITS V adds some elements of the AIFMD to UCITS, mainly as regards the separation between the depositary and fund manager, and the remuneration of fund managers. Amid growing recognition that the UCITS framework needs a full recast to achieve modernization and simplification, the European Commission launched a consultation in 2012. The future UCITS VI framework may take the form of a regulation and address the use of derivatives and indices, leverage limits and access to less-liquid asset classes.

The UCITS framework is probably one of the bright stories of European integration but the single market for UCITS funds remains evasive, given the lack of progress at EU level in addressing the distribution and infrastructure bottlenecks. Member states are adopting their own solutions, addressing in particular conflicts of interest in retail distribution, building sensible but divergent frameworks that act as barriers to the cross-border business. The situation is unlikely to be resolved unless EU standards were to converge to the highest national denominator.

The 1985 UCITS directive was the forerunner of a wave of EU rules governing the free provision of financial services across borders under home country rules. The directive introduced harmonized *product* regulation for investment funds that were allowed for cross-border sales in the EU (and the countries of the European Economic Area). It was followed in the early 1990s with directives defining the terms under which the banking, insurance and investment services sectors could 'passport' their *services* across the EU on the basis of authorization from their home state regulator (Appendix). The UCITS Directive was amended and expanded in 2002 and, later in 2009, to become more of a horizontal asset management directive to reflect the increasing convergence of the core sectors of the financial services industry. The last sector to undergo cross-border liberalization was pension funds in 2002. The directive on institutions for occupational retirement provision (IORP) has had limited success so far – there were only 84 cross-border IORPs in Europe in 2011 – and will be revised to incorporate risk-based supervision. In the meantime, the new wave of the financial services action plan (FSAP) had started to come into effect, most importantly with the market in financial instruments directive (MiFID). In 2012, the alternative investment fund managers directive (AIFMD) came to set the framework for all non-UCITS managers in the pursuit of a level-playing field and more transparency toward both supervisors and investors.

The UCITS framework itself has transformed over time. In 2002, key amendments expanded the scope of activities that were possible under the original UCITS directive. The so-called 'UCITS III' product directive widened the scope of eligible assets for funds, to include derivatives and indices, under certain conditions. It also facilitated new formats, such as funds of funds, money market funds, cash funds or index tracker funds. A second directive – the UCITS III management directive – detailed minimum standards, including the introduction of a minimum level of own funds to be held by the management company and broadened its permissible activities. It also introduced a simplified prospectus, the predecessor of today's key information documents (KIDs). The UCITS III directive granted the 'single license' to fund management companies in the broad sense of the word. It comprises not only the management of investment funds – the core services – but also other activities related to portfolio management, such as pension funds for individuals, investment advice and administration of investment funds, which are seen as noncore or ancillary.[2]

In 2009, at the deepest phase of the financial crisis, UCITS IV brought a further set of amendments, implemented in July 2011. These facilitated a genuine European passport for UCITS management companies, allowing for the separation between the location of the company and the jurisdiction where funds are registered. UCITS IV also facilitates the cross-border mergers of UCITS, which makes it possible to increase the average size of European funds. In the same vein, it allows for master-feeder structures, that before were specifically excluded due to concerns for portfolio diversification. Entity pooling should generate scale economies and thus contribute to a consolidation of the sector serving end-users. However, the uptake has been limited so far, since barriers remain, notably with respect to taxation. Finally, UCITS IV further eases cross-border marketing of UCITS by simplifying administrative procedures. The home supervisor notifies directly the host authorities, which can monitor commercial documents but cannot refuse access.

UCITS has also served as a laboratory for EU investor protection, in particular for disclosure rules. UCITS IV created the first EU standard format of summary pre-contractual disclosure. The 'key investor information document' or KIID was an important step forward in helping consumers choose and understand their purchases. It is currently being reviewed in the context of its extension to other (packaged) retail investment products (PRIPs). The new standard will help to compare UCITS with other investments such as unit-linked insurance policies, personal pensions and bank structured products, but the challenge of comparability should not be underestimated.

Yet, the investor protection credentials of UCITS suffered a great blow with the Madoff scandal. In response to it, the European Commission proposed a stricter separation between the depositary or custodian and the fund manager. Madoff revealed that some European asset managers had not properly applied the separation between manager and depositary, which is a strict obligation under UCITS, but also that the UCITS rules on deposits were only principle-based and had not been correctly implemented in several EU member states (ESMA, 2010). The issue is also that once certain derivative financial instruments are allowed to be used in UCITS, a 100% separate holding certainty is illusory since derivatives cannot be held in custody as transferable securities can. The draft UCITS V directive (proposed in July 2012) will bring the depositary rules in UCITS in line with those in the alternative investment fund managers directive (AIFMD).

The duties of fund depositaries in EU regulation may be boiled down to three: i) control the title of any assets received by the fund, ii) keep assets in custody or, where this is not possible, keep their records and iii) monitor cash flows and other oversight functions. The difference between *custody* and *record-keeping* is fundamental, given the different standards of responsibility that apply. Custody involves holding a security, either physically or electronically, while record-keeping only concerns taking note of the given right or contract. The AIFMD imposes strict liability for the loss of an asset kept in custody while liability in record-keeping arises in the case of negligence or intentional failure. The gist is in determining which assets can be *kept in custody* instead of *kept in record*. Only transferable securities, money market instruments and fund units capable of being held in an account in the name of the depository can be held in custody. Less clear cut is the situation arising in cases of collateral arrangements, securities lending and repos. The assets will exit custody only if there is a transfer of ownership away from the alternative fund manager. Therefore, one needs to look at each transaction. Indeed, the collateral directive distinguishes 'title transfer' and 'security' arrangements – under a security arrangement there is no transfer of title so the assets remain in custody. But without harmonized securities and bankruptcy laws, problems will continue to arise in practice. The key difference between the depositary rules for UCITS and AIFs will lie in the ability of (professional) investors in AIFs to renounce some of the guarantees offered by the directive (in relation to the restitution of lost assets) in a limited number of circumstances, catering in particular for investments in emerging economies.

16.4   Creating an EU regime for 'alternative' funds

The financial crisis crystallized the consensus that European and global regulation of alternative funds was necessary. Before 2008, regulatory approaches varied across European jurisdictions, from registration-only to more detailed frameworks. The crisis changed this view rapidly, and although initially much politicized and strongly contested by the industry, the new regime is now seen as an opportunity for business growth. And as for UCITS, a single passport now exists for alternative fund managers in the EU, albeit restricted to professional clients.

The London G-20 summit (April 2009) agreed that 'all systemically important financial institutions, markets and instruments should be subject to an appropriate degree of regulation and oversight.' Leaders of the world's main economies intended to put an end to regulatory arbitrage, seen to be one of the drivers of the crisis. The G-20 stated that hedge funds and other asset managers should be registered and disclose information about their leverage to supervisors. In addition, they should be subject to effective risk management.

The proposal for an EU directive on alternative investment fund managers (AIFMD) was under preparation before the crisis and was published very soon after the London G-20. The problem was to find a comprehensive way of regulating the sector, given its diversity and the risk of relocation to off-shore jurisdictions. The EU directive applies to managers of alternative investment funds – wherever they are registered – and formally not to the funds. In contrast with UCITS, the AIFMD does not contain product structuring rules, such as restrictions on eligible assets, issuer concentration or leverage limits. In this sense, and by adding a reciprocity provision, the EU ensures that the whole nonharmonized fund sector that falls outside the scope of the UCITS directive is covered, including also private equity, commodity and real estate funds. Managers of funds domiciled in third countries will be able to benefit from the EU passport after an uncertain transition period, provided they comply with the directive (de Manuel and Lannoo, 2012, p. 95 and Annex 2).

The AIFMD directive follows to a great extent the spirit of the provisions in UCITS and the markets in financial instruments directive (MiFID) on the conduct of business, organizational, reporting and prudential requirements. The directive added elements that have come up in the crisis, such as the need for appropriate liquidity management, strict segregation of assets, and additional reporting requirements for highly-leveraged funds. It adopts a tough stance on delegation and outsourcing to limit circumvention.

The AIFMD applies a partial exemption to managers with under €100 million in assets under management or €500 million if investors are locked-in for five years and in the absence of leverage. Managers under this threshold will be requested to register and provide simplified reporting to authorities to enable more effective financial stability oversight. The transparency threshold for private equity managers with stakes in nonlisted companies is 10% for disclosure to competent authorities and over 50% of voting rights for disclosure to other shareholders.

Although intensely criticized by the industry, which claimed it would lead to high costs for investors and a flight of fund activities out of the EU, the directive creates a single license for non-UCITS funds and their managers in the EU, which did not exist before. In sum, the AIFMD represents a consistent framework for the regulation of the wider asset management industry from a prudential policy perspective by introducing minimum common rules. In particular, it addresses: i) prudential oversight, ii) leverage and pro-cyclicality, iii) maturity and liquidity transformation and iv) links with the banking system. It is also aimed at improving transparency and service obligations toward professional investors but relies on the buy-side prudential rules to enforce full transparency on the underlying (e.g., the look-through principle in Solvency II). More clarity within the non-UCITS sector will benefit users, supervisors and the industry as well.

16.5   Money market funds

Money market funds (MMFs) were by most accounts the sector of the asset management industry worst affected by the financial crisis. The run on US money market funds in 2008 demonstrated not only their importance for the economy but also the lack of any specific EU framework for MMFs other than UCITS. Divergent national requirements allowed the use of the denomination 'money market' for funds with stable and fluctuating net asset values (NAVs), funds investing in longer maturities and even funds investing in nonmoney market instruments (usually called cash+funds). In stark contrast, US MMFs were narrowly defined by the Investment Company Act of 1940 (2a-7 rule) as stable-NAVs complying with specific requirements on credit quality and maturity, among others.

The situation was addressed by the European Securities and Markets Authority (ESMA), the successor of the former Committee of European Securities Regulators (CESR), in 2010 by issuing guidelines on the common definition of MMFs in the EU. The guidelines introduce two categories of money market funds: i) *short-term MMFs* subject to the same maturity constraints as MMFs in the US, after the 2010 revision of 2a-7 rule; and ii) *MMFs* invested in longer-term securities under a fluctuating NAV.

Stable-NAV MMFs are at the centre of the international discussions on 'shadow banking' led by the Financial Stability Board (FSB). It is proposed that the stable-NAV MMFs would either have to provide sufficient capital to back their 'promise' of liquidity at face value or otherwise completely abandon such a 'promise' and move into fluctuating NAVs. Fierce opposition by the industry, coupled with the fear of placing further stress on money markets in the currently weak economic circumstances, have frustrated reform by the US Securities and Exchange Commission (SEC) so far. The stable NAVs associated with US MMFs is not prevalent in Europe where even 'short-term MMFs' tend to have fluctuating NAVs. But the EU is likely to lead action in this front by banning stable-NAV MMFs, as the pressure mounts on the European Commission to open the debate and bring the ESMA (CESR) guidelines into law.

16.6   The interaction with MiFID

Whereas UCITS strictly speaking regulates products and the AIFMD managers, the markets in financial instruments directive (MiFID) regulates investment services, affecting the wider asset management industry, except the insurance sector. Adopted in 2004, MiFID updates and replaces the 1993 investment services directive (ISD). It allows for the free provision of investment services all over the EU with a single license, subject to conduct-of-business and organizational provisions. The problem for the industry is to deal with the interaction between these three pieces of legislation.

MiFID brought more competition to exchanges in equity trading, by abolishing their monopoly, and through the introduction of alternative trading facilities. In return, it imposed stricter requirements on firms in securities transactions, through best execution, client categorization (suitability and appropriateness test), conflict of interest and transaction reporting requirements, which have been harmonized to a high degree. These measures reduced transaction costs, but the benefits to users have so far failed to materialize (Valiante and Lannoo, 2011).

Conduct-of-business rules in MiFID apply to asset managers when they provide discretionary asset management and investment advice, as well as to the providers of back-office services such as custody and administration. MiFID applies therefore to product originators, in this instance fund managers, to the extent that they also carry out the distribution of their products. These rules are, above all: organizational requirements, in particular regarding conflicts of interest; and conduct-of-business obligations, in particular client suitability and best execution.

An important issue for the fund management industry is the regime for inducements under MiFID. Inducements are payments by an investment firm of a fee, commission or non-monetary benefit that could place the firm in a situation where it would not be acting in compliance with the MiFID principle of 'acting honestly, fairly and professionally in accordance with the best interest of clients'. The current MiFID rules require distributors to demonstrate that inducements paid by the originator do not result in bias and facilitate an enhanced service for customers. The difficulties to enforce this approach in practice are driving the revision of the directive discussed below.

In effect, conflict of interest provisions create difficulties for widely accepted distribution practices in the fund management industry, namely the retrocession of fees from originators to distributors. In some instances product providers and intermediaries may be contemplating significant fees as a condition for the products being placed on the distributor's panel or recommended list. Such fees are unconnected with, and additional to, conventional commissions which are paid on the sale of particular products. Such fees are thus incompatible with the fundamental principle that a firm must not conduct business under arrangements in conflict with its fiduciary duty to its customers.

Following the financial crisis, some aspects of MiFID were opened for review in 2011. This review concerned the extension of the pre-trade price transparency provisions to the non-equity markets, particularly bond and derivatives markets and the clarification of the rules applicable to in-house matching by investment banks ('dark pools'). To better ensure accurate implementation, these elements will be part of a regulation (MiFIR), whereas the organizational and conduct-of-business rules for trading platforms, brokers and data vendors are part of an update to the directive (MiFID II). The most important change thereby is tighter rules for investment advice in order to better protect investors in the sale of complex financial products. Clients should be able to assess how 'independent' the financial advice they are receiving is and fees must be unbundled.

The proposed label for independent advisers and the disclosure of the costs linked to distribution should help investors make more informed decisions but the questions of quality of advice and professional standards remain unaddressed. Some member states have adopted bolder structural solutions to conflicts of interest in distribution (notably banning inducements) but EU legislation is unlikely to follow suit. In the absence of structural solutions, much will depend on the effective application of the directive in practice. Many blame poor supervision for the dismal record of MiFID I in improving investor protection. The new supervisory setup, discussed below, is expected to improve the situation.

MiFID II is also called to address the increasing complexity of some UCITS funds, following the expansion of eligible assets and practices enabled by UCITS III in 2009. Under MiFID I, all UCITS benefit from a blank categorization as 'non-complex' financial instruments. This means that UCITS can be sold without any intermediary assessment of the adequacy of the product to the individual investor. This so-called 'execution only' regime is an exception to the generally applicable MiFID suitability and appropriateness tests. The growing complexity of UCITS products has challenged this exception: The evidence that investors do not understand nonmarket risks (such as counterparty risk) embedded in the use of derivatives calls for a cautionary approach in the sale process. Most retail investors purchasing an 'investment fund' still expect to hold the underlying securities and would need professional advice to understand, for instance, the benefits and risks of accessing the returns of the same basket of securities through a total return swap. But the question remains whether the issue should be tackled by reforming MiFID or UCITS itself.

Product proliferation within UCITS has rendered its future uncertain, in particular after the adoption of the alternative investment fund managers directive (AIFMD). Much bespoke brand fragmentation is already a reality. Not only do markets speak of 'alternative UCITS' but the UCITS rules themselves distinguish categories of UCITS such as sophisticated, structured, exchange-traded and money market. The introduction of the AIFMD as a horizontal legislation for all non-UCITS managers has increased the pressure to restrict the UCITS brand to traditional practices.

16.7   Impact of the changing supervisory setup

The financial crisis finally made Europeans realize that the form of supervisory cooperation they had was not up to their degree of market integration. Under the new setup, supervision is much more coordinated, with the implementation of conduct-of-business rules being monitored by the European Securities Markets Authority (ESMA), the successor of CESR, and prudential control of banks placed almost entirely in the hands of the European Central Bank (ECB) from 2014 onwards under the single supervisory mechanism (SSM). How the interaction between both will work in the future remains to be seen.

The financial crisis revealed serious shortcomings in the oversight of financial markets, which initially led to the recommendations contained in the 2009 de Larosière report, and later in 2012 to the calls for a full banking union. The de Larosière report created the European System of Financial Supervisors (ESFS), comprising three functional authorities covering banking, insurance and securities markets, and a European Systemic Risk Board (ESRB), administered by the ECB. These authorities have the formal responsibility to enforce EU rules and supervise its application by national supervisors, and should thus contribute to eliminate some of the problems raised above. The end-goal is to have a single rulebook, which means that exactly the same rules will apply in all member states across the Union. A single rulebook is also the objective of the ECB's single supervisory mechanism, although it is too early to judge how this will work in practice.

In the field of asset management, the responsibilities reside clearly in the field of ESMA, whose role has not been questioned as a result of the sovereign crisis. ESMA has the formal responsibility to mediate between supervisory authorities, and to delegate supervisory powers in the supervision of fund managers, for example. The role of ESMA appears of particular importance in providing technical guidance to the European Commission to implement the post-crisis legislation and as a standard setter and supervisor of coordination mechanisms, with powers of direct intervention only in exceptional circumstances.

16.8   Towards a horizontal asset management regime

A comparison of various national regimes within the EU covering retail investment products reveals an immense diversity, with a patchwork of different obligations on distributors regarding disclosure and investor protection, different forms of prudential supervision and a high degree of variation in marketing and advertising rules (Appendix 1, see Table 16.1). The major challenge for the years to come is to work out a coherent regime for retail investment products across sectors at EU level. The crisis has however reinforced the tendency for the fragmentation of the different regimes. The

2012 initiative on packaged retail investment products (PRIPs) is expected to level the playing field from the perspective of distribution but abstains from otherwise imposing a more comparable structure.

From a prudential perspective, diverse business models and promises to investors warrant distinct treatment. Guaranteed insurance products are to be based on capital requirements (per Solvency II) while nonguaranteed products, where the full market risk falls on the investor, barely need any capital backing. Examples of the latter are investment funds and defined contribution pensions. Defined benefit pensions and hybrid arrangements will be subject to distinct rules that will take into account the promises made to beneficiaries and the steering mechanisms available, including the ability to raise contributions, cut benefits or rely on sponsor support. These changes will be operated under a revised directive on institutions for occupational retirement provision (IORPs). No framework exists yet in Europe for third-pillar pensions, but the European Commission asked EIOPA in 2012 to deliver technical advice by 2015 – a process on which the future of the European asset management industry largely depends.

Product structuring and authorization rules remain very much fragmented despite the fact that the similar economic functions of retail products called for a consistent approach. Today, unit-linked insurance products are not subject to EU rules on structuring while bank structured products are even less regulated. The introduction into MiFID II of so-called 'suitability at product design' could provide the foundation for a uniform framework based on the responsibility of senior management to approve the policy governing the services and products offered by the firm, in accordance with the characteristics and needs of the clients to whom the products will be offered or provided (see Commission proposal). The extension of this principle to insurance (in the insurance mediation directive) and its practical implementation remain however uncertain at this stage.

As for distribution, the level of mandatory fiduciary care afforded to retail investors as well as the degree of supervision undertaken by regulatory authorities may vary depending on the distribution channel through which they access investment products, even if, in terms of outcomes or payoff profiles, the products are broadly similar. Pre-contractual disclosure will be harmonized in the form of key investor documents (KID) for investment funds, unit-linked insurance policies, structured products and third-pillar retirement schemes (de Manuel, 2012b). Plain vanilla securities have to comply with the prospectus directive, which will sooner or later be reconciled with the KID standard. Sales practices will be governed by MiFID II except for unit-linked insurance products, which will remain under the insurance mediation directive (IMD). Rather than creating a single framework on sales practices superseding both MiFID and IMD, the EU has chosen to keep both frameworks alive and separate, albeit converging. As for private placements, MiFID will continue to apply to the

Table 16.1   EU regulatory framework for retail investment products (long-term)

	UCITS	Non-UCITS (AIFs)	Life insurance (also unit-linked)	Listed security	Structured products
Marketing and selling practices	MiFID UCITS	MiFID AIFMD	IMD	MiFID	MiFID
			Distance Marketing of Financial Services Directive		
Disclosure	– PRIPs – UCITS – MiFID	– PRIPs (retail) – AIFMD – MiFID	– PRIPs – Solvency II – IMD	– PRIPs (?) – Prospectus directive	– PRIPs – MiFID
Asset allocation	– UCITS		– UCITS (unit-linked)		
Prudential	– UCITS	– AIFMD	– Solvency II		– CRD

Source: Authors' own elaboration.

extent that the securities are placed via investment firms in the sense of the directive (banks, brokers or financial advisers).

In view of the above, the framework for investment products remains too complex even for an informed investor. Some products are tightly regulated at EU level, whereas for others, there is only general service level regulation. The problems raised by the interaction of a product directive (UCITS) with the rest of the framework (not based on product rules) indicates that many questions remain to be answered, possibly by developing a strong set of product-to-market principles and supervision, based on the responsibility of the originator to design products generally suitable for the investors they target, as discussed above.

An additional complexity is added to the exercise by the fact that many constituent elements of the retail investment product regime are shared competences between the EU, the member states and the industry, which militates against the emergence of a coherent framework. Properly addressing these concerns would probably require the creation of a stand-alone regulation to cover the distribution of all investment products, mechanisms to further ensure consistency of national implementation of EU legislation, and the elaboration of pan-European industry codes of conduct.

16.9   Conclusion

A well-developed regulatory framework is in place for the asset management industry in the European Union. Two basic regimes are emerging, one for retail investment products under UCITS, and the second under the AIFMD for professional investors. This has levelled the playing field between both. At the same time, the more integrated EU supervisory structure should lead to a stricter enforcement of rules, most notably with regard to the conduct-of-business rules enshrined in MiFID. But much still remains to be done to bring full coherence to these frameworks.

Post-crisis, the challenges for the industry and policymakers are to restore confidence and allow a re-diversification of the savings of households. The 2008 market turmoil, coupled with the increase of deposit guarantees by governments and the bail-out of the banking system pushed more savings towards banks. This is however an unhealthy situation, as much for households as for the economy as a whole, since the transfer of savings to productive investments is hindered. The asset management industry strives today to deliver long-term value propositions to investors, looking beyond UCITS into balanced funds and retirement savings.

In the medium to long run, the objective should be to create a more coherent framework for the retail investment product regime across sectors and for long-term investments. Too many differences remain in the rules applicable to the fund business and other product originators despite the recent initiatives. This creates distortions of competition, but leads also to inefficiencies and maintains the vertical structure of the financial industry as we know it today. A more open architecture of the financial industry should be the imperative across the board, in the interest of consumers and the public at large.

Appendix Stylized overview of selected aspects in the EU financial services directives

	Capital requirements directive (CRD I – IV)	Solvency II	Pension funds directive (IORP)	MiFID I	UCITS III and IV	Alternative investment funds managers (AIFs)
Initial capital	– Minimum €5 million	– Minimum capital requirement or MCR	– Capital depends on the sort of guarantee (if any) provided to beneficiaries and the presence of steering mechanisms (under upcoming revision of directive)	– Minimum €125,000, may be reduced to €50,000 for local firms or €25,000 for investment advisers (Directive 2006/49/EC)	– €125,000 per management company – Plus 0.02% of AuM exceeding €250m – Max. €10m capital	– €300,000 for internally managed AIFM or €125,000 for externally managed AIFM + – Plus 0.02% of AuM exceeding €250m – Max. €10m capital
Additional capital requirements	– Minimum 8% of risk-weighted assets (Basel Accord) or VAR for trading book (under review)	– Solvency capital requirement of SCR – Risk-based solvency charges based on standard formula or approved internal models	– Risk-based solvency charges (under upcoming revision of directive)	– Function of trading book (Directive 2006/49/EC, under review)	– Capital requirement shall never be less than required under Art. 21 of Directive 2006/49/EC	– Capital requirement shall never be less than required under Art. 21 of Directive 2006/49/EC
Permissible activities (non-exhaustive, only when related to asset management)	– Portfolio management, safekeeping and administration of securities, trading in and underwriting of securities	– Life insurance (including group insurance) – Nonlife insurance (large and mass risk)	– Management and investment of funded occupational pension schemes	– Individual portfolio management, securities brokerage and order execution activities	– Management of investment funds – Discretionary asset management (including pension funds)	– Management and marketing of non-UCITS – EU AIFMs – Non-EU AIFMs if they manage an EU AIF or market a non-EU AIF in EU

Continued

	Capital requirements directive (CRD I – IV)	Solvency II	Pension funds directive (IORP)	MiFID I	UCITS III and IV	Alternative investment funds managers (AIFs)
					– Investment advice – Safekeeping (custody) and administration of UCITS	
Asset allocation	– Holdings in non-financial institutions limited to 60% of own funds, and 15% for a single holding – Large credit exposures to single clients are limited to 800% of own funds and 25% for a single exposure	– Quantitative restrictions abolished by Solvency II, and replaced by a risk-based regime	– Investment limits based on minimum harmonization – Member states may set more stringent rules for institutions active on their territory, but within certain limits – Investment in sponsoring undertaking is limited to 5% of the technical provisions	– Rules on large exposures	– <10% of assets in single security, except for public debt, and <40% for single investments of 5% – <10% nonlisted securities – < 10% of same body for money market instruments, and <20% for investments in single other funds and deposits with credit institutions – Special rules for master-feeder structures	– No requirements – Liquidity towards investors in line with liquidity of underlying – Special reporting requirements to supervisors for certain leveraged AIFs
Conduct of business	– Host country rules on advertising and 'general good'	– Responsibility and governance – Conflicts of interest	– Conflicts of interest – Host country social and labour rules	– Harmonized, but host country in charge of enforcement of rules for branches	– Host-country conduct-of-business rules (unless subject to MiFID rules for noncore);	– Conflict of interest – Risk and portfolio management functions

	Banking	Insurance	Pensions	Investment services	UCITS	Alternative investment funds
Disclosure	– Pillar III	– Conduct of business specific to life and nonlife activities – Valuation – Public disclosure – Disclosure to supervisors – Disclosure to clients	– Disclosure of investment policies, risk and accrued benefits to fund members	– Extensive, full price transparency (for equity securities), unbundling of cost of transactions	– Key Investor Information (KII)	– Host country advertising and marketing rules – Annual report, disclosure of investment strategy, risk management, depository, fees and charges – Reporting to authorities – Controlling stake notification rules – Delegation and outsourcing – Valuation – Remuneration
Investor compensation	– Deposit guarantee directive	– Insurance guarantee fund		– Investor compensation schemes directive	– Investor compensation schemes (depending upon national implementation)	– Not applicable
Final date for implementation	– 2014	– New framework (Solvency II) by 2014	– 2004	– November 2007	– July 2011 (UCITS IV)	– July 2013
Technical adaptations	– European Banking Committee (EBC), limited	– European Insurance and Occupational Pensions Committee, limited	– European Insurance and Occupational Pensions Committee, limited	– European Securities Committee (ESC), extensive	– European Securities Committee (ESC), limited	– European Securities Committee (ESC), extensive

Sources: Authors.

Notes

1. Other forms of portfolio management, i.e., management of pension fund portfolios or those of individuals, are presented as a form of derogation from the central objective of the directive, which is the management of investment funds as authorized under the directive (Art. 5).
2. A feeder UCITS is a UCITS or an investment compartment thereof that invests at least 85% of its assets in one other UCITS, called the master UCITS.

References

BCG (2011) *Global Asset Management 2011: Building on Success*. Boston: Boston Consulting Group.

Casey, J-P. and Lannoo, K. (2009) *Pouring old wine in new skins? UCITS and Asset Management after MiFID*, Centre for European Policy Studies, Brussels.

de Larosière, J., Balcerowicz, L., Issing, O., Masera, R., Carthy, C.M., Nyberg, L. Pérez, J. et al. (2009) *Report of the High-Level Group on Financial Supervision in the EU*, European Commission, Brussels.

de Manuel Aramendía, M.J. (2013) *Prepare for profound AIFMD changes, Financial Times*, 7 January 2013, London.

de Manuel Aramendía, M.J. (2012a) *Clues in shadow banking and UCITS debates, Financial Times*, 10 September, London.

de Manuel Aramendía, M.J. (2012b) *Will the PRIPs' KID live up to its promise to protect investors?* ECMI Commentaries, 06 July, European Capital Markets Institute – Centre for European Policy Studies, Brussels.

de Manuel Aramendía, M.J. (2010) *Third Country Rules for Alternative Investments: Passport flexibility comes at a price*, ECMI Commentaries, 16 December, European Capital Markets Institute – Centre for European Policy Studies, Brussels.

de Manuel Aramendía, M.J. and Lannoo, K. (2012) *Rethinking Asset Management: From Financial Stability to Investor Protection and Economic Growth*, CEPS Task Force Reports, 19 April, European Capital Markets Institute – Centre for European Policy Studies, Brussels.

ECB (2011) Statistical Data Warehouse, European Central Bank, Frankfurt.

EFAMA (2011) *Asset Management in Europe: Facts and Figures*, European Fund and Asset Management Association, Brussels.

EIWG (European Investors Working Group) (2010) 'Restoring Investor Confidence in European Capital Markets', European Capital Markets Institute (ECMI), Brussels.

ESMA (2009) *Guidelines on a Common Definition of European Money Market Funds*, CESR/10–049, European Securities and Markets Authority, Paris.

ESMA (2010) Mapping of duties and liabilities of UCITS depositaries, CESR/09–175, European Securities and Markets Authority, Paris.

ESMA (2012) Guidelines on ETFs and other UCITS Issues, ESMA 2012/474, European Securities and Markets Authority, Paris.

European Commission (2006) *White Paper on Enhancing the Single Market Framework for Investment Funds*, COM (2006) 686 final, European Commission, Brussels.

European Commission (2009) *Communication on Packaged Retail Investment Products*, COM (2009) 204 final, European Commission, Brussels.

European Commission (2012a) *Proposal for a Directive amending Directive 2009/65/EC on the coordination of laws, regulations and administrative provisions relating to undertakings for collective investment in transferable securities (UCITS) as regards depositary func-tions, remuneration policies and sanctions* (UCITS V), COM(2012) 350 final, European Commission, Brussels.

European Commission (2012b) *Consultation on Undertakings for Collective Investment in Transferable Securities (UCITS) with respect to Product Rules, Liquidity Management, Depositary, Money Market Funds and Long-term Investments.* 26 July 2012, European Commission, Brussels.

European Union (2011) *Directive on Alternative Investment Fund Managers*, 2011/61/EU, Brussels.

FSA (2009) *Distribution of retail investments: Delivering the RDR.* Consultation Paper 09/18, Financial Services Authority, London.

FSB (2011a) *Shadow Banking: Scoping the Issues.* Financial Stability Board, Basel.

FSB (2011b) *Shadow Banking: Strengthening Oversight and Regulation. October.* Financial Stability Board, Basel.

ICI (2011) *Investment Company Fact Book.* Investment Company Institute, Washington, D.C.

Insurance Europe (2012) *The European Life Insurance Market in 2010.* European Insurance and Reinsurance Federation, Brussels.

Moody's (2010) *Sponsor Support Key to Money Market Funds.* Moody's Investor Service.

OECD (2011) 'Fostering Long-term Investment and Economic Growth: A Long-term Investor's View', *Financial Market Trends,* (1): 1–4, Organisation for Economic Co-operation and Development, Paris.

OEE (2011) *The Importance of Asset Management to the European Economy.* Observatoire de l'Eparge Européene, Paris.

PWGFM (2010) *Money Market Fund Reform Options.* US President's Working Group on Financial Markets.

SEC (2011) *Use of Derivatives by Investment Companies Under the Investment Company Act of 1940.* Securities and Exchange Commission, Release No. IC-29776, File No. S7–33–11, Washington, D.C.

Valiante, D. and Lannoo, K. (2011) *MiFID 2.0 Casting New Light on Europe's Capital Markets.* Centre for European Policy Studies, Brussels.

17
The Asset Manager's Guide to Sustainable Regulatory Advantage

Anders Bidsted Andersen and Carsten Kunkel

17.1   Introduction

Regulatory changes are possibly the greatest source of change in the asset management industry today. Regulatory-driven legislation is multiplying continuously, with the scope of regulatory changes extending deep into system infrastructures and operational processes. The operational impact is significant: the cumulative projected two-year IT spending for implementing major regulatory initiatives for buy- and sell-side institutions worldwide is estimated to be in the region of $11–15 billion.[1]

Driven by a legislative offensive in the tailwind of the 2006–09 financial crisis, these immense changes and enforced processing and system adaptations by industry incumbents make a clear statement that commitment to compliance must be continuous. On the market-side, most companies are feeling the hot breath of regulatory pressure: a survey among 1,330 CEOs in 68 countries across the globe showed that more than 900 of the polled CEOs (or 69%) are concerned that their growth prospects are threatened by over-regulation.[2]

The pressing importance of this challenge was further illustrated by the prioritization of topics at the latest meeting of the World Economic Forum in January 2013, where addressing weaknesses in the international financial system and navigating regulatory environments while pursuing growth opportunities were at the top of the global and industry agenda.

For the asset management industry, the key to maintaining and increasing competitive advantage in these difficult conditions is to maintain an agile business infrastructure, with effective change management covering organizational and operational structure, as well as supporting systems. With this chapter, we explore strategic opportunities for asset managers to obtain operational gains from a timely and cost-efficient adaptation of regulatory changes.

The ambition is to capture value through:

- shorter time-to-market solutions;
- avoiding opportunity costs associated with passivity;
- focusing attention where it matters during the processing of regulatory initiatives;
- increased agility to compete with world-class competitors in today's global marketplace.

In a nutshell, it is our objective with this chapter to provide concrete opportunities for readers to leverage competitive advantage from a regulatory approach that is proactive.

17.2   A history of regulation

We have compiled the following brief history of regulation to offer readers an overview of some of the events we think were instrumental in the progressive regulatory evolution driving major changes through the entire financial services industry.

In this section, we provide accounts of the meta-view of the deregulation and lowering of trading barriers in the global free-trade zones, cycles of regulation and deregulation in the European financial markets and a chronological review of the major drivers and events characterizing the latest global financial crisis.

17.2.1   From national to supranational regulation

The second half of the 20th century was dominated by a process of lowering hurdles in goods trading and cash transfers in order to reach a state of free trade. This process began with bi-lateral or regional free trade zones, like the North American Free Trade Agreement (NAFTA) in North America, the European Union (EU) and the European Free Trade Association (EFTA) in Europe, and the Southern Common Market (Mercosur) in Southern America.[3, 4, 5]

At the same time, it became clear that regulation of supranational markets could not be performed on a national level only. Consequently, regulatory moves for entire markets were initiated on a regional or global level. Examples here are banking regulation introduced by the Bank for International Settlements (BIS) in the way of the Basel accords, or the worldwide drive to regulate the international derivatives markets as initiated by the G20 summit in Pittsburgh in September 2009.

17.2.2   The cycles of decreasing and increasing regulation

Historically, the European financial markets have been regulated very differently on a national level. The process of harmonization in the EU has resulted in a continuous deregulation in all member states over the late 1980s and 1990s. This is especially visible when looking at the investment fund market in Europe, which began to be regulated on a pan-European level in 1985, with the publication of the original Directive on Undertakings for Collective Investment in Transferable Securities (UCITS).[6]

UCITS regulation has evolved over the past 30 years, with further steps in the form of UCITS III Directives (2001/107/EC and 2001/108/EC) and UCITS IV Directive (2009/65/EC), to reach the point where UCITS-regulated funds today are allowed to invest in a broad range of financial products using different management approaches, including in recent years the opportunity to wrap hedge-fund strategies into UCITS funds, known as 'NewCITS'.

The financial crisis and public scandals, such as the Madoff fraud scandal in 2008, were motivating factors in the conclusion that some unregulated fund types should be made subject to common European regulation, paving the way for the consultation process leading to the Directive on Alternative Investment Fund Managers (AIFMD).[7] Lately, the European Securities and Markets Authority (ESMA) has also issued guidelines clarifying previously discussed questions, such as requirements for collateral covering counterparty risk in OTC derivative positions, thereby taking concrete action to reduce risk in the market.

17.2.3   The RNA sequence of financial disruption

Comparing the global financial crisis of 2006–09 to that of 1907–09, an article by Professor Robert F. Bruner concludes by stating: 'There is no "silver bullet", single explanation, for financial crises. The thoughtful person must embrace a variety of factors explaining crises.'[8]

However, looking into the chain of events leading up to the actual 'financial dislocation', as Bruner describes it in his article, it is possible to shed some light on the main motives, initiatives, events and corporate and investor behavior, which – if not giving rise to – then at least accelerated the events that eventually produced the dislocation. Observing the timeline, it also describes the rise and fall of investment banking.

We start our account of events in 1980, with the landslide victory for US Republican President Ronald Reagan, who started his presidency amid the full-blown stagflation that his Democrat predecessor Jimmy Carter had tried to fight without success.

Deregulation 1980–2005

In 1980, US Congress passed the Depository Institutions Deregulation and Monetary Control Act (DIDMCA), which effectively removed caps on interest payments for depositors, created competition for deposits and motivated banks to look for assets with higher returns. Two years on in 1982, DIDMCA was expanded with another initiative in the form of the Alternative Mortgage Transaction Parity Act (AMTPA), which gave mortgage-engineering free and spurred new loan types, such as balloon payments, interest-only and adjustable-rate mortgages (ARMs), which allowed unpaid interest to be added to the loan principal.[9] In the period from the 1980s to the 2000s, deregulation of credit/ debt ratings rolled through the financial industry, rating agencies replaced government regulators, and capital requirements were now based on security ratings by Fitch, S&P and Moody's, all of whom were facing incentives to do both and the risks of doing so.

In 1999, the Glass-Steagall Act of 1933 was partly repealed by the Gramm-Leach-Bliley Act (GLB), which enabled deposit-taking banks to engage in investment activities and removed the barrier between bank savings and investment holdings. In 2001, after incumbent US President George Bush signed the third-largest tax cut in US history, ARMs lowered barriers to capital for borrowers. Next door, investment bankers bundled subprime ARMs into residential mortgage-backed securities (RMBS) products with a higher debt rating and where the risk mark-up on the interest rate was lower. Securitization made it virtually impossible to value the assets that backed the securities, which in turn increased the products' sensitivity to variation in values of residential properties bundled into the RBMSs.

The securitized loan market became increasingly liquid, and whipped-up demand was needed to absorb the liquidity. Requirements for borrowers were reduced with new and more liberal credit ratings (like 'Stated Income') and with borrowers allowed to self-adjust credit approval by stating income without any verification, with the result that predatory lending began to flourish. In one of the first cases of predatory lending in 2005, Ameriquest, the largest US subprime lender, set aside $325 million for attorney-general investigations in 30 US states.

Collapse of the credit market 2006–2009

In this period, the crisis began to speed along at full throttle. In 2006, Ameriquest Mortgage closed all its retail offices and shifted loan business to mortgage brokers. A significant driver of the financing motor was the securitization of residential mortgages, which were packaged and sold as mortgage-backed securities (MBSs). Also in 2006, after a five-year legislative process, US Congress increased liquidity in the market by passing the Financial Services Regulatory Relief Act, which allowed interest payments on Federal Reserve Bank balances, opened the possibility of lowering required reserve ratios for transaction accounts, and allowed member institutions 'to count as reserves the deposits in other banks that are "passed through" by those banks to the Federal Reserve as required reserve requirements.'[10] The Relief Act effectively lowered the minimum capital requirements for banks and and thereby increased lending capacity with the same capital requirements.

Late in 2006, US house prices began to fall. Speculators and risky borrowers began to default on their payments in rising numbers, the buy–sell house price spread went negative for many home owners, illiquidity made many miss their mortgage payments and forced them into selling at a loss. This drained liquidity out of the market and induced a snowball effect with mounting failures and losses in the first half of 2007. As the snowball effect on subprime mortgages grew larger, demand for securitization dried up, credit ratings were downgraded, and funds and asset managers specializing in MBSs began to close down. The effects backfired through the feeding channels from the investment banks to the commercial banks, and in the summer and fall of 2007, commercial banks began to report large write-offs on loans and the closing of special subprime investment vehicles. This triggered the first real bank run on Northern Rock in the UK, and recession in the US was officially announced.

Toward the end of that year, industry pressure increased exponentially and in January 2008, US Congress passed a stimulus package. In February, the first real 'too-big-to-fail' collective rescue of mortgage insurer AMBAC was executed by a group of banks; in March 2008, Bear Sterns had to seek cover under the wings of the Federal Reserve Bank of New York and was subsequently sold to JPMorgan Chase. In April, Citigroup, Wachovia and Washington Mutual all had to start raising external capital from investors. Over the summer of 2008, MBIA and AMBAC's ratings were downgraded, and the SEC intervened actively to relieve pressures on Fannie Mae and Freddie Mac, while Californian IndyMac was seized by the Federal Deposit Insurance Corporation.

In August and September 2008, the crisis escalated with a liquidity freeze, when banks started fleeing the inter-corporate loan market due to fears of solvency risk, and this effectively shut down the credit market. The US government seized direct control of Fannie Mae and Freddie Mac, and Lehman Brothers declared bankruptcy, which sent an important signal to the market as to what could happen without intervention. The message was delivered and received, fears spread, market confidence dropped, and expectations and thus market values plummeted. A wave of emergency consolidations rolled through investment banking, emergency loans were administered, and in late September 2008, the two large remaining independent US investment banks, Goldman Sachs and Morgan Stanley, applied to become bank holding companies shortly after the Federal and US Treasury announced measures to support money market mutual funds.

International ripple effects

Amid the dramatic series of events, October 2008 witnessed the start of banks and financial institutions around the globe being nationalized, receiving emergency relief loans or filing for bankruptcy. The crisis continued to spread unabated and infect open economies globally. A few of the many national examples were: in the UK, nationalization continued with Bradford and Bingley Bank; in Iceland, the largest banks Landsbanki, Glitnir and Kaupthing were nationalized with the help of IMF emergency loans; in Germany, the state rescued Hypobank when threatened with insolvency; and similarly in the Netherlands, banking and insurance group ING Groep and insurer Aegon, which as owner of US insurer Transamerica was facing rapidly rising impairment charges, were bailed out by the Dutch government rescue fund.[11] In Japan, life insurer Yamamato filed for bankruptcy, and Pakistan and Turkey received emergency loans. The Russian stock exchange closed for several days to stem market panic. In the remainder of 2008, the US financial sector was restructured, while the big three US auto-makers were extended emergency loans under the government-sponsored Troubled Asset Relief Program (TARP).

To fight the crisis, the US government in November 2008 made financial commitments in the neighbourhood of $8.2 trillion, of which the government disbursed $3.9 trillion and invested $375 billion under TARP. Bankruptcies in the USA were up 40% from 2007 levels and the stock market was down 38.5%, resulting in a global value loss for equity investors of $30 trillion.

The day of 9 March 2009 marked the decade low for the US stock market with an accumulated drop of almost 50% since 2007, and the largest drop in value since the 1930s.[12] A few days later, on 19 March, IndyMac was acquired by Californian OneWest Bank Group LLC. But the American Recovery and Reinvestment Act of 2009 (ARRA), enacted in February 2009 by President Barack Obama, began to have an effect. By the end of 2009, the S&P had regained 60%.

Reregulation 2010

Early in 2010, the *Wall Street Journal* (WSJ) quoted University of Chicago professors Becker, Davis and Murphy arguing that the economic stimulus package deployed would do little but soften the recessionary impact and that the resulting increase in money supply would only stimulate inflation. Their point was that stimulating the monetary system must wait until the economy had fully emerged from recession.[13] But shortly after in 2010, US Congress passed and President Obama signed into law the Dodd–Frank Wall Street Reform and Consumer Protection Act, marking the most sweeping overhaul of US financial market regulations since the Great Depression and ending the period of tax-payer funded bailouts.[14] ARRA proved as hard to anchor as growing tall trees on rocky ground, and market pressure resulted in much of the imposed regulation being neutralized by the Jumpstart Our Business Startups Act, signed into law in April 2012.

As of writing in February 2013, with the residual effects of market volatility still embedded in the spinal cord of the financial industry, markets remain wary of any fresh signs of trouble, and confidence needs to be rebuilt. But on 1 February 2013, the Dow Jones Industrial Average closed above 14,000, only missing 1.1% from stealing home on the previous record of 14,164.53. Notwithstanding this positive development, investors are cautioned that markets are not clear of the tentacles of the crisis yet.[15] Based on the rapid rebound of the market and asset price increases, more attention is now directed at the systemic proportions in the global markets, and economists are discussing whether the current rapid increases in asset prices are driven by healthy economic fundamentals or are a product of financial bubbles driven by capital availability.[16]

In case of the latter, this is water on the mills for further regulation, and it is clear that this kind of momentum and inertia in regulatory bodies will not come to a standstill overnight. Some might also argue that industry maturity will need a few, well-designed nudges along the way in order to stay competitive. But to stay competitive, system providers and market incumbents must engage efficiently in a commitment to collaboratively comply with continuous regulatory change.

17.3   Impact of regulation on the operations of asset managers

Asset managers around the globe today face an increasing volume of regulations, which have implications for the entire asset management value chain, extending beyond that and impacting underlying business models, organizational and operational structures, as well as the supporting IT infrastructures. The difference between some 30 or 40 years ago and the recent three to five years is not so much the challenge of becoming compliant with the single initiative, rather that the increased volume of regulation, combined with increasingly aggressive regulatory deadlines, exposes the industry to massive pressure.

For individual companies, this requires regular reviews of the active business models, organizational and operational structures, as well as the supporting IT infrastructures, in order to secure timely identification and application of required changes at relevant levels. The main tactical challenge of today is that companies do not only have to monitor one or two regulations at a time; instead they have to manage a portfolio of ongoing regulatory initiatives and analyze the impact on portfolios and on business lines – both globally and locally. The key to successfully managing the regulatory portfolio is to identify the right sources to monitor, select the relevant initiatives to follow, prioritize them according to business impact and timing, and at the same time drive timely implementation of identified requirements. We examine this in greater detail later in the chapter.

The increasing frequency with which new regulatory initiatives are released on the market requires companies to be far more agile now than previously.

The requirement for agility must be reflected in the underlying governance models and structures covering:

- active business models;
- organizational and operational structures;
- supporting IT infrastructures.

From a regulatory perspective, the requirements for the active business models are that they be monitored on a continuous basis to identify compliance gaps in new or upcoming regulatory initiatives. Now and in the future, asset managers must design their business models to be adaptive to new regulation without compromising operational continuity for the organization, hardly a trivial task.

With more adaptive business models, fewer adjustments to organizational and operational structures are required, which over time will allow the organization to achieve higher productivity levels. But even when having adaptive business models in place that accommodate the vast majority of regulatory initiatives, we will see certain regulations containing specific requirements, enforcing changes in the organizational and operational structure of a company. Recent examples of deep-impact initiatives like this are Dodd–Frank and EMIR regulation, prescribing changes down to the business-process level.

Adaptive business models and organizational/operational structures generate friction with the supporting IT infrastructure, because they require the IT organization to meet the asset manager's conflicting objectives of a highly adaptive yet at the same time scalable IT infrastructure. In modern financial services business, this is one of the most frictious and probably also most discussed business challenges: the impact of regulatory initiatives can be systemic to the IT infrastructure. However, this chapter focuses on the impact of regulatory change on investment management operations, and we are not going to explore the IT infrastructure challenges further here.

17.4   Implications of regulation for software design

About 2,500 years ago, Greek philosopher Heraclitus had his now world-famous epiphany that the only constant is change, and ever since then generations of regulators have confirmed Heraclitus' insights through a continuous flow of new regulation. Especially during recent decades, investors' rising demands for returns has increased the appetite for risk in the capital markets. This in turn has spurred a wave of financial innovation in search of sophisticated algorithms to eliminate or delineate and ultimately control risk exposure. This innovative movement has attracted regulators' attention, and an increasing number of new or changed regulatory requirements has been imposed on the financial industry worldwide.

17.4.1   Regulatory selection

Measured as the increase in regulatory events, including everything from speeches to final binding rules, worldwide regulatory activity has jumped by 52% in the period 2008–11; 35% of compliance teams spend more than seven hours a week on average tracking and analyzing regulatory development.[17] With the double-digit growth in regulatory activity during those years, bid-ask spreads have narrowed and volume predictions from options have increased, with foreign exchange and now also fixed-income algorithmic trading representing a growing share of the total trading volume.[18] Future margin performance will depend on increasing mathematical and technical sophistication, and on businesses' ability to control and reduce the cost of regulatory compliance with standardized solutions. In this environment, it is fair to assume that compliance teams can expect heavier workloads, as attention from regulators rises with trading volume and product complexity.

With this kind of outlook for continuous change in a heavily system-supported industry, asset management industry software providers must gear up for intensified change management and regulatory governance with close and attentive monitoring of regulators and regulatory initiatives worldwide.

This makes investment management software design more challenging than ever, not due to the individual requirements or the design of individual functionalities, but because of the systemic properties of ratified legislation. For software-supporting legislation, and successive deployment of legislation of the likes of Dodd–Frank, every new instruction or function is required to integrate and be fully compliant with the existing functionality. Today, when it comes to software providers to the financial industry, it is fair to say that the original drivers of competitive advantage – product innovation and efficiency – have found a fast-growing sibling in regulatory compliance.

Also, taking the velocity of regulatory change into consideration, and if we look at investment management software provider challenges in a past, present and future perspective, one can rightfully argue that among these software providers, the future winners will be picked out, not by natural selection but by regulatory selection. Here are some of the main characteristics:

17.4.2   Past

Solutions were designed and developed to enable individual companies to leverage competitive advantage and become compliant with national legislation. Software was creatively engineered, hard to maintain, with many individual adaptations and hard-coded functionality, often with a limited international perspective.

Solutions were designed in the first place to meet national regulatory requirements and left little or no flexibility to cater for other markets as well. Slow-growing legislative maturity enabled market leaders to leverage intellectual capital and hasten to realize legal and economic arbitrage opportunities, and even small features made a large difference.

For investment management software providers, several factors contributed to complicate scaling and leveraging volume-driven advantages: relatively limited standardization; fragmented systems often consisting of poorly integrated functional islands; databases distributed among several systems with different data structures; and client- and provider-specific integration protocols enabled through a proprietary mix of technologies/system architectures.

17.4.3   Present

Solution providers are under rapidly mounting pressure from increasing demand for regulatory compliant solutions, both in terms of software and service-based solutions. With the swiftly progressing development of new algorithmic trading solutions, STP processing, high-performance computing and data transmission, not to mention the increasingly automated processing of even the most stubborn manual tasks in the trade-processing flow, the industry has come to a point where it is natural to ask how many processes should be allowed to remain manual in an increasingly connected future.

In answering the question if anything should remain manual, it is necessary to consider both the system providers' ability to automate trade-processing flows end-to-end and clients' and system providers' abilities to test and control automated end-to-end flows, systems of automated flows and systems of systems of automated end-to end flows. The new challenges posed by the combination of automation and processing speed in the full value chain offer a complexity on a higher level in terms of staging and execution of business testing.

But particularly in terms of validating results, performing root cause analysis and explaining differences, system providers and asset managers will face a new set of rules and consequences of significantly larger proportions. We have had the opportunity to sneak a peek of this through a few of the reality checks we have seen so far. These include the US stock market $862 billion flash crash of 2010, Knight Capital's suicidal black eye to Wall Street in 2012, and Mumbai Nifty-Fifty's 15.6% $60 billion flash crash of October 2012 nudged by Mumbai-based Emkay Global under the suspicion of 'fat-finger mistake' in entering a $125.7 million trading order.[19] [20]

These events are all painful lessons showing all sides of any table that convergence is needed, and that the recipe for success is collaboration, mutual learning and a continuous improvement culture that is resistant to failure.

17.4.4   Future

The truth in nuclear physicist Niels Bohr's classic small vent of frustration that 'it is hard to predict, particularly about the future' is realized on a daily basis by traders and investment managers throughout the financial services industry.

Disruptive financial innovation, systems managed by systems, new tech-nologies leveraging quantum graphs and spectral geometry, self-perpetuating nano objects, multi-dimensional fault tolerant algorithmic structures, neural interfaces – our wildest guesses will not even come near the real world or they will surpass the real world by decades. As we have been taught by evolution so far, we are (still) only human.

But what we currently believe and can state with some confidence is that investment management systems will become the default vehicle for regulatory compliance if regulatory progress continues at the current or faster pace.

Apart from technologies, speed requires proximity and connectedness offered only by integrated systems built on scalable database management systems. The next frontiers will also move technology out of the 'engine room' as standards converge and systemic global regulation evolves from global trading and gov-ernment collaboration on taxation of cross-border capital and employment.

On the development side, new internationally and globally ratified regu-lation will drive research and development efforts in the direction of inter-faces, multi-dimensional accounting, multiple variable attributes, distributed common data repositories plus tax distribution and reconciliation – to name just a few of the developments.

On the system provider side, the increased speed of new regulatory initia-tives will drive efforts to fix current glitches in scaling of agile approaches, enabling methodology and tools to be both adaptive to new requirements and rapid to market at reasonable and controllable cost. Key to faster adoption and ratification is automation of quality improvements, consequence analysis and early adoption. In an increasingly automated world, system providers are key to enabling this by committing to closer and earlier involvement in legis-lative processes.

17.5   Fundamental concepts

Cost-effective responsiveness to regulatory changes is highly-correlated with insight into the local legislative processes, as well as monitoring activity in national, regional, international, continental and global regulatory bodies. There are a number of important perspectives that our tracking of the regu-latory processes has shown to be key to capturing value faster from regulatory change.

In this section, we highlight the most important keys to leveraging regu-latory change by proactively aligning with the regulatory process.

17.5.1   The Curve of Uncertainty

For asset managers, the Curve of Uncertainty holds the key to a cost-efficient approach to regulatory compliance. Starting from the first touchpoint between new regulation and market participants (not counting lobbying organizations) through to new regulation in action, the resource commitments for monitoring and involvement differ significantly over time. Timing the resource commitments are key to both controlling operational costs and maximizing acceleration of regulatory efforts.

The obvious first choice for many is to encapsulate regulatory complexity in a organizational unit with a name that indicates a solution to the problems, e.g., a 'Regulatory Compliance Unit', then staff this unit with legal/regulatory specialists, and launch it as an enterprise-wide service on a shared platform. And this might not be such a bad idea as long as the regulatory workload justifies this.

However, as over time the workload tends to vary considerably with legislative progress, and as business focus shifts from monitoring to gap analysis, design, development, deployment and maintenance – so do resource (and competency) requirements. This is where the usual internally shared services setup runs into problems, because the required breadth in competencies widens quickly, slimming coverage and obstructing scaling advantages. The main steps of the general legislative process for regulatory initiatives have been set out by SimCorp Strategic Services and Solutions Research (see Figure 17.1).

Step L1	Step L2	Step L3	Step L4	Step L5	Step L6	Step L7
Initial proposal for new regulation	Hearing	First proposal	Revised proposal	Regulation in place	Regulation in action	Regulation clarification and adjustment

Figure 17.1 High-level illustration of main steps in legislative process for regulatory initiatives

Source: SimCorp Strategic Services and Solutions Research.

As these main steps indicate, the process is very much driven by local, regional and global regulatory bodies. This is also what is driving variation in compliance requirements, and which is why competency coverage becomes stretched and outside help is required.

The initial proposal for new regulation is often conceived and drafted by committees or central regulatory bodies (see Step L1). The significance of their work is that they are indicating in/from which direction change will be coming; monitoring the output of these entities is like looking into a strategic kaleidoscope – it provides strategic indications.

Proposals go into public hearing processes (see Step L2), typically with dead-lines of up to 12 months for feedback, and based on the feedback from market incumbents, industry groups and lobbyists, a first proposal is drafted (see Step L3), with a shorter time of typically six months for questions and market responses. Should substantial change requirements arise from the hearing process, typically within a three-month timeframe, they are included in the revised proposal (see Step L4), which is normally the last frontier before the regulation is in place (see Step L5). Often changes are not included between when the final revised proposal is published and when the regulation is in place.

Step L4 will iterate a number of times through the process, depending on the type and scope of legislation. In engagement of industry and business organi-zations with legislative initiatives, such as IFRS 9 and Solvency II, we have seen proposals to regress from fairly late in the process, even though preparations were fairly solid and good proposals were put forward. For Solvency II, EIOPA is now running the sixth Quantitative Impact Study (QIS).

During the first phase the regulation is in action (see Step L6), typically stretching over a 12-month period, reactions are monitored and actions accumulated for a first amendment to the regulation in place (see Step L7). Additional amendments are added according to market needs and conditions.

From a solution provider's perspective, the process of monitoring the steps a given piece of regulation takes is quite interesting, as the flow of the regulatory initiatives through Steps L1–L7 promotes a distinct sequence of product devel-opment activities required to maintain product compliance. This sequence of product development activities runs from positioning over solution proposal, through build and launch activities, to solution support and updates. SimCorp Strategic Services and Solutions Research has also mapped the product devel-opment activities to the seven-step regulatory flow (see Figure 17.2).

Step L1	Step L2	Step L3	Step L4	Step L5	Step L6	Step L7	
Initial proposal for new regulation	Hearing	First proposal	Revised proposal	Regulation in place	Regulation in action	Regulation clarification and adjustment	
	Positioning		Solution proposal	Solution development and launch		Support	Maint.
	Step PD1		Step PD2	Step PD3		Step PD4	Step PD5

Figure 17.2 Mapping a five-step product development flow to seven-step legislative process

Source: SimCorp Strategic Services and Solutions Research.

For solution owners and solution providers, the key to leverage compliance effectively lies in the ability to enable seamless synchronization of the five-step product development flow with the seven-step flow of regulatory initiatives.

The structure of the five-step product development flow is less granular than the flow that regulatory initiatives go through, as the objective of the development flow is business-side tracking of the initiatives and matching the final outcome with an adequate service and/or solution.

An important feature of the product development flow is that the initial step (PD1) frontloads the process with a high burst of legal and commercial focus. The burst ensures that the bearing on the regulatory initiatives is zeroed in, and that tracking of in-progress regulatory initiatives is enabled. Value capture in the positioning phase ensues through three core themes: 1) rapid anchoring of a global position; 2) background monitoring of regulatory progress and verification of expected vs. actual progress; and 3) preparation of and handover to solution proposal phase (see Step PD2). In the event of a significant deviation from expected progress, experts are scrambled for recalibration of position and the process is re-engaged.

With Step PD2, the proposal phase assesses whether requirements are best covered by system functionality or by process. An initial solution design is generated as the basis for the first post-hearing proposal, with the objective to anchor solution scope, interface requirements and potential timing dependencies. As soon as the final revised proposal is published by the regulatory authority, solution scope is locked in, and development initiated (see Step PD3).

The initiation of solution development directly out of Step PD2 enables solutions to be developed and delivered just in time for when new regulatory initiatives are launched. This type of on-time compliance requires a clear split of system support and manual processes, timed to launches of individual regulatory initiatives. Following the launch in Step PD3, support and maintenance (see Steps PD4 and PD5) require continuing monitoring, adjustment of regulatory solutions and change management of document repositories.

The duration of the positioning phase extends over a period of up to 12–24 months, followed by a two- to six-month solution proposal and review phase and a four- to six-month development and launch phase. The sequence of activities, however, is not the strongest enabler of a speedy process – a rapid elimination of uncertainties and maturing of the final form of regulatory initiatives are more important.

Maturing of regulatory initiatives in the USA and in Europe each follow their own distinct path. While the US path is longer, US initiatives are launched relatively quickly but at a lower maturity level, with more processing to be done over a longer period of time. The European process aims at launching at a higher maturity level after the review periods to eliminate most of the major uncertainties and avoiding backflows. Both approaches have pros and cons, but obviously the European front-loaded approach can deliver solid initiatives with their first-time-right approach, while the US approach can execute rapid launches of new solutions in market segments and start to collect feedback for improvements.

As the uncertainty level is correlated with risk, and as the gradually more detailed specifications of the regulatory initiative take form, the requirements reduce owner and supplier risk at an increasing pace. In the EU, it is slower but with a steep decline after the hearings; in the US, it is at a slower but steadier pace spread over a longer period of time (see Figure 17.3).

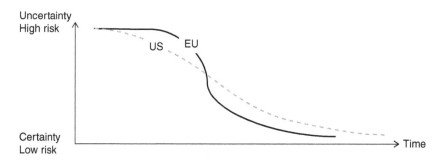

Figure 17.3   Mapping US and EU Curves of Uncertainty
Source: SimCorp Strategic Services and Solutions Research.

Taking a step back and coupling the process-flow profiles of the legislative process, the product development flow, and the Curve(s) of Uncertainty, we can combine the pictures into one, illustrating the major progress levers of regulatory initiatives.

In Figure 17.4, it becomes more obvious when to advance actively and when to monitor progress passively. The objective of the curve is to be able to adjust effort dynamically to the uncertainty curve of any specific regulatory initiative, which is possible with this model by learning about the published schedule for the particular regulatory initiative, estimate and then align phases accordingly in the following order: 1) Curve of Uncertainty; 2) Timing of legislative process; and 3) Positioning and product development flow.

Mapping the Curve of Uncertainty is a strong framework for increasing efficiency in planning and execution of regulatory initiatives, both for solution providers and customers.

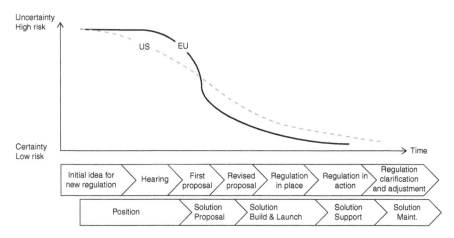

Figure 17.4   Illustration of the Curve of Uncertainty merged with legislative process and product development flow

Source: SimCorp Strategic Services and Solutions Research.

For the solution provider, the following goals should be kept in mind when dealing with regulatory requirements:

- Provide cost-efficient regulatory compliance solutions
- Manage the uncertainty of regulatory process efficiently
- Enable flow, don't waste time on static positions
- Build flexibility into solutions by design.

In order to achieve the above-mentioned operational goals, the rethinking of already taken positions periodically is key to avoiding getting trapped in disadvantageous situations where the risk of ending up with the wrong solution design and facing costly rollbacks is high.

17.5.2   The pyramid of influence

We have modeled the sources of regulatory activities into a hierarchy, enabling companies to gauge the most effective hierarchical level of regulatory interaction. In this section, we argue in favor of using this model to pursue cost-efficiency in regulatory activities. Our hierarchical structure is a five-layered 'champagne fountain' model of the primary global sources of regulatory information, and it serves two main purposes: 1) Providing an operational structure for the sources of regulatory information, ordered according to the sources' proximity to the legislative process; and 2) Serving as a map to businesses with regard to where to link up to get regulatory information feeds according to business needs.

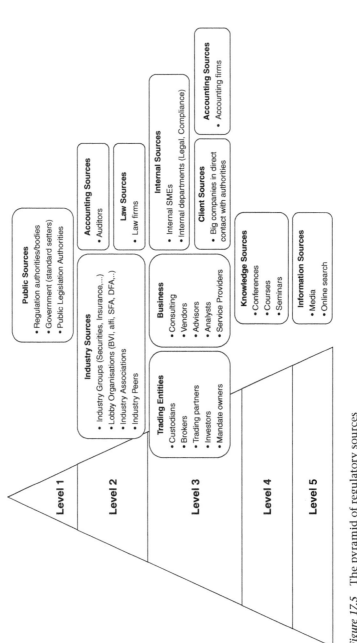

Figure 17.5 The pyramid of regulatory sources

Source: SimCorp Strategic Services and Solutions Research.

The five levels in our model represent main sources of regulatory information: 1) Public Sources; 2) Industry Sources; 3) Business and Internal Sources; 4) Knowledge Sources; and 5) Information Sources (see Figure 17.5). Looking at the five layers in more detail, they all serve distinct practical purposes.

Level 1 in the model is the official source of new regulatory initiatives, including international regulatory bodies outlining initiatives and proposing concrete legislation, government entities ratifying initiatives, adapting international legislation and formulating national laws according to local market conditions. Tapping into Level 1 means hooking up to flows of raw information from legislative entities. Linking up at this level requires high-volume legislative screening and processing capacity and capabilities. This is costly but also the source of competitive advantage.

At Level 2, we have the legislation pre-processing layer where we have placed three large groupings: industry groups/associations, lobby organizations and professional service providers. Industry groups and associations working on behalf of businesses and trading entities operate, monitor, filter and pre-process regulatory initiatives in order to evaluate the operational aspects of legislation and make regulatory information digestible. Lobby organizations representing industry groupings and individual businesses work directly with regulators on behalf of groups or businesses to inform and influence policymakers, governing entities and regulatory bodies. Professional service providers, primarily within the spheres of law and accounting, need constant updates of forefront knowledge and professional capabilities to both keep own basis service deliverables current and leverage knowledge into advisory capabilities. Tapping into Level 2 typically means hooking up to a continuous flow of processed information from industry groups or professions. The cost of obtaining information from Level 2 sources is significantly lower than from Level 1.

Level 3 represents commercially available sources of information. At this level, legislative information is typically bundled with products or services and targeted either for internal use or for certain business segments or industry groups. Tapping into the Level 3 sources means hooking up to asynchronous information flows, subject to change over time. The cost of obtaining information is low for high-volume sources, but pre-processing plus internal processing, specialization and commercialization make that information often specific to business purposes. A multitude of Level 3 sources may be necessary to generate a complete picture, complicating the task of information scrubbing.

Level 4 depicts knowledge sources available via professional training and knowledge providers. The content is pre-processed, interpreted and zeroed in on specific purposes through courses, conferences and seminars. Hooking up to Level 4 sources means hooking up sporadically to information bursts at times of convenience. The purpose is to obtain pre-processed and interpreted information and access to experts and peer groups through course/seminar participation.

Level 5 takes the form of self-service information gathering and heavily depends on the quality of the information sources and the gatherer's ability to verify the facts and condense them into a solid analytical basis. Hooking up to Level 5 sources means asynchronous searches in generally available information of varying quality. The purpose is light ad hoc research and individual analysis.

The costs (and risks) of information vary significantly across Levels 1–5 in the model, which is why it matters where in the hierarchy one hooks up. The cost of information access and risk variation across access levels in our model can be seen in relation to one another (see Figure 17.6).

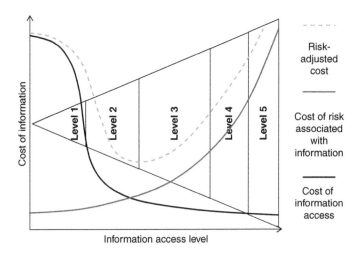

Figure 17.6   Illustration of relationship between pyramid of regulatory sources (levels) and cost of information

Source: SimCorp Strategic Services and Solutions Research.

When access to information offers a competitive advantage, the value of (new) information is high and an extended regulatory affairs setup can be justified by the competitive gain and strategic arbitrage opportunities offered by having first access to new regulatory requirements.

Key to an efficient regulatory affairs approach is clarity on own business requirements and the ability to tap directly and efficiently into the relevant level/source in the Pyramid of Influence. Dimensioning a regulatory setup is hence dependent on competitive requirements for access to regulatory information. If time criticality of regulatory information is not a competitive parameter, then the most efficient approach is to hook up to Level 2 (or Level 3 if access to regulatory experts is not critical).

17.6 Applying the fundamental concepts in practice

To apply the fundamental concepts in practice, asset managers must split activities into strategic and tactical components according to time horizon and purpose.

17.6.1 Strategic vs. tactical point of view

In order to deal efficiently with regulatory challenges, it is normal industry practice to divide the regulatory responsibilities among two corporate functions which interact heavily with business and systems people in realizing regulatory solutions:

Regulatory Affairs

and

Regulatory Compliance.[21, 22]

The two functions are distinguished by two main criteria:

- Time horizon → long-term vs. short- to mid-term;
- Purpose → influence regulatory discussion vs. implementation of regulatory requirements.

The two functions will have overlapping areas of interest and responsibility. As a consequence, implementing these two functions as one organization in a practice structure is done differently from company to company.

17.6.2 Regulatory affairs

Challenges and organization

A Regulatory Affairs unit is in charge of monitoring the national and international regulatory environment relevant for the company in order to be able to identify important initiatives at an early stage. One of the main challenges for this unit is always the question of identifying the regulations that need to be monitored more closely, those that can be dealt with at a lower priority and those that can be defined as out-of-scope for the company. Due to the fact that regulation is becoming more and more supranational, as described earlier in the chapter, it is fair to question how much future national regulation will still be relevant to monitor. Taking a closer look, however, it becomes apparent that national regulation will remain an important work area for Regulatory Affairs. Here are a few reasons:

- taxation remains a national topic (even in the EU);
- supranational regulations, such as the Basel accords or the UCITS regime in the EU, are transposed into national jurisdiction that needs to be monitored and implemented.

Added to that, when examining a little more closely the challenges for Regulatory Compliance, one sees that the size of the challenge is influenced by some key variables:

- in what **industries** is the company active?
- in what **countries/regions** does the company operate?
- what specific **business models** are being operated by the company?

In contrast to a Regulatory Affairs unit, the focus of a Regulatory Compliance unit must extend across all targeted business combinations in order to be both a business enabler and at the same time be able to identify and decide how, at what stage and when to engage the regulatory process most efficiently. It must also provide implementation support for regulatory initiatives directly to business units. From a going concern perspective, the protection and support offered by the Regulatory Compliance unit is vital when regulatory initiatives and changes influence the underlying business models of the firm.

On the other hand, the Regulatory Affairs units of financial service institutions are mainly tasked with engaging at a very early stage in impact assessments and participation in anything from political processes to professional discussions on the financial implications of regulatory initiatives. The focus of the Regulatory Affairs unit must span national and supranational regulation; in most companies, the staff of Regulatory Affairs units are contributing at one and the same time to their relevant representative industry organizations (i.e., BVI or GDV in Germany, ALFI in Luxembourg, and EFAMA on a European level) in order to bring business perspectives and practical consequences into the political discussion about regulation.

The main business objectives for a Regulatory Affairs unit are:

- an **early involvement** in political discussion; in order to
- **bring practical experience** to the table; and
- **influence** regulatory processes to synchronize them better with existing business models.

The basic questions that the Regulatory Affairs unit must focus on are:

- Will a certain regulation impact the company at group level, at business-line level or at local branch level?
- To what extent will a regulatory initiative require changes to the underlying business model?

Why care about software?

The effective deployment of regulation in modern financial markets is entirely dependent on supporting software solutions. With this in mind, the current setup where regulatory discussions are often dominated by legal practitioners is clearly suboptimal and poses an increasing financial and operational risk for asset managers. When discussions and consultations on early levels in the regulatory process focus solely on regulatory intent and consequently omit the operational impact of regulations on IT, processes, systems and costs, the proposed regulatory initiatives turn south – as was recently the case with the proposed reclassification of holdings in the transition from IAS 39 to IFRS 9 reporting. The crush of accelerated technological development and financial innovation during the latest financial crisis has alerted regulators and asset managers to a few new regulatory hotspots, notably:

- derivatives
- high frequency trading (HFT)
- tracing and detecting toxic trading patterns.

To avoid a situation where process and systems implications of regulatory initiatives become unbridgeable gaps in the discussion between regulators and the market, asset managers and solution providers must implement certain mechanisms. One practical measure is to introduce feedback loops to pump lessons learned from practical implementation by the Regulatory Compliance units back into the Regulatory Affairs units to spur, fuel and value focus discussions with regulatory bodies. The IFRS 9 case is a good example of this feedback loop when operated successfully. When assessing where and how to link up in the regulatory process, the Pyramid of Influence provides pointers to what entry level in the regulatory hierarchy should be engaged to obtain the required effect/return (see Section 17.5.2).

17.6.3   Regulatory compliance

Whereas Regulatory Affairs units focus on assessing the long-term strategic implications of regulatory initiatives at an early stage, Regulatory Compliance units can best be described as regulatory governance functions, focused on handling the practical consequences of regulatory initiatives and how to design and implement adequate and cost-efficient solutions for the prevailing set of individual initiatives. Regulatory Compliance should not only focus on a single initiative but on the given set of initiatives in order to create synergies wherever possible. At the point when Regulatory Compliance picks up on a regulatory topic, the first round of political discussions and lobbying activities has already rolled, and a first draft of the regulatory text is typically available. At this time, the regulatory initiative may still be in draft form and hence associated with a relatively high degree of uncertainty with regards to practical compliance requirements. Lobbying and discussions about the regulations intensify at this stage, and Regulatory Affairs and Regulatory Compliance units typically overlap in the monitoring and impact analysis stages to enable real-time positioning and impact analysis as input for decision-making. The Regulatory Compliance unit's focus must hence span the entire value chain, ranging from background monitoring, impact analysis, Q&As of solution proposals, guidance in the implementation processes to advisory support in the operations and maintenance phases (numbers in headlines refer to numbering in Figure 17.7).

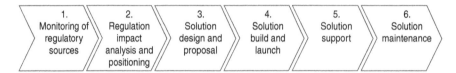

Figure 17.7 High-level illustration of supported business activities for a Regulatory Compliance unit

Supporting activities are explored further in the following sections.

The 'Position' phase (1. + 2.)

The 'Position' phase is Regulatory Affairs territory, but Regulatory Compliance already starts to get involved at this stage, gradually assuming responsibility for the regulatory initiatives in the regulatory portfolio that need monitoring.

To manage the regulatory portfolio efficiently, the use of regulatory 'heatmaps' is helpful to increase portfolio transparency regarding the impact of the single regulatory initiative and its time criticality (see Figure 17.8). To create the heatmap, the following questions must be answered:

- How will the regulatory initiative impact the product portfolio? (depth/breadth)
- What product properties will be impacted by the regulatory initiative? (scope)
- Can the regulatory initiative be enabled by changes to existing products and solutions or do entirely new products and solutions need to be built? (Δ)

The underpinning idea and practical purpose with the regulatory heatmap is to project data from research institutions, such as CEB TowerGroup, through the lens of internal research and strategic ambition in order to provide an company specific operationally prioritized snapshot of all relevant regulatory challenges at a given point in time. With this design, repeated snapshots of regulatory heatmaps can be used to generate a time-dependent high-level view

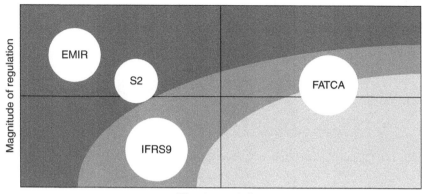

Figure 17.8 Example of a heatmap

Source: 'Perspectives on Regulation: Regulatory Update, Estimated Spending and Implications for IT', CEB TowerGroup, September 2012.

of the evolution of the monitored regulatory initiatives and proactively track and predict changes in risk levels for monitored initiatives.

The regulatory heatmap is used as a basis for commercial pre-emptive positioning with timely involvement of relevant stakeholders. Typical stakeholders to be included are marketing, product management, services, presales and postsales, and client representatives/relationship managers from the market-facing parts of the organization responsible for products and delivery.

The 'Solution Proposal' phase (3.)

The focus of the activities in the 'Solution Proposal' phase is for Regulatory Compliance to take over initiatives from Regulatory Affairs and to draft, refine and finalize proposed solution concepts with due attention to legal and technical restrictions.

In this phase, after anchoring the final solution concept with Regulatory Affairs, the scope of the required changes to processes and systems and the timeframe available will often provide the solution provider (internal or external) with reaction times that are too short to propose and create fully stand-alone solutions in one go. In such cases, a successive design and delivery approach implying a temporary or short-term solution is required to provide both the necessary regulatory compliance for asset management operations and to allocate the extra time and resources to solution providers to build a complete solution. Here the key to smooth transitions and cost-efficient solutions is to carefully design and plan the migration from a temporary to a final solution. Failure to do so is a major cost driver.

To leverage from solution design, it pays off to apply a modular design when designing solutions for regulatory initiatives (see Figure 17.9).

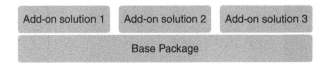

Figure 17.9   Regulatory solution 'base plus add-on' structure

A default product structure like the one illustrated is particularly useful for regulatory areas with successive changes requiring fairly configurable processing and system platforms. The basic idea is to configure and implement a common base solution, which can be reused as a basis to provide an advantage when implementing final or successive add-on regulation.

During this phase, the frequency of interaction between Regulatory Affairs and Regulatory Compliance teams increases significantly in bursts in order to secure:

* Proper and due clarification of all the necessary business requirements;
* Maximum leverage of a standardized solution approach for the majority of clients.

The result of this phase is a solution proposal that is aligned with the requirements as identified by Regulatory Affairs and scoped and modelled by Regulatory Compliance into a standardized regulatory solution proposal that covers basic requirements for compliance and is prepared for successive regulatory adjustments and amendments.

The 'Solution Build & Launch' phase (4.)

This section highlights solutions for the primary challenges that exist when execution of solution build processes must take into account that the factual foundation is incomplete and information and decisions are lacking.

Challenges in the 'Build' part.   Developing regulatory solutions faces the same challenges as any other project in respect of managing time, cost and quality, as the traditional project management triangle reminds us. But on top of the 'regular' requirements for regulatory solutions, risk is a major driving factor and there are a few more interdependencies in the model for solutions covering regulatory initiatives (see Figure 17.10).

Figure 17.10   Solutions for regulatory initiatives expand project management triangle

One of the key challenges for regulatory solutions is standardization, as also mentioned earlier. While solution conceptualization and builds are prepared and engaged, the regulatory process may still be ongoing and final require-ments for regulatory solutions are thus not available. This high degree of uncertainty embedded in the process requires asset managers to apply mature internal project risk management processes together with strict cost man-agement focus in order to realize the two core goals:

1. Immediate and full regulatory compliance.
2. Enabling the solution well before the regulation becomes binding in order to prepare and ramp up production.

To code or not to code.   One of the core challenges in the build phase is to decide on solution-scoping because scoping determines the proportions of software-enabled automation through coding, configuration and manual or service-enabled processing. These are the basic options:

• design and code a new (or enhance an existing) regulatory software solution;
• design and implement pre-configurations and/or supporting tools;
• design and run manual process flows.

As the business's 'last line of defence' against regulatory pressures, Regulatory Compliance, when dealing with any given piece of regulation, must make a qualified recommendation for the final decision on the appropriate (succes-sive) solution configuration(s) over time.

The 'Solution Support' and 'Solution Maintenance' phases (5. + 6.)

After deployment, when a regulatory solution is launched and 'in operation' over the short- or long-term, the Regulatory Compliance unit must make sure that the solution package is maintained continuously and that all clients remain cued to the same standardized version of a solution. Failing that, findings and updates must be synchronized at regular intervals.

When regulatory solutions are designed to employ a standardized and stepwise approach as discussed earlier in this chapter, it is particularly important to ensure consistent deployment across all initiatives and initiative add-ons. This ensures that standardized migration procedures can be employed to guarantee consistently good results.

Putting the Curve of Uncertainty into practice

We have recently made several interesting observations concerning different supranational regulatory processes, such as IFRS 9 (connected with the update of IFRS 4) and Solvency II:[23, 24]

- The regulatory requirements were continuously changing over a long period of time owing to intense lobbying activity by industry organizations and/or certain countries with specific interests or representing specific interests.
- Due to the ongoing changes in regulatory requirements, the originally planned timelines were postponed multiple times.

The increased uncertainty stemming from constantly changing requirements and an unclear timeline make planning for asset managers and their solution providers additionally complex. The concept of the Curve of Uncertainty was conceived to offer guidance and a reference in order to cope with complexity surrounding regulatory changes and updates.

For future regulatory processes, it is reasonable to expect that asset management industry organizations will be forced to increase their lobbying intensity, and that consequently the risk facing solution providers in terms of increased regulatory volatility from the lobbying pressure will increase. Hence, two key lessons learned for solution providers dealing with regulatory change are:

- Not only monitor regulatory bodies or standard setters but also always keep an eye on the strongest interest groups for the regulation or market in question.
- If possible, become a member of the relevant industry organizations/interest groups.

17.7   Regulatory lessons learned

Throughout our professional careers and through the consolidation of experience in this chapter, we have accumulated lessons learned and conclusions drawn across regulatory topics. In this section, we recapitulate the major points regarding: client interaction along the Curve of Uncertainty; task differences between Regulatory Affairs and Regulatory Compliance units; profiles needed to run these units; and the need for continuous client interaction.

17.7.1 Regulatory affairs and regulatory compliance on the Curve of Uncertainty

In general, two major focus areas apply to regulatory units, namely, the overall monitoring of regulatory activity, involvement in lobbying and political initiatives, screening for relevance and significance (Regulatory Affairs), and the activities related to actual implementation of the relevant and prioritized regulatory initiatives of strategic importance (Regulatory Compliance). Objectives have been discussed earlier in the chapter and here we will elaborate on the key principles for organizing the work in the functions to ensure that all phases of the Curve of Uncertainty are sufficiently and timely covered and coordinated (see Figure 17.11).

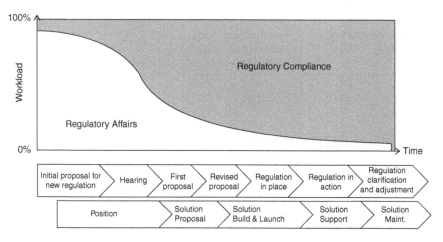

Figure 17.11 Distribution of workload between Regulatory Affairs and Regulatory Compliance units relative to the Curve of Uncertainty

Efficient organization of the regulatory processes along the entire Curve of Uncertainty is a recurring headache for many organizations today. But the big question of whether or not to establish a dedicated Regulatory Affairs unit can be answered simply by evaluating the amount of business touchpoints and added value in terms of product development acceleration and risk mitigation such a unit would be engaged in. The more the touchpoints, the more the acceleration opportunities, the larger the risks to be mitigated, the more the value is directly captured by such a unit.

17.7.2 Same, same, but very different...

The two organizational entities Regulatory Affairs and Regulatory Compliance work on some of the same topics and partly at the same time, as shown in the preceding chapters but their tasks and responsibilities are very different (see Figure 17.12).

	Regulatory Compliance	Regulatory Affairs
Influence political discussion	No	Yes
Evaluate impact on business model	Only to a limited degree	Yes
Focus on implementation & operational impact	Yes	No
Contribute actively to consultations	Partly in later stages	Yes
Monitor market for updates	Yes (mostly focusing on minor releases or changes to interpretations)	Yes (mostly focusing on big changes and new regulation)

Figure 17.12 Comparison between Regulatory Affairs and Regulatory Compliance

17.7.3 Which profiles are required?

After having discussed the differences between Regulatory Compliance and Regulatory Affairs with regards to their responsibilities in the entire regulatory management process, a comparison of the skillsets required for successfully running the two units shows that there is a set of core competencies that everyone involved in regulatory management should share. These are the likes of sound market and client knowledge, communication skills and a basic understanding of the legal background. But also note that the complementing competencies of the two areas are rather disjunct (see Figure 17.13).

17.7.4 Continuous interaction with stakeholders

Besides the regulatory interaction with regulators, industry organizations or other influencers, direct contact with and/or feedback from users are essential activities for any asset manager in order to ensure fully compliant regulatory solutions. Over the lifetime of a regulatory initiative, the frequency of interaction between solution provider and clients varies considerably (see Figure 17.14).

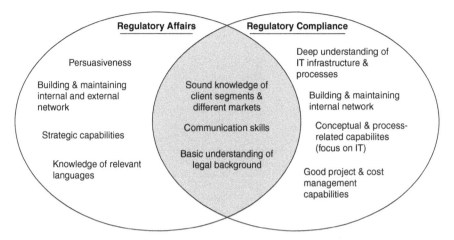

Figure 17.13 Common and different skills for members of Regulatory Affairs and Regulatory Compliance units[25]

Depending on the phase of the lifecycle, the communication mix differs:

- During the 'Positioning' phase, clients require regular updates on the regulatory discussion with the current positioning of the company toward the single regulation.
  → Client Interaction Index: Low
- The 'Solution Proposal' phase involves expert meetings with interested clients and the solution provider. The phase typically ends with formation of a 'Client Focus Group' consisting of first movers among the entire client group.
  → Client Interaction Index: Medium
- The 'Solution Build & Launch' phase is characterized by frequent meetings with the Client Focus Group to continuously improve the solution.
  → Client Interaction Index: High
- During the 'Solution Support' phase, the implementation of the solution at the client is facilitated by direct communication through/with the project team.
  →Client Interaction Index: High
- After implementation of the solution, the 'Solution Maintenance' phase concludes the Curve of Uncertainty. In this phase, communication is event-driven and primarily consists of service updates that are handled through established client-support channels.
  → Client Interaction Index: Low

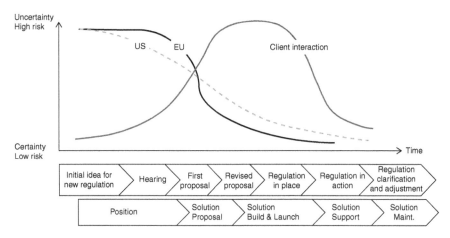

Figure 17.14   Curve of Uncertainty vs. Client Interaction Index

In mapping client interaction to the Curve of Uncertainty, it becomes apparent that both communication efforts and focus vary considerably over the individual phases of the regulatory lifecycle. Only part of the regulatory lifecycle involves client communication. Successful regulatory solution providers adopt their communication and intense client involvement to fit with lifecycle progress and status of individual regulatory initiatives.

17.8   Summary

We embarked on writing this chapter with the objective of providing necessary information for designing, building and running efficient IT-enabled regulatory units available in the future, when professionals like ourselves will be looking for inspiration on how to ensure continuous efficient regulatory compliance. We know and we regret that we have not been able to cover all the bases, but hope that what we *have* done will provide inspiration and enable cost-efficient, scalable approaches to regulatory compliance.

There is no escaping the hard lessons learned and ripple effects from the years 2006–09: the systemic proportions of the global financial support systems cannot be ignored. Providing the right-scoped, right-sized regulatory unit setup and ensuring lean and up-to-date IT support for providing continuous systematic monitoring of direct and indirect risk exposure are what need to be uppermost in the mind of every financial services business leader today.

We have seen how the progress from struggling with enabling free trade has turned into a global hunt for capitalizing network effects of free trade through malicious, predatory regulatory initiatives in the form of Tobin tax schemes and the like. This risks crowding out the very same arbitrage opportunities that ensure we have globally interconnected financial markets today.

We have reached a historic plateau in the world, where regulators globally must decide between hoping that business growth can be stimulated by governmental intervention like John Maynard Keynes claimed, or else believing in Adam Smith's invisible hand and leverage the power of free markets. Globally, we see a lot of oscillation in the continuum between the two extremes represented by Keynes and Smith.

Hence, the reregulation of the free markets is almost a negation, which offers food for thought, especially when regulatory activity in the world is rising as rapidly as is currently the case. After all, a 63% increase in regulatory activity from 2008 to 2011 is significant. To compete today, it is imperative to be aware of the nature of regulatory lifecycles, and to leverage from the right information sources.

With this chapter, our aim was to provide keys to efficient regulatory compliance, both by highlighting the Curve of Uncertainty and by introducing the Pyramid of Influence, with the goal of enabling better decisions with timely access to the right knowledge and support of a state-of-the-art IT infrastructure.

Winning in today's competitive world requires strategic and tactical engagement in the regulatory lifecycle via the right mix of regulatory affairs and regulatory compliance activities, from regulation-impact assessment, monitoring and solution design to timing of communication and market-launch activities.

We hope that the concept of the Curve of Uncertainty and the underlying phases for regulators and asset managers will stimulate more timely, focused and cost-efficient global approaches to regulatory compliance. We strongly believe that tomorrow's winners will be those asset managers who are able to map out and balance on their curves of uncertainty, and use them to chart the critical path to regulatory compliance.

There is no doubt that IT is a key enabler for any asset manager addressing the various regulatory challenges in today's global financial services industry. We believe that in choosing your solution provider you need to consider their commitment to the ongoing investment and strategic focus on regulatory compliance that are required to take on joint requirements at eye-level.

Finally, we have shared some learning experiences from a lifetime of supporting the asset management industry in the hope that the shared learning will enable smoother communication and acceptance of the concepts and experience-based recommendations proposed in this chapter.

Continuous business involvement is the most important enabler of all when the structural and practical effects of regulatory changes are addressed. We believe that the future winners among asset managers will be picked out by regulatory selection – and investing in regulatory compliance can really make a difference when positioning yourself for fighting it out in the financial food chain.

Notes

1. 'Perspectives on Regulation: Regulatory Update, Estimated Spending and Implications for IT', CEB TowerGroup, September 2012.
2. PricewaterhouseCoopers, PwC 16th Annual Global CEO Survey, 2013.
3. NAFTA was founded in 1992 with Canada, Mexico and the USA as members. See also http://www.nafta-sec-alena.org.
4. EFTA was founded in 1960. See also http://www.efta.int.
5. Mercosur was founded in 1991. See also http://www.mercosur.int.
6. The original UCITS Directive was published under 85/611/EEC.
7. AIFMD is set to be transferred into national law by EU member states in 2013.
8. Apart from our own research of the 2006–09 events, this section primarily draws on the article 'Dynamics of a Financial Dislocation: The Panic of 1907 and the Subprime Crisis' by Robert F. Bruner, Dean and Charles C. Abbott Professor of Business Administration, Darden Graduate School of Business Administration, University of Virginia in Larry Siegel (ed.), *Essays on the Panic of 2008* Charlottesville: Institute for Chartered Financial Analysts, Laurence B. Siegel, 2010; and for the timeline before 2007 also on the book 'How Markets Fail', John Cassidy, Penguin 2010.
9. CNN Money, 'How Congress helped create the subprime mess', 31 January 2008.
10. Federal Reserve Bank of Philadelphia, 'The Financial Services Regulatory Relief Act of 2006', Q2 2007.
11. insurancedaily.co.uk, 'Aegon taps Dutch Government rescue fund for €3bn', 29 October 2008.
12. Federal Reserve Bank of Atlanta, 'Stock Prices in the Financial Crisis', September 2009.
13. *The Wall Street Journal*, 'Uncertainty and the Slow Recovery', 4 January 2010.
14. *The Wall Street Journal*, 'Obama Signs Financial-Regulation Bill', 21 July 2010.
15. Forbes.com, 'Dow Over 14,000 For First Time Since October '07, Eyes All-Time Record', 1 February 2013.
16. Federal Reserve Bank of San Francisco: 'Asset Price Booms and Current Account Deficits', 5 December 2011.
17. Thomson Reuters Accelus, 'Special Report: The State of Regulatory Reform 2012', 2012 and 'Cost of Compliance Survey 2013', 2013.
18. The Economist, 'Special Report: Financial Innovation, High-frequency trading: The fast and the furious', 25 February 2012.
19. *The New York Times*, 'Flood of Errant Trades Is a Black Eye for Wall Street', 1 August 2012.
20. Bloomberg, 'India's NSE Says 59 Erroneous Orders Caused Stock Plunge', 6 October 2012.
21. Regulatory Affairs, often referred to as 'Strategic Management of Regulations'.
22. Regulatory Compliance, often referred to as 'Operational Management of Regulations'.
23. The 'International Financial Reporting Standards' are being defined and published by the International Accounting Standards Board (IASB).

24. Solvency II is the upcoming insurance and occupational pension regulation in the European Union and the European Insurance and Occupational Pension Authority (EIOPA) is one of three European Supervisory Agencies driving the process.
25. Korte, Andrea (2012), WM-Seminar 'Regulierung als Prozess', 25 September 2012.

References

Bloomberg, 'India's NSE Says 59 Erroneous Orders Caused Stock Plunge', 6 October 2012, http://www.bloomberg.com/news/2012–10–05/nse-probing-freak-trade-that-caused-price-error-on-bourse.html

Bruner, R.F. (2010) 'Dynamics of a Financial Dislocation: The Panic of 1907 and the Subprime Crisis', in Latty Siegel (ed.), *Essays on the Panic of 2008*, Charlottesville Institute for Chartered Financial Analysts, 2010.

Cassidy, J. (2010) 'How Markets Fail', Penguin.

CEB TowerGroup, 'Perspectives on Regulation: Regulatory Update, Estimated Spending and Implications for IT', September 2012.

CNN Money, 'How Congress helped create the subprime mess', 31 January 2008, http://money.cnn.com/2008/01/30/real_Estate/congress_subprime.fortune/

Federal Reserve Bank of Atlanta (Gerald P. Dwyer, Director) 'Stock Prices in the Financial Crisis', Notes from the Vault, September 2009, Center for Financial Innovation and Security, http://www.frbatlanta.org/cenfis/pubscf/stock_prices_infinancial_crisis.cfm

Federal Reserve Bank of Philadelphia (Chris Hahne, Assistant Examiner) 'The Financial Services Regulatory Relief Act of 2006', SRC Insights: Second Quarter 2007, http://www.phil.frb.org/bank-resources/publications/src-insights/2007/second-quarter/q2si3_07.cfm

Federal Reserve Bank of San Francisco (Paul Bergin), 'Asset Price Booms and Current Account Deficits', 5 December 2011, FRBSF Economic Letter, http://www.frbsf.org/publications/economics/letter/2011/el2011–37.html

Forbes.com, 'Dow Over 14,000 For First Time Since October '07, Eyes All-Time Record', 1 February 2013 https://www-staging.forbes.com/sites/steveschaefer/2013/02/01/dow-over-14000-for-first-time-since-october-07-eyes-all-time-record/, and for the timeline before 2007 also the book 'How Markets Fail' by John Cassidy, Penguin 2010.

insurancedaily.co.uk: 'Aegon taps Dutch Government rescue fund for €3bn', 29 October 2008, http://www.insurancedaily.co.uk/2008/10/29/aegon-taps-dutch-government-rescue-fund-for-e3bn/

Korte, A. (2012), 'Effizientes Regulierungsmanagement für den Finanzsektor', WM-seminar 'Regulierung als Prozess', factor-i GmbH, 25 September.

PricewaterhouseCoopers (2013) 'PwC 16th Annual Global CEO Survey', 2013.

The Economist, 'Special Report: Financial Innovation, High-frequency trading: The fast and the furious', 25 February 2012.

The New York Times, 'Flood of Errant Trades Is a Black Eye for Wall Street', 1 August 2012, http://www.nytimes.com/2012/08/02/business/unusual-volume-roils-early-trading-in-some-stocks.html?pagewanted=all&_r=0

The Wall Street Journal, 'Uncertainty and the Slow Recovery', 4 January 2010, http://online.wsj.com/article/SB10001424052748703278604574624711732528426.html

The Wall Street Journal, 'Obama Signs Financial-Regulation Bill', 21 July 2010, http://online.wsj.com/article/SB10001424052748704684604575381120852746164.html

Thomson Reuters Accelus, 'Cost of Compliance Survey 2013', 2013.

Thomson Reuters Accelus, 'Special Report: The State of Regulatory Reform 2012', 2012.

Part V
Operational Processes and Costs

18

The Interrelationships between Processes, Costs, and Risks in Asset Management

Michael Pinedo

18.1 Introduction

The global asset management industry can be divided into two broad categories, namely institutional asset management and retail asset management. These two categories have fairly different cost characteristics, productivity metrics and risk metrics. The institutional asset management groups include traditional investment advisory firms (such as UBS Asset Management), hedge funds (such as AQR), as well as private equity funds (buyout or venture capital such as Blackrock). This category of asset management firms deals directly with large institutions and is not concerned with the complexities of the retail business. The retail category includes the mutual fund companies (such as Fidelity and Vanguard) as well as the pension funds (such as TIAA–CREF); this category must maintain individual accounts for individual people with the number of retail clients usually being very high. The retail category requires, therefore, a higher level of technology than the institutional category (more elaborate websites, larger call centres etc.). This in order to deal with individual account registration, maintenance, accounting, and a host of other activities (see Duran 2013). There are also a number of asset managers who deal with both institutional and retail clients.

The asset management industry in general has undergone some major changes over the last two decades. These changes took place in several phases. During the phase from the early 1990s until around 2008, Assets under Management (AUM) skyrocketed due to the high liquidity in the global financial markets caused by abundant credit and ever-increasing personal asset valuations (for example housing prices). This phase also witnessed the formation of hedge funds. The hedge funds are typically asset managers who have a smaller

345

number of clients, a smaller total amount of money to manage (in the tens of billions) and who can take very risky positions and make bets that may yield substantial returns. These hedge funds continue to play a major role in the financial markets, mainly because of their ability to act fast and take advantage of arbitrage opportunities. Recently, advances in software and system technologies resulted in significantly lower transaction costs, enabling hedge funds to go into high frequency trading. The high frequency trading strategies depend very much on the development of the new systems and innovative software. However, errors in the software design or bugs in the system may exhibit themselves suddenly without any warning and cause a significant amount of damage.

During the financial crisis of 2008–2009 many of the largest asset managers saw their AUM suddenly drop 30–40%, not only because of a decline in asset prices (which had a major impact on the funds), but also because of clients who were withdrawing their money either out of necessity or due to concerns regarding the financial health of their asset managers. The crisis brought regulatory failures to light, such as the Bernie Madoff case (one of the largest operational risk events in history). Many investors close to retirement lost their pensions, not only because of market conditions but also because of a lack of caution and a lack of responsible risk management at their pension funds.

After the credit crisis, the sector suffered tremendously for several years, as financial markets all over the world tumbled, and liquidity, once abundant, became either very restricted or non-existent. Hedge funds that had been set up all over the world had been closing in droves. The recovery after the crisis has been gradual, but slow. The asset management industry is finding itself now in a new phase and is still undergoing major changes. Even with the markets recovering, the level of liquidity and wealth is recovering only very slowly. A sector that only a few years ago thrived in a vast sea of liquidity, faces today a very different reality.

Before the recent crisis, most asset managers were not too worried about operating costs or operational risk, as ever-increasing personal wealth made their AUM grow at a steady pace. Excessive costs and errors were buried under the increasing revenues from a growing asset base, and under the solid profits that were generated by high returns in world markets. Nowadays, asset managers have started to focus heavily on their operating costs since returns and profit margins have declined considerably making every cost element count.

In this overview chapter on processes and costs, we first have a general discussion concerning the processes, costs, productivity and operational risk issues that are of importance in industry in general and examine the interrelationships between these factors. We then proceed with a discussion regarding these same factors within the asset management industry. We furthermore discuss the trade-offs and optimization issues asset managers have to deal with. In the very last section we provide an outline of important directions for future research.

18.2 Processes, costs and risks in general

Processes, costs, productivity, operational controls, and total quality management have been studied extensively in many industries, in particular in the manufacturing sector, where these issues are nowadays fairly well understood. Large manufacturing companies, such as IBM and Toyota, have extensive cost accounting as well as productivity measures and quality measures in place. In service industries, operational aspects are harder to analyze than in manufacturing industries; costs, productivity and quality tend to be harder to measure. Nevertheless, various service industries have made real progress over the last couple of decades with regard to their operational controls, as well as with regard to costs, productivity and quality measurements. In particular, the transportation (aviation), health care and hospitality industries have made solid advances; they appear to be ahead of the financial services industry. It seems that the financial services sector can learn a lot from various other industries, including aviation and health care (see Cruz and Pinedo, 2008, 2009). For example, the reliability theory used in the design of fault tolerant processes and systems in the aviation and the aeronautics industry can also be useful in the design of processes and procedures in the asset management industry; the concept of optimal redundancy has been studied extensively in the aeronautics industry. Optimal redundancy involves trade-offs between additional investments and the resulting reductions in probabilities of failure. Such a concept is very useful in the asset management industry as well. The procedures used for productivity improvement and for Total Quality Management (TQM) in manufacturing and services operations turn out to be very similar to procedures that can be used in the management of operational risk in financial services.

In the manufacturing industries, the trade-offs between investments, productivity, and quality control are all fairly well understood. On the one hand, the larger the investments in human resources and in technology, the higher the productivity and the better the quality control. On the other hand, the more stress the system is subject to (e.g., a sharp increase in output), the lower the quality of the product (i.e., an increase in risk). Similar relationships hold in the asset management industry. Productivity in an asset management firm could, for example, be measured by the number of trades made by a trader in one day or the number of research reports produced by an analyst in one year. Quality could be measured either by the percentage of trades that were executed with errors or by the total financial impact of the errors.

18.3   Processes, costs, and risks in asset management

The new reality has forced asset managers to develop a much stricter discipline with regard to their operational processes; in particular with regard to their costs, productivity and risk management. These factors, which, historically, have played a very important role in manufacturing, began to play a more significant role in asset management only over the last decade. Each one of these factors has started to receive attention in academic literature (see Harker and Zenios 1999, 2000; Melnick, Nayyar, Pinedo and Seshadri 2000; and Hatzakis, Nair and Pinedo 2010) however, the interdependencies and trade-offs between costs, productivity and operational risks have not yet been thoroughly analyzed (see Figure 18.1). For example, it is very likely that any reduction in costs, with the goal of increasing productivity, can without proper planning substantially increase exposure to operational risk.

In financial services in general, the type of firm (whether it is a retail firm or an institutional firm) and its organizational structure (i.e., its corporate structure, its line management, etc.) have a significant impact on costs, productivity and risk management. For a retail asset manager the organizational structure is as important as it is for an institutional asset manager, and many strategic decisions have to be made with regard to the organizational structure. How much should a firm invest in human resources and how much should a firm invest in new technologies? To what extent should a firm be outsourcing and/or 'offshoring' its operations? These decisions affect both the cost structure and the

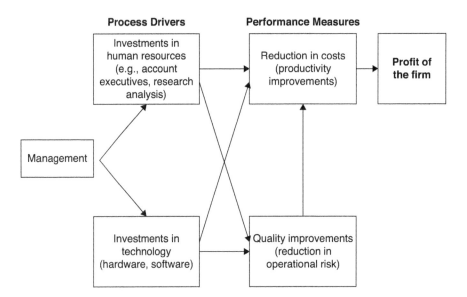

Figure 18.1   Process drivers and performance measures in asset management

operational risk profile of the firm. In subsequent chapters, these factors and their interdependencies are considered in more detail.

In the financial services industry, it has been primarily the retail firms that have been at the forefront of productivity and quality measurements and improvements. For example, retail banks often perform extensive cost and productivity analyses of their branch networks and call centres. On the other hand, trading operations in financial services typically pay more attention to risk management in general and operational risk management in particular. The same is true in asset management: retail asset managers have focused more attention on costs, productivity and customer care, whereas institutional asset managers have focused more on the operational risk profile of their trading operations. Nowadays, however, it has become clear that even institutional asset managers with large trading operations have to keep their costs under control.

Asset managers in general are susceptible to various forms of risk, the primary risks being market, credit and operational risk. These different forms of risk are not independent of one another (e.g., large fluctuations in the market may bring about an increase in operational risk events due to an increase in human error rate). These risks can manifest themselves in two ways: they may have either a direct or an indirect impact on the asset manager. Asset managers can be impacted directly by, for example, operational risk events caused by wrong assumptions in the underlying operating models, by errors in processing trans- actions, or by failures in abiding by government regulations. Errors in processing transactions or systems failures also can cause severe damage and can impact the balance sheet of the asset manager. Failures with regard to compliance of local regulations or with regard to business ethics may also generate large oper- ational losses and result in serious reputational damage. Asset managers can be impacted indirectly by the client funds being subject to market and credit risk. Market risks are due to the daily fluctuation of asset prices, and credit risks are due to the possibility that some counterparties, with whom the funds have business dealings, can go bankrupt, rendering certain financial assets worth- less. Such losses would have an indirect impact on the asset manager's revenue, as dwindling funds result in lower commissions; however, the main losses are still carried by the clients.

The most important cost and operational risk factors in both categories of asset management firms (institutional as well as retail asset management) can be summarized as follows:

- the costs and risks related to human resources (e.g., portfolio managers, administrators, research analysts and call-centre operators);
- the costs and risks related to system development and transaction processing (e.g., algorithm design, software implementation);

- the costs and risks related to customer contact centres and distribution channels (e.g., physical assets).

The following chapters deal with all three cost and risk factors mentioned above. These three factors are clearly intertwined in both categories of asset management firms. It is evident that the first factor is important for both types of asset management firms. The operational risks asset managers are subject to include risks with regard to rogue trading as well as risks with regard to insider trading. Over the last couple of years it has become clear that it is not easy for asset managers to curb rogue trading or insider trading. Several well-known asset managers have recently been prosecuted and convicted for insider trading.

The second factor also is important for both categories of firms. However, the emphasis on IT infrastructure and system development in a retail firm may be slightly different from that of an institutional firm. In a retail firm, the systems development often centers around Customer Relationship Management (CRM) activities, including call-centres and customers' Internet access. The emphasis on systems development in an institutional firm (such as a hedge fund) may, for example, be on transaction processing at high frequency (see Lopez de Prado, 2012). Over the last couple of years several glitches have manifested themselves in high frequency trading, which resulted in very serious losses.

The third factor is clearly more important in a retail firm than in an institutional firm. There are interesting aspects that play a role in this domain concerning capacity management and queueing. The firm has to decide on the number of account managers and call-centre operators to hire assuming a certain amount of demand. However, this demand may fluctuate significantly over time (often, because of exogenous factors) resulting in significant customer delays and a deteriorating quality of service.

18.4   Trade-offs and optimization in asset management

With regard to each one of the cost and risk factors mentioned in the previous section, asset managers are concerned with the trade-offs between, on the one hand, costs and productivity and, on the other hand, quality management and operational risk (in a way that is similar to such trade-offs in manufacturing industries and other service industries). A fair amount of research has been done in many different industries on the optimization of the trade-offs between, on the one hand, productivity and costs of processing and, on the other hand, quality control and customer service level. Since these two objectives are typically measured in different types of units, the minimization (maximization) of total costs (profits) is not that easy.

There are several issues that make this optimization problem in practice quite difficult. First, the problem is highly nonlinear. One can assume that the vulnerability toward operational risk decreases convexly with an increase in investments in human resources (e.g., the number of personnel employed) and technology, see Figure 18.2. Second, in practice it is not a deterministic problem but rather a stochastic problem with a fair amount of randomness (uncertainty). The total objective not only has to be optimized in expectation – the tail effects have to be analyzed as well (i.e., probabilities of catastrophic events occurring). Third, one can make a distinction between investments made in human resources and investments made in technology. A right balance has to be struck between these two different types of investments in order to achieve the maximum benefit in a reduction of operational risk exposure (since the effects of the two different investments clearly depend on their interaction). Taking into account that the organization is also subject to budget constraints, the resulting constrained optimization problem is not very easy. (This sort of nonlinear stochastic optimization problem may at times be referred to as a resource allocation problem.)

In the trading world often decisions have to be made where to invest in order to increase profitability as well as quality control. Investments can be made in human resources (e.g., hire additional personnel to reduce exposure to operational risk events) or in technology (e.g., purchase computer equipment and/or software for the development of new products that would generate additional profits). There is clearly a limited budget. This problem in its simplest form is a standard resource allocation problem.

For example, we may have the following basic investment allocation problem that has as its goal the minimization of total expected costs, including total investment costs and total costs due to expected losses caused by operational risk events:

minimize $(x_1 + x_2 + g(x_1 + x_2))$
subject to
$x_1 + x_2 \leq B$

Here the decision variables x_1, x_2 represent the amounts invested in the two types of resources, say, personnel and technology (clearly, there may be more types of resources). We can argue that the costs of the investments are linear in the amounts being invested. In practice, there is typically a limited budget B, which may be a tight constraint. We may also assume that the $g(x_1, x_2)$ function represents the expected losses caused by operational risk events which is a function of the amounts invested in the various different resources. We may assume that the function $g(x_1, x_2)$ is decreasing convexly in both x_1 and x_2. It is to be expected that the reduction in the total expected losses caused by operational risk events should have the convex property shown in Figure 18.2, since it will become harder and harder to reduce the total expected losses through

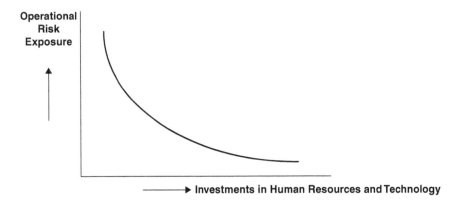

Figure 18.2 Convexity of relationship between investments and operational risk exposure

an additional increase in investments. Unfortunately, the function $g(x_1,x_2)$ may not be separable; normally, there is an interaction between the different kinds of resources requiring investments, so the function $g(x_1,x_2)$ has to include the synergy effects as well (in practice, the more balanced the investment is the greater the reduction in operational losses).

Moreover, this type of optimization problem with the goals of minimizing operational costs and maximizing the expected reduction in operational risk exposure (which is already highly nonlinear and stochastic) also has to take into account possible actions that can be taken in the form of financial hedging and insurance (e.g., rogue trader insurance).

If the budget is not limited, then the optimal amount spent on each one of the resources may very much depend on the amount of randomness the firm is subject to. For example, the number of daily trades, which is a random variable, may affect the expected profits as well as the exposure to the expected losses caused by operational risk events. The more randomness the system is subject to (which can be measured by, for example, the variance in the number of daily trades), the higher the expected capital allocation to the various resource types should be. Actually, the optimal capital allocations tend to increase convexly in the variance of the number of daily trades (see Xu, Pinedo, and Xue 2012).

18.5   Conclusions and new research directions

The area dealing with the interactions between costs, productivity and risks is clearly an important and interesting one. Several important new directions for future research and development have become apparent. One direction could be a study of the interrelationships between the various different aspects of global asset management which may be more empirical and experimental: For example, an analysis of the relationships between the management structure, the various cost factors (i.e., human resources, information technology, etc.), the operational risk exposures, and the relative performance of a fund. Another direction may be more of a modeling nature. As stated before, the general problem being considered is a nonlinear stochastic resource allocation problem subject to certain financial constraints. Making certain assumptions with regard to the nonlinearity and the stochasticity, would it be possible to show certain theoretical properties of optimal solutions?

References

Cruz, M. and Pinedo, M.L. (2008) 'Total Quality Management and Operational Risk in the Service Industries', Tutorials in Operations Research, chapter 7, pp. 154–169, INFORMS.

Cruz, M. and Pinedo, M.L. (2009) 'Global asset management: costs, productivity and operational risk', *Journal of Applied IT and Investment Management*, (2), SimCorp.

Duran, R.E. (2013) 'Financial Services Technology – Processes, Architecture, and Solutions', Cengage Learning Asia Pte Ltd, Singapore.

Harker, P.T. and Zenios, S.A. (1999) 'Performance of Financial Institutions', *Management Science*, (45)9: 1775–1776.

Harker, P.T. and Zenios, S.A. (eds) (2000) 'Performance of Financial Institutions – Efficiency, Innovation, Regulation', Cambridge, UK: Cambridge University Press.

Hatzakis, E.D., Nair, S. and Pinedo, M.L. (2010) 'Operations in Financial Services – An Overview', *Production and Operations Management*, (19)6: 633–664.

Lopez de Prado, M.M. (2012) 'Advances in High Frequency Trading Strategies', Doctoral Thesis, Faculty of Economics, Complutense University, Madrid, Spain.

Melnick, E.L., Nayyar, P.R., Pinedo, M.L. and Seshadri, S. (eds) (2000) 'Creating Value in Financial Services – Strategies, Operations and Technologies', New York: Springer.

Xu, Y., Pinedo, M.L. and Xue, M. (2012) 'Operational Risk in Financial Services from an Operations Management Perspective', Technical Report, IOMS Department, Stern School of Business, New York University.

19

A Best Practices Framework for Operational Infrastructure and Controls in Asset Management

Ümit Alptuna, Manos Hatzakis and Reha Tütüncü

19.1 Introduction

The financial crisis of 2007–2009, which caused US households alone to suffer a $13 trillion decline in wealth, and accelerated the contraction of the investment management industry that has been taking place since 2000 (Investment Company Institute, 2012), created opportunities to identify, study and remedy weaknesses in the asset management process that can be linked to poor operational and control practices on the part of asset management institutions.

Most asset managers aim to implement operational and control best practices. Industry experience suggests that the firms that succeed in properly implementing and adhering to these practices have typically established a strong governance process, and undertaken substantial investments in operational infrastructure, such as technology and skilled personnel. In this regard, asset management firms and hedge funds with a commitment to strong governance and the willingness and ability to make such capital investments, will have an inherent operational advantage.

In this chapter, we present an operational and control framework for asset management organizations that is based on industry-wide best practices and that incorporates lessons learned from the current financial crisis.[1] Our framework is flexible enough to allow firms to modify it on the basis of their size, resources, and structural and operational complexity.

Our discussion of operational and control best practices often focuses on hedge funds, because research indicates that their current practices are in substantial need of improvement.[2] The explosive growth of hedge funds in recent years, and the fact that they are often subject to less restrictive regulatory

354

regimes, may, to a certain extent, account for their shortcomings. However, we believe that our framework is still relevant to mutual funds and other well-regulated structures with more crystallized operating practices because the industry landscape and regulatory regimes continually evolve. Time and events constantly shape and refine best practices as well.

19.2   The importance of governance in the investment management process

Before we begin to outline our proposed framework, we must address the issue of governance. We cannot over-emphasize how crucial and catalytic the role of governance is in effecting best practices in an organization. Extensively documented analysis of financial institution failures during the 2007–2009 period points to weak governance as the root cause of many of these failures (see, for example, O'Hara, 2009; Smith, 2007). In a recent study (2011), Pozen and Hamacher show that an asset management firm's governance structure is the main predictor of its success in the fund industry.

At a very high level, quality governance begins with sound principles. It is incumbent upon each organization to demonstrate an unwavering commitment to these principles and ensure that they take root in the firm's culture. An influential set of governance principles that investment professionals are encouraged to adhere to is the CFA Institute's Code of Ethics and Standards of Professional Conduct (2010a). The CFA Institute has developed a handbook that enables in-depth study and interpretation of its Code and Standards (2010b), and a Code of Professional Conduct specific to Asset Managers (2009).

Implementing a principle-centred governance process requires addressing a multitude of known issues and anticipating potential unknown ones that could emerge. Governance in the investment management process is so important that the CFA Institute has taken official positions on specific governance issues and communicated them to regulators and other entities in the US and elsewhere (found on the CFA Institute Centre website).

The CFA Institute's official positions on governance are summarized below (see CFA Institute Centre (2009) for details).

Board independence

An investment fund's board of directors must be an independent force in fund affairs, and at least two-thirds of its members must be independent. Since the board must safeguard the interests of investors, it must be structured to support independent decision-making and mitigate potential conflicts of interest. A super-majority of independent directors helps ensure that business issues affecting investors' interests can be addressed and important decisions can be made without undue influence from the fund manager or other interested parties.

Independent review committee

Members of the independent review committee have a duty to act in the best interests of fund investors. They must address the conflicts of interest inherent in the agreement between a fund and its investment manager. They should be compensated with fund assets, and not by the fund manager, to help reduce the manager's influence and reinforce their independence. Furthermore, the fund should clearly and prominently disclose compensation figures for committee members, and how such compensation is determined, in their annual reports. The committee should have the authority to effect implementation of its recommendations by the fund so that investors' best interests are served. Committee members' liability should be based on a 'reasonable person' standard, so as not to deter highly-qualified individuals from filling independent review committee positions. The committee should maintain adequate records and make those available to fund investors.

Transparency

Funds should disclose any sort of revenue-sharing arrangements they may have involving brokerage commissions. They must provide detailed information on adviser compensation, including benefits related to marketing efforts and long-term compensation related to an account. Fund expenses and sales loads for each share class should be clearly and prominently communicated. With regard to stock lending, firms should require clients to acknowledge, in writing, that they have received and understood information stating that the firms may lend clients' shares to third parties, and that doing so may cause the clients to lose voting rights.

Market-timing arrangements

Overall, funds should not permit their employees and clients to engage in market-timing practices, since such practices are detrimental to long-term investment goals. If applicable, funds should have to disclose to investors the risks of frequent purchases and redemptions, and their policies with respect to such practices, and explain in clear terms why market timing leads to long-term suboptimal investment outcomes. Funds that permit market timing should have to clearly explain how, and why, some investors engage in market-timing strategies, and under what circumstances such strategies are allowed. Funds that do not permit market timing should disclose their policies and procedures for detecting and preventing such practices and clearly explain how such policies and procedures will be effective.

Soft commissions and directed brokerage

As a general principle, brokerage is the property of the client. Managers should have to disclose to their clients that they may enter into bundled brokerage or soft commission arrangements prior to engaging in such activities, and subsequently provide full and fair disclosure of how clients' transactions are handled and commission benefits used. Plan sponsors and plan trustees should disclose all arrangements they have with investment managers and brokers. Managers should address conflicts of interest inherent in soft commission or bundled brokerage arrangements through a combination of increased disclosure and more precise definitions of what goods and/or services may be acquired under these arrangements. Managers should not use directed brokerage to reward a broker for selling the fund's shares to investors. For more detailed guidance, please refer to the CFA Institute's Soft Dollar Standards (CFA Institute (2004; revised 2011)).

Conflicts of interest

Investment firms should prohibit reporting structures that could create conflicts of interest between corporate finance and trading departments, as well as between agency and proprietary trading desks. They should manage their conflicts of interest in ways that not only avoid self-dealing, but also avoid all outcomes that work against clients' interests. The fiduciary duty of investment firms to obtain best execution for their clients may be compromised if firms pay brokers to market funds to investors. Investment firms should adopt procedures to address certain conflicts created by personal investing, including restrictions on participation by investment personnel in the IPOs of equity or equity-related securities.

Proxy voting

Fund managers should enable clients to evaluate how proxy voting is handled, and should be held accountable for adopting proxy-voting policies in alignment with investors' own objectives, so long as disclosures do not reveal how the fund manager intends to vote on particular issues prior to completion of the proxy process. Managers should designate a policymaking body, or individual, to recommend a proxy-voting policy and monitor its implementation. The policymaker should develop clear proxy-voting guidelines and processes and be held accountable for their proper administration.

As an additional note on the topic of governance, we believe that a robust internal audit function will strengthen the governance process and will lend credence to it. The infrastructure of an asset management firm can be highly complex, especially if the firm offers a wide variety of products and maintains a global footprint (see Figure 19.1 for an illustration of the operational and

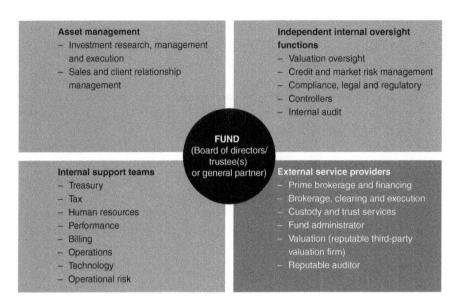

Asset management
- Investment research, management and execution
- Sales and client relationship management

Independent internal oversight functions
- Valuation oversight
- Credit and market risk management
- Compliance, legal and regulatory
- Controllers
- Internal audit

FUND
(Board of directors/trustee(s) or general partner)

Internal support teams
- Treasury
- Tax
- Human resources
- Performance
- Billing
- Operations
- Technology
- Operational risk

External service providers
- Prime brokerage and financing
- Brokerage, clearing and execution
- Custody and trust services
- Fund administrator
- Valuation (reputable third-party valuation firm)
- Reputable auditor

Figure 19.1   Typical structure of an asset management organization

control functions in asset management organizations). For this reason, external investors and operational due diligence managers may find it difficult to map out the entire governance process within an asset management firm, and determine whether the process is truly integrated and functions as intended. At best, these external parties can gain comfort in key areas such as valuation, cash controls and settlement. Because of their superior knowledge about the workings and structure of the asset management organization, an internal audit team is often best positioned to uncover problems and weaknesses in the organization's governance process. Internal audit best practices include a rolling audit process that covers the entire asset management business, and a review from the start of the trading process down to the settlement cycle. The audit should generate a clear list of actionable items with an indication of the seriousness of the control weakness. These items are typically separated into risks that are mitigated by secondary and tertiary controls, and risks that are in need of immediate remediation. Equally important is a clear list of the actions undertaken by management to remedy the issues that surfaced during the audit, within a prescribed time frame.

19.3   Key issues pertaining to operational best practices

Best practices should not be viewed as an end in themselves, but as the means to address the objectives of stakeholders in the asset management process.

The ultimate goal of best practices is to serve the interests of investors. Our discussion will focus on the interests of large institutional investors and High Net Worth (HNW) individuals, because these groups have access to hedge funds and other alternative investments where both anecdotal evidence and systematic analysis[2] show that operational best practices are less prevalent. Small retail investors are somewhat sheltered from poor operational practices because the investment vehicles available to them (mutual funds, for example), are subject to more rigorous regulatory oversight and legislation, such as the Investment Company Act of 1940.

Large institutional investors and HNW individuals must evaluate the ability of asset managers to serve their needs. In a Model Due Diligence Questionnaire for Hedge Fund Investors, proposed by the Managed Funds Association (see 2009), three key issues pertaining to operational best practices are highlighted:

Infrastructure and controls for supporting the integrity of the Net Asset Value (NAV) cycle

What is the organization's current trading, portfolio management, and post-trade reconciliation and accounting infrastructure? Is third-party software used for the above? How are trades executed? What types of controls are typically used to prevent unwanted executions? What segregation of responsibilities is employed in the post-trade reconciliation process? How are cash or other assets transferred, both internally and externally? What types of controls are used to prevent unwanted transfers? How are trading errors handled? Who is the fund administrator, if any? Who are the main prime brokers used by the fund? Is there a written business continuity, disaster recovery (BC/DR) and crisis management plan? If not, how does the firm plan to maximize its ability to recover from business interruptions?

Valuation

What is the valuation process of the fund's positions, including positions that do not have a market price? What is the frequency of valuation? Are any third-party services employed in the valuation process, and, if so, how are these third parties monitored? Has the fund had any material restatement of its financial statements or any prior results since inception? Was the restatement the result of an audit by an external auditing firm?

Risk management

What is the organization's risk management philosophy, and what approach is used in the management of the fund's: exposure to equity, interest-rate, currency and credit risk (as applicable); financing and counterparty risk; and operational risk?

To present best practices related to each of the three key issues above, we draw on the body of available research within the investment management industry, such as Alternative Investment Management Association (2007a, 2007b) Asset Managers' Committee to the President's Working Group on Financial Markets (2009), Managed Funds Association (2009).

19.3.1   Infrastructure and controls

A robust operational infrastructure and control environment is increasingly necessary, due to heightened competition among managers, globalization, complex investment and trading strategies, and the likelihood that regulatory requirements will become more and more stringent. In developing an operational and control framework, managers must take into account the size and complexity of their activities, and the requirements of their investment strategies. Essential elements of such a framework include (Asset Managers' Committee to the President's Working Group on Financial Markets (2009), Managed Funds Association (2009):

- policies and procedures to provide for appropriate checks and balances on operational systems and accounting controls, such as: counterparty relationship selection and management; cash, margin and collateral management; key service provider selection and a formal vendor management function; robust infrastructure and operational practices; robust operational and accounting processes, including appropriate segregation of business operations and portfolio management personnel; and a BC/DR process;
- systems, infrastructure, and automation in proportion to the manager's scale of business and trading operations, including regular review of such infrastructure to assess operational risks in light of internal and external changes;
- a member of senior management vested with the responsibility of managing business operations, supported by internal personnel, or, where appropriate, external resources with the appropriate levels of skills and experience corresponding to the manager's operations; this senior manager, who can be a chief operating officer (COO), or a person with similar responsibilities, should coordinate and partner with investment professionals and senior legal, risk and compliance managers.

In the remainder of this section, we will discuss in greater detail certain issues that a manager's operational infrastructure and control environment should seek to address.

Counterparty selection and management

Typical counterparties include executing and prime brokers, banks, custodians and over-the-counter (OTC) derivative, stock loan, repo and cash management counterparties. Key factors in selecting counterparties include: creditworthiness, reputation, experience, identity, and the legal and regulatory regime (for example, insolvency laws and customer protection rules) of the counterparty, its parent company and affiliates, if appropriate; the level of service that the counterparty can provide in light of the manager's business needs (including complexity of products and frequency of trading), such as efficient transaction processing, reporting, clearing, and settlement; adequate financing capabilities; appropriate staffing to support the manager's business; and stability of the terms which the counterparty is willing to extend (such as term-funding lock-ups for prime brokers). The manager should negotiate and maintain, with all counterparties, signed agreements governing the terms of the relationship (with regard to, for example, account opening, prime brokerage, stock lending, ISDA, custodial arrangements and give-up agreements). Risks embedded in such agreements (such as terms that can increase collateral requirements) should be carefully evaluated.

Cash, margin and collateral management

The manager should have an effective framework, consistent with industry practices, for managing cash balances and processing margin or collateral calls from its prime brokers, financing and OTC derivative counterparties. Compliance with credit agreements, and amounts and types of collateral needed to support positions, should be understood and monitored. Marks used by counterparties to value the fund's positions for collateral purposes should be verified; and margin calls must be verified and met in a timely manner. Investing excess cash should include the analysis of credit risk of relevant counterparties.

Key service provider selection and oversight

Key service providers should be selected based on reputation, expertise and the experience needed to support the manager's business, and include: providers of accounting, consulting and proxy services; IT vendors; legal counsel; fund administrators (where applicable); sub-advisers; and external portfolio managers. Selection and monitoring of service providers should take into account a provider's independence and control over its activities. Agreements with service providers should clearly delineate the service levels to be provided, and ensure that they are appropriate for the manager's internal infrastructure and complexity of operations. The manager should monitor the quality of services offered by providers and be prepared to replace a provider whose quality of services becomes inadequate. Responsibility for any outsourced parts of the process must remain with the manager under all circumstances. The manager should appoint members of senior management to implement and monitor oversight procedures for outsourced activities.

Development and documentation of infrastructure and operational practices

The manager must develop and document infrastructure and operational practices tailored to its business, which will depend on the types of investments, frequency of trading, and the need for manual processing as opposed to the availability of automated systems. Implementation of the latter may be appropriate to reduce settlement risk, depending on the size and complexity of the organization. Reporting policies must be established for resolving material breaks, errors, or other potential causes of loss to the fund. Business process monitoring, analysis and optimization techniques should be employed to identify and address breaks and inefficiencies. If practical, the manager must aim to cross-train personnel or otherwise have appropriate back-up, so that key operations functions are not solely dependent on one individual.

Clearance, settlement and wire transfer procedures

As a minimum, the manager must adopt operational procedures for clearing and settling transactions, and for wiring funds. Such procedures may address: position and cash account reconciliation across prime brokers, futures clearing accounts, the fund administrator and front office, including prompt resolution of failed trades; authorized signatories, checks and balances, and other issues involved in cash movements; segregation of duties between investment and operational personnel, including sending confirmations to non-trading personnel; use of industry utilities and software tools to automate OTC derivatives processes, and central clearing houses and/or exchanges for OTC contracts, if applicable; corporate actions, such as mandatory and voluntary elections, dividends, splits, and reorganizations; and management of positions with expiration dates, such as options, warrants, rights and conversions.

Trading of derivatives and other complex instruments and strategies

The manager must adopt additional infrastructure and operational practices, depending on its involvement and trading in OTC derivatives, and other complex markets, such as bank loans, mortgage-backed securities/collateralized mortgage obligations, structured credit, private transactions and transactions in overseas markets. Operational procedures for such activities are discussed in more detail in Asset Managers' Committee to the President's Working Group on Financial Markets (2009) and Managed Funds Association (2009). The manager should regularly assess the appropriate level of staffing and resources for complex or unique trading strategies from an operational and business risk perspective, and be willing to maintain that level.

Accounting procedures

The manager needs to have appropriate systems, processes, and personnel in place so that the trading activities of its funds, and all related contractual arrangements and agreements, can be properly recorded from an accounting perspective to allow for the calculation of both fund-level and investor-level net NAV as well as for the production of other important financial data necessary to meet investor, risk, financial statement, and tax reporting requirements. Systems should be in place that: maintain trading-related data (including quantity, cost basis, market value, realized and unrealized trading gains and losses, interest and dividends, and fees and expenses); summarize, in a general ledger format, trading and non-trading-related data, such as management fees and expenses; allocate fund-level results to the individual investor level; properly record, from an accounting perspective, non-trading related activities such as management and incentive fees, or other fees and expenses. A month-end-close process should be implemented to: verify the recording of any material valuation adjustments and non-trading-related activities; allocate fund-level NAV to individual investors; and prepare and distribute account statements to investors. Annual processes should be in place to produce: financial statements and related footnotes to be audited by the fund's independent accounting firm; and investor-level tax information, as needed by investors, according to the regulations promulgated by the relevant tax authority. Operational controls should be periodically assessed in light of changing business needs, particularly where there have been changes to the activities of the organization. The manager should retain responsibility and oversight for any outsourced parts of the process. A daily profit and loss reconciliation process that is undertaken internally and that shadows and duplicates many of the functions that a Fund administrator performs, is also advisable. When repeated daily, this reconciliation process should lead to a month-end NAV process that has fewer exceptions, and to less sizable adjustments between the estimated monthly performance figure calculated intra-monthly and the official monthly performance figure established at the month-end close.

Information technology

The manager must establish policies and procedures to control changes to any information technology, including software, data, hardware, and infrastructure, as well as for information technology security.

Best execution and soft dollar arrangements

The manager must seek best execution in its trading activities for the benefit of each fund it manages. Factors to consider for best execution include, but are not limited to: prompt and reliable execution; the financial strength, integrity, and stability of the broker or counterparty; the quality, comprehensiveness, timeliness, and frequency of available research and market information provided by the executing broker; the executing broker's ability to execute transactions (and commit capital) of size, in liquid and illiquid markets, with minimal or no disruption to the market for the security; the competitiveness of commission rates in comparison with other brokers satisfying the manager's other selection criteria; and the ability of the executing broker to maintain confidentiality. Soft dollar (commission management) arrangements, including directed brokerage and commission-sharing agreements, may impact the evaluation of best execution. Therefore, a manager should determine whether brokerage and research services fall within the safe harbour as set forth in section 28(e) of the Exchange Act (Securities and Exchange Commission, 1998). If soft dollar arrangements fall outside the safe harbour provided by section 28(e), the manager should ensure that such arrangements are consistent with its duties to its funds, and determine whether the products and services received fall within the disclosed usage of soft dollar arrangements. All soft dollar arrangements should be fully disclosed to investors in the funds' offering documents and Form ADV, if applicable. More comprehensive guidance about soft dollar arrangements is offered by the CFA Institute's Soft Dollar Standards (CFA Institute, 2004; revised 2011).

Business continuity/disaster recovery (BC/DR) plans

The manager should establish a comprehensive BC/DR plan to mitigate financial loss in the event of disaster or other business disruption. The plan should include a business impact analysis to identify and prioritize critical processes. It should clearly articulate business recovery and resumption objectives. It may also include written procedures and documentation, test plans and test scenarios, and other procedures for addressing unforeseen events in an emergency. Business continuity planning should cover all operational business functions and not be limited to technology-based BC/DR.[3]

Anti-money laundering (AML) programs

Anti-money laundering is becoming an increasingly important consideration to be addressed by best practices. In the United States, section 352 of the USA PATRIOT Act requires financial institutions to establish AML programs (Department of the Treasury, 2002). At a minimum, such programs must include: the development of internal policies, procedures and controls; designation of a compliance officer; an ongoing employee training program; and an independent audit function to test programs. Managers should adopt and implement AML programs consistent with section 352 as a matter of sound business practice. The AML program must be tailored to the manager's business and operations, including the nature and location of investors, relationships with third parties and applicability of AML rules to non-US jurisdictions.[3]

19.3.2   Valuation

If there is a single area that has the potential to expose poor operational and control practices in the eyes of the investor, it is valuation.[4] At all times, but especially during periods of market stress, investors are concerned about illiquidity and the mispricing of securities. As part of the pre-investment due diligence process, investors should be looking for hard evidence of a real valuation process, documented by policies and procedures, and monitored and enforced by a team that is separate from the portfolio management team. Because valuation issues are so important to investors, managers should strive to implement best-in-class policies and procedures in this area.[5]

The best valuation practices, as industry-wide evidence suggests, involve a layered approach that engages multiple parties both internal and external to the fund. In our view, best practice in this area is always associated with an uncompromising mark-to-market discipline that is operative at all times, not just during the month-end NAV cycle. Key to the integrity of the process is the strict segregation of pricing and verification duties, which should be performed by independent teams. External service providers need to be utilized. Independent prices can be sourced by the fund administrator or custodian. If hard-to-price assets are included in the portfolio, the services of reputable third-party valuation firms need to be retained. In such situations, the external valuation provider should offer a valuation range for the assets being priced independently, rather than a negative assurance letter that references a valuation estimate generated by the investment manager. The portfolio and key controls must be audited by a reputable external auditing firm.

Valuation issues related to hedge funds assume greater importance because incentive fee arrangements are often present. Such arrangements enable hedge fund managers to participate alongside investors in the fund's performance, often in an asymmetrical, non-linear manner.[6] Incentive fees (also referred to as performance fees) align the interests of managers and investors and enable hedge funds to attract and retain top investment talent. If they are improperly structured, however, incentive fee arrangements create the potential for conflicts of interest between managers and investors.[7] Conflicts that may arise due to valuation and performance data may be mitigated, potentially, through the use of third-party providers to source such information.

The types of assets, in which a fund invests, will determine the nature and severity of the valuation issues that may arise, such as those listed below:

Liquid exchange-traded securities

Valuation issues are generally minimal or do not exist for such investments, since market price information is, in almost all cases, widely available and valuations are readily and independently verifiable.

Illiquid exchange-traded and OTC securities

If an investment has limited or non-existent trading activity, establishing its price is problematic and this will complicate the fund valuation process.

Such securities include OTC derivatives where pricing information can only be obtained from brokers that deal in those derivatives. In some cases, the only pricing sources are the fund's trading counterparties.

Private investments

Such investments may not have a readily ascertainable market value after the initial transaction has been made, and may not have that until the investment is realized or redeemed. Potential valuation conflicts may arise with such investments.

Investors must understand what portion of a fund is comprised of hard-to-value assets. FASB Topic 820 – Fair Value Measurements (Topic 820 of the Financial Accounting Standards Board's Accounting Standards Codification), defines a hierarchy of assets according to the reliability of available pricing information: Level 1 assets have observable market prices to a large extent, such as equities trading on major exchanges; Level 2 assets have observable market prices to some extent, such as OTC derivatives for which broker quotes are relied on for pricing; and Level 3 assets have largely unobservable market prices, such as private equity investments. Managers must report to investors the percentage of the fund in Level 2 and 3 assets at least quarterly, which is more stringent than the annual frequency that Generally Applicable Accounting Principles (GAAP) will soon require. If pricing models have to be used to value Level 2 and 3 assets, the quality of these models must be assessed by the independent team responsible for valuation, using analyses such as back-testing employed internally or by third-party providers.

Hedge funds increasingly use a mechanism called a 'side pocket' to separate illiquid assets with no readily available market value from more liquid investments. Investments placed in a side pocket are available to current, but not future, investors in the fund. Redemptions from side pockets are generally not permitted until an investment is removed from the side pocket upon realization of a gain or loss. The purpose of side pockets is to protect investors by avoiding the need for them to enter or exit illiquid and unreliably priced investments. Most managers do not earn incentive fees on investments in side pockets until an investment is deemed realized and some type of market-pricing information becomes available. The use of side pockets must be governed by clearly-defined guidelines that must state, among other things, if and when an asset should be moved into and out of a side pocket. Relevant considerations include the availability of evidence of value (for example, through market prices or broker quotes), the inherent difficulty in establishing a value for an investment, the nature of the market and the anticipated ability to enter or exit an investment. Valuation policies of side-pocketed investments should be the same as those for other investments.

19.3.3 Risk management

An investment manager must establish a comprehensive and integrated risk management framework that takes into account the size, portfolio management process and investment strategies of its funds. All potential sources of risk inherent in the manager's investment styles or processes need to be identified, understood, and, as far as possible, translated into relevant, measurable risk factors. Typically, a risk measure should estimate the impact of an event on the portfolio and the probability of this event occurring. Categories of risk could be widely recognized ones such as liquidity risk (including both asset and funding liquidity), leverage risk, market risk, counterparty credit risk, operational risk, legal, regulatory and compliance risk (each discussed below), or more specialized ones as applicable to a given portfolio. The impact of each risk factor on the portfolio should be measured under both normal and stressed market conditions. This impact also needs to be evaluated using both quantitative and qualitative criteria.

Although senior management should retain overall responsibility for risk management by empowering a chief risk officer (CRO) or a Risk Committee, industry-wide evidence suggests that risk management needs to be addressed in a holistic manner. We envision a process that does not reside within a single department, but involves multiple areas throughout the organization. Among the groups that need to interact continuously to define and monitor potential exposures quantitatively and qualitatively are 'Treasury', 'Operations', 'Legal', and 'Compliance'. Such activity can only occur in an organization that enjoys strong governance, and which removes organizational barriers that impede necessary communication so that all the relevant groups can be brought together. The risk monitoring and management process should not be outsourced; senior management should maintain overall responsibility for it. If specific risk measurement functions are outsourced, senior management must ensure adequate understanding of the outsourced parts of the process and maintain responsibility for them.

The investment manager must ensure the integrity of the risk management function. Where practical, there needs to be segregation of duties, with different people responsible for the risk management function and for the investment management function. Periodic reviews by independent personnel or external parties must be performed to evaluate the continued robustness of the risk management process and ensure that controls and limits are being adhered to.

Principal categories of risk that the risk management process must address include those listed below:

Liquidity risk

This refers to the ability of a fund to meet its need for cash. A manager should evaluate the impact of factors that contribute to liquidity risk, including: (i) funding provided by lending counterparties, including terms of margin borrowing, (ii) redemption rights by investors and the amounts of capital involved, (iii) market liquidity conditions that could affect the manager's ability to sell securities with minimal adverse price impact.

Leverage risk

This refers to the practice of using borrowed funds to trade and invest. A manager should manage leverage carefully. For portfolios without derivatives, leverage may be defined as the market value of assets relative to the portfolio's capital. Leverage for more complex portfolios or portfolios containing derivatives may be estimated by analysing the risk of different strategies and understanding the potential for extreme losses arising from those strategies.

Market risk

This refers to the financial risk resulting from changes in the market price of a fund's positions. A manager should identify the size, direction and rate of change of portfolio exposures to market risk factors, including equity indices, interest rates, credit spreads, currency exchange rates and commodity prices. Scenario analyses and stress tests should be conducted on portfolios at appropriate frequencies. Historical, forward-looking, or ad hoc scenario analyses must be used only after the advantages and limitations for each are clearly understood. Stress tests measure the vulnerability of a portfolio to shocks of single or multiple market factors by constant amounts or percentage moves. The manager must periodically review the performance of market risk models in use and adjust assumptions, inputs and model structures to better represent current reality.

Counterparty credit risk

This refers to risk of loss because of changes in creditworthiness or solvency of prime brokers, custodians, derivative dealers and lending, trading, cash management and depositor counterparties, as applicable. A manager must carefully monitor a fund's exposure to counterparties and understand the impact of potential counterparty loss of liquidity or failure, including the risk of business disruption. Diversifying through the use of multiple prime brokers and other counterparties should be weighed against the increased complexity and practicality of settlement, reconciliation and daily collateral management.

Operational risk

This refers to the risk resulting from inadequate or failed internal processes, people, and systems, or from external events.[8] A member of senior management not associated with the investment management process, a COO or similar, should oversee all operational areas. The manager should implement and maintain strong internal controls to minimize the potential loss resulting from operational risk. These controls may include, as applicable: (i) the use and maintenance of a centralized position data set; (ii) the adoption of trade capture devices; and (iii) the prompt reconciliation of trading information with the fund's prime broker or settlement agent and fund administrator (if any). A fund should monitor its overall level of operational risk, either internally or by using third-party reviewers. Elements subject to review could be (as applicable): (i) assets and products; (ii) staffing and resources; (iii) infrastructure (including information technology resources, BC/DR planning); and (iv) compliance and regulation.

One key aspect of operational risk is the notion of *implementation risk*, namely the risk of the implemented investment strategy differing from what is articulated to the clients in disclosures and investment management agreements due to issues in systems, data, and software used for the implementation. Implementation risks can be more pronounced in systematic strategies where investment decisions may rely on quantitative models with complex data and software infrastructure requirements. Following SEC's focus on these issues (Securities and Exchange Commission, 2011), the review and oversight of investment models and their implementation are being held to the stricter standards and scrutiny applied to financial disclosures and statements.

Compliance, legal and regulatory risk

This refers to the risk of loss resulting from litigation or regulatory non-compliance. A manager should develop a comprehensive manual that will include all compliance policies to be adhered to in key operational areas to limit or mitigate the risk of regulatory non-compliance. A chief compliance officer (CCO) must be appointed to be responsible for ensuring that compliance policies are followed and enforced. A well-developed legal infrastructure is particularly important for asset managers that operate on a global basis. The legal team must ensure that the asset manager's legal entity structure is sound from a tax and regulatory perspective in the different jurisdictions in which the manager operates. The establishment of a new products committee that includes representatives from operations, technology, controllers, valuation, compliance, regulatory and legal groups is another best practice within the industry. This committee is tasked, in part, with reviewing each product before it is launched to ensure that the necessary infrastructure is in place and that legal, and regulatory, requirements and limitations are understood and accounted for in advance of the product's launch. The legal team must also monitor the ever-changing regulatory landscape on a global basis, so that managers can modify their strategies, policies and operational practices when necessary. Recent revisions to short-selling rules in many jurisdictions are an example of regulatory change that has had a profound impact on the investment strategies and operations of certain hedge funds.

19.4   Operational and control issues related to the management of multiple portfolios

So far, our discussion has focused on operational and control issues encountered in the management of a single fund. Additional issues arise in the management of multiple portfolios, such as separately managed accounts (SMAs) that share a common portfolio construction approach and may trade simultaneously.[9] We describe some of these issues in the subsections below.

19.4.1   Increased operational complexity

Managing multiple funds increases operational complexity for the investment manager. Data aggregation, trade allocation, selecting third-party service providers and working with multiple prime brokers are some of the key considerations.

The level of complexity is a function of how control over portfolio operations is apportioned between the asset manager and the asset owner (for example, the separate account holder). Generally, the asset manager must deploy more extensive infrastructure in cases where the asset owner exercises a lot of control over the selection of third parties, such as prime brokers, ISDA counterparts and fund administrators. In classic SMA structures, more control will rest with the asset owner, while the overhead will be more pronounced for the investment manager. Greater investment in technology and personnel will be required to address issues such as: investment restrictions for the SMA that differ from those that apply to the main fund; additional disclosure requirements, such as position transparency; and management of derivative counterparts and trading flows.

19.4.2   Fairness

Managers must adhere to fairness principles to ensure equitable treatment of all portfolios under management. On the trading side, at the very minimum, fairness dictates that any accounts that are trading the same security in the same direction on a given day with the same execution benchmark, will receive the exact same average execution price.

19.4.3   Cross-trades

One of the important issues that arises in the management of multiple portfolios is the possibility of a cross-trade, which is defined as the sale of an asset from one portfolio and the purchase of the same asset into another portfolio where both portfolios are under the control of the same manager.

The Employee Retirement Income Security Act (ERISA) prohibits cross-trades in portfolios representing ERISA plans, unless they are consummated pursuant to an exemption (Federal Register, 1998). When portfolio rebalancing needs require the manager to trade on opposite sides for two separate ERISA accounts, the manager must ensure that these trades are strictly separated and are channelled through different brokers to comply with the ERISA legislation.

19.4.4 Market impact

The market impact of a trade generally refers to the change in the price of the traded security as a direct result of that particular trade. While most of the market impact from individual trades is temporary and negligible, larger trades in illiquid securities may have a permanent market impact. When a manager trades a particular security for one of the portfolios it manages, it is inevitable that the market impact of that trade will affect the values of other portfolios under the manager's discretion that hold active positions in that security. Therefore, trading in one account has the potential to adversely affect other accounts managed by the same firm. While this does not constitute a violation of fairness, the manager must disclose this possibility to all its clients. In addition, the manager must ensure that each account has an equitable share of the trading opportunities based on new information so that market-impact effects from trades across all accounts are also equitably experienced. This can be achieved by rotating the order in which the accounts are traded when implementing each new trading idea.

19.4.5 Portfolio construction

Managers of multiple portfolios must ensure that the trade ideas that result from their expertise and analysis are shared equitably among all managed portfolios. This is often easier said than done. Not every trade idea the manager generates is appropriate for all accounts under management, since individual clients typically have unique objectives, risk tolerances, benchmarks and other considerations. Even when the same idea can be applied to all accounts, the order in which the idea is implemented across the accounts may lead to different outcomes in individual portfolios as a result of market movements. A systematic, model-based approach that integrates an unbiased, rotating rebalancing schedule and a relatively nondiscretionary portfolio construction process with appropriate checks and safeguards often provides the best platform for addressing such fairness concerns.

19.5 Outsourcing investment management operations

Investment managers rely increasingly on third-party providers to perform a variety of investment operations. The main advantage of outsourcing is cost effectiveness, since third-party providers develop and operate platforms to service multiple firms and thus create operational and technological efficiencies. Results of benchmarking studies, as reported by State Street in a study on outsourcing (State Street, 2009), show that outsourced operations are on average 9% more efficient than in-house operations, and that new arrangements achieve savings of 15–22%. Most of the middle-office and back-office operational functions shown in Figure 19.2 (which was adapted from State Street's article (State Street, 2009), can be outsourced, freeing up managers to focus on their core competency, which is generating returns.

In addition to cost savings, outsourcing of investment operations offers the assurance of quality, since the third-party providers develop core competencies and expertise, and, out of competitive necessity, focus on providing superior service for the functions outsourced to them.

Another advantage of outsourcing is the independence of a third-party provider. This provides assurance to the investors that investment management and operational duties are segregated in critical functions such as NAV calculation and reporting. In light of recent investment scandals (for example, Madoff, (Arvedlund, 2009)), asset managers are finding it necessary to employ a reputable, independent firm to clear and price assets.

Front office	**Asset management**
	– Sales and client
	– Relationship
	  management
	– Investment research
	– Portfolio and risk
	  management
		Trade execution
		– Trade order
		  management and
		  execution
		– Financial Information
		  eXchange (FIX)
		  connectivity	

Middle office	**Investment operations**
	– Transaction
	  management
	– OTC derivatives
	  processing
	– Data management
	– Cash administration
		– Performance and
		  analytics
		– Corporate actions
		  processing
		– Portfolio recordkeeping
		  and accounting
			– Reconciliation
			  processing
			– Client reporting
			– Billing
			– Client data
			  warehouse

Back office	**Fund accounting**
	– General ledger
	– Security pricing
	– NAV calculation
	– Reconciliation
	– Daily, monthly, and
	  ad-hoc reporting
		Global custody
		– Assets safekeeping
		– Trade settlement
		– Cash availability
		– Failed trade reporting
		– Reconciliation
		– Income/tax reclaims
			Transfer agency
			– Shareholder
			  servicing

Figure 19.2   Investment management process functions

For any outsourcing arrangement to succeed, the investment manager must retain overall responsibility for any functions outsourced to third-party providers. The investment manager must hold designated internal personnel accountable for outsourced activities, and a member of the senior management team, such as the Chief Operating Officer, should be charged with overseeing all outsourced operations. A pure outsourcing model, with only a skeletal in-house crew employed by the investment manager, must be avoided.

Managers that offer separately managed accounts (SMAs) need to consider the additional infrastructure, resources and effort needed to manage relationships with multiple external providers. They must also contend with the increased operational complexity required to effectively integrate their own service platforms with those of third-party providers such as custodians, prime brokers, fund administrators and ISDA counterparts, especially where clients control the selection of such providers.

19.6 Summary and conclusions

In this chapter, we present a best practices framework for operational infrastructure and controls in asset management organizations. Although our framework focuses on best practices with regard to hedge funds, we believe that more mature vehicles, such as mutual funds, could borrow from it as well.

Operational and control best practices are the means to address the objectives of stakeholders in the asset management process. Their ultimate goal is to serve the interests of investors. Sophisticated investors should seek to determine whether their investment managers employ best practices in the key areas of (i) infrastructure and controls, (ii) valuation, and (iii) risk management. Managers may be interested in exploring outsourcing solutions for certain operational functions that enable them to benefit from the expertise and experience of third-party providers, while reducing costs and improving the quality of service offered to investors.

A manager that wishes to adopt best practices can access free and open industry resources, such as the Managed Funds Association's Sound Practices for Hedge Fund Managers (Managed Funds Association, 2009), the Report of the Asset Managers' Committee to the President's Working Group on Financial Markets (Asset Managers' Committee to the President's Working Group on Financial Markets, 2009), The Alternative Investment Management Association's Guide to Sound Practices for European Hedge Fund Managers (Alternative Investment Management Association, 2007a) and the CFA Institute's Asset Manager Code of Professional Conduct (CFA Institute, 2009), among others.

As a final note, we offer a word of caution regarding 'check-the-box' approaches to operational and control activities. It is straightforward to obtain information about best practices (anyone with an internet connection may do so), but it can be challenging to put them into practice effectively. Successful implementation of best practices across an asset management organization is often a function of experience, investment and strong governance. Managers that seek to introduce best practices in their organizations should first ascertain that they have a sound, principle-based governance structure in place before they embark on such an initiative. This will help ensure that appropriate parties are held accountable for critical activities and processes, and that communication between essential functions across the firm proceeds smoothly.

Acknowledgements

We extend our sincere thanks to Jeff Byrne, Suzanne Escousse, Olaniyi Mabogunje, David May, Keri Minichiello, Michael Pinedo, Andrea Raphael and especially Jay Reingold for reviewing this chapter and providing insightful comments that greatly improved its content and readability. We would also like to thank Priscilla Eng for greatly enhancing the appearance of the two figures in the chapter.

Notes

1. Report of the Asset Managers' Committee to the President's Working Group on Financial Markets (2009), Managed Funds Association (2009), Alternative Investment Management Association (2007a), CFA Institute (2009).
2. Kundro and Feffer (2003) report, from the findings of a study initiated in mid-2002, that 54% of failed hedge funds had identifiable operational issues, and that 50% of failures could be attributed to operational risk alone.
3. More comprehensive guidance is given in Managed Funds Association (2009).
4. Kundro and Feffer (2010) report, from among the findings of a study undertaken earlier in the decade, that 57% of valuation issues implicated in hedge fund failures can be attributed to fraud or misrepresentation, 30% to process, systems, or procedural problems and 13% to mistakes or adjustments.
5. Useful guidance can be found in Alternative Investment Management Association (2007b), as well as in Managed Funds Association (2009), and Asset Managers' Committee to the President's Working Group on Financial Markets (2009), among other resources.
6. Stulz (2007) provides a plain explanation of incentive fee structures in the hedge fund industry, and their differences from those available in mutual funds.
7. Anson (2001) discusses potential misalignments between the interests of managers and investors resulting from the use of some incentive fee structures. Asness (2006) suggests improvements in hedge fund fee structures.
8. Brown, Goetzmann, Liang, and Schwartz (2009) propose a quantitative operational risk score ω for hedge funds that can be calculated from data in hedge fund databases. The purpose of the ω-score is to identify problematic funds in a similar manner to Altman's z-score, which predicts corporate bankruptcies, and can be used as a supplement for qualitative due diligence on hedge funds.In a subsequent study (Brown et al. 2012), the same authors examine a comprehensive sample of due diligence

reports on hedge funds and find that misrepresentation, as well as not using a major auditing firm and third-party valuation, are key components of operational risk and leading indicators of future fund failure.

9. A separately managed account (SMA) is an investment account owned by a single entity (typically an institutional or an HNW investor) and managed by an investment management firm. SMAs were developed in the 1970s to satisfy the needs of investors whose investment objectives did not match those of available mutual funds. Compared with mutual funds, SMAs offer investors flexibility through portfolio customization, greater control of flows in and out of the portfolio, a certain degree of transparency, which increases investors' level of comfort with managers and their strategies (Black. 2007), as well as greater tax efficiency. These benefits often come at the cost of higher fees.

References

Alternative Investment Management Association (2007a) 'Guide to Sound Practices for European Hedge Fund Managers', May. (Retrieved from http://www.aima. org/en/knowledge_centre/sound-practices/guides-to-sound-practices.cfm on 2 December 2012).

Alternative Investment Management Association (2007b) 'Guide to Sound Practices for Hedge Fund Valuation', March. (Retrieved from http://www.aima.org/en/knowledge_centre/sound-practices/guides-to-sound-practices.cfm on 2 December 2012).

Anson, M.J.P. (2001) 'Hedge Fund Incentive Fees and the "Free Option"', Journal of Alternative Investments, (4)2: 43–48, Fall.

Arvedlund, E. (2009) 'Too good to be true: the rise and fall of Bernie Madoff', Portfolio Hardcover, New York: Penguin Publishing, 11 August.

Asness, C. (2006) 'The Future Role of Hedge Funds', CFA Institute Conference Proceedings Quarterly, (23)2: 1–9, June.

Asset Managers' Committee to the President's Working Group on Financial Markets (2009) 'Best Practices for the Hedge Fund Industry: Report of the Asset Managers' Committee to the President's Working Group on Financial Markets', 15 January. (Retrieved from http://www.amaicmte.org/Public/AMC%20Report%20 -%20Final.pdf on 2 December 2012).

Black, K. (2007) 'Preventing and Detecting Hedge Fund Failure Risk through Partial Transparency', Derivatives Use, Trading & Regulation, (12)4: 330–341, February.

Brown, S.J., Goetzmann, W.N., Liang, B. and Schwartz, C. (2009) 'Estimating Operational Risk for Hedge Funds: The ω-Score', Financial Analysts Journal, (65)1: 43–53, January/February.

Brown, S.J., Goetzmann, W.N., Liang, B. and Schwartz, C. (2012) 'Trust and Delegation', Journal of Financial Economics, (103)2: 221–234, February.

CFA Institute (2004; revised 2011) 'Soft Dollar Standards: Guidance for Ethical Practices Involving Client Brokerage'. (Retrieved from http://www.cfapubs.org/doi/abs/10.2469/ccb.v2004.n1.4005 on 2 December 2012).

CFA Institute (2009) 'Asset Manager Code of Professional Conduct', Second Edition. (Retrieved from http://www.cfapubs.org/doi/pdf/10.2469/ccb.v2009.n8.1 on 3 August 2009).

CFA Institute (2010a) 'Code of Ethics and Standards of Professional Conduct'. (Retrieved from http://www.cfapubs.org/doi/pdf/10.2469/ccb.v2010.n14.1 on 2 December 2012).

CFA Institute (2010b) 'Standards of Practice Handbook', Tenth Edition. (Retrieved from http://www.cfapubs.org/doi/pdf/10.2469/ccb.v2010.n2.1 on 2 December 2012).

CFA Institute Centre (2009) 'About Investment Management: Governance'. (Retrieved from https://www.cfainstitute.org/centre/topics/im/governance.html on 17 August 2009).

Department of the Treasury (2002) 'Treasury Department Issues USA PATRIOT Act Guidance on Section 352', 25 October. (Retrieved from http://www.treas.gov/ press/ releases/po3580.htm on 22 August 2009).

Federal Register (1998) 'Cross-Trades of Securities by Investment Managers', (63)54: 20. (Retrieved from http://www.dol.gov/ebsa/regs/fedreg/notices/98007271.pdf on 27 August 2009).

Investment Company Institute (2012) '2012 Investment Company Fact Book', 52nd Edition, (Retrieved from http://www.ici.org/pdf/2012_fact book.pdf on 2 December 2012).

Kundro, C. and Feffer, S. (2003) 'Understanding and Mitigating Operational Risk in Hedge Fund Investments', Capco Institute, White paper series, March. (Retrieved from http://www.capco.com/content/knowledge-ideas?q=content/research on 31 August 2009).

Kundro, C. and Feffer, S. (2010) 'Valuation Issues and Operational Risk in Hedge Funds', Journal of Financial Transformation, (10): 41–47.

Managed Funds Association (2009) 'Sound Practices for Hedge Fund Managers'. (Retrieved from https://www.managedfunds.org/wp-content/uploads/2011/06/Final_2009_complete.pdf on 2 December 2012).

O'Hara, N.A. (2009) 'Asleep at the Switch? Corporate boards' culpability in the 2008 financial crisis', The Investment Professional, (2)3: 60–65, Summer.

Pozen, R. and Hamacher, T. (2011) 'Most Likely to Succeed: Leadership in the Fund Industry', Financial Analysts Journal, (67)6: 21–28, November/December.

Securities and Exchange Commission (1998) 'Section 28(e) of the Exchange Act: Inspection Report on the Soft Dollar Practices of Broker–Dealers, Investment Advisers and Mutual Funds', September 22. (Retrieved from http://www.sec.gov/ news/studies/ softdolr.htm on 22 August 2009).

Securities and Exchange Commission (2011) 'SEC Charges AXA Rosenberg Entities for Concealing Error in Quantitative Investment Model'. (Retrieved from http://www.sec. gov/news/press/2011/2011-37.htm on 10 January, 2013).

Smith, R. (2007) 'Merrill's $5 billion bath bares deeper divide', The Wall Street Journal, 6 October.

State Street (2009) 'Outsourcing Investment Operations: Managing Expense and Supporting Strategic Growth', State Street Vision Series, May. (Retrieved from http:// www.statestreet.com/knowledge/vision/2009/2009_oio.pdf on 22 August 2009).

Stulz, R. (2007) 'Hedge Funds: Past, Present, and Future', Journal of Economic Perspectives, vol. (21)2: 175–194, Spring.

Topic 820 of the Financial Accounting Standards Board's Accounting Standards Codification, as amended. (Source: www.fasb.org. Requires registration).

20

Managing Costs at Investment Management Firms

Adam Schneider

20.1 Overview

The investment management industry is facing tremendous obstacles. After a long period of excellent financial performance, the industry is now challenged by volatile markets, changing revenue models, and substantial client faith and trust issues. As a result of the 2007–2009 financial crisis, many investment management firms are facing significant pressures including revenue declines, issues with product performance, cost pressures, and the need to adjust business strategies to changing conditions. Managing these pressures, retaining clients and restoring acceptable levels of financial performance are substantial issues.

In many cases, investment management firms have experienced significant asset decreases due to relative underperformance. Asset decreases can easily lead to a revenue shortfall, and affected firms have been forced to actively manage their cost structures. However, in our experience cost management in the industry is a bit of a 'black art'. While many other types of firms can translate their expenses into standardized unit costs and compare them over time or can use benchmark studies that include competitors, it is difficult for most investment management firms to obtain the proper information, and even harder to assess it in an industry-wide context. Part of this is due to the owner-operator mentality present in many firms, and part is due to the difficulty in comparing firm costs on an even basis.

This chapter is based on a wide variety of projects and exercises conducted over the past 20+ years throughout the investment management industry and covering many firms. During the course of these projects, investment manager-specific cost issues were examined in detail and a framework for analysis was designed to effectively allow firms to compare their cost performance with that of other investment firms.

The key issues faced when examining and comparing the cost structures of investment management firms include the following:

- while a firm's total cost is known, it is difficult to measure true cost at the investment strategy or functional levels, where management action can most readily be taken;
- firms have generally focused on gathering assets and growth rather than cost management, so basic reporting or analysis of costs may not be in place;
- with the emergence of investment managers at the trillion-dollar assets under management (AUM) range, the impact of scale can dominate the cost discussion and effectively distort unit costs for smaller firms;
- one of the larger expenditures, information technology (IT), has an unclear impact on investment manager productivity and is notably difficult to allocate to business activities;
- the industry has a quite logical belief that increased investment performance and increased client service, both measures of success, come at a price. For example, increased performance may require proprietary research, investment analysis and technology, raising the question of how high cost but high-performing managers should be evaluated;
- there are significant management trade-offs between worker productivity (the work accomplished per person) and the cost of an employee, which tends to vary with geography and seniority.

It should be pointed out here that we are discussing the *costs* of the core investment management capability focusing on internal activities and cost drivers. We are not addressing cost from an *investor* perspective: if an investment management firm charges investors 100 basis points annually for its product, that is *revenue* to the firm, not cost. Often, the industry talks about 'low-cost' investment management from an investor perspective – not the focus here. In addition, this discussion relates to the cost of the core investment activities and does not include the cost of retail distribution such as loads, sales commissions to agents, and other distribution charges.

20.2   Key issues in examining investment management firm cost structures

20.2.1   Measurement difficulties, especially at product and functional levels where action can be taken

While many investment management firms are relatively small, they may also be very complex. Each firm generally has a full range of *business functions* such as marketing, sales, research, portfolio management, Information Technology and back-office processing; investment management firms generally manage different, asset type-based *investment strategies* such as growth equity, value equity, cash, mortgages or index trackers; these strategies are packaged into a variety of *products* such as separate investment accounts, mutual funds or hedge funds. We make a distinction between *functions, strategies* and *products,* because assigning costs appropriately is important for cost management. While capturing a firm's total costs may be straightforward, the allocation or assignment of cost of the specific functions, strategies and products is challenging to calculate, but essential for comparing cost structures, calculating profitability and measuring efficiency.

At the same time, total costs are rarely helpful for comparative purposes and unit costs are more effective. The question is how to 'unitize' incurred costs. After performing numerous studies, including detailed activity-based costing (ABC) examinations, it seems that external functions such as sales and marketing are best measured in terms of accounts or assets gained (for example, net inflows), while core investment management functions such as research, trading and back-office operations are best measured in terms of cost-per-AUM. This type of structure enables significant comparisons and 'normalization' between firms to be made.

Comparing costs at increasing detail is correspondingly more difficult. For example, there may be enough cost and AUM such that cost for a major strategy, such as 'Fixed Income', can be determined. However, 'Fixed Income' is a misnomer; it is an umbrella term that incorporates disparate investment areas such as cash management, corporate bonds, government bonds (often segregated by duration), mortgage-backed securities, high-yield securities and a wide range of synthetic investments. Developing unit costs at the more detailed (and more actionable) level is less precise and more subject to interpretation. Given the wide variety of strategy definitions, investment philosophies and diversity of scale, it is increasingly difficult to structure an accurate cost study at this level.

20.2.2   Impact of focusing on asset gathering versus managing costs

Most investment management firms expend significant resources obtaining new clients, building new products, developing new distribution channels and other growth activities. The trade-off between asset acquisition and asset management is a management decision that has more to do with business opportunity than cost. If a particular firm is focused on maximizing investment performance, it may choose to spend heavily in investment research. Equally, a firm focused on asset growth may concentrate spending on marketing, advertising or increasing commission payments to distributors. These are choices, not inherent costs; hence, when comparing investment management firm cost structures, it is typical to distinguish activities focused on business growth from those aimed at the actual management of investments.

It is possible to think of investment management firms as having two different businesses under one roof. The first, the actual 'investment' business, manages existing products and clients; this business could easily be very profitable if managed and measured separately. The second, the 'client acquisition' business, is charged with growing assets, finding new clients and introducing new strategies or products; this is typically unprofitable per se, but vital to the strategic health of the firm. The management balance between these two sets of activities is based on the relative economics of asset acquisition versus asset management. Many firms spend as much as three or four years of revenue attributable to new assets, believing that investment assets are 'sticky' and worth a significant investment.

20.2.3   Impact of scale on unit cost

The asset management business has been consolidating for a number of years, and for good reason: there are often large-scale economies in areas such as branding, distribution and product management. In addition, mergers have been a major trigger for firm asset size to growth. Even when focusing on investment activities, it is hard for an investment management firm with $10 billion in assets to have the same cost-per-asset as a firm with $100 billion. A wide variety of fixed costs can be spread over the larger asset base, including costs of sales, marketing, portfolio management and various types of IT costs.

That being said, larger firms also experience some diseconomies of scale. At the largest firms, standards for automation, quality, error resolution and client support are very high and correspondingly expensive. Larger firms typically spend more on product design and legal and compliance functions and generally maintain state-of-the-art IT systems. For example, smaller investment firms may have little to say on a subject like business continuity, while the largest have formal plans and capabilities.

The AUM of an individual strategy also affects comparisons since, given the impact of scale, it is very difficult to measure the cost efficiency of a new strategy. For example, for an investment management firm to decide it will launch a new strategy it must generally assign or hire portfolio managers and traders, establish a research function and gear up back-office capabilities before there are any significant assets. As a result, for subscale strategies, unit costs are often extraordinarily high and therefore not comparable with a mature firm in the same strategy. It is probably more appropriate to treat costs of this nature as 'market entry' costs, as opposed to ongoing 'ok to compare' costs.

20.2.4   Impact of technology expenditures on productivity

Perhaps the type of expense most difficult to assess is that of Information Technology. Technology expenses are difficult to characterize, as much of the expense goes toward shared infrastructure, operational requirements or special-purpose projects. Compounding the measurement difficulty is that many IT 'projects' are in fact multi-year in nature, and expenses in a given year may more accurately be relevant to future benefits rather than to current products or strategies.

Investment management firms can normalize their IT expenditure in several ways:

- 'Firm projects' that require extraordinary spending, such as relocating to a new building, can be separated from ongoing costs. (Although, while this may seem reasonable, we have seen that at many firms 'one-time' expenses still recur every year and, over time, the business must be able to fund them.)
- IT organizations can often measure and allocate costs back to the strategy or functional areas (such as allocating the cost of an equity trading system back to that strategy, or a compliance system back to that function).
- Remaining IT costs that are not directly assignable can often be allocated on another measure that is viewed as being fair or representative, such as on a per-person or per-square foot basis.
- Management at investment management firms may consider cost allocation hard to understand, so it is valuable to analyze cost both 'with' and 'without' allocated costs such as IT. The analysis 'with' costs shows detail of fully-loaded costs, while 'without' allows a focus on those costs that are more directly controllable by the area in question.

By utilizing these techniques, we have generally been able to provide insight into the IT costs of investment management firms.

20.2.5 Relationship between increased client service, increased investment performance and cost

A limited production sports car is not expected to have the same market price, or cost-per-car, as a high-volume sedan. There are many who believe the same is true for the investment business and that choices such as 'high-touch' client service and/or a goal of 'high-performance' in investment strategies inherently 'cost more' than others with less ambitious goals might spend. And there are clear cases where that is true: certainly no one would expect an actively managed strategy to cost the same as a passive strategy.

Ultimately, the decision to focus additional resources on improving client service or investment performance is a management issue beyond the bounds of 'cost'. The key considerations for this type of focus include revenue needs, market positioning, meeting client expectations, long-term requirements for scale and product profitability.[1]

20.2.6   Trade-offs between productivity and labour costs

In this era of offshoring and outsourcing, it is common to think in terms of labour cost arbitrage moving selected processes to lower-cost areas or to specialized firms with unique capabilities. Investment management firms have a wide range of choices, not only concerning the number of people involved per function (normalized to, say, per $1 billion in assets) but also the ways in which labour costs per-person can be structured.

For many functions, including back office processing and Information Technology, there are many alternatives, including nearshore locations, off-shore locations or outsourcing. Functional decomposition can be used to understand the work performed and the appropriate way to structure labour cost. This type of work management is common at this point.

Mainline investment activities are different. In addition, there is another reason to study these labour costs: the relatively high cost per-person for those performing investment activities. It is not unusual for the cost of investment activities to approach 50% of the total cost base, although these activities are carried out by a much smaller percentage of total personnel. Since this is 'the actual product' and senior investment professional compensation is involved, direct and careful management is typical.[2]

20.3   Value chain, processes and functions

Managing costs in the investment industry requires the ability to define what work is being done, so as to appropriately segregate work activities and costs. Relying on experiences with a number of firms, a representative investment management firm value chain follows in Figure 20.1.

The value chain attempts to summarize core activities into a universal framework and define key functions and processes required. When analyzing investment firms for cost opportunities, one can use a framework of this type to normalize the type of work being performed. This type of analysis finds similar work across the organization and groups together the work, people and related costs.

The major advantage of using a functional, standardized view of activities is that it enables the identification and segregation of the work performed, people involved, technology utilized and the related costs, anywhere in the organization. The approach is useful for such purposes as:

- internal assessment of who is performing what type of work;
- consolidation of similar activities;
- developing specific functional and per-unit costs;
- comparison/benchmarking with potential improvements, such as outsourcing or offshoring;

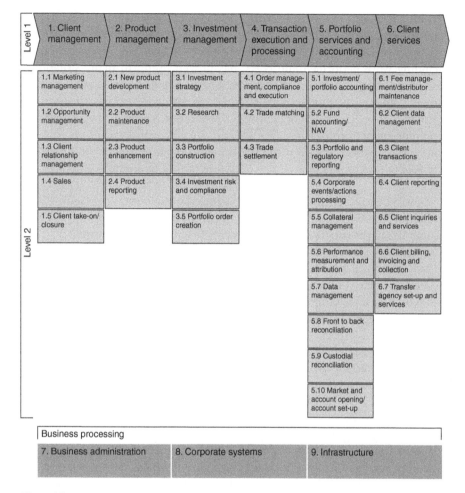

Figure 20.1   Investment management value chain and standardized processes

- re-engineering existing processes to provide better accountability, improved control and lower cost;
- automation of key functions.

20.4   Cost management and benchmarking

One question that we are asked: Is a functional approach valid, or does it obscure important organizational details and make analysis of cost and implementing change more difficult?

Over a twenty-year period, the functional model approach has been used to compare the unit cost and productivity performance of over 50 different investment management firms. These firms have had widely differing organizational structures and approaches to the investment process, and AUMs ranging from as little as $500 million to over $1 trillion. The analysis process, including work performed and costs, has proven useful in many situations. Since the functional model is organizationally neutral, it can be effectively used to compare the productivity, staffing and unit costs of investment management firms regardless of how firms are organized or where, in each, various functions are performed.

A typical analysis process using the function model includes the following activities:

- identifying discrete investment management functions (as per Figure 20.1);
- quantifying the resources used to perform those activities;
- organizing the functions and resources into a common structure;
- segregating special activities that are not typically performed by investment management firms from the 'core' comparisons;
- defining a set of business measures that are used to 'normalize';
- developing a series of comparisons against relevant measures (other firms who have gone through this process, existing benchmarks or profitability goals).

When benchmarking investment management firms, it is useful to assess them across four dimensions as follows:

- **Business profile**
  For scaling and to confirm applicability, the benchmark process starts by summarizing the investment firm's overall business profile and key information such as strategies, products, and current AUMs. This is done to ensure firms are similar enough to each other to be meaningfully compared and to provide 'hard facts' by which to view any cost analyses. Typical summary statistics include:
  - structure of the firm in terms of management and organization;
  - overall investment philosophy;
  - AUMs, by strategy, product and distribution channel;
  - internal views of relative capability and maturity of processes, technology, and asset management capabilities;
  - key investment statistics such as supported asset classes, number of portfolios, asset universe, transaction volumes, portfolio turnover and average transaction size.
- **Expense by strategy and by function**
  There is no substitute in a cost management exercise for actual direct expenses. These expenses are typically known from financial reporting and

are then adjusted to produce basis point costs based on AUM. For example, an organization spending $100,000,000 on equities but managing $100 billion in equity values would have a cost for equities of 10 basis points. Key to this expense assignment is an assignment process based on financial reporting but translated to the standardized value chain. Typical 'cuts' of the cost structure would include:

- by function, including investment activity, accounting, reporting, legal and systems, as per the value chain;
- by strategy, such as equity, fixed income, private placement, real estate equity, real estate debt and international;
- in some cases, depending on size and scale, by asset class within strategy, such as money market within Fixed Income.

- **Productivity**
  Comparative measures are then produced that measure productivity, which we generally define as AUM per full-time employee. For example, an organization with $100 billion in AUM and 100 investment management employees would have productivity of $1 billion per employee. The productivity measures are generally also calculated by function and by strategy as above (and in the case of 'submeasures', actual assets rather than total assets must be used). For example, one firm in which we worked asked for relative costs for function 5.5 Collateral management. Since only a portion of the firm's assets utilized this service, costs incurred by this function were divided by the actual assets 'using' the function.

- **Staff cost efficiency**
  The last measure of comparison is cost efficiency per-person, also calculated by function and by strategy. We have seen analyses of this sort leading to many different types of management action, including the appropriateness of compensation programs, location of work being performed, potential for outsourcing selected functions and potential for offshoring work to lower-cost locations.

In light of the industry's consolidation in some circumstances, it may be appropriate to develop and compare investment managers in other ways. For example, a larger firm may have multiple, independently-managed subsidiaries and need a value chain analysis for each. Other firms may rely heavily on outsourced service providers, and the costs of these providers will need to be considered in detail.[3]

20.5   Cost management and benchmarking in practice

After the gathering, collection and analysis of data, there are multiple ways to review benchmarking information. Generally, the two most effective ways are by investment strategy or function. Figure 20.2 shows a typical high-level summary of investment management firm costs by strategy, and Figure 20.3 shows a high-level summary by function.

The data indicated is real: it is derived from surveys covering over a dozen sizable investment management firms and shows the lowest cost found, the highest cost found, and the average weighted by AUMs, all in basis points versus relevant AUM. While the data provided here is real, there are some limitations: most of the studied managers are single-country firms, and most costs represent the cost for supporting local domestic products. For similar firms,

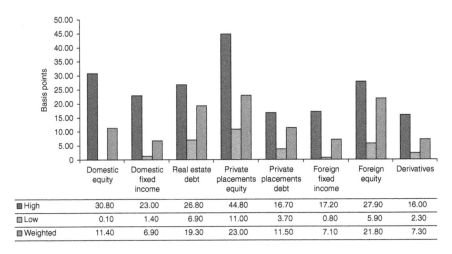

	Domestic equity	Domestic fixed income	Real estate debt	Private placements equity	Private placements debt	Foreign fixed income	Foreign equity	Derivatives
High	30.80	23.00	26.80	44.80	16.70	17.20	27.90	16.00
Low	0.10	1.40	6.90	11.00	3.70	0.80	5.90	2.30
Weighted	11.40	6.90	19.30	23.00	11.50	7.10	21.80	7.30

Figure 20.2   Investment management costs by strategy (in basis points)

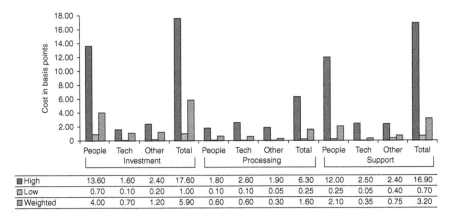

| | People | Tech | Other | Total | People | Tech | Other | Total | People | Tech | Other | Total |
	Investment				Processing				Support			
High	13.60	1.60	2.40	17.60	1.80	2.60	1.90	6.30	12.00	2.50	2.40	16.90
Low	0.70	0.10	0.20	1.00	0.10	0.10	0.05	0.25	0.25	0.05	0.40	0.70
Weighted	4.00	0.70	1.20	5.90	0.60	0.60	0.30	1.60	2.10	0.35	0.75	3.20

Figure 20.3   Investment management costs by function (in basis points)

or relevant parts of more global firms, the weighted-average cost is usually a good benchmark for appropriate cost levels. Investment management firms with widely differing cost levels are candidates for a cost control program such as re-engineering, automation or outsourcing.

Significant insight can be gained by comparing a given firm's cost structure with the averages. In the case of a review by strategy, this provides a high-level basis for evaluating product cost, related product profitability (if some assumptions can be made about average revenue rates) and comparisons with peers. Note that costs in this case, by strategy, include all of the value chain; for example, they include the cost of each of the functions identified in Figure 20.1 as applicable to the relevant strategy.

The functional view, which includes detailed costs for people, technology, and 'other' (such as office space), allows one to compare the relative efficiency of actual core function areas. For example, in this case, average cost for back office processing was found to be 1.60 basis points across all assets and strategies. A firm's cost base that exceeds this level by a significant amount, unless it is providing an unusual mix of services, service levels, or supporting an unusual asset mix, would indicate that firm is a candidate for structural change such as re-engineering or outsourcing.

20.6   Investment manager cost control

Generally speaking, firms with 'high costs' may choose to implement a formal cost management program. How can such programs be structured effectively?

Cost management programs can be approached narrowly by focusing on a particular function or strategy that is identified as needing improvement or more broadly, often firm-wide. This is a management choice. At one time, a firm might have focused on specific improvements such as process re-engineering, setting up an offshore centre, automation, or outsourcing. The firm would use cost data to set a baseline for improvement.

Over time we have seen firms take a more holistic view of cost management.[4] Investment management firms have been attempting a long-term program that can sustainably reduce cost, including building a supportive internal culture. A long-term-oriented cost management program should address four key principles:

– **Align objectives with financial imperative** Set overall target cost reduction objectives and focus efforts on cost areas that are aligned. In practice, this means that the largest and most significant cost pools are directly targeted.
– **Balance requirements and resources** Firms should employ a clearly-defined cost reduction process that includes a balanced set of time frames, resources, scope, and analytical requirements.

- **Motivate the organization** Firms need to create an environment in which executives, management and staff understand the financial imperative and support the stated objectives. This often requires significant communications and explanation, and can be the hardest part of the program.
- **Aim for sustainable benefits** Firms need to establish an ability to not only identify and implement savings, but also to sustain them.

A broadly focused cost management program includes analysis of essentially all activities with a long-term goal of finding more efficient ways to run the entire organization. However, this is difficult. Techniques for managing *external* spend such as supplies and travel are well known and include consolidating vendors, establishing price and rate cards, and using online vendor management tools. However, when the discussion shifts to the broader topic of lowering *internal* costs, firms face hard decisions about which work should be performed, how people should be paid, and what can be consolidated or performed differently. Investment management firms often struggle with their own scale, complexity, and with the difficult human capital decisions involved.

Across the value chain, there are some typical cost management strategies employed for each major portion. Following is a brief summary of strategies commonly employed in the marketplace, organized by the value chain in Figure 20.1.

20.6.1 Client acquisition

Of all the elements of the value chain, the activities we label 'client acquisition' are among the most difficult to measure and value. 'How much is that client worth?' is a perennial question that must balance the difficulty and cost of attracting clients with their long-term value. Related to client acquisition are some key factors. In practice most investment clients above a minimum threshold are profitable, muddying the conversation on 'which clients' to accept. Second, investment firms are usually competing for clients and it may be necessary to offer a range of strategies rather than focus just to retain the client at all. Third, the distribution strategy may demand that certain types of clients be accepted.

That being said, firms can pursue successful cost management strategies for client acquisition by:

- quantifying the value of a new client *and* managing the new client acquisition process according to that value. Some firms segregate acquisition cost and planned revenue (or profitability) for new clients in an effort to ensure their overall costs do not exceed actual client value;
- eliminating strategies, sales channels and marketing efforts with low historic return on investment;

- automating customer relationship management activities and proposal-generation activities in an effort to improve close rates;
- improving servicing systems so that client take-on is easy and efficient.

20.6.2 Strategy and product management

Many investment management firms have a wide variety of investment strategies, embedded within a number of externally offered products, sold through a wide variety of sales channels. For example, a simple 'growth equity' strategy capability may be part of a mutual fund sold through a brokerage channel, an institutional separate account sold by a dedicated team, and the 'long' strategy part of a long-short hedge fund product.

Many firms end up with various strategies, products, and channels, but have less ability to understand the profitability dynamics of each of these. The key to product management is often in recognizing the products the firm is good at providing, is profitable at offering, and which can be sustainable over the long term. One key concept we have employed is that of 'no hobbies'. Either firms have significant scale, or can see the way it can be achieved, or it is time to consolidate. Given the industry's significant scale economies, strategies, products or channels that do not meet size, growth and alignment criteria should be candidates for consolidation or elimination.

20.6.3 Investment management

Investment management is arguably the most expensive single part of the value chain in many firms, particularly at institutional firms which do not support retail clients. The area is composed of professionals who are generally diligent and extremely knowledgeable about their strategies, performance, competitive positioning, and of course, the overall investment marketplace.

There are two primary strategies for cost management in this area: ensure that the investment professionals are aligned and effective; and provide a sufficient level of automation for administrative efficiencies.

For managing investment professionals, the use of activity-based costing and/or a direct review of strategy profitability are effective tools to review and understand efficiency. Given the industry's scale economies, the analysis may be able to focus on strategies with smaller AUM. It is also important to think through relative strategy performance when considering any aspect of cost management (for example high cost may be required to generate high relative performance).

In terms of administration and automation, many firms have implemented automated portfolio, rebalancing, investment compliance and trading tools. Many strategies, such as index funds, are dependent on them. They generally improve the portfolio management process in terms of efficiency, as well as lowering the probability of trade or guideline errors.

20.6.4   Transaction execution and processing

Cost management in this value chain activity is essential, often dominated by what is needed for investment management firms to trade assets successfully. This area features a complex mix of costs for portfolio management capabilities, trading, and access to additional sources of liquidity. Many consider there to be an 'arms race' between investment management firms and their competitors in terms of trading technology and capabilities.

In addition, there are nonfirm costs paid for by the asset owner in terms of transaction costs, market impact and other factors. Please see Chapter 22 for a leading-edge discussion of the costs of transaction execution.

20.6.5   Portfolio services and accounting

Portfolio services is a complex, operationally intensive activity that has grown increasingly sophisticated over time. As firms add strategies, products, and channels, specific requirements for processing, service, and support technology follow. Configuration of processing capabilities varies greatly, depending on firm history and strategy, and the way these have evolved over time.

Given the variety, many firms have a complex environment with a series of parallel infrastructure capabilities. For example, firms generally need to perform portfolio accounting for their own 'books and records' but may hire a bank to perform a different type of accounting to determine the NAV if that same portfolio is also a mutual fund. There are many similar examples of parallel infrastructure, including specialized accounting for insurance clients, specialized accounting for hedge funds and tax-aware accounting for personal accounts. For global firms, there are also many country-specific requirements and tax-specific requirements.

Strategies for cost management of this area include re-engineering of processes, consolidation of investment accounting platforms, offshoring to a lower-cost environment, consolidation of multiple environments where possible, and automation of manual activities.

Efforts of this sort are often large, expensive and complex projects. In recent years another alternative has developed, the outsourcing of many of these activities to an asset servicing institution, generally a bank. The major providers have built a series of processing and accounting technologies and operations capabilities which have significant integrated competencies and which can be very cost effective. We have seen investment managers achieve cost reductions through these types of strategies.

20.7   Summary

Cost reduction programs are significant undertakings and typically to be effective must last for many years. It is important to structure the effort in ways that can be successful in the long term. To do so, investment management firms must balance the value of the initiatives versus the cost of implementation versus the administrative and management process required. Ideally, cost management is a sustainable, reinforcing process:

- Identifying initiatives is analytic in nature and fundamentally starts with benchmarking: typically, an analysis team identifies opportunities, but the realization is dependent on the investment management firm culture.
- Cost reduction implementation requires focused project resources, deadlines, a degree of centralized management or coordination, and reinforcement of objectives over time.
- Sustainability is possible when cost reduction activities become part of the culture, including budget, incentive compensation, annual goals and promotion criteria.

These key factors are summarized in Figure 20.4.

Lastly, it is essential to structure cost management efforts for success. In terms of focus, this includes a specific plan to obtain 'quick hits' as well as build a long-term sustainable program. In terms of team, it requires senior

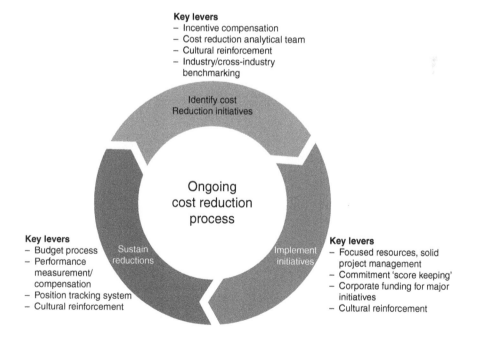

Key levers
- Incentive compensation
- Cost reduction analytical team
- Cultural reinforcement
- Industry/cross-industry benchmarking

Identify cost Reduction initiatives

Ongoing cost reduction process

Key levers
- Budget process
- Performance measurement/ compensation
- Position tracking system
- Cultural reinforcement

Sustain reductions

Implement initiatives

Key levers
- Focused resources, solid project management
- Commitment 'score keeping'
- Corporate funding for major initiatives
- Cultural reinforcement

Figure 20.4 Sustainable cost reduction

management oversight, a highly-capable project manager and analysis teams staffed with well-respected, analytical and objective personnel.

Notes

1. See 'Reconnecting for Profit: Strategies for Building Sustainable Profits in Wealth Management', http:// www.deloitte.com/assets/Dcom-UnitedKingdom/Local%20 Assets/Documents/UK_FS_Reconnectingforprofit.pdf
2. For a fuller discussion in light of recent market events, please see 'Altering Compensation Approaches to Reflect the Changing Financial Services Landscape', https://www.deloittenet.com/CM/ThoughtLeadershipHub/FinancialServices/default.htm
3. For a fuller discussion of potential outsourcing choices, see 'Evolving operating models within the hedge fund industry', https://marketplace.deloitte.com/MPContent/NR/rdonlyres/A4EABB87-B0B7–4DDA–8DDD-82535552E1B9/74909/us_fsI_IM_EvolvingmodelsHF_may09dcs2790143_7.pdf
4. One of the outstanding business and cost management questions in light of recent events is the state of investment firms' risk management procedures. For approaches to risk management, please refer to 'Global Risk Management Survey: Sixth Edition – Risk Management in the Spotlight', https://marketplace. deloitte.com/MPContent/NR/rdonlyres/84D830AC-6EE1–4B00–8BDD-B9ABF106E070/72460/DeloitteGRMS6thEdition_final_high.pdf

21

Strategic and Tactical Cost Management in the Asset Management Industry

Marcelo Cruz

21.1 Introduction

The financial crisis that started in 2008 made the global asset management industry face challenges it has not seen in decades. The industry was accustomed to high margins and substantial profits (particularly in the years 2000–2007, due to the availability of excess liquidity). As the market climbed over the last 30 years, occasional dips notwithstanding, asset managers became used to the steady increases in their assets under management (AUM) and almost certain yearly profits in a relatively low risk environment. However, in the wake of the biggest downturn since the Great Depression, a slow recovery has left many firms struggling. Even in 2012/2013 the recovery seems stalled, as the crisis still lingers to a certain extent, the highly volatile environment and macroeconomic uncertainties (more particularly high unemployment rates in most of the world) still do not allow customers to build wealth which is crucial for the asset management industry to grow.

Major structural changes are not new in this industry. If we consider only the past two decades, we can broadly break down these changes into two distinct phases. In the first phase, which took place from the 1990s until 2008, AUM in the sector skyrocketed, mostly due to the high liquidity in the global financial markets that was caused by abundant credit and ever-increasing personal asset prices (for example stocks and house prices). This phase also witnessed an exponential increase in the number of hedge funds asset managers who typically have a smaller number of wealthy clients, and who can take very risky positions and bets that have a tendency to offer substantial returns. Such hedge funds were often established by either star traders from investment banks or asset managers looking for independence in a less regulated environment. These funds continue to play an important role in the financial markets by exploring arbitrage opportunities, although this subsector of the industry is also bound for significant changes as many hedge funds are going out of business.

The asset management industry is now experiencing the second phase of major changes. After the credit crisis, the sector suffered tremendously as world markets tumbled across the globe, and liquidity, once abundant, became either very restricted or non-existent. Even with the markets recovering, it cannot be expected that the same level of liquidity and wealth will be available.

During the 'golden years' of abundant liquidity, most asset managers were not overly worried about the costs incurred in running their operations and did not pay close attention to the risks involved, since the continuous growth in personal wealth steadily increased their AUM. Expansion and global growth were the order of the day. Errors and high operating costs were buried under the increased revenues from a larger asset base and the profits that came from high returns in the world markets.

Immediately after the 2008 financial crisis, the situation has changed dramatically. Large asset managers have seen their AUM go down by 30% or 40%, not only because of the drop in asset prices but also because clients are withdrawing funds, either from the necessity to cover debts, because they fear that the stock markets will take a long time to recover, or out of concern for the financial well-being of the asset managers. The crisis also showed regulatory failures, like the Bernie Madoff case (this case is one of the largest operational risk events in history). Many investors close to retirement lost their pensions, not only because of the market conditions, but also because of a lack of caution and risk management from pension fund managers.

This new economic environment is forcing asset managers to develop a much more careful discipline around costs, risk management and productivity. Each of these factors has received widespread attention in the media. Productivity is a concept usually associated with manufacturing, but it can also play an important role in asset management.

In this chapter, we argue that, within the options available to them for returning to their former profitability levels, asset managers will have to take a very careful look at their cost structure and risk management frameworks. The next section of this chapter analyzes how the global asset management industry is faring since 2007/2008. In the section 21.3, we will analyze the cost structure of asset managers and describe strategic/tactical options to reduce costs on an item-by-item basis. In the last section, we describe how a well-tailored and well-implemented risk management program can impact an asset manager's bottom line.

21.2   Survivor mode: analyzing how asset managers are faring in the long winter after the crisis

The 2008 financial crisis has affected the industry in a much deeper way than previous downturns have. As the link between wealth and economic growth is obvious, as the economic environment is taking time to have a solid growth, the industry growth itself has stalled. To illustrate this point, in 2007 the global value of AUM was around EUR 38 trillion. By the end of 2011 this figure was pretty much the same. Just as a comparison, the pre-crisis period in between 2007 and 2011 followed an average annual growth of 12% between 2000 and 2007.

The struggle that the global asset management industry has been going through since the crisis can be seen in Figure 21.1. These graphs, showing the performance for the US asset management industry, clearly show that they are struggling to recover. These graphs have 2007 indexed at 100, and we can see that the industry revenue in the US is 96% of what it was in 2007 (the same decline seen in AUM); however, costs are 8% higher compared to 2007 which reflects in profits at only 81% of the 2007 levels.

Difficult economic environments, particularly when lasting for such a long period, have also an impact on investor behavior which subsequently affects the asset management industry. This happens for two reasons. Firstly, investors who lost a significant amount of their savings in the financial crisis will tend

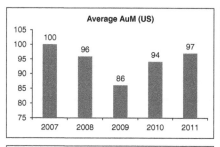

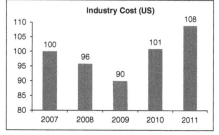

Figure 21.1   AUM, profits, revenues and costs of US asset managers

to be more cautious in the next few years. This behavior has been confirmed in previous recessions and also by recent client surveys. The second reason is that most clients (particularly, but not exclusively, in the US) are in a deleveraging process, since a large proportion of the population is deeply indebted. They now face the worst job market in decades with unemployment around 8% in both the US and most of Europe (some countries have rates above 10%). This process tends to slow down economic growth and may make the stock markets less attractive for a long time. Based on these two factors, clients are looking for more conservative, risk-averse funds that, typically, do not offer high margins. Although fund charges vary from country to country, asset managers usually receive an administration fee that is a fixed percentage of the AUM. This fee is in most cases somewhere between 1% and 3% (depending on the type of fund). In the most sophisticated and risky funds there is also a performance fee of around 20–25% on the returns exceeding a given benchmark. Therefore, funds that take more risk can have much higher margins than relatively risk-averse funds.

A second important factor that affects the industry is that the financial crisis that took place in 2008 is often considered to be a result of the greediness of investment bankers and asset managers who were looking for better returns in assets with extreme, and often misunderstood, risks. For this reason, the regulatory pressure is now considerably higher. For example, hedge funds that were basically unsupervised by the authorities are seeing a completely different environment ahead of them. The costs that this prospective new regulatory overhaul bears are driving a number of the smaller hedge funds out of business or forcing them to consolidate. Regulators are also pushing for a more robust risk management framework, an area that few asset managers can claim to have fully developed and one that can be quite costly.

All these factors (summarized in Table 21.1) forced asset managers to consider strategic and tactical alternatives. The important strategic questions that they need to face are, for example, whether or not they should change their business models by focusing on a particular asset (fixed income, equities etc.), whether or not they should merge with competitors to reduce costs through economies of scale, and how the company might be downsized to adapt to the new environment without losing clients or being forced to shut down. These questions offer a different perspective from those of a year ago, when strategic decisions would be mainly concerned with international expansion and growth in different client segments. The focus now is on survival and managing a declining financial bottom line.

To illustrate the impact of the crisis on the financial bottom line in this industry, we assess the impact on company profitability, measured in basis points. The average profit (operating margin) for an asset manager fell from 38 points at the end of 2007 to 34 at the end of 2008 and in 2011 this figure was at about 28 points as can be seen in Figure 21.2. Most players in the industry are

Table 21.1 Economic crisis impact on the fundamentals of the asset management industry

Factor	Description	Impact/reaction
Change in client behavior	Client risk-averse behavior, preferring simpler, transparent products	Development of new products with lower margins
Regulatory pressure	Increasing regulation demands that AMs enhance transparency through risk disclosure and maintain capital requirements through balance sheet management	Higher compliance costs
Change in industry structure	Sharper differentiation based on chosen business models, increase in the number of independent firms, as well as larger players, due to consolidation	Immediate strategic decisions need to be taken and, based on that, a new focus for tactical decisions
Higher costs in developing robust risk management	Risk management will enter a new paradigm, shifting from client risk reporting to protecting the institution itself, requiring asset managers to develop new tools and techniques	Higher focus on risk management
Pressure on the financial bottom line (revenue, profits and costs)	Fundamental shift in cost structure (toward more variable costs and 'industrial' processes) necessary to address profitability challenges; pressures on revenue and profits due to threat from substitute products; and margin pressure from shifting product mix and lower volumes	Cutting costs

also suffering from a substantial decrease in AUM either because of a decrease in asset value or because of client withdrawals. For this reason, their financial bottom line is being severely impacted, and the most tactical way to try to return to a higher level of profitability is via cost cutting and by developing a robust risk management framework. We examine these two options in detail in the next two sections.

21.3 Cost reduction programs at asset managers

Considering the recessive economic environment, the more controllable of the options for asset managers (shown in Table 21.1) would be to cut costs in order to return to their previous levels of profitability. It would be unlikely that asset managers at this stage will succeed in attracting new clients to more profitable products. Even if we assume that the economic conditions in 2009–2011 are

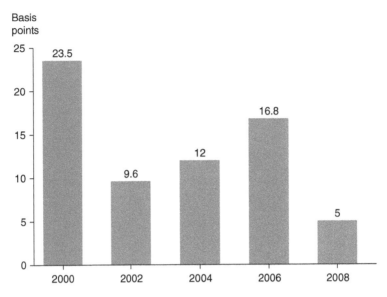

Figure 21.2 Operating profits of European asset managers (in basis points)
Source: Wall Street Journal, NY Times, Pensions & Investment Magazine and funds web sites.

no worse than those in 2008 and that their revenues remain at the same level, asset managers would still have to cut their current costs by 50% to return to their 2006 profitability levels. This cost-cutting exercise would need to be accomplished in a much tougher regulatory environment, with regulators keeping close tabs on asset managers to ensure that non-revenue-generating back office functions like risk, legal and compliance (usually some of the first to be cut in tough times) remain in place. On the positive side, such cost optimization exercises were long overdue. Most asset managers preferred not to face these issues while they were focusing on an expansion of their funds; however, these new lean times are now forcing them to make such adjustments.

The industry has indeed been quick to react to this new reality. However, as usual, the 'lowest-hanging fruit' is a reduction of headcount, which a number of firms had already been doing, as shown in Figure 21.3. These cuts show companies adapting to the new environment with lower margin products and less demand.

While the initial focus was a reduction of headcount, asset managers can optimize their operational platforms significantly in order to decrease costs. These platforms were mostly developed and implemented when the industry was growing at double-digit rates per annum and companies were scrambling to keep up with AUM and geographical expansion. Cost containment was not

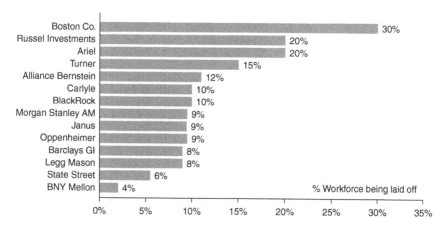

Figure 21.3   Asset managers that publicly announced workforce layoffs (as % of current workforce)

Source: Wall Street Journal, NY Times, Pension Investment Magazine and funds websites.

the highest priority in these good times; it was consistently of lesser importance than the speed of development.

The cost structure in asset management can basically be broken down into two main components, namely compensation and non-compensation expenses (NCE). Figure 21.4 depicts the breakdown in these major components, which are almost evenly distributed. It is more difficult for firms to balance the cuts in direct compensation, since, as in any financial services organization, rewarding portfolio managers and investment and quantitative research analysts is key for having good performance and attracting new business. If cuts are too deep in these areas, then firms run the risk of losing their key performers to competitors; therefore, they hesitate to make heavy cuts on the revenue generating side.

Many firms have already made adjustments on the NCE side of their costs in view of the impact that the recession is having on their businesses. A sample of three very large asset managers in the US (see Figure 21.5) shows how they have been reducing their NCE. BlackRock, for example, in spite of an unusual increase in revenue from 2007 to 2008, reduced its NCE by $171 million, and its NCE/revenue ratio fell from 37% to 32% in 2008. Legg Mason reduced its NCE in absolute value by $168 million (very close to BlackRock); however, as its revenue declined 16% in one year, its NCE/revenue ratio actually increased to 43% in 2008. Franklin Templeton also had the same problem; although it made a cut in its NCE, its revenue decrease more than offset the NCE cut. This illustrates how deep the cost cuts have to be in order to return to higher levels of profitability.

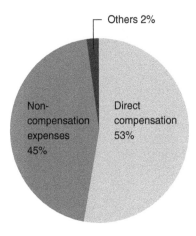

Figure 21.4 Breakdown of asset managers' expenses
Source: Largest five asset managers' financial statements.

	BlackRock	Legg Mason	Franklin Templeton
2007 AUM	1.357	999	644
Revenues	4.845	4.707	4.228
Non-compensation expenses (NCE)	1.784	1.874	923
NCE/Revenues (%)	37%	40%	22%
2008 AUM	1.154	711	400
Revenues	5.112	3.935	3.711
Non-compensation expenses (NCE)	1.613	1.706	849
NCE/revenues (%)	32%	43%	23%
Deltas Variation NCE/revenues	−5%	3%	1%
Decrease in AUM	−203	−288	−244
Variation in revenues	6%	−16%	−12%
Variation in NCE	−171	−168	−74

Figure 21.5 Examples of cost cutting in non-compensation costs in three major firms (in $ millions)
Sources: Companies' websites.

In order to design optimal cost reduction programs, we need to break the NCE down into more detailed categories. We did this by analyzing the cost breakdown of the largest 50 global, US and European asset managers as a percentage of their total costs (see Figure 21.6). Occupational expenses (real estate, rents etc) represent slightly more than a quarter of the total NCE.

A branch network usually entails a significant real estate cost. A network of branches is useful if the asset manager is focused on retail clients. A branch may be useful in attracting new clients by facilitating a first face-to-face contact. (Later on, an investor may communicate with the asset manager through one of the other channels of communication.) If the asset manager is focused on the institutional side, then an extensive network of branches is not necessary. (An asset manager may be content with having a small number of offices only in big cities.) If the asset manager has a large number of smaller individual investors, then a larger and more extensive network of branches may be advantageous. When cutting these costs, a firm needs to bear in mind the strategic consequences when it comes to attracting and retaining clients.

The second largest expense would be in technology and telecommunications. Given their importance, most of the cost savings would have to come from these categories, but cost cutting in these areas is never easy.

Personnel-related cuts are also important, but firms need to be careful to cut only in areas that are directly related to the volume of business. Changes that were not made in previous years because of accelerated growth, like de-layering levels of hierarchy inside the firm, should now be a priority, as this can cut headcount by up to 30%. In Table 21.2, we summarized a few cost reduction activities by type of cost, considering the time they would take to be achieved and the average savings they would produce. IT and real estate cost cuts, for example, are extremely relevant, but would take longer to achieve results. Reducing these costs usually demands investment, as breaking or renegotiating leasing contracts, for example, commonly command fees and charges. The same applies to IT optimization, which needs to be implemented very carefully to avoid serious operational problems in the future.

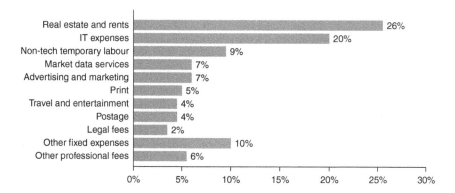

Figure 21.6 Breakdown of non-compensation expenses (NCE)
Sources: Largest five asset managers' financial statements.

Table 21.2 Cost-cutting activities

Cost	Possible cost-cutting activities	Average savings*	Timeline
IT	Outsourcing programs Re-evaluate IT and telecommunication needs due to the new activity levels. Reassess redundancy. Server consolidation and right-size laptop and PC ratios.	10–20%	1 year
Personnel – organization	Cut layers of hierarchy. Push activities to lower cost personnel ('empowering').	5–10%	3–6 months
Personnel – headcount	Cut headcount across the board, adapting to the new level of activity.	10–30%	Immediate
Products range	Optimize the product range to better use investment teams, portfolio managers and research.	15–20%	3–6 months
Operations, securities settlement	5–40%	3–6 months	1 year
Real estate	Close facilities and/or renegotiate leases. Increase use of outsourced resources that do not demand real estate use. Use shared services. Consolidate functions.	5–20%	6–12 months
Marketing and advertising	Consolidate marketing functions across the firm. Shift spending to the most efficient vehicles. Cut advertising spending.		

Note: * *Average savings, considering only their base cost.*

The industry has been quick to react to this new reality. For example, a large independent US asset manager has already put in place several measures to reduce costs, by sharing services in its distribution and administration departments to reduce costs across geographies. This same firm has also launched an initiative to reduce its NCE by 20% in 2009, with the development of an inter-company committee to determine which expenses will have to be eliminated.

A European-based global firm decided to reduce the amount of product offering and the development efforts for a few products where it can build competitive advantage on a global scale. This firm also decided to immediately implement a plan, which had been on the shelf for many years, to streamline its operational platforms on a global basis. Currently, each geographical location

Table 21.3   Most common types of cost-cutting programs

Type	Definition	Situation
Cost blitz	Companies start cutting costs immediately in a desperate fashion.	Sudden market changes that caught companies unprepared. Quick loss of profitability.
Category specific	Focus on only one category to cut costs – for example cutting IT costs seen as the solution.	There is an obvious need for cost reduction in this expense category that market conditions aggravate.
Deep dive/ transformation programs	A more analytical and holistic way to optimize costs and spending.	As the economic environment keeps deteriorating, companies see the need for a more structural change in their cost management.

(and sometimes within the same country) has its own platform with different vendors and frameworks to process securities. Another US-based global firm followed the same path, creating and developing global centers of excellence in an attempt to provide their clients with the best possible service.

There are a few ways to perform such cost-cutting programs. Firms tend to go through all of them in recessionary times. These types are shown in Table 21.3.

When suddenly hit by a very serious crisis, as in September 2008 with the demise of Lehman Brothers, a company may often go immediately on a 'cost blitz', which may result in a major round of layoffs. As the current situation does not seem to improve, many firms now also have to manage costs in specific categories, such as closing locations that are not profitable and are only viable if experiencing accelerated growth. Some firms still focus all their efforts on the IT category. As the current economic downturn seems to be lasting longer than initially expected, quite a few firms are now cutting their costs dramatically. These transformation programs tend to be longer, but usually present long-lasting results.

On a positive note, these changes are coming at a good time, as the previous fast growth meant that these firms did not use these resources in an optimal way. The crisis is therefore a good opportunity to check all these costs, and, when growth returns, this may stimulate large productivity increases.

21.4   Using risk management as a productivity tool for asset managers

As mentioned earlier in this chapter, asset managers are now expected by regulators to review their risk management frameworks. This will certainly require not just investments, but also greater management time and attention. However, we will show in this section that better risk management, particularly operational risk management, can also bring opportunities to reduce costs.

Asset managers are susceptible to all forms of risks, namely market, credit and operational risks. These risks manifest themselves in two ways: they either impact client funds, thus affecting the asset manager indirectly, or they impact the asset manager directly. Client funds are subject mainly to market and credit risk. Market risks are due to the daily fluctuation of asset prices, and credit risks are due to the possibility that some counterparties with whom the funds do business might default and make a financial asset worthless. These eventual losses would have an indirect impact on the asset manager's revenue, as any loss to the client funds entails lower commissions; however, most of these losses are borne by the fund's clients. (These market and credit risk-related losses would impact the quotas and NAVs, so the client would take a direct hit; the asset manager would just have less fee revenue in these cases.) Asset managers themselves are particularly subject to operational risk. Operational risk is an amalgamation of many different types of risks under the same umbrella (Cruz, 2002). It involves anything from transaction processing errors to internal and external frauds and terrorist attacks. For asset managers, errors in processing transactions or a system failure can cause severe damage and impact the balance sheet of the asset manager. Consistently failing to comply with local regulations, or with very basic business ethics, can generate very large operational losses and subsequent reputational damage. Clients can also sue for poor performance. A sample of recent losses is shown in Table 21.4.

Operational risk can be modeled in a few different ways. It particularly affects factors like people (human resources) and IT systems. In what follows, we elaborate on these two risk factors and how good risk management can translate into a positive impact on the bottom line.

21.4.1 People risk: operational risk in human resources

As a service sector firm, any type of asset manager needs to hire top talent in order to provide the best return and service for its clients. Human resource talent is needed for:

- general management (portfolio managers etc.);
- administrative personnel (operations settlements, accountants etc.);
- research (equity, bond and currency analysts, risk analysts etc.);
- technologists (IT specialists, for example);
- sales force.

As in many financial firms, asset managers have to make sure that they are able to attract and retain, above all, portfolio managers with an established

Table 21.4 Sample of recent large operational risk losses by asset managers

Year	Risk failure	Event	Financial impact	Asset manager
2008	Failure to comply with copyright laws	Reached settlement for alleged regulatory and supervisory violations that led to employees' improper acceptance of gifts.	$12m	Fidelity
2007	Legal and compliance failure to KYC ('Know Your Customer')	Czech government agency reclaimed funds that were either arguably embezzled or mishandled.	$24m	UBS
2007	Insufficient hedging due to system model error	Flagship global alpha fund suffered very large losses.	$3 billion	Goldman Sachs
2007	Failure to comply with business ethics	Alleged insider trading at UBS O'Connor	$10m	UBS O'Connor.
2004	Legal and compliance failure	Improper trading – market timing and improper mutual fund trading	$288m	Janus Capital
2004	Legal and compliance failure	Settlement for allegations that investors who traded rapidly were favoured at the expense of longstanding shareholders.	$450m	Invesco

track record and a potential to bring in clients and provide high returns to their funds. Such people are the face of the firm to the outside world and are a basis for attracting clients. Compensation of such personnel is one of the highest costs of an asset manager (as seen in Figure 21.5). Losing top talent is very costly and also increases the susceptibility to operational risk. There is a learning curve for apprentices and, during this period, the probabilities of error are higher. Asset managers are, therefore, highly exposed to key personnel risk. Particularly in the US, but also in other countries, funds are often named after their portfolio managers. Typically, these portfolio managers have developed such a track record and reputation that clients want to invest with them. These funds linked to a name can hold many billions of dollars in investments, and the asset manager may become very dependent on this particular person. The risk of losing such a portfolio manager may represent a loss of revenue of many millions per year in administration and performance fees.

In the front office, sales people need to follow procedures and local regulations to sell pension and other types of funds. Several pension mis-selling cases have occurred in different countries. Probably the most infamous case of pension mis-selling was the situation that arose in Britain between 1988 and 1994, after British regulators decided to allow individuals to buy pensions from private sector providers. The regulators determined at that time that pension investors should have the choice of who provided their pension (not necessarily their employer) and that they should be allowed to invest, in effect, in a retail pension fund. Many who decided, or who were persuaded, to buy a retail fund should not have done so. High-pressure tactics by commission-based salespeople led to tens of thousands of people purchasing products that proved to be entirely unsuitable. High fees and charges and poor investment returns combined to shrink the retirement savings of these investors. Many found themselves locked in and unable to switch to more appropriate products without incurring very high exit fees. The result was a nightmare for investors, pension providers and the government. After a long legal process, the funds were told to reimburse the investor for mis-selling these pensions. Until 2008, an estimated £11.5 billion (nearly $20 billion) had been paid in compensation for mis-selling by certain asset managers that operated in this market.

The British experience serves to illustrate what can go wrong when, even with the best intentions, a choice is given to people who are unprepared for it. It also shows how greedy salespeople can exploit unsuspecting consumers, and how something that starts out as a good idea can turn into a major financial liability to asset managers if not properly conducted.

Operational risk can also manifest itself in back office personnel. For example, risk managers, auditors and accountants play an important role, since they have to guard the firm against the likes of rogue traders, accounting frauds and Ponzi schemes (like the aforementioned Madoff case). It is important that the reporting lines of the traders and risk managers are kept separate.

21.4.2   Systems risks: operational risk in systems development and transaction processing

Scale plays an important role in asset management. The larger the portfolio, the lower the cost per transaction. However, the optimal size of a managed fund is often a balance of various trade-offs. For example, whereas an overall larger scale for an asset manager is preferred because of economies of scale, a small fund would be more agile to move a fund's allocation in reaction to market movements, and would probably be better able to outperform the competition. This is the case with hedge funds. Another aspect that has an impact on the optimal size of a fund is the error rate (operational risk), which is a function of the transaction frequency. It is to be expected that the probability of error increases with an increasing frequency in the rate of transactions. A larger fund, in order to meet its benchmarks, will have to take bigger bets. So, for each type of fund there is an optimal size and an optimal focus. Historically, several funds that reached a size deemed to be larger than optimal decided to close entry for new clients, such as Fidelity's Magellan.

Financial institutions in general, and asset managers in particular, have traditionally never been as careful with costs as other industries have been. In several industries, like car manufacturing, error rates are extremely low and very well-controlled by very analytical quality control departments, which are usually one of the most sophisticated areas within an organization except for research (or product) development. On the other hand, in the financial services industry, the most analytical departments are located either in the front office or on the revenue side. Financial derivatives are priced taking only market opportunity costs (and rarely transaction costs) into consideration; even if transaction costs are taken into account, the analysis is not very deep. In the portfolio aggregation of these products, the final effects of processing are never considered. In this section, we try to briefly depict how a more sophisticated cost analysis can be developed for financial products based on a traditional microeconomic analysis.

Economic theory postulates that, for a firm to maximize its results, it is necessary that it produces such a quantity that allows an equilibrium between the variation of the total cost and the variation of the total revenue. In economic terms, there are three types of revenue: total, average and marginal. The total (or gross) revenue is simply the result of multiplying the price p of a certain product by the quantity q negotiated. It can be represented by

$$R_{GROSS} = p \cdot q$$

The average revenue is defined as the result of the division between the total revenue and the quantity negotiated. It is represented analytically by

$$R_{Average} = \frac{R_{GROSS}}{q} = \frac{p \cdot q}{q} = p$$

The third representation of revenue, the marginal, corresponds to the variation of the total revenue in relation to the quantity sold. It is represented by

$$R_{Mg} = \frac{dR_{GROSS}}{dq}$$

Assuming that the variation of the quantity and the gross revenue can be admitted as infinitesimal (this works in theory, but is unlikely to be the case in business practice), the marginal revenue can be determined by the first derivative of the gross revenue in relation to the quantity sold.

In asset management, the increased number of transactions (the 'production') will bring about an unexpected variable cost that is an increase in operational error (human and system factors would not perform the same when subject to a higher volume of transactions). The relationship between the number of operational errors and the transaction volume can be estimated through multifactor models. The entire analysis of revenues, production and costs based on (micro)economic theory is complex, and there is a vast literature on the subject. We will not delve into more detail in this section, but strongly recommend understanding these relationships when developing any growth strategy. It is worth noticing that perhaps the most important conclusion from these relationships is that profit will be maximized when

$$C_{Mg} = R_{Mg}$$

The above relation means that profit will be maximized when the marginal cost and the marginal revenue are exactly the same. This relation will hold for all cases and should be the objective of the firm's strategy.

In what follows, we present a very simple stylized example to illustrate the above theory. Suppose a particular fund trades a single product with a very tight margin that is stable at 0.006% per unit trade (one unit = \$100,000 notional) as seen in Table 21.5. We can, therefore, simulate the revenue, which we do from 200,000 to 700,000 transactions processed per day. In general, the fund trader would only see the trades from the revenue side and would be happy seeing the revenue grow \$4,200,000 when 700,000 units are traded. This is a very general view, but revenue generators will not bother about the costs incurred to achieve that revenue.

Let us now analyze the costs. We divide the costs into two components: processing cost and error cost. The processing cost is expected to be stable at \$5 per transaction. The error cost is \$1.81, with a standard deviation of 3.89. Developing a 95% confidence interval for the error cost, we find that it would be \$9.43. Therefore, on average, it would cost you \$5 to correctly process a transaction and \$12.43 to reprocess because of errors.

We can also find a loss ratio. For this exercise, we assume a simple linear model to relate the loss ratio to the number of transactions processed. The model is given by

Loss Ratio = 0.0094957 + 1.15573E – 07* Transactions R2 = 89.12%

Table 21.5 Cost structure for a fund

	Revenue					Costs					
Quantity	Profit	Marginal profit	Revenue	Marginal revenue	Average revenue	Total cost	Total management cost	Total average cost	Processing cost	Error cost	Marginal error cost
200,000	138,497		1,200,000			1,061,503	5.31	5.31	1,000,000.00	61,503.20	0.308
205,000	140,842	0.47	1,230,000	6.00	6.00	1,089,158	5.53	5.31	1,025,000.00	64,157.88	0.531
210,000	143,133	0.46	1,260,000	6.00	6.00	1,116,867	5.54	5.32	1,050,000.00	66,867.06	0.542
220,000	147,551	0.44	1,320,000	6.00	6.00	1,172,449	5.56	5.33	1,100,000.00	72,448.89	0.558
230,000	151,751	0.42	1,380,000	6.00	6.00	1,228,249	5.58	5.34	1,150,000.00	78,248.69	0.580
240,000	155,734	0.40	1,440,000	6.00	6.00	1,284,266	5.60	5.35	1,200,000.00	84,266.46	0.602
250,000	159,498	0.38	1,500,000	6.00	6.00	1,340,502	5.62	5.36	1,250,000.00	90,502.21	0.624
260,000	163,044	0.35	1,560,000	6.00	6.00	1,396,956	5.65	5.37	1,300,000.00	96,955.92	0.645
270,000	166,372	0.33	1,620,000	6.00	6.00	1,453,628	5.67	5.38	1,350,000.00	103,627.61	0.667
280,000	169,483	0.31	1,680,000	6.00	6.00	1,510,517	5.69	5.39	1,400,000.00	110,517.27	0.689
290,000	172,375	0.29	1,740,000	6.00	6.00	1,567,625	5.71	5.41	1,450,000.00	117,624.90	0.711
300,000	175,049	0.27	1,800,000	6.00	6.00	1,624,951	5.73	5.42	1,500,000.00	124,950.50	0.733
310,000	177,506	0.25	1,860,000	6.00	6.00	1,682,494	5.75	5.43	1,550,000.00	132,494.08	0.754
320,000	179,744	0.22	1,920,000	6.00	6.00	1,740,256	5.78	5.44	1,600,000.00	140,255.62	0.776
330,000	181,765	0.20	1,980,000	6.00	6.00	1,798,235	5.80	5.45	1,650,000.00	148,235.14	0.798
350,000	185,152	0.17	2,100,000	6.00	6.00	1,914,848	5.83	5.47	1,750,000.00	164,848.09	0.831
400,000	189,805	0.09	2,400,000	6.00	6.00	2,210,195	5.91	5.53	2,000,000.00	210,194.95	0.907
427,000	**190,052**	0.01	2,562,000	6.00	**6.00**	2,371,948	**5.99**	5.55	2,135,000.00	236,948.08	0.991
450,000	189,009	(0.02)	2,700,000	6.00	6.00	2,510,991	6.02	5.58	2,250,000.00	260,991.11	1.016
500,000	182,763	(0.12)	3,000,000	6.00	6.00	2,817,237	6.12	5.63	2,500,000.00	317,236.54	1.125
600,000	153,925	(0.29)	3,600,000	6.00	6.00	3,446,075	6.29	5.74	3,000,000.00	446,075.27	1.288
700,000	103,289	(0.51)	4,200,000	6.00	6.00	4,096,711	6.51	5.85	3,500,000.00	596,711.15	1.506

By using the model above, we are able to verify that, if the loss ratio is estimated to be 3.26% when the number of transactions is 200,000, when the number of transactions grows to 700,000, the error rate climbs to 9.04%!

Following traditional optimization analysis, the maximum profit condition – $C_{Mg} = R_{Mg}$ – will be reached, given the current costs, at 427,000 units traded. If we trade more than that, we have declining profits and need to adjust our processing capacity likewise. This type of modeling also offers us conditions to verify our capacity and see how an improvement in the process (system improvement, training process, hiring employees etc.) will benefit the organization and increase productivity.

In our example, when $C_{Mg} = R_{Mg} = \$6$, the profit will be maximized at $190,052.

Therefore, the average number of transactions was 239,815, given our current environment and capacity conditions; we would maximize our potential by trading 427,000 units per day. If the asset manager has any strategy of trading more than that, it will also have to take the costs into consideration.

We also performed a simulation with these data, supposing that we were able to cut the processing costs by 20%, from $5 per transaction to $4 per transaction, due to economies of scale. The modification is substantial. The maximum profit condition in this case is reached at 900,000 units per day, more than duplicating our optimal capacity, as can be seen in Table 21.6.

In another simulation, the loss ratio was cut proportionally to around 3%, due to operational risk reduction (for example by training employees and improving systems), and the error cost was reduced proportionally throughout the table. The maximum profit condition was reached at around 600,000 units per day. Therefore, the simple fact that we reduced the operational risk in a business unit increased our optimal capacity by 40%. We had a dramatic productivity gain by managing the operational risk better. See Table 21.7 for more details.

There are several other factors that affect the costs and risks of transaction processing. Transaction processing can be outsourced (however, usually not offshore, but preferably to some firm relatively close by, so that any form of operational risk does not increase too much). Another important factor is manual versus automated transaction processing (for example SWIFT). Automated transaction processing clearly has a higher productivity than manual transaction processing. However, automated transactions can only be done with regard to standard, plain vanilla transactions, not with regard to more complicated esoteric transactions. Even though one may think that automated processing is more reliable and less susceptible than manual processing to operational risk, it is not clear that this is actually the case (for example, automated transactions are still subject to typographical errors, which have often cost managed funds millions).

Table 21.6 Cost structure for a fund: reducing processing costs to $4 per transaction

	Revenue				Costs						
Quantity	Profit	Revenue	Marginal revenue	Average revenue	Total cost	Total management cost	Total average cost	Processing cost	Error cost	Marginal error cost	Average error cost
200,000	338,497	1,200,000		6.00	861,503	4.31	4.31	800,000.00	61,503.20	0.308	0.308
205,000	345,842	1,230,000	6.00	6.00	884,158	4.53	4.31	820,000.00	64,157.88	0.531	0.313
210,000	353,133	1,260,000	6.00	6.00	906,867	4.54	4.32	840,000.00	66,867.06	0.542	0.318
220,000	367,551	1,320,000	6.00	6.00	952,449	4.56	4.33	880,000.00	72,448.89	0.558	0.329
230,000	381,751	1,380,000	6.00	6.00	998,249	4.58	4.34	920,000.00	78,248.69	0.580	0.340
240,000	395,734	1,440,000	6.00	6.00	1,044,266	4.60	4.35	960,000.00	84,266.46	0.602	0.351
250,000	409,498	1,500,000	6.00	6.00	1,090,502	4.62	4.36	1,000,000.00	90,502.21	0.624	0.362
260,000	423,044	1,560,000	6.00	6.00	1,136,956	4.65	4.37	1,040,000.00	96,955.92	0.645	0.373
270,000	436,372	1,620,000	6.00	6.00	1,183,628	4.67	4.38	1,080,000.00	103,627.61	0.667	0.384
280,000	449,483	1,680,000	6.00	6.00	1,230,517	4.69	4.39	1,120,000.00	110,517.27	0.689	0.395
290,000	462,375	1,740,000	6.00	6.00	1,277,625	4.71	4.41	1,160,000.00	117,624.90	0.711	0.406
300,000	475,049	1,800,000	6.00	6.00	1,324,951	4.73	4.42	1,200,000.00	124,950.50	0.733	0.417
310,000	487,506	1,860,000	6.00	6.00	1,372,494	4.75	4.43	1,240,000.00	132,494.08	0.754	0.427
320,000	499,744	1,920,000	6.00	6.00	1,420,256	4.78	4.44	1,280,000.00	140,255.62	0.776	0.438
330,000	511,765	1,980,000	6.00	6.00	1,468,235	4.80	4.45	1,320,000.00	148,235.14	0.798	0.449
350,000	535,152	2,100,000	6.00	6.00	1,564,848	4.83	4.47	1,400,000.00	164,848.09	0.831	0.471
400,000	589,805	2,400,000	6.00	6.00	1,810,195	4.91	4.53	1,600,000.00	210,194.95	0.907	0.525
427,000	617,052	2,562,000	6.00	6.00	1,944,948	4.99	4.55	1,708,000.00	236,948.08	0.991	0.555
450,000	639,009	2,700,000	6.00	6.00	2,060,991	5.02	4.58	1,800,000.00	260,991.11	1.016	0.580
500,000	682,763	3,000,000	6.00	6.00	2,317,237	5.12	4.63	2,000,000.00	317,236.54	1.125	0.634
600,000	753,925	3,600,000	6.00	6.00	2,846,075	5.29	4.74	2,400,000.00	446,075.27	1.288	0.743
700,000	803,289	4,200,000	6.00	6.00	3,396,711	5.51	4.85	2,800,000.00	596,711.15	1.506	0.852
800,000	830,856	4,800,000	6.00	6.00	3,969,144	5.72	4.96	3,200,000.00	769,144.16	1.724	0.961
850,000	836,465	5,100,000	6.00	6.00	4,263,535	5.89	5.02	3,400,000.00	863,534.59	1.888	1.016
900,000	836,626	5,400,000	6.00	6.00	4,563,374	6.00	5.07	3,600,000.00	963,374.31	1.997	1.070
950,000	831,337	5,700,000	6.00	6.00	4,868,663	6.11	5.12	3,800,000.00	1,068,663.31	2.106	1.125
1,000,000	820,598	6,000,000	6.00	6.00	5,179,402	6.21	5.18	4,000,000.00	1,179,401.60	2.215	1.179

Table 21.7 Cost structure for a business unit: reducing the cost of errors

	Revenue						Costs				
Quantity	Profit	Revenue	Marginal revenue	Average revenue	Total cost	Total management cost	Total average cost	Processing cost	Error cost	Marginal error cost	Average error cost
200,000	195,077	1,200,000			1,004,923	5.02	5.02	1,000,000.00	4,923.20	0.025	0.025
205,000	198,837	1,230,000	6.00	6.00	1,031,163	5.25	5.03	1,025,000.00	6,163.38	0.248	0.030
210,000	202,542	1,260,000	6.00	6.00	1,057,458	5.26	5.04	1,050,000.00	7,458.06	0.259	0.036
220,000	209,789	1,320,000	6.00	6.00	1,110,211	5.28	5.05	1,100,000.00	10,210.89	0.275	0.046
230,000	216,818	1,380,000	6.00	6.00	1,163,182	5.30	5.06	1,150,000.00	13,181.69	0.297	0.057
240,000	223,630	1,440,000	6.00	6.00	1,216,370	5.32	5.07	1,200,000.00	16,370.46	0.319	0.068
250,000	230,223	1,500,000	6.00	6.00	1,269,777	5.34	5.08	1,250,000.00	19,777.21	0.341	0.079
260,000	236,598	1,560,000	6.00	6.00	1,323,402	5.36	5.09	1,300,000.00	23,401.92	0.362	0.090
270,000	242,755	1,620,000	6.00	6.00	1,377,245	5.38	5.10	1,350,000.00	27,244.61	0.384	0.101
280,000	248,695	1,680,000	6.00	6.00	1,431,305	5.41	5.11	1,400,000.00	31,305.27	0.406	0.112
290,000	254,416	1,740,000	6.00	6.00	1,485,584	5.43	5.12	1,450,000.00	35,583.90	0.428	0.123
300,000	259,919	1,800,000	6.00	6.00	1,540,081	5.45	5.13	1,500,000.00	40,080.50	0.450	0.134
310,000	265,205	1,860,000	6.00	6.00	1,594,795	5.47	5.14	1,550,000.00	44,795.08	0.471	0.145
320,000	270,272	1,920,000	6.00	6.00	1,649,728	5.49	5.16	1,600,000.00	49,727.62	0.493	0.155
330,000	275,122	1,980,000	6.00	6.00	1,704,878	5.52	5.17	1,650,000.00	54,878.14	0.515	0.166
350,000	284,167	2,100,000	6.00	6.00	1,815,833	5.55	5.19	1,750,000.00	65,833.09	0.548	0.188
400,000	302,965	2,400,000	6.00	6.00	2,097,035	5.62	5.24	2,000,000.00	97,034.95	0.624	0.243
427,000	310,850	2,562,000	6.00	6.00	2,251,150	5.71	5.27	2,135,000.00	116,149.78	0.708	0.272
450,000	316,314	2,700,000	6.00	6.00	2,383,686	5.73	5.30	2,250,000.00	133,686.11	0.733	0.297
500,000	324,213	3,000,000	6.00	6.00	2,675,787	5.84	5.35	2,500,000.00	175,786.54	0.842	0.352
550,000	326,664	3,300,000	6.00	6.00	2,973,336	5.95	5.41	2,750,000.00	223,336.27	0.951	0.406
600,000	323,665	3,600,000	6.00	6.00	3,276,335	6.01	5.46	3,000,000.00	276,335.27	1.005	0.461
700,000	301,319	4,200,000	6.00	6.00	3,898,681	6.22	5.57	3,500,000.00	398,681.15	1.223	0.570
800,000	257,176	4,800,000	6.00	6.00	4,542,824	6.44	5.68	4,000,000.00	542,824.16	1.441	0.679
850,000	226,930	5,100,000	6.00	6.00	4,873,070	6.60	5.73	4,250,000.00	623,069.59	1.605	0.733
900,000	191,236	5,400,000	6.00	6.00	5,208,764	6.71	5.79	4,500,000.00	708,764.31	1.714	0.788
950,000	150,092	5,700,000	6.00	6.00	5,549,908	6.82	5.84	4,750,000.00	799,908.31	1.823	0.842

21.5   Conclusions

The financial and economic crisis has changed the asset management industry landscape completely, and this now presents many challenges for asset managers all over the world. Senior management and boards at these companies are using the best possible tactics to return to higher levels of profitability, in some cases even in order to survive. Probably the most straightforward way to improve profitability these days, given a stagnant market, is through cost reduction programs. Finding the optimal cost structure in the current environment without losing clients for poor quality of service is key. These cost optimization programs in asset management firms were overdue. As they were concerned only with expansion in the last few years, there are usually a number of legacy systems that need to be closed (duplicate processing, unnecessary office locations etc.), which would make these firms leaner and more productive. Costs, productivity and operational risk are strongly intertwined. For a firm to optimize its investments and operations, all possible factors and trade-offs have to be taken into account. Such an optimization process is an analytical task that needs to be carefully executed. However, asset managers who survive this crisis will be much stronger when markets recover.

References

Cruz, M. (2002) *Modeling, Measuring and Hedging Operational Risk,* NJ: John Wiley & Sons.

Cruz, M. and M.L. Pinedo (July 2009) 'Global asset management: costs, productivity and operational risk', *Journal of Applied IT and Investment Management,* Sim-Corp, (1)2: 5–12.

Judd, C. (2009) 'The future of the asset management industry', white paper, Watson Wyatt Consultants.

Merrill Lynch/CapGemini World Wealth Report, June 2009.

Shank, J. and Govindarajan, V. (2008) *Strategic Cost Management: A New Tool for Competitive Advantage,* Free Press.

22
Transaction Costs and Asset Management

Yakov Amihud and Haim Mendelson

22.1 Introduction

Asset management firms engage in three major types of activities: the core activity of making and implementing investment decisions, client acquisition, and development and support efforts that facilitate and enable the other two activities. Transaction costs link all three activities. As we show in this chapter, the judicious management of transaction costs creates opportunities to increase investment returns, improve profitability and better target investor clienteles.

Transaction costs are the variable costs of trading. As such, they are directly related to the implementation and support of asset managers' core investment activities. Like other cost items, they are important because they affect asset managers' net revenue and profit. But unlike many other cost items, transaction costs cannot (or at least should not) be viewed as being separate from the underlying investment process, as they directly affect both the gross and the net returns on the asset manager's investment portfolio. Thus, as important drivers of investment decisions, they play both a role similar to other operating costs and a role similar to risk.

Recent trends in the asset management industry underscore the importance of liquidity and the management of transaction costs. Fee compression and industry consolidation make cost containment important for asset managers, with transaction costs playing a key role. In the United States, direct-contribution retirement plan sponsors controlling $5 trillion in assets in 2012 are increasingly focusing on transaction costs and fees as part of their fiduciary duty to plan participants. In all segments of the asset management industry, investors have failed to receive positive compensation for the risk they have taken in recent years, and the assets they held proved to be much less liquid than they had assumed. As a result, investors increasingly emphasize quality, safety and liquidity as key characteristics of the investments they are seeking. In 2010, equities comprised 27% of the portfolios of high-net-worth individuals worldwide, compared with

33% in 2007, and cash and fixed income increased from 44% in 2007 to 60% in 2010. The 2009 Investment & Pensions survey of institutional asset managers in Europe found that 'the need for safer havens encouraged investors to invest twice as much in bonds as equity, reversing the previous trend, with an overall allocation to cash almost doubling' (IPE, 2009), and in the 2011 survey, 'the flight to safety continues with fixed income gaining more ground with investors', although some investors have begun to make riskier investments (IPE, 2011). Many industry participants expect the asset management industry to become more commoditized, with loss aversion being rife for the foreseeable future and client investment choices being largely driven by the desire for capital protection (Rajan, 2009). This leads investors to focus on low return, low risk and highly liquid assets (Rajan, 2009). In this environment, transaction costs account for a substantial percentage of overall returns, and managing them properly can make the difference between the success and failure of an investment strategy. However, this does not mean just holding highly liquid assets in the portfolio. Rather, it calls for making intelligent trade-offs between liquidity and expected returns, given the portfolio's investor clientele.

In what follows, we first present the nature and structure of transaction costs. We then show how transaction costs affect investment returns. Lastly, we consider the implications of our findings for asset managers.

22.2   What are transaction costs?

Transaction costs are the variable costs of buying or selling securities. Some of these costs are directly measurable, as they involve an explicit cash outlay by the asset manager: brokerage commissions, variable telecommunications cost, clearing costs, exchange and regulatory fees, and the variable costs of trading room operations.[1] However, there is another component of transaction costs: the costs of effecting transactions in the capital markets, which include the bid-ask spread (the difference between the buying and selling price for quoted-size transactions) and the market-impact cost (the extent of price change caused by trading, per unit of the quantity traded).[2] These costs are typically not paid separately; rather, they are reflected in the prices at which securities are bought or sold by the asset manager.

Most of the trades executed by (or on behalf of) asset managers take place on continuous markets where securities can be bought or sold instantaneously. Because each transaction requires a counterparty that is ready and willing to trade on the other side, the operation of continuous markets involves designated market makers or a mechanism that enables investors to provide liquidity through limit orders. Market makers continuously quote prices at which they are willing to trade.[3] Most trading in the US as well as in stock exchanges around the world is done in electronic order-driven markets, where traders place limit orders at which they will buy or sell securities. Other market partici-pants can trade against these limit orders at any time, and the traders who placed the limit orders are required to honor them. Effectively, the traders who place the limit orders provide market-making services. In each of these cases, the market (or the trading platform) posts the best prices at which investors can buy or sell securities: the best bid (the highest price at which an investor can sell the security instantaneously, up to a specified quantity) and the best offer or ask price (at which the investor can buy the security, up to a specified quantity). The ask price is always higher than the bid price, and the difference between the two, the *bid-ask spread,* represents a cost to the asset manager, or a compensation to the market maker, for providing liquidity to the market and for taking a risky position in the security.

The best bid or offer prices are available only for limited quantities, which can range from 100 shares for illiquid stocks to 1,000 shares for many other stocks, and to 10,000 shares or more for liquid stocks. If an asset manager wants to trade a larger position, as is often the case, he/she will need to pay a price premium on buying or give a price discount on selling; the larger the position the asset manager wishes to accumulate or liquidate, the larger the price premium or discount, especially if the asset manager wishes to trade quickly. The costs of trading a large position are called *market-impact costs,* as they reflect the impact of the trade itself on the market price, which always works against the party who initiated the transaction.

The costs of effecting transactions in the capital market (bid-ask spread and market-impact costs) reflect both the risk incurred by the market maker in taking a position and the effects of *adverse selection*: when a trader wishes to accumulate a large position in a security, this may well reflect non-public infor-mation which indicates to the trader that the security's price is likely to go up. But if the trader gains by trading on such information, he would do so at the expense of the market maker who took the other side of the transaction. Market makers protect themselves against adverse selection losses by increasing both the bid-ask spread and the market-impact cost. That is, they charge a greater premium for providing immediacy and absorbing the order quantities.

Given that, say, liquidating a large block of securities may result in a large market-impact cost, asset managers may choose to break the block into smaller pieces and gradually sell their position into the market in the hope that the cumulative discount on selling the smaller pieces will be smaller than the cost of liquidating the entire block quickly. However, this results in another com-ponent of transaction costs: *search-and-delay costs.* These costs are incurred when asset managers engage in an active search process for counterparties in order to find better prices or to reduce the market impact of their trades.[4] Asset managers who successfully reduce the market impact of their trades by selling them in smaller pieces over time, bear instead the cost of delay – the opportunity costs and risks of holding the positions that they wanted to liquidate for a longer period of time. For example, if an asset manager wanted to sell a stock in the belief that its price would decline, such an anticipated decline may well happen while the position is still being liquidated, lowering the proceeds of the sale. The asset manager thus trades off the benefit of a lower price-impact cost against the risk that the market will turn against him/her.

As the last example illustrates, there are trade-offs between the different components of transaction costs (in this case, market-impact costs versus search-and-delay costs). Asset managers may execute their trades on different trading venues depending on whether they prefer faster execution at the current price or a slower execution at a potentially improved price. Or, asset managers may outsource the implementation of a trading strategy such as accumulating or liquidating a large position to a broker who will 'work the trade' on their behalf. In that case, asset managers may pay a higher brokerage commission, while reducing the market-impact cost of their trades, the delay cost and risk associated with implementing trades over a long period of time, or the cost of maintaining a sophisticated in-house trading operation.

The different components of transaction costs are substitutable, but they are also highly positively correlated across assets: assets with high price-impact costs also tend to have high bid-ask spreads, search-and-delay costs and brokerage commissions. This means that empirical work can often use a component of transaction costs, such as the market-impact cost or the bid-ask spread, as a proxy for the full transaction cost.

22.3   The structure of transaction costs

The per-share cost of buying or selling q shares of a security, $C(q)$, can be represented by the linear relationship

$$C(q) = k + \lambda q \tag{1}$$

where the coefficient λ is the market-impact cost per share and k reflects all other variable costs. The market-impact coefficient λ can be estimated for each security following the methodology developed by Glosten and Harris (1988), which builds on the well-established linear model of Kyle (1985) and uses transaction-by-transaction trades and quotes. Glosten and Harris (1988) suggest estimating for each security the regression

$$dP_t = c\,(I_t - I_{t-1}) + \lambda I_t\,V_t \tag{2}$$

In equation 2, dP_t is the price change between transaction t and transaction $t-1$, I_t equals 1 for a buy or -1 for a sell transaction (estimated by whether the trade was at the ask or at the bid price, respectively), and V_t is the transaction size. The coefficient c estimates the bid-ask bounce, and the coefficient λ estimates the market-impact cost per unit of trading in the security.

Unfortunately, the transaction-by-transaction trade and quote data needed to estimate this model are often unavailable. Amihud (2002) has proposed a methodology that estimates the market impact cost coefficient λ of a given security based on *daily* data on closing prices and volumes, which are more readily available. Amihud's (2002) estimate is given by

$$\lambda = |R|/DVOL \tag{3}$$

where R is the daily return on the security and $DVOL$ is its dollar volume, obtained as the product of the stock's daily share volume by its price. Intuitively, Amihud's estimate of λ measures by how much a given dollar amount of trading moves the stock price.

All other variable costs are reflected in the proportional transaction-cost coefficient k, which includes half[5] of the bid-ask spread per share, the per-share brokerage commission, and all other direct per-share trading costs incurred by the asset manager.

22.4   Transaction costs and asset returns

Transaction costs are different from traditional back-office operating costs, as they directly affect the asset manager's investment strategies. The reason is that, as first shown by Amihud and Mendelson (1986a,b), transaction costs affect asset returns. As a result, transaction costs link the cost and value sides of asset management.

To study how transaction costs affect asset returns, we developed a model (Amihud and Mendelson, 1986a) that characterizes assets by their transaction costs and investors by their investment horizons. Each investor maximizes the expected present value of the cash flows his investment portfolio generates, taking into account his/her transaction costs. We first found that, in equilibrium, the return on each asset should be an increasing function of its transaction cost. The intuitive reason is that investors require compensation for bearing transaction costs: if an asset had both lower transaction costs and a lower (or the same) return as another asset, investors would prefer to buy it, bidding up its price and lowering its return. Further, the relationship between transaction costs and asset returns is increasing and *concave*, as the compensation for transaction costs increases at a decreasing rate.

We tested these predictions using stock returns and bid-ask spreads for stocks traded on the New York and American Stock Exchanges over the years 1961–1980. Our transaction-cost measure was the relative bid-ask spread (the ratio of the dollar spread to the stock price).[6] To test the spread effect, we divided stocks into seven portfolios based on their bid-ask spread, and, within each, into seven portfolios ranked by their systematic (β) risk coefficient, for a total of 49 (7x7) portfolios. In a cross-sectional estimation of the average return on each portfolio as a function of the bid-ask spread, as well as firm size and unsystematic risk, we found that average portfolio returns were significantly higher for stocks with higher bid-ask spreads. The functional relationship was increasing and concave, as predicted by our model. The following formula (Amihud and Mendelson, 1986b) summarizes the relationship between expected return, bid-ask spread and systematic risk:

$$R_j = 0.0065 + 0.0021 \ln(S_j) + 0.001\beta_j \tag{4}$$

where Rj is the monthly return on portfolio j in excess of the 90-day Treasury bill rate, Sj is the portfolio's relative spread, and βj is its systematic risk. The logarithmic form means that the extra return needed to compensate for a given spread differential is lower at higher levels of the spread. For example, the same excess return of about 0.15% per month (approximately 1.8% annually) is needed to compensate investors when the spread increases from 1% to 2%, or from 2% to 4%.

The concave (logarithmic) form of the relationship between excess return and bid-ask spread represents another prediction of the model of Amihud and Mendelson (1986a): assets with higher transaction costs are purchased by investors with longer investment horizons, over which they can depreciate their transaction costs. In contrast, investors who trade more frequently acquire more liquid assets, so the transaction costs they pay repeatedly will be lower. This implies that there is a *clientele effect*: the more frequently an investor trades, the more likely he/she is (other things being equal) to hold more liquid assets in his/her portfolio. Thus, assets with higher transaction costs are held by traders who trade less frequently and, as a result, demand lower compensation for the transaction costs they bear. This means that while higher transaction costs are associated with higher expected returns, the marginal compensation required for transaction costs is lower when the level of transaction costs is higher, leading to a concave relationship.

Our results also show that the effect of transaction costs on asset prices is large. The reason is that while the transaction costs of a single transaction are low relative to the asset price (for publicly traded stocks, they are of the order of 1%), what matters is their *cumulative* effect on value, which is large. Consider, as an illustration, a risk-free bond that pays out 5% a year in perpetuity, and assume that the risk-free rate is also 5%. Absent transaction costs, this bond will be priced at face value. If, however, the bond incurs a transaction cost of 1% of its value and is traded once a year, the cash flow stream associated with the transaction costs has a present value of 21% of the bond's value.[7]

Subsequent studies consistently support the theory that stocks with higher transaction costs have higher expected returns after controlling for risk and other characteristics[8]; see a review in Amihud, Mendelson and Pedersen, 2013. This relation, which is consistent with the theory, holds up with different measures of transaction costs in different markets and is highly robust.

The positive relationship between transaction costs and returns (or yields) also holds in the bond market. We tested this relationship by studying the differences between US Treasury bills and notes with less than six months to maturity (Amihud and Mendelson, 1991). For these maturities, both securities are discount instruments and, when their maturities are matched, they are completely identical, except that Treasury bills are much more liquid than Treasury notes. The average bid-ask spread on bills in our sample was 0.00775% compared with 0.0303% for notes; the brokerage fees were $12.5 to $25 per million dollar value for bills and $78.125 per million dollar value for notes. Similarly, notes have a higher price-impact cost than bills. Because notes are less liquid than bills with the same maturity, our theory predicts that their yields should be higher. We tested this effect for 37 randomly selected days between April and November 1987, matching notes with bills so they had the same maturities.[9] As predicted, we found that the annual yield to maturity for notes was 0.43% higher than for bills with the same maturity.

Corporate bonds are known to have, on average, higher yields than government bonds of a similar maturity and, within corporate bonds, lower rated bonds have higher yields. This yield differential was traditionally attributed to differences in the risk of default, which is higher for corporate bonds and higher still for lower rated bonds. However, if transaction costs are higher for corporate bonds and for riskier bonds, part of the yield differential should reflect compensation for higher transaction costs. Chen, Lesmond and Wei (2006) estimated the illiquidity cost of corporate bonds and found that it is generally higher for bonds with lower rating. They then estimated the effect of transaction costs on bond yields across bonds, controlling for risk, issuer characteristics and the bond's special features, and found that transaction costs had a strong positive and robust effect on bond yields. For investment-grade bonds, an increase in the bid-ask spread of one basis point increases the yield spread (over US Treasuries) by 0.42 basis points. For speculative-grade bonds, which are riskier and therefore more sensitive to liquidity, an increase of one basis point in the bid-ask spread results in an expected increase of 2.29 basis points in the yield spread.

22.5   Implications for asset managers

We next consider the implications of our findings for asset managers.

22.5.1   Portfolio construction and fund scope

We have shown above that transaction costs affect asset values: for any given level of risk, securities with higher transaction costs have lower prices or higher expected returns. Transaction costs are pervasive. They cannot be eliminated, but they can, and should, be managed. For example, just as asset managers can diversify risk by holding securities with different risk levels, so too can they hold securities with different levels of transaction cost, ranging from cash-equivalents (the most liquid) to small, infrequently traded stocks and bonds. By reducing the frequency of trading in the least-liquid securities, the asset manager's portfolio can enjoy their higher return while not bearing their full transaction costs. When the asset manager needs cash, he/she can liquidate the most liquid securities first, thereby reducing the portfolio's overall transaction cost. Because more liquid instruments yield, on average, lower returns, the asset manager needs to continuously manage the trade-off between liquidity, risk and return, given the pattern of cash outflows and inflows experienced by the portfolio managed. Asset managers should take these factors into account in addition to traditional portfolio construction strategies, which focus on managing the risk of gross returns (before transaction costs) and ignore the effects of transaction costs.[10]

Transaction costs also affect the size and scope of investment funds. Consider a fund of Q dollars in assets under management with an annual portfolio turnover μ. The turnover reflects both the fund's investment clientele and its investment style. Assume that the fund is managed so that a fixed percentage of its value, t_i, is allocated to asset i ($i = 1,2,...,n$). We adjust the units of measurement so that each of the n assets is priced at one dollar.[11]

The per-share transaction costs for each asset i are given by Equation 1, namely $C_i(q_i) = k_i + \lambda_i q_i$ for $i = 1,2,...,n$, where q_i is the transaction order size. Assuming that all purchases and sales follow the fund's asset proportions t_i, the fund's annual transaction-cost rate arising from transactions in asset i is proportional to $\mu Q \left[k_i t_i + \lambda_i t_i^2 Q \right]$, and the fund's net risk-adjusted[12] annual investment profit π is given by

$$\pi = Q \left[\sum_{i=1}^{n} R_i t_i - \mu \sum_{i=1}^{n} (k_i t_i + \lambda_i t_i^2 Q) \right] \tag{5}$$

where R_i is the risk-adjusted expected return on asset i. Note that the net investment profit π first increases in the fund's size Q, but then starts decreasing. The reason is that market-impact costs give rise to diseconomies of scale, as transaction costs increase in transaction sizes, which in turn increase in fund size. From Equation 5, the profit maximizing fund size is given by

$$Q^* = \frac{\sum_{i=1}^{n}(R_i - \mu k_i)t_i}{\mu \sum_{i=1}^{n} \lambda_i t_i^2} \tag{6}$$

If all n assets have the same weight in the portfolio, Equation 6 takes on the simple form

$$\frac{Q^*}{n} = \frac{\bar{R} - \mu\bar{k}}{\mu\bar{\lambda}} \tag{7}$$

where Q^*/n is the average investment in each asset and $\bar{R}, \bar{k}$, and $\bar{\lambda}$ are the mean values of R_i, k_i and λ_i. Then, the optimal fund size per asset is given by the ratio of the average return, net of proportional transaction costs, to the product of the fund's turnover rate and the average market-impact coefficient of the assets in the fund's portfolio.

The greater the fund's turnover rate μ, the smaller the optimal fund size (for a given set of assets in which it intends to invest).[13] And, higher average trading costs – both proportional and market-impact costs – reduce the desirable size of the fund. However, the two components of transaction costs affect the optimal fund size in different ways. For the proportional transaction cost component, the optimal fund size is driven by the simple average of the per-share (proportional) transaction cost. In contrast, the market-impact effect is weighted by the square of each asset's portfolio allocation, so assets with a larger weight in the portfolio dominate the market-impact effect. Further, while the sum of the individual asset weights t_i is always unity, the sum of t_i^2 ranges from $1/n$ for an equally-weighted portfolio of the n assets to 1 when the portfolio is concentrated in a single asset. Thus, as discussed above in qualitative terms, diversification can partially mitigate the market-impact cost and its effect of fund size.

Adding a new asset $i=(n+1)$ to the portfolio with a small weight Δ increases the net annual investment profit π by

$$\Delta[(R_{n+1} - k_{n+1}\mu) - (\bar{R} - \bar{k}\mu)] + 2\Delta Q\mu\bar{\lambda} \tag{8}$$

As long as the expected return on the new asset, net of proportional transaction costs, is greater than or equal to the average expected fund return net of proportional transaction costs, adding the new asset to the portfolio will always be beneficial (assuming the other costs of doing so are negligible. The reason is that, with more assets for a given fund size, the market-impact of the fund's trades per asset is smaller.

In actively managed funds, adding assets to be tracked and managed by the fund is expensive because of the costs of analysis and research. Further, such funds will tend to have higher transaction costs: unlike passive funds, which by their very nature do not trade on new information about the assets in their portfolios, actively managed funds do, so the adverse selection problem of trading against them is more severe – and so is the compensation required by market makers, as long as they can identify or infer the source of these trades. Passive funds can take advantage of the fact that they do not trade on new information by trading on specialized venues with lower market-impact costs, which are not available to actively managed funds. They (or the broker trading on their behalf) can sometimes disclose the fact that they are passive and command lower transaction costs that reflect the lower extent of adverse selection in trading against them. Further, when an active fund discovers an investment opportunity in an asset – say, it finds that an asset is undervalued – it will allocate a large amount (t_i) to invest in it, thereby increasing its market-impact cost, which increases in t_i. In addition, once an opportunity for a profitable investment is discovered, speed is of the essence (active funds' opportunity and delay costs are high), which further increases their transaction costs, especially the market-impact cost λ_i.[14] Finally, the portfolio turnover μ of actively managed funds is higher as well, because they turn over the assets they hold once the information they traded on was incorporated into the asset's price (or they turned out to be wrong). As a result of all these factors, the transaction costs incurred by actively managed funds tend to be large, which limits their potential size,[15] hence the adage 'size is the enemy of alpha'. When considering the addition of an asset to their portfolios, actively managed funds should take into account, in addition to the new asset's potential contribution to the fund's alpha, the effects of adding the asset on the fund's overall market-impact cost and on its proportional transaction costs. This is in addition to the obvious diversification effect of adding a new asset to the fund. Asset managers should explicitly analyze the transaction-cost structure of the assets they manage and take that into account when structuring their investment portfolios.

Consider, for example, an actively managed fund whose portfolio consists of n assets. The fund is considering increasing its investment capacity to $(n+1)$ assets at an annual cost F, which reflects the incremental costs (of research, analysis, stock selection etc.), which are not sensitive to the actual investment sizes. The fixed cost F introduces economies of scale in the fund management, and thus the fund faces a trade-off: Investing more in the incremental asset lowers the annual fixed cost per dollar invested but on the other hand it raises the market-impact cost per dollar invested, which means diseconomies of scale. The resulting investments are expected to have an incremental return of $\Delta\alpha$ over and above the expected market return. Assuming an incremental investment of q, the resulting increase in the fund's expected annual net investment profit is given by

$$qR_{n+1} - F - \mu q\,(k_{n+1} + q\lambda_{n+1}) \tag{9}$$

where the expected return R_{n+1} reflects both the incremental return (expected to be $\Delta\alpha$) and the market's compensation for transaction costs. If the fund's expected transaction costs were identical to those reflected in R_{n+1}, the decision would depend on the relationship between $\Delta\alpha$ and F/q, where q is determined by the fund's investment policies or by the optimal transaction-cost driven level $[R_{n+1} - \mu k_{n+1}/(\mu\lambda_{n+1})]$, analogous to Equation 7. However, it is likely that the market compensation for transaction costs is lower than an active fund's actual transaction costs, since the former typically reflects a longer investment horizon. Further, the fund will need to act quickly to be able to realize the return on its information and research, which will increase its transaction costs and, in order to amortize the fixed cost F of new information and research, it is likely to acquire a larger position than the marginal investor, which again results in a larger market-impact cost. Naturally, if on the other hand the fund possesses superior trading technology which lowers its transaction costs below the average market's, then investing in less liquid securities may produce a higher alpha.

22.5.2 Trade implementation

Money managers usually focus on stock selection and market timing. However, the managers' skill in buying and selling the positions they manage has a substantial effect on portfolio performance. For example, suppose a fund wants to sell a large position in a security. Dumping the entire quantity in a single transaction would obviously lead to a large price-impact. Selling the entire quantity in a negotiated block transaction can reduce the cost, but is also costly due to commissions and search-and-delay costs. A third alternative is to split the order and sell it in pieces. Here, it is possible to construct a model that takes as input the quantity to be sold, the price-impact per unit, and the cost of delay or time constraints to liquidate the position. The model would provide an optimal, cost-minimizing way to sell the position. If the fund wishes to sell a position in a number of securities whose returns are correlated, a further complication ensues, which can be worked into the model. Skilled buying and selling of securities, aimed at minimizing illiquidity costs, has a substantial impact on investment performance.

22.5.3 Cash management

Cash holding by a mutual fund that competes for performance is unreasonable in a world without transaction costs because of the zero return on cash. Also, a passive index tracking investment has no room for cash holdings, because this would generate tracking error and underperformance versus the index. However, a fund is subject to variations in the inflows and outflows of cash, either coming from investors buying new units or redeeming them, or from the cash flow generated by the financial assets (such as dividends and coupon payments). If the fund immediately invested its excess cash in securities or sold assets to accommodate redemptions, it would incur high transaction costs. Instead, the fund can refrain, within some limit, from investing excess cash and, instead, hold a cash position to accommodate redemptions. The optimality of refraining from trading in securities in order to save on transaction costs was developed by Constantinides (1986). He assumes a risk-averse investor who wishes to hold fixed proportions of a risk-free asset that has no transaction costs, and a risky security having proportional transaction costs. The investor faces a trade-off: frequent portfolio rebalancing will keep his/her portfolio at the desired ratio of risky/riskless assets, but entails high cumulative transaction costs. Constantinides proposes a solution of setting a boundary around (above and below) the optimal asset ratio, within which the investor refrains from trading, even though the risky/riskless assets ratio deviates from the desired one. When the ratio is outside the boundary, the investor transacts to the nearest boundary. The width of the no-trade region increases in the risky security's transaction costs, and thus higher transaction costs lead to less trading but a higher opportunity loss for the investor, due to the deviation of the actual asset ratio from the desired one.

Connor and Leland (1995) apply this idea to mutual fund management with cash. They point out that a cash position in a mutual fund lowers expected transaction costs because its transaction cost is nil compared with that of ordinary securities. They propose an optimal cash-management policy of setting an upper limit on the cash position in the fund. If cash inflows cause cash to exceed this limit, the fund manager should invest the excess cash so that the weight of cash in the portfolio is restored to its upper limit. Similarly, when redemptions by investors deplete the available cash below the assigned weight, the fund does not trade its securities until the cash position hits zero, in which case any additional cash outflow leads to selling securities in the proportions that befit the fund's investment policy (for example, in line with the weights of the securities in the index that the fund is tracking). Connor and Leland show that the optimal upper-bound of the cash level is particularly sensitive to the proportional transaction costs and to the volatility of cash inflows and outflows. As the values of these two variables rise, so does the maximum cash position. Thus, higher transaction costs and higher cash inflow volatility increase the tracking error of the fund and worsen its performance relative to the index benchmark.

Now, suppose that an investment fund wants to hold two classes of risky assets, as well as cash in some target proportion, and it is subject to cash inflows and outflows, as well as to fluctuations in asset values. Trading in the risky assets entails proportional transaction costs. The investor is averse to the

426 Yakov Amihud and Haim Mendelson

magnitude of the tracking error of his investment return compared with the return he would have if the assets were always at their target weights, which means that it is costly for the investor to deviate from the optimal weights. A common practice in such a case is to periodically rebalance all the assets in the portfolio to keep them at their target proportions. The reason for periodic (rather than continuous) rebalancing is to save on transaction costs.

However, Leland (1999) shows that this is inferior to an optimal trading policy that works as follows. The fund determines a no-trade region around the target proportions of these assets and allows the actual proportions to fluctuate within this region. If an asset proportion moves beyond the region's boundary, trading is undertaken to move it back to the boundary. Also, this strategy requires trading a single asset, rather than all assets. Under some reasonable parameter values, Leland shows that this strategy can optimally reduce turnover by about 50%, and thus reduce transaction costs.

The initial investment in assets depends on their transaction costs and on the covariance between their returns. If two risky assets have different transaction costs and their returns are highly correlated, the fund will under-invest (hold less than its target weight) in the asset with the higher transaction costs and overinvest in the other asset, whose transaction costs are lower and can serve as a substitute in case of a need to reduce the investment in the high-transaction-cost asset. While these deviations from the target weights may be costly to the investor, holding initially more of the asset with lower transaction costs is beneficial because it is less costly to liquidate the asset which is less costly to trade, should the need arise. Thus, the higher correlation between the assets' returns makes them partial substitutes, while the lower transaction cost on one asset makes it preferable.

More generally, cash holding is not always the best way to accommodate liquidity needs because of the low return on cash. Funds may prefer to hold highly liquid equities, which provide better tracking of the benchmark index that the fund wishes to outperform, and earn a higher return than cash because of their higher risk. Going beyond Leland's (1999) example of two risky assets that differ in their liquidity, funds that are subject to liquidity needs may choose to accommodate these needs by investing in highly liquid equities in proportions that exceed those dictated by their investment objectives, which ignore transaction costs. The preference for liquid equities over illiquid equities is consistent with the prediction of Amihud and Mendelson's (1986a) model that assets with lower transaction costs are in higher demand and thus they have lower expected returns in equilibrium.

22.5.4 Liquidity management in mutual funds

Mutual funds manage their liquidity not only by choosing between cash and equity investments, but also by selecting securities according to their liquidity.

SEC Rule 35d-1 mandates that a mutual fund should 'invest at least 80% of its assets in the type of investment suggested by the name', that is, cash holding is constrained to 20% in funds that declare their investment to be in certain types of securities. Holding cash imposes an opportunity cost on the fund if it forgoes investing in securities with positive risk-adjusted returns for the sake of holding liquidity in cash. Fund managers may therefore manage their fund's liquidity by selecting the securities that comprise the fund not only on the basis of their excess returns but also by taking their liquidity characteristics into account. If they want to increase their fund's liquidity, they will tilt the fund's holdings toward securities that satisfy the fund's investment policy and have greater liquidity. Massa and Phalippou (2005) study the liquidity of actively managed mutual stock funds and find that larger funds and funds with greater turnover (μ in our analysis) hold stocks that are more liquid on average. Also, consistent with our theoretical analysis, portfolio concentration induces a preference for fund investment in more liquid stocks. The preference for investing in more liquid assets when the fund's turnover is higher can also be inferred from our result (7) above, which shows that there is a trade-off between the weight of a single security in the fund's portfolio and its liquidity, for any given risk-adjusted return that it generates. For given transaction costs, the fund reduces the amount that it holds in each security in order to reduce its price impact costs. If not for transaction costs, the fund would have concentrated on investing in securities that are the best by its analysis of their fundamental value. Massa and Phalippou (2005) find that funds do indeed actively manage the liquidity of their portfolios. If some fund characteristics change, they respond by changing their portfolio composition (changing the weights of the stocks they hold) in a way that would provide the desired liquidity. And, if the average fund liquidity changes due to changes in the values of the stocks it holds, the fund again changes its portfolio composition to re-establish the desired level of liquidity.

22.5.5 Dynamic liquidity management

Asset liquidity changes over time with liquidity shocks being negatively correlated with asset returns (Amihud, 2002). Also, greater volatility in the market induces redemptions from mutual funds. Thus, a fund may want to manage its liquidity by holding more liquid securities when it expects an increase in redemptions, so as to reduce the transaction costs of selling securities. The need for greater liquidity in times of high volatility is highlighted by the fact that in times of high volatility, market liquidity declines. Huang (2008) analyzes the features of liquidity management by mutual funds, observing that funds do indeed increase their holdings of liquid stocks when there is a rise in expected stock volatility (measured by the VIX). The switch into liquid stocks in times of higher expected volatility is particularly strong in low-load funds, where the likelihood of withdrawals is higher in bad times, and where these funds therefore need to be ready with more liquid assets in place, which they can divest at lower cost. The increase in the portfolio weight of liquid stocks when expected volatility rises is also stronger for funds with greater volatility, for growth funds compared with income funds, and for funds with greater turnover, where liquidity is more valuable.

Liquidity management by mutual funds improves their performance. Huang finds that, while larger holdings of liquid stocks generally lower the fund's alpha because high-liquidity stocks earn lower risk-adjusted returns (Amihud and Mendelson, 1986a), liquid holdings strongly improve performance when stock volatility is expected to increase.

Simutin (2013) finds evidence of liquidity management in actively managed equity mutual funds. Funds whose portfolio constitutes riskier or less liquid stocks hold greater amounts of cash. Higher levels of cash are also associated with lower operation costs. Simutin (2013) also finds that funds with greater excess cash holdings have better performance, but this is traced to managerial stock selection skills: stock purchasing decisions are more profitable in funds with greater cash holdings.

Another evidence of liquidity being a factor in the management of mutual fund investments is provided by Shawky and Tian (2011). They find that small-cap mutual funds earn excess return by buying less liquid stocks and selling more liquid stocks, with this pattern being pronounced in value funds. Similarly, Idzorek, Xiong and Ibbotson (2011) find that 'mutual funds that hold relatively less liquid stocks from within the liquid universe of publicly traded stocks outperform mutual funds that hold relatively more liquid stocks' (p. 16), after controlling for the funds' investment styles and risk variables. These findings are consistent with the liquidity-based asset pricing theory of Amihud and Mendelson (1986a) and the analysis here.

Evidence that hedge funds manage their investment to accommodate liquidity changes is presented by Cao et al. (2013), who find that fund managers adjust the exposure of their portfolio to the market according to market liquidity conditions. When market liquidity is high, funds increase the market exposure of their portfolio, and reduce this exposure when market liquidity is low. This strategy is employed mainly by funds whose holdings are less liquid, which are exposed to greater illiquidity risk, whereas funds whose holdings are liquid tend to react to past market liquidity rather than time it ex ante. The relation between market illiquidity and market exposure is asymmetric. Hedge funds react more strongly to unusually high market illiquidity, in which case they reduce their market exposure, whereas when illiquidity is unusually low they do not increase their market exposure. Altogether, the evidence shows that market liquidity is an important consideration in hedge-fund strategies.

The importance of managing funds' liquidity risk is underscored by Sadka (2010) for hedge funds and by Dong, Feng and Sadka (2012) for mutual funds. Sadka (2010) shows that across funds, those with higher exposure to unexpected liquidity shocks have higher returns, after controlling for risk factors, and Dong et al. (2012) find similar evidence for stock mutual funds, although there, the effect of liquidity risk on fund performance is smaller.

22.5.6   Client acquisition and development

Our results show that investment decisions depend on the investors' investment horizons. As a result, there is an optimal clientele for each portfolio, depending not only on the portfolio's risk and traditional investment style but also on its liquidity. Thus, client acquisition and development should reflect not only the firm's traditional investment style but also its liquidity or transaction-cost profile. Alternatively, firms may need to segment their clients based on their transaction-cost characteristics.

Indeed, the 2009 asset manager survey by Investment & Pensions Europe found that 'for anyone managing pension fund and other institutional portfolios investing over the long term, the investment horizon is now to be the key objective in looking at internally managed assets. "Investment horizon" has jumped from its ranking of fifth position in last year's survey to first this year.'[16] This implies that both asset management activities and client development should target the client's investment horizon as a key characteristic.

Investment horizons are indeed strongly connected with the type of securities that investors select. Naes and Odegaard's (2009) study of all investors on the Oslo Stock Exchange finds that more liquid stocks attract individual investors with shorter holding periods. In general, financial investors have shorter holding periods, individual investors have longer holding periods, and foreign and corporate (non-financial) investors are in-between. Furthermore, stocks with greater volatility and larger capitalization attract owners with shorter holding periods. Similarly, Uno and Kamiyama (2009) find that, in Japan, the weighted average holding period of a stock, calculated from the investment horizon of the constituent shareholders of each stock, is positively related to the stock's illiquidity.

By this analysis, investors self-select into load and no-load funds according to their planned holding periods and personal trade-off between liquidity and return. In no-load funds, short-term investors freeload on those who intend to invest for a long period, because the cost of liquidation to accommodate redemptions is borne by all fund investors. Also, the need to hold more liquid securities to accommodate redemptions erodes the return that accrues to all investors in the fund. In contrast, mutual funds with load payments should expect to attract investors with longer investment horizons. The reduced need to accommodate frequent redemptions enables the fund to engage in a less costly liquidity-management policy, and can enhance the fund's performance. The fund will be less compelled to give up excess return in order to maintain greater liquidity of its assets. Therefore, investors who do not expect to liquidate their position soon would opt for load funds. Some privately managed investment funds with limited clientele go as far as restricting or limiting liquidations within a certain period, which is even more attractive for long-term investors and enhances the range of investment opportunities that the asset manager may consider.

22.6   Concluding remarks

In this chapter, we introduced the nature and structure of transaction costs, studied how they affect asset prices, and examined their implications for asset managers. We have shown how transaction costs affect portfolio construction, fund scope and size, trade implementation, cash and liquidity management strategies, and customer acquisition and development.

We defined transaction costs as the variable costs of buying or selling securities. Some of these costs (such as the bid-ask spread) are incurred in the market where the security is traded. Other transaction costs are operational in nature – the (variable) costs of telecommunications, direct costs of execution, variable personnel costs, internal technology investments etc. Both types of cost affect asset mangers' performance, and both are constantly driven down by the continuous decline in the cost (and the corresponding increase in the capacity and functionality) of information and communication technologies.

Will we then reach a point where transaction costs become negligible, rendering them irrelevant? We think the answer is 'no'. A decline in both internal and market-wide transaction costs leads to an increase in trading volumes and enables the creation of new and innovative trading instruments and the design of new trading strategies. Just as the decline in the cost of processing power did not lead to the demise of the computer industry (in fact, it made the industry and its applications, grow), we may observe a similar effect on asset markets as transaction costs continue to decline.

As recent events have shown, transaction costs may actually spike as a result of the increased complexity of financial instruments, the higher volatility of financial markets, and global interconnectivity. The same factors that drive trading costs down drive up speed, complexity, volume and risk, and, with them, the continued importance of transaction costs.

Notes

1. The variable cost of trading room operations may not be directly available, but it can be calculated using standard cost-accounting techniques.

2. As discussed later, another transaction-cost component is search and delay costs.
3. The New York Stock Exchange assigns specialists to each stock; they continuously provide quotes. On the NASDAQ stock market, broker–dealers make markets in multiple stocks.
4. When the trader's intention is disclosed, some market participants may engage in front-running, which further exacerbates the market impact. Such practices may be illegal, and traders will usually select broker–dealers who do not engage in them.
5. The bid-ask spread represents the cost of a 'round-trip' transaction of buying and selling the stock, hence the average bid-ask spread cost per transaction is half the spread.
6. Recall that the different components of transaction costs are highly correlated.
7. In this example, $0.01/1.05 + 0.01/1.05^2 + 0.01/1.05^3 + 0.01/1.05^4 + \ldots = 0.21$.
8. Amihud, Mendelson and Lauterbach (1997) show that the relationship also holds when the liquidity of a stock changes over time.
9. More precisely, each note was straddled by two bills, one maturing just before and the other just after the note.
10. In addition, liquidity risk, which considers the co-variation of an asset's illiquidity with market illiquidity, was shown to be priced (see a review in Amihud, Mendelson and Pedersen, 2013). This calls for portfolio construction strategies that also take liquidity risk into account.
11. We assume here that the number of assets is fixed. We later consider how the fund's cost structure changes as the number of assets n increases.
12. Without loss of generality, we adjust the constant of proportionality to 1.
13. Empirical evidence for active equity mutual funds shows that there is negative correlation between their size (total net assets) and turnover; see Amihud and Goyenko (2013).
14. Engle, Ferstenberg and Russell (2012) present estimations of the trade-off between speed of execution and transaction costs.
15. Indeed, asset managers stop receiving assets into actively managed funds once they reach a certain size. In addition to liquidity considerations, the fund manager faces the prospect of worse performance as the fund exhausts its superior investment opportunities.
16. IPE European Institutional Asset Management Survey, June 2009, p. 6.

References

Amihud, Y. (2002) 'Illiquidity and stock returns: cross-section and time series effects', *Journal of Financial Markets*, (5): 31–56.

Amihud, Y. and Goyenko, R. (2013) 'Mutual fund's R² as predictor of performance', *Review of Financial Studies*, (26): 667–694.

Amihud, Y. and Mendelson, H. (1986a) 'Asset pricing and the bid-ask spread', *Journal of Financial Economics*, (17): 223–249.

Amihud, Y. and Mendelson, H. (1986b) 'Liquidity and Stock Returns', *Financial Analysts Journal*, (42)3: 43–48.

Amihud, Y. and Mendelson, H. (1991) 'Liquidity, maturity and the yields on U.S. government securities', *Journal of Finance*, (46): 1411–1426.

Amihud, Y., Mendelson, H. and Lauterbach, B. (1997) 'Market microstructure and securities values: Evidence from the Tel Aviv Exchange', *Journal of Financial Economics*, (45): 365–390.

Amihud, Y., Mendelson, H. and Pedersen, L.H. (2013) *Market Liquidity: Asset Pricing, Risk and Crises*. Cambridge University Press, New York, NY.

Cao, C., Chen, Y., Liang, B. and Lo, A.W. (2013) 'Can hedge funds time market liquidity?', *Journal of Financial Economics*, (109): 493–516.

Chen, L., Lesmond, D.A. and Wei, J.Z. (2006) 'Corporate yield spreads and bond liquidity', *Journal of Finance*, (62): 119–149.

Connor, G. and Leland, H. (1995) 'Cash management for index tracking', *Financial Analysts Journal*, (71)6: 75–80.

Constantinides, G.M. (1986) 'Capital market equilibrium with transaction costs', *Journal of Political Economy*, (94): 842–862.

Dong, X., Feng, S. and Sadka, R. (2012) 'Liquidity risk and mutual fund performance', working paper.

Engle, R., Ferstenberg, R. and Russell, J. (2012) 'Measuring and modeling execution cost and risk', *Journal of Portfolio Management*, (38)2: 14–28.

Glosten, L.R. and Harris, L.E. (1988) 'Estimating the components of the bid/ask spread', *Journal of Financial Economics*, (21): 123–142.

Huang, J. (2008), 'Dynamic liquidity preferences of mutual funds', working paper, NUS Business School.

Idzorek, T.M., Xiong, J.X. and Ibbotson, R.G. (2011) 'The liquidity style of mutual funds', working paper, Morningstar Investment Management.

IPE European Institutional Asset Management Survey (2009), *Investments & Pensions Europe*, June.

IPE European Institutional Asset Management Survey (2011), *Investments & Pensions Europe*, June.

Kyle, A.S. (1985) 'Continuous Auctions and Insider Trading', *Econometrica*, (53): 1315–1335.

Leland, H.E. (1999) 'Optimal portfolio management with transactions costs and capital gains taxes', working paper, The Haas School, University of California, Berkeley.

Massa, M. and Phalippou, L. (2005) 'Mutual funds and the market for liquidity', working paper, Insead.

Næs, R. and Ødegaard, B.A. (2009) 'Liquidity and asset pricing: Evidence on the role of investor holding period', working paper, University of Stavanger.

Rajan, A. (2009) *Future of Investment: the next move?* Create-Research, Tunbridge Wells, UK.

Sadka, R. (2010) 'Liquidity risk and the cross-section of hedge-fund returns', *Journal of Financial Economics*, (98): 54–71.

Shawky, H.A. and Tian, J. (2011) 'Small-cap Equity mutual fund managers as liquidity providers', *Journal of Empirical Finance*, (18)5: 802–814.

Simutin, M. (2009) 'Cash holdings and mutual fund performance', *Review of Finance*, forthcoming.

Uno, J. and Kamiyama, N. (2009), 'Ownership structure, liquidity and firm value: Effects of investment horizon', working paper, Waseda University.

Part VI

Operational Platforms and IT Strategies

23
Operational Platform and Growth: A Strategic Challenge

Jacob Elsborg

23.1 The consequences of lacking an operational platform strategy

The global financial crisis has been tough, and experts have varying views of future prospects. Some of the more optimistic analysts believe that the markets will surpass the 2007 levels in 2013 or 2014. The only possible conclusion to be drawn from comparing the various analyses is that the markets are not yet stable and that the higher level of volatility seen in the markets over the past couple of years will continue.

In this chapter, it is questioned how well asset managers in general are prepared for growth or at least a positive change in the financial markets. Searching the literature, none of the contributions have (to this author's knowledge) proposed ways to change the operational platform strategy to reflect changes in the business strategy caused by the financial crisis. This indicates that asset managers may be preparing for growth and/or change, but none of them have considered changing the operational platform accordingly to support new business goals. This lack of alignment between an operational platform strategy and the business strategy is seen far too often. In fact, a proper operational platform strategy is extremely rare.

The following definition of an operational platform (Elsborg, 2008) is applied in this chapter: *An operational platform in the asset management industry is where the management of an organization's data and information takes place, together with the execution of decisions.*

The situation of a market set for change and growth opportunities puts a great deal of pressure upon asset managers. What are they to expect and do in a market like this? Unfortunately, there is no room for what would no doubt be an exciting discussion of the strategic initiatives taken by asset managers during the global financial crisis and how they have prepared for the future. What is interesting, as stated above, is that looking for evidence of changes to operational strategies, operational platform strategy or IT strategy (IT strategy is included here because many asset managers have no operational strategy) as an answer to changes in business strategy caused by the financial crisis, there are very limited results to be found in the available literature on the subject (close to none).

The conclusion that can be drawn from this is that any alignment of operational strategy with business strategy (investment strategy) is rare and that the operational platform is not usually a part of the response to changes in the market.

This situation illustrates a common problem in the industry. Many asset managers do not differentiate between an IT strategy and an operational platform strategy. Far too often, making no differentiation between these strategies causes the operational set-up and the development of this set-up to be based upon technical considerations stated in the IT strategy (if there is one). By contrast, an operational platform strategy – as defined in this chapter – is formulated by the business unit using the platform, which ensures that the management of an operational platform becomes an integrated part of the business. An operational platform strategy includes processes and the functional set-up of investment management operations. The difference between the operational platform strategy and operational strategy is that the former includes the functional set-up.

Once the operational platform strategy is defined, the underlying technological processes such as network, communications and hardware are managed within the framework of the IT strategy, which must of course be aligned with the operational platform strategy. The author of this chapter acknowledges that management of IT strategy is of equal strategic importance (and often more complex).

The approach of strategic management of the operational platform, however, can be more or less sophisticated, e.g., the basic model can be developed further according to the results of the analysis; the analytical approach is extendable; and the strategies and drivers of the platform are equally extendable. It is all a question of how complex a business the operational platform must support.

The value of defining and strategically managing the company's operational platform, however, exceeds the cost, with the following main benefits:

- Management buys into the development of the operational platform through working with alignment of the operational strategy with the business strategy.
- Development of the operational platform is not driven by a day-to-day approach, but by defined long-term business goals.
- The platform development processes become more precise and timely due to the integration on a strategic level with the business strategy, which leads to a decrease in cost.

- A more stable platform results from the long-term perspective development and it is thus less of a 'putting-out-the-fire' platform.
- A better understanding develops between the users and developers of the operational platform due to the strategic alignment.
- On a strategic level, IT and operational management are separated, leaving the purely technical strategy and decisions to the technical staff and the operational strategy and decisions to the business unit.

The conclusion is obviously that the choice and design of an operational platform is not an isolated technical decision, but a strategic management tool that either supports the development of the business or creates obstacles if not well-managed. The operational platform can be seen as a way to gain competitive advantage from cost-efficient design, reliability, flexibility and scalability. In short, the main goal for strategic management of the operational platform is to create alignment of the operational development with the development of the business so that it supports the strategies of the business and thus enables growth.

23.1.1 Case: order management

To illustrate the concept of defining an operational platform strategy, the following example shows how the order management process in its simplest form is strategically based (Figure 23.1).

Order management in its simplest form consists of the following elements requiring action/decisions:

a) instrument trading
b) legal contracts/financial security
c) pre-trade compliance
d) order generation
e) order execution
f) trading system
g) interface to other systems
h) data repository
i) connectivity
j) IT security

An investment strategy defines what instruments are to be handled within the framework of order management and how the legal aspects of order management are handled. The objectives and strategy of pre-trade compliance, order generation and order execution are handled within the framework of an investment strategy, whereas the processes and integration executing the orders are defined in an operational platform strategy.

Strategic framework			
Elements requiring action/ decision	Investment strategy	Operational platform strategy	IT strategy
Case: order management			
Instruments traded	×		
Legal contracts/financial security	×		
Pre-trade compliance	×	×	
Order generation	×	×	
Order execution		×	
Trading system	×	×	
Interface with other systems		×	×
Data repository		×	×
Connectivity		×	×
IT security			×

Figure 23.1   Strategic order management framework

An operational platform strategy should specify which instruments (instrument classes are defined later in the chapter) are to be handled electronically, and the choice of system must be aligned with the investment strategy. The integration processes and functional set-up (pre-trade compliance, execution, data storage, etc.) are handled within the operational strategy and again aligned with the objectives of the investment strategy.

An IT strategy should cover physical tasks such as communication, both the internal interface between trading system and treasury system (if the systems are separate) and the handling of the external communication, e.g., whether all external communication is through a broker. The IT security set-up and processes are also included in the IT strategy.

It is obvious that if there is no operational platform strategy, the strategic framework of both the investment strategy and the IT strategy must be widened to cover what is defined in an operational platform strategy. As a consequence, both strategies will be less focused, and the management owning the strategy will manage areas that are not part of their core business. In this case, the investment strategy ought to be defined by the investment professionals focusing on markets, instruments and business opportunities. Having to define operational processes and platform strategies covering all the aspects of operations will indeed make the strategy broad and unfocused.

The same thing happens with an IT strategy that has to cover aspects that are not an integrated part of a general IT strategy: it will lack focus.

Thus the operational platform strategy is a necessity if one wants to focus both the investment strategy and IT strategy. An operational platform strategy will also support the managerial focus on the operational side of the business.

Far too often, the areas that ought to be defined as part of the operational platform are left in a strategic vacuum covered by no strategy at all. In such a situation, the operational platform is relegated to day-by-day development with no real management.

23.2 The strategic framework

A business strategy is the foundation of any successful organization. A strategic framework depends upon many factors: company type (e.g., pension fund or hedge fund), size of company, corporate culture and investment universe. The discussion above focused on the problems that arise when a firm has no operational platform strategy.

The definition of a business strategy derives from the usual steps: analysis followed by definition of vision/mission, objectives, strategy and tactics (VMOST) (Sondhi, 1999), which again leads to the definition of an investment strategy (it has been seen that the strategy and tactics definitions of the business strategy are the definition of the investment strategy). This is the main strategy for the entire organization and, depending upon the size of the company, may also be a high-level strategy.

For the most part, implementation of an investment strategy as the strategy/tactics of the company strategy is not an appropriate way to define the strategic framework, except for companies that have asset management as their only activity; otherwise this kind of strategic mixing often leaves a gap between investment strategy and operational strategy and an unclear strategic direction. Thus a proper strategic framework ensures that an investment strategy is defined, and this strategy supports the overall business strategy.

It is upon this basis the operational platform strategy is defined. The implementation of the operational platform strategy thus becomes an integrated part of the implementation of the business strategy. Some asset managers define an operational strategy as the strategy that incorporates the tactics and processes that support the investment strategy. The operational platform strategy expands the operational strategy by including the overall functional set-up as a part of this strategy. Sometimes the functional set-up is defined within the framework of the IT strategy, but, far too often, the functional definition is left in a no man's land (not a part of any strategy).

It is outside the scope of this chapter to define a business or investment strategy, which means it is impossible to define a specific operational platform strategy. However, it is possible to define basic operational drivers without

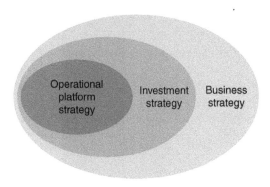

Figure 23.2   Strategic alignment

having the precise strategic scope of the business, the investment or the operational platform strategy. Creating a successful operational platform strategy requires accurate market assessment and subsequently identification of actions required to achieve the goals of the investment strategy (see Figure 23.2).

23.3   Model framework of an operational platform

To implement a strategic approach to managing an operational platform, a functional model must be defined and in place. This model is the main starting point in conducting analyses and setting up a strategy for an operational platform.

Defining the activities of an asset manager within the concept of a value chain (Sondhi, 1999) forms the basis of the functional model (Figure 23.3).

The value chain consists of three primary activities, which are the investment processes:

a) decision making
b) transaction processing
c) information delivery.

Using this definition of the activities of an asset manager with respect to an operational platform, a model in its simplest form can be used to show where the management of an organization's data and information takes place, together with the execution of decisions (Figure 23.4).

In order to define a strategic approach to managing an operational platform, the primary activities in the value chain have to be defined separately. The next part of this chapter is an analysis of the primary activities of an operating platform. Figure 23.5 gives a brief presentation of a functional model

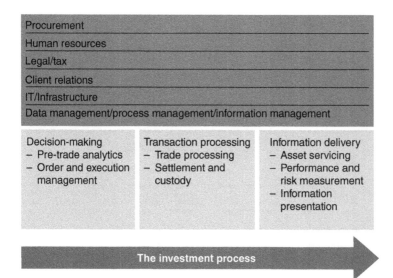

Figure 23.3   Value chain

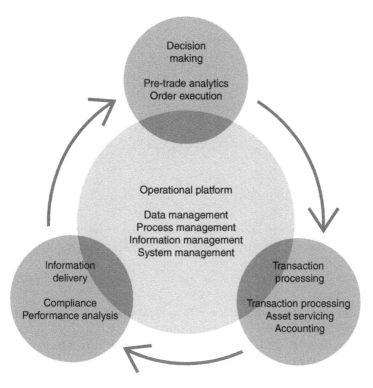

Figure 23.4   Operational platform

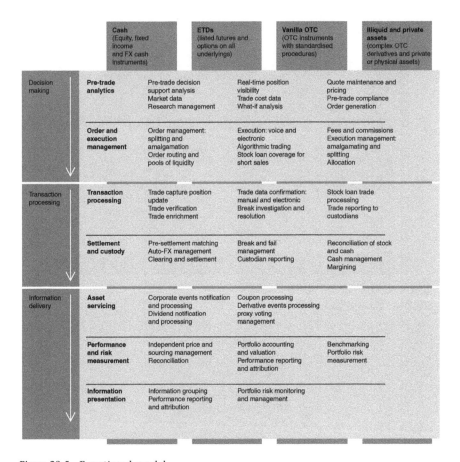

Figure 23.5   Functional model

framework (Heyes, 2007; Elsborg, 2008) for the defined activities of an operational platform.

Within the framework shown in Figure 23.5, a differentiation based upon the characteristics of the instruments is suggested. The asset classes are:

1) **Cash.** Cash instruments are equities, fixed income and FX cash instruments.
2) **Exchange-traded derivatives (ETDs).** ETD instruments are listed futures and options on all underlying instruments.
3) **OTC (named 'Vanilla' OTC)** OTC products are instruments with standardized procedures.
4) **Illiquid and private assets.** Illiquid and private assets are complex OTC derivatives and private or physical assets.

The assets within each group have the same characteristics in terms of their defined main functions, and they are thus useful when analyzing the operational platform. It is not the intent of this chapter to discuss in detail the characteristics of each asset class or how to use the various instruments in terms of portfolio management; however, one must be aware of the differentiation when defining a strategic model of an operational platform.

23.4   The basics of an operational platform analysis

The basic analysis of the operational platform is centered on the objectives and strategic direction of an operational platform, which is again based on the overall business strategy. The basic analysis is therefore defined as the strategic analysis of the operational platform, and the analysis is performed as a standard basic analysis of a strategy (Henley Management College, 2002). The critical success factors (CSFs) and the main operational drivers of the platform can be determined from this process, along with the key performance indicators (KPIs) (Henley Management College, 2002). Figure 23.6 illustrates the flow of the analysis.

The analytical steps for the model presented in Figure 23.6 are:

1) operational platform strategy, objectives
   – strategic direction
2) definition of critical success factors (CSFs)
3) main operational drivers
4) key performance indicators (KPIs).

Strategic analysis forms the basis for information and process analysis. For this reason, analysts must be careful when defining CSFs, main operational drivers and KPIs: some of them have dual uses (used in both information and process analysis), but many of them have only a single use.

Figure 23.6   Strategic analysis of operational platform

23.4.1   Operational platform strategy: objectives and direction

To conduct a proper information and process analysis, its strategy/objectives must be defined. As stated above, this strategy is based upon the business strategy.

It is vital that the objectives of the operational platform cover the three main functions defined above.

The strategic direction of the operational platform should be defined by developing an operational platform strategy. A useful framework for defining the strategic direction of the operational platform is Michael Porter's competitive strategies (Porter, 1985; see Figure 23.7).

The alignment of the strategic direction of an operational platform with the business strategy is crucial because this direction has a direct impact on all levels of an operational platform strategy.

Several drivers (which are not the same drivers as the operational drivers) are reflected in an operational platform strategy; they depend on the business strategy on which the operational platform strategy is based. Three main drivers that should be considered when developing an operational platform strategy are:

- flexibility
- scalability
- technology.

These drivers are highly dependent on the strategic direction defined for an operational platform.

As identified within the competitive scope above, costs can be considered as a separate driver or simply as a function of the drivers defined above.

Having defined a functional model and strategic direction/drivers for a platform, a strategy for an operational platform can then easily be defined. Afterwards, a strategic fit between the existing operational platform and the strategy should be determined in order to decide on the future development of the operational platform.

Competitive scope	Advantage	
	Low-cost	Differentiation
Broad	Broad low-cost	Broad differentiation
Narrow	Focussed low-cost	Focussed differentiation

Figure 23.7   Michael Porter's competitive strategy
Source: Porter 1985.

Before starting the information and operational analysis, the main operational drivers, CSFs and KPIs should be defined. All three definitions are then used in the information and operational analysis.

23.4.2 CSFs

There are many different approaches to defining CSFs. According to the approach developed by Sondhi (1999), the CSFs determine the success of an application for the organization. CSFs can be product-oriented (e.g., higher product quality or innovative design), development process-oriented (e.g., a more efficient and effective development process), or standards-oriented (e.g., the product complies with standards), or they may have societal goals (e.g., a product that can be used by people with special needs).

In other words, the CSFs are the critical activities a business must undertake to be successful (Sondhi, 1999). Identification of these factors has its origins in the strategy and the strategic direction.

23.4.3 Main operational drivers

The main operational drivers can be defined as the factors that cause changes to the platform. Again, it is crucial that the identification has its origins in the strategy and the strategic direction. Various operational drivers are defined in the literature, and they are extremely dependent on the business, of course. What follows is a list of some of the most common operational drivers in the industry.

Number of decision-makers (e.g. portfolio managers)

The number of decision-makers is defined in the business strategy and is typically based upon the number of markets the asset manager chooses to be in and the variety of instruments used. This is an important number because the infrastructure of the platform is dependent on where and how many clients it has to serve.

Number of geographical representations

This mainly concerns the infrastructure of the operational platform because it has great impact on the infrastructure if you are running a 24-hour business spread across the globe compared with only one location.

Instruments traded on the platform

The complexity of the operational platform depends on the number of instruments traded on the platform. No instruments are the same, so the degree of complexity rises almost proportionally with the number of instruments handled on the platform.

Number of transactions

The number of transactions is as specific as the other numbers mentioned above. The possibility for bulk processing of trades exists, so it is vital to be aware of how the various transactions are to be processed.

Other operational drivers (Solvency II, number of clients, reporting, etc.) can also be defined, depending on the strategic business goals of the asset manager. The five operational drivers defined above are simply examples that are often used.

23.4.4   Key Performance Indicators (KPIs)

The KPIs help organizations achieve the goals for their operational platform through the definition and measurement of progress (Sondhi, 1999). The key indicators are measurable indicators that will reflect the critical success factors. The KPIs selected must reflect the goals of the operational platform; they must be key to its success, and they must be measurable. KPIs are usually long-term considerations for the platform.

23.5   The analysis

A basic analysis can be defined based on the KPIs defined above. The analysis comprises two steps based on two questions:

- What information is required at what level? (Kanter and Miserendino, 1987)
- Is the operational platform capable of performing the task? (Wild, 2002)

To answer these questions, the basic analytical model is structured in three parts (Figure 23.8).

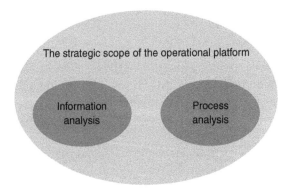

Figure 23.8   Main function analysis model: basic framework

As illustrated above, the basis for the model is the strategic direction definition of the operational platform that was presented above. The analysis consists of an information and operation analysis performed on this basis. The analysis is outlined below.

23.5.1 Basic analytical framework: information analysis

The main purpose of information analysis is to define what information is required at what level (Kanter and Miserendino, 1987). This process must be performed for each of the main functions defined in the functional model (Figure 23.5). Also, the second target is to conduct a gap analysis to define the informational need (Henley Management College, 2002).

The information requirement very much depends on the business strategy. If the business aims for growth targeting new markets or products, it is vital that the operational platform includes the generation of the new information requirements.

The analysis is based on the KPIs defined in the strategy analysis outlined above. The structure of the analysis is described in Figure 23.9.

23.5.2 KPIs

The KPIs derive from the strategic analysis mentioned above, and they are used to determine the information requirements. These requirements are expressed as critical information sets (CISs) based on the KPIs. (A model for analysis is Anthony's Triangle [Kanter and Miserendino, 1987] (see Figures 23.10 and 23.11).)

23.5.3 Information requirement/CISs

In attempting to categorize how and where information is applied, it is useful to define a taxonomy of terms. The starting point was to define the KPIs,

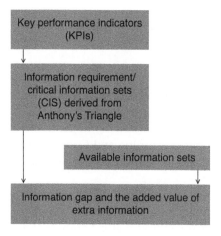

Figure 23.9 Basic information analysis

Level	Hackathorn	Turban
Strategic planning	– Definition of goals, policies – Determination of organisational objectives	Defining long-range goals and policies for resource allocation
Management and tactical	– Acquisition of resources, tactics etc. – Establishment and monitoring of budgets	The acquisition and efficient use of resources in the accomplishment of organisational goals
Operational planning and control	Effective and efficient use of existing facilities and resources to carry out activities within budget constraints	The efficient and effective execution of specific goals

Figure 23.10   Anthony's three management levels

Figure 23.11   Anthony's Triangle

Note: The framework is often shown as a management pyramid, in which a few are engaged at the strategic level while many more are involved at the tactical and operational levels.

Source: Hackathorn 2002.

and the next step is to 'build' a framework using Anthony's Triangle, which diagrams operational activities, management control and strategic planning. These three levels of management activity in the model are defined by Robert Anthony in his 1965 book 'Planning and Control Systems: A Framework for Analysis'. Richard Hackathorn (2002) and Turban et al. (2004) summarize the three levels as follows:

The problem solving and decision making domain extends right across an organization at all management levels. Anthony's Triangle provides a framework that allows something that is highly complex to be broken down into easier-to-understand parts (Hackathorn 2002).

	Levels (Anthony's taxonomy)		
Information characteristics	**Strategic**	**Tactical**	**Operational**
Information users	Management (CIO, CRO, COO)	Portfolio managers, middle managers	Operational staff
Nature of decisions	Investment-strategic decisions	Investment decisions	Analytical and process decisions
Scope	Broad	Intermediate	Narrow
Term focus/ Time horizon	Future-oriented (1 year +)	Within the current plan (3 to 12 months)	Day-to-day, usually with immediate ramifications

Figure 23.12   Anthony's Triangle: basic terms of information use

In Figure 23.12, the framework is applied in basic terms to information use and other aspects using Anthony's model in this framework, based on a broad and general definition of terms. These definitions can vary from company to company.

Other writers and authors have also taken Anthony's taxonomy and used it as a basis for characterizing information at different management levels.

The next step is simply to define the critical information sets (CISs) that can be derived directly from Anthony's information needs for each level.

23.5.4   Available information sets

The available information sets need neither method nor model to be determined. The term is simply used to define what information is available and provided by the operational platform (Henley Management College, 2002).

23.5.5   Information gap

To conclude the analysis, the information gap is defined as the residual between the CITs, which are the information sets the users of the operational platform need, and the available information sets provided by the operational platform (Henley Management College, 2002).

Taking a look in the rearview mirror at some of the financial crises from the past, it is obvious that not all asset managers had all the right information available on their operational platform, or the information was at least not available in a form useful to the decision takers. If a firm wishes to grow or is targeting new markets or products, information analysis is crucial to success, because it is a way to ensure that the right information is generated and made public on the operational platform.

23.6   Basic analytical framework: process analysis

The basic process analysis of the operational platform has the same foundation as the information analysis: it is also based on the strategic analysis of the operational platform as defined above.

The analysis defined below is a simple process analysis, and it would only determine the basic parameters for the operations. To bring the analysis to a higher level would depend on the actual operational platform, so the choice of analysis is dependent upon that as well.

The main approach differs from the one used in the information analysis, because the process analysis is made in parallel with the strategy analysis. For this reason, a gap analysis of the KPIs is performed.

Figure 23.13 illustrates the flow of the analysis, which must be performed for all the main functions outlined in the functional framework defined above.

The operational flow is defined on the basis of Slacks' framework (2002) and Wild's system structure (2002). These frameworks were chosen because of the simplicity they represent. In general, asset management operations are extremely simple compared with those of manufacturing companies because the former involve no actual physical transactions (no inbound or outbound logistics). The analysis has two main layers (Wild 2002):

1) Process mapping
2) Capacity analysis.

These two analytical methods/models will be defined in the section below, and then the conclusion that can be derived from them will be defined and reviewed.

23.6.1   Process mapping

Process mapping is defining each process that takes place on the operational platform. The processes must be mapped to analyze how capacity against fluctuation in demand is handled. Multiple mapping designs exist (Wild

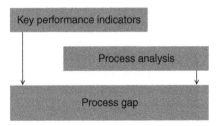

Figure 23.13   Process gap analysis

2002) and it is not important in this connection which mapping design is chosen (see Figure 23.13).

The aim of this part is to define what and how conclusions can be drawn based upon the mapping of the processes.

The mapping process is defined for each service on the platform. Figure 23.14 shows the high-level process mapping of an order or transaction process. It is a well-known fact that the complexity is in the detail, so the analyst must be aware of the level of detail included in the mapping. The level depends on what the intended use of the analysis is.

Some conclusions that can be drawn from this analysis after having mapped all flows are how sufficient the flows are and whether the degree of straight

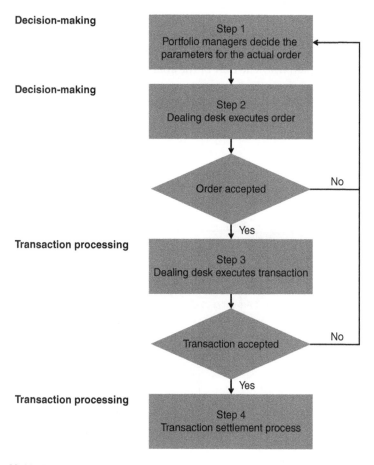

Figure 23.14 Process mapping
Source: Wild 2002.

through processing is acceptable. With respect to changes in the business, another aspect of the analysis is whether the process can include the new business the asset manager intends to take in. This has to be held up against the objectives of the operational platform.

23.6.2   Capacity analysis/management

The capacity analysis/management is about handling the flow of information, orders, transactions and data. Wild (2002) has defined this as follows: 'The determination of capacity requires not only the estimation of steady-state or average demand levels but also decisions on how best to deal with demand level fluctuations.'

The scope of the capacity analysis is to define where there are bottlenecks and how they are managed. A simple approach is the 'decision tree' used in the selection of capacity management strategies. The tree is taken from an original by B. Melville at the University of Waikato in New Zealand (Wild 2002; see Figure 23.15). The capacity analysis has to be done for each service defined upon the operational platform. The flow of the analysis is as follows (Wild 2002):

*   Are the objectives and KPIs for the service defined with a primary goal of resource utilization or as a customer service?

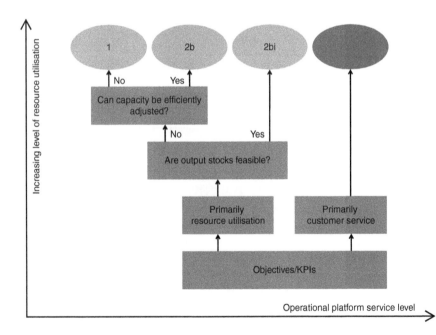

Figure 23.15   Capacity tree

- If the primary goal is customer service, i.e., that the service can be used as needed, then the service has to be maintained with excess capacity. One example is transaction processing: the platform must be able to execute the transactions made by the portfolio manager (2a).
- If the primary goal is resource utilization, another question arises: Are the output stocks feasible?
- If yes, a stock has to be built up to absorb demand fluctuation (2bi). – If no, there are two ways to handle the fluctuation in demand:
  - with a fixed upper capacity: there is a maximum level of how much the users can utilize the service (2b).
  - by providing an efficient adjustment of the capacity (1).

Employing this approach with all the services on the operational platform, the steady state of each can be determined and bottlenecks can be identified and dealt with.

23.6.3   How to align business and the operational platform on a daily basis

As stated earlier in this chapter, it is impossible to calibrate IT strategy with business strategy without considering the role of the operational platform. The clearest analogy to draw is that an IT strategy is a 'sticky' or 'gluey' strategy, whereas an investment strategy is fluid or volatile. The operational platform is considered the core of an effective investment organization today and hence must be viewed as a vehicle to transport business value, driving rather than merely supporting value creation across all the business lines. With this in mind, it is obvious that maintaining the operational platform and maintaining its alignment with the business platform is not only a task subject to analysis conducted every second or third year, but is an ongoing process that must form part of the managing processes within the company. Figure 23.16 illustrates the process that ATP has established in order to secure the daily alignment between business strategy, operational platform strategy and IT strategy.

23.7   Conclusion

Defining and implementing a strategic approach is not an easy task, which is why many asset managers instead choose using a technical IT strategy or some general statements as guidelines instead.

Taking a strategic approach to managing the company's operational platform is fairly time consuming, not only with regard to defining the first strategy, but also with regard to aligning the business strategy and operational strategy with the gap analysis and maintaining the functional model of an operational platform.

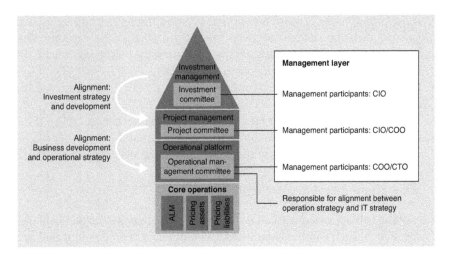

Figure 23.16   Investment management rocket

The value of defining and strategically managing the company's operational platform, however, exceeds the cost, and if the operational platform is left in a strategic vacuum, it is not an integrated part of the business and thus not an active asset when changes occur.

To support growth, management has to buy into the development of the operational platform by defining and implementing an operational platform strategy that is aligned with its business strategy. The separation on a strategic level between IT and operational management (in two separate but aligned strategies) provides both the business and its IT management with clear and focused strategies, leaving the business strategy decisions to the business management and the purely technical strategy/decisions to the technical staff.

The development of the platform changes from being a day-to-day driven approach into one with long-term defined goals, when having defined these goals within the operational platform strategy and ensured the alignment with the business strategy. This ensures sufficient support of the business growth strategies. This is a cost-efficient development approach rather than a constant 'fix-the-burning-platform' one, and this focuses both time and development resources on development that supports the firm's business goals. Aside from these advantages, a well-defined development process will also increase the stability of the operational platform (see Figure 23.16).

Depending on the size of the business, a strategic approach to management of the operational platform is beneficial in terms of development, stability and cost, and will support a firm's business goals in a timely manner.

References

Anthony, R.N. (1965) 'Planning and Control Systems: A Framework for Analysis', Harvard Business School, Division of Research.

Elsborg, J. (2008) 'The Operational Platform – A Way to Gain Competitive Advantage', dissertation, Henley Management College.

Hackathorn, R.D. (2002) 'The BI Watch: What Do We Do with What We Know?', *DM Review*.

Henley (2001) 'Managing Performance', Henley Management College.

Henley (2002) 'Managing Information', Henley Management College.

Heyes, R. (2007) 'Example operating principle', UBS Prime Brokerage Services.

Kanter, J. and Miserendino, J. (1987) 'Systems architectures link business goals and IS strategies', *Data Management Magazine*, November.

Porter, M.E. (1985) 'Competitive Advantage: Creating and Sustaining Superior Performance', Free Press.

Slack, N.D.C. (2002) 'Operations Strategy', London: *Financial Times*/Prentice Hall.

Sondhi, R. (1999) 'Total Strategy', Airworthy Publications International Limited.

Turban, E., Aronson, J.E. and Liang, T.-P. (2004) 'Decision Support Systems and Intelligent Systems', (7th edition), London: Prentice-Hall.

Wild, R. (2002) 'Operations Management', Cengage Learning.

24

Addressing the Data Management Challenge in Asset Management

Howie San

24.1 Introduction

24.1.1 Historical perspective

The need for good data is not new. Ever since the Assyrians invented accounting 7,000 years ago, reliable data has always been a key requirement for running a business. In that respect, the investment management industry is no different. Even before computers arrived on the scene in the 1960s, reliable information, such as closing prices or positions, had always been a critical driver of business success. The market ticker tape was invented in the 1870s precisely in order to deliver stock price information in a quicker way to market participants so that they could trade more rapidly and frequently. It was the failure of that ticker to keep up the pace that spawned investor panic in the stock market crash of 1929. Later, in the 1960s, the market data company Datastream grew out of UK stockbroker Hoare Govett's internal data management operations.[1] Data has always been one of the indispensible requirements for investing.

24.1.2 Recent developments

Nowadays, however, the need for good data is more pressing than ever. This has been driven by a number of recent developments as examined in more detail below.

Risk management

The collapse of Lehman Brothers in 2008 required a great deal of work by other firms to assess their exposure to the failed bank. The complexity of the situation, evidenced by the fact that Lehman Brothers comprised over 7,000 individual legal entities in more than 40 different countries, demonstrated that many of them had systems that were inadequate, and thus required a great deal of manual work and time to pull all the required information together.[2]

Since then, the trouble experienced by other parties – whether sovereigns like Greece and Cyprus or corporates like AIG – has meant that similar exercises have had to be performed time and again.

Unsurprisingly, the events of recent years have sharpened the focus on risk management. This greater prominence has in turn increased the need for reliable supplies of clean and timely data, without which risk measures are late, suspect and unreliable.

Regulation/compliance

Additionally, the growing regulatory burden means that firms must be able to report on far more than was previously the case. There are numerous examples of this. In the USA, the Dodd–Frank Wall Street Reform and Consumer Protection Act has led to hedge funds now being obliged to file form PF disclosing basic information regarding their investment strategy, assets under management (AUM), performance and counterparty exposures. 'Know your customer' remains a constant corporate concern, as the recent regulatory cases against Standard Chartered and HSBC for allegedly trading with Iran, demonstrate.[3, 4]

Client demands

With the recent market upheavals, clients are paying much closer attention to where their funds are invested and how those investments are performing.

Eying profits

Investment firms are looking to profile many clients more accurately in order to screen and identify opportunities to cross-sell complementary products. Additionally, the search for profit in difficult markets continues. All of these activities require increasingly large volumes of accurate data.

Cost control

Data can cost in many ways. Investment management firms are voracious data consumers, and the costs of subscribing to the products of market data vendors like Bloomberg and Thomson Reuters can be significant. There is also the cost of bad data. Some studies indicate that financial firms can lose up to 20% of their operating profit through bad data. Such costs, although very difficult to quantify or obtain information about in the public domain, are obviously very significant. Reductions in either types of cost could generate significant additional profits.

Shifting horizons

What is more, the nature of the data is changing. Firms can expect to:

- *Consume greater volumes of data.* The trend, especially with using more quantitative techniques, is to consume larger amounts of data.

- *Experience greater velocity.* Data is coming in faster as latency between event and receipt of the data is reduced. At one end of the spectrum, some trading firms seek to reduce information latency by micro-seconds. Further along the spectrum, firms are moving from end-of-day batch feeds to intraday and near real-time data feeds.
- *See more unstructured data.* Data is increasingly coming in unstructured as well as structured formats. Unstructured formats, such as emails, tweets, instant messaging conversations and even voice and video recordings, are much more difficult to manage than traditional data feeds.
- *Cope with more connections.* With the greater adoption of industry utilities like SWIFT, FIX or services like MarkitSERV and also of outsourced services like custody, there is an increasing need for investment management firms to connect to multiple external services, each with their own formats and ways of connecting.

24.2   The current data problem(s)

In many firms, however, the underlying data architecture and organization are simply not up to the task of responding appropriately to all of these additional demands. Typical problems include:

24.2.1   Data fragmentation/disparate systems

More often than not, a firm does not have a single data repository. Instead, key data is stored in a number of different data silos. This complicates the workflow unnecessarily since any system needing access to this data is required to interface to a number of different data repositories.

Insufficient standards

Although there are scattered localized standards of how data is compiled and published, there is still a long way to go. Many important entities, such as legal entities or complex derivatives, lack internationally accepted and openly available standard-identifying codes. Data purporting to be the same measure may in fact be calculated using different methodologies, such as the difference in the accounting procedures used by different jurisdictions.

Different formats

There are very few standards published for the formats in which data is stored and transmitted. Most systems tend to use their own proprietary designs for data models and the format of data files and messages. Although the increasing adoption of standards such as ISO 15022, 20022 and FPML has made some positive impact, when interfacing to other systems developers normally have to transform the data from various formats to their own internal format. Even if standards like ISO 15022 exist, it is often the case that different systems and different organizations have different interpretations of what data goes in what field, rendering a supposedly standard message unique to them and opaque to others.

Divergent codes

Different systems often use divergent codes to identify the same entity. For entities where no internationally accepted coding system is currently in place, such as legal entities, individuals or derivative contracts, then any coding system used will normally be unique. However, even where there are standard codes, there can still be divergence. Take security coding, where an instrument may have an ISIN, SEDOL, CUSIP, WKN number, ticker or RIC – to name just a few. Different coding systems need to be cross-mapped and cross-checked, which is time consuming and costly to set up and maintain.

Duplicate data

Especially in a best-of-breed architecture, where firms run disparate systems with their own data repositories, a large duplication of datasets is certain to arise. This leads to a substantial duplication of effort in maintaining these duplicate datasets. In addition, there is normally a cast-iron rule in IT that duplicate datasets maintained independently will inevitably drift out of synchronization, so that there will be little or no consistency of data between the various independent best-of-breed systems.

Different teams

Often different teams maintain the data on different systems. It is often difficult to identify who actually owns and who is responsible for maintaining an individual data item.

Varying procedures

With different teams come varying procedures for maintaining data. Different teams may follow different rules and treat changes with varying levels of urgency. Two datasets that are theoretically identical will soon drift out of synchronization if they are maintained with varying sets of procedures.

Multiple suppliers

Market data is expensive. Yet, especially in larger organizations there is often a 'cat's cradle' of data feeds and data supply agreements with multiple vendors. Different vendors, or even the same vendors, may be supplying the same data to different departments or different locations. Different sales offices of the same vendor may be supplying the same data at different prices. Different departments may hold contracts. In cases where there are two separate suppliers,

640Howie San

this normally creates double work since the two suppliers will have different formats, different codes (e.g. Reuters RIC vs. Bloomberg Ticker), different delivery methods, different contracts, payment terms, contractual terms and limitations. While it is good practice to have dual supplies for business critical data, often firms have duplicate supplies of the same data from the same vendor because two departments have ordered their data independently and in ignorance of one another.

Poor quality

With the best will in the world, the era of universally high-quality data seems far off, despite the major advances made in data technology over the last 25 years. Data sources vary significantly in their quality. Data may be inaccurate, it may be incomplete, or it may arrive too late. Different markets and jurisdictions often differ in the standard of the data they produce. Trusting any data source by default is unwise. Any data should be subject to significant validation until a high degree of trust is won through real experience.

Inadequate security

There is evidence to suggest that in instances where big information repositories are developed, their custodians are very keen to drive up utilization by making their information available to all comers. However, this approach is fraught with danger and really is inadvisable. Data is valuable and it should be ensured that only the right people have access to it. This is for a variety of reasons.

First, a lot of data is confidential. It may be client data that by law needs to be protected against unauthorized access. Or national regulations may insist it is physically stored and only accessible within a certain legal jurisdiction. It may be confidential company information. It may need to be segregated from certain parts of an organization. Or it may be commercially valuable and which you do not wish to divulge. Inadvertent or premature disclosure can cause significant problems. One example of this in the public domain was the premature publication of Google's third-quarter 2012 earnings in October 2012, which sparked a suspension of trading in the stock and to which we refer in more detail below.

Another reason to apply robust data access controls is that the externally sourced data may only be licensed for use in certain processes or departments or locations. Market data vendors guard their intellectual property closely. Often licenses are very proscribed, identifying specific purposes and user groups to use that data. Redistribution of market data outside the firm is a particularly sensitive topic, and rigorously policed. Breach of contractual terms can lead to significant retrospective charges, lawsuits and potentially having the market data service cut off.

No transparency

It is increasingly becoming important to be able to establish the provenance of a data point if required. There are many cases where there are alternative sources of data, derived from different means, and where the decision of what to choose can be subjective. Take the example of marking to market securities with very low liquidity and hence no public market quotation. A firm can use a number of different prices including historical prices, evaluated prices from a market data vendor, theoretical calculated prices, prices of proxies or consensus guessestimates. The process by which a price is chosen, and then being able to understand how and why that price was arrived at, should be something a firm can answer if challenged by auditors, regulators or clients.

Lacking support

Historically, data management has never figured as a major focus area for senior executive management, being viewed as just another technology issue or on a par with utilities, such as power and water. Submitting data to effective management control has not been seen as a business priority, consequently attracting less resources than other areas deemed more important for business success.

Inaccessible state

While data must be protected against unauthorized access, it is the converse rule that data needs to be made available to those systems that need it. However, it is far too often the case that highly valuable data is trapped in a single silo and hence cannot be reused where it is really needed. This leads to duplicate supplies being put in place or complex integration projects having to be undertaken. Data needs to be made available where it is required, in good time and in a format that can be readily consumed.

Nurturing data

Data is like everything else in life. If no one owns it or holds responsibility for it, it gets neglected, and quality wanes. On the other hand, if someone or a team values and looks after a dataset, it is likely they will seek to improve the quality by various means.

   A slightly different problem arises where too many owners are at play. Here the problem again is to find someone who is responsible for ensuring data quality, with the natural human tendency being to always pin the blame on someone else when something goes wrong.

Inadequate knowledge

Often there is very little information (i.e. metadata) about the data itself. Hence, it becomes very difficult to identify what is the correct data item, or whether it needs any correction or conversion to make it consistent and applicable.

24.3　The inevitable consequences

The typical problems arising from the underlying data architecture and organization's lack of ability to absorb all of the additional demands outlined earlier have inevitable and often damaging repercussions. These include:

Unauthorized access

Allowing persons access to data they should not have can produce serious consequences. Regulators the world over take a dim view of firms that cannot keep their client data secure. There is the example of one investment bank where the national regulator threatened to revoke its banking licence for sending client reports to the wrong clients.

Another example is the premature disclosure of Google's third-quarter 2012 results, which led to the internet company's shares being suspended from trading and the subsequent reputational damage for both Google and its financial printer RR Donnelley.[5]

Unauthorized access to data can lead to accusations of insider trading. As well as controlling data access, controlling access to the data an organization publishes is very important. At the time of writing this chapter, Barclays, RBS and UBS have all had heavy fines to pay, amounting to hundreds of millions of dollars to settle allegations that some of their employees manipulated benchmark interest rates such as the London interbank offered rate, known as Libor, and Euribor.[6]

Bad data

Bad data architecture produces bad data. Period.

More cost

Rectifying the consequences of badly managed data can be expensive. In the straight-through processing (STP) world of finance, a failed trade that has to be manually corrected can be expensive to fix. The resulting costs of a failed or wrong transaction can be substantial, be it a missed corporate action, the wrong allocation in an IPO or a lost trade. As described above, the costs of data security breaches can run into the millions. Bad data can cost a lot of money.

Costs are not just financial. Inadequate data management can also inflict reputational damage. If a firm fails to respond to a regulator's request, it runs the risk of incurring heavy penalties. If a firm cannot react to a client's request in the appropriate manner, its reputation and relationship with that client can be damaged. Working with bad data is incredibly frustrating and can hurt the morale of those staff affected.

Unnecessary data duplication also costs. Data is expensive to source and expensive to maintain. Maintaining multiple copies of the same data incurs unnecessary expense. There are many cases of firms taking expensive data feeds and then not using them at all. In one instance, a large global investment bank was paying a large market data vendor over $150m per annum to take a feed of data that was hardly ever used.[7]

No change

The complexity and fragility of many firms' data architectures risk having the effect that implementing the changes necessary to support the business is costly, uncertain and slow. These firms then suffer from the inability to change their business operations to embrace new products, new procedures, and new markets – or do existing things better than they do them today.

Too little

As business activities evolve and change, so will the underlying data requirement. A firm with a limited data architecture that is difficult to use will simply not have all the relevant data available.

Too late

Late data serves no purpose. End-of-day valuations that arrive too late to be incorporated into a net asset value (NAV) worksheet have no use. In algorithmic trading, data that arrives seconds after the rest of the market has received the same data is worthless. Risk is not calculated frequently enough because the data cannot be made available in time.

24.4   The Answer(s) to the problem(s)

The answer – or answers – to all these problems makes for hardly earth-shattering news. While the solution may be easy to identify, it is not so easy to implement. The main thing to bear in mind is to take data management seriously and give it the priority it deserves within your organization. If having reliable, accurate and timely data is critical for your firm's wellbeing, then you should give data management the necessary high priority.

24.4.1   What is data management?

This chapter defines data management as a rigorous and structured approach to managing the key datasets of a firm. It is not just technology, although technology does play a major part. It is more akin to the way a firm manages other major areas, such as finance or risk. It is a question of putting the resources, the methodologies and the systems in place to control a complex and dynamic asset class.

Key aims of data management

For data management to be successful, it needs to contain a number of elements that we now attempt to describe point by point in more detail.

Top management sponsorship

While smaller projects can be undertaken successfully without the knowledge and backing of top management using tactical resources or recourse to 'black' projects, any larger scale data management initiatives need senior executive sponsorship. The reasons are many:

- Larger projects will require larger amounts of resources to complete.
- Senior management sponsorship and approval are usually required for expenditures of that magnitude.
- Human nature being what it is, there is some level of resistance to be expected to the significant changes often arising from data management projects.
- Senior management leverage may be needed to force people to cooperate and agree to change.
- When differences in opinions and approach cause disagreement and conflict, senior management intervention may be required to resolve the issue.
- The necessary cooperation and participation from departments may not be forthcoming unless clearly mandated by senior management.

Data governance

Defined simply, data governance is the process of management and operations used to ensure that the objectives for effective data management are realized.[8] Data governance requires a clear structure of tasks and responsibilities within various functional areas, and seniority levels within an organization. Such a structure would typically include:

- definition of the ownership and responsibility levels of data;
- customer engagement to ensure that the consumers of data get maximum value from it;
- the proper operational management model defining the processes and procedures not only for onboarding new data sources, but the daily tasks and procedures required to maintain an uninterrupted flow of high-quality data;
- a structure to track and manage the costs;
- ways and means of measuring service quality.

The structure would typically have three layers:

1. the senior management data governance committee,
2. the data management working group, and
3. the data operations team.

The senior data management committee serves as the senior level sponsor of data management. The committee sets the data management strategy and oversees its execution, while also acting as the face of senior data management to the rest of the organization, raising visibility especially at board level.

The data management working group controls the overall data management program and ensures that it is in line with the overall data strategy. Additionally, it manages external vendors to ensure that they deliver at agreed service levels. It is also responsible for the development of data management processes.

The data management team conducts the operational aspects of data management, including the day-to-day operations to ensure that the data flows smoothly, and the processes of extending and enhancing the data universe, such as onboarding new data sources.

Data supplier management

The aim here is to manage your suppliers proactively and rationalize them for what you realistically need and can afford. Ideally, all market data supply should go through a nominated individual and department, preferably with experience in the field, who then has a complete picture of where the firm buys its data. The big banks and the market data companies themselves, which have to manage hundreds of different data suppliers, do this as a matter of course.

Unnecessary duplication of feeds should be eliminated to save costs. Data is generally cheaper when bought in bulk, so look to merge multiple contracts with a vendor into a single overarching contact and look for a price reduction. Leverage the intense competition between the vendors to get a good price. Look at substituting vendor products, such as Vanguard did recently when it substituted its existing index providers for another in a move that is 'expected to result in considerable savings'.[9, 10]

Security is paramount

As described earlier, unauthorized access to data can cause significant financial and reputational damage. Therefore, it is essential to have the correct controls in place. These will generally include ensuring that all users have their own profile to describe the datasets, records and even fields they are entitled to read or update. Accompanying such a security scheme should be a rigorous level of authentication and access control to ensure that the user is actually who they say they are. For sensitive datasets such as client data, this may require access control methods beyond the normal user ID and password, such as dual factor authentication, potentially using hardware devices like the data fobs manufactured by RSA SecurID.[11]

Another issue to be aware of is the jurisdiction where the data is physically stored. Several countries like Luxembourg place restrictions on where client data can be stored and from where it can be accessed. Such data stored outside an approved jurisdiction may often need to be encrypted or may need a waiver from the relevant regulator. For firms outsourcing some of their operations, they need to know where their provider stores copies of their data and what security measures are in place to protect it. Just uploading it into the 'cloud' is not to be recommended.

Price transparency

In view of the widening range of financial assets that investment management firms invest in, the complexity of some of these assets, the illiquidity of many financial instruments, and the various different types of prices available, it is now increasingly important to be able to identify the provenance of a price and why it was used.

Data consistency

The much quoted ideal in data consistency is to have a single master database in which the golden copy, i.e., the master record of every significant piece of business information, resides. In the real world, however, unless an investment management firm has a system designed from the start with a single data store philosophy, such as SimCorp Dimension where the concentration into a single golden copy is delivered 'out of the box', implementing such massive data warehouse projects has often proved very costly and drawn out with little real benefit delivered. A more modest objective would be to identify the golden source for every important piece of data, and endeavor to concentrate all data maintenance on that golden source, using it to feed other systems that require the same pieces of data.

Agility imperative

Benjamin Franklin remarked that only two things in life are certain: death and taxes. After the events of the past five years since 2007, a third certainty is warranted: change in financial markets. The pace of change appears to have accelerated sharply in this time. Firms need to change their business to meet the new circumstances, such as changing market infrastructures, and it is essential that data management too can change and evolve. Any system you implement must be agile enough to handle the changes, be it new instrument types, changing workflows or procedures. The data management architecture is there to support the business – not to constrain it.

Data ownership

Every dataset should have an owner. The group or team that holds the responsibility and accountability for the data's quality must be charged with ensuring that it is maintained correctly and for extending and improving it when and where necessary. By giving designated persons this control, they become motivated to improve the quality of their datasets and a source of subject matter experts will develop. Conversely, if quality falls below standard, it becomes easier to identify those who are responsible for rectification. A suggested preference is to have business owners, who have a stake and direct interest in maintaining data quality.

Linkage concept

A key concept of financial data is the relationships or linkages between the various different types of entity and therefore data. These linkages reflect the reality of complex and interrelated financial markets. For example, when asked the question: 'What is our exposure to Japan?' the system should be able to show all the relevant assets such as:

- all JPY cash balances;
- all JPY derivative contracts;
- all instruments issued by the Japanese government;
- all JPY denominated instruments;
- all Japanese-listed equities and equity derivatives;
- all instruments issued by a Japanese-domiciled entity;
- all Japanese clients or counterparties;
- any indices with substantial Japanese constituents;
- all assets held with Japanese institutions such as banks or custodians;
- the amount of business transacted in Japan;
- the number of staff domiciled in Japan;
- all investments in instruments in forms with substantial operations in Japan.

Hence, data management systems should manage and expose these relationships, as well as data about the entities themselves.

Service monitoring

The data management architecture should enable monitoring of the various data processes and also the various data suppliers and sources to ensure long-term service continuity. Hence, two types of monitoring are required:

- *Operational.* This monitors the various processes and jobs to ensure they are running successfully and in good time. If they do not, the system should raise alerts to the appropriate individuals with the necessary information to allow them to intervene and rectify the issue hopefully without serious impact to downstream processes.

- *Commercial, i.e., KPI/SLA.* This monitors data supplier performance against pre-agreed criteria, such as service level agreements (SLAs). This information can be used to track performance trends and emergent issues (such as an increasing number of data errors or late deliveries), to make claims for compensation from SLAs or to grade suppliers.

24.5   Making the impossible possible

Implementing all of the points described above may look daunting at first, and it is indeed a major undertaking. However, within the financial sector today there exists a group of companies that have gone most or all of the way to implementing total data management. These are the market data companies, such as Thomson Reuters, IDC and Rimes.[12] Since data is their business, there has always been a senior management commitment to 'get it right'.

Look around the typical market data company and you will see most of the hallmarks that distinguish data management. It will have a central team of data procurement experts, who actively manage all the commercial aspects of their myriad data suppliers. It integrates data from a variety of different sources into a single coherent standardized data set. It has teams of data specialists responsible for discreet data sets. It has robust data management systems for the collection, aggregation, cleansing, organization and publication of data.

Wherever possible, the market data company generates a single golden copy of the data for use across multiple different products. It makes its data available in a number of different formats in order to make it accessible to as many different systems and consumers as possible. It has a strong system of access control so that only those authorized to access the data can do so. The data is documented and support is available for all customers. It has an established commercial model that captures the value of the various datasets published.

All in all, the experience of the market data firms shows how very large volumes and velocities of data can be managed effectively. Although they handle amounts of data that are a magnitude larger than what an investment management firm would ever encounter, their experience and the operating models they have evolved serve as a very useful template for the investment management industry as it rises to the challenge of managing data more effectively and efficiently.

24.5.1   Systems available

As hopefully gleaned from earlier in this chapter, data management is not just another system; it is much more than that. Having said this, data management does require robust data management systems in order to be able to deliver many of the features described above. Over the years, two different operating models have emerged for data management within an investment management scenario. They are:

1. integrated, and
2. distributed.

Integrated

The integrated operating model uses a technical architecture where there is a single data platform and repository into which all the different functional modules plug to retrieve and publish their data. A market leader in this area is SimCorp. Its integrated front-to-back solution includes products and services for virtually all the major business functions of an investment management firm, all driven from a single and consistent data store. This means that there is only one golden copy of the data that all products draw from. The SimCorp solution comes with extensive data cleansing tools to manage the aggregation of multiple external data sources, such as market data for example.

Distributed

The alternative operating model is one of distributed systems – each with their own data store. This proliferation of data stores causes many of the data problems described earlier. To support data management in this operating model, the enterprise data management (EDM) system has evolved.[13] An EDM system takes in data from multiple publishers, both internal and external, scrubs it and then publishes the golden copy to all subscribing systems.

Stated very simply, an EDM system sits as a central data hub of all the disparate systems, collecting and scrubbing data from various publishers to create the golden copy, and then distributes this single source of truth to all the subscribers

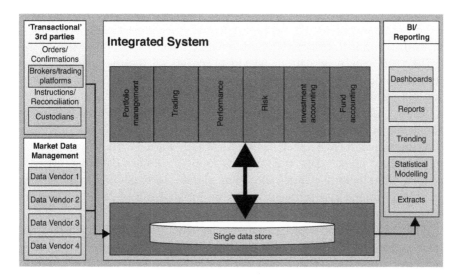

Figure 24.1   Example of a fully integrated system

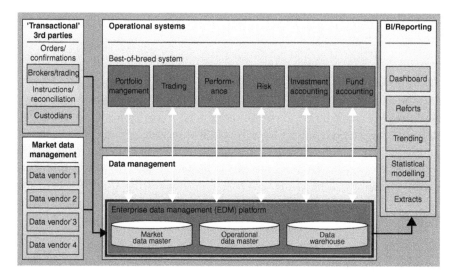

Figure 24.2   Example of an enterprise data management (EDM) system

who require it. This approach promises much, supposedly giving the dispersed system architecture the same single data view as the fully integrated solution.

However, such an approach has its drawbacks. Integrating all the different data sources to the EDM system to create a single overarching data model can be highly complex work. There is anecdotal evidence of several large, expensive high-profile projects over-running budgets, taking much longer than expected to implement, and failing to deliver the anticipated benefits. Perhaps as a reflection of this, there is a discernible trend away from huge enterprise-scale projects and back to more focused and limited solutions with less benefit but far less risk and cost.

The term 'enterprise data management' covers all the relevant data types that are critical to an investment manager. However, historically the datasets covered by such systems have evolved organically. Looking at the financial industry, observers have noticed a distinct pattern in the way that firms have adopted data management.

As illustrated in Figure 24.3, firms have usually started with managing externally sourced market data, then moving to more complex data like corporate actions, then looking at internally sourced data, such as client/counterparty records, positions and transactions in the form of the so-called investment book of record (IBOR).

Whereas the first four categories are relatively mature and established, the IBOR concept is relatively new.[14] The need for IBOR arises when a firm runs separate trading and accounting systems with two different data stores, as illustrated in Figure 24.4.

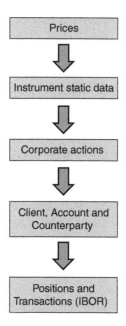

Figure 24.3 Sequential development in adopting data management

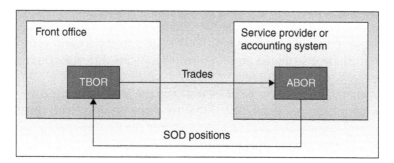

Figure 24.4 TBOR versus ABOR in a target-operating model based on outsourcing investment operations

The trading system – otherwise known as trading book of record (TBOR) is normally fed from the accounting system with the latest positions at the start of every day. During the day, it tracks transactions in real time but does not account for corporate actions or other drivers of position value, such as valuations, interest payments, etc.

The accounting system – or accounting book of record (ABOR) – provides the end-of-day view including all transactions, trades and corporate actions. However, it does not include intraday transactions, simulations or pending trades since it is generally an end-of-day system. Worse still, where a firm has outsourced its accounting operations to multiple vendors, the accounting position is fragmented across multiple systems.

All in all, in a precarious situation like this there is no real-time updated golden source record of the firm's positions. This is a major drawback for those firms looking for more up-to-date and accurate position data to drive their investment decisions in a fast-moving financial world.

The answer proposed to resolve this dilemma (again arising from the separation of trading and accounting systems and their respective data stores) is IBOR, which in reality is a capability for maintaining a near real-time view of all current positions and expected positions.

There is ongoing debate where IBOR functionality should sit. Some argue that it sits best in the trading system. Others urge that it should be an extension of ABOR, while a third viewpoint is that it should be a standalone independent and separate system. Two points are worth noting in this debate.

First, ABOR is arguably better functionally equipped to handle all the different types of events that IBOR needs to cover since it covers more transaction types than TBOR, which would need to have a large amount of completely new functionality, such as corporate actions, added into the trading system.

Second, where there is fragmentation of TBOR (e.g., where there are multiple different trading systems for different asset classes) or ABOR (for example, where the accounting is outsourced to multiple providers), it makes less sense to extend those fragmented systems to IBOR. Rather, it may make more sense to insert a separate new IBOR system to collect and consolidate data from these distributed and fragmented systems into a single coherent picture.

All in all, IBOR appears to be in increasingly the focus for many investment management firms, especially those that have chosen to go with distributed systems architecture and that seek to overcome the data integrity challenges that such an approach inevitably incurs.

24.6   Conclusions

The investment management industry has always treated data as an essential component in its business operations. But the vast majority of firms still struggle to integrate and transform their terabytes, if not petabytes, of data. Rapidly changing financial requirements and technological pressures, including the era of exponentially rising data volumes, will only exacerbate this problem.

Firms need robust and responsive investment management systems that have the necessary technology to address these requirements and pressures, delivering tangible operational, financial and business benefits. For many companies, however, data has not been managed to the degree warranted by these imperatives, and there remains some way to go before they achieve the necessary control over their data assets.

This chapter has sought to describe some of the typical data problems experienced by investment management firms and the necessary steps to be taken to reduce these problems by adopting a holistic approach to managing these data assets.

There is definitely no magic formula or quick-fix solution. It is more a question of applying some common-sense methodology, the appropriate technology, and a lot of hard work. For those firms that are prepared to take this route, it is our hope that this chapter has shed some light on the paths they should be taking.

Notes

1. Now part of Thomson Reuters.
2. PricewaterhouseCoopers, 'Lehman Brothers' Bankruptcy – Lessons learned for the survivors', August 2009.
3. Bloomberg.com (2012), 'Standard Chartered Pays $327 Million on U.S.–Iran Transfers', http://www.bloomberg.com/news/2012–12–10/standard-chartered-pays-327-million-in-u-s-iran-transfers-case.html
4. The US Department of Justice (2012), 'HSBC Holdings Plc. and HSBC Bank USA N.A. Admit to Anti-Money Laundering and Sanctions Violations, Forfeit $1.256 Billion in Deferred Prosecution Agreement', http://www.justice.gov/opa/pr/2012/December/12-crm-1478.html
5. FT.com (2012), 'Google panic over results bungle', http://www.ft.com/intl/cms/s/0/710240e6–1945–11e2–9b3e-00144feabdc0.html#axzz2Opzsjdc8
6. Reuters.com (2013), 'Exclusive: RBS fined $612 million for rate rigging', http://www.reuters.com/article/2013/02/06/us-rbs-libor-idUSBRE91500B20130206
7. 2010. Private conversation between author and data manager of large investment bank.
8. SimCorp (2013b), # Journal of Applied IT and Investment Management, 'Data governance: key contributor to successful data management strategy', Volume 5, No 1, January 2013, for a fuller exploration of data governance.
9. Vanguard (2012), https://pressroom.vanguard.com/press_release/2012.10.02_benchmark_change.html
10. Screen Consultants (2012), http://www.screenconsultants.com/dmdocuments/vendor_comparison.pdf as an example of an outsourced vendor management service.
11. EMC (2013), http://www.emc.com/security/rsa-securid/rsa-securid-hardware-authenticators.htm
12. SimCorp (2013a), 'Best practices: learning from the pioneers in financial data', *Journal of Applied IT and Investment Management*, Volume 5, No 1, January 2013.
13. Citisoft (2012), 'Enterprise Data Management: Implementing the Components of an EDM Strategy', March 2012.
14. SimCorp (2013c), 'The investment book of record: one version of truth from front to back office', *Journal of Applied IT and Investment Management*, Volume 5, No 1, January 2013.

References

Bloomberg.com (2012) 'Standard Chartered Pays $327 Million on U.S.-Iran Transfers', retrieved April 10, 2013,http://www.bloomberg.com/news/2012–12–10/standard-chartered-pays-327-million-in-u-s-iran-transfers-case.html

Citisoft (2012) 'Enterprise Data Management: Implementing the Components of an EDM Strategy', March.

EMC (2013) 'RSA SecurID Hardware Authenticators', retrieved April 10, 2013,http://www.emc.com/security/rsa-securid/rsa-securid-hardware-authenticators.htm

FT.com (2012) 'Google panic over results bungle', retrieved April 10, 2013,http://www.ft.com/intl/cms/s/0/710240e6–1945–11e2–9b3e-00144feabdc0.html#axzz2Opzsjdc8

PricewaterhouseCoopers (2009) 'Lehman Brothers' Bankruptcy – Lessons learned for the survivors', August.

Reuters.com (2013) 'Exclusive: RBS fined $612 million for rate rigging', retrieved April 10, 2013,http://www.reuters.com/article/2013/02/06/us-rbs-libor-idUS-BRE91500B20130206

Screen Consultants (2012) 'Vendor Services Selection', retrieved April 10, 2013,http://www.screenconsultants.com/dmdocuments/vendor_comparison.pdf

SimCorp (2013a) # Journal of Applied IT and Investment Management, 'Best practices: learning from the pioneers in financial data', (5)1, January.

SimCorp (2013b) # Journal of Applied IT and Investment Management, 'Data governance: key contributor to successful data management strategy', (5)1, January.

SimCorp (2013c) # Journal of Applied IT and Investment Management, 'The investment book of record: one version of truth from front to back office', (5)1, January.

The US Department of Justice (2012) 'HSBC Holdings Plc. and HSBC Bank USA N.A. Admit to Anti-Money Laundering and Sanctions Violations, Forfeit $1.256 Billion in Deferred Prosecution Agreement', retrieved April 10, 2013,http://www.justice.gov/opa/pr/2012/December/12-crm-1478.html

Vanguard (2012) 'Vanguard to change target benchmarks for 22 index funds', retrieved April 10, 2013, https://pressroom.vanguard.com/press_release/2012.10.02_bench-mark_change.html

25

The Use of Advanced Technology in Global Asset Management

Anders Kirkeby

25.1 Introduction

If we view investment management as a classic industrial activity, the firm produces service products from a resource stream containing people, money and other financial assets, regulation and technology. Technology makes it possible to do new things, and competitors' use of technology may force others to use a particular technology simply to remain competitive. Changes in the regulatory regime may provide compelling events to review and further optimize the target operating model of the firm; this in turn may also have implications for the new technology and operational systems involved.

When the Web took off in the mid-1990s, it sparked a torrent of software innovation and a slow but steady migration of data and processing from the firm's own hardware. Over the same time-span, we have seen virtualization become mature with minimal overhead and subsequent commoditization, and now virtualization is evolving into multiple forms of cloud service offerings.

Hardware innovations in the very fluid and competitive space of mobile phones have generated a substantial and rapid change in the mix of current end-user computing devices, with smartphones far outselling PCs now and tablet sales soaring. The pace of this innovation has made it increasingly hard for enterprise IT organizations to keep up with users' evolving demands; a great example of this is the bring-your-own-device (BYOD) trend, which has seen employees show up at work with their own iPhones and iPads expecting them to be useful tools for daily work tasks.

This chapter delves into the current technology trends that are most relevant to the investment management industry: various types of cloud computing and cloud-based service models; global operating model considerations in view of cloud offerings; how to cope with increasing volumes of fast-moving data from multiple sources and, perhaps more important, not just cope, turn it into a competitive advantage; user and customer experience are assuming ever more importance especially on the Web and via tablets and smartphones; and finally security concerns are becoming even more important as systems open up to offer user experience improvements.

These are the technology trends that are of most relevance to the investment management industry at this point in time. It should not be viewed as a shopping list; nor should it be viewed as a comprehensive IT checklist for solutions. Rather it aims to be an overview of what the selected technologies can do for the investment management enterprise to enable growth through innovation or to reduce cost and risk in operations. What are the pertinent questions to ask both the business stakeholders and the technologists who are involved in designing the concrete solutions?

A substantial part of the discussion is essentially framed in the context of customer or user experience to emphasize that technology is merely an enabling resource. What matters are the end product or service and the strategic target operating model that delivers it. But some appreciation of the pertinent possibilities and limitations of specific technologies is required to make effective and timely decisions on the use of new technology in the investment management industry.

This chapter attempts to define the key new technology concerns to keep in mind while making decisions whether to acquire new investment management software or prolong the use of legacy systems. Some of the new technology discussed can be layered on top of legacy systems with some compromises and custom integration work. But a strategic interest in these technologies should prompt a review of what legacy systems might be holding back the use of new technologies and services.

Leading technology research and advisory companies like Gartner and Forrester are more than happy to provide annually updated lists of the technologies and memes they consider to be important at any given point in time across all industries. Gartner also has the hype cycle concept to temper the excitement about new technology and remind us that, while IT is a fast-moving industry, more often than not it takes years for most technologies to penetrate the enterprise.

A particular new technology does not necessarily move at the same pace in the investment management industry as it does in other industries and applicability will vary too. But these technology shifts create new opportunities, which should not be ignored in the investment management industry. However, many also introduce new security challenges.

This chapter provides a current overview of where these specific technology trends are going, how the opportunities can be characterized for the investment management industry, and how to frame the discussion of relevant security aspects. The confluence of these technologies combined with the overall market conditions of 'the new normal' create both opportunity and pressure to bring about new competitive advantages.

25.2 Cloud computing

The apparent value of cloud computing as such is obvious: instead of individual companies hosting their own tens or hundreds of servers, they effectively pool all or a substantial part of their hardware with a cloud operator to save on the capital expenditure side and be better placed to respond to periodical and ad hoc shifts in demand for computation. The cloud operator can achieve a different economy of scale by running thousands or tens of thousands of servers from the same location. There is also an important economy of scale in the skills required to manage the large data centers.

Across all types of cloud computing, Celent has estimated that the global capital markets spent around $2.3 billion in 2012 (Celent, 2012a) with a view to saving 10–15% in costs alone. CEB TowerGroup estimates up to a 4–6% reduction in costs and only over a few years (Shahrawat, 2012). These numbers are quite far from the potential cost savings known from the kind of web-based B2C businesses that gave rise to the notion of cloud computing. However, this does not mean that cloud computing is irrelevant for the investment management industry. It merely means that we need to apply it with discretion and more importantly look at the cloud categories that are not solely about cost savings based on scale.

25.2.1 Public clouds

On top of the basic economy of scale, companies can choose to pay for just the right number of servers at any given time to match peaks and troughs in demand over the course of a day or month. End-of-period reporting, in particular annual reporting, is a computationally heavy process. So to the extent that the systems can scale out, it makes perfect sense to bring more cloud-based servers on line at times of peak demand. When demand drops again, some of the servers are released back into the pool and the company pays only for what it uses and when it uses it.

In the traditional setup, a company has two ways to handle peaks in demand: either accept that peaks will cause bottlenecks, or keep sufficient headroom. In reality, most companies will aim for a combination of both. But regardless of the model, without the cloud there will be costly idle hardware in the data centre.

The cloud operator views hardware as a substitutable commodity. There is enough redundancy built in so that when a problem occurs with a particular server, it is simply powered down and in due course a technician will replace it. This means that as a cloud customer you cannot have any dependency on a particular piece of hardware. One of the great features of cloud computing is that it allows metered use of servers according to an elastic demand. Both aspects mean that it should be a straightforward automated task to set up a new server to run the required services.

Another consequence of such dynamic assignment of hardware is a concern over what happens to data stored in a machine when it stops being used by a particular client. Databases obviously leave a footprint in storage, but files being exchanged and caching can also leave data on disks. An investment manager looking to leverage the public cloud must therefore seek very clear and auditable guarantees of full destruction of recoverable data when a particular server is released again.

25.2.2   Private and hybrid clouds

The current perceived lack of sufficient guarantees of data security in public clouds has severely limited the uptake of public cloud computing in the investment management industry (Celent, 2012a). An alternative is the private cloud. The public cloud offers optimal cost reduction by continuously matching demand with just the right amount of servers. The private cloud on the other hand is a set of permanently allocated servers with some level of isolation from other servers if hosted in a shared data centre.

The private cloud may or may not be in a shared data centre. What is important about the private cloud is that it is the continuation of the virtualization trend with the inherent scalability of the cloud. But it does not offer dynamic server resources on-demand. An answer to that can be a hybrid approach where everything by default runs in a private cloud, but certain processes are processed in the public cloud. This requires that the data involved is either non-sensitive or that it can be obfuscated on the way out of the private cloud. The data is then processed in the public cloud using a dynamic demand-based set of servers. Upon return, an internal set of keys and algorithms is then used to remove the obfuscation again.

25.2.3   Opportunities in the cloud

Extrapolating from the above views on cloud-based services, it is fair to say the whole space is still very fluid. This brings uncertainty, but also opportunity. The cost-saving aspects should only be one of the reasons for moving into the cloud. Getting access to industry-relevant services that may form part of hybrid clouds can be leveraged to release more resources for differentiating activities that are more core to the business. Collaborating with cloud vendor services could prove to be a very effective path to innovation and differentiation through some level of business process outsourcing to the vendor.

Some solutions will come directly from a system vendor; others will be offered via investment management-process outsourcing firms. But regardless of this, a suitable system is one that can be deployed on standard commodity hardware. The legacy mainframe is unlikely to make it to the cloud.

To make the most of the cloud requires software that is relatively simple to deploy in a system with limited access and control over the environment. To make the most of cloud-based services requires a modular system that is easy to integrate.

25.3   Global business architecture

When pondering cloud options, there are a couple of important geographical concerns to carefully consider: the intended global target operating model and the legal implications for data in a global setup.

25.4   Global operating models

For the global investment manager, there is a need to provide operational systems to trade and settle across different markets in different time zones. But he also needs to be able to produce all regulatory reporting figures and other analytics in a timely fashion for local regulatory compliance. A common approach is to run independent systems for each major geographical area that makes all the time and regulatory constraints self-contained.

Another approach is to run everything out of a single location in some cloud variant that can provide the most cost-effective approach. But a single location does make the fully centralized system subject to the combined set of regulations across the locations where trading operations take place. The central solution, for instance, must be able to produce timely reporting data for all the relevant time zones from a single system. This must be done for up to seven workdays a week when operating across particular country combinations, which substantially reduces the scope for having global batch-processing windows where the data in the system is otherwise at rest.

For a business operating in Asia, Europe and North America, for example, all the hours in a 24-hour day would see the system supporting users creating trades and processing transactions as and when they occur. If the trading volume or activity in general is highly asymmetrical among the different locations, some make do with the time zone of the dominant location. But in recent years, obtaining complete views of risk has become very important; there is a strong trend toward being able to do comprehensive risk reporting without the delays or gaps in coverage that are typically created by data residing in the silos of individual poorly integrated legacy systems.

A third alternative is to have a hub-and-spoke architecture, where a central system acts as the master for part of the data in the value chain or as the final reporting and accounting location. The local systems thus take on the bulk of local regulatory requirements. This is a more complex setup, but may in some cases offer the best of both worlds. This mixed setup has the added benefit of offering the best interactive system performance, as users will be physically close to the operational systems. The physical distance and network switching along the way can be a problem, for instance, for users based in Australia if they connect to a central system based in Europe.

The challenge is to find the right operational systems that are able to provide a robust hub-and-spoke model with the right interfaces between local and central systems. It is also a way to centralise or outsource activities, where efficiencies can be released as cost reductions or centers of excellence. An example of this is to have local front office and portfolio accounting systems but with the trade processing handled by a shared service operating from a single location – or the work can be outsourced to an asset servicing firm perhaps offering this service via a hybrid cloud model.

25.4.1 Legal concerns surrounding global operations

The other geographical concern is to do with data protection legislation and regulation. Countries and supranational blocs like the EU are enacting increasingly strict legislation and regulation to protect the use and dissemination of the data of individual citizens.[1] For an investment management system located outside the EU but serving EU individuals, this raises issues, as the investment manager will have to ensure that no data identifiable to any EU residents is transported out of the EU. This is hardly a trivial requirement to abide by (Desai, 2013), and similar legislation is appearing in other parts of the world as well.

Another angle to this concern is the right of many governments to request data from a company subject to their legislation about foreign individuals and companies regardless of geography. An example of such national legislation is the USA's US Foreign Intelligence Surveillance Amendment Act (FISAA) of 2008. While relatively obscure, some clients may not be comfortable with such rights of foreign governments because of either client confidentiality or tax reasons. In such a case, the cloud option may not be appropriate, or the cloud operator must at least be able to demonstrate how it is not subject to specific instances of such legislation.

25.4.2 Global operating model opportunities

Local market conditions and regulatory shifts will drive changes in how investment management companies do business. This provides an opportunity to review and optimize the operating model over the medium to long term via a revised global target operating model that must factor in a sourcing strategy for the different services required. Should a particular part of the value chain be done locally or centrally, should it be outsourced, or should other work in fact be insourced?

It is very hard to provide general prescriptive guidance on global operating models without delving into the specific needs of the firm. But any investment management enterprise will do well to have a system that affords substantial flexibility to accommodate different geographical needs as they evolve over time, and good relations with a system vendor or consultancy with substantial practical experience covering all the affected markets.

25.5   Data and analytics

A fact of life in investment management, as in any other industry that is heavily dependent on IT, is the growth of data that needs to be processed or calculated. In recent years, new regulation and work to improve the quality of risk measurement have been the greatest sources of increased analytical workloads. The currently proposed Potential Future Exposure, for instance, will require substantially more calculation than the current common exposure measures. Generally, the underlying transaction and market data volumes are largely unchanged but the calculation load is growing fast.

25.5.1   Database appliances

Cloud computing is all about exploiting the ever increasing commoditization of computer hardware, not least to provide scalability in the form of cheap and on-demand horizontal scalability. Horizontal scalability over multiple smaller machines is one way to keep up with computational demands in the investment management industry. Vertical scalability is another option, where the focus is on making fewer units of hardware do more computation. The two approaches to scalability are complementary – together they solve different system performance challenges.

One class of specialized hardware is the database appliance, where the Oracle Exadata Database Machine is a very capable example. These are heavily optimized non-commodity systems with an attractive mix of high throughput and low latency. But because they are non-commodity, they are slow to enter the general-purpose clouds. Their cost and capacity put them at odds with cloud economics. This is a shame since the combination of cheap commodity resources in the public or hybrid cloud, coupled with the throughput and low latency of a database appliance, would be very beneficial to the investment management community. The data volumes and types of interrelated hierarchical aggregation that are typical in performance calculation and risk analysis are not served particularly well by a generic parallelized model, where the work is spread over many independent servers, as they keep having to correlate with other chunks of the data in order to complete the task.

25.5.2   Specialized computer chips

In the specialized hardware category, we also find more esoteric hardware, such as GPUs and FPGAs. Both are essentially chips that are optimized to do just a few things but to do them very fast on one large dataset at a time. Both GPUs and FPGAs are relatively hard to program and this factor is holding back their widescale adoption.

Their raw speed has seen both technologies becoming popular in the sell-side industry, but they are still a rare sight on the buy-side. GPUs and FPGAs are not generally available on the major cloud platforms, with Amazon being an important exception on the GPU side. However, the computational power they offer means it is a technology to watch.

25.5.3   Big data

'Big data' is a rather loosely-defined approach to analyzing data. It is not necessarily about big volumes, but recognizes that data volumes are growing and that some of the data may not naturally exist in the transactional databases and data warehouses of the day.

The poor fit with regular database platforms can be due to the change frequency and data volume that do not need to be held for posterity. Historical market data must typically be kept accessible, for instance, to calculate historical performance. Such data is part of the heavily regulated usage for tax and transparency reasons, where there is little or no proprietary intellectual property (IP) in the processes – everybody is essentially taxed the same way on the same transaction. However, in the big data space we find data that can be considered disposable and which is used in entirely bespoke ways that may well be considered the proprietary IP of the specific investment management firm.

An example of this is high frequency trading (HFT), where few would bother to retain the full-tick market data history that made the algorithms employed take specific decisions. Another emerging example is aggregation of various data sources, including unstructured text, such as news feeds or social media feeds for sentiment analysis to drive investment decisions. In a later section touching on security, there is also an argument for using pattern analysis based on Complex Event Processing (CEP) for early detection of fraud and other malicious intent. Big data analytics in this context can be found both on large data sets 'at rest' on a disk, or on streaming data that may never come to rest.

In the investment management industry, everybody is accustomed to using systems that provide the absolute truth – as can be calculated from available data. It is entirely possible that big data could introduce a new paradigm of statistically significant likelihood in response to some of the new complex regulatory requirements being discussed, especially in areas where a documented process weighs more heavily than financial figures, for instance, in areas to do with operational risk.

25.5.4   BI, KPIs and analytics

Reporting is an extremely important part of data processing in the investment management firm and regardless of whether it be internal risk measures or external NAV values, they tend to have a very slow change frequency, not least because many are based on regulatory or best practice frameworks. But there is more to data analysis than just counterparty exposure or NAVs. There are many more open-ended questions about the business that can be answered by analyzing the data available across the operational platform – assuming these systems are able to share data.

Scorecards and key performance indicators (KPIs) are a common management information (MI) tool to overcome information overload by carefully identifying key metrics that reflect the salient measurable aspects of a system or process. A common KPI in the investment management industry is the straight-through processing (STP) rate, where the size of the gap to 100% is a measure of inefficiency in terms of required manual intervention with a largely direct correlation to trade processing costs.

Different parts of an organization will require different KPIs to reflect how their performance is measured. A department that represents a single activity in the value chain will have KPIs spanning that value chain activity. Company-level KPIs, on the other hand, are likely to cover the entire value chain end-to-end. If the operational platform consists of multiple independent operational systems, it is important to be able to capture KPIs across these systems. Some KPIs cannot just be inferred from the regular transactional data, but require process telemetry. It is therefore very important to the quality of the KPIs that the operational systems are able to emit sufficient process information.

The business intelligence community has been pushing the use of different kinds of OLAP cubes and supporting databases and data warehouses for a long time. This can be powerful technology for simple sums and other linear aggregations. But this technology is typically very constrained in the types of custom parameterized aggregation it can perform, which is a key requirement for the hierarchical data splits required to assess risk or performance. Further, traditionally cubes have been relatively static due to their technical nature and the way they optimize response times.

As a response, there is now substantial innovation going on in the analytics space that sometimes overlaps with big data in terms of underlying technology, but that is somewhat different in purpose. More often than not, data is at rest but retained on purpose-built database-like platforms. These are configured and optimized for online queries and use a combination of column-orientation for fast aggregation on individual fields and large in-memory databases (IMDB) to save the roundtrip to far slower mechanical drives or solid state drives (SSDs) that classical database platforms normally have to do (Ovum, 2011; 2012).

The right analytics solution on top of modern systems is one that is able to pull together data from separate systems and answer interactive users' questions in real time while they wait. It should no longer be necessary to take a coffee break while the system prepares the report.

25.5.5   Opportunities in data

We will still be using Online Transaction Processing (OLTP) databases 10 years from now. Data warehouses and marts will also remain very useful for reporting purposes if they have not merged with databases in more integrated solutions by that time. But the technologies cited above will prove not just useful but if used correctly will have substantial potential to enable new differentiators for the innovative investment management firm.

The hardware options can bring us the next order of magnitude in cost-effective throughput. Advanced analytics technology will empower users to slice and dice more online data in real time. And big data approaches will offer ways to stand out in an increasingly regulated and commoditized investment management service industry.

First and foremost today, an investment manager must have modern systems of record at the core of the operational platform. A fully integrated investment book of record (IBOR) across all functional silos is desirable, not least from a cost point of view. Data crunching analytics are then generated in other modules or systems on top of the IBOR or other systems of record.

When looking for a new performance attribution, risk solution or accounting solution, it is critical for an investment manager that these can continue to scale with the task. There are inherent challenges to scalability in some of these domains. But if the current system in one of these time-critical, computationally heavy areas does not allow for more hardware to be added as demand grows, then it is time to consider replacing that system.

Such bottlenecks may hold back regulatory compliance, not simply because of the increased load alone but also in restraining growth by putting artificial constraints on the business. A modern solution in any computationally heavy aspect of investment management must be able to scale by adding hardware incrementally; and it should have at least some of the above technologies in its future roadmap. If it does not, it may not prove a viable platform a few years down the road.

25.6   End-user application platforms

For many years there was little choice; if you had to provide end-users with a user interface for a reasonably advanced application, you would develop a Windows application. This has changed more recently with the explosive growth of smartphones and tablets, as well as the latest generations of web browsers that have become viable application platforms.

25.6.1   Web

The web browser as a viable end-user application platform has been promised almost ever since the Web took off in the mid-1990s. Some software categories have seen this happen. But in many others, the promise has been held back by a combination of poor performance, lack of stability and the limitations of the sandbox environment in which secure browsers run applications.

However, with the renewed competition in the browser space in recent years and the rapid growth of mobile non-Windows platforms, we have seen a new breed of browser appear that is far more robust and performs, by some metrics, two orders of magnitude faster. The next version of the standards used to define web pages – HTML5 – has become the rallying beacon for this movement. HTML5 and adjoining technologies, such as CCS3 and various popular open-source JavaScript libraries, are on a path to deliver on the promise of the Web as a serious enterprise application platform.

This does not mean that all enterprise software will be migrated to become web applications overnight. But it does mean that it has become easier to expect an enterprise software vendor to either offer parts of their software via a browser or at least have concrete plans to do so. Any system that is not on a path to becoming at least partially web-enabled is likely to end up being a legacy platform that is not viable in the long term.

Table 25.1 shows different approaches to delivering investment management system functionality into the hands of the user. For a long while the only real option has been to deploy a Microsoft Windows application. As web browser capabilities improve, serious consideration should be given to pushing at least some functionality to the web browser for wider reach through easier deployment – everybody has a web browser. It is still a bit too early to expect a good web-based user experience for all tools such as complex investment decision making tools. But this will change. For now it is worth looking at providing web-based reporting, especially for clients as well as using the web browser as a way to facilitate collaboration with partners and allow greater flexibility for employees with more readily available process tools.

Predefined web-enabled reporting capabilities can sometimes be bolted onto legacy systems at an acceptable cost. But the full potential of web-based enterprise software capabilities will typically require a suitable architecture that is optimized for use across networks. The heavy calculation that is often required here is best done close to the data, with ample processing resources and not inside the browser with potentially limited processing capabilities.

The large data volumes that are often in play mean that data that is not visible should stay in the data centre – both because of the volume to be transported across varying networks but also for security reasons. Lastly, the expectations

Table 25.1 Advantages and disadvantages of different ways to deliver investment management system functionality to end-users

Scope/Platform	Advantages	Disadvantages	Alternatives
Windows application	Rich user experience in a largely safe environment	Hard to deploy outside own organization	Web-based applications
Fully web-enabled	Lower cost of providing remote access	It is still too expensive to be practical for most vendors to offer everything on the Web with a good user experience	Application and desktop virtualization infrastructure, e.g., Citrix XenDesktop
Web-based client reporting	Great for wealth management clients who can have a great empowering user experience through a dynamic online reporting tool	None	Static posted paper-based or emailed PDF file reports
Web-based partner collaboration	Cheap way to extend part of a system to a partner for effective collaboration, e.g., both sides of a business process outsourcing arrangement	Chance of scope-creep when never quite having enough of what is available in the full application	Application and desktop virtualization infrastructure, e.g., Citrix XenDesktop, but requires exchange of login details, documentation and network details
Web-enabled overviews and tasks	Likely to provide much of what is required for most people most of the time	The functionality available in a browser may continue to just fall short of expectations despite increases in scope	Full Windows application

for the web-based user experience are different compared to Windows applications. Users are less patient and they expect simpler functionality in a personalized user experience (Celent, 2012b).

25.6.2 Tablets and smartphones

Hardware innovations in the very fluid and competitive mobile phone space have generated a substantial and rapid change in the mix of current end-user computing devices, with smartphones far outselling PCs and tablets rapidly gaining on PCs. The pace of this innovation has made it very hard for enterprise IT organizations to keep up with users' demands, and in the last few years we have seen the significant bring-your-own-device (BYOD) trend become an accepted fact in many enterprises.

The BYOD trend is already starting to have an impact on IT application strategies in enterprises across different industries. That is a profound change in itself, but the potential for unlocking new business capabilities should really be the focus. Putting the right tools in the hands of a mobile workforce may be leveraged to bring out new efficiencies and effective ways to engage clients (Camargo and Fonseca, 2012).

For the early movers, there are potential new differentiators to bring to market. Later joiners may soon feel a more urgent pressure to mirror the functionality employed by the early movers. The entire software and business architecture may need adjustment to support modern tablet and smartphone user experiences properly.

It is far preferable to decide to make such changes as part of a strategic plan aligning various business strategic aims with a coherent technology change program. Later joiners may not have the luxury of time to keep the clients happy and may be forced to make tactical investments that are poorly aligned with the target operating model.

Many apps for smartphones and tablets may seem like gimmicks at first sight, but that is changing rapidly. The opportunities for the investment management industry should not be ignored. But with the opportunities come new security challenges that will be discussed in a later section.

25.6.3   End-user platform opportunities

Employing web, tablets and smartphones can also improve many entirely internal processes; the following scenarios, albeit not specific to the investment management industry, are probably the most important to consider:

- managers who are not daily users of the system and with little desire to train to use the system in light of their needs;
- users who spend a lot of time away from their desks;
- users with lighter meeting loads but with time-critical tasks that may arise at short notice;
- all users – the work/life boundary gets increasingly blurred because of email and smartphones.

Options abound. The key task is to identify what touch points are appropriate for the target operating model and ensure the systems strategy is in place to support these capabilities with the right user experience and integrity of the data. Table 25.2 gives an overview of the relative usefulness of a given platform to solve needs for specific operating models.

By far the most important element of mobile applications is ease of use (CEB TowerGroup, 2013). This probably means a slightly different use of data and functions than the one we know from desktop applications. An underlying operational platform for web and mobile clients in particular must have as few data silos as possible, since the data is likely to be combined in new ways

Table 25.2 The overall usefulness of different application delivery platforms for a few key scenarios using the web, tablet and smartphones

Business model	Scenario	Content	Utility of platform in scenario		
			Web	Tablet	Smartphone
Private banking (also wealth management in general and family offices)	Client self-service	Interactive reports on investment performance, typically for defined periods, e.g., monthly	High	High	Low
	Advisory session	Investment strategy and asset allocation modeling – impact analysis	Medium	High	Low
Asset manager	Sales situation with institutional investor	Empower sales team including portfolio managers and risk specialists with the ability to answer most questions in the natural flow of the meeting	High	High	Low
Asset servicer	Daily operations	Extend interface between service provider and client to facilitate timely responses, e.g., corporate actions where the asset servicer does not have the mandate to make the financial decision on, say, a stock split, or where an active investor client has particular responsible investment policies to be applied	High	Low	Medium

on-the-fly, and new actions on different sets of data require functional flexibility or good integration tools.

Further, in areas that are used directly to service clients via web or mobile devices like tablets or smartphones, it is fair to expect system vendors to either have systems in place or to be in the process of building them.

The systems of a target operational platform that face clients for self-service purposes should be expected to have some or at least be working on a level of built-in support for use via web and mobile devices, such as tablets and smartphones. If the involved systems providers are not already working on this support, they are behind the curve. Older legacy systems on minimum investment life-support are destined to become increasingly sore points in the system as attention shifts to web and mobile devices in particular.

25.7   Security and operational risk

25.7.1   Internal risks and cyber security in general

Cyber security is a growing problem globally. Table 25.3 outlines the major sources of threats to an investment management system and how to mitigate the particular threats.

Authorization is the first line of defense. The operational systems that together make up the investment management operational platform used by the enterprise must sufficiently support granular access permissions to both functions and data. It is also crucial to be able to report on who has access to what on a regular basis. This is also becoming a regulatory requirement, for instance, with Pillar II of Solvency II.

Having regular audits on authorizations in place helps to motivate getting the right tools and processes set up. Spot testing of authorization and of potential alternative ways (exploits) to gain access is a sensible secondary measure to prove the validity of the audit report. Done right this should go a long way to prevent the large fraud losses brought on by overreaching individuals like the trader Kweku Adoboli at UBS (FSA, 2012); the FSA also found a contributing factor was poorly integrated systems that made it hard to track the problems across multiple systems. A single integrated backend system is far better placed to enforce appropriate authorizations across functional areas.

Security training of employees is another critical part of the defense against crime (FSA, 2008). Employees may be clever, but they also need to trust their colleagues; they are busy and most tend not to perceive new acquaintances as adversaries. Security awareness training can help employees spot when they are being asked something that is not right from an IT security point of view. The IT security industry is full of anecdotes about just how much an adversary can persuade the average employee to reveal through social engineering.

Table 25.3 Some of the main types of cybercrime relevant to the investment management industry, divided primarily along motive, method, impact and prevention line

Perpetrator	Intent	Motive	Method	Reputational risk	Monetary risk	Prevention
Individual employee	Non-intentional	None	Authorized use	Low	Medium	Authorization and audit
Individual employee	Intentional	Revenge	Authorized use and some system or social exploit	Medium	Medium	Authorization and audit, tests, training
		Cover prior actions	Authorized use and a system or social exploit	High	High	Authorization and audit, tests, training
		Steal assets	Authorized use and a system or social exploit to funnel assets away	Low	Low	Authorization and audit, tests, training, pattern analysis
Criminal organizations	Intentional	Steal assets	Social engineering and hacking	Medium	High	Penetration testing, training, pattern analysis
		Blackmail	Social engineering and hacking	High	High	Penetration testing, training, pattern analysis

Pattern analysis that is increasingly based on Complex Event Processing (CEP) technology can be a very effective component of spotting potential crimes early and to allow timely counter-measures to be taken. Such pattern analysis will analyze particular streams of data and events to look for suspicious patterns as a secondary control mechanism on top of audits. While common in the retail banking space, this technology has not, at least for now, found itself translated into standard investment management software – quite possibly because the problem remains underestimated.

> *Underreporting of cybercrime is a fundamental issue that only makes it harder to educate about cybercrime in order to prevent or at least reduce the risk of an attack. There are voluntary networks for sharing cybercrime intelligence, but it is being considered to make companies legally bound to report attacks to the relevant authorities. The current underreporting is basically caused by concerns regarding reputational risk by being more open about any attacks or losses sustained. This behavior is very understandable in the financial services industry, where reputational risk is a very important concern. But it is a disservice to the industry as a whole. Everybody loses.*

25.7.2   Single sign-on and single point of control

An enterprise employing many separate operational systems runs a substantial risk by allowing each system to require separate credentials (user name and password) to gain access to each system. The main issue here is that users tend not to be able to remember many unique passwords. As a result, most users will opt for one of two strategies:

Either they begin to write down the passwords – the password written on a yellow sticky note attached to the user's monitor is a classic sight in offices across the world. The risk here is obvious: internals and externals can simply gain physical access to the office and glean enough information to impersonate another user.

Alternatively, they use the same password across several systems, which is very common behavior, well-known and expected by hackers. The implication of this behavior is that the security of all the operational systems the user has access to may be down to just one of the systems. A hacker may be able to find a way to obtain a clear-text password from the weakest protected system.

There are two complementary solutions to the problem: reducing the number of individual systems to reduce the number of individual points of authentication and attack surfaces, and adopting a single sign-on (SSO) architecture. This is far from supported by all systems currently in use, but it should be on the requirements list when looking at new systems.

With the SSO concept, the user logs in to authenticate just once, typically against the operating system, and each SSO-enabled system will subsequently ask the operating system for an authenticated user. SSO also affords another key capability in that it allows all main user control to be centralized. Central control over users means that new users can be created across systems in a structured consistent manner and users can be disabled from a single point, which helps reduce a disgruntled employee's potential to do damage.

25.7.3   Remote access

Authenticating users accessing an investment management system via a web browser from inside the corporate firewall can be based entirely on the SSO capabilities provided by the existing identity infrastructure, such as Microsoft Active Directory. Smartphone and tablet users accessing the system from inside the firewall can also be done securely with widely used technology.

When users connect from these platforms from outside the corporate firewall, encrypted communication is required on top of robust authentication mechanisms. Reasonably mature technology solutions exist to address these issues. However, some organizations will be challenged to effectively persuade themselves that these technologies in fact can be combined to form an environment that is secure enough for handling sensitive client data and executing transactions with material financial impact.

One of the new features introduced to standard web technology with HTML5 is to allow web-based applications to work offline from cached code and data. However, this is still very new and has to prove itself on the market. So far a key differentiator between mobile apps and a regular website is the ability to work offline.

Mobile devices are frequently lost or stolen and, as a consequence, many enterprises enforce the use of pin codes or similar and enable remote wipe – even with 'bring-your-own-device' devices. However, these features are not a guarantee against data loss, merely a reduction of the risk. Hence it should be considered very carefully whether the value of allowing the user to work offline on a mobile device really outweighs the risk of the potential loss of data.

25.7.4   Security opportunities

As we expose systems to the cloud and via browsers and mobile devices, we increase the overall surface that is open to attack. These technical challenges are hurdles to be overcome, but they do not offer much in the way of opportunities in their own right. The one exception may be that success with mobile, and to a lesser extent, web applications depends on striking the right balance between security and ease of use. Too secure and it may become too hard to use. Very easy to use and it may not be secure enough.

More generally, modern operational systems must have a granular authorization model that is robustly enforced, quite likely through the use of a single integrated system, or at least a small set of modern systems.

25.8 Conclusions

The investment management industry is one of the business sectors with the very largest IT budgets. But despite a heavy reliance on IT, or maybe in fact because of it, the investment management industry by and large remains conservative when it comes to adopting new technology. This is probably due to generally very mature IT change risk modeling – driven by necessity; for instance, if a security issue resulting from being an early mover on a particular new technology becomes public news, it might represent a very substantial reputational risk or it could carry high financial costs.

A recommended path to reconcile the risk adversity and be able to leverage new technology is to rely on standard systems, where the system vendor takes on the risk and integrates the new technologies in an evolutionary fashion. Operational systems that do not benefit from substantial investment in continuous research and development are likely to lag behind technologically. This may not be a problem at present, but sooner or later, it is likely to reduce agility by preventing a new idea to be acted upon quickly at a known cost and risk.

It may be tempting to try to ride out this period of high market uncertainty and low margins by cutting IT budgets and sticking to existing systems and capabilities, and this may work better for some than others, but generally it is risky path – it will leave the firm unprepared for the raft of new regulation underway. The firm will be poorly positioned both to benefit from cloud services for cost savings and for the option to replace a capital expenditure model with an operational expenditure model.

It also means playing catch-up with competitors to provide the right data and applications on the right integrated platforms to offer the user or customer the experience expected tomorrow. Companies with little prior experience in the web and mobile area should not underestimate the size of the change project to fully embed web and mobile capabilities in the organization.

Few medium to large investment management businesses are created as such from scratch. Rather they tend to grow from a small beginning or evolve from another line of business. That means layers of evolving technology and processes to support the business have been added over time. It may be necessary to replace key legacy systems to unlock data stuck in silos and to enable new uses and timely combinations of the data locked in each system.

With a modern configurable operational platform based on a well-integrated single or small set of operational systems, it is generally possible to incrementally add new technology to gain better risk control, improve cost efficiency in business or IT operations, or offer clients or internal users innovative solutions to drive growth.

Note

1. For instance, we see this in the EU Data Protection Directive that is to be superseded by the EU General Data Protection Regulation, which in fact is more sensitive to globalization and technology concerns than the original directive is.

References

Camargo, A. and Fonseca, I. (2012) 'Mobile Applications for Advisors: A Study of the European Market', Celent.

CEB TowerGroup (2013) 'Top 10 Technology Initiatives in Capital Markets for 2013: Preparing for Major IT and Operations Projects Across Securities and Investments', 12 February.

Celent (2012a) 'Cloud Computing Capital Markets'.

Celent (2012b) 'IT Trends and Spending Implications for the Securities & Investment Industry: Finding Opportunities Amidst the New Realities', 8 October.

Desai, D. (2013) 'Beyond Location: Data Security in the 21st Century', in *Communications of the ACM*, January, (56)1.

FSA (2008) 'Data Security in Financial Services', Retrieved 2013/02/10, http://www.fsa.gov.uk/pubs/other/data_security.pdf

FSA (2012) 'FSA fines UBS £29.7 million for significant failings in not preventing large scale unauthorised trading', Retrieved 2013/02/10, http://www.fsa.gov.uk/library/communication/pr/2012/105.shtml

Ovum (2011) 'In-Memory Databases in the Capital Markets', Strategic Focus.

Ovum (2012) '2013 Trends to Watch: Financial Markets Technology'

26

Fit-For-Future Enterprise Architecture: Supporting Strategic Business Challenges

Marc Schröter

26.1 Introduction

Since 2007, the asset management industry has been undergoing major changes. Asset values declined steeply in 2008 and 2009 and even though assets have recovered, profits are still significantly lower than in 2007. The period has seen ongoing financial turmoil and market volatility, as well as increasing regulatory requirements and client demands.

In this market environment, asset managers are evaluating their business model to see how they can improve their products and services and bring these to market rapidly, while at the same time having efficient operations. To support their business model, they are looking for an operating model that provides robust, scaleable and yet flexible operational platforms that enable growth, optimize operational processes to minimize costs and at the same time provide first class risk management and business control support. The operating model defines how the asset manager operates across processes, people, organizations and technology in order to support the business model in an optimal way and typically involves considerations of core versus non-core business, outsourcing, shared services, process optimizations and supporting software systems.

The technology part of the operating model covers many aspects including hardware, software, networks and more. In this chapter, we will primarily focus on software systems in the IT infrastructure, here referred to as 'enterprise architecture'. Often the enterprise architecture is regarded as the result of decisions related to business model, process and organization. However, the enterprise architecture may also be a limiting factor in achieving the optimal target operating model and thereby realizing the desired business objectives. Here we analyze how enterprise architectures can best support the desired target operating model and what asset managers need to be aware of when deciding on the overall enterprise architecture as well as its individual components.

We start with describing some of the current major strategic business and operational challenges for asset managers. Next, some of the main characteristics of what we have chosen to call 'traditional enterprise architectures' are described, along with their capabilities in supporting the strategic business and operational challenges. Subsequently, we propose an enterprise architecture, which is prepared for handling the strategic challenges, and finally we discuss how best to go from As-Is to the desired To-Be state.

26.2 Post-crisis strategic business challenges for asset managers

Let us first take a look at some of the high-level financial figures for asset managers, starting with the 2012 McKinsey North American Asset Management Benchmarking Survey, summarized in Figure 26.1.[1,2] In the period since 2007, assets under management (AUM) declined sharply but have now recovered to approximately the same levels as before the crisis. During the period 2007–11, net fund flows were almost zero, meaning that market appreciation is the main driver for the increase in AUM. The revenues follow the same curve as AUM, whereas profits are significantly under pressure. This is due

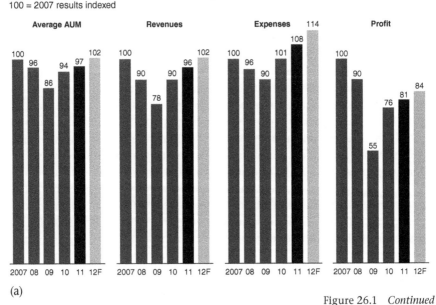

(a)

Figure 26.1 *Continued*

Prices for most institutional products continued to decline

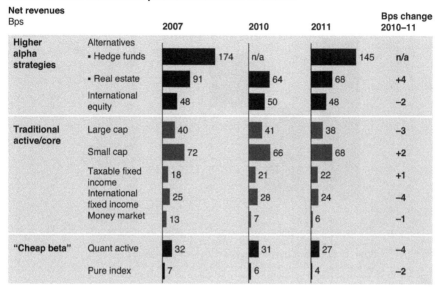

Net revenues Bps		2007	2010	2011	Bps change 2010–11
Higher alpha strategies	Alternatives				
	• Hedge funds	174	n/a	145	n/a
	• Real estate	91	64	68	+4
	International equity	48	50	48	–2
Traditional active/core	Large cap	40	41	38	–3
	Small cap	72	66	68	+2
	Taxable fixed income	18	21	22	+1
	International fixed income	25	28	24	–4
	Money market	13	7	6	–1
"Cheap beta"	Quant active	32	31	27	–4
	Pure index	7	6	4	–2

(b)

Many asset managers experienced negative operating leverage, with costs rising across all functions

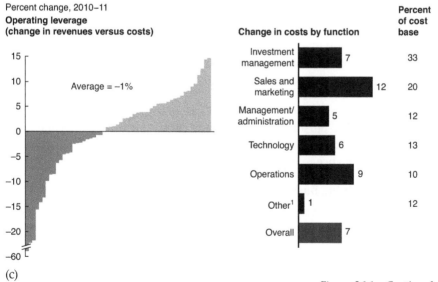

Percent change, 2010–11

Operating leverage (change in revenues versus costs)

Average = –1%

Change in costs by function

		Percent of cost base
Investment management	7	33
Sales and marketing	12	20
Management/ administration	5	12
Technology	6	13
Operations	9	10
Other[1]	1	12
Overall	7	

(c)

Figure 26.1   *Continued*

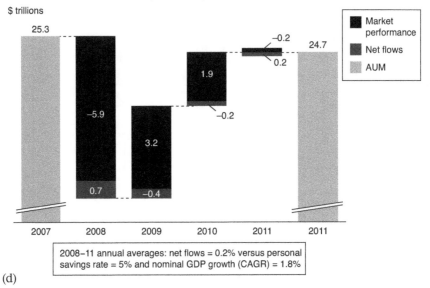

(d)

Figure 26.1 Summary of AUM, revenues, expenses, and profit figures for North American asset managers

Source: McKinsey, 'The Asset Management Industry: Outcomes are the New Alpha', Report on the '2012 McKinsey North American Asset Management Benchmark Survey'.

to a number of factors. Firstly, prices have been declining for both traditional active management, and passive/index tracking, whereas they have risen for alternatives. Secondly, expenses have increased significantly due to increased costs and reduced productivity. The main sources of cost increases are sales and marketing, but also investment management, operations and technology costs have all increased. In addition, asset managers have experienced a negative operating leverage, i.e., costs have grown faster than revenues (in fact, every year since the financial crisis began).

In order to improve their profitability, asset managers are adjusting their business models to pursue growth opportunities and are tuning their operating models to optimize costs, while at the same time improving risk management, ensuring compliance to new regulations and developing client services.

26.2.1 Redefining business models

During the last few years, net flows have been shifting from traditional active relative return funds to passive funds, alternative investments and so-called solutions.[3,4]

A number of studies, such as the S&P Indices versus Active Funds Scorecard, for example, has showed that active management is struggling to outperform passive index tracking funds or low cost ETFs over time.[5] On the other hand, the low interest environment, as well as the ongoing market turmoil and volatility, means that alternative strategies, such as hedge funds, private equity and structured products that incorporate hedging, inflation and volatility, for example, have become increasingly attractive to investors.[6]

The third category of products that has seen an increase in net flows takes the form of so-called solutions. These are products that are engineered to address a specific need, such as retirees reaching their 'target dates' and who are therefore looking for solutions that generate income while also protecting their principal. Another example is directed benefit pension plans, which are looking for solutions to reduce volatility and produce more consistent returns. Generally, solution products are outcome-oriented rather than benchmark-oriented and are constructed by packaging a range of investment strategies and financial products depending on the purpose (derivatives, inflation, volatility, absolute return, etc.). As much as 85% of asset managers rate solutions as a top-3 growth priority and they expect that solutions will represent 25% of flows and 15% of profits by 2015.[7]

All in all, this means that asset managers are adjusting their business models to shift from traditional relative return products to either passive products, alternative investments or solutions.

26.2.2   Risk management

Investors lost huge sums of money during the financial crisis, market uncertainty and volatilities remain high and events, such as the collapse of Lehman Brothers and Bear Stearns (and many subsequent bank bailouts around the globe), as well as scandals like the Madoff fraud case, have really pushed risk management to the top of every investor's agenda. Risk management is also a key focus area for regulators and is being addressed by regulations, such as Solvency II and the Dodd-Frank Act. Asset managers are implementing improved risk management to satisfy both regulators and investors, but also because there is a general acceptance that risk management needs to be improved in light of the difficulties experienced during and after the financial crisis.

As just illustrated by the examples earlier in this chapter, good risk management needs to look at risks across all risk types, such as market, credit, liquidity and operational risk, as well as systemic and reputational risk. Hence, risk management is now about much more than complex market risk calculations. Rather it involves having a holistic view across the enterprise – for example, on counterparty risk, how to decompose the risk of structured products, or how to account for complex assets according to fair value. Data quality management is a key aspect for risk management. Risk calculations and assessments rely on key data, such as prices, exchange rates, yield and volatility curves, but also on security classifications, counterparty identifiers and online and validated position data.

Another aspect is that risk management is no longer being considered as just an 'after-the-event' measurement but is increasingly becoming an integrated part of the investment decision-making process.

All this means that asset managers are implementing improved risk and data management procedures, hence giving the risk function more power, which is a trend that is expected to continue.

26.2.3   Compliance with new regulations

The last few years have brought a 'tidal wave' of new regulations that asset managers must adhere to. The Dodd-Frank Act, EMIR, FATCA, UCITS IV, AIFMD, Solvency II and MiFID II are just a few of these. Complying with each of these regulations requires a significant investment in processes and IT infrastructure in order to handle the regulation, as well as the derived consequences of it (see Figure 26.2). For example, EMIR and Dodd-Frank aim to reduce counterparty risk by introducing clearing via a central counterparty (CCP). This involves building processes and IT infrastructure to integrate to the CCPs and matching platforms, but there are a number of consequences,

ESTIMATED IT COSTS OF EIGHT MAJOR REGULATIONS ON THE BUY-SIDE

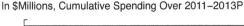

In $Millions, Cumulative Spending Over 2011–2013P

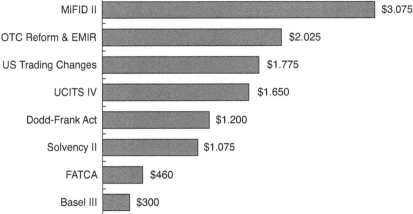

MiFID II	$3.075
OTC Reform & EMIR	$2.025
US Trading Changes	$1.775
UCITS IV	$1.650
Dodd-Frank Act	$1.200
Solvency II	$1.075
FATCA	$460
Basel III	$300

Figure 26.2   Estimated IT spending on eight major regulations on the buy-side

Source: CEB TowerGroup Research, 'Responding to Risk, Cost and Growth Issues in the Investment Industry: CEB, 2012'.

such as new processes for raising cash for margin payments and significantly expected increases in collateral messages for bilateral trades, which again increases the need for automation and solutions to support this. The new regulations also introduce additional requirements for data, such as legal entity identifiers (LEIs).

Compliance with new regulations is a major focus area and concern for asset managers globally. First priority is of course to comply with current and upcoming regulations. But it is just as much a case of being well prepared for additional regulations in the future.

26.2.4 Client services

The massive declines in asset values during the financial crisis mean that investors are lacking trust and confidence in their asset managers. Therefore, along with the regulators, clients are now also demanding increased transparency into investment strategies and risk management, compliance and business controls, as well as improved services, such as higher reporting frequency, quality and level of detail. Information relevant to investors must be more readily available, perhaps even online, and be of much higher quality than before. Asset managers can no longer spend days or even weeks validating the content of client reports before presenting it to the client.

A recent survey shows that in 2013, 86% of asset managers are concentrating on client-focused initiatives, such as providing timely and accurate information to clients, delivering more information on investment decisions and more personalized business intelligence with more self-service capabilities.[8] One of the main reasons is regulatory reform that is aimed at protecting investors – so there is a clear link between client and regulatory demands. The other main reasons are increased competition to win new clients and increased requirements from existing clients.

26.2.5 Operational efficiency

With regards to cost optimization, asset managers initially have focused on short-term solutions, such as lay-offs, restructuring and renegotiation of vendor contracts. But as these possibilities have become exhausted, they are turning to longer-term structural solutions, such as process optimization, system consolidation, shared services and outsourcing.

Previously, outsourcing was a case of either running investment operations in-house or outsourcing them. Today, a range of options exists, where both the traditional administrators, as well as software and solution providers, offer a range of options for outsourcing IT or business operations (see Figure 26.3). Some analysts expect an increase in outsourcing over the coming years, but bad experience has also led to some major institutions bringing operations back in-house again. Also, the expectations are different depending on the

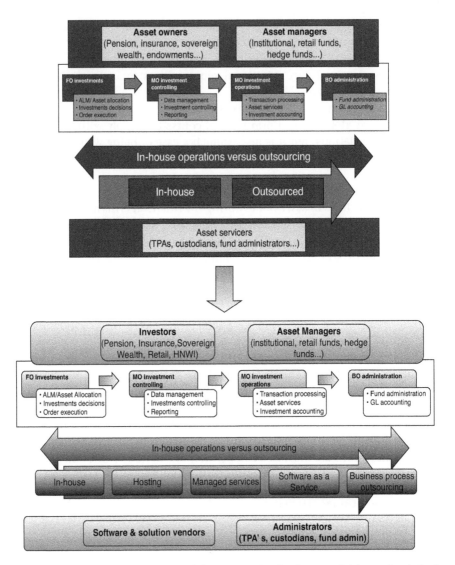

Figure 26.3 A high-level overview of the outsourcing landscape, which previously had few options and service providers

Note: Now it has been extended by software and solution providers, who offer a range of options for outsourcing IT or business operations.

type of outsourcing and whether it is business process outsourcing, managed services, hosting, etc.[9]

Another way to optimize costs is to achieve a better scale in operations. Average fund size is significantly larger in the USA than in Europe and, supported by the UCITS IV fund merger framework and cross-border master-feeder constructs, one can expect a consolidation of funds in Europe.[10] On a global level, the last few years have also showed that AUM for the largest asset managers has increased significantly.[11]

Finally, asset managers are looking to optimize their most inefficient and costly processes, such as corporate actions, collateral management and derivatives processing. Many of these inefficient processes involve communications with external parties and, while asset managers can make an effort to streamline the processes themselves, the real driver for automation is introduction of market standards. There are a number of initiatives, for example: within corporate actions notifications and election flows; collateral messaging formats; derivatives clearing; and ISDA CSA documents.

26.3   Traditional enterprise architectures

Technology has always been important in the finance industry as an enabler of both growth and cost optimization – so the enterprise architecture is paramount for meeting current and future strategic business challenges.

While CTOs are aware of this, many asset managers have enterprise architectures that are not prepared for supporting the strategic business challenges. First of all, changes in business model and risk management, as well as increased requirements from clients and regulators, must be supported. But equally important, this must be done in an efficient way in order to restrain costs and preserve profits. It is no longer an option to implement inefficient and manual processes based on disparate systems or in-house build solutions that are costly to operate, error-prone and increase the operational risk. In fact, CTOs are faced with the problem that they have to 'do more with less'.

CTOs must ask themselves two questions. First, is the enterprise architecture 'fit-for-purpose', that is, how well does it support the current business and operating models? Secondly, is the enterprise architecture 'fit-for-future', in other words, is it robust, scaleable and flexible enough to incorporate the necessary changes in order to support the future business and operating models?

A few examples from recent SimCorp polls point to some of the challenges.[12]

- 30% of asset managers need days or weeks to get an overview of their exposures across all holdings and financial instruments (for example to evaluate counterparty exposure). An additional 40% need hours to do this, whereas ideally this should only take minutes.
- More than half do not believe their accounting system is able to accurately record all events in the transaction lifecycle of, for example, OTC derivatives.

- Two-thirds say that there is a significant effort required to reconcile data between disparate systems.

In the following, we will look at some of the characteristics of what we call 'traditional enterprise architectures' and see what implications they may have.

26.3.1   Multiple disparate systems

Based on market surveys, SimCorp estimates that on a global scale about one-third of all asset managers have a so-called best-of-breed systems strategy, i.e., a collection of disparate systems from different vendors and often of different incompatible technologies that are connected via multiple integration points (see Figure 26.4).[13] For some asset managers, this is a result of additions and adjustments to the enterprise architecture over a number of years, where new systems have been introduced to solve specific problems. For others, it is a deliberate strategy to use the system that provides the most comprehensive set of features for each specific business function rather than optimizing system support for the whole value chain with regards to costs and efficiency.

Some of the main challenges with this strategy are:

1. Due to the many integration points, the architecture requires a huge reconciliation effort and it is a substantial task to keep all systems compatible through their individual upgrade cycles.

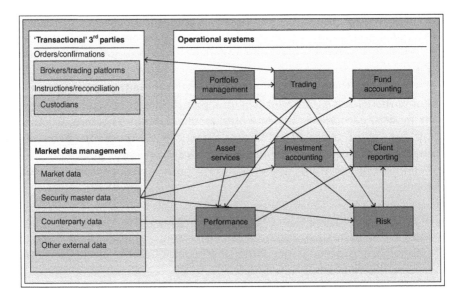

Figure 26.4 A typical architecture with many disparate operational systems from different vendors or other sources connected via multiple integration points

2. The same data is duplicated in multiple systems with the risk – indeed inevitability – of inconsistencies. Similarly, each system holds some data but no system holds all data and, as a result, there is no clear identification of the 'one version of the truth' that is required, for example, to obtain a full overview of counterparty exposure.
3. Introduction of new financial products or instruments is a significant task since it must be implemented in all systems, such as front office OMSs, settlement and accounting, as well as risk and performance.

26.3.2 Legacy systems

Enterprise architectures with multiple systems are unlikely to be stronger than the weakest link, which is often a legacy system. Legacy systems are systems where developer and support resources are both scarce and expensive, where there is a minimal investment in R&D, where there is no roadmap, and where there have been no significant updates in years. Hence, these systems are ill-equipped to deal with necessary updates due to changes in business or operating model. Legacy systems therefore represent a significant business risk.[14]

Based on the market surveys referred to earlier, SimCorp estimates that up to 25% of all asset managers have legacy systems bought from software vendors and an additional 10% have in-house built systems as central components in their architecture. In all, this adds up to an estimated one-third of all asset managers!

The strategic business challenges require updates of central systems in the enterprise architecture for most asset managers. New financial products and instruments must be rolled out across all systems across the value chain. If one of these systems does not handle, say, private equity funds, OTC derivatives or structured products, the consequences may at best be inefficient operations and at worst the new products cannot be implemented and must be discarded by the business.

Often the new products, such as alternatives or solutions, require updated risk management to decompose risk into the underlying components, for example. This is not just an update to the risk system, but an update to the system(s) holding core instrument and position/contract information, as well as front-office, performance and valuation systems.

The flood of new regulations also calls for changes to systems across the enterprise architecture. Dodd-Frank and Solvency II require the ability to assess counterparty risk in a timely manner (intra-day). EMIR and Dodd-Frank introduce CCP clearing, which requires new types of information, such as Legal Entity Identifiers (LEIs) or unique contract identifiers. FATCA introduces additional data points, such as entity identifications, while UCITS IV/V allows for a completely new master-feeder fund construct.

If we look at MIFID, it led to increased market fragmentation by introducing multilateral trading facilities (MTFs), which has made the search for liquidity more complex. This results in smaller trade sizes and increased trading volume that must be handled by software systems. MIFID also introduced additional data requirements in the form of documentation of best execution and reporting of trades to central trade repositories.

With Dodd-Frank and EMIR, asset managers must clear interest rate swaps (IRSs) and credit default swaps (CDSs) centrally through electronic integration to matching engines and CCPs. The process requires margin processing on a daily basis via new communication flows. For bilateral OTC trades, it is expected that collateral messaging will increase significantly. This requires optimization of the information flows to counterparties via electronic communication using standardized message types.

These are just a few examples of the regulatory requirements and business model changes that impact systems across the enterprise architecture. Any legacy or internal system that may not be able to support these changes in a timely manner imposes a serious business risk.

26.3.3   Separate book of records for trading and accounting

Another characteristic of traditional enterprise architectures is that the fundamental differences between front office and investment operations views on portfolios are exposed by the enterprise architecture.[15] On the one hand, investment operations and accounting functions are primarily concerned about end-of-day processing (EOD) and closing the books accurately according to fund domicile EOD. Front office, on the other hand, requires correct start-of-day (SOD) balances according to where the portfolio is managed. It needs an accurate view on positions and investable cash and to have portfolios updated with intra-day changes due to trading activities, corporate actions, collateral management events, resets and more.

This leads to a typical architecture as illustrated in Figure 26.5. Accounting systems maintain EOD records – records that are also referred to as an accounting book of record (ABOR). Each morning, the front-office systems receive SOD positions based on an ABOR and overnight events, such as coupons or redemptions. Intra-day, the front-office systems handle the impact of trading activities, often called a trading book of record (TBOR).

The challenge with this architecture is that neither the TBOR nor the ABOR holds the entire truth. The TBOR is first of all dependent on the quality of the SOD positions and it holds no position history nor captures all intra-day events not originating in the front office, such as collateral events or intra-day corporate actions. On the other hand, an ABOR lacks information about simulated trades or pending orders and often intra-day trades are not updated online.

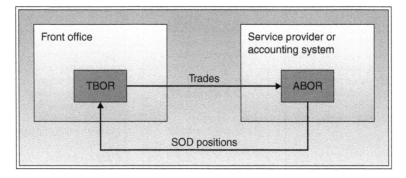

Figure 26.5 Typical architecture with intra-day versus end-of-day view on positions

Note: Service providers or accounting systems hold the correct end-of-day balance that is used to feed the front- and middle-office systems each morning with start-of-day (SOD) positions. The front-office systems then maintain an intra-day view of positions.

As a result of this, front-office investment decisions are based on an inaccurate and incomplete view on positions available for trading. From a risk management perspective, this architecture does not provide a single source from which to obtain a consolidated and consistent overview as the basis for risk assessments. Hence, risk assessments are also based on inaccurate and incomplete information. Investment decision-making and risk management are the core functions of an asset manager; it is therefore of serious concern if there is a risk of making wrong decisions based on incorrect data.

26.3.4 Operational impact of outsourcing

Many asset managers outsource part of their investment operations at various degrees as illustrated in Figure 26.6. As well as cost containment, considerations in outsourcing normally stem from a strategy geared toward retaining core and value-adding business processes in-house and outsourcing non-core and non-value adding processes. Drivers also include improved efficiency, access to improved technology and scale, as well as reduction of staff risk.

These are all valid considerations and, depending on the situation, many benefits can be gained from outsourcing. However, there are also some consequences that asset managers need to be aware of.

* Standardization versus flexibility. The third-party administrator (TPA) wants standardization and achieves cost efficiency via scale in controlled environments using global centralized processes and systems and often has an accounting-centric view on portfolios and funds (see earlier ABOR description). The asset manager wants flexibility, bespoke solutions with local autonomy and quick response times and always has an investment-centric

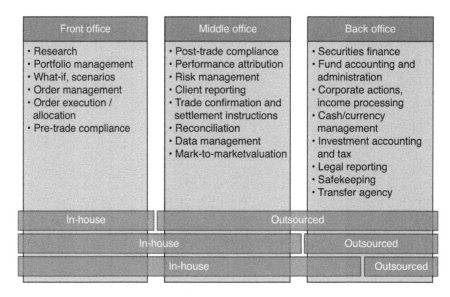

Figure 26.6   Various degrees of outsourcing

view on portfolios and funds. Hence, there is a fundamental contradiction between asset managers and TPAs that needs to be managed.

- Costs savings may be less than expected. Surveys indicate that there is as little as 10% difference in costs between outsourcing and in-house operations.[16] Hence, cost savings should not be the only or main driver for choosing outsourcing arrangements, as has frequently been the case.

- Ultimately, asset managers are accountable to regulators and clients. A survey by Beacon Consulting suggests that up to 40% of asset managers who have outsourced their operations have felt the need to invest in a high level of oversight, such as full shadow booking or review of all service provider output.[17] The most important reasons are to ensure quality and understanding, undo past errors by service providers and soften the impact of inexperience and turnover of service provider staff. It is clear that this level of oversight erodes the very reason for outsourcing in the first place.

- Asset managers may want to reduce risk toward the service provider. In a recent letter from the FSA in the UK to 'CEO's of Asset Managers', they highlight their concern over outsourcing arrangements and dependency on the service provider. Among other things, the FSA advises asset managers to have adequate contingency plans in place to deal with expected as well as unexpected termination of outsourcing contracts.[18] This should prompt asset managers to consider their outsourcing agreements and weigh up options, such as using multiple service providers and having an enterprise architecture (and operating skills) that enables continuation of business if the outsourcing agreement is changed.

- Outsourcing arrangements also impact management and control of master data. Figure 26.7 shows that if critical functions, such as fund accounting and client reporting, are outsourced, the master records are split between the asset manager and the TPA. Often, the TPA actually maintains the master version of business critical information, such as portfolio holdings. This creates a dependency on the TPA in terms of quality of data but also timely access to data – for example, in the case of intra-day calculation of counterparty risk (see earlier TBOR/ABOR description). Since the TPA has an accounting-based view on portfolios, it may not be able to provide data at the necessary level of granularity, for example, positions per manager or strategy versus fund or general ledger account. If the asset manager has multiple TPAs, a consolidated and consistent overview is out of the question. Even if there is only one TPA, this very argument excludes the possibility of having several TPAs at a later point in time.

26.4   A fit-for-future enterprise architecture

In the previous section, we looked at some of the challenges of traditional enterprise architectures. In this section, we will propose an enterprise architecture that is better prepared to support the current and future strategic challenges of asset managers and therefore is both fit-for-purpose and fit-for-future.

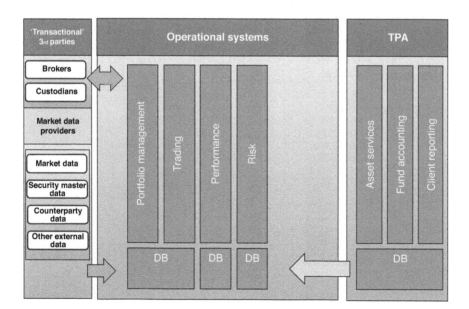

Figure 26.7   Outsourcing of business processes leads to 'outsourcing of master data'

Figure 26.8 shows a high-level overview of the main components of such an enterprise architecture. The architecture can be implemented in a number of ways, which will be discussed later in this section.

26.4.1 Main components

On a high level, the enterprise architecture consists of three types of components:

- An investment book of record (IBOR) as foundation for all operational processes across the value chain covering market, reference and client data, including integration with data vendors, positions and transactions and derived analytics, such as market values and cash forecasts.
- Operational system(s) supporting all processes in the asset management value chain, including integration with external parties, such as brokers and custodians.
- Reporting and Business Intelligence (BI) for analyzing and distributing information to both internal stakeholders, such as management, and external stakeholders, such as clients and regulators.

IBOR

The IBOR is used as the foundation for all processes across the value chain, from front-office decision support, over middle-office risk and performance

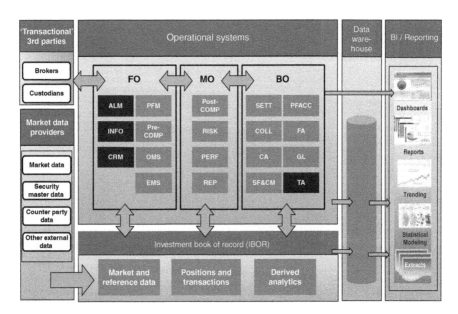

Figure 26.8   Proposed high-level enterprise architecture component

measurement, to accounting and reporting. In this way, there is only 'one version of the truth', and all operational systems use the same data as the basis for processing.

The IBOR contains online data, which is both distributed to and updated by the operational systems. This differs from a data warehouse, which primarily holds offline and validated data.

At the core of the IBOR are the positions and transactions combining the front office's intra-day trading book of record (TBOR) and the accounting-based end-of-day book of record (ABOR) in a complete and up-to-date view on current positions, including all events no matter what their origin. Also included is transaction lifecycle management, as well as historical balances on securities, derivatives contracts and cash. This part of the IBOR is the core foundation for front-office decision-making and risk assessment at all times. The IBOR is the foundation of the whole business, and in principle the asset manager should be able to rebuild everything from the transactions as well as existing and future positions.

There are different views on whether the IBOR should contain derived data, such as market values and cash forecasts, as opposed to calculating this information in the operational systems. Keeping this information in the IBOR has the advantage of ensuring consistency and reducing reconciliation efforts, assuming that the information is used for the same purpose across the value chain.

For example, the cash forecast used by treasury and portfolio managers should preferably be based on the same methodology and data. Similarly, end-of-day risk and performance figures, as well as portfolio valuation, would typically be based on the same market values. In this case, market values would be held in the IBOR, whereas performance time-weighted return or attribution would be retained in the performance system.

For calculating market values, the IBOR needs market information, such as prices, exchange rates and yield curves. Forecasting cash and security balances requires registration of security and contract event schedules, dividends and income, corporate actions, redemptions, resets, option dates and much more. Hence, the IBOR also needs a comprehensive security master file.

In addition, the IBOR should also hold other types of information used across operational systems, for example, client data or counterparty identifications, such as LEIs. Typically, the same benchmarks are used in several systems, such as front office, risk and performance, but also in fund accounting for validating change in the fund's net asset value (NAV) versus change in benchmark. Hence, a natural option, also, would be to maintain indices and benchmarks in the IBOR.

Much of this data is typically sourced from data vendors or data service providers via integration solutions. Many asset managers consider it best practice to source data from several vendors and use validation rules for comparing the data and create a so-called golden record, which is more reliable than just deriving the data from a single source. This method has to be weighed against the cost of acquiring and cleansing the data from multiple sources.

Some may have architectures in which market and security data are sourced from the data vendors, validated and loaded into the data warehouse and distributed from there rather than from the IBOR. This could also be a viable setup, so external market data can either be sourced from data vendors into the IBOR and distributed from there (including to the data warehouse), or sourced from the data vendors into the data warehouse and distributed from there (including to the IBOR).

On the surface, the IBOR may look like a traditional data management system, but in fact the IBOR is much more than this.[19] It contains advanced business logic for event-handling across instrument types, including OTC and exchange-traded derivatives (ETDs), and structured products or alternative investments, such as private equity or property. It contains position management for securities, cash and contracts, including historical records.

The IBOR must also be able to handle back-dated changes to transactions due to settlement errors, wrong corporate actions, missing dividend notifications and all the other events that occur on a daily basis and impact both historical and current positions. Forecasting capabilities must also be included for both cash and securities, as well as valuation methodologies and key ratio calculations,[20] including theoretical valuation for illiquid securities. Figure 26.9 illustrates the elements of an IBOR that can handle these requirements.

A traditional data management system is unlikely to provide these features; rather, this much more resembles the functionality of an integrated portfolio management system covering front and middle office, investment operations and accounting functions.

Operational systems

All the main processes in the asset management value chain must be supported by the operational systems. Traditionally, these systems have been categorized as front-, middle- or back-office systems to be used by the typical end-user roles of asset management organizations. Figure 26.8 also illustrates this structure.

However, there are many different opinions on what is handled by front office versus middle office, middle office versus back office, with some using the term investment operations instead of back office and so on, all of which makes the definitions somewhat unclear.

In addition, traditional front-, middle- and back-office processes are becoming more and more integrated. A process that used to be handled entirely by one organizational role using one system is now often a shared process, where roles from different parts of the asset management organization need to have

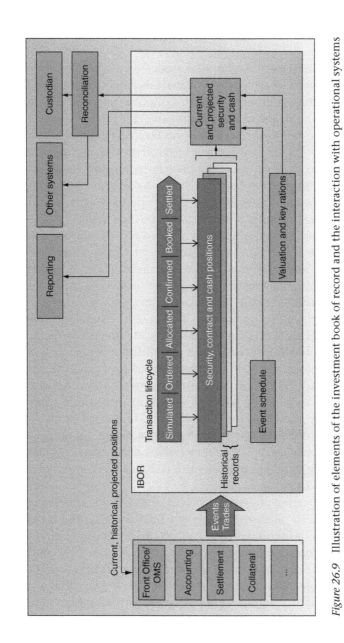

Figure 26.9 Illustration of elements of the investment book of record and the interaction with operational systems

exactly the same view on data and a process that runs smoothly across the organization in order to achieve efficient operations. Figure 26.8 illustrates this process with the arrows between front, middle and back office.

Some examples of cross-organizational processes:

- Collateral management used to be considered a back office after-the-event task, which involved calculating collateral requirements, exchanging information with the counterpart, managing disputes, selecting eligible collateral and exchanging this with the counterpart. This process is now starting to move into the front office, where portfolio managers and traders want to have a view on collateral to decide which collateral is needed to best support their activities. Instead of collateralizing every single trade, counterparts will make agreements across their trades leading to netting possibilities. Traders can then look at their entire trading position with each counterpart and use that to determine where to place the next trade.

- Performance attribution was historically based on accounting systems, since these held the transaction history necessary for calculating time-weighted return (TWR) and other performance key ratios. Today, it is often the case that funds and portfolios are managed by several managers according to different investment strategies for asset allocation, security selection and currency overlays. Performance attribution must measure the effect of the investment decisions on each of these levels and therefore needs to combine information of both front office and accounting systems.

- Corporate actions elections is a process that goes across front and back office. The back office calculates entitlements based on corporate actions notifications and current positions. Based on this information, the portfolio manager makes the election, which is then used by the back office to instruct custodians. Each custodian has different cut-off times, so that the portfolio manager and corporate actions administration processes must run effectively intra-day and must also be based on positions that are completely up-to-date (online).

- Instead of allocating money to different strategies, some asset managers allocate risk via so-called risk budgeting. Total portfolio risk is decomposed and allocated to each asset class and portfolio manager with set risk limits (budgets) using tracking error, for example. So, the front office must be able to see the current utilization of risk budget and also see the effect of a given portfolio rebalancing on the risk budget before trades are placed in the market. All this requires a tight integration between front office and risk departments and systems.

Previously, it was very common (particularly in the front office) to have different systems for each asset class, which also reflected the typical organizational split between equities, fixed income and asset allocation. This is to some extent still the case: for example, asset managers often have separate systems for alternative investments or commodities that are distinct from the systems handling the traditional asset classes. However, asset managers are increasingly implementing cross-asset class systems in order to have one common view on their overall portfolio.

For example, counterparty risk must include all positions held in securities issued by the counterparty across asset classes, all unsettled trades with the counterparty, all derivatives contracts with the counterparty, all derivatives contracts on underlying indices or baskets with securities issued by the counterparty, as well as any collateral exchanged with the counterparty. It is very difficult to produce this overview in a timely manner without an IBOR and with different systems per asset class and different systems holding information on collateral, unsettled trades (not just intra-day) and held versus ordered positions.

When it comes to asset class coverage, therefore, most asset managers consider it best practice to use cross-asset class systems, whereas it is still common to operate different systems to support different processes in the value chain. As previously noted, SimCorp estimates that on a global basis around one-third of all asset managers has a systems strategy that involves many disparate systems. This proportion varies between regions: for example, in North America and the UK the figure is much higher. However, many of the same arguments favoring cross-asset class systems can also be made when it comes to 'cross-process' or 'cross-organizational' integrated systems.

Reporting

Operational systems are based on data structures that are optimized for online transactional processing (OLTP) and data is typically organized in a normalized relational database. Data warehouses, by contrast, optimize data for reporting by organizing data in so-called data marts per 'topic' (as cubes or star-schemes), and data is extracted from the OLTP and loaded into the data warehouse with a certain frequency. This makes it easier to create reports and analysis by business users, thereby making them less dependent on IT support. Also having a separate data warehouse, heavy analysis does not impact the operational systems. Finally, the data warehouse typically also holds historical data, for example, information about historical client reports. Reports and BI tools then typically draw data from the data warehouse.

However, the escalating demands from regulators and clients for more transparency and timely access to ever more detailed information are increasing the requirements for reporting and BI. Traditional enterprise architectures may have a data warehouse that is updated with new and validated information perhaps once a day. This has been the customary setup for many years, where being able to validate data once every day is still very ambitious. In fact, most asset managers need several days before they have reliable data for sending out monthly reports to their clients. This is often a consequence of the traditional enterprise architecture, where data must be collected from many different systems into the data warehouse, the same data resides in multiple systems and therefore needs to be reconciled and validated, and data is often in general of such a low quality that it cannot be trusted.

The paradox here is, if data for client reports cannot be trusted without thorough validation, how can the same data then be trusted for making investment decisions on a daily basis? A fit-for-future enterprise architecture supports efforts to achieve high-quality online data for daily operations via the IBOR and, since the IBOR is the common foundation for operational systems, data coming from different systems will be much more consistent. This structure supports more reliable and timely available data for reporting.[21]

To meet the demands from regulators and clients, reporting must provide a more real-time view on data. Modern data warehouses contain both real-time data views (sometimes called advanced analytics) on operational data, as well as the end-of-day validated data for official reports and historical records that document the content of past reports.

Therefore, an enterprise architecture prepared for future strategic business challenges will contain not only traditional data warehouse and BI elements for end-of-day reporting and documentation of historical reports, but also a real-time view on data, which is based on a tight connection between the data warehouse, the IBOR and the operational systems that provide advanced calculation services, such as performance and risk figures, where totals are not simple sums but require advanced calculations that cannot be provided by the data warehouse.

Since many of the reporting requirements originate from regulators and clients, it is also important to give these stakeholders access to the information via efficient distribution channels, such as internet and mobile devices.

26.4.2   Implementation options

In the previous section, we described the main components in a fit-for-future enterprise architecture and how these components interact. There are different approaches to implementing such an enterprise architecture based either on a complex architecture with many disparate systems or a more simple and lean architecture based on one or a few integrated systems. This is a general discussion not only within asset management but also across industries, and it is not the purpose of this chapter to discuss the pros and cons of the two approaches in detail.

Generally, selecting a system for each business process provides the potential to focus on feature richness in that particular area. Reduced dependency on a single vendor is also a commonly heard argument for this strategy. On the other hand, integrated systems offer lower TCO, because the integration and reconciliation effort is much less and because the platform is much easier to maintain and upgrade.[22] This is in contrast to a complex architecture, where many disparate systems must be made compatible across patches and upgrade cycles. To simplify, one could argue that end-users focus on their own specific requirements, whereas C-level decision makers focus on lower TCO and more efficient processes across the value chain.

There will always be different sentiments toward either approach. However, given the current and future strategic business challenges, there are a number of factors that point to a trend toward the consolidation of systems across the enterprise architecture and an increased preference for a more integrated approach.

Firstly, strategic business challenges mean that many enterprise architectures must be updated to comply with new regulation, to handle new asset classes, to meet increased client demands, etc. Hence, many of the core systems in the enterprise architecture must be updated more frequently than before in order to meet these requirements in a timely manner.

Secondly, architectures with clusters of disparate systems make it very costly to ensure that all systems are compatible across upgrades: more upgrades mean higher costs. At the same time, we know that many asset managers are under pressure to improve profits and that costs are increasing across investments and operations, which would indicate that low TCO is going to take priority over feature richness in the coming period.

A consolidation of systems is likely to save costs, as there are typically large-scale effects to be gained in addition to the arguments cited earlier. For example, hardware resources can be better utilized, operational staff require less training with only one system, and it is easier to maintain fewer vendor relationships.

The previous section described a number of areas, where core business processes involve several roles, and are therefore difficult to support optimally with a traditional split between front-, middle- and back-office systems. As mentioned earlier in this chapter, there has been a similar debate about replacing 'single asset class' systems with 'cross-asset class' systems, now a generally accepted best practice. In many ways, this is a comparable situation to replacing 'single process' systems with 'integrated cross-process' systems. Integrated data, as well as integrated workflows, will in many cases better support the strategic business challenges.

The trend is also supported by the fact that many software vendors across front, middle and back office are broadening their offerings to cover the tighter integration of processes across the value chain.

Having said all this, few software applications cover the entire value chain to an extent where they fulfil all the asset manager's requirements. While this section argues that integrated systems strategies are best positioned to fulfil the asset manager's strategic business challenges, the most likely choice for many asset managers is to have one main system as their core solution, covering as much of the value chain as possible and then having a number of add-on systems to fill the gaps.

26.4.3   Benefits of the fit-for-future Architecture

The IBOR solves many of the problems of traditional enterprise architectures, because it consolidates information in one place to produce a common and complete view across front, middle and back office.

For the front office, the benefits of an IBOR reside in minimizing the risk of wrong investment decision-making owing to poor quality, incomplete or imprecise position data, and of having an inaccurate and incomplete picture of risk exposures.

The IBOR also provides the foundation for better risk management as well as supporting legislation, such as Dodd-Frank, EMIR or Solvency II, all of which have highlighted the need for having an accurate, online view of risks in the form of counterparty exposures across all asset classes including collateral and exposures to the underlying assets of derivatives.

For the back office, the benefits of having an IBOR are related to having an independent view of positions. The IBOR provides a basis of control for having multiple service providers, since it serves as a single point of aggregation and alignment across service providers.

Furthermore, should the business need arise and depending upon the operating model employed, individual outsourced business functions can be brought back in-house, retained functions can be outsourced, or migration from one outsourced service supplier to another is facilitated. Finally, the IBOR also provides the basis for reconciliation against custodians or accounting systems.

The fit-for-purpose enterprise architecture does not have any legacy systems and is based on one or a few systems supporting the entire value chain. This enables the asset manager to achieve more efficient workflows across the value chain to better support the processes that are shared between organizational units. It will also simplify the architecture in terms of integration points and number of systems that have to be maintained on a daily basis and across upgrade cycles, and this in turn will save costs.

By having fewer systems and integration points and no legacy systems, the asset manager will be in a much better position to support changes to the business model where new products and financial instruments can be implemented faster and more easily. This also goes for implementation of legal requirements, expansion into new markets and increasing volumes.

26.4.4   Migration paths

The first important decision for CTOs is to acknowledge whether or not there is an issue with the existing architecture. If some of the problems outlined in this chapter prevail, it is simply not an option to do nothing.

The next thing to consider is how to shift from the current enterprise architecture (As-Is) to the fit-for-future enterprise architecture (To-Be). This is not a trivial question, as CTOs will be weighing expected outcome against costs and implementation risks.

There are two fundamentally different approaches.

Data warehouse on top of legacy architecture

One approach that might be tempting at first glance is to leave the existing architecture as it is but adding a data warehouse on top of it that consolidates data for reporting to provide the missing overview (see Figure 26.10). This approach basically says 'impose order on the chaos by adding a layer on top'.

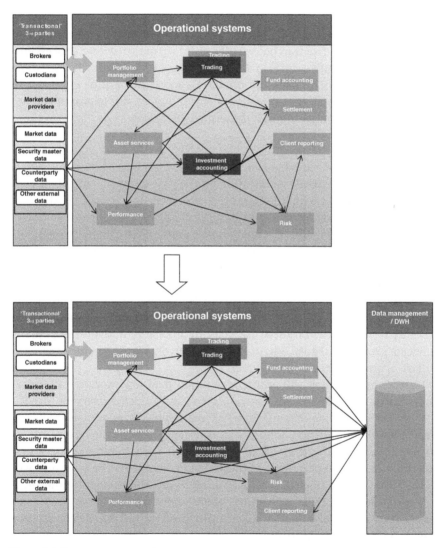

Figure 26.10 Introduction of a data management system to solve issues with legacy architectures

But a range of critical problems persists. Legacy systems will still impose a severe business risk of not being able to change a business model with new financial products or adapt to new regulation. Adding a data warehouse layer hardly solves the basic problem of data everywhere and multiple versions of the truth. The data warehouse may provide data for reporting purposes, but there will still be silos of operation using their 'own' data.

Combining the data warehouse with market data management is a step in the right direction, but there will still be 'multiple versions of the truth' in terms of positions, transactions, valuations, forecasts, etc. Operational inconsistencies, errors and reconciliation issues will remain.

The ensuing operational infrastructure complexity is a cost escalator and increasing it with a data warehouse will only make matters worse. Process efficiency will not improve, since cross-organizational processes will have to go through a number of systems and interfaces, and it will still be expensive to operate and upgrade all the disparate systems. All in all, this approach will not enable the asset manager to reach the desired To-Be state.

Clean up legacy architecture

The alternative approach is to identify the root cause – which is the unwelcome complexity of the current architecture and legacy systems – and then consolidate and replace with future-proven system(s). In contrast to the first approach, this alternative says 'get rid of the chaos by replacing it with order'. It places the asset manager in a much better position for driving the business forward and addressing the strategic challenges the business faces.

Replacing a host of systems in one step may of course introduce undesirable risks. However, there is no need to take such a 'big bang' approach. Any concrete guidance for the order of implementation would always depend on the specific pain points. Typically, it would be a priority to replace legacy systems in order to reduce the business risk of being unable to develop the business model or satisfy regulators. This process could involve consolidation of systems to save operational costs.

Introducing an IBOR will ensure a common data repository for all operations across the value chain, providing the consolidated overview needed for improved decision-making and risk management, as well as reducing dependency on third-party administrators. When replacing the legacy systems in Figure 26.11's step 1, it should be done in such a way that it serves as a first step in implementing an IBOR, as illustrated in steps 2–4. The asset manager may further reduce implementation risk by instead implementing the IBOR as the first step and replacing legacy systems and consolidation as the second step. This is also a viable approach bearing in mind the risk associated with still having legacy systems as part of the architecture.

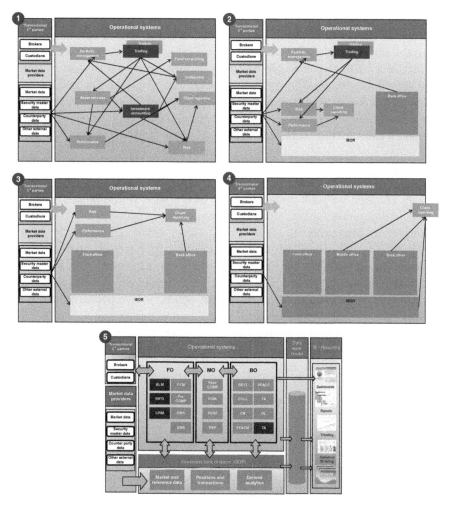

Figure 26.11 Simplified illustration of migration path toward the desired To-Be architecture

Finally, a robust reporting architecture should be introduced to provide transparency and timely distribution of information to clients and regulators (Figure 26.11's step 5). The exact reporting requirements should be evaluated and it should be decided what type of reporting is to be run off the data warehouse and how best to achieve a more real-time view on data as well. The IBOR is obviously instrumental here, since it provides online positions and transactions; but other types of information, such as online calculations of performance and risk figures, would have to be sourced directly from these systems as an online service. All this is quite ambitious, however, and it should of course be assessed how important this requirement is.

In the end, the order of implementation always depends on the specific pain points of a particular enterprise. Some solutions, as in the case of SimCorp Dimension, can be used to solve most of the challenges of traditional enterprise architectures. By using one integrated solution, it may be easier to let the next phase of the implementation build on the preceding step in order to achieve a clean architecture with as few systems as possible.

26.5   Conclusion

In this chapter, we have described some of the strategic business challenges asset managers are facing, along with some of the problems of traditional enterprise architectures.

We propose a leaner fit-for-future enterprise architecture that is better prepared to support changes in business and operating models.

It is important not to fall into the trap of trying to solve the problems by introducing a data warehouse as yet another component in the architecture, as this just adds to the complexity.

Instead, asset managers are recommended to clean up their architecture by replacing legacy systems, introducing and investment book of record and a robust reporting infrastructure.

The implementation should proceed in measured steps in order to manage project risks, where each step builds on the previous to arrive at the desired architecture.

Notes

1. McKinsey, 'The Asset Management Industry: Outcomes are the New Alpha', Report on the '2012 McKinsey North American Asset Management Benchmark Survey'.
2. A similar picture emerges for European asset managers, according to the '2012 McKinsey/US Institute Asset Management Survey.'
3. Deloitte: 'Alpha or Beta? Challenges and opportunities for traditional active managers', 2010 (http://www.deloitte.com/assets/Dcom-UnitedKingdom/Local%20Assets/Documents/Industries/Financial%20Services/UK_FS_Alpha_or_Beta.pdf).
4. McKinsey: 2012 McKinsey North America Asset Management Benchmark Survey.
5. Forbes: 'Indexes Beat Active Funds Again in S&P Study', 11 October 2012 (http://www.forbes.com/sites/rickferri/2012/10/11/indexes-beat-active-funds-again-in-sp-study/).
6. Russell: '2012 Global Survey on Alternative Investing', June 2012 (http://www.russell.com/institutional/research_commentary/alternative-investing-survey.asp?wt.mc_id=altsurvey2012).
7. McKinsey: 2012 McKinsey North America Asset Management Benchmark Survey.
8. Investit: 'Investment Management Firms Prove Clients are at the Top of Their Agenda in 2013', 30 January 2013 (http://www.investit.com/investment-management-firms-prove-clients-are-at-the-top-of-their-agenda-in-2013/#more-2329).

9. CEB TowerGroup: 'Outsourcing: Vendor Analysis', 2012.
10. Efama, 'Worldwide Investment Fund Assets and Flows: Trends in the third quarter of 2012', January 2013.
11. Ibid.
12. SimCorp polls are based on specific questions for an invited audience typically in connection with webinars. The results are indicative rather than statistically verifiable.
13. SimCorp regularly conducts comprehensive market surveys based on responses from a significant representation of asset managers globally.
14. Woodbine Associates: 'Maximize Alpha of Investment Accounting Platforms', 15 February 2013 (http://www.iss-mag.com/news/woodbine-associates-maximize-alpha-of-investmen).
15. Schröter, Marc: 'The investment book of record: one version of truth from front to back office', *Journal of Applied IT and Investment Management*, vol 5, no 1, January 2013.
16. Investit: 'The Future of Investment Operations in Australia', November 2011.
17. Beacon Consulting Group: 'Beacon PeerView: Oversight Q3', 2011.
18. FSA's 'Dear CEO' letter of 11 December 2012 about contingency plans for outsourcing arrangements http://www.fsa.gov.uk/library/communication/ceo
19. Schröter, Marc: 'The investment book of record: one version of truth from front to back office', *Journal of Applied IT and Investment Management*, vol 5, no 1, January 2013.
20. For example, duration, yield to maturity, delta vectors, convexity, delta, gamma, etc.
21. Systems and architectures do not guarantee high data quality in its own right – this requires good data governance as well.
22. Raul L. Katz, Ph.D and Juan Pablo Pereira: 'Assessing TCO for Best-of-Suite Versus Best-of-Breed Architectures in the Communications Service Industry', 2007.

References

Beacon Consulting Group, Inc. (2011) 'Beacon PeerView: Oversight Q3'.
CEB TowerGroup (2012) 'Outsourcing: Vendor Analysis', 2012.
Deloitte (2010) 'Alpha or Beta? Challenges and opportunities for traditional active managers'.
Efama (2013) 'Worldwide Investment Fund Assets and Flows: Trends in the third quarter of 2012', January, http://www.deloitte.com/assets/Dcom-UnitedKingdom/Local%20Assets/Documents/Industries/Financial%20Services/UK_FS_Alpha_or_Beta.pdf
Forbes (2012) 'Indexes Beat Active Funds Again in S&P Study', 11 October., http://www.forbes.com/sites/rickferri/2012/10/11/indexes-beat-active-funds-again-in-sp-study/
Investit (2013) 'Investment Management Firms Prove Clients are at the Top of Their Agenda in 2013', 30 January. http://www.investit.com/investment-management-firms-prove-clients-are-at-the-top-of-their-agenda-in-2013/#more-2329
Investit (2011) 'The Future of Investment Operations in Australia', November.
Katz, R.L. and Pereira, J.P. (2007) 'Assessing TCO for Best-of-Suite Versus Best-of-Breed Architectures in the Communications Service Industry', April.
McKinsey, 'The Asset Management Industry: Outcomes are the New Alpha', Report on the '2012 McKinsey North American Asset Management Benchmark Survey'.

Russell (2012) '2012 Global Survey on Alternative Investing', June, http://www.russell.com/institutional/research_commentary/alternative-investing-survey.asp?wt.mc_id=altsurvey2012

Schröter, M. (2013) 'The investment book of record: one version of truth from front to back office', *Journal of Applied IT and Investment Management*, (5)1, January.

Woodbine Associates (2013) 'Maximize Alpha of Investment Accounting Platforms', 15 February.

http://www.iss-mag.com/news/woodbine-associates-maximize-alpha-of-investment-accounting-platforms

Part VII
Future Challenges and Growth

27

The Strategic Imperative of Creating and Capturing Value

Paul Verdin

27.1 Introduction: uncertain and challenging times

These are uncertain times. That is the understatement of the last few years, if not of the last decade. While this could also apply to the political, social, demographic and even the scientific, technological and climate front, what has happened on the financial and economic scene in the past couple of years is unprecedented in terms of magnitude and global coverage, even if the underlying mechanics and principles were not without parallel or historical basis and bias.[1]

The causes and the results of the financial crisis have by now been aptly and widely described.[2] The full consequences, however, have certainly not been well understood or played out – not for the financial markets and the (dys) functioning financial system, nor certainly for the economy in general. We avoid here the term 'real' economy – as if the financial markets were rather imaginary or virtual, i.e., not real (if anything the experience of the last few years has blatantly illustrated how 'real' they actually are) or as if one could function without the other (no economy except the most rudimentary barter economy could exist without some kind of financial market).

The financial markets seem to have recovered significantly from their deepest contraction and have found a renewed type of stability. Risk appetite has returned in a shape and form that sometimes makes one wonder about the kind of amnesia that may be governing our current markets. Liquidity has been restored, although not quite across the entire spectrum of markets and instruments. Volatility is down again to almost pre-crisis levels, although this should not be confused with a possible decline in underlying risk – the different types and interactions of which we have just been reminded in the darkest days of recent market debacles.

In fact, it might well be argued that it was a substantial neglect of or at least underestimation of the correlation between different types of risk on the one hand, and the confusion between actual *risk* (and how it may affect underlying value) and *volatility* (as measured by the latest market transaction prices) on the other, that was at the root of many of our troubles.[3]

In addition, we were reminded that 'markets' or 'financial systems' only function through people who are sometimes subject to very strange and not always predictable swings in moods and behaviors, thereby giving a firm boost to the relatively recent field of 'behavioral finance': the study of how human behavior affects the (dys)functioning, particular opportunities and outcomes of financial markets and investing strategies, as well as their potential implications for new product development and design.[4]

Financial markets remain fragile, however, as they are still sustained by the vast amounts of government support, actual or implicit. Very little, if any, structural reform has taken place so far, and the 'too big to fail' syndrome has propelled the previously rather academic concept of 'moral hazard' to the forefront of concerns for the immediate if not the distant future. In addition, the banking system is still not providing the amounts and especially the conditions for credit that borrowers would like to see, while both lenders and borrowers are still taking part in a massive de-leveraging in large sectors of the economy.

The adjustments in the economy are still working their way out and may need a lot more time if history is anything to go by – perhaps years to come. Inadequate or untimely government 'exit strategies' remain a delicate and unpredictable threat, while concerns about the public sector deficits have thrown financial markets already back into heavy turmoil and questions remain about a 'private credit bubble' having been replaced by a 'public' one.

Is the 'real economy' recovery for real? The free fall has been halted, but is what we have seen more than just a bounce-back on its way to a 'double dip' (a W-type, assuming we recover after the second dip)? Or is it the beginning of sharp recovery (a 'V', most likely not for most economies given the available data) or a modest if sustained recovery (a full-fledged or asymmetric 'U', or 'amputated U or V' as some commentators call it)? Even an 'L' or protracted 'U' is not entirely out of the question in some places.

The resumption of growth in the 'emerging' economies has certainly been impressive, up to the point that questions persist about its sustainability and it becoming the possible source of the next downturn, particularly in view of the overdue correction of global imbalances. Structural adjustments by nature or definition are difficult and painful, as fundamental shifts and changes are always hard to accomplish. They are hard to make real in the corporate world, and they are even harder to decide on and implement on a global scale, especially in the public sector.

'Predictions are hard to make, especially about the future', it is often said. We should not be spending much time or effort on predictions, for at least two reasons. First of all, the actual track record of economic forecasts and predictions is generally very poor. Several studies tracking the validity of forecasts against actual developments have confirmed this, and those studies include the possible 'self-fulfilling prophecy' bias potentially associated with any generally regarded and accepted forecasts, as planners, strategists, investors may base their decisions to some extent on the forecasts made, thereby helping them to become reality. Even so, most forecasts do not go further than extrapolating on the past (if not in trend, then in the structural model that is behind it) and they break down completely when confronted with the kinds of events that we have just witnessed. For this reason, we would argue to ignore the forecasts, but – given the high degree of uncertainty – keep a close eye on the actual data. Who was it who said, 'In God we trust; everybody else, give us data' (not forecasts)?

Secondly and more importantly, from a business and corporate point of view, it is not the economy or the overall environment that will determine your success for the most part, but rather the other way around. *Companies are successful because of what companies do (and don't do)* in their own business, in their market, in their own organization and strategy and not primarily because of what 'the economy' or even 'the market' or 'the industry' did or will do.

Likewise, 'the economy' is the result of what companies do – and not the other way around – a simple fact some economists (especially macroeconomists of the 'old' school) sometimes seem to forget. Several studies over the last several years have illustrated or proven that point with a variety of approaches and data.[5] Similar results have been obtained on 'the way down' – i.e. what makes companies stumble or fail.[6] 'Firms don't fail because of what the world does to them but because of what they do to themselves', as Jim Collins stated in the middle of the crisis.[7] Or exactly the opposite of what President Clinton used to say about his success in the elections: 'It's the economy, stupid'. But now and for us in the business world it is the *company*, stupid![8]

This is both good and bad news. It means we cannot just blame a poor performance on the economy or the sector – and we cannot or should not hope for the sector or the economy to take us out of the doldrums. The good news is that much of our success lies in our own hands – certainly over the long haul. And this is what strategy and a strategic perspective are all about.

27.2 An increasingly competitive business

What does this all mean for the asset management business? As with many sectors, it certainly means that a quick return to (easy) growth is not in the cards, whatever some upbeat commentators and analysts are pretending.[9] Waiting for 'back to business as usual' will certainly not be our method. If anything it should be 'back to the basics of the business'. But what is the business about? And what is it that will make us successful going forward? How will we outperform in what might be a sloppy and probably also bumpy market environment?

Major regulatory changes are on the horizon or have already been enacted. A discussion and update is provided in Karel Lannoo's contribution to this volume (Chapter 16). There are calls for more transparency in the products, in the processes and in the organization, and clearer guidelines on governance. Clients are becoming more demanding on liquidity and more sensitive to potential conflicts of interest within the organizations that asset managers often belong to.

And, last but not least, they are taking a closer look at fees, commissions and costs, especially as they are eating away a larger share of their return in a low-interest, low-return (and possibly also higher-tax, given the state of public finances) environment. In addition, as evidence is mounting throughout the crisis about the overall underperformance of the average active investment management business as compared to passive and low-cost or other focused operators, the need for a clear reassessment of strategy and strategic choices is apparent. Earlier in this volume (Chapter 2), Massimo Massa provides a chilling and sobering picture of what his and other academic experts' recent research shows us on this front.

One thing is clear as a result of all this: the business is certainly becoming more – rather than less – competitive and challenging. There has been, and could be a further, trend toward consolidation and a few large global players dominating the scene. However, there are equally important trends toward downsizing, particularly on the banking scene, and the shifts in preferences and power of the client as well as regulation could open clear opportunities for newcomers and focused 'niche players' or outperforming 'boutiques'.

Other industries have been in such a situation before. For years, we could see the easy money flowing and the likely crisis coming. For a long time, nothing happened and everyone wondered why questions are raised about the sustainability – and then, often in an unexpected fashion or due to an unexpected shock, major shifts take hold, and the business is shocked and taken apart. We may be on the verge of such a situation in asset management, or we may not (yet) be. At any event, now is the time to start asking (or repeat) the basic strategic questions. How will we be successful in the future? How will we do better than the business next door? How and where will we find the growth?

To illustrate the questions and challenge facing the industry and as a push to start thinking about the possible answers, we turn to a simple framework we have developed over years of strategy-making in a variety of sectors and industries, not only in financial services.[10] What we are witnessing in the asset management business is not unlike the challenges many other businesses have been facing, especially those that used to be run on the basis of a rather limited competition, protected by regulatory conditions, stable technology, local market conditions, poor customer scrutiny and, as a result, the relatively strong power and mutual understanding of major players.

Such was the situation in the 'old' telecoms world and other not-so-old 'utilities' such as electricity, gas, water production or distribution, traditional pharma, and indeed in major areas of financial services and insurance industries. They found themselves earning a (more than) decent return without too much competition, able to capture a great deal of value (for shareholders or stakeholders such as management, employees or even the public sector) while only creating the minimum value for customers or the market. This situation is illustrated by the first position in Figure 27.1(lower right-hand corner): in many ways the good old 'dream' of many businesses.

While the first position seems like a dream, enjoy it while it lasts, because dreams don't last forever. Sooner or later competition catches up, (de)regulation strikes, technology shifts or the market changes. We have observed this in many industries. It may occur much later or more slowly than expected, e.g., in different parts of financial services and asset management, or it may strike with a bang as in the 'Big Bang' of deregulation in the eighties and the beginning of the nineties or, most recently, through the financial crashes.

Not that we could not see it coming if we were honest. There has undoubtedly been ample opportunity for the 'value-capturing' game in asset management, as bluntly stated by David Swensen, the celebrated manager of the Yale University Endowment:

> *The overwhelming number of investors fail because the fees charged by the investment management industry are egregious relative to the amount of value that is added. It is really quite stunning.*[11]

Worse still, long before the crisis struck, I remember some asset managers (from some of the banks that later were hammered by the crisis) confessing to me 'we seem to be off the chart!!' by which they meant 'we are earning good money by capturing value but actually we are not even creating any value for our customers', referring to the average underperformance of active asset managers compared to their benchmarks or the indices. That indeed would put them even below quadrant no. 1 in Figure 27.1 above, destroying value for clients – while still making handsome returns for managers and shareholders of the asset management companies involved. According to the former CEO of Credit Suisse Asset Management:

> *I have long believed customers are not getting a good deal from asset managers.*[12]

The immediate reaction of market participants to increased competition or deregulation, however, often starts with denial, which turns into inertia or a

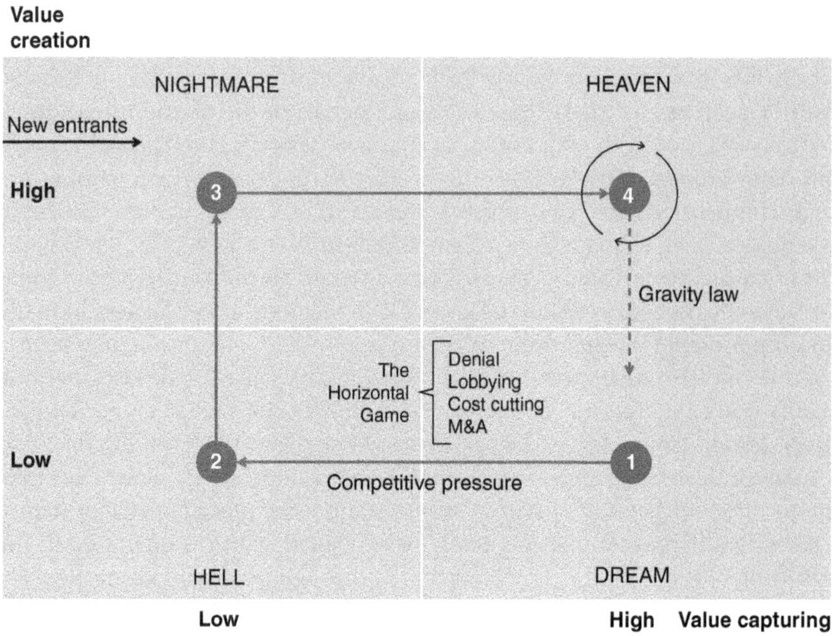

Figure 27.1   The dynamics of the value creation-capturing framework
Source: Paul Verdin, 2009.

slide back into old habits and tricks. It often moves further to outright attempts to restore the past and engage in defensive moves. 'It won't happen to us', they say. 'We are different.' Or perhaps repeating, 'This time is different', 'It won't happen so soon', 'We will worry about it later' or 'Professor, you don't understand. This does not apply to us: *we are a Swiss insurance company!*' (This was before the investment management side almost killed them.) Then again, there is the 'knowing-doing gap': 'We'll change tomorrow; let's enjoy the ride while it lasts' and 'Let's hope we can ride again when markets recover.'

We can try and fight back, and hold onto privileged dominance through lobbying or other defensive tactics as embedded in 'strategic' alliances, (anti) competitive practices, and mergers and acquisitions inspired by 'buying competitors rather than beating them', 'capturing market share' or 'industry consolidation' (based on not-so-well-understood economies of scale, elusive synergies, or just a way to keep a too-high cost base in place).

Deliberate attempts to reduce transparency or sneak-in price increases in the wake of mounting competition are very popular choices, as sometimes preached by desperate consultants or practiced by short-term opportunists, especially in today's high-pressure environment. I like to call this 'playing the horizontal game', i.e., trying to move back on the horizontal axis to position 1, just like one-off cost-cutting or restructuring programs, even if unavoidable in certain areas and conditions.

Sooner or later, however, we risk being pushed into the lower left-hand corner (position 2) – this is not an enviable situation, as value added or value creation for clients is still under pressure and the possibility of capturing any of it is drastically reduced. This is typically the situation of commodity businesses or commodity traps. 'We are stuck.' How can we escape? It is hard, but not impossible: through the long, hard work of arduously climbing the mountain of value creation through innovation, moving up along the vertical axis.

This is exactly what CEOs were referring to when asked about their top strategic priorities in a 'survey of surveys', we carried out right before the crisis.[13] While acknowledging that increased competitive pressure was seen as the overarching concern across a variety of industries, including the financial sector, top priorities were aiming at growth and innovation. It is interesting to note that both were seen to go hand in hand.

'Either you innovate or you are in commodity hell', declared Samuel Palmisano at IBM following Lou Gerstner's dramatic turnaround starting from the customer. According to Jeff Inmelt, CEO of GE: 'Constant reinvention is the central necessity at GE. ... We're all just a moment away from commodity hell.' These sentiments were echoed by many more, at least before the crisis. And while the crisis may have made this challenge all the more demanding, the fundamental requirements have not changed. 'One of the biggest mistakes that can be made right now is to slash investments in innovation. ... If you fail to fund the future, all you'll be left with is a really lean company trying to churn old ideas into new business', as aptly put by Anne Mulcahy, now chairman of Xerox.

The most recent McKinsey Global Survey confirms: 'Executives expect that the most powerful effects on their companies will be increased innovation, greater consumer awareness and knowledge, and increased product and service customisation.' [14]

27.3 Value creation and innovation

Value creation in competitive markets requires continuous innovation in order to provide ever more value to the client. There is no other way, however much our current effort and attention may be focused on short-term fire-fighting or cost-cutting. In fact, *the more competitive your market gets, the less you should focus directly on your competition,* because the only way to beat that competition is to deliver better value to clients.

Even today there are really only two ways to consistently create value and innovate: either go for 'cost innovation', the continuous, relentless innovation in your business model, value or supply chain so that you can continuously offer ever-lower prices to clients, or go for 'value innovation', the continuous search to offer ever-better and -greater (and possibly different bundles of) value to customers, based on the drivers and attributes of value they perceive and appreciate most. Current recessionary times may provide a renewed impulse and opportunity to select this last option by forcing further improvements in value-for-money strategies.[15]

Climbing up the wall of innovation, however, still does not offer easy solace, as it makes us go through a nightmare (position 3 in Figure 27.1), even if we manage to please the client and add real or perceived value. Eventually, we need to be able to translate the higher value into higher margins: through higher prices, in the case of a value innovation strategy, or through higher volume driven by lower prices, in the case of cost innovation strategies. Both strategies will lead to profitable and healthy growth. But growth is not the driver of the strategy – it is the result of it. Most – in fact, all – successful companies actually reach the point (position 4) of being able to add good value and capture enough of it in the process in a consistent and continual way.

We need to keep working at it, if only because of competitive pressure constantly trying to diminish or devalue our competitive advantage. Otherwise, we may start slipping, losing sight of the client, cutting innovation and eventually falling down into the lower right-hand quadrant. The law of gravity will take over. Blinded as we will be by our own success or our own strong position, we will be trying to hold onto value capturing while losing our value creation potential, jeopardizing our long-term strategic health and thus sustainable growth.

IBM, Microsoft and Intel, to name but a few, have gone through this cycle at least once before. Fighting antitrust authorities is often part of the final stages, and time has come to face the next competitive cycle. The only way to avoid this ordeal is to focus again on innovating and facing up to competition rather than obstructing it.

In asset management as anywhere else, defensive 'value-capture strategies' have not quite fallen out of fashion, as illustrated by the following statement signalling a possible back-tracking from the 'open architecture' distribution model adopted at many banks before the crisis under increasing competition:

> *The current recession means many institutions are pushing their own products, in an attempt to keep all possible earnings from selling funds in-house.*[16]

The question remains, however, whether such a move back is even sustainable in today's more competitive environment. Indeed, we hear many more wake-up calls than ever before, urging us to face up to the innovation and value creation challenge:

The asset management industry understands it needs to align itself better with investors' interests.[17]

We don't think enough with our clients and for our clients.[18]

Some observers are clearly pushing further, linking the need for a renewed focus on clients back to questioning the appropriate governance model:

Being created to think solely about the investor has been critical. We don't have to worry about family, shareholders, or partners. It is a wonderful business model.[19]

This argument was made by Vanguard, referring to their corporate governance model going hand in hand with a distinct client value proposition and business model (See also Figure 27.2).

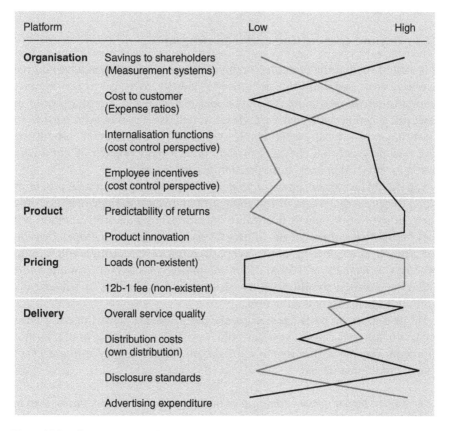

Figure 27.2   The Vanguard Value Curve

In conclusion, a successful strategy should always be guided by creating perceived value for the client and the market, while of course also being able to capture at least some of that value through pricing (fees, commission, basis points, etc.) in a continuous and consistent way. An undue or unbalanced focus on either one of those two basic dimensions of strategy invariably leads to problems or even disaster, particularly over the medium-to-long term. This is exactly what strategy and growth should be concerned with.

Beyond risk management and cost-cutting, the next if not more important challenge for long-term success is to identify the relevant drivers or attributes of value for the groups of clients or segments we want to serve and explore new ways of delivering that value in a better, more efficient way than ever before. Growth can thus never be simply more of the same or a return to the past. In these trying times, it is a golden opportunity to examine these questions again and to go beyond the easy games of value capturing, merging and acquiring, or just riding the market booms which have benefited, but also equally blinded, many a provider in recent times.

27.4   Beyond cost-cutting and lean programs

It is very likely that the preceding boom and asset price inflation have allowed excessive costs and non-value activities to flourish, covered by easy revenues from an increasing volume of assets under management. The sharp drop in asset prices compounded with a decrease in net asset flows or even outflow of assets has exposed many asset managers' profitability. A focus on cost-cutting and lean programs has therefore already proven quite popular, if not a condition for survival or short-term profitability for many.

You should be warned, however, that an overly eager focus on such programs when not properly framed in the context of an overall strategy may not only turn out to be non-strategic (tactical or operational in pure survival mode) but may become even antistrategic – if they divert attention from a proper focus on the required strategic focus of the company going forward. Unless you want to become the 'Ryanair' or 'Wal-Mart' of the industry, a focus on customer value and value creation should drive the strategy, not a mindless or strategically unfounded focus on cost reduction.

While a focus on costs has been understandable in today's lingering crisis environment, you cannot cost-cut your way out of the crisis and even less grow your way out of the crisis by cutting costs. Anne Mulcahy, former CEO of Xerox, put it quite nicely:

> *One of the biggest mistakes that can be made right now is to slash investments in innovation. ... If you fail to fund the future, all you'll be left with is a really lean company trying to churn old ideas into new business.*[20]

More specifically, one should be careful not to smuggle in cost strategies – which are only sensible when accompanied by a consistent low-price strategy – where, in most cases, value strategies should be aimed. Pure size, scale or leverage strategies are not a suitable answer either, as leveraging or scaling up a poor business or inadequate business model only lands you with a bigger bad business or a business model still performing poorly. In other words, as you cannot hope to grow your way out of an overhead that is too high, you cannot grow your way out of a bad business model or a poor strategy, either.

In addition, an ill-conceived growth strategy involves a risk of increasing your overall 'strategic risk' while not delivering any substantial benefit (as argued by Mathias Schmit and Lyn-Sia Chao in Chapter 8 of this book).[21] This should be a stern warning in view of the observation which emerged from the recent 'Global Investment Management Growth Survey 2010' by SimCorp StrategyLab that most asset managers are looking for growth (growth ranked as a top priority by 2/3 of those surveyed). Yet an equal number of respondents (that is, 2/3) do not have a particular framework as a concept for achieving such growth.[22]

27.5 A renewed focus on creating value for the customer

If a renewed focus on value creation for customers is the message, the question arises of what that really means. What constitutes 'value' to customers? As in other sectors and businesses, value is usually a multidimensional concept, a 'catch-all' that must be deconstructed and analyzed in greater detail. The crisis has only made such analysis even more pressing:

> *Customers used to focus only on returns. Now they are asking questions about liquidity and transparency.*[23]

> *Everyone is fundamentally re-thinking their approach to investing and manager selection.*[24]

To illustrate a useful approach to this question, let us take a popular example: a car. What are you looking for when you are in the market for a new car: speed, status symbol, safety, comfort, fuel efficiency, versatility, ease of use, experience, or – who knows – perhaps even transportation (positive attributes to be maximized)? Or are you looking for low cost, environmental friendliness, least damaging to pedestrians, or quietness (negative attributes to be avoided or minimized)? Of course, this list of 'attributes' runs much longer and should be further broken down into much greater detail, e.g., what do you mean by 'safety' (active or passive, for whom, under what conditions, etc.) or 'speed' (acceleration from zero or from a higher point, maximum speed, etc.)? What kind of comfort are you looking for (quietness, sound system, seat quality, dashboard, etc.)? Thus one can arrive at the long list of features and/or gadgets that end up decorating our cars, some 'standard' and others 'options'.

Clearly not all value attributes are equally important (for all customers). Some are much more prevalent than others. Some are so important they are to be considered 'basic' or 'must haves'. Others are more secondary and a means of differentiation from the competition. Note that competition takes place not always on the most important or crucial attributes, but often only on secondary ones. For example, safety for airlines may be seen as a top attribute for most customers but is generally well established and comparable across airlines, and (let's hope) most airlines do not actively compete on safety, in part because it is regulated but also because it is considered basic and essential by everyone.

Furthermore, not all attributes are equally valued by all customers. This leads us to an intuitive and useful definition of what may constitute a 'segment': a group of customers that value the same (selection of) attributes – and are willing to pay for it. Conceptually the 'willingness to pay' (a condition for 'value capturing') may be distinguished from the actual 'received' or 'perceived value' by the customer (the value created for the customer). In practice, however, value 'delivered' for which the customer will not pay is quite esoteric and in fact useless or a waste of resources from the company's (or even a society's) point of view.[25]

The strategic choice for any company therefore refers to (i) deciding which particular (bundle of) attributes to focus on and to offer profitably to its customer (segments) – by relating its offer to targeted customers' preferences of attributes – thus also deciding which attributes to ignore, and (ii) distinguishing its particular offer in any meaningful and sustainable way from that of any (existing or potential) competitor.

In order to do this profitably, of course, our offer should also refer to our particular strengths, assets, resources, competencies or capabilities, allowing us to deliver a superior offer to customers in a more profitable way than anyone else. Naturally, the basic tests for a good strategy remain valid: (i) how can we be better than the competition in any sustainable way and (ii) do we have what it takes?

Along these lines, Figure 27.2 provides a possible illustration of the Vanguard Value Curve (orange line) as compared to a representative competitor (brown line) on a number of selected attributes.[26]

This also implies that we constantly should strive to improve our value offer, as competition is bound to erode any advantage we may have on any (combination of) relevant attributes. Thus we should not only focus on delivering well the attributes 'as is' (as they are today) but also on the 'to be' (where we strive for and aim to improve going forward), setting out the direction of our strategic ambitions in very specific terms.

This is illustrated in the accompanying chart (Figure 27.2) which shows, for illustrative purposes only, a list of (positive/negative) attributes, our 'current offer' to customers (as is), and our current (closest or most relevant) competitor offer, all of which should be the result of a simple, but structured strategy process within your own company. In a more complete process, we should also include our 'to be' value curve, a validation with actual and potential customers, and of course the link to the required and available resources, competences or capabilities to be able to deliver the chosen attributes.

Various aspects of this approach have been covered in the illuminating and almost concurrent work by Gunther-McGrath & MacMillan and Kim & Mauborgne.[27] A focus on attributes leads to the conclusion that 'products are not products' – they are the (sometimes transient) carriers or conduits of attributes as the source of (perceived) value to the customer. Most, if not all, products thus are only valuable insofar as they are the source of delivering value attributes to the customer. And this reasoning may be extended to 'services' such as financial or investment or asset management services.[28]

More than ever, it is clear that strategy, then, is about choosing which value attributes to deliver and which to ignore or leave to the competition. We cannot be or do all things for all people. And then, of course, we have to deliver those attributes extremely well, i.e., focus on operational excellence and superior execution in the context of a well-conceived and suitable business model.

An adequate and working IT platform and support function can either be an enabler for delivering any chosen attributes or, indeed, could be more at the forefront of the specific value proposition or attributes that (segments of) clients are looking for (e.g., transparency, speed and clarity of information, risk management information, etc.)

Where does price (charges, fees, commissions, etc.) come into the picture? Contrary to some popular representations, I believe that unless you are aiming to be the single-minded price leader in the industry, price is best *not* to be seen as an attribute (even if clearly a negative one usually[29]): rather it is the net result of all the attributes you are aiming to deliver, which is what lies behind the popular expression 'value for money' referred to above. 'Differentiation strategies' therefore require you to determine which (bundle of) attributes to target and what the value *proposition* is resulting from that target.

27.6 From value attributes to value proposition

A value proposition undeniably almost always contains price as a key component, as 'the other side of the equation' and is thus not in and of itself a value attribute.[30] Differentiation strategies almost always refer to the potential of a multitude of attributes to highlight, and therefore can be considered as 'multidimensional' in most cases, in contrast to 'low-price' (read: low-cost) strategies, which are single-mindedly focused on just one variable or dimension: price (for customer or consumer).

Whereas this approach is very much in line with the clear 'dichotomy' between cost and differentiation strategies as largely popularized by the work of Michael Porter[31] (it is *either* cost or differentiation *or* 'stuck in the middle'), it quickly becomes clear that the 'middle' may prove a very fertile ground for various kinds of differentiation or segmentation based on the choice of which potentially new attributes to focus on. This reminds us of the third variant or 'focus' strategies as put forward by Porter – only in Porter's case this was dismissed somewhat as a possible 'niche' strategy, whereas we can see it as being applicable in a much wider context.[32]

In other words, 'price' is where 'the rubber hits the road' or the 'moment of truth' for checking whether the value bundle proposed at a given price holds up toward clients – as compared to relevant competition, obviously.

Further elaborating on what exactly constitutes 'price', however, the distinction between 'price' (or cost) and 'differentiation' strategies quickly becomes blurred, while we take into account such concepts as 'cost of ownership', 'lifetime user cost', service and maintenance costs, and, yes, even durability, reliability and serviceability, leading us to realize that even 'differentiation' strategies often come down to 'low-cost' propositions for the client, if one takes the broader and more long-term view of what constitutes 'price' or cost to the client.

In other words, quite a few 'differentiation strategies' then may prove to be more sophisticated 'low-cost' strategies, especially in professional or business-to-business markets in which the customer is a company, a business or an organization that runs on budgets and accounts – with a long-term time horizon. Why would these customers ever pay more for 'differentiated' products or services? In fact, they would do so because they turn out to be cheaper in the long run, all things considered, for their own business or that of their customers.

This approach thus forces us to take a more in-depth as well as a more integrated, holistic and strategic view of the value proposition for the customer and the basic strategies that go with it. They also lead the way toward taking a customer's perspective much more explicitly into account, with the implication that we believe that a 'value (innovation) strategy' is probably a better term than 'differentiation'. Likewise a 'low-price strategy' seems a better term than 'low-cost' – if only because a differentiation strategy ends up representing low cost to the rational or professional customer, at least over the long haul, whereas a 'value' strategy is clearly different from a low-price strategy.

27.7 Value attributes and the dynamics of competition

Value attributes and their relative importance naturally evolve over time – not only because of shifting customer preferences, but first and foremost due to the effects of competition (and the impact of regulation and/or the general progress in know-how, technology and economic possibilities). What were once 'differentiators' or even 'exciters' (e.g. turbo engine, airbags, ABS brakes or electronic traction controls) in terms of value attributes may soon be considered basic or neutral (for positive attributes), and what were once tolerable negatives (e.g. a diesel car that won't start in very cold weather) may turn into real 'dissatisfiers' or 'enragers'.[33]

As a result, competition will constantly try to devalue the (relative) value of an offer and thus eliminate or decimate any differentiation that is not based on a sustainable advantage or continuous improvement, as some observers have recently reminded us in the wake of the current crisis:

Weaker institutions that cannot differentiate themselves on product, service, or any other critical factor will slowly disappear.[34]

This is further illustrated in Figure 27.3,[35] where the red arrow running from the positive north-eastern corner of the graph down to the middle and then down

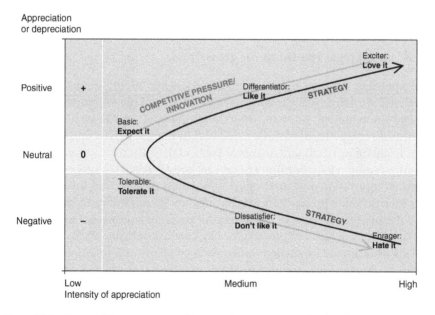

Figure 27.3 Competitive pressure and innovation strategy in the Attributes Map
Source: Adapted from Gunther McGrath-MacMillan (2005). © Paul Verdin 2010.

into negative attributes in the south-eastern corner of the graph represents the continuous pressure from competition constantly devaluing any potential temporary competitive advantage from a particular value attribute, while the blue arrow starting in the south-eastern corner pushing in the opposite direction represents the challenge of any dynamic competitive strategy constantly trying to reduce the impact of possible negative attributes or even turning them into outstanding positives.[36]

In other words, the value curves and their relative position as illustrated in Figure 27.2 tend to move, and the relevant list of attributes themselves may also change. Indeed, innovation does not only pertain to the strength of a particular (bundle of) attribute(s), but even more so to the continual development and discovery of new attributes that customers may value. This means that, while listening to customers is always a useful and good thing to do, limiting yourself to the known and express needs of your current customers obviously can be quite a constraint as well. 'If I had only listened to my customers. … all they ever wanted was a faster horse!' is a well-known saying attributed to Henry Ford.

Even more confusing is the fact that what customers say is not necessarily what they actually do, and what they say they want is not necessarily what they really need. More subtly still, they may prefer not to express their preferences, and this does not seem at all that far-fetched in such intangible and complicated areas as investment management, as Alistair Byrne illustrates brilliantly in his contribution to this volume.[37]

27.8   A strategic roadmap for growth

The approach outlined, while not rocket science or highly sophisticated, was intended to chart a roadmap for strategic growth and the milestones that must be laid out in order to get there. It hits at the basics of any successful strategy in increasing competitive markets. It requires in-depth analysis and close attention to changing needs and drivers of value to the customers: creation of value as a precondition for continuing to capture good value in the process. From the need for innovation and value creation, we must go deep into the elements of our specific value proposition, the business model necessary to make it work and the unique assets, systems, strengths and core competencies required to make them work – and to provide the basis for a sustainable advantage.

This work should be carried out by each company as a function of its own position, its assets and resources, and its ambitions. As much as in any other competitive market, this will require continuous improvement and refinement of the value proposition, which must be delivered in a consistently excellent manner, underscoring the importance of operational excellence and superior execution.

DOs	DON'Ts
Stay close to your core	Just extrapolate or multiply
Understand your core	Jump too far too fast
What are we good at? Really?	Go for size or growth per se
Leverage your strength	Spread yourself too thinly
Can we manage?	Make too many changes at once
Do we have the right resources?	Lose your identity
Know what you stand for	Lose sight of customer value
Continuously assess and improve the value created	Just 'capture' value

Figure 27.4   Some dos and don'ts for successful growth
Source: Paul Verdin 2009.

While not rocket science, it seems there is a great deal of room for improvement and opportunity: according to Massimo Massa's original contribution to this volume on the mutual fund industry, many funds lack even some of the most basic components to deliver the required basic value to clients – he even calls them 'cars without engines'. Before elaborating on the more sophisticated value attributes, there may be room to go back to some of the basics. Renewed calls for passive, index-based and low-cost investing are, of course, a logical consequence of the weaknesses of many a player in the sector.[38]

On the other hand, the doubtful recovery and economic prospects may precisely call for a more micro-based and company-focused value investing, and the simultaneous and unprecedented collapse of a wide range of markets, supposedly previously uncorrelated and a good basis for diversification, may have questioned even some of the most basic rules of asset allocation and may even have extended the potential need and reach of active investment management.

Let us conclude by reminding ourselves of some of the do's and don't's for successful growth:

27.9   Conclusion: are you 'ready for growth'?

Good strategy leads to growth: if your strategy is successful, then it will lead to growth. For this reason, it is important to be ready or 'fit' for growth in terms of the scaleability of your business model and supporting systems. An appropriate, flexible and scalable IT platform with supporting systems is then a must: a condition for growth. Companies must thus ask themselves 'how ready are we for growth?'. In our view, such growth should not be expected so much from an easy return to the favorable macroeconomic and external circumstances, but more from a keen understanding and implementation of a successful strategy adapted to the increasing and changing requirements of delivering sustained and focused customer value in an increasingly competitive market.

If we are successful in our existing activities, we may also be looking for ways to leverage or extend our success and explore new avenues in terms of products, customers (or segments) and geographic markets. However, such strategies can only be successful if they are based and built on a keen understanding of our existing core strengths and competencies. Expansion, diversification and internationalization can only be successful if built upon a position of strength and success, not on weakness or underperformance in a search for a cover-up or an escape to 'the grass that is always greener' (on the *other* side).[39]

The more competitive your business becomes, the more you should realize that sustained value creation and profitable growth will result from strategies that are aimed at creating and delivering superior value to clients – rather than entering a race to 'capture value' in existing markets or from pre-determined 'profit pools'.[40]

Long-term success, the essence of sustainable growth, will be as much of our own making as the result of spotting the right trends and riding the waves. 'The real test is not whether a company has been smartest about predicting the timing of the recovery but whether it has been truly competitive in its preparation.'[41] It will depend primarily on our taking our business into our own hands. And that requires a keen understanding of the present and the future, of the actual and potential needs of our customers and clients, of what it is that creates value for them as they see it, and of how we will be able to deliver that value better, cheaper and faster than our competitors in a truly sustainable way.

Notes

1. See some of the 'classics' on the subject, e.g. Galbraith (1954), Kindleberger (1978) and the work by the late Hyman Minsky.
2. Also in the first volume by Thomsen et al. (2009) in this SimCorp StrategyLab series.
3. We thus refer to the issue of partial risk models that take insufficient account of 'the big picture' or, in more technical terms, underestimate explicitly and especially implicitly the potential correlations between different risk classes or types of risk, especially in the case of rare but extreme events (the famous black swan or the long tail). We also refer to the role of 'mark to market' rules as they were applied and as they were at least in part responsible both for provoking and exacerbating the crisis and for possibly creating the conditions for the emergence of the next one.
4. Behavioral finance is represented in this volume particularly in the contribution by Alistair Byrne (Investit, London) and his rather novel treatment of it from the point of view of product design as distinct from the more 'traditional' interpretation of it as a factor in explaining 'anomalies' and detecting opportunities for outperformance on the investment management side. For a recent overview of the academic literature on this subject see e.g., Byrne and Brooks (2008), or for a more popular and pragmatic treatment aimed at the individual investor, see e.g., Montier (2010).

5. See our own studies, for example, which are currently in the process of being updated with new and the most recent data, both for the US and major European countries: Hawawini, Subramanian and Verdin (2005, 2004, 2003).

6. Corporate Executive Board found that most companies' growth stalls at some point (and dramatically so) due to 12% uncontrollable external factors, with the remaining 88% due to their own strategic (70%) or organizational (18%) factors (2008); see also the Harvard Business Review (2008).

7. Collins, J. (2008), 'The Secret of Enduring Greatness', Fortune, May 5. This article provides an update to the author's best-selling books 'From Good to Great' and 'Built to Last', reporting on the key success factors of a large sample of outperforming companies over the long term.

8. Such was Peter Lynch's (1994) answer even from the point of view of an investor (one of the most successful of our times), considering the (ir)relevance of 'industry' or 'sector' much along the lines of the same argument: 'If it's a choice between investing in a good company in a great industry or a great company in a lousy industry, I'll take the great company in the lousy industry any day. It's the company, stupid.'

9. Examples have been quoted in our earlier article 'Reinventing value for growth in global asset management' included January 2010 in the publication 'Enable growth strategies with SimCorp Dimension' (SimCorp, 2010).

10. An overview has also been presented in Verdin (2009).

11. Swensen, D. (2009), *Financial Times,* 26 Jan.

12. Norman, D. (2010), *Financial Times,* 18 Jan.

13. Our survey carried out in the summer of 2007 covering studies by Bain, BCG, IBM, McKinsey, PwC and the Economist Intelligence Unit, right before the crisis hit. Presented at EFQM 'Executive Roundtables' held in Athens in October 2007, Brussels in February 2008 and Paris in October 2008.

14. McKinsey Quarterly, May 2010.

15. Williamson and Zeng (2009); Kim and Mauborgne (1997).

16. Garland, R. (2009), *Financial Times,* 7 Sept.

17. Bolmstrand, N. (2009), *Financial Times,* 14 Sept.

18. Du Toit, H. (2009), *Financial Times,* 25 May.

19. McNabb, N. (2009), *Financial Times,* 4 May.

20. Mulcahy, A. (2009), *Fortune,* May 4.

21. Schmit and Chao (2010).

22. Results from the 'Global Investment Management Growth Survey 2010' performed by SimCorp Strategy-Lab and The Nielsen Company, Spring 2010.

23. MacLeod, J. (2009), *Financial Times,* 7 Sept.

24. Walkerm, G. (2009), *Financial Times,* 7 Sept.

25. This does not diminish my earlier argument, developed through the 'value creation-capturing' framework, that in a competitive market any value captured can only be based on and driven by value created, or that we cannot hope to capture any value if we do not focus on creating any for the customer. In fact, it is precisely because we cannot measure or monitor the value 'created' for the customer directly and unequivocally that we must resort to 'willingness to pay' or actual price paid as a proxy or a measure, and therefore we often fall into the trap of only focusing on the price and the capturing – thereby ignoring the creating part.

26. See Koza (2002).

27. MacMillan and McGrath (1996); McGrath and MacMillan (2005); Kim and Mauborgne (1997, 2005).

28. The somewhat simplistic if not superficial distinction between 'goods' or 'products' and 'services' and a similar distinction between 'production' and 'service' sectors therefore evaporates again, as it had also been rightly questioned from a complementary perspective such as that developed by Teboul (2006) in 'Service is Front Stage: Positioning services for value advantage' (INSEAD Business Press/Palgrave MacMillan, 2006).
29. Price is the sacrifice made by the customer and therefore obviously in most cases a 'negative' value attribute. However, even if this seems obvious in most cases, it could be argued that in some (end) consumer markets, as well as in highly intangible services markets, price may sometimes act as a positive attribute (as with so-called Veblen goods) insofar as price signals (otherwise unmeasurable) quality and/or price plays with a 'snob effect' or a 'show off' factor for high-end customers.
30. Except in the cases referred to above, in the previous footnote.
31. Porter (1985).
32. A similar argument has been developed in the current recessionary environment in the recent article by Williamson and Zeng (2009).
33. Referring to the different types of attributes as proposed by MacMillan and McGrath (1996).
34. BCG Global Asset Management Report 2009, 'Conquering the Crisis', July 2009.
35. My own adaptation of the attribute map developed by MacMillan and McGrath (1996).
36. The colors used are more in line with the 'red' ocean of competition on existing or known attributes discussed in Kim and Mauborgne (2005) versus the 'blue ocean' of new attributes that may allow you (at least temporarily) to avoid or outsmart the most competitive arena in your market.
37. Byrne (2010).
38. See e.g., Malkiel and Ellis (2010).
39. As amply argued and supported in the path-breaking work by Zook and Allen (2001) and by Zook (2004).
40. While the notion and the definition, measurement and distribution of a 'profit pool' in any given industry or market is an extremely useful concept – ex-post – as originally introduced by Gadiesh and Gilbert (1998), it should in our view not be taken as a pre-determined or given factor that is external to the (successful) strategies and dynamics in that industry, as we have argued and illustrated elsewhere based on our large-scale empirical studies quoted above: Hawawini, Subramanian and Verdin (2003).
41. 'Innovating for the upturn', Accenture Report, 2003.

References

Accenture Report (2003) 'Innovating for the upturn'.

BCG Global Asset Management Report (2009) 'Conquering the Crisis', July 2009.

Byrne, A. (2010) 'Designing products for reluctant investors: applications of behavioural finance', Chapter 7 in 'Growth and value creation in asset management', SimCorp StrategyLab.

Byrne, A. and Brooks, M. (2008) 'Behavioral Finance: Theories and Evidence', The Research Foundation of CFA Institute.

Gadiesh, O. and Gilbert, J. (1998) 'Profit Pools: A Fresh Look at Strategy', *Harvard Business Review*, May–June.

Galbraith, J.K. (1954) 'The Great Crash of 1929', Houghton-Miffon.

Hawawini, G., Subramanian, V. and Verdin, P. (2003) 'Is performance driven by industry – or firm-specific factors? A new look at the evidence', *Strategic Management Journal*, 24(1): 1–16.

Hawawini, G., Subramanian, V. and Verdin, P. (2004) 'The Home Country in the Age of Globalization: How Much Does It Matter for Firm Performance?', *Journal of World Business* (formerly Columbia Journal of World Business), 39(2): 121–135.

Hawawini, G., Subramanian, V. and Verdin, P. (2005) 'Is performance driven by industry – or firm-specific factors? A Reply to McNamara, Aime and Vaaler', *Strategic Management Journal*, 26(11): 1083–1086.

Kim, C. and Mauborgne, R. (1997) 'Value Innovation – The Strategic Logic of High Growth', *Harvard Business Review.*

Kim, C. and Mauborgne, R. (2005) 'Blue Ocean Strategy: How to Create Uncontested Market Space and Make the Competition Irrelevant', Boston: Harvard Business School Press.

Kindleberger, C.P. (1978) 'Manias and Panics: A History of Financial Crises', New York: Basic Books

Koza, M. (2002) 'Vanguard Inc. – Value Innovation in the Mutual Funds Business', INSEAD – CEDEP Case Study, 09/2002 – 4827, Teaching Note, p. 9.

Lynch, P. (1994) 'The Stock Market Hit Parade', article.

MacMillan, I. and McGrath, R.G. (1996) 'Discover Your Product's Hidden Potential', *Harvard Business Review.*

Malkiel, B. and Ellis, R. (2010) 'The Elements of Investing', New Jersey: John Wiley.

McGrath, R.G. and MacMillan, I. (2005) 'Market Busters: 40 Strategic Moves that Drive Exceptional Business Growth', Harvard Business School Press, Boston.

McKinsey Quarterly (2010) 'Five forces reshaping the global economy: McKinsey global Survey results', May.

Montier, B. (2010) 'The Little Book of Behavioral Investing', NJ: Wiley.

Porter, M. (1985) 'Competitive Advantage', New York: Free Press.

Schmit, M. and Chao, L. (2010) 'Managing growth and strategic risk', Chapter 10 in Growth and value creation in asset management', SimCorp StrategyLab.

SimCorp StrategyLab (2010) 'Report on Global Investment Management Growth Survey 2010'.

Teboul, J. (2006) 'Service is Front Stage: Positioning services for value advantage', INSEAD Business Press. London: Palgrave Macmillan.

Thomsen, S., Rose, C. and Risager, O. (2009) 'Understanding the financial crisis: investment, risk and governance', SimCorp StrategyLab.

Verdin (2009) 'Time to return to growth?', *Journal of Applied IT and Investment Management*, 1(2): July 2009, pp. 21–26.

Williamson, P. and Zeng, M. (2009) 'Value-for-money strategies for recessionary times', *Harvard Business Review*, March.

Zook, C. and Allen, J. (2001) 'Profit from the Core', Harvard Business School Press, Boston.

Zook, C. (2004) 'Beyond the Core. Expand Your Market Without Abandoning Your Roots', Harvard Business School Press, Boston.

28

Check or Checkmate?
Game-Changing Strategies for
the Asset Management Industry

Martin Huber, Philipp Koch and Johannes Elsner

28.1   Introduction

Has somebody got it wrong? Representatives of the asset management industry and commentators alike are talking about the ongoing crisis of the asset management industry with increasing margin pressure, high levels of volatility and shrinking investor asset pools since 2007. Yet at the same time, 2012 and 2013 seem to be turning out as record years with growth outlooks in the region of up to 11% until 2014.

Has somebody got it wrong? An unprecedented number of regulatory initiatives with potentially significant impact on the industry is under way (e.g., FATCA, AIFMD, UCITS IV, MiFID). Representatives of the asset management industry and commentators alike weigh the potential benefits and game-changing nature of such regulatory intervention. Yet at the same time, business models are unchanged and the industry landscape in general does not look much different than in 2010 when we wrote this chapter in the previous edition.

Somebody indeed has got it wrong. How can we bring perception and reality together again? To find an answer, two facts are worth further consideration: First of all, the industry's (unexpectedly fast) recovery in 2012 and 2013 was largely driven by capital markets, not new client money. Secondly, not all asset management players will be equally affected by regulatory changes: the extent will depend significantly on the company's business mix and its underlying business and operating model.

The explanation for the strikingly bad mood in the industry is that volatility and ambiguity are there for many, yet benefits are reaped by a precious few. An increasing 'lateral stretch' between winners and losers is clearly evident, intensifying the 'winner takes it all' paradigm. The top-quartile players raised their share of the overall profit pool from 50 to 58% between 2007 and 2011. The forecast for 2013 could bring this figure up to 70%. As a consequence, speaking in terms of averages no longer makes sense. This will lead to significant change in the competitive landscape (called the industry 'chessboard' in the following), requiring industry players of all types – scale players, specialist players, boutiques, and captive players – to prepare themselves for the new reality.

What can the industry make out of this? Undoubtedly, this is the time of big opportunities. The question is which asset managers will be able or courageous enough to make winning moves. Some players will retreat and others will come to pick up their client franchise. Players in all segments therefore urgently need to refine and reinforce distinctive competitive advantages. The quest to position themselves for growth will require asset managers to review their business and operating models fundamentally, and to deliver on a clear product and distribution strategy.

To succeed in this stretched environment, however, the task will be to deliver a true performance transformation in the midst of unparalleled volatility and an increasingly perforated safety net. The good old days for the asset management industry on average have gone. This intensified structural change leaves many players confronted with the overwhelming question: 'check or checkmate?'

28.2 Analyzing the state of play

Back in 2007, before the global financial crisis hit, McKinsey applied the analogy of a chessboard to formulate a vision for the future of asset management, using it to describe the industry frontiers, the players, and the nature of competition between them.

Since then, the world has experienced repeated financial crises of unexpected magnitude. Looking back at the projections of four years ago, however, the industry has by and large been moving in the direction predicted. Yet as 2012 has been a strong year, it is tempting to think that the industry is merely going through a cycle with shorter and more brutal swings. Looking at the underlying figures, it becomes clear that a cycle can be ruled out: The question is whether the financial crisis has changed the industry fundamentally, or whether the high volatility is merely masking and amplifying the effects of more fundamental changes that have been reshaping the competitive structure and economic foundations of the industry for quite some time already.

28.2.1 The wrong 'average industry' perspective

On average, it is clear from the facts that the industry has faced unprecedented levels of volatility. After the crisis years of 2008 and 2009, the asset management industry bounced back in 2010, judging by averages based on 2007 index levels, only to dither again in 2011 and come back in 2012: Total third-party AUM in Western Europe grew from EUR 7.3 trillion to EUR 7.9 trillion (8%) from 2009 to 2010, yet stalled again in 2011, although levels surpassed those of 2007 (EUR 7.7 trillion). Profits remained under pressure in 2011 after initial signs of recovery in 2010: the 2011 profit pool amounted to only 67% of 2007 levels.

The root cause of this decrease in profits was volatility on the revenue line. While the revenue pool returned to 90% in 2010, it faltered at 88% again in 2011. On the cost side, no significant adaptations to the cost base since the onset of the crisis were apparent.

Since the renewed 2009/2010 upswing resembled the recovery pattern of the post-crisis period from 2002 to 2004, one could argue that 2011 constituted another mere 'bump' on the road to longer-term recovery. And asset managers' individual medium- to long-term plans suggest that the industry considers growth to be feasible again.

However, not only does the mere comparison of figures reveal a deviation from the previous post-crisis recovery: a closer look at industry developments also calls into question such an interpretation. Looking beneath the surface at the sources of the 2009/2010 recovery, it becomes evident that the (average) health of the industry is actually very feeble. The continuing viability of the dual growth model based on net inflows and market appreciation effects can no longer be taken for granted. Figures show that since 2007, the asset management industry as a whole has hardly seen any financial inflows. 2011 actually witnessed zero net inflows. Preliminary estimates based on mutual funds data show inflows of around 2.5% until Q3 2012. This is in stark contrast to the recovery in early 2000.

The bottom line is that the recovery was driven almost entirely by developments on the capital markets, leaving the industry's growth model entirely on the drip feed of capital markets. There are no signs of a strong return of net investor inflows on the horizon. These developments combined with the macroeconomic uncertainty have left the asset management industry – again, on average – increasingly exposed to the new reality of the market rollercoaster.

Looking beneath the 'on average' volatility, an even more striking insight comes to light. Only a limited number of business models are demonstrating growth and profitability while the rest are facing significant pressure. This widening gap between winners and struggling players could be termed a 'lateral stretch': When comparing net revenue levels by different performance quartiles, it becomes clear that the gap between different market players has been widening significantly since 2008. Currently, the net revenue levels for the top-quartile players are 25% higher compared to the market average across Europe.

The gap is also widening to unprecedented levels when analyzing the development of net inflows – the future source of profitability – between independent and bank-owned players. The former have managed to generate significant inflows over the last few years, in contrast to the latter. Indexing flow levels in 2006, independent players have managed to increase their inflows beyond that level, reaching 125 % in 2010. Bank-owned players have failed to maintain their inflows, experiencing net outflows in 2008 and 2010.

What are the drivers behind this change? Five trends are permanently reshaping the industry and its underlying economics. Asset managers need to consider these going forward:

- Increasingly brutal competitive pressure in the retail business: Even though the share of mutual funds as a fraction of total personal financial assets has declined from roughly 14% in the mid-2000s to only around 12% by 2011, growth opportunities of biblical proportions are emerging in the long-term savings field. The entire retail revenue pool accounted for EUR 14.6 billion by the end of 2010 and could increase to EUR 18 billion in 2014 again, driven by retail investors seeking long-term savings products. Competition is retreating from this area: Life insurers are struggling to meet their return needs and payout their obligations. After deposits were all that mattered in the past 5 years, banks are struggling to repair their advisory processes and re-enter the field of investment advice. Other forms of investment – cash, structured products, alternatives – struggle to compete against risk-managed and regulated long-term asset management products.
- Swing to solutions and services for institutional investors: In contrast to the retail segment, the global institutional arena has seen cumulative growth since 2008 – even if 2011 was not as resilient as in the past, 2012 yielded strong results. Going forward, at least moderate growth is anticipated. Generally this growth is anticipated to come via two concentrated pockets of opportunities, both of which are expressing an increasing professionalization of the industry. First, there is the trend toward stronger use of outcome-oriented investment solutions such as asset allocation strategies, inflation-sensitive strategies, and absolute-return strategies. Second, in light of the growing complexity in the current environment, institutional investors are increasingly seeking services from external providers. Portfolio construction services as well as risk and liquidity management are top of their agenda and expected to provide growth opportunities for asset managers.
- Squeeze and polarization in asset classes: Switching from a client to a product perspective, the alpha-beta product separation of recent years has continued throughout the crisis, characterized by a strong demand for passive products. Many institutional investors now have over 50% of their assets in passive products. Exchange-traded funds (ETFs) are experiencing accelerating

growth, reflected by a rise in volume from EUR 103 billion in 2008 to EUR 241 billion in Q3 2012 in Europe. Solutions and high-alpha products have been growing moderately while traditional instruments have been losing market share. Although the bulk of the assets is still in the traditional arena, we see this trend not just continuing: it will move ahead full steam.

- Growing emerging markets opportunity from globalization, both in terms of products and markets: Where products are concerned, investors in mature markets are showing a strong appetite for global and particularly emerging market exposure. In 2010, the demand for emerging markets (measured by AUM allocated globally) reached EUR 350 billion: EUR 100 billion in the retail business and EUR 250 billion in the institutional segment. Asset allocations are still at a level of 6 to 7%, but many experts foresee a move toward 10% at least. With regard to new markets, the Chinese asset management market is already number 5 worldwide with a profit pool of EUR 1.9 billion, followed by the Brazilian market with EUR 1.6 billion. Both are higher than the figure for France, which was EUR 1.2 billion in 2011. The markets are already extremely crowded, with intensive competition and no middle ground.

- No longer uncertain strategic challenge from the regulatory environment: A wave of regulatory initiatives is approaching the asset management industry. More than 25 initiatives are pending that are of high relevance for the industry; the peak of implementation is anticipated for 2014/15. McKinsey has identified ten initiatives to be of particular strategic relevance and may result in significant change to the industry structure as well as shifts in the relative attractiveness of various business models.

  1. The first four of these prioritized initiatives are the Alternative Investment Fund Managers Directive (AIFMD), Undertakings for Collective Investment in Transferable Securities (UCITS) IV and V (especially with their implications on cross-border operating models and the implied opportunities for centralization), and the Investor Compensation Scheme Directive (ICSD), all of which particularly target the asset management industry.

  2. The list goes on to include Basel III, the Markets in Financial Instruments Directive (MiFID), Packaged Retail Investment Products (PRIPs), the Insurance Mediation Directive (IMD), Solvency II, and the Foreign Account Tax Compliance Act (FATCA), which are designed for financial markets in general and will thus have an indirect impact. Despite this indirect nature, these initiatives will have potentially game-changing effects by increasing transparency on risks and economics contained in products.

  3. Of particular interest in the context of the industry structure is the potential impact of a ban of sales commissions, which the European Commission is currently discussing as part of MiFID II and IMD. The

regulative objective of these measures is to abolish a long-standing conflict of interest between the distributor as sales-incentivized adviser and the retail customer as less-informed buyer. Several countries have already taken this route or are considering such action: In India, the regulator (SEBI) implemented a comprehensive ban on sales commissions in 2009 that led to a push toward insurance products (exempted from the ban) and a decline in industry profitability as asset managers started to pay commissions to distributors from their own account. The regulator in the UK (FSA) took a similar approach with the Retail Distribution Review (RDR), becoming effective December 31, 2012, by introducing a ban of all inducements and demanding higher professional qualifications for financial advisers. In Switzerland, the Swiss federal court recently ruled that kickbacks concerning funds used in discretionary mandates have to be passed on to investors. For now, the regulator (Finma) has only demanded that all banks establish transparency on kickbacks received in the last 10 years. Finally, the regulators and Finance Ministeries in the Netherlands (AFM) and Germany (BaFin) are considering a potential ban of commissions from 2014 on, even if MiFID will not contain such provisions. These regulatory intentions have already led some players to voluntarily abolish sales commissions and to explore commission-free products or changes in management fees.

4. The impact of such a ban of commissions on the industry structure in Europe would likely be profound: overall industry profitability could decrease due to a potential shift toward insurance products and lower cost products (e.g., ETFs which also are more transparent) and new ways of profit-sharing between producers and distributors; independent advisers could come under significant pressure and experience an accelerated consolidation; and banks could be facing asset managers pushing toward direct distribution (which especially the independent scale players will be considering) at a time where they are already struggling to sell asset management products.

5. In the end, not all asset management players will be equally affected by these looming regulatory changes. The extent will depend significantly on the company's business mix and its underlying business and operating model. Research also reveals that the regulatory initiatives will particularly impact revenues rather than the cost base. An in-depth assessment of possible repercussions is required to ensure that asset managers are optimally prepared for the upcoming changes.

28.2.2 New reality – new game?

In light of the volatility that the industry has come to terms with, it appears reasonable to assess strategic options using a scenario-based approach. Margins came under pressure again in 2011, falling from 12.5 basis points in 2010 to 10.7 basis points. If the capital markets stabilize, estimates suggest a growth in profit margins of up to 13.6 basis points in 2013. If volatility remains at the present levels but no major capital market meltdown occurs, profit margins are still expected to maintain some ground, resulting in an estimate of 11.9 basis points for 2013. Even more important, however, is to recognize that – as a result – speaking in terms of averages no longer makes sense. Examining the underlying distribution of the profit pool, the lateral stretch phenomenon is already tearing apart established structures.

Applying the trends just described to these economic estimates, this concentration of the profit pool appears set to accelerate. Predictions for 2013 and beyond are that the share of top-quartile players could increase to up to 70% of a potentially further contracting profit pool. This shift will put further pressure on the business models of the remaining competitors. At the outset, we posed the question: check or checkmate?

These analyses suggest the developments under way could bring even midfield players perilously close to being checkmated. Fundamental changes to the industry have already taken place and are increasingly separating the wheat from the chaff. Rooted in these changes, the intensified volatility is only the context, not the cause. The entire asset management ecosystem is at a point of radical change, not simply in a cycle. As a consequence, the industry as a whole and its players individually will need to strengthen their position to secure a winning position as the new constellations take shape. Strategic investments in growth opportunities will be vital, whether bespoke investment solutions and services or new geographies.

All these changes, however, will need to be underpinned by sound organizational redesign – something the industry on average has historically shied away from. Riding on the long periods of high growth and profitability it has enjoyed, the industry has traditionally felt that organizational realignment could demotivate the entrepreneurial talent it is so highly dependent on. Correction of this belief has long been overdue and is now all but too late, as the next chapter will describe.

28.3   Aligning to the new chessboard

What constellations are likely to populate the asset management chessboard of the future? What new rules will apply if players wish to avoid a weak business model that fails to compete in the new market environment?

Four different types of players are emerging, each with their specific change agendas: scale players, specialist players, boutiques, and captive players. The factors that will ensure success on the new board of the future vary by segment.

28.3.1 Scale players: the industry spearheads

Without a doubt, players able to build and sustain scale will spearhead the industry, while the amount of scale will depend on their relevant market context. This segment will consist of retail power brands from Europe and the US as well as large-scale institutional solution providers. A number of players will continue to grow, as some have demonstrated impressively over recent years. Others in this segment will feel the pressure and find it hard to retain their current asset base. The key to sustainable success lies in the ability for constant renewal of scale organizations:

- A flexible and scaleable operating model: the ability to capture scale effects will require a centralized and consolidated design of middle- and back-office activities. While local presence will remain important, cross-border infrastructure functions and services delivery will have to replace the conglomerates of historically grown local offices.
- Product portfolio optimization: winning clients going forward will require innovation in solutions and services that truly meet the specific needs of retail and institutional investors. To stay ahead in the stagnating retail segment, players have to again and again renew their offering by closing no longer profitable or scaleable products. In the institutional segment, scale players will need to make sure that they provide excellent solutions and services along the entire investment process to tap additional sources of growth.
- Diversification: Some of the scale players face significant cluster risks following their breathtaking growth over the last few years. They will have to find new avenues to diversify their business mix in order to sustain their competitive positioning. This diversification could take place in the product and solution arena or be of a geographic nature.
- Organizational effectiveness: Having built such scale either organically or via acquisitions over recent years, scale players will have to address questions on how to sustainably reduce complexity in their organizational structure and processes, often across countries. They also will have to reinforce a strong entrepreneurial management and business culture and to develop and retain the successful managers of the future.

28.3.2 Specialist players: a distinct industry segment

This second distinctive industry segment consists of players with a specialty in product and/or solution categories, investment styles, asset classes, or geography. The difference between a specialist player and a boutique is generally determined by size – AUM and people – as well as distribution approach/reach, not depth and breadth of offering. We anticipate great vigor in this segment, as this specialist status is well appreciated in the institutional and retail arena, with many assets likely to be channeled to this category of players. Their key success factors diverge from those of scale players in a number of key areas:

- Expanded distribution reach: In contrast to scale players that are able to tap into large networks with a full variety of services, specialists have to remain focused in order to build their pipeline for growth. This focus can relate to selectively expanding regionally, but also in terms of client segments and channels, as long as they are able to maintain the unique value proposition. This maintenance will require investments in sales and marketing capacity as well as talent that can provide access to new asset pools.
- Selective product/service extension: To mitigate the concentration risk and stay ahead of competition, specialists could also examine the opportunities of selective product and service extension. Innovation would help diversify what is typically a very concentrated business mix. Balancing the future sources of growth and profitability will help specialists to be a very competitive industry segment in the asset management world.
- Institutionalized capabilities: Success for these players in the past was to a significant extent driven by the quality and reputation of single talents. To replicate the success of the past and mitigate the business risk of losing individual capabilities, specialists will have to find ways to ensure that such capabilities are institutionalized. This can be achieved via the rigorous application of formal mechanisms and processes, training and routines, but also via a more values-oriented culture and systematic approach to talent development.
- World class human resource management: New talent in distribution and investment management that facilitates growth and expansion aspirations requires attractive development opportunities. Significant top management attention will therefore be key to establishing a proposition and performance culture sufficiently distinctive to attract and retain the talent so crucial to unlocking new sources of growth.

28.3.3   Boutiques: vibrant niche operators

Boutiques are set to be a very vibrant asset management segment in the future. As in the past, new boutiques will enter the chessboard, bringing their new investment ideas to investors, particularly in the institutional sphere, but increasingly also to parts of the upper retail arena. Other boutiques will exit or grow out of the boutique status and eventually become specialists. The following priorities are anticipated in this dynamic landscape to sustain competitiveness in the industry environment going forward:

- Exclusive distribution access: For boutiques, a great focus will be on securing sustained distribution access to ensure that their investment ideas find their way into investor portfolios. The ideal approach is to secure exclusive or semi-exclusive shelf-space. The retail distribution partners will ask for effective, hands-on sales and marketing support, and a specialized distribution team will be required to succeed in serving institutional investors.

- Risk management excellence: Given the size of boutiques and the market volatility, potential investors are naturally concerned about their risk management capabilities. Boutiques will have to credibly demonstrate their control of investment and operational risks to allay these apprehensions. Focused investments in upgrading current capability levels will be needed to remain competitive in the demanding institutional arena.
- Tailoring: Players in this segment will have to offer some degree of (perceived) individualization both in terms of products and in terms of client service to avoid being squeezed out. The challenge of this customization is to manage operational complexity in order not to lose valuable scale benefits, and to remain able to continuously add new themes to the product development pipeline without fragmenting the value proposition and sales story.
- Organizational flexibility: Targeted organizational design will be of huge relevance to boutiques. Management capabilities will have to focus on building an efficient organizational set-up able to cope with growth momentum, but also to retain and attract the quality talent that will drive future success or failure more than in other industry segments. Maintaining a start-up spirit will be critical to encouraging external hiring opportunities while at the same time formalizing organizational structures and processes.

28.3.4 Captive players: playing a catch-up game

This industry segment is under the greatest pressure to renew itself. In the past, captives could rely on their parent organization. The urgent need now is to carve out a differentiating and relevant value proposition vis-à-vis investors in the retail and institutional sectors, and most notably toward the parent company. In 2009 and 2010, more than 75% of captive players across Europe were confronted with outflows. The four following points stand out as crucial to ensuring survival and competitive positioning:

- Clear positioning vis-à-vis channel: Captive players will have to address the key decisions on their future sources of value creation. Along the lines of the expected business model restructuring, captive players will need to make great efforts to clarify their positioning vis-à-vis their proprietary channel. The future role of captive players can take a wide variety of shapes and forms. Crucial for success will be a clear commitment to the asset management business from top management and an investment in understanding end customer needs in order to design compelling investment solutions hand in hand with channels.

- Selection/advisory capabilities: In cooperation with proprietary channels, captives could expand their business scope by strengthening the advisory activities of their parent organizations. They could leverage their capabilities in asset allocation strategies, portfolio construction, and research to carve out a strong position in selection and advisory services toward the channel and their customers, bolstering their overall role.
- Product range optimization: Consistent with the previous priority, there is no doubt that captive players will have to significantly review their product range, removing products that no longer suit the claim of greater client centricity in channels. They will also need to step up the development of solutions such as outcome-oriented or absolute-return products as well as 'new balanced' and selective alternative products (leveraging the in-house expertise of their parent) to ensure the continuous capture of inflows from retail investors.
- Complexity reduction: In accordance with the priorities outlined above, captive players should also remove complexity – often based on legacy processes and systems inherited from the parent organization – along all areas of the value chain to structurally rebuild profitability. It will be a challenge to gain sustained commitment from their parent company without demonstrating the management competence to renew their set-up.

28.4   Mastering the changing chessboard

In light of the changes outlined in the previous chapter, the asset management industry will experience a remarkably different landscape over the next five years. For the first time, this industry will have to come to terms with a stagnating market environment, especially in the retail field, which has been the major source of profitability in the past. The evolving lateral stretch between business models will put pressure on some segments more than others, particularly on captive and specialist players with a less clearly defined value proposition. The regulatory wave of initiatives also raises a big question mark over how to react and has the potential to wipe out traditional distribution and business models.

In effect, there will be no middle ground to provide shelter anymore, so the time to act is now. Naturally, top management needs to take the right strategic decisions, positioning their organizations deftly in this evolving landscape to cope with the business challenges outlined above. Reviving retail segments, introducing new investment approaches/asset classes, and building solutions/ services for institutional clients will all be crucial. Entering emerging markets and adapting to the new regulatory environment will require a carefully crafted strategy, too.

However, the agenda will also have two different dimensions:

- First, in a maturing environment where players have to fight hard for growth, operational excellence and execution capabilities become paramount. Such capabilities still have not been developed sufficiently over the last years in the industry:
  - Transparency: insights into economics and performance drivers have to be significantly improved by automation and consistency, allowing an action-oriented view on revenues and costs. In this context, data availability (e.g., customer data, flows, cost units, employees) and accessibility has to be made a central part of the management agenda.
  - Forward looking statements: information systems and processes have to be clarified and populated with consolidated databases. These systems have to be supported by new management routines of operational diligence and supervision allowing for 'ex ante' management, i.e., anticipation of bottlenecks and errors, as opposed to the traditional quarterly review.
  - Automation: User-friendly new technological support solutions (e.g., iPad apps, data models, interactive presentations) have to be introduced and rolled out, especially to improve interfaces such as sales, sales support and production/fund management and introduce a 'deliver or explain' culture, based on informative performance dialogues.
  - Performance review: Target setting and review processes have to be standardized and individualized, while these activities themselves have to be consequently performed and a greater differentiation in objectives, incentives and evaluations has to be achieved.
  - Activation: Agenda setting is also essential, identifying priorities for management to focus on, such as international expansion, consolidation, cost reduction, or a performance turnaround.
- Secondly, asset managers are not familiar with successfully managing change, and now the safety net of loyal parent companies, loyal customers, healthy profit pools, and benevolent regulators is crumbling away. The task is to initiate and complete a successful transformation journey in the middle of an unprecedented crisis to prepare for the future and succeed in the new environment. Asset managers need to find powerful new ways to ensure their organization is on the winning side. Given the magnitude of change we anticipate for many players within the asset management industry, in the end it all comes down to one simple but important question: is the organization willing and able to transform?

According to McKinsey research, successful transformations were always driven by three factors:

- Aspirational and courageous leadership by top management: As market volatility grows, leaders have less and less time to achieve their transformation targets. Organizational choices have to be made top down, such as whether the company will operate profit centers, divisions with shared services, or an integrated model. At the same time, CEOs and their team need to exemplify a strong decision making culture to ensure progress in implementation along the roadmap. This will reduce the instability in organizations that typically arises in transformation periods and diminishes the open-mindedness to change.
- Activation of the organization: Analyzing failed transformations, the vast majority – over 70% – were caused by factors related to organizational health, such as negative employee attitudes and inadequate management behavior. The next essential is therefore to manage the 'soft underbelly' of change: enabling all operating units and management levels, that should ideally contribute to the transformation story, to actually do so. This process needs to focus on three areas primarily:
  - Identifying change agents: Social network analysis can be used to identify opinion leaders, who can then serve as change agents with their own communication roles and feedback rounds. The top team should embed the new objectives in a consistent, compelling, and tailored change story for the entire journey, with different divisions taking on responsibility for detailing the section relating to them, ensuring a clear 'from-to' progression. Alignment workshops may also be performed to create a shared language around the cornerstones of the management agenda, investigating cultural root causes of reluctance to break from old patterns.
  - Installing developmental talent management: Another crucial element is defining a systematic talent management process. Asset management is a prime example of a 'people business'. As one CEO pointed out: 'It's about putting people in the right suit: you have to place people where they are going to be successful. Some people are business builders, some are business drivers, and some are journeymen: you need all three.'
  - Inspiring entrepreneurship and innovation: Good managers demonstrate trust in their people to trigger deep-rooted innovation, whether in terms of new products, new approaches to distribution (such as direct sales and client communication), or new ideas to make processes and operations more flexible. Staff needs to feel their contributions matter and are valued. 'If you don't have trust, then you can't have open debates and encourage controversial ideas,' as one of the CEOs in our discussions emphasized.

- Formal mechanisms to reinforce change: The third requirement is to put a number of formal mechanisms in place that enable leaders to manage transformation with the appropriate rigor and discipline. The overt ingredients are of course vitally important, whether organizational realignment with new reporting lines, project structures, steering committees with strong decision making powers, or incentive systems. However, a structured communication is even more important as a mechanism to support change. Involving staff in dialog via the exchange of ideas and perspectives is key. This can take the form of regular town hall meetings, off-sites, the use of digital channels, or newsletters with interviews, portraits, and success stories. It is important to remember that social media and other technologies have raised the bar for communication. Now that employees have access to multiple sources of information and can share perceptions instantly, they will swiftly form an impression of ongoing efforts from the digital grapevine. A bi-weekly 'pulsecheck' barometer is also an effective means of tracking mood/momentum. Chat rooms and online forums can stoke up enthusiasm with new routines.

28.5   Outlook

The coming years will undoubtedly be challenging for the asset management industry as a whole and for some players in particular. The recent macroeconomic upheaval has revealed how prone the market remains to volatility. Developments since summer 2011 have shown how difficult the overall environment is likely to remain in the foreseeable future.

The 'average' volatility of the industry clearly disguises the evolving lateral stretch between players, ownership models, and markets. The game for asset managers is becoming ever more specialized and competitive, accelerated by the five forces described earlier. Asset managers need to take up the challenge of this game by continuously working on their competitive positions – no matter whether they turn out to be scale players, specialist players, boutiques, or captive players.

Given the context, it is only a matter of time before it becomes evident which players evolve into grandmasters and which end up on the verge of checkmate. The potential of asset management is still enormous – new markets are opening up substantial opportunities. In the end, the winner's game will hinge – as it always does – upon smart moves embedded in a coherent, far-thinking strategy and relentless willingness to constantly reinvent the game.

29
Designing Products for Reluctant Investors: Applications of Behavioral Finance

Alistair Byrne

29.1 Introduction

Behavioral finance is often held out as offering an explanation why financial markets are inefficient and holding the prospect that an understanding of it can help active fund managers 'beat the market'. This chapter[1] argues that a more important use of behavioral finance is in understanding and meeting the needs and wants of your clients. The chapter focuses particularly on the case of defined contribution (DC) pension plans, which represent a growing part of the asset pool in many countries. It argues that most DC plan members can be characterized as 'reluctant investors' who do not want to make detailed investment choices and would prefer investment decisions to be made by experts on their behalf. Trends within pension plan provision mean these members typically have to operate without guidance from expert advisers and need to navigate the investment decisions on their own. Reluctant investors have limited interest in investment matters, are easily confused or put off by investment choice, and exhibit inertia that prevents them following through with decisions and actions. An understanding of the behavior of DC pension plan members can allow an investment manager to offer better products to these clients and drive business growth. Typically, this means offering simple, transparent products, avoiding excessive choice and communicating clearly what the product is intended to do for the client rather than the intricacies of its manufacture.

29.2 The growing importance of Defined Contribution

Defined Contribution (DC) is becoming the most common type of pension plan in the UK private sector and in many other markets. In defined benefit

(DB) plans, the employer bears the investment and longevity risk. In DC these risks are transferred to individual members, who must make complex decisions about which funds to invest their contributions in. It is unusual for employers to pay for face-to-face investment advice, and this lack of member-specific *advice,* as opposed to generic information and guidance, means most members end up in the default fund. Figures vary from plan to plan, but the 2007 NAPF annual survey found that, on average, 94% of members end up in the default fund (NAPF, 2007).

Most DC members can be described as 'reluctant' or 'disengaged' investors. By this we mean that these are individuals who, for a range of reasons, are not prepared to make an active investment choice and instead *passively accept* the default fund. The high proportion of plan members who passively accept default arrangements raises important questions for asset managers about the structure of the default fund and how to best serve the needs of these clients.

DC plans in the UK can be trust-based ('occupational DC'), in which case the employer establishes the plan under trust law and there is a board of trustees whose job it is to act in the members' best interests and negotiate on their behalf with service providers, including asset managers. The alternative is contract-based DC, and here the contractual arrangement is directly between the individual member and the provider, typically an insurance company.

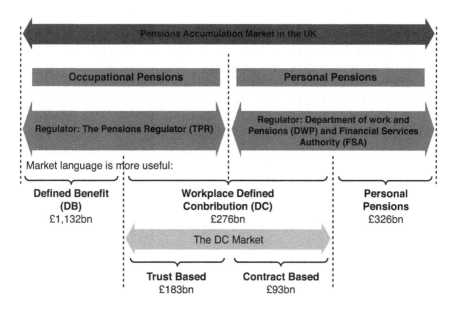

Figure 29.1   Types of private pension provision and estimated total assets in 2011
Source: Spence Johnson Ltd (www.spencejohnson.com). Reproduced with permission.

The key difference between these two structures, therefore, is that in contract-based DC there is typically no entity recognized in law or regulation that acts solely on the members' behalf. Contract-based plans do, however, fall under financial services regulation and Financial Services Authority (FSA) requirements for providers to 'treat clients fairly'. Our research found that the trend in the private sector is not only from DB to DC, but also from occupational DC to contract-based plans. Figure 29.1 shows an outline of the UK pension market and an estimate of the asset sizes as at 2011.

The primary factors that determine the outcome of a DC pension plan during the accumulation phase are the level of contributions and the investment strategy – principally asset allocation. This chapter focuses on the latter: the investment strategies offered by DC plans and, in particular, the default fund provided for members who do not want to make an active choice.

The remainder of this chapter is organized as follows: Section 29.3 explains our research method, while Section 29.4 discusses governance of DC investment. Section 29.5 focuses on default funds, while Section 29.6 looks at issues in investment choice and is followed by a brief conclusion.

29.3   Research method

In the fourth quarter of 2006, we undertook a thorough analysis of the DC investment strategies available to private sector employees in the UK. This research was supplemented by an online survey, which was completed by 54 experienced professionals from the DC pensions market. Respondents included individuals who work for fund management companies, pension plan providers and pensions consultancy firms, as well as pensions lawyers and professional trustees.

We also conducted interviews with over 60 pension and investment experts, either face-to-face or by phone. In many cases, these are the same individuals who participated in the survey, but the interviews allow for a more in-depth understanding of their views. Comments from individual respondents in this research are non-attributable, but we indicate the professional role of the interviewees. From these interviews we were able to build up a clear picture of the framework in which employers introduce DC, the advice they receive, current trends and innovations, and the nature of the problems that concern all parties involved in the design and delivery of plans for the reluctant investor.

29.4   Governance of DC investment?

29.4.1   Survey results

Of the pensions experts we surveyed, 69% say that the typical investment arrangements in UK DC pension plans do not meet most members' needs.

Respondents, on average, think that only 10–15% of DC plan members understand the investment risks they face. Over half put the figure at 10% or less.

In this section we ask the question, 'what constitutes appropriate governance in the context of DC pension plan investment?' For members, understanding basic investment fundamentals and the confidence to make decisions are quite separate characteristics. Even where a member has a reasonable understanding of investment issues, putting this into action is a separate task. It is important not to underestimate the member's fear of making the wrong decision. This is a major factor that explains the concentration of members in the default fund, which further implies that additional information and communications, although very important, will not by themselves convert a reluctant investor into an active one. Our research suggests that what most members want is not more information, but rather to have an expert make the investment decision for them.

The main problem arising from this situation is that many investment 'experts' do not want to make decisions on behalf of DC members for fear of liability. As we discuss later in this chapter, this applies to various aspects of DC investment, including the selection of default funds, the decision on how much investment choice to offer to members, and the nature of information and advice provided to members. We have the perverse outcome that experts – who have the skill and knowledge to make investment choices on behalf of members – prefer not to make them because of fear of liability if the decision turns out to be wrong. The consequence is that decisions are made instead by the members – that is, those who, on average, have very limited investment knowledge. We argue below for changes to law and regulation so that employers, trustees and others who are in a position to support members of DC plans have less to fear from using their expertise provided they can show appropriate standards of care.

29.4.2   Differences in governance between trust-based and contract-based plans

Trust-based DC typically is used by larger employers and can be established with a high level of governance via the trustee board. In theory at least, therefore, a plan with a trustee board is better placed to ensure the member makes appropriate investment decisions. The trustees are responsible for meeting relevant investment regulations and investing funds in a manner consistent with the members' best interests. Their approach to this should be set out clearly in the statement of investment principles. In practice, however, the effectiveness of the trustee board can and does vary from plan to plan.

In some cases, trustees probably do not give DC the attention it deserves. Many trustees of occupational DC plans are also trustees of a DB plan, and the latter presents the most pressing problems at present due to underfunding and the prescriptive requirements of the Pensions Act 2004. Consultants report that

DB issues dominate trustee meetings and that DC is frequently sidelined almost to the point where it becomes an issue listed under 'Any Other Business'.

> *Trustees sometimes neglect DC. They have their head buried in DB problems.* (Consultant)

> *Trustee meetings for DC are inefficient. With DB the investment decisions affect the employer. With DC they affect the employee.* (Consultant)

Some plans may benefit from having a separate group of trustees who oversee the DC plan from those responsible for the DB plan. This would suggest having a separate trust, which is the case in many, but not all, DC arrangements. That way, the DC plan may get more consistent attention. A DC subcommittee is another possible option.

As regards governance of contract-based plans, several advisers and consultants put forward the idea of establishing a board or executive who would undertake some of the responsibilities of trustees. This could oversee the selection and monitoring of investment managers and funds, and take a role in determining the information and guidance provided to members. The employer could invite employee representatives onto the committee and invite advisers and providers to report to the committee. However, such a committee would lack formal legal responsibility for the pension arrangements – which are contracts between the employees and the provider – and this might limit its effectiveness.

> *While employers want to help employees make sensible decisions, they don't want any legal responsibility for the outcome. The answer is to establish a pension committee for the contract plan, which can do everything that trustees did but without actually giving advice to members and having any legal responsibility.* (IFA)

> *Trustees are not always best placed to supervise DC arrangements, but there should be a strong governance committee. Trustees often are reluctant to do much with what is members' money. I'm a big fan of intelligent governance, but I'm not convinced a board of trustees is the right way to deliver this.* (Consultant)

As regards the role of investment consultants, some respondents suggested that trust-based DC gave the consultant the same commercial advantages as DB, in that they could advise but would not have to take responsibility for dealing with individual members.

> *Few people want to take responsibility for the end user in DC. Who wants to 'own' the compliance? The big consultants are the worst, and the life companies have an advantage there.* (Asset manager)

29.4.3   The role of the employer

Many employees would like to turn to their employer for guidance on what to do with their DC pension investments. Employers, though, are often reluctant to help for fear of falling foul of financial services regulation or incurring other liabilities if the guidance they offer causes some disadvantage to members. There would seem to be merit in looking at what can be done to encourage employers to take a more active role.

> *I am in favour of making the law easier for employers to stick their neck out a bit in what they can say to employees without fear of being penalized by a regulator or an ombudsman.* (Pensions lawyer)

The traditional way for the employer to offer support is to establish a trust-based plan with a board of trustees. However, as noted above, trust-based plans are in decline as employers move to the simpler contract-based arrangement. It is a very attractive proposition to employers weary of the trust-related admin-istration, cost and liabilities.

> *Employers are switching to contract DC to put a distance between themselves and the plan outcome, so that all they have to do is collect and forward contributions – they don't want to be involved in the fund choice.* (IFA)

> *We have virtually no new business enquiries for trust-based DC. We have lost trust-based clients to contract-based plans. The life companies' pitch is that they offer a more straightforward platform.* (Asset manager)

While employers are moving from trust-based to contract-based plans to reduce their responsibilities, there are some indications that the regulators may wish to see employers take more direct responsibility for the oversight of contract-based plans. The section below highlights some important issues raised in The Pension Regulator's 2006 consultation paper on DC regulation.

29.4.4   The regulation of DC investment

In November 2006, The Pensions Regulator (TPR) published a consultation paper (TPR, 2006) setting out how it intends to regulate DC pensions. The paper notes four issues that TPR believes could contribute to poor investment practices:

- inadequate processes for the selection and ongoing review of performance of investment managers and funds
- provision of an inappropriate fund or range of funds
- inappropriate design of the default fund
- lack of member understanding.

In terms of fund choice, the paper notes that the investment range must allow members to make choices that suit their circumstances, but that providing too wide a range increases complexity and may increase the risk of administrative errors being made.

TPR says that it intends to offer guidance on good practice in the following areas:

- effective processes for selecting and reviewing investment managers
- effective processes for the review of investment funds
- how to offer a well-designed fund or range of funds to suit member demographics – examples of different approaches to the design of default funds
- examples of investment options, including diversification
- examples of clear and simple information that can be provided to members.

Perhaps the most important part of the consultation paper is the section covering the TPR's 'expectations', which can be viewed as a description of the standards that need to be met. The stated requirements are that:

- there is a robust selection process for investment managers and funds, and regular performance reviews
- a suitable fund or range of well-managed funds is offered, especially in respect of the default fund
- steps are taken to help raise members' understanding of investment decisions, level or risk and potential impact on benefits.

The TPR's guidance on DC investment issues can play a key role in helping employers and trustees to design their DC arrangements in a manner that is helpful for members. If employers and trustees can show they have followed TPR's guidance, then that may have some impact on any discussion of liability for poor investment results. However, formal safe harbor provisions might be more beneficial.

29.4.5   Implicit and explicit advice

Many of the problems in DC investment could probably be solved by providing members with individual investment advice. However, this is quite rare due to the cost. Generic guidance has a role to play, but some of the professionals we interviewed noted that it was typically not sufficient to enable members to make confident investment decisions.

> *I believe that most people actually need far more than generic financial advice at points in their lifetime, for example on joining, transferring or retiring.* (Consultant)

Employers and trustees are wary of giving advice, but members would like guidance from an expert. Furthermore, what the FSA defines as advice is a long way from the definition most employees would use. Many members will regard aspects of the design of their plan as implicit advice. This is particularly true of the default fund, which members can easily regard as being chosen as suitable for them.

> *The selection and monitoring of the default fund or funds is absolutely critical to the success of the plan and to good governance. It doesn't matter that the regulations do not regard this process as 'advice' in the technical sense. Effectively it is advice, since most members take the default option on the assumption that it has been selected specifically for those who do not want to make investment decisions.* (Trustee)

29.4.6   Safe harbor

One prospect for improving governance of DC plans is that each party to the plan – and this could include any combination of the employer, trustee, adviser, consultant, plan provider and asset manager – should be set clear regulatory responsibilities. In exchange for taking a greater fiduciary role, they should be protected through the introduction of safe harbor rules.

By safe harbor, we mean provisions that relieve the employer, trustees or other party from liability for the investment outcome, provided the decisions they take conform to the standards set out in the regulations. Details of safe harbor provisions used in the US are set out in the section beginning at the bottom of this page. It is not compulsory for employers and others to follow the safe harbor guidelines, but doing so provides important protections which many will be reluctant to forgo.

Our argument is that provision of a safe harbor could encourage employers, trustees and advisers – the relative experts on investment – to provide more support to members in investment decision making. Key areas of application include specifying and selecting default funds, choosing appropriate ranges of investment choice, and providing members with appropriate information and guidance.

Obviously, care needs to be taken in developing and specifying the safe harbor provisions. They are likely to drive behavior, and if they are poorly thought out, that behavior may be no better than the situation we have today. Nevertheless, we recommend the safe harbor approach as a possible way of ending the process of employers, trustees and advisers distancing themselves from investment decision making in DC plans.

29.4.7   US safe harbor provisions for DC default funds (QDIA)

The US Employee Retirement Income Security Act (ERISA) provides relief from liability for investment outcomes for sponsors ('fiduciaries') of DC pension plans, typically 401(k) plans, where members make their own investment choices from an appropriate range of funds on offer. This relief is known as a 'safe harbor'.

Some plan sponsors have worried about potential liabilities arising from the performance of default funds on the basis of an interpretation that default funds are not 'chosen' by members. Many have responded by either refusing to have a default fund or choosing a low-risk fund, such as cash, as the default to minimize the chances of short-term losses. These decisions can create a number of adverse consequences such as discouraging employees from joining (because they must make a fund choice), preventing use of automatic enrolment (which requires a default fund), and encouraging recklessly conservative investment strategies.

The Pensions Protection Act of 2006 contains several measures designed to support the use of automatic enrolment, one of which is an amendment to the ERISA safe harbor provisions. The new provisions create a safe harbor where:

- assets are invested in a Qualified Default Investment Alternative (QDIA);
- members have been given an opportunity to provide investment direction but have failed to do so;
- members have been given notice 30 days before the initial investment and again 30 days before the start of each plan year about how their assets will be invested in the QDIA;
- the plan offers a broad range of investment alternatives;
- members are able to switch out of the QDIA into the other funds.

The regulations also provide requirements for the QDIA:

- it must not impose any transfer penalties on switching to other funds;
- it must be managed by a registered investment manager or investment company;
- it must be diversified so as to minimize the risk of large losses;
- it may not invest employee contributions directly in employer-issued securities;
- it may be a lifecycle fund, a target-date fund, a balanced fund or a professionally managed account.

A key point about safe harbor provisions is that they are not compulsory for sponsors to follow. The sponsor is free to choose an alternative course of action. The provisions do, though, give sponsors a firm steer as to what approach the government regards as appropriate. If the provisions are well-designed, they provide a powerful indication of best practice.[2]

29.5   Default funds

In this section we examine what constitutes good default fund design. We also discuss lifestyle funds, given that lifestyle is a common approach for the default fund.

29.5.1   Survey results

Of the pensions experts we surveyed, 89% think that a DC plan should have a default fund.

Respondents, on average, say that, where a plan has a default fund, typically 82% of members invest in it. Of respondents, 57% think DC plans should offer a lifestyle fund as the default, while 39% think lifestyle should be available as an option members can choose.

The results of our survey, together with other surveys such as the NAPF 2006 Annual Survey (NAPF, 2007), show that typically more than 80% of plan members accept the default fund, many of them passively. Default funds, therefore, are essential for the reluctant investor, who is deterred from joining if membership involves making complex, often incomprehensible, investment choices. Default funds are obviously also required where automatic enrolment is being used.

> *It is tempting to suggest that a default should not be offered in order to force people to make a decision. However, thinking realistically, it is unlikely that we will, in the foreseeable future, get many people to engage with this decision, so I think a default is necessary and may produce better/less volatile results than would be true for people forced to make a choice.* (Insurance company)

The NAPF 2006 survey reports that 83% of DC plans have a default fund. Despite this widespread use, our research revealed growing concern among some advisers about the potential liability of employers, trustees and advisers for any problems arising in the default fund.

> *The real purpose of the default is to encourage people to join. Without it, people will see that they have to make complicated choices and will not join. But, there is a trend away from defaults in occupational DC because the trustees are afraid they will be held accountable for the outcome.* (Asset manager)

> *I am increasingly of the view that providers and employers can't escape liability for the outcome where there is a very large number of people in a default fund. Members who accepted the default will claim that they didn't actively choose it.* (Insurance company executive)

29.5.2   Choosing the default fund

Many of the professionals we interviewed believe that members generally see the default fund as implicit advice. We investigated the selection process for the default fund and found that employers using contract DC usually delegate the choice to their adviser. The adviser in turn tends to recommend the default fund put forward by the selected provider. Historically this has been either a balanced managed or index-tracking fund, depending on the provider's areas of specialization. This means that the default fund is not driven by buy-side needs, but by sell-side expediency.

> With stakeholder plans the main driver is cost – so the default fund will be the life office's cheapest option. So, if you have an L&G stakeholder the default will be passive; a Scottish life company's default will be the active balanced managed fund. The [members'] 'choice' therefore, is illusory. Generally the consultant or IFA will select the provider, so the default is not a major consideration. (Asset manager)

The TPR consultation on DC governance notes the intention for the regulator to provide guidance on the process for selecting a default fund. This would seem likely to include issues such as considering the risk tolerance of members, the appropriate means of managing risk as members approach retirement, and the effective management of costs. As we argued above, it may make sense to go further and establish safe harbor provisions that protect the employer from liability for the outcome of investment in the default fund, provided that appropriate care has been taken in the selection decision.

29.5.3   Lifestyle funds as the default

Lifestyle (or lifecycle) funds switch members' pension fund assets from equities to bonds and cash as the planned retirement date approaches. A lifestyle overlay is a common component of default options, and it serves two important purposes. First, it ensures that members are invested predominantly in equities, or other growth assets, for most of the accumulation years. Secondly, it ensures that members gradually switch from risky to safer assets in the few years before retirement to avoid the potentially disastrous impact of a market crash at a time when earned income is expected to cease shortly.

The lifestyle approach is common in practice, with the NAPF (2007) survey reporting that it is used as the default in 63% of DC plans. However, there are disputes over:

– the length of the lifestyle switching period
– the exchange of assets involved in the switch
– whether lifestyling is even an effective strategy at all.

There is also a concern that where there is only one lifestyle default fund, this gives rise to an over-concentration of members in a single fund. As mentioned earlier, this poses potential problems for employers, in particular if members are dissatisfied with the outcome and complain that they were 'directed' into an inappropriate fund.

The variety of different lifestyle mechanisms that are in use across the DC market suggests that opinions vary about what is most effective. Different providers operate lifestyle mechanisms that start the switch into safer assets at any time from three to ten years (and in a few cases more) prior to the expected retirement date. Equally, the growth vehicle in use for the early years of membership varies across providers and can be a UK equity fund, a global equity fund or some form of balanced fund, with additional variations in terms of active or passive management. (Byrne et al., 2007)

> *Lifestyle hasn't changed or developed for a decade. The thinking varies. Some argue that a three-year switch is optimal to allow for maximum growth, but in practice it does not work. This is largely because people don't know when they are going to retire and three years doesn't give enough flexibility – nor does five in many cases. The current trend is toward an earlier start for switching. One of our clients decided to err on the cautious side and recently changed from five to ten years because of the uncertainty over actual retirement dates.* (Consultant)

The decision on the switching period is driven by two main considerations. The first relates to managing market risk: a longer switching period provides greater protection from losses, but on the other hand imposes a cost in terms of reduced expected return, given the longer period in low-risk/low-return assets. The other consideration relates to uncertainty in relation to the member's retirement date. A short switching period may mean that a member who is forced to retire a few years early is still heavily invested in equities – and hostage to market conditions – at that point.

Traditional lifestyle funds switch the member's investments from risky assets, such as equities, to safer assets such as bonds, as the planned retirement date approaches. Typically, this is achieved by switching the units of the funds the member is holding from, say, the equity fund to units in the bond and cash fund. An alternative method that simplifies unit holdings is the target-date fund.

Target-date funds work on a similar principle to conventional lifestyling, but the switching occurs within each dated fund. So, for example, a member expecting to retire in 2040 would buy the '2040 Fund'. This would have an internal lifestyling mechanism and would start to switch into safer assets in, say, 2030 so that by 2040 the fund is 75% in fixed income and 25% in cash. Target-date funds may be easier for members to understand: they simply choose the fund that coincides with their planned retirement date, and the manager does everything else. In this way they focus the member on the final outcome rather than on shorter-term performance. The Personal Accounts Delivery Authority[3] charged with designing a new national DC scheme for the UK has suggested that target-date funds will be appropriate for its target membership of low- and middle-earners without access to existing work-based pension plans.

Target-date funds may be appropriate for use as the default in a DC plan. As with many forms of funds, providers may take different views on what is an appropriate asset allocation to support the target date. This diversity is not bad in itself, but given diversity in the underlying asset allocations, employers, trustees and advisers need to make their selections very carefully with the member profile in mind.

29.5.4   Changing the default fund

In trust-based plans, trustees select the default fund and the investment range. An important issue arises when they decide the existing arrangements are no longer appropriate, for example due to sustained poor performance by the investment manager.

Where trustees decide to make a change, they need to think about how to deal with members' existing holdings in the fund that has been removed. Often the approach taken is to inform members of the change and invite them to switch. Trustees often seem reluctant to close fund options entirely and force members to switch. The result can be large numbers of members invested in legacy funds, with complications in administration, communication and ongoing monitoring.

> *Trustees are not bold enough. Where they do change an underperforming manager, many fail to ensure members automatically transfer. Instead they send a letter saying that there is now a new manager – and they leave it up to the member whether or not to switch. The result is that most members stay put and end up with underperforming legacy funds.* (Consultant)

An alternative is to create a range of funds in the employer's name – for example the XYZ UK equity fund. This is sometimes known as a 'white-labelled' fund, where the asset manager provides the manufacturing on an unbranded basis. The trustees and/or their adviser can then appoint one or more managers per fund and monitor them, replacing managers where necessary. This avoids the above problem because members don't have to make any decisions – they are automatically moved to the new managers.

This approach would appear to have benefits from a governance point of view and from an administrative perspective. It should be possible in contract – as well as trust-based arrangements. However, employers and trustees may be reluctant to adopt this approach for fear of liability, should their investment decisions turn out poorly. Again, there may be a need for safe harbor provisions that reassure the decision makers that they will not be held liable for the outcome, provided that they followed appropriate steps in taking the decision.

29.6   Investment choice

29.6.1   Survey results

Most of the pensions experts we surveyed think that DC plans should offer a relatively narrow range of funds for members to choose from. The respondents' views on the appropriate number of funds to offer can be contrasted with data from the NAPF 2006 Survey (NAPF, 2007) on the choice actually provided by DC plans (See Figure 29.2). Beyond the default, most DC plans offer a range of funds for active investors to choose from. The NAPF 2006 survey reports that 94% of DC plans provide members with investment choice. Twenty-three per cent of plans offer members 20 or more funds to choose from, and 10% of plans offer 40 fund choices or more.

Today most advisers and consultants recognize that wide choice can confuse members and that a small range of funds is preferable, but they do not always feel confident, from a liability perspective, in narrowing down the choice. Our interviews revealed that the selection of an appropriate range of fund choices in relation to membership profiles is hampered by the fear that the selection and elimination process could create a liability if it goes wrong. The concern is that members could later claim that they suffered because better funds were denied to them.

There have been a lot of articles recently on the inadvisability of providing choice. I have to say, having just joined my own firm's group personal pension plan, which had over 200 funds to choose from, I agree with this. (Pensions lawyer)

It is difficult for employers to pare down fund choice. Typically they will want their consultant to do it. Consultants are wary of cutting funds out of predetermined ranges – there is 'regret risk' that the ones they exclude will do well. (Asset manager)

Number of funds	Survey: % of respondents	NAPF data % of plans
1	0%	6%
2–5	17%	14%
6–10	57%	35%
11–20	9%	21%
20+	15%	23%
Don't know	2%	N/A

Figure 29.2   The appropriate number of funds to offer according to respondents and the choice actually provided by DC plans

Source: Pensions Institute report 'Dealing with the reluctant investor' (see Note 1) and NAPF 2006 Survey.

We appear to have the unfortunate situation whereby experts believe that a small range of funds is appropriate but what is offered frequently is a much wider choice, even though this is confusing and unhelpful for most members.

Beyond the reluctant investor, there may be members who want and need a wider fund choice. If pension plans want to provide choice for this group, it is important they do so in a manner that does not impose costs and complexity on the vast majority of members with simpler requirements. One option would be to establish an appropriate filter system for the investment range. This would involve creating two or three layers of fund choices, so that members with basic requirements need only consider the simple choice offered in the first tier, and the wider range is only displayed to those who request it.

29.6.2   Risk-graded multi-asset funds

As we have discussed above, it is unlikely that a single default fund will meet the risk/return preferences of 80%+ members of the plan. The issue may be that the default fund is the only 'packaged' option and moving from that to 'do-it-yourself' asset allocation using individual funds is too intimidating for most members. One alternative to this, which is growing in use, is to offer a small number of packaged options that members may choose from. For example, the plan could offer either three or five multi-asset strategies differentiated by the balance between risky and safer assets, with some form of lifestyle overlay to manage risk through time. Members can choose from among them based on their perceived attitude to investment risk, and the funds can be described or categorized on that basis.

One way to characterize the funds is to give them names such as 'Adventurous', 'Balanced' or 'Cautious' (the 'ABC' approach). These names attempt to differentiate the funds for the reluctant investor. Underlying the classification can be a more objective measure of risk, for example where each fund has a target range for its value-at-risk or volatility parameters. An example is provided in Figure 29.3.

Members can be provided with a risk profiling questionnaire to help them consider their attitude to risk. Some providers suggest that this type of approach

Asset class	Asset allocation		
	Cautious fund	Balanced fund	Adventurous fund
UK equities	30%	40%	50%
Overseas equities	30%	40%	50%
Fixed income	40%	20%	–

Figure 29.3   Asset allocation of risk-graded managed strategies

Source: Hypothetical example developed based on a review of fund options available in the UK pensions market.

has been helpful in reducing the percentage of members who end up in the default fund. The key is in making the fund choice more manageable for the non-expert, although it is fair to say that inertia remains strong and many members will, in any case, end up in the default fund.

> *Risk profiling of members can be advantageous. You're more likely to offer a suitable fund range and to get positive member feedback. But it's labour intensive and there are regulatory risks.* (IFA)

While the ABC approach appears to have merits, employers, trustees and advisers need to make sure the provider's interpretation of risk profile matches their own view. It is unlikely that many members will be able to do so for themselves.

One issue raised by a number of our contacts was whether these types of funds should have descriptive names, such as 'Cautious' or names based on factual aspects such as the equity content (e.g. 'The 75 Fund', which has a 75% equity allocation). The argument for the latter is that there is less risk of members being misled, for example by interpreting 'Cautious' in a way that is different from the provider's view. However, elsewhere we make the argument that members will be better served by communicating funds based on *what they are expected to achieve* rather than on the asset allocation and investment style.

Finally, it is worth noting that the ABC approach does not remove the need for a default fund: some members won't complete the risk profiling questionnaire, and some that do so still won't make an active choice of one of the three funds. It should, though, reduce the proportion of members going into the default *on a passive basis* by providing a simpler menu for active choice.

29.7   Recent trends

Since the initial research in 2007, the UK DC market has continued to grow. This has been driven in large part by defined benefit (DB) schemes being closed, firstly to new members and more recently to future accrual by existing members. Many of the employees for whom DB plans are no longer available have become members of DC plans. While scheme closures initially affected smaller companies, the trend is now entrenched in larger employers. The 2012 Towers Watson FTSE 100 DC Survey shows:

Pension Arrangements	% of companies 2012	% of companies 2009
DC for new employees; DB for existing employees	67	81
Now have DC for all employees	22	5
Only ever offered DC to all employees	11	14

The overall size of the market was estimated to be £276 billion in 2011 (Source: Spence Johnson) – this includes trust-based and contract-based workplace pension schemes, but not personal pension schemes arranged by individuals. As large schemes continue to close to new and existing members, cashflows into DC schemes will increase significantly and some estimates suggest that the DC asset pool will triple in size over the next ten years.

One driver of growth in the DC market will be legislation requiring employers to automatically enrol their employees (age 22+ and earning more than £8,000 per annum) into a workplace pension scheme. The employee has the right to opt out, but if they choose to remain in the scheme, the employer must make a minimum level of contributions on their behalf (1% rising to 3%). The requirement took effect from 1 October 2012 for the largest employers (120,000+ employees) and will be phased across progressively smaller employers over the period to 2017. The expectation is that the changes will introduce between 5 million and 8 million new savers into the pension system and the vast majority of these will be enrolled in DC schemes. Some will be enrolled in the National Employment Savings Trust (NEST) set up on behalf of the government, while others will be enroled in existing workplace DC schemes.

Automatic enrolment has created a renewed focus on the governance of pension schemes and the responsibilities of sponsors, trustees, advisers, plan providers and asset managers. There is a particular focus on default funds on the basis that employees who are automatically enrolled are likely to be even less engaged (or more reluctant) than existing members and hence more likely to end up in the default fund. The result has been significant regulatory activity.

The Investment Governance Group is a body set up comprising key stakeholders in the DC market (government, regulators, investment managers, investment advisers, trustees) to provide guidelines on best practices in scheme governance. Their guidance (IGG, 2010) sets out high level principles for schemes to follow:

Stage I: governance structure

Principle 1: Clear Roles and Responsibilities – identifying who makes which decisions
Principle 2: Effective Decision Making – decision makers have sufficient information, time and resources

Stage II: investment choices and monitoring

Principle 3: Appropriate Investment Options – to meet the needs of the range of scheme members
Principle 4: Appropriate Default Strategy – with clear objectives and based on the needs of members

Principle 5: Effective Performance Assessment – regular monitoring of investment performance

Stage III: communications

Principle 6: Clear & Relevant Communications – to enable members to make informed choices

The Department for Work and Pensions has also issued guidelines (May 2011) focused on ensuring default funds are appropriate and well-governed. These do not have legislative force, but there has been comment that if the industry does not comply with the guidelines, legislation could follow.

> *It is likely that the vast majority of individuals being automatically enrolled will end up in the default option. Therefore the design, governance and communication of the default option will play an important role in securing good outcomes for members.*
>
> *The default option should take account of the likely characteristics and needs of the employees who will be automatically enrolled into it. It is likely that employees in the default fund will not be engaged in financial decisions. Decisions will need to be taken for them about their risk profile. As such there should be an appropriate balance between risk and return for the likely membership profile and the charging structure should reflect this balance.* (DWP, 2011)

The guidance also states that the suitability of the default should be subject to regular review and that care should be taken that the charges are reasonable.

A number of the investment innovations discussed earlier in this chapter have taken greater hold, although they are far from universal. There is growing use of Diversified Growth Funds (DGFs) in DC schemes. These are widely diversified multi-asset funds intended to have equity-like returns, but lower volatility. Many have actively managed asset allocations, although a number of lower-cost passive options exist. The Towers 2012 FTSE 100 survey found 70% of schemes offering a DGF to members, with 15% of schemes using the DGF as part of the lifecycle default strategy.

There also appears to be growing acceptance that a smaller, more focused fund range is easier for members to use. Trust-based schemes, where trustees take fiduciary responsibility for the fund choice offering, have tended to have narrower ranges. In the Towers Watson FTSE 100 survey most trust-based schemes have between 5 and 15 fund choices. Contract-based schemes tend to have wider ranges, in some cases 50+, but there is a growing trend to having narrow core ranges, alongside wider full ranges, to allow most members just to focus on the core funds. A number of providers have introduced risk-graded multi-asset portfolios, to allow members to focus their decision on how much risk they want to take rather than detailed asset allocation decisions.

Nest's own investment arrangements may provide a benchmark for DC investment arrangements more generally. They have chosen to offer annual target-date funds as the default. These are multi-asset, with the underlying assets mostly passively managed. Interestingly, the target-date funds for younger members who are a long way from retirement have quite cautious asset allocations. This is contrary to theory and industry convention that such members are able to take significant amounts of risk, but Nest's approach has been based on the idea that investment volatility in the early years of membership might unnerve members and cause them to opt out of the scheme. The target-date funds take more risk when the member has been in the scheme for a few years, before reducing again closer to retirement. Outside of the default there is a limited fund range consisting of a higher risk growth fund, a lower growth fund, a pre-retirement bond fund, an ethical equity fund and a Shariah-compliant equity fund.

29.8   Conclusion

Most of the pensions professionals we interviewed regard the majority of DC plan members as reluctant investors with limited investment knowledge and even less desire to engage with investment choices. Asset managers looking to grow their business in the DC market need to take account of this behavioral characteristic in their product design and marketing. Innovation for this market is not more and more complex products, but rather a few well-designed and effective products. Communication should focus on the details of the benefits the product delivers for the investor, rather than esoteric information on the manufacturing process. These are not approaches that come naturally to many providers in the asset management industry.

The growth and changing nature of the DC market presents some interesting challenges for asset managers. Most will be investment-only providers to the market, supplying funds but not providing the scheme 'wrapper' and member record keeping. A few will have a parent or affiliate in the record keeping business. For the investment-only providers one question is whether they want to offer broad (typically multi-asset) solutions to DC members or whether they want to provide best-in-class asset class components in other providers' solutions. This is against a background of market segmentation whereby smaller schemes may buy off-the-shelf funds from managers and/or scheme providers, while larger schemes build bespoke solutions for their members using the advice of large investment consulting firms. The market dynamic also creates distribution challenges for managers and lack of clarity about who is the client. While the assets belong to the member and the final investment decision may rest with the member, many will accept default funds selected by trustees or providers. In turn those default funds rest on decisions made by scheme providers, sponsors and advisers. All of these parties are 'clients' of the asset manager to an extent and need to be serviced appropriately.

The precise path of the UK DC market over the next few years is not entirely clear. There will be growth and asset managers and other providers will have to adapt and invest in their offerings to benefit from that growth. However, the basic premise of the this chapter – to consider the needs and behavior of the underlying customers in designing investment offerings – will remain true. The managers that are best able to do this are likely to see the greatest growth.

Notes

1. The chapter is based on the Pensions Institute report 'Dealing with the reluctant investor' by Alistair Byrne, Debbie Harrison and David Blake. See www.pensions-institute.org.
2. For more details see http://www.dol.gov/ebsa/newsroom/fsdefaultoptionproposalre-vision.html.
3. PADA is the predecessor organization to Nest (National Employment Savings Trust)

References

Byrne, A., Blake, D., Cairns, A. and Dowd, K. (2007) 'Default Funds in UK Defined Contribution Pension Plans', *Financial Analysts Journal*, July/August.

DWP (2011) 'Guidance for offering a default option for defined contribution automatic enrolment pension schemes', London: Department for Work and Pensions.

IGG (2010) 'Principles for investment governance of work-based DC pension schemes', The Pensions Regulator, Brighton.

NAPF (2007) 'National Association of Pension Funds Annual Survey 2006', National Association of Pension Funds, London.

Towers Watson (2012) 'FTSE 100 Defined Contribution Pension Scheme 2012 Survey', Towers Watson, London.

TPR (2006) 'How The Pensions Regulator will regulate defined contribution pension plans in relation to the risks to members', The Pensions Regulator, Brighton.

30

Current and Future Challenges Faced by Investment Funds

Martin J. Gruber

Investment funds, principally open-end mutual funds comprised of shares, fixed-income securities and other assets, have been one of the most successful innovations in the global financial architecture. Properly structured, fund shares are easy to buy and sell at relatively low cost. They open a wide variety of active management styles and asset exposures to ordinary investors, including specific sectors of the economy and a broad range of international markets. They are relatively transparent in terms of their net asset value (NAV) and the composition of their holdings. They are tracked in terms of performance, expenses and risk profiles by various investor information services around the world.

In addition, they are competitive with respect to the costs paid by the investor, which makes it possible to compare across funds, including an increasing array of passive, or index funds and exchange-traded funds (ETFs), which involve lower costs and often improved tax-efficiency as well. And they are fairly well regulated in most countries, so that a reasonable level of investor protection is provided – the European Union's UCITS approach stands out in this regard, proving benefits for the investor and the investment fund industry alike. In countries like the US, regulatory integrity has become even more important as the shift from defined benefit to defined contribution pension plans has further accentuated the importance of open-end funds as investment vehicles.

The history of investment funds, of course, has not been without its share of controversy. A perennial question is whether the expenses associated with owning investment fund shares are justified by fund performance. These include trading costs, front loads, marketing charges, operating costs and advisory fees that are paid out of the pool of fund assets and erode total returns to investors. Since these charges have a probability of one and have to be benchmarked against uncertain total portfolio returns, they are a key concern for investors.

There is ample empirical evidence in this regard, much of it controversial with respect to the research methodologies involved. This has become even more apparent with the risk of extremely low-cost passive investment vehicles, and evidence that the investment funds community as a whole failed to protect its clients during the recent financial crisis any better than passive funds would have done. The certainty is that investment management organizations live and die by the size of their AUM, and so they are in a never-ending game of convincing the investing public that they are indeed adding value.

Nor have regulatory challenges of fostering efficiency, innovation, competitiveness and fairness in the investment community been universally successful. Many observers found it virtually inconceivable that investment fund managers would allow hedge funds to engage in late trading (at stale prices used to calculate fund net asset values) in mutual fund shares holding the retirement savings and household assets of millions of investors, as revealed in the early 2000s in the US.

This gross violation of fiduciary duties, resulting in large regulatory fines, class-action suits and reputational losses by some of the most prominent names in the industry, called into question some basic assumptions about transparency and integrity. The same was true of market-timing trades in fund shares, which facilitated arbitrage but at the same time increased fund trading costs as well as cash balances required in fund operations. Many of these practices have been addressed, and they certainly did not infect all fund managers, but memories are long and continued vigilance in governance and regulation is required.

Given the investment management industry's evolution around the world and its continued patterns of growth – the money has to go somewhere, and the investment management industry can be expected to capture a substantial share of net new money – this chapter focuses firmly on the future. What are the major challenges the industry faces in its three key dimensions – risk management, cost control and growth? Each is examined in terms of its central aspects – what are the issues, the lessons of history, likely future prospects and indicated management options for strategic success?

In the risk domain the focus is, as always, on market risk and benchmarking risk-adjusted fund performance. But issues of credit risk, operational risk and regulatory risk are also considered in some detail. With respect to costs, efficiency is the name of the game given its importance in driving net risk-adjusted returns to investors, and the discussion focuses on key issues such as technology platforms, the use of outsourcing, fee shrinkage under stiff competitive conditions, and patterns of cost and earnings allocation.

The growth discussion starts with the retirement–provisioning use of investment funds as a central demographic driver, including the need to tailor products in a more granular way to this critical sector, as well as the need to retarget strategies geographically to where the growth will be going forward. Readers will find this chapter to be a thoughtful, comprehensive and balanced discussion of the evolving competitive landscape for investment funds.

30.1   Introduction

The most pressing challenge facing the investment funds sector today is the challenge to growth as triggered by the financial crisis of 2008–09. The crisis resulted in money flowing out of funds (although it has started to flow back in), and people switching funds both within and between fund complexes, reacting rapidly to short-run moves in the market. The crisis has also increased the threat of new regulation as to how investment funds can or should function. All of this has heightened the uncertainty for investment fund management.

In the discussions forming the basis of this chapter,[1] we found that one way investment funds can start to meet this challenge is to work on their public relations. The investment fund industry has a really good track record, and if the last three financial crises are examined, we have found that while the industry suffered temporary losses as a result of each crisis, when the crisis was a year past the industry bounced back to previous levels.

While there is a threat of increased regulation, the point also has to be made that regulation is a cost but also one of the biggest advantages for the industry, because regulation in combination with the industry's self-determination has led to a tremendous transparency in the investment fund business; more transparency in our view than is offered by any other financial intermediary. This is one of the major advantages of investment funds that has to be promoted.

The most discernible opportunity facing the industry today comes out of a very large social challenge. If we look around the world today, the demographics in every country mean that we have fewer working people supporting more retired people. This means that we have to have better and better schemes for retirement planning.

In the US, 70% of the people owning investment funds, when asked why they own such funds, gave retirement as the principal reason. The private retirement system has to grow all over the world, but particularly in Europe. Investment funds are a natural product for the retirement industry and can also be crafted into a platform that will actually help people plan for retirement. We see this as representing a tremendous opportunity for the development of products and systems and one that the industry finds advantageous.

30.2   Risk challenges

The four key challenges for the immediate and medium-term future related to risk issues in the investment funds sector were discussed in our group under the headings of market risk, valuation and credit risk, regulatory risk and operational risk. Taking each one in turn:

30.2.1 Market risk

Market risk was identified as the prevailing financial market instability and heightened volatility, as unleashed by the collapse of Lehman Brothers in September 2008 and which has resulted in a loss of confidence both in financial markets and in investment funds and diminished fund industry growth. This instability is accentuated by investors switching between investment funds intent on chasing short-term performance at the expense of continuity and stability.

In a sense, investment funds were oversold. The diminished industry growth is reflected both in a decline in AUM (which has since corrected itself) and in the reduced number of households owning investment funds (which has yet to recover).

The discussed and agreed responses to this challenge are itemized below:

1) Investor confidence has to be restored. This involves providing both better 'education' about the purpose of investment funds and also better and more easily understood data on the performance of funds. Investment funds provide investors with the ability to own a share in the capital markets with lower transaction costs, less expensive diversification, professional management and more transparent and audited results than owning individual securities or other financial intermediaries.

2) Education should start at the aggregate level. Programs and reports should be developed that present, in easily understood form, a clear picture of the performance of funds on an aggregate level. This involves performance statistics for all funds, perhaps disaggregated by country and type (e.g., growth, income funds, etc.). In addition, the performance has to be put in the perspective of a long-term investor, not that of a short-term trader. Because of their ability to offer low-cost diversification, good performance, and the ability to overcome short-term movements in market levels, investment funds are a preferred instrument for an investor planning for his or her future. The investor has to be educated about the favorable risk characteristics of funds and shown that simply return chasing or buying a small portfolio of stocks cannot produce results as favorable as those produced by owning funds.

Part of this process has to be the development of the appropriate and easily understood benchmarks to judge fund performance. External information providers, such as Morningstar, will and do produce benchmarks for the investor. It is important that the industry plays a role in the development and dissemination of benchmarks. If it does not do so, it will find that it is judged by criteria, which may or may not be relevant. Only if the industry sets realistic and appropriate standards can it be assured that at least some third-party providers will supply appropriate criteria for judging the industry as well as for judging individual funds.

3) Work to develop transparency and consistency. While the industry has done a good job of creating transparent return data, work still remains to be carried out in developing external and internal transparency and consistency. It is of key importance that marketing and sales personnel do a careful and objective job of presenting fund information. If a good product is portrayed inaccurately at the point of sale, the purchaser may be dissatisfied. Controls need to be exercised on all marketing and sales materials.

4) Switching has pros and cons. The ability of fund holders to switch their investments at low or no cost between funds in the same complex or between funds in different complexes is both a major advantage of and hindrance to funds. It is an advantage because it has appropriate appeal to the serious investor. The serious investor will want, and should have the right, to switch funds across types of investments. Switching is logical and has economic rationale as an investor's circumstances change because of health, age, or employment. It is also logical because relative returns may result in an investor having too large a percentage of his or her portfolio invested in a category of funds that has done well over a long period of time. These types of trades should not be discouraged. However, the short-term trader is damaging the funds. The trader that tries to exploit short-term returns imposes costs on longer-term fund holders. Such switches can be particularly costly in times of crisis in the financial markets.

5) Need to develop new solutions. Mechanisms have to be developed that penalize frequent traders without imposing high cost on long-term investors. Measures are needed to handle the liquidity and dilution problems that occur at times of crisis. The impact of solutions such as entry and exit fees, switching fees for intervals shorter than a specified time period, and swing pricing have to be investigated and IT systems developed to study and implement these alternatives.

The industry has to position itself with respect to increased competition between active funds, index funds, exchange-traded funds (ETFs), hedge funds, and money market funds. The risk–return characteristics of each of these instruments need to be examined along with the appropriateness of each instrument for different types of investors. For example, ETFs may be a superior product for the frequent trader but not for the longer-term investor. The existence of ETFs might actually help investment funds by siphoning off frequent traders.

The fund industry (especially the UCITS brand) needs to promote itself more. With the industry facing strong competition from related products (i.e., ETFs, structured products, etc.), the industry needs to explain to clients the advantages of entering UCITS funds. These advantages include: strong risk control (UCITS risk limitation, value-at-risk (VaR) stress testing on sophisticated funds); strong governance; high liquidity (daily liquidity and limitations on illiquid securities); high transparency (KID risk indicators that are volatility based); and fair valuation (daily mark-to-market and net asset value (NAV) calculations).

Finally, in examining performance and developing the risk–return characteristics of individual products, appropriate measures of tail risk and (VaR) need to be developed. These models, properly implemented, can be used to understand worst-case scenarios and serve as a useful addition to mean variance analysis. These measures should be incorporated into investment management systems.

30.2.2   Valuation and credit risk

Valuation and credit risk was discussed in the group on the basis of price discontinuities and disparities, which pose problems associated with valuation and credit assessment, and the failure of some instruments held by a fund. An additional lesson from the crisis is how massive new fund flows in a market with increasing spreads can lead to significant dilution effects in a 'single-NAV universe', damaging fund performance.

Ideally a bid-offer NAV would mitigate most of the risk impact, but instead measures such as swing pricing and antidilution levies have been introduced, which may not prove effective. Liquidity risk and its appropriate management is another area that has received a great deal of attention. As certain asset classes turn less liquid, managers may be forced to sell liquid assets when investors are redeeming the funds, leaving the remaining investors with less attractive and more illiquid assets. If proven business and IT models to manage and/or monitor liquidity/eligibility and investor behavior are not in place, the risk of acting too late becomes all the greater and carries with it significant related financial and reputational risks.

The first steps in meeting these challenges are: to identify a more reliable and transparent valuation process; develop models for determining prices for non-publicly traded securities; and models for publicly traded securities when markets are closed.

Closely aligned with this is the development of internal credit models. Independent credit ratings are now required in the US. Both valuation and credit models will require the development of procedures to monitor the implementation of the process and to assess the accuracy of the results over time.

Systems must be developed to monitor risk-control measures and compliance functions at each stage of the transaction process and management chain. This involves implementation from front to back office, distribution, asset management, private wealth and advisory services. If risk is controlled in the investment process, but not at the final point of sale, the risk-control function will not be properly implemented. To ensure consistency, straight-through-processing (STP) and algorithmic trading must be used.

Risk management strategy and IT solutions must involve assuring and determining the integrity of the data, models and processes. This must be done at every stage of the investment distribution and sales chain.

30.2.3   Regulatory risk

Identified here was the increased pace of regulatory reform, which is creating initial uncertainty and dislocation. For the investment management industry, by and large, the regulatory and compliance challenges in the years ahead will be unprecedented. Among the manifold changes to be taken into account at the strategic, tactical, systemic and operational levels are the new regulatory framework and demands of the landmark Wall Street Reform and Consumer Protection Act (Dodd-Frank Act) in the US, AIFMD, MiFID conduct of business, PRIPs, Solvency II and UCITS IV (and soon UCITS V) in the European Union (EU), as well as, on an international level, the new tax rules and standards primarily embodied in IFRS 9.

Regulation is both good and bad in the sense that it endows the industry with a great deal of credibility but it remains uncertain what the future holds.

It was generally agreed that regulatory risk will in the long run engender greater product and market transparency as described in more detail below.

We also agreed that the industry should be spurred into becoming less reticent and more forthcoming by engaging in dialogue with regulators to find common ground on issues of compliance and legal requirements. Good regulation is advantageous to the industry. Furthermore, becoming part of the regulatory process will provide more lead-time in adjusting to the future legislation. Self-regulation is in the best interest of the industry. The fund industry offers perhaps the most transparent product available to the public. Nevertheless, funds should: a) tighten consumer protection and fiduciary standards; b) exert a greater influence on management to exercise caution in decision-making; and c) clarify or dispel uncertainty surrounding new regulations.

It is in the interests of the industry to simplify its structure. In order to add both more transparency and simplicity, the industry should advocate standardizing tax requirements to reduce change and administrative burdens, ease restrictions and reduce the complexity of fund structures.

Finally, the industry should recognize that extending regulation to the hedge fund industry entails a structural shift that could pose a potential risk to the investment fund industry, in the sense that investment funds might become more like hedge funds, and vice versa, marring the distinctions between the two.

30.2.4   Operational risk

Operational risk involves the business-related risk associated with investment fund liability for investor obligations. For the purposes of this discussion, we defined operational risk as a risk arising from execution of an investment fund company's business functions. It is a very broad concept, which focuses on the risks arising from the people, systems and processes through which a company operates.

It also includes other categories such as fraud risks, legal risks, physical or environmental risks. A widely-used definition of operational risk is the one contained in the Basel II regulations. This definition states that operational risk is the risk of loss resulting from inadequate or failed internal processes, people and systems, or from external events. In this context, the group agreed that there was a need for investment fund organizations to take the steps as outlined below:

1) Start by accepting that people, processes and systems are imperfect and that errors can arise at every level of internal operations as well as in the interface with the public.
2) Then, assess the size of acceptable loss appetite for operational risk.
3) The next step is a commitment to a level of expenditure in order to develop monitoring and control systems to ensure that the desired level of risk is not exceeded.
4) Eliminating any chance of loss would be prohibitively expensive if not impossible. Holding risk of loss to the low level achieved in the past involves:
   a. Assessing the assets held in the funds and ensuring to the extent possible that they are appropriate, given the investor behavioral pattern.
   b. Pursuing transparency in all stages of the investment process. This is particularly important at the point of sale: basic interface with the client.
   c. Reviewing and improving transparency and accuracy of product offering. Investors should be helped to understand the rewards from, and even more important, the risks associated with any product requirements. Failure to meet disclosure requirements is a risk that should be minimized.
   d. Proceeding with the development of systems and processes to comply with disclosure.

30.3   Cost challenges

The four key challenges for the immediate and medium-term future related to cost issues in the investment funds sector were identified and examined in our group under the categories of industry concentration, external outsourcing, fee shrinkage and cost/profit allocation. Taking each in turn:

30.3.1   Industry concentration

Cost considerations must take into account the investment fund industry's increasingly concentrated structure that arises because of the market power of the largest players and the increasing costs of entering the industry. Measuring the economies of scale for both individual funds and fund complexes remains incomplete. Studies indicate that European asset/fund managers have very different cost structures. Some have lower IT backbone costs but higher marginal costs due to less efficiency and scalability. Others have higher IT backbone costs but lower marginal costs due to investments in efficiency and scalability.

On the one side, the industry is facing tough cost competition, lower margins, more volatile outflows, and rising regulatory demands. At the same time, meeting client needs with more complex products will put more pressure on the industry. The number of yearly fund launches needs to be reduced and at the same time the success rate of new fund launches needs to be increased.

Therefore, the resources invested in developing new funds will increase and the development time will lengthen. The fund industry must develop tools that provide a planning process and follow-up culture, enabling the industry to learn from past experiences and failures and also obtain a much clearer picture of client needs before developing new products (i.e., adopting a client-driven approach instead of product push). Further, the complexity also requires a much stronger project culture, enabling companies to run complex projects as fast and as cheaply as possible.

One of the key lessons to be drawn from the studies is that if the investment has yet to be made and the wish is to become more scaleable, an investment fund company can either team up with an operational outsourcing partner or invest in an in-house platform and organization. But if the investment has already been made, then the company will be better off the more volume it adds to a scalable platform. However, caution has to be exercised about where to focus efforts and services, and the company must not lose sight of how to channel the right products to the right clients in the most cost-effective way. The agreed responses to this challenge are listed below:

1) Economies of scale at the fund level and fund complex level are not as well understood as they might be. At the individual fund level, more analysis is needed of the trade-off between the impact of increased fund size on the need to find more profitable investments and the necessity of larger transactions and the impact of this on transaction costs, versus the ability of large funds to hire better managers and gain name recognition in the market place.

2) For fund families there can be a tension between economies and diseconomies of scale, but the advantages of larger size are more compelling than the advantages at the fund level. The advantages of size for more efficient IT operations, more professional trading desks, reputational recognition and sales and distribution functions are easily recognized. Of course at some point, problems of span of control, managing larger organizations and

supervising the actions of a large number of employees may overtake the advantages of size.

3) Given the advantages of size, particularly at the fund family level, increased concentration in the investment fund industry is likely to occur. This concentration of funds has proceeded rapidly in the US and in Europe. The advantage of large size, together with the increases in the cost of market entry, has resulted in fewer investment funds. The largest funds have to monitor the impact of size on costs. They must refrain from monopolistic behavior with respect to distribution and costs, or they may face the threat of more regulation.

4) Funds in Europe have structural barriers to their obtaining the full benefit of economies of scale. Technical and fiscal barriers continue to impede the free and unrestricted flow of investment funds across borders. Funds are fragmented by legal restrictions in cross-border sales and by tax regimes in different countries. These frictions need to be addressed.

5) Finally, fund managers should review their business models in light of the new opportunities under UCITS IV (i.e. mergers of funds, master-feeder funds, management company passports), and they should attempt to find solutions to optimize performance.

30.3.2   External outsourcing

Outsourcing in terms of benefits and costs poses challenges as well as opportunities. Functions being outsourced include: distribution, back-office operations, IT and portfolio management. In outsourcing it is necessary not only to look at the direct costs, but also the quality of the service obtained and the cost of monitoring quality.

Emerging from the discussion was agreement on the need for investment fund organizations to take the following steps:

1) Examine areas for outsourcing. In considering areas that might be outsourced, the fund complex should examine whether it has a competitive advantage in the area. Does it do something better than an external supplier can? Does it have special skills or knowledge that an outside supplier does not have? If so, the functions should not be transferred, or at the very least, the cost of sharing the complex's special skills with others should be considered.

2) Assess costs and benefits of outsourcing. Models and methods should be developed to evaluate outsourcing. These methods should include more than an examination of costs. They must include an analysis of the quality of the products and services that may be outsourced.

3) Monitor the performance of outsourced functions. Construct metrics and systems to continuously monitor important functions that have been

outsourced. The easiest part of the process is monitoring costs. The more difficult problem is designing metrics that measure quality. This is particularly important in those functions where quality has a direct impact on the product that funds deliver.

All of these processes require IT solutions that, based on the individual investment management company's business requirements, can assist in evaluating and monitoring outsourced functions.

30.3.3 Fee shrinkage

Regulatory action, market competition and company restructuring are resulting in declining investor costs, including reduced fees. Fees should naturally come down owing to increased competition both within the industry and across product lines.

The question is: do fees shrink to the degree that investment no longer is channeled into the activities that are of benefit to the industry? When the markets head south, the first thing that investment fund companies tend to do is to jettison the services they really need in the long run, i.e., educational services; they tend not to put money into systems at the very point they really need those systems to safeguard against risk.

The industry must prepare for increased pressures on fees. Active managers in particular are under fee pressure from index funds and ETFs, as well as from government coercion. The industry has to educate the public to examine fees, but also to look beyond fees to performance. Given a fixed level of management performance, higher fees mean lower returns to investors. However, better investment performance before fees can result in a fund offering higher returns to investors even if fees are higher.

Funds have to examine fees and consider fee levels in the context of investor returns and competitive lower fee products (i.e., index funds).

Fees in the active fund industry have declined and are likely to continue to decline over time. This means that management has to place increased emphasis on controlling costs and pricing products correctly. Cost control systems will have to be designed to increase flexibility, not only over time, but also in response to changes in inflows and outflows to the fund complex.

In times of stress, management should avoid cutting resources to the very areas that allow the fund to compete successfully in the long run. There is a tendency when resources are tight to trim resources to the key areas that do not immediately affect the bottom line. Often, resources are decreased for IT and analytical control functions at the time when they are most needed.

It is a categorical imperative to design flexibility into systems so that they can respond both in terms of costs and services to short-run changes in the industry.

30.3.4   Cost/profit allocation

Companies operating multiple funds and/or multiple products find it difficult to define the cost and profit of a particular fund, creating problems related to cost allocation and assessment. Fund companies must learn to transform cost into product profitability. Concerns remain regarding proper principles for allocation of common costs that ensure fair treatment of investors, as well as gauging entry and exit charges of swing pricing elements.

Fund management companies need to develop a prudent cost allocation and income overview, ensuring that profitability is properly measured. It is of vital importance that fund companies obtain fund information that takes into account the entire cost which originates from the production value chain. This will enable the fund company to close down loss-making funds (or re-engineer the funds), and hereby free up running capacity. In addition, the industry should be able to develop more transparent benchmarking tools that give the ability to benchmark efficiency in the fund production platforms spanning the industry.

Fund families must develop more robust models of cost allocation. The distinction between marginal and average costing is very important in the investment fund business, because so many costs are joint costs. The marginal cost of adding a fund to a complex is low and on that basis a particular fund may look profitable. This can easily lead to a situation where each fund more than covers its marginal cost, but the fund complex does not cover total cost.

Costs are marginal (variable) only with respect to a particular decision. Models have to be developed to not only measure the marginal cost of any decision but also to see if that decision covers both marginal costs and a rational allocation of joint costs. This means that investment management systems have to be developed that allow the alternative cost structure of any decision to be evaluated.

The level of overall cost has to be decreased. There are several areas where cost savings can be achieved. The level of automation and STP applications within the European investment fund industry is too low. Inefficiencies and potential for cost savings are most apparent in the cross-border distribution of funds. The growing importance of open/guided architecture exacerbates the ensuing operational costs for fund families and investors.

Increasing the level of automation and back-office operations offers one of the best strategies for fund managers to control costs and risks. All key players along the value chain, particularly fund distributors, must coordinate to increase the benefit of automation.

Part of cost allocation and profit attribution has to be the development of better performance measurement techniques. What should be the proper way to measure performance? Should it be on an absolute basis, relative to a peer group of products, or relative to index funds? Risk as well as return metrics must be considered in any evaluation model.

There is a growing body of evidence that past performance is somewhat pre-dictive of future performance. There is also strong evidence that investors track performance and place more money into funds that have done well in the past one to three years, while they remove money from funds that have done poorly. This creates problems for poorly performing funds, because their diminished size results in an increase in expense ratios and exacerbates the problem of reversing poor performance. On the other hand, large amounts of new money flowing into an investment fund can create problems of investment allocation even while it results in the spreading of fixed costs.

30.4   Growth challenges

The four key challenges for the immediate and medium-term future related to growth issues in the investment funds sector were identified in our group as private retirement savings, products and planning, emerging markets, and scale and internationalization. Taking each one in turn:

30.4.1   Private retirement savings

As a result of changing demographics, increased private retirement savings will represent a major source of growth. The tendency to save more and retire later will spur growth in the industry. In a recent US survey, 75% of inves-tors in mutual investment funds stated that their primary purpose for holding funds was for retirement. At this point in time, 36% of the assets in US mutual funds arise from formal retirement accounts. This amount is more than US$4 trillion.

Secondly, the trend in pension funds is shifting more and more away from defined benefit plans to defined contribution plans. Further, given the demo-graphics of population in almost every developed country, the need to set aside savings for retirement is certain to continue growing. This represents a tremendous opportunity for investment funds, as they are a natural vehicle for retirement savings and pension funds because of transparency and daily valuations.

The impact of this will be discussed in further detail below.

The fact that in almost every country around the world, life expectancy is increasing means that there will be fewer working adults to fund more retired workers. Paying for retirement, while allowing retired people to live with dignity, will be a major problem around the world.

The solution will involve encouraging more savings at an earlier age and the education of all employees. This is an area where investment funds can and should play a leading role. It not only represents a tremendous business oppor-tunity; it represents an area where the investment fund industry can make a significant contribution to society.

Investment funds are a natural component of a retirement system, because they offer transparency in general, but particularly with respect to valuing the collection of assets in the fund, flexibility in design and the ability to change the mix of funds. This latter factor allows the participant to achieve goals as his or her particular circumstances change.

Investment funds should be encouraged to take a leading role in educating the public and policymakers on the need to save for retirement and the need for incentives to encourage such savings. On an overall level, the industry should advocate the kind of tax policy that encourages savings for retirement. It should also be a strong advocate for portability in pensions, both within and between countries. These two steps are necessary for a country to gain traction on the increasingly critical problem of providing its population with sufficient resources for retirement.

Given current demographics, the creation of a private pension system should mean that there are large inflows to the system, inflows that should exceed outflows for many years. The investment fund industry should benefit from this as long as it develops in a way that both encourages the use of fund products that are attractive as well as serve an economic purpose. There are several steps that the industry should take:

1) The industry should both use existing channels and establish new distribution channels (third party or direct) that offer products and services that are investment fund related. A large part of the success of investment fund companies will depend on the design of products and services that meet the needs of participants in pension funds.

2) While product design is important, the real breakthrough will be in advising participants on how to plan for retirement: what asset allocation is appropriate given the participant's wealth level, predicted income path, and planned retirement age. This requires advice at every stage of a participant's working life but particularly at retirement. Here investment fund companies should provide related pension services such as annuities, financial planning advice, record keeping, etc.

3) The industry should develop products that are designed to meet retirement needs. While advice on the right product mix is important, some products can either be a replacement or a starting point for individual choice. One product class that can start this process is a stable of life-cycle funds. These funds serve as an asset mix vehicle for pension holders at different stages of their working and retired life. The guidance they provide is important. The concept and its implementation are still relatively new and need to be refined.

4) Participants in pension funds differ in wealth and planned retirement age, but they also differ in their attitude toward risk. Products should be

developed that serve these different clienteles. They include, at a minimum, products that are designed to offer an inflation-protected return and products that are designed to offer an absolute return.

30.4.2   Products and planning

New products and financial planning (with an emphasis on saving more and retiring later) will spur growth. Innovation has always been one of the investment fund industry's strong points. The industry has traditionally tended to think in terms of product in the hope of attracting capital and making a profit. Investment fund companies take the world of securities and slice and dice them into any one of several ways to form investment funds.

The most aggregate way to partition funds is into active funds and passive funds (i.e., index funds). Passive funds are growing in importance. In the US, 13.7% of mutual fund assets are held in passive funds. These funds have much lower fees than actively managed funds. Funds are also formed by asset characteristics (e.g., growth, value, or income or stable funds).

Designing active funds generally involves determining areas in which the fund company has special ability, funds that will have market appeal, or funds needed to fill out a product line to compete with other fund families. The industry is now thinking more in terms of delivering a process rather than a product.

Business is being generated by offering financial planning at different levels – partly as a way to sell product but also as a very useful tool in itself. More and more organizations have financial software packages that are aimed at delivering a useful product to the client and helping him or her plan. This includes everything from full-scale private banking for very wealthy clients to tax planning for small-scale clients. Here are the steps that must be taken.

1) The industry has done a good job of designing funds that partition securities according to their type (growth, value, income, small or large securities, etc.). Funds are also frequently designed to appeal to a set of tastes or social goals; e.g., green funds, energy funds, funds that avoid socially undesirable products, such as tobacco. A fund complex should consider the economics of these funds as well as the label. For example, are green funds held because people feel good about holding the stocks in these funds or are the stocks in these funds projected to have a high return because of their investment philosophy?

2) Fund complexes are starting to think about funds not simply as an aggregation of securities by security characteristics, but as an aggregation of securities to satisfy customer needs. The ability to expand the types of funds offered with the emphasis on investor needs will be a major engine for growth. New developing products to meet investor needs include:

lifestyle funds, absolute return funds, inflation-protected funds and structured funds.

3) Associated with new products to satisfy investor financial needs and risk tolerances will be an increase in financial services designed to help investors pick the right funds and make appropriate asset allocations. This will involve a change in the industry, with fund complexes delivering both a service and the products to accompany that service.

4) Fund complexes run the gamut from large complexes, which offer a large number of investment funds covering almost every conceivable division of the market, to boutique complexes offering a small number of funds, which tend to concentrate on a specific area of the market. Large funds can and should deliver advisory services. Smaller specialized fund complexes will be under increased pressure to find a mechanism to become part of an organizational structure that can meet investor needs.

5) As process becomes more important to the industry, the value chain of an organization, and its complete management from advisory to distribution outlets, will assume far greater prominence in efforts to gain and maintain competitive advantage. Investment management companies with a retail banking network at their disposal have a built-in advantage in selling financial products based on advice, whereas products sold through third-party distribution channels are much more volatile and dependent on short-term performance criteria and quality of advice to investors.

30.4.3 Emerging markets

Emerging markets will represent a significant growth opportunity for the industry as a source of new products and new customers. There will be a very rapid growth in wealth, and a tremendous savings capacity in countries like China and India. As the share of emerging economies in global economic output keeps increasing, these markets will become an essential source of demand for investment products and management.

The challenge is that competition between European funds and funds domiciled in Asia, the Middle East and Latin America is likely to increase with the help of local regulators to promote the developments of a local industry replicating the success of the EU's UCITS provisions, at times with the tacit support of global fund management companies. One of the possible consequences of AIFMD will be to drive fund managers into managing outside the EU, a set of alternative management funds targeted at clients located outside Europe. Steps that should be taken to achieve this include the following:

1) The industry should propose solutions to promote cost efficiency and competitiveness of European investment funds. It should promote their attractiveness in terms of regulation and risk-adjusted performance and ensure

that this promotion remains a priority for the industry and European policy.

2) Fund complexes should examine and decide whether or not to establish a presence in a market where competitive advantage is not immediately self-evident. Where they decide to enter a market, they should consider market penetration tactics, such as joint marketing arrangements, partnerships, or outsourcing to local players as a means to safeguard against domestic political uncertainties and economic vagaries. Funds must be aware of and overcome cultural and institutional difficulties with emphasis on objective and neutral product offerings and service provision. They must apply a global approach combined with local skills and expertise with a view to extending the investment fund franchise into targeting emerging markets.

3) Part of a global approach is to create provisions against liquidity issues, such as massive outflows and other disruptive financial influences. The bigger the worldwide dispersion of a fund complex's investors, the better the competitive advantage.

4) Funds should identify other emerging markets that are closer to home with greater cultural and linguistic affinities; i.e., Eastern Europe, Latin America, etc.

5) Finally, they should roll out the global investment management and distribution platform and interface this with every local outlet for subscription and redemption purposes. This involves applying and, where necessary, adopting the in-house savings concept and other advisory mechanisms through the local market.

30.4.4   Scale and internationalization

The scale and internationalization of the industry will grow in strength but challenges will arise because fund products are not standardized and standardization is hindered by several influences, particularly tax policy.

A key question related to the success (or failure) of internationalization efforts is whether in future the bank-affiliated investment fund model widely seen in Europe or the more independent mutual investment fund provider devoid of conflict of interest as prevalent in the US (i.e., Fidelity, Franklin Templeton, etc.) will prevail. Here the opinion remains divided over what the best operating method is to achieve competitive advantage in a climate of growing internationalization.

For some, full integration with a self-owned distribution channel is the preferred method; others opt for third-party distribution and open architecture. Others still, view distribution via bank channels at least as important as distribution through independent channels. In the US, for example, only 9% of mutual investment funds are distributed through banks; in Europe, the proportion is overwhelmingly larger (in some countries above 80%). The group's overall consensus is summarized as follows:

1) It is now widely recognized that the industry's competitive landscape has changed. There is a need to understand the reasons why some sectors of the investment fund industry have experienced less growth and to identify the major factors behind this slowdown in growth.
2) It would help growth in the industry if similar fund products were merged, particularly in the European market place, which remains prone to fragmentation. More concentration among major players has occurred in the market, particularly where new funds are concerned. And more concentration has occurred among those players that are operating across markets.
3) Industry players need to assess whether their respective fund platforms and volumes are scaleable, particularly where consolidation enters the picture. Size and scale together are more or less good for the organizations that have the necessary resources and integrated platforms; however, it is bad for the small players that cannot afford scale. It may be good for the industry as a whole, but will probably make it more difficult for small players to enter the market and succeed.
4) Finally, the value proposition of those companies that succeed needs to be identified. Cross-border organizations have probably recovered better than their local-based counterparts in Belgium, the Netherlands and Spain, for example. Anywhere between 80 and 90% of asset inflows are captured by 20% of firms operating in the industry.

30.5 Conclusions

The preceding discussion can be summarized in four main conclusions:

First, business issues related to risk, cost and growth factors are interconnected and impact investment funds in varying degrees of significance.

Second, increased market volatility, financial instability and regulatory change have become permanent features of the global industry landscape, creating challenges as well as opportunities for industry players. Although the outlook for the investment funds industry remains broadly optimistic, the ability to manage risk, cost and growth respectively will separate the winners from the losers.

Third, changing demographics (i.e. aging populations) will alter investment funding patterns, creating new cost challenges but also growth opportunities for the investment management industry as a whole.

Finally, internationalization and the right choice of investment management system are key determinants in controlling risk of both a market and a regulatory nature, curbing costs whether in the IT or operational sphere and spurring growth in terms of both business and product.

Note

1. This chapter is based on discussions within the Investment funds group at the SimCorp StrategyLab Copenhagen Summit 2011 held 22–23 February 2011. Members included Martin J. Gruber (head), Professor, (Leonard N. Stern School of Business, NYU); Dr Massimo Massa, Professor, INSEAD; Ulrik Modigh, Head of Asset Management Operations, Nordea Savings & Asset Management; Brian S. Jensen, Head of Business Processes, Nordea Savings & Asset Management; Peter Hertel, Domain Manager, Fund Accounting, SimCorp; Bernard Delbecque, Director of Research and Economics, European Fund and Asset Management Association (EFAMA); and Merele A. May, Senior VP Investment Operations, American Century Investments.

31

Current and Future Challenges Faced by Asset Managers

Stephen J. Brown

With few exceptions, asset managers emerged from the recent financial turbulence with their reputations among clients severely tested.[1] Many failed to
protect their investors against the broad market decline and increased volatility that accompanied the crisis. Others sold investors financial products they
themselves clearly failed to understand – and could not explain adequately
to clients – while several major funds locked in their customers to prevent
redemptions in disorderly markets. Still others failed in key areas of due diligence and risk management.

The alternative asset management industry as a whole was found lacking
in transparency as well as effective risk control and operating efficiency,
compounding the traditional challenge of producing significant and durable
excess returns. Consequently, the post-crisis era has begun with the industry
facing skeptical, sharp-eyed and cost-conscious investors who have not for-
gotten their recent experience, together with low-cost asset management alternatives and demanding regulatory changes.

The discussions reflected in this chapter consider in some depth operational
risk issues that reached their peak in the Madoff and Bear Stearns episodes,
including the need for serious external audits by firms exposed to high levels
of reputational risk, stress-testing for both liquidity and earnings streams, the
structure of incentives, and the problem of risk aggregation in its transmission
to senior management and boards. Legal and regulatory risks are part of this
mosaic, as is the application of a good dose of commonsense alongside traditional and proprietary risk modeling.

Equally important are rigorous cost accounting discipline – an area where
the firms have often been found wanting in their rush to boost AUM – as
well as operating leverage in the face of high fixed costs and variable revenues, and trading costs and uncertainty over the importance of economies of
scale. Given the difficulty of persistent outperformance in returns, costs are a
critical competitive element and require imaginative outsourcing, application

601

of world-class technology, and in some cases serious dialog with clients about appropriate fee structures.

Asset management has bright growth prospects worldwide. But unless issues of risk and efficiency are addressed more effectively than in the past, it is the rapidly evolving competition that will be the main beneficiary of that growth.

This chapter provides a compelling diagnostic of these key drivers of the asset management industry in the second decade of the 21st Century and their implications for competitive performance and strategic direction going forward. It points to the challenges of rebuilding confidence while at the same time dealing with intensified competition from several quarters and formulating a constructive set of responses to the inevitable increase in regulatory pressure – some of which remains highly uncertain – that just as inevitably follows financial trauma.

The emphasis here is on improved transparency at all levels – products, processes, costs and compliance – and a fundamental reconsideration by top management of these issues as sources of competitive advantage rather than purely defensive challenges. Asset managers able to meet these challenges in the face of rigid non-traditional competitors are likely to be most prominent among the winners in a world where 'business as usual' is unlikely to produce the kind of growth, risk profile or operating efficiency the industry has enjoyed in the past.

31.1   Introduction

The greatest challenge for the asset management industry since the global financial crisis is to rebuild confidence. Confidence has been shaken, regulators have been stirred, an increasing groundswell of regulation is in the pipeline, and the industry has to get to grips with these issues. Last but not least, clients are concerned and the industry must develop procedures and techniques to deal with this crisis in confidence.

What clearly emerged from discussions with industry representatives is the need for asset management companies to increase transparency at all levels: transparency in terms of the cost structure as many companies do not fully comprehend their own individual cost structures; and the need to increase transparency in business processes – if the companies fail to fully understand some of the products they are selling, how can they explain them to the clients?

In the period before the crisis the asset management enterprise was very different from what it is today. Businesses were able to survive with very high cost structures. Now we are seeing a need to control costs and a need to be transparent within the organization on the nature of the products being sold and the magnitude of the costs necessary to provide those products.

For the asset management business as a whole, the most pressing challenge is the crisis in confidence resulting from the financial crisis. On top of this, there is increased competition from low-cost providers as well as increased government regulation and intervention in the markets.

The opportunity for growth lies with those enterprises that are most able to meet these challenges by providing transparency to their clients, their stakeholders and in particular their regulators. Those enterprises that can meet this challenge will be the ones that will be the most effective in meeting future challenges. They will be the winners in this new and different environment.

The purpose of this chapter is to summarize discussions with industry representatives with a view to examining in some detail the challenges the asset management business must confront as it approaches issues of risk, cost and the opportunities for growth in this sector. In a separate and final discussion we examine the interactions and main drivers that influence these challenges. Under each of these headings, we examine industry best practice designed to address the challenges that asset management faces in the years ahead.

31.2   Risk challenges

The expert group identified four key risk challenges for the asset management sector in the immediate and medium-term future. These fall under the headings of operational risk, market risk, regulatory risk and legal risk. We now examine each in turn.

31.2.1   Operational risk

Operational risk is the most significant risk factor facing the asset management business at this time. We adopt the Basel definition that holds operational risk as the risk of direct or indirect loss resulting from inadequate or failed internal processes, people or systems, or from external events excluding market or reputational risk.[2] To address this risk, the asset management industry needs to bring to bear state-of-the-art operational due diligence practices at every level of the organization.

First and most importantly, every asset management firm must understand that operational due diligence is central to its business model. This understanding goes beyond merely increasing the budget allocation to due diligence. Prior to the Madoff scandal, operational due diligence was seen as a necessary cost imposed by regulators on the asset management business.

Since Madoff, operational due diligence is seen as part of the value proposition, indeed as a source of alpha. This is particularly true in a delegated funds management context. In a context where some fund failures are highly predictable, not doing the necessary operational due diligence can have very serious consequences indeed. There are advanced information technology solutions that are emerging to address this critical need.

One often overlooked aspect of operational due diligence is the necessity to perform an external audit of information technology infrastructure on a periodic basis. With the growing complexity of instruments and markets, it is a constant challenge to update legacy information technology platforms to adapt to this ever-changing investment environment.

The May 2010 flash crash shows that failures in the information technology infrastructure can have widespread ramifications. It is therefore important to conduct external audits of the information technology infrastructure to ensure that this infrastructure is robust enough to meet the challenges posed by this changing market environment.

The increasing complexity of the trading environment implies the need for substantial improvements in counterparty and collateral management specifically with respect to over-the-counter (OTC) derivatives. This is an area where there is great potential for advances in information technology. Standard practice to this point has been to concentrate attention on the immediate counterparties to each transaction. However, the experience of the recent financial crisis has shown the importance of accounting for the systemic risk of those counterparties and the extent to which a liquidity crisis will negatively impact their ability to deliver on the terms of their contracts.[3]

The collapse of Bear Stearns, Lehman Brothers and other major financial institutions in the U.S. has emphasized the importance of using independent asset valuations wherever this is feasible. Given that illiquid assets are frequently marked to model rather than marked to market suggests the importance of external and independent valuations of fund assets.

Not only is this an important due diligence function – any increase in the transparency of the valuation process not only increases the confidence of outside investors but also of those responsible for managing the in-house trading function.

Related to the importance of independent asset valuation is the critical role played by the use of well-resourced and recognized external auditors. The Madoff case is the best possible example of the perils that follow from relying on the advice of small auditors. It is not merely that large accounting firms are more skilled and have access to tools and techniques unavailable to smaller accounting firms. It is also because large accounting firms have significant reputational capital at stake and perform their own internal operational due diligence before accepting asset management companies as clients.

The due diligence function itself needs to be rethought. The standard approach typically relies on a check-box bottom-up analysis of reports collected at local levels. There are many ways that processes, people and systems can fail, and the sheer volume of information in due diligence reports that filter up the management chain become so general as to be of limited use.

An operational failure that involves a conflict of interest at a local or branch office may have limited impact on the asset management firm taken as a whole. However, the aggregated information may become so general as to miss important operational failures at the headquarters of the organization.

Part of the problem here is that the operational due diligence function is typically designed to meet the bare minimum regulatory requirements that may not have been designed to meet challenges not thought of when these requirements were established. These minimal standards would not in general match the specific problems faced by a particular asset management firm. For this reason, operational due diligence designed to meet specific regulatory mandates was not regarded with great seriousness by many asset management firms.

But the challenge facing the industry now and in the future is to improve investor confidence. The most effective way to do this is to improve operational transparency. One way of accomplishing this objective is to convince investors, regulators and other stakeholders that the asset management firm takes operational due diligence very seriously.

31.2.2   Market risk

We define market risk from the point of view of the enterprise rather than the point of view of the investor/client. For this reason, it is important to expand our view of market risk, going beyond market volatility to consider extreme or tail events that can impact the viability of the enterprise. The group discussions defined various ways of doing this as follows:

1) To address market risk, we must refine our stress-test analysis beyond standard value-at-risk (VaR) technologies.
2) We must re-examine short-term incentives of managers throughout the organization.
3) Finally, we must improve transparency at all levels of the organization.

Events of the recent financial crisis have emphasized the importance of developing advanced approaches to the use of stress-tests for worst-case scenarios. Extreme market events can cause a significant drawdown of assets under management (AUM), not merely because of the revaluation of assets, but also because of investor withdrawals.

This can significantly challenge the business model of asset managers in two ways. The organization can face a liquidity crisis as it attempts to meet current and anticipated investor withdrawals. At the same time, revenues – determined as a fraction of AUM – suffer a substantial decline. As such, the stress-tests must accommodate both contingencies.

Standard approaches to stress-testing involve VaR measures computed either using historical data or Monte Carlo approaches. These approaches can be very mechanical in application and rarely consider revenue loss and liquidity demands that can challenge the viability of the asset management firm. Indeed, when we consider market risk at the enterprise level, VaR can become part of the problem rather than part of the solution.

Mechanically applied VaR controls can have the adverse consequence of providing supervision with a false sense of security. For example, a manager can be lulled into a degree of complacency by a string of persistent positive returns that necessarily precede a significant drawdown of AUM in a negative market environment when there are no effective risk management practices in place. Perhaps this is why many managed funds missed the massive Madoff fraud. Standard VaR analysis of the suspiciously persistent positive returns would have indicated that Madoff was an extremely low-risk asset manager.

In the aftermath of the recent financial crisis, many observers have pointed to the undue reliance on short-term incentives as a leading cause of the crisis and the failure of many large and respected financial enterprises. As a consequence, there are many regulators who are calling for a re-evaluation of incentive contracts in the financial sectors.

The asset management business is not immune from this concern. Short-term incentives can encourage allocations to assets, which generate persistent short-term profits at the expense of significant tail risk for the enterprise as a whole. Beyond this there is the issue of soft-dollar accounts and the adverse short-term incentives these create for portfolio managers and others involved in the asset management function.

Concern about incentives raises a more general issue relating to transparency, particularly relating to the complexity of many of the financial product offerings of asset management companies. Events of the recent financial crisis revealed that many managers did not understand the characteristics of the complex financial products they were selling to clients and did not appreciate the risk they were taking in the name of the firm.

Either they did not know or they chose not to understand, given the focus on short-term profits and remuneration that these products generated. Greater transparency is just good business practice, not only in terms of client relations, but also in terms of enterprise risk management within the firm.

31.2.3   Regulatory risk

Financial regulation is of course by itself not a source of risk for the asset management enterprise. However, in Europe, the US and Asia the regulatory environment is in a state of flux. As a result, uncertainty about future regulations is a significant source of risk both for its potential impact on investor flows and for its impact on competitiveness.

This concern speaks to an important role for industry associations in mediating the relationship between regulators and the industry and resolving regulatory uncertainty at a time when the industry is challenged by reduced revenues and increasing costs of doing business.

This mediatory role can provide information in a two-way direction. After all, regulatory risk is largely a result of a lack of transparency in the rule-making process. By becoming actively involved in this process, the industry association can more effectively transmit industry concerns to regulators. In return, the association can give industry participants advance notice of prospective changes in rules and regulations that may affect the way they operate and the terms under which investors may commit funds.

Of course, the role of the industry association is not limited to that of being a conduit of information. The industry association can take a proactive role in influencing the nature of the regulatory environment in which firms operate. According to a report published in the New York Times in March 2007, one enterprise, Goldman Sachs in the US, spent more money lobbying the US Congress on proposed changes in laws governing the asset management business than did the entire asset management industry taken as a whole. It is not surprising then that the asset management industry had only limited influence in shaping the regulatory agenda that followed from the US financial crisis.

Another important role for the industry association is to urge regulators to give advance notice to individuals in the industry regarding future regulatory initiatives. There should be no surprises that would adversely affect the risk calculations and exposure of asset management entities. By the same token, a positive relationship between the industry and the regulators can foster and promote the development of effective self-regulatory mechanisms. The development of strong and robust self-regulatory mechanisms will offset any incentive on the part of regulators to institute mandatory requirements, which may not be in the interest of the industry or its clients.

Finally, one of the most important roles for the industry association is to advocate harmonization of standards and regulations that affect the asset management industry, certainly throughout Europe. Without harmonization there is the possibility of regulatory arbitrage and a flight to the least restrictive jurisdiction. This would be precisely counter to the objective of increasing investor confidence and transparency.

31.2.4 Legal risk

In this context, we define legal risk as the risk that arises when the asset management firm faces liabilities arising from its relationship with its investors, where these liabilities are implied but not explicitly defined in the contractual obligations of the firm to its investors.

An obvious response to this risk is to strengthen the legal and compliance functions within the asset management firm. Without a strong culture of compliance, individuals and groups within the asset management firms may create products and engage in sales and marketing activity that lead to significant costs and adverse legal obligations for the asset management firm.

As with all dimensions of risk, transparency is key. An important way in which one can reduce legal risk is to carefully review product-offering terms to clarify and improve transparency. In some instances, firms do not completely understand the characteristics of products being offered to clients. As a result, clients may not be well informed about these characteristics and create a legal liability for the firm should events occur that lead to a loss in value of these products.

31.3   Cost challenges

In the discussions with industry representatives the consensus emerged that, in the current operating environment, the business model of many asset management firms is challenged by the fact that costs are rising while the revenue base is not keeping pace. This has focused attention on the general lack of transparency in the cost structures of the asset management business. There is the need to deal with operating leverage that arises due to the fact that costs are fixed and do not scale to AUM, a prime determinant of revenue for the firm. Finally, the asset management business needs to deal with the fact that costs are rising as the business becomes more complex and more heavily regulated. Identified as four main challenges by the group, then, were cost structure, operating leverage, trading costs, and regulatory compliance costs. Taking each in turn:

31.3.1   Cost structure

Many asset management firms face the challenge of understanding and measuring their cost structure both for internal and external stakeholders. It would appear that the asset management business is unique in the difficulty it faces in appropriately allocating costs across different product lines.

In an environment of reduced revenue and increasing costs, it is imperative that the firm adopts transparent managerial accounting practices to understand and control costs through the entire value chain. The group identified various approaches to this as follows:

1) The first and most obvious point is to apply cost accounting disciplines that are common in other industries but that have not been generally applied in the asset management industry up to this point. When revenues were strong and positive across all product lines, there was not a great incentive

to examine costs and pricing across different products. The recent financial crisis has emphasized the importance of controlling costs and determining an appropriate basis for pricing product offerings.

2) In the same spirit, it is essential to examine and reappraise costs broken down into product, market data and customer along the entire value chain. Product pricing must reflect the cost of providing that product, and products should be re-examined where the cost of providing the product exceeds the revenue that product generates.

3) There is an obvious need to manage the client relationship in order to understand the cost of servicing that client. In the past, the focus has been on increasing AUM seemingly at any cost. Too little recognition has been given to the issue of appropriately managing the client service function and the fact that certain products require much greater customer servicing than others. An appropriate analysis of costs and revenues might lead to a pruning of the product offerings, concentrating on those products that yield the highest revenue per unit cost.

4) A related point is the importance of implementing effective transfer pricing within the organization so that the products are effectively costed-out. In the past, common costs associated with research and especially information technology functions were arbitrarily assigned to product lines. Sometimes there was no cost allocation of any kind. This inevitably leads to the result that weaker products are cross-subsidized by stronger product offerings.

5) One common cost that is extremely difficult to allocate appropriately is the hidden cost associated with maintaining embedded information systems technology. Managers often fail to recognize that this technology in many instances has a very short shelf-life, given recent and rapid changes in the trading environment. It is often more costly to maintain otherwise obsolete technology than to invest in new technology. However, since the necessary maintenance expenditures are not costed-out appropriately, managers will maintain the old systems rather than invest in new systems. They need to understand the magnitude of these costs and how they impact processes they use and the product mix they offer.

31.3.2   Operating leverage

Operating leverage arises because the asset management business is typically characterized by high fixed costs set against a highly variable revenue base. Since most AUM fee structures imply that revenues are tied to AUM, this implies the possibility of significant economies of scale in the provision of asset management services.

On the other hand, a market downturn that leads to a swift reduction in AUM both through revaluation and through investor withdrawals can challenge the business model of the asset management industry. To examine this question in any depth, it is necessary to study with some care both the cost structures and the extent to which revenue does indeed depend on the scale of operations.

Since the benefits of operating leverage are given by economies of scale in the provision of asset management services, it is important to develop techniques to measure accurately how large these economies might be and just how big one must be to build on the resulting cost advantage. This depends in turn on an accurate assessment of the cost structure associated with each product and how scaleable the investment function actually is. In many cases, there are capacity constraints that limit the potential gains from these economies of scale.

On the downside, there is the priority of at least considering outsourcing back-office functions in the event that AUM and the associated revenue fall below the fixed costs of providing these functions in-house. Outsourcing does allow otherwise fixed costs to be scaled to the size of the enterprise. However, there is a critical scale at which it makes sense to bring these functions back in-house.

In the past, the assumption has generally been made that the interests of the asset management company are best served by increasing the amount of AUM it has regardless of how much it costs to service those assets. In the past five to ten years, there has been a shift in the focus of the enterprise from maximizing the size of AUM to a consideration of what offerings are more or less profitable. This leads to the importance of entering into a dialog with clients about what fee structures are most appropriate in this context.

An important new development is the recognition that new and sophisticated products that are now coming to market imply higher personnel costs in terms of new hires or training existing staff. As we observe, these costs should be applied against the new products being offered instead of being just added to the general administrative cost overhead. At the same time, they simply add to the fixed costs of the enterprise unless the new products represent a net increase in AUM.

On the other hand, many of these new products are not fixed costs but vary with AUM. Examples of this are new quant products that rely extensively on the use of market data and information costs (i.e., index costs). These costs are frequently scaleable as they are typically charged as a function of AUM.

One approach to the operating leverage problem is to consider alternative product delivery vehicles, such as managed accounts in the context of institutional business. The problem of operating leverage arises because in the majority of cases, fees are locked into an AUM structure, while costs are relatively fixed. It is difficult and/or costly to re-examine fee structures at this point, although some clients are likely to push the industry down this path. Offsetting the potential advantages from alternative revenue bases, the asset management company needs to question the legal and regulatory costs associated with alternative product delivery vehicles.

31.3.3 Trading costs

Trading costs have generally risen in the period subsequent to the financial crisis, as trading and liquidity have not yet returned to levels experienced before the crisis. These costs extend beyond commissions and market impact to include the costs associated with the information technology necessary to adapt to the trading environment that is currently emerging. This cost challenge can best be addressed by adapting the trading function within the asset management firm to this new trading environment. The group discussed and identified a number of steps to rise to this challenge as outlined here:

1) The first and necessary step toward accomplishing this goal is to reduce trading costs by lessening the reliance on legacy information technology infrastructures to handle new trading environments. Too often the solution is to merely adapt existing information technology platforms to the new patterns of trading. This is costly, inefficient and possibly ineffective. Rather than just throw money into old technology, it may be a better idea to develop new information technology infrastructures to deal with the changing technological environment.
2) A second approach is to consider alternative trading strategies such as algorithmic trading, as well as methods and platforms that can reduce commissions and market-impact charges. A good example is the fact that high-conviction managers can boost capacity limitations through the use of dark pools and other trading technologies. Another and related approach is to develop and implement STP functions across the entire value chain.
3) It is important to unbundle research and transaction services. By eliminating soft-dollar accounts and separately outsourcing the research and investment services functions, we can not only control trading costs but also appropriately cost out and attribute the service function costs to each product area. In addition, the existence of soft-dollar accounts creates an adverse incentive to trade when it is not strictly necessary to do so.
4) With asset management firms becoming global operations with trading functions around the world, an important element of cost control is to professionalize, automate and integrate the trading functions across developed and developing markets. Given the internationalization of asset management firms, there is the opportunity of introducing best-practice techniques across the enterprise rather than to delegate the monitoring and control to each regional unit.

In summary, while trading costs have risen due to changes in the trading function in the period subsequent to the financial crisis, asset management firms can take advantage of the new opportunities presented to actually reduce trading costs significantly by adapting to these new circumstances.

31.3.4   Regulatory compliance costs

In response to the financial crisis, regulatory compliance costs have increased. In some cases the costs have increased substantially. These costs are unavoidable and are a necessary burden of doing business.

In light of this, there is an opportunity for the industry to treat regulatory compliance in a positive and constructive way to re-establish investor confidence in the industry and to encourage transparency. In order to achieve this objective, it is necessary to frame the regulatory compliance as providing a long-term confidence-building exercise for the individual company's clients and stakeholders.

One unintended consequence of the more strictly enforced compliance regime is to provide an opening to the industry associations to urge upon regulators the priority of harmonizing investment company regulations across national boundaries. This will eliminate the possibility of regulatory arbitrage and create a level playing field for all.

In addition, the existence of a uniform international regulatory regime can only help increase investor confidence in the industry that was badly shaken by the financial crisis and the Madoff fraud, which crossed international boundaries and exploited differences in regulatory regimes.

31.4   Challenges

In the aftermath of the financial crisis, challenges and opportunities for growth have emerged. The ability to adapt to these changes is key to survival in this industry. There has been a significant increase in competition in the industry from low-cost providers, and this will necessitate a repositioning of the product mix for most of the asset management business. The low-cost providers depend on economies of scale and the question arises whether and to what extent existing product offerings are scalable. Finally, there is the need to consider how to correctly position the product mix in this new business environment. Accordingly, the group discussions resulted in four main clusters under the headings of challenges and opportunities, increased competition, size and positioning. Turning to each in turn:

31.4.1   Challenges and opportunities

These challenges arise from the fact that the environment for the asset management business has changed as a result of the global financial crisis, and 'business as usual' may no longer be an option for most companies. A number of considerations are worth discussing in this respect:

1) The first and most obvious point is to identify solutions that address legitimate client concerns arising from the global financial crisis. Asset

management companies need to place more of a focus on constructing such solutions and putting them on the market. Risk management solutions directed at the retail customer base are one example of a product that should be offered by most asset management companies.

2) One of the most common complaints from retail customers of their investment advisers is why they need to pay them a fee when their account has not risen in value over what it was five years ago. Part of this is education, and in particular the need to explain the unrealistic expectations made plain by the global financial crisis. The important point is to explain the necessity to save and invest, and part of the responsibility of the asset management business is to engage in dialog in order to rebuild customer confidence; and improving operational transparency is a necessary part of this process.

3) Distribution channels have been dramatically impacted by the global financial crisis. There have been dramatic regulatory changes in all financial jurisdictions. These changes have had a significant effect on distribution channels and it is important to assess how the product mix needs to be adapted to address these changes. In addition, demographic changes in both developed and developing markets have changed patterns of investing and saving, and again we need to consider how to adapt the product mix to meet this new reality.

4) In addition, new markets have developed in the last several years. Commodity-rich emerging markets and the growth of sovereign wealth funds around the world represent new markets and new opportunities for asset management companies. The question is whether existing asset management companies will be able to adapt to serve these markets or whether new and more specialized companies will take their place.

31.4.2 Increased competition

One important development in the last five years has been the dramatic increase in competition from low-cost providers, particularly index funds and exchange-traded funds (ETFs) adapted to many different investor clientéles. This competition represents a significant challenge to the revenue base of the more traditional asset management companies.

In this context, it is vitally important to consider precisely what the given product has in the way of a competitive advantage, and to shift the emphasis away from the product to the value-chain solutions that highlight the enterprise's competitive advantage. In addition, the existence of these low-cost providers highlights the importance of cost containment, the consolidation of product lines internally, and cost control on external service providers.

31.4.3   Does size help?

The industry needs to challenge the presumption that increased scale alone will decrease costs per unit of AUM and/or increase revenues. This raises several important issues that need to be recognized. Taking each in turn:

1) It is the low-fee section of the market that has the highest degree of economies of scale. This raises the issue of where economies of scale are most likely to be found. These economies are most pronounced in the administrative, compliance and distribution functions.
2) In addition, marketing expenses imply that the largest companies have the highest degree of market penetration. On the other hand, investment platforms can scale very well up to the point of capacity. The issue arises as to what determines how scaleable the investment function really is.
3) Scalability of the enterprise depends on many things. Investment style (in particular active versus passive), the asset universe, and asset research coverage are important considerations.
4) Also, scalability depends on the nature and availability of human capital to the enterprise. For this reason, it is not immediately clear that high-conviction management can be scaled significantly – the best managers may leave for boutique funds in cases where a cultural conflict arises, and the corporate philosophy, environment or investment style change. If taken too far, increasing the scale of the enterprise can lead to staff and business fall-out. This is particularly true, given the sometimes fragile balance between the size of AUM and the creation of alpha.
5) Finally, growth through mergers and acquisitions on the one hand can lead to operational efficiencies but on the other can be harmful to human morale and have a disruptive effect on many levels of management.

31.4.4   Positioning

How can a company best position itself for growth in light of challenges posed by diminished confidence as a result of the financial crisis and the weaknesses that crisis exposed? The clear answer to this question is to emphasize the central importance of transparency in product description, fee structure and the investment process. The financial crisis in general and the Madoff scandal in particular reflected the truth that some asset management companies failed to fully understand the nature of the products they were offering to their clients. If the asset management firm does not understand the product, it cannot explain it to the client.

The group discussions identified a number of remedial actions to rectify this state of affairs. Taking each in turn:

1) While transparency is often promoted as an issue limited to the relationship between the client and the asset management organization, a first step to

providing transparency to the client is that the organization is internally transparent and that it understands the nature of the product it is offering to the client.

2) The second most important response is to develop a focus on client satisfaction as an important criterion for managers at all stages of the value chain. This includes – but is by no means limited to – an emphasis on education, not only of the client but also education of the intermediary who services the client, particularly in managing unreasonable expectations. In this context, the experience of the global financial crisis was an important learning experience for everyone in the asset management industry.

3) The third response is to encourage a proactive involvement of the industry associations in developing industry standards for product descriptions and risk. This is perhaps the most important task as it relates to the difficult relationship between the industry and its regulators.

31.5 Interconnection of risk, growth and cost

In a separate discussion held as part of the main session, group participants examined how the identified risk, cost and growth factors were interconnected and interrelated. To do so, each member of the group had to select his top three drivers for a relation 'A drives B most' scenario. The results were then aggregated to the top level of risk, cost and growth, respectively.

For example, under the heading 'risk', a member could choose from a) operational risk; b) market risk; c) regulatory risk; or d) legal risk, the one category he considered to be the most important driver impacting one of four categories under 'growth' – a) challenges and opportunities; b) increased competition; c) does size matter? or d) restoring confidence) – and/or under 'cost' one of the four categories a) transparency; b) high operating leverage; c) trading costs; or d) regulatory compliance.

Following on from this, a member could then decide by way of example that under 'risk', the category of market risk was driving challenges and opportunities under 'growth' the most; that under 'growth', the category of challenges and opportunities was driving high operating leverage under 'cost' the most; and finally that under 'cost', the category of regulatory compliance was being driven the most by regulatory risk under 'risk'.

Another option was for a member to choose two categories under the same heading, i.e., that under 'growth', the issue of restoring confidence was driving challenges and opportunities the most.

Weighing up all the evidence provided by the participants, it turned out that the working group members were generally of the opinion that categories under the 'cost' heading were driving categories under 'growth' the most. Here the main emphasis was on cost transparency driving the processes of challenges and opportunities as well as restoring confidence under 'growth'.

This was followed by categories under 'risk' driving categories under 'cost' the most, with the emphasis on regulatory risk driving regulatory compliance the most.

Another individual driver regarded as key was high operating leverage under 'cost', which was seen as most impacting the question of whether size matters under 'growth'. This driver was in fact the individual top scorer among all the participants. In joint second place were cost transparency driving challenges and opportunities as well as restoring confidence under 'growth', although equal weight was also given to restoring confidence driving transparency under 'cost'.

Bearing this outcome of the discussion in mind, it seems reasonable to conclude that when formulating a strategy, issues in an order of A, B and C should be examined and discussed with top consideration given to 'growth' as the core factor, heavily influenced by 'cost' and 'risk' as determining satellite factors in that order of magnitude.

31.6   Conclusions

The four main conclusions to emerge from the group discussions were the importance of rebuilding investor trust; the important role of increasing transparency at all levels as a means to that end; the difficult challenge posed by increasing competition from low-cost providers; and finally the extent to which the factors that influence risk, cost and growth interrelate. Here are the main conclusions in more detail:

First, clearly emerging in this process of interaction, the greatest challenge since the global financial crisis is to rebuild confidence. Confidence has taken a severe knock, regulators have been put on notice, and there is an increasing groundswell of regulation in the pipeline. The industry has to come to grips with this reality. Last but not least, clients are concerned and the industry must develop procedures and techniques to deal with this crisis in confidence.

Second, the most effective way in which to rebuild eroded confidence is for asset management companies to ensure that their investment management systems embrace transparency at all levels: transparency in terms of really understanding and comprehending their own individual cost structures as well as the need to increase transparency in business processes and products for sale.

Third, the crisis in confidence is also associated with increased competition from low-cost providers as well as increased government regulation and related challenges. The opportunity for growth lies with those enterprises that are most able to meet these challenges by providing transparency to their clients, their stakeholders and in particular their regulators.

Finally, these factors are all interrelated, but there is a common theme here. The global financial crisis is the greatest challenge the industry has ever faced. It is the central reason for the crisis in confidence, and operational due diligence and increased operational transparency are a necessary first step to win back that confidence.

Notes

1. This chapter is based on discussions within the Asset Management group at the SimCorp StrategyLab Copenhagen Summit 2011 held 16–17 March 2011. Members included Dr Stephen J. Brown (head), Professor (Leonard N. Stern School of Business, NYU); Dr Marno Verbeek, Professor, Rotterdam School of Management (Erasmus University); Lester Gray, CEO, Schroders Asia; Michael Jarzabek, Chief Representative, LBBW Asset Management Investmentgesellschaft mbH; Lars Eigen Møller, Executive Vice President, Dansk Capital; Dr Matthäus Den Otter, CEO, Swiss Funds Association (SFA); Dr Ralf Schmücker, Managing Director, SimCorp Central Europe; Peter Engel, Senior Sales Manager, SimCorp Central Europe; and Dushyant Shahrawat, Senior Research Director, Tower Group.
2. 'Working paper on the regulatory treatment of operational risk', BCBS Working Paper No. 8, September 2001.
3. One approach to this problem has been to define a methodology to quantify the extent to which each financial institution is exposed to systemic risk. See, for example, V. Acharya, C. Brownlees, R. Engle, F. Farazmand and M. Richardson, 'Measuring Systemic Risk', in V. Acharya, T. Cooley, M. Richardson and I. Walter (eds) (2011), 'Regulating Wall Street: The Dodd-Frank Act and the New Architecture of Global Finance', Hoboken NJ: John Wiley & Sons.

32

Current and Future Challenges Faced by Pension Funds

Massimo Massa

In this chapter we assess and evaluate the main points to emerge from an expert group discussion on pension and insurance funds, highlighting the main challenges facing the sector.[1]

By the end of 2013, the global population will have surpassed 7 billion, and current demographic projections put the number at 9 billion by 2050. The dire warnings of Thomas Malthus (1766–1834) have been tested many times over the years, and have so far been inaccurate for a host of reasons, most having to do with productivity growth and technology advance. But as mothers often warn their children, 'just you wait...' Sooner or later, demographic pressures may well exceed sustainability constraints, although the pacing is likely to be closer to a boiling frog than a catastrophe.

Meantime, there are plenty of things to worry about as global population growth masks dramatic geographic and sectoral changes, which will put pressure on economic and social systems long before any demographic tipping point is reached. Between now and 2050, the global population under age 25 is expected to hold steady at about 3 billion, but the population exceeding age 60 is projected to increase by 1.25 billion – the product of high fertility and past declines in child mortality in developing countries, a population cohort that is now rapidly aging. While dependency rates in these countries have been falling, they will increase dramatically in the years ahead, joining the dramatic growth of dependency in Europe, Japan and the rest of the developed world where the ratio will double by 2050. Only southeast and south Asia, the Middle East and Africa are likely to escape the dependency pressure-cooker in this timeframe.

The overall demographics are further clouded by increased levels of consumption on the part of older people, largely driven by increased costs of medical and long-term healthcare. As higher incomes and public policies such as tax and social support systems have encouraged earlier retirement, the result in many countries has been to both increase dependency and redeploy population from lower to higher consumption cohorts. The impact, however, has varied widely by country and how the resulting 'life-cycle deficits' are financed – through public-sector support, intergenerational transfers within families, or accumulated assets, for example. Recent studies suggest that public transfers and personal assets finance most of these deficits and will continue to do so.

Most endangered are national pension systems that rely heavily on public-sector support and depend on current retirement contributions (so-called pay-as-you-go systems), some of which incorporate fictitious 'trust funds' invested in government debt securities. Many such systems were established under political conditions that encouraged generous retirement promises and were built on optimistic economic growth assumptions. Such systems now confront a stark reality. They can either break their promises to retirement beneficiaries by reducing payouts via later retirements, tax increases on pension benefits, or by reducing benefit indexation to reduce the value of benefits in real terms. Or they can significantly raise pension contributions on the part of the workforce, which increases intergenerational transfers and runs into the reality of adverse demographics.

The least vulnerable are well-provisioned pension systems that combine a baseline public benefit program with dedicated, pre-funded pools of financial assets provided either by employers or individuals, or both. Employers may provide defined benefit pension plans, which oblige them to maintain asset levels sufficient on an actuarial basis to meet their obligations, usually backed by guarantees to manage the risk that the employer will be unable to make good on its obligations – in which case the asset pools turn out to be underfunded.

Alternatively, employers can sponsor defined contribution plans for their employees, with various alternative investment options. Key developments in the employer-sponsored sector have covered replacement of defined benefit with defined contribution plans in order to shift the pension funding risk to employees, as well as a broader range of choice for beneficiaries, including reduction or elimination of the employers' own shares from investment options.

In addition to public baseline and employer-sponsored plans, well-structured pension systems also include individual defined or voluntary contribution programs encouraged by favorable tax treatment for contributions, accumulated assets and/or withdrawals. Set at realistic levels under conservative assumptions about demographics, economic growth, and financial returns – and permitting broad portfolio diversification options – such 'three-tier' systems are likely to be most capable of meeting their commitments and are least vulnerable to future shocks.

Given these realities, it is astounding how great the variation is among countries in terms of the design of their pension systems. Among developed countries they extend from rock-solid systems like the Nordic countries and Switzerland, to disaster-prone systems like Spain and Greece. Even rich countries like France and Germany are looking at major funding gaps down the road.

Among developing countries, many of which benefit from much better demographics at least in the medium term, existing systems extend from well-provisioned mandatory approaches like Singapore and Chile to nationalization of private pensions in Argentina and virtual non-existence in much of Africa and parts of Asia. Fortunately, the slower progression of population aging gives many of these countries time to design properly funded and managed pension schemes.

In the end, the amalgam of national pension systems and the absolute necessity of properly funding them to avoid serious economic and political repercussions paints a very bright picture for the future growth facing suppliers of pension services. Expansion of viable pre-funded public and private pension systems is by far the least-cost alternative for countries confronting their demographic realities. And they stand to reap big dividends as disproportionate growth in pension pools spurs the development of broader and deeper capital markets that are likely to produce additional growth dividends. This chapter surveys the key issues confronting the global pension fund industry in terms of risk, cost and growth. It explains the central risks, ranging from demographic change and increased regulation to stiffer competition and adequacy of investment returns.

Equally important are costs and efficiency, both in supporting adequate pension benefits and distinguishing among competitors in an industry where durable performance advantage is not easy to achieve. This depends heavily on coherence in investment processes, economies of scale and outsourcing, the on-site transactions and asset management infrastructure as well as application of state-of-the-art information technology.

The final chapter of this book examines the inevitable sources of growth in the industry, as discussed here, including issues related to internationalization and consolidation, and not least regulation. In combination, the key drivers of the industry examined here will ensure that the pension sector will be one of the most dynamic in global financial services going forward.

32.1   Overarching issues

The biggest challenge facing pension and insurance funds today is the rapidly aging population. This will force funds to provide participants with payouts for a longer period of time. Pension and insurance companies will be required to provide high returns and at the same time stable cash flows for the retiring population.

In other words, the industry is under pressure to provide higher returns, presumably adopting an increasingly client-centric approach with more customized services, and, at the same time, lower risk and greater dependability. This will increase demands on the companies. In the next 10–20 years, the entire industry has to restructure itself in order to simultaneously better manage risk, provide stable cash flows and meet more and more the tailored needs of their corporate sponsors and participants.

In the discussions forming the basis of this chapter, our expert group found that one of the key factors that could lead the industry to a successful future is consolidation. The simultaneous requirement of higher performance, lower risk and more stable cash flows can be met in a better way mostly by bigger financial groups that can invest across many different asset classes and perform stable and reliable risk management by acquiring the right asset management system to enable and support this.

No doubt, the biggest opportunity facing the industry is the switch from a pay-as-you-go system to a new one based on three pillars. Pillar I is mainly pay-as-you-go, usually defined benefit and redistributive; Pillar II is privately funded, almost always defined contribution; and Pillar III is the privately funded, voluntary and supplementary, preferably defined contribution.

Next to the government-provided funds, private funds will participate in the growing business of providing coverage to an increasingly aging population. Both the company-sponsored plans and the employee-funded funds will be mostly in the private domain. Private pension funds and insurance companies will be competing to exploit this new opportunity.

The discussion on which this analysis is based comprises an excellent basis for looking at these challenges and opportunities. It is very rare to find a situation in which representatives of the pension fund industry, regulators, academics and the technology community can gather around a table and exchange views about the industry and its strategic development and outlook for the future. What follows are some key points and considerations that emerged from this very positive initiative.

32.2   Risk challenges

The group identified four key challenges for the immediate and medium-term future related to risk issues in the pension and insurance funds sector. The ensuing discussion can be summarized under four major headings: aging population, increased competition, regulatory risk and investment risk. We will now address them in turn.

32.2.1   Aging population

The aging population represents one potential source of risk. It is estimated that by 2025, nearly 30% of the population in the Western world will be over 60.

This will require more effective retirement plans and saving schedules. At the same time, life expectancy in the developed world (and in many other parts of the world) was on the increase, and from 1980 to 2010 the actual retirement age – at least in Europe – was on the decrease, although this is expected to swing into reverse as national governments raise the mandatory retirement age to augment depleted budgets.

In this environment, pension savings have failed to grow at the same rate of speed as the average number of years in retirement. As the population turns older, pension coverage has to be extended. This has put pressure on both national and private pension schemes. Attempts to restore some balance have proved politically controversial.

In terms of fixed-benefit agreements, given the low yields obtainable in current market conditions, there is a very real risk of funding deficits arising (i.e., as seen in France and Germany). In terms of guaranteed pension agreements, a large number of pension schemes are in their core of a defined contribution character, but accompanied by a guaranteed minimum yield or minimum payment.

These pension schemes also have a potential funding problem in the current market conditions. When reserves are tight and a funding problem is looming, the regulator will typically insist on safe, conservative investments, which – while less risky – will limit the return pension savers expect to see.

The group discussed and agreed on several potential responses to this challenge. The main idea here is that the industry has to recognize that the growth of private collective and independent pension schemes represents a continued broad-based trend to exploit. The responses are itemized as follows:

1) A first response involves the adoption of measures that provide highly dedicated and specialist solutions to accommodate the aging population trend in the pension area, turning this into a source of competitive advantage. Assuming that the expected change in retirement lengths or dependency ratios are dictated by demographic patterns or governments, innovative solutions imply dealing with uncertain retirement ages and with uncertain life expectancy. The former are related to the flexibility offered to pensioners in when to take their pensions and the rewards for delaying, while the latter is related to the ability to hedge longevity risk or spread it in different ways among pension scheme members.

2) A second response revolves around the needs for the industry to employ an active and professional management of the increasing complexity required by the investors. This involves better risk and liquidity management, more effective portfolio allocation as well as greater effort to 'educate' customers about the fact that pension and insurance products are more complex than banking products and require a higher risk-taking in order to deliver the required performance.

3) A third response is the development of a proper process to benchmark performance. This has to be developed at the industry level with a coordinated effort. It would help to not only provide higher transparency to the investors, but also be instrumental to an appropriate implementation of IT applications and processes.

32.2.2 Increased competition

Most reformed pension systems nowadays combine elements of three pension pillars as defined above. These three different pillars best serve different functions, and single pillar pension systems may not be the best approach to achieving the central policy goals of a pension system. Different pillars are exposed to different risks and the correlation between those risks is far less than 100%.

A key policy issue for governments designing pension and social insurance systems is to balance redistributive, savings, and insurance functions. Each pension pillar serves these three functions in different ways. Depending on a country's situation, combining the approaches into a three-pillar pension system may be the most effective way of balancing pension objectives.

However, the case for multipillar pension schemes raises the prospect of increased competition from new providers, which represents a major source of risk for the established providers of pension schemes. This competition would be healthy and beneficial to customers in the case of a level playing field among funds and countries. However, there is a real danger of the lack of such a level playing field because regulation can skew and distort the market in favor of some and against others. This can become worse as competition emerges in a sharper form, when tax incentives are eliminated and pension wrappers disappear.

Competition will enhance the role of operational platforms. An operational platform in the pension industry is where management of the organization's data and information together with the execution of decisions takes place. The situation could arise that a big player is subsidized because it has the right operational platform and is able to defray its costs by being affiliated with a major financial conglomerate, whether in the insurance, pension or bank sector.

The more appropriate responses to the challenge induced by competition vary. Taking each in turn:

1) First, scaling up to a dimension that allows the scale economies of the platform to be reaped. This would create a sort of barrier to entry to ward off competition from new market entrants.
2) Second, introducing value-management mechanisms to monitor each link in the investment management chain. For this purpose, the implementation of business and IT-related measures would help to increase the competitiveness of front- to back-office functions, distribution, asset management, private wealth and advisory services to secure and enhance transparency.

3) Third, the adoption of straight-through-processing (STP) and other automatic functions will help to ensure that product, data and valuations remain synchronized among all the parties engaged in the value chain.

4) Finally, a critical factor is the coordination with other products offered by the same financial conglomerate. Here, the focus is on examining and deciding whether more investment fund products should be added to the pension and insurance fund product portfolio to enhance competitiveness.

32.2.3 Regulatory risk

The introduction of new regulation and the increased pace of regulatory reform pose risks for the industry in the sense that they foster initial uncertainty and oblige a risk-related response from the industry as it takes on the new burden. For the investment management industry, by and large, the regulatory and compliance challenges in the years ahead will be unprecedented. Among the manifold changes to be taken into account at the strategic, tactical, systemic and operational levels are the new regulatory framework and demands of the Wall Street Reform and Consumer Protection Act (Dodd-Frank Act) in the US, AIFMD, MiFID conduct of business, EMIR, PRIPs, Solvency II and UCITS IV in the European Union (EU), as well as on an international level the new tax rules and standards primarily embodied in IFRS 9.

Regulation is both good and bad in the sense that it endows the industry with a great deal of credibility but it creates regulatory uncertainty and increases complexity. Many responses to this challenge can be envisioned. Here we examine each one:

1) The first involves the introduction of internal regulatory compliance procedures and mechanisms to deal with the burden of increased regulation. In this context, the choice of the right operational platform that is sufficiently agile and flexible to take all the existing and forthcoming regulatory changes into account and apply them to the business process may be the key operational response to this challenge.

2) The second response to the challenge implies exerting a greater influence on management to exercise caution in decision-making. This can translate in clarifying or dispelling uncertainty surrounding new regulations (i.e., UCITS IV, AIFMD), standardizing tax requirements, especially internationally across major geographical areas (i.e., the EU), and tax jurisdictions to reduce change and the administrative burden. This also involves the design and construction of appropriate operational and IT structures and platforms that are more flexible and attuned to change in the event of new regulations and standards and reviewing marketing material and making it clearer.

3) The third major response entails involving the regulators. This translates into exercising lobbying-power more to ensure that regulatory decision-making and implementation of new standards reflect the knowledge and experience of industry participants.

Overall, there is a sense that transparency is not always necessarily good and that there is a lot of work ahead for the industry to coordinate with the regulatory authorities to settle on the optimal amount of regulation and transparency as well as on the type of transparency that is required – i.e., regulation-driven, reputation-driven, industry-driven or a combination of all three.

32.2.4 Investment risk

The investment risk covers a very broad area. It involves the market- and business-related risks of pension and insurance fund liability for investor obligations. There are at least four types of risk: the traditional one of setting money aside for retirement in the form of reserves; the market risk in terms of volatility and various forms of diversification; fat tail risks (i.e. popcorn, domino and tsunami effects); and short- and long-term risk. While market trends in products and prices cannot always be forecast accurately and in time, risk can be identified with varying degrees of success. Therefore, a successful risk management model must be able to comprise dynamic risk budgeting in a fast-changing and volatile world in order to secure reserves.

Diversification represents one way of reducing risk. However, tails are fatter and occur more often than almost all models predict. Not all value-at-risk (VaR) models have the desired effect of reducing investment risk. In the hazardous hunt for alpha when the basic, safe return is low, there is an inducement to take higher risks. This goes for the pension institution as well as for the pension investments controlled by the individual pension saver.

In this context, it is clear that there is a need for pension and insurance fund organizations to recognize that new market trends (e.g., absolute versus relative) are all part of the process of a market place in constant flux and that to this effect asset management must be effectively and efficiently aligned with IT and process strategies. The industry has to be able to identify the risks that are most harmful and diversify in order to reduce the risk.

This process involves the need to examine how well the industry fares in relation to risk/return, assessment of tail risk and implementation of suitable VaR models supported and assisted by integrated IT platforms. It also implies the adoption of appropriate investment strategies to guard against risk (options, hedging, short and long positions, etc.). These investment strategies should be part of an overall strategy that also examines both the asset and liability side, offering pension schemes and insurance policies that are appropriately tailored to the assets and liabilities of the individual sector company.

There is a question of whether the pension investment horizon is long enough to allow pension funds to reap the benefits of a long-term strategy and whether this implies that pension funds can enjoy lower investment risk (i.e., reduced sensitivity to liquidity and fire-sales risks). Designing appropriate risk management strategies for institutions with very long investment horizons is critical.

The concern is that with inappropriate strategies, sharp deteriorations in the investment climate may force institutions to rebalance their portfolios just when the costs of rebalancing the portfolio are highest. The industry should be able to identify which types of risk actually become diversifiable within the longer time frame that would not be diversifiable for short-term traditional asset managers. Whether or not this is a source of competitive advantage remains unclear.

Finally, it is important to ensure more industry-driven transparency of operating procedures to help identify best practice, in the process strengthening the regulatory compliance function supported and assisted by the appropriate IT solutions. In this context, it is worth stressing the importance of measures and exercises to benchmark best practice in the industry, thereby more clearly defining parameters and barriers to competition.

32.3   Cost challenges

The group identified four main key challenges for the immediate and medium-term future related to cost issues in the pension and insurance funds sector. These were discussed and grouped under the categories of technology and infrastructure, investment processes, general outsourcing, and scale and consolidation. We will now examine them in turn.

32.3.1   Technology and infrastructure

This category combines a number of cost-related factors: technology management and infrastructure costs; manual processing costs; and processes to manage change and flexibility.

In order to control costs effectively, the individual pension and insurance fund organization's platform needs to be managed extremely well. In the area of technology management, far more difficult and complex products and services need to be handled than in the past. For example, investment in illiquid structures requires more data and is more costly than traditional liquid investments. Also, the more widespread use of derivatives increases costs due to clearing access and margining. This calls for a more flexible platform to ensure strategic management of the operational platform.

In the area of infrastructure, costs have increased associated with implementation of internal cost controls and introduction of customized operational practices tailored for the asset management business (i.e., reduction of settlement risk). Manual processing is still widespread in the pension and insurance funds sector, ranging from corporate actions handling, over various reconciliation processes to communication with the end-client.

To cope with this challenge, the pension and insurance fund organizations need to stress the importance of having an adaptable and flexible platform that provides the corporate decision makers with the information they need at all times in the most cost-effective way. They should also attempt to promote cost-effectiveness with the careful and calculated selection, choice and implementation of an operational platform strategy and secure alignment of the platform with business and IT strategies over a longer horizon. This involves an increase in the rate of automated workflows, STP and client communication services.

However, this does not mean reduction in human investment. Indeed, a key factor of success is to recognize that it is becoming increasingly difficult to manage various asset classes and that there are manual processes that cannot be downsized or streamlined. In fact, an increase in relevance of less liquid asset classes increases the need for direct manual management.

So the challenge here is to try and standardize processes as much as possible, accepting the need for a long-term development of human resources. This requires efficient cost management (the group calculated that 85% of a company's resources are tied up in human capital and is a major source of cost, with 15% going to the rest, i.e., IT platforms, technology, etc.).

Finally, it is important to acknowledge that the regulatory environment and the market place itself are in a state of constant flux and that flexible processes to manage this changing environment need to be in place to ensure effective operational cost management.

32.3.2 Investment processes

New international regulations and rules currently going into effect pose cost challenges in terms of the investment processes undertaken by companies operating in the pension and insurance funds sector. For example, Solvency II brings a fundamental change to the regulation of insurance companies in the EU. In the short and medium term, the data management and data quality requirements resulting from Solvency II will pose a huge cost challenge for insurance companies and their asset management.

As higher risk requires higher solvency capital, insurance companies will generally aim for low investment risk. This will alter the asset allocation strategy and will also have an impact on the industry as a whole. The complexity of asset management for insurance companies is high due to the differences in the individual investment portfolios of insurance companies and the resulting different levels of granularity of the requirements. Examples of data required include: quoted market prices and yields of bonds and equities; detailed information on derivatives; geographical data on the individual assets; and information on guarantees.

Apart from Solvency II, asset managers in the insurance fund sector will face additional legal and regulatory requirements, which increase the importance of an early response. An efficient, timely and structured approach can save costs and resources.

The main response to this challenge is the definition of an investment strategy/policy that takes account of analyzing securities, minimizing portfolio risk, evaluating performance and revising the portfolio in as cost-effective and automated a way as possible without jeopardizing the integrity of the investment process. This implies several steps:

1) Identification and application of more reliable and transparent investment processes;
2) Adoption of a cost-efficient operational platform;
3) Introduction of an effective way to measure, monitor and manage appropriately the liquidity risk involved in investment processes;
4) Establishment of viable risk-return profiles and benchmarks to determine allocation in the investment process.

Ensuring that performance measurement plays a pivotal role in the investment process and supporting and strengthening the risk management system with the appropriate integrated IT solutions are key factors for this purpose.

The successful pension and insurance company should be able to recognize that risk management constitutes an integral part of the overall investment process, as well as being capable of assessing and determining whether the need to provide transparency and ensure the integrity and consistency of the data and models used in the investment process rank at the top of the list of any risk management strategy.

32.3.3   General outsourcing

Many pension and insurance fund operators continue to use a combination of in-house asset management for domestic and other more familiar assets and external asset managers for more specialized investments. This raises challenges as well as opportunities in cost terms. Functions being outsourced include: distribution, back-office operations, IT and portfolio management.

In outsourcing it is necessary not only to look at the direct costs, but also the quality of the service obtained and the cost of monitoring quality.

If outsourcing solutions are to be sought out, they must be able to integrate state-of-the-art technology with unparalleled business-specific knowledge, equating to top-of-the-line performance and uninterrupted operations.

This yields reliable and flexible management tools and operational workflow systems, which focus on quality processing. This goal is often achieved by developing in-house systems based on an open architecture as a continued investment process to support market and distribution demands. These factors will separate the winners from the losers in the pension and insurance funds industry.

These considerations suggest that pension and insurance organizations should identify the areas designated for outsourcing and find the right partners with which to cooperate. This involves defining areas, where the pension and insurance organizations do not define themselves as having a competitive advantage, and then defining the screening and selection process. They should define and examine methods to evaluate outsourcing and whether it is the right course of action. This is primarily a front-office and due-diligence function.

Building systems to monitor and measure the quality of the product or service that is subject to outsourcing as well as determining ways to measure outsourcing and in what areas it would best be applied are also critical factors required in the industry. Outsourcing should be assessed not only in terms of cost savings but also the impact on quality, flexibility and control. This drive towards the implementation of standardized and efficient solutions should not make us forget that the key ingredient to success is the ability to maximize customization.

32.3.4 Scale and consolidation

The pension and insurance funds sector is increasingly becoming concentrated owing to the market muscle of the largest players and rising market-entry costs. The asset management industry in general is consolidating and the pension institutions embedded in insurance companies are no exception.

However, when applying mergers and acquisitions as a technique to spur consolidation and concentration, it has to be noted that stand-alone pension institutions are typically not organized as commercial companies and can therefore not be acquired. This raises the question of what is the 'optimal' level of competition and also raises a number of cost-related issues.

Another cost challenge is to examine and identify cheaper distribution channels for pension savings products. In this area, competition has only limited capacity to drive down costs because charges are opaque, and savers poor at comparing products. Existing low cost distribution channels (i.e., company pension schemes) are increasingly under threat with employers having little interest in providing pensions, and inhibited in doing so for fear of potential legal liabilities if things go wrong.

So the industry is already more or less converging on a relatively higher scale in terms of centralized technology and optimal work processes but remains biased in its ability to grow larger and reap the benefits of economies of scale.

Technical and fiscal barriers to market entry continue to impede consolidation across borders, particularly in the EU, and these obstacles need to be overcome in order to reduce acquisition costs.

However, those pension and insurance fund companies that have already recognized these challenges, and have built and integrated the necessary asset management platforms based on appropriately applied and flexible IT processes to accommodate scale and consolidation, will emerge among the industry's winners.

There are several answers to this challenge. First and foremost, the pension and insurance companies should adopt a clear course of action with the 'endgame' firmly in mind as a source of strength and with cost synergies playing a secondary yet still important role. They should examine and identify the processes and systems that scale well to take on more volume to apportion costs better. Indeed, while it is attractive to obtain higher volume through growth, the attainable growth is not always enough to fully utilize the capacity.

There are two main paths to improved capacity utilization: consolidation and cooperation. Many organizations remain reluctant about consolidation (unless they are the larger party); cooperation (i.e. by setting up joint operation companies) may appear more appealing as it is less threatening. However, consolidation can lead to a discount when pursued in a functional direction, generating a geographical premium.

From a general welfare perspective, the cost of market entry will rise, creating problems for small players and new entrants, while increasing the prospect of monopolistic behavior and a concomitant rise in investor fees as competitors are squeezed out of an increasingly competitive and cost-driven market. This poses the question whether scale should take the form of a complete package offered to more interested parties or many alternative packages.

32.4   Growth challenges

Another important area of analysis is the industry growth scenario and the challenges faced. Also in this case, the group picked out four key challenges for the immediate and medium-term future related to growth issues in the pension and insurance funds sector. These were grouped under the headings of changing demographics, benefits and competition, internationalization and regulation. We will now study them in detail, taking each in turn:

32.4.1   Changing demographics

Increased private retirement savings as a result of changing demographics will represent a major source of growth and opportunity for pension and insurance funds. Save more and retire later will spur growth in the industry. With the trend shifting more and more away from defined benefit to defined contribution schemes, this represents a major source of growth, and a structural shift.

Yet it also poses a major risk as it opens up space for other competitors and competing products, such as open-ended funds and so on. The demographics of population in almost every developed country, compounded by the need to set aside savings for retirement, is certain to continue growing. This represents a tremendous opportunity for pension and insurance funds, as they are a natural vehicle for retirement savings and de facto pension funds in terms of transparency and daily valuations.

Other factors to be taken into consideration in this context, particularly in the European sphere, are younger people having to save earlier and later mandatory retirement ages owing to people living longer. This creates the framework for a bigger market and increases the scope for expansion. One of the other major challenges is filling the gap caused by underfunding in the Pillar I area of public, defined benefit schemes.

This involves a proper definition of the market that is best suited to the individual organization; a clear setting of the strategic direction, operational structure and cultural inclinations (i.e., national, regional or global); the utilization of existing or the establishment of new distribution channels (third-party or otherwise) that are specifically geared to the pensions sector in the way of offering attractive, off-the-shelf and cost-effective products; the adoption of a corporate policy of systematic implementation and execution based on the starting point of an auditable view; the effort to promote a greater degree of flexibility in the choice of funds that are geared to pension schemes and insurance policies, particularly in Europe where the current situation is rigid.

The goal is to take the value chain, break it into its constituent components, and figure out the global dimensions of each part of the chain. In one part the 'global dimension' is probably zero; in another part it may be extremely important. This should ensure that funds are specifically tailored to meet investors' varying retirement needs.

32.4.2 Benefits and competition

If, as all appearances suggest, the majority of the industry is seeking to move from defined benefit to defined contribution, and the risk is passed on to the investor, perhaps the best way for the investor to evaluate how good a provider is – given that the risk is now on the side of the investor – is a standard performance-based measure. So possibly one of the major structural changes at the point of inflection is the shift from defined benefit to defined contribution, and a corresponding shift in the risk – these also entail a shift in the characteristics so that relative return is assessed in terms of defined benefit and absolute return in terms of defined contribution.

The fixed-benefit pension model is under pressure and the fixed-contribution pension model is expanding. There is a market opportunity in offering these pension schemes and in offering supporting services. At least in Europe, national (fixed-benefit) pension schemes are being reduced and the population is being encouraged to make additional pension savings. In this way, the traditional pension fund is reduced to an ordinary investment fund, depending on the degree of the collective risk-sharing. These add-on pension schemes come both as individual pension contracts and as collective pension schemes through e.g., an employer or a trade union.

These individual pension contracts are made directly with a pension institution, while the collective pension schemes either will contract with a pension institution or build their own pension institution and contract for supporting services. Many countries see a rapidly increasing role for private defined contribution plans to fill the gap as state and employer provision declines. But how this growth will occur is less clear. One of the challenges will be to work out how best to market a pension plan to ordinary savers – as a saving plan with a well-defined current value, or as a promised or expected pension flow from a certain age.

Related to this is the design of guarantees. While in principal guarantees look attractive, they often look much less attractive in retrospect (i.e., a minimum return guarantee looks attractive ex ante but ex post the saver's benchmark is likely to be more what he thought he was going to get than some calculation based on historic contributions). Depending on the business strategy, some pension funds have serious defects, such as lack of liquidity and pursuing what is likely to be a non-optimal investment strategy.

On the asset side, there is scope for widening the set of assets held within pension plans. Many risks can be marketed; recent suggestions include longevity bonds that pay off according to mortality rates within a cohort, and social bonds that pay off according to the success of some remedial program.

All these new products and services (with an emphasis on saving more and retiring later) will spur competition in the market place.

With the industry now thinking more in terms of delivering a process rather than a product, this represents a competitive growth opportunity; growth in the industry as it is of value to users, and growth for the individual companies that emerge as early competitive players and who will hence rank among the winners.

Competition will increase across the entire spectrum of products and services that are related to defined contribution, possibly at the expense of defined benefit, opening up possibilities of expanding market share in that segment but also exposing the more traditional pension fund providers to sharper competition.

The industry has to decide whether it wishes to base itself on absolute or relative performance. It will have to identify and obtain the right product mix that clients want to have in each pension market segment, whether defined benefit or defined contribution, and here time-to-market will play a significant role.

Product innovation will be a key factor in promoting industry growth, with an increased focus on investment funds as a vehicle for pension and retirement savings plans on the part of the larger players. Products will have to be designed to take investor profiles into account (i.e., risk profiles as well as fiscal profiles).

The entire value chain of a pension or insurance fund business, and its complete organization from advisory to distribution outlets, will assume far greater prominence in efforts to gain and maintain a competitive advantage.

32.4.3 Internationalization

Internationalization entails both the internationalization of the market for pension products and the internationalization of the investment universe. With capital flows becoming more and more international and transparent, it is possible to transact portfolio allocation on a worldwide scale and this presents manifold opportunities for growth, while simultaneously exposing industry players to a more integrated market.

Some countries like France, Italy, Spain and Portugal are massively underfunded and these are potentially new markets for pension fund product-offerings. In this general context of growing internationalization, emerging markets also represent a potential growth opportunity for the industry as a source of new products and new customers. China, India and many of the previously poorer countries are developing at very fast rates, boosted by private consumption. Latin America, with Brazil, Chile and Mexico in the lead, is already building up a huge asset management industry.

Here, the main bone of contention is whether these markets will be sufficiently mature for European players to enter or not mature enough to make it worthwhile. While in terms of the market in general, the potential is enormous, the markets themselves are very heterogeneous. So there is a potential conflict between homogeneity and heterogeneity. There will be a very rapid growth in wealth, and a tremendous savings capacity in countries like China and India.

However, the challenge is that competition between European pension and insurance funds and equivalent funds domiciled in Asia, the Middle East and Latin America is likely to increase with the help of local interlocutors to promote the establishment of a local industry. So the challenge will be market penetration and whether to grow organically or acquire a local distribution channel or player.

As the share of emerging economies in global economic output keeps increasing, these markets will become an essential source of demand for investment products and management. This will spur a global relocation of portfolios prompted by several factors, including tax, globalization and population shifts. National regulations – especially tax differences – make many pension markets difficult to penetrate, but with IFRS and – at least in Europe – with demands to synchronize financial policies in the Euro zone, it should become less difficult in the coming years. Business developments will be moving too fast for traditional IT models, and business technology (BT) leaders will need to partner with business colleagues to create business and technology strategy simultaneously.

In particular, the winners will be those that are capable of accepting and acting on the fact that at one level below the pension institutions – their various suppliers – they are already operating internationally and that this tendency will probably increase. They will not lose sight of the ability to act and transact in accordance with objectives and supported by marked-to-market procedures, as well as risk management/dynamic risk models. They will also recognize that flexibility and scalability are the key success factors for any strategy. For example, a flexible operational platform enables innovation and growth.

Also, they should be able to ensure that the trend of financial institutions with an international presence advertising pension retail services globally is maintained, securing the correct alignment between business and operational strategy in order to ensure the ability to change the business according to changes in business strategy.

A critical factor to success is the ability to apply a global approach combined with local skills and expertise with a view to extending the pension and insurance fund franchise into the targeted market. This should translate into the creation of a global investment management and distribution platform and to interface this with every local outlet to accommodate local market tastes, customs and traditions.

32.4.4   Regulation

Although the pension and insurance funds sector will bear all the hallmarks of increasing internationalization, it will face challenges of a more national and regulatory character. One is that it is not sufficiently standardized and another is that it remains impeded by national tax barriers and hindrances.

Regulation has three dimensions: one is the regulatory overlay itself; the second is asset selection; and the third is market entry. So it is a combination of micro and macro factors. With unparalleled regulatory activity and more stringent rules on the horizon, achieving growth will entail that pension and insurance fund companies make the right investment management system and platform choices in the current environment.

The changes resulting from the regulatory imperative are at the strategic level; they are not at the business unit level anymore or at the product level. Whereas in the past, the approach was more tactical in orientation, the present circumstances call for more of a strategic reappraisal to take account of not only one aspect of regulatory change, if the Dodd-Frank Act in the US is taken as an example, but a whole host of other regulatory measures (i.e., AIFMD, MiFID, EMIR, Solvency II, UCITS IV, etc.).

As a consequence, and in view of this all-encompassing and wide-ranging change, regulators expect to see, and indeed demand, a comprehensive, custom-built and sophisticated regulatory compliance program with full testing, use of technological tools and applied IT expertise.

Separating the winners from the losers in the area of increased regulation will be those companies that are able to diagnose the prevailing regulatory trends correctly, anticipate the changes that are coming and are prepared to implement the necessary measures to accommodate the new regulation.

In particular, it is now widely recognized that regulation is altering the contours of the industry's competitive landscape. It would help to provide an impulse to growth if pension and insurance fund products were more stand-ardized, particularly in the European market place, which remains prone to heterogeneity and fragmentation. Increased regulation may help spur product standardization.

More concentration has occurred in the market as a result of regulation, at least in terms of the major players, and more concentration in those players that are operating across markets. Industry players need to assess whether their respective fund platforms and volumes are scalable, particularly where consoli-dation as a result of increased regulation enters the picture.

Size and scale are good for the organizations that have the necessary resources and integrated operational platforms; they may be good for the industry as a whole, but probably make it tougher for small players to enter the market and succeed. The value proposition of those companies that succeed to meet the demands of growing regulation needs to be identified. Cross-border firms are probably better equipped to deal with regulation on a pan-European or indeed global scale than their local-based counterparts.

32.5 Conclusions

The Pension and insurance funds group discussions generated four main conclusions, which were as follows:

1) Changing demographics (i.e. aging population) will alter pension funding patterns, creating new cost challenges but also growth opportunities for the pension and insurance funds industry as a whole.
2) Greater market volatility, increased financial instability and more regu-latory change are creating challenges as well as opportunities that are not necessarily always in equal measure. The main drivers for success in the

pension and insurance funds sector will be flexibility in implementation and adaptability in operation.

3) Scale, internationalization and the right choice of investment management software system are key determinants in mitigating risk, controlling costs and promoting growth. It is not only the investment side of handling assets under management that is to be considered but also a software system for handling assets and liabilities; therefore an appropriate investment management system for the entire business should be considered.

4) The investment management software system is the common denominator running through all the themes discussed. It is beneficial in ways to reduce cost, promote flexibility and create a huge barrier to entry for others intent on entering the industry. If sufficient resources are forthcoming and the company is big enough, the right operational platform (operational set-up, procedures, staff as well as IT solutions) effectively helps create a special niche and fend off competition.

Note

1. It is based on discussions within the Pension and Insurance Funds Group at the SimCorp StrategyLab Copenhagen Summit held 24–25 February 2011. In addition to the author of this chapter, participants included Dr Anthony Neuberger, Professor (Warwick University); Ingo Walter, Professor (Leonard N. Stern School of Business, NYU), Director of SimCorp StrategyLab; Marc van den Berg, COO PGGM; Arne E. Jørgensen, Domain Manager, Accounting, SimCorp Group; Jacob Elsborg, Head of Technology ATP Investment Area; Dr Annukka Paloheimo, CEO Scandinavian Financial Research; and Dr Frank Wellhöfer, Managing Director MEAG MUNICH ERGO Asset Management GmbH.

Index

Printed and bound in Great Britain by
CPI Group (UK) Ltd, Croydon, CR0 4YY